Student Solutions Manual
Laurel Technical Services

NINTH EDITION

Introductory
Mathematical Analysis
for Business, Economics, and the Life and Social Sciences

Ernest F. Haeussler, Jr.   Richard S. Paul

PRENTICE HALL, Upper Saddle River, NJ 07458

Executive Editor: Sally Simpson
Managing & Supplements Editor: Gina M. Huck
Editorial Assistant: Sara Beth Newell
Special Projects Manager: Barbara A. Murray
Production Editor: James Buckley
Supplement Cover Manager: Paul Gourhan
Supplement Cover Designer: Liz Nemeth
Manufacturing Buyer: Alan Fischer

© 1999 by Prentice-Hall, Inc.
Simon & Schuster / A Viacom Company
Upper Saddle River, NJ 07458

Printed in the United States of America

10 9 8 7 6 5 4

ISBN   0-13-934209-5

Prentice-Hall International (UK) Limited, *London*
Prentice-Hall of Australia Pty. Limited, *Sydney*
Prentice-Hall Canada, Inc., *London*
Prentice-Hall Hispanoamericana, S.A., *Mexico*
Prentice-Hall of India Private Limited, *New Delhi*
Prentice-Hall of Japan, Inc., *Tokyo*
Simon & Schuster Asia Pte. Ltd., *Singapore*
Editora Prentice-Hall do Brazil, Ltda., *Rio de Janeiro*

Table of Contents

Table of Contents

Chapter 0

Exercise 0.2

1. True; -7 is a negative integer.

3. False, because the natural numbers are 1, 2, 3, and so on.

5. True, because $5 = \dfrac{5}{1}$.

7. False, because $\dfrac{4}{2} = 2$, which is a positive integer.

9. True, because 0 and 6 are integers and $6 \neq 0$. *Note:* $\dfrac{0}{6} = 0$.

11. True

Exercise 0.3

1. False, because 0 does not have a reciprocal.

3. False; the additive inverse of 5 is -5 because $5 + (-5) = 0$.

5. True; $-x + y = y + (-x) = y - x$.

7. True; $\dfrac{x+2}{2} = \dfrac{x}{2} + \dfrac{2}{2} = \dfrac{x}{2} + 1$.

9. False; the left side is $x + y + 5$, but the right side is $x + y + x + 5$.

11. distributive

13. associative

15. commutative

17. definition of subtraction

19. distributive

21. $5a(x + 3) = (5a)x + (5a)(3) = 5ax + (3)(5a)$
    $= 5ax + (3 \cdot 5)(a) = 5ax + 15a$

23. $(x + y)(2) = 2(x + y) = 2x + 2y$

25. $x[(2y + 1) + 3] = x[2y + (1 + 3)] = x[2y + 4]$
    $= x(2y) + x(4) = (x \cdot 2)y + 4x = (2x)y + 4x$
    $= 2xy + 4x$

27. $a(b + c + d) = a[(b + c) + d]$
    $= a(b + c) + a(d)$
    $= ab + ac + ad$

Exercise 0.4

1. $-2 + (-4) = -6$

3. $6 + (-4) = 2$

5. $7 - (-4) = 7 + 4 = 11$

7. $-8 - (-6) = -8 + 6 = -2$

9. $7(-9) = -(7 \cdot 9) = -63$

11. $(-1)6 = -(1 \cdot 6) = -6$

13. $-(-6 + x) = -(-6) - x = 6 - x$

15. $-12(x - y) = (-12)x - (-12)(y) = -12x + 12y$
    (or $12y - 12x$)

17. $-2 \div 6 = \dfrac{-2}{6} = -\dfrac{2}{6} = -\dfrac{1}{3}$

19. $4 \div (-2) = \dfrac{4}{-2} = -\dfrac{4}{2} = -2$

21. $3[-2(3) + 6(2)] = 3[-6 + 12] = 3[6] = 18$

23. $(-5)(-5) = (5)(5) = 25$

25. $3(x - 4) = 3(x) - 3(4) = 3x - 12$

27. $-(x - 2) = -x + 2$

29. $8\left(\dfrac{1}{11}\right) = \dfrac{8 \cdot 1}{11} = \dfrac{8}{11}$

31. $\dfrac{-5x}{7y} = \dfrac{-(5x)}{7y} = -\dfrac{5x}{7y}$

33. $\dfrac{2}{3} \cdot \dfrac{1}{x} = \dfrac{2 \cdot 1}{3 \cdot x} = \dfrac{2}{3x}$

35. $(2x)\left(\dfrac{3}{2x}\right) = 3$

37. $\dfrac{7}{y} \cdot \dfrac{1}{x} = \dfrac{7 \cdot 1}{y \cdot x} = \dfrac{7}{xy}$

39. $\dfrac{1}{2} + \dfrac{1}{3} = \dfrac{3}{6} + \dfrac{2}{6} = \dfrac{3+2}{6} = \dfrac{5}{6}$

41. $\dfrac{3}{10} - \dfrac{7}{15} = \dfrac{9}{30} - \dfrac{14}{30} = \dfrac{9-14}{30} = \dfrac{-5}{30}$
$= -\dfrac{5 \cdot 1}{5 \cdot 6} = -\dfrac{1}{6}$

43. $\dfrac{x}{9} - \dfrac{y}{9} = \dfrac{x-y}{9}$

45. $\dfrac{2}{3} - \dfrac{5}{8} = \dfrac{16}{24} - \dfrac{15}{24} = \dfrac{16-15}{24} = \dfrac{1}{24}$

47. $\dfrac{\frac{x}{6}}{y} = \dfrac{x}{6} \div \dfrac{y}{1} = \dfrac{x}{6} \cdot \dfrac{1}{y} = \dfrac{x}{6y}$

49. $\dfrac{7}{0}$ is not defined (we cannot divide by 0).

51. $\dfrac{0}{0}$ is not defined (we cannot divide by 0).

Exercise 0.5

1. $(2^3)(2^2) = 2^{3+2} = 2^5 (= 32)$

3. $w^4 w^8 = w^{4+8} = w^{12}$

5. $\dfrac{x^2 x^6}{y^7 y^{10}} = \dfrac{x^{2+6}}{y^{7+10}} = \dfrac{x^8}{y^{17}}$

7. $\dfrac{(x^2)^5}{(y^5)^{10}} = \dfrac{x^{2 \cdot 5}}{y^{5 \cdot 10}} = \dfrac{x^{10}}{y^{50}}$

9 $(2x^2 y^3)^3 = 2^3 (x^2)^3 (y^3)^3$
$= 8x^{2 \cdot 3} y^{3 \cdot 3} = 8x^6 y^9$

11. $\dfrac{x^8}{x^2} = x^{8-2} = x^6$

13. $\dfrac{(x^3)^6}{x(x^3)} = \dfrac{x^{3 \cdot 6}}{x^{1+3}} = \dfrac{x^{18}}{x^4} = x^{18-4} = x^{14}$

15. $\sqrt{25} = 5$

17. $\sqrt[5]{-32} = -2$

19. $\sqrt[4]{\dfrac{1}{16}} = \dfrac{\sqrt[4]{1}}{\sqrt[4]{16}} = \dfrac{1}{2}$

21. $(100)^{1/2} = \sqrt{100} = 10$

23. $4^{3/2} = \left(\sqrt{4}\right)^3 = (2)^3 = 8$

25. $(32)^{-2/5} = \dfrac{1}{(32)^{2/5}} = \dfrac{1}{\left(\sqrt[5]{32}\right)^2} = \dfrac{1}{(2)^2} = \dfrac{1}{4}$

27. $\left(\dfrac{1}{16}\right)^{5/4} = \left(\sqrt[4]{\dfrac{1}{16}}\right)^5 = \left(\dfrac{1}{2}\right)^5 = \dfrac{1}{32}$

29. $\sqrt{32} = \sqrt{16 \cdot 2} = \sqrt{16}\sqrt{2} = 4\sqrt{2}$

31. $\sqrt[3]{2x^3} = \sqrt[3]{2}\sqrt[3]{x^3} = x\sqrt[3]{2}$

33. $\sqrt{16x^4} = \sqrt{16}\sqrt{x^4} = 4x^2$

35. $2\sqrt{75} - 4\sqrt{27} + \sqrt[3]{128}$
$= 2\sqrt{25 \cdot 3} - 4\sqrt{9 \cdot 3} + \sqrt[3]{64 \cdot 2}$
$= 2 \cdot 5\sqrt{3} - 4 \cdot 3\sqrt{3} + 4\sqrt[3]{2}$
$= 10\sqrt{3} - 12\sqrt{3} + 4\sqrt[3]{2}$
$= -2\sqrt{3} + 4\sqrt[3]{2}$

37. $(9z^4)^{1/2} = \sqrt{9z^4} = \sqrt{3^2(z^2)^2} = \sqrt{3^2}\sqrt{(z^2)^2}$
$= 3z^2$

39. $\left(\dfrac{27t^3}{8}\right)^{2/3} = \left(\left[\dfrac{3t}{2}\right]^3\right)^{2/3} = \left[\dfrac{3t}{2}\right]^2 = \dfrac{9t^2}{4}$

41. $\dfrac{x^3 y^{-2}}{z^2} = x^3 \cdot y^{-2} \cdot \dfrac{1}{z^2} = x^3 \cdot \dfrac{1}{y^2} \cdot \dfrac{1}{z^2} = \dfrac{x^3}{y^2 z^2}$

43. $2x^{-1}x^{-3} = 2x^{-1+(-3)} = 2x^{-4} = \dfrac{2}{x^4}$

45. $(3t)^{-2} = \dfrac{1}{(3t)^2} = \dfrac{1}{9t^2}$

47. $\sqrt[3]{7s^2} = (7s^2)^{1/3} = 7^{1/3}(s^2)^{1/3} = 7^{1/3}s^{2/3}$

49. $\sqrt{x} - \sqrt{y} = x^{1/2} - y^{1/2}$

51. $x^2 \sqrt[4]{xy^{-2}z^3} = x^2(xy^{-2}z^3)^{1/4}$
$= x^2 x^{1/4} y^{-2/4} z^{3/4}$
$= \dfrac{x^{9/4} z^{3/4}}{y^{1/2}}$

53. $(8x - y)^{4/5} = \sqrt[5]{(8x - y)^4}$

55. $x^{-4/5} = \dfrac{1}{x^{4/5}} = \dfrac{1}{\sqrt[5]{x^4}}$

57. $2x^{-2/5} - (2x)^{-2/5} = \dfrac{2}{x^{2/5}} - \dfrac{1}{(2x)^{2/5}}$
$= \dfrac{2}{\sqrt[5]{x^2}} - \dfrac{1}{\sqrt[5]{(2x)^2}} = \dfrac{2}{\sqrt[5]{x^2}} - \dfrac{1}{\sqrt[5]{4x^2}}$

59. $\dfrac{3}{\sqrt{7}} = \dfrac{3}{7^{1/2}} = \dfrac{3 \cdot 7^{1/2}}{7^{1/2} \cdot 7^{1/2}} = \dfrac{3\sqrt{7}}{7}$

61. $\dfrac{4}{\sqrt{2x}} = \dfrac{4}{(2x)^{1/2}} = \dfrac{4(2x)^{1/2}}{(2x)^{1/2}(2x)^{1/2}} = \dfrac{4\sqrt{2x}}{2x}$
$= \dfrac{2\sqrt{2x}}{x}$

63. $\dfrac{1}{\sqrt[3]{3x}} = \dfrac{1}{(3x)^{1/3}} = \dfrac{1(3x)^{2/3}}{(3x)^{1/3}(3x)^{2/3}} = \dfrac{\sqrt[3]{(3x)^2}}{3x}$
$= \dfrac{\sqrt[3]{9x^2}}{3x}$

65. $\dfrac{\sqrt{32}}{\sqrt{2}} = \sqrt{\dfrac{32}{2}} = \sqrt{16} = 4$

67. $\dfrac{\sqrt[4]{2}}{\sqrt[3]{xy^2}} = \dfrac{\sqrt[4]{2}}{x^{1/3}y^{2/3}} = \dfrac{\sqrt[4]{2} \cdot x^{2/3}y^{1/3}}{x^{1/3}y^{2/3} \cdot x^{2/3}y^{1/3}}$
$= \dfrac{2^{1/4}x^{2/3}y^{1/3}}{xy} = \dfrac{2^{3/12}x^{8/12}y^{4/12}}{xy}$
$= \dfrac{(2^3 x^8 y^4)^{1/12}}{xy} = \dfrac{\sqrt[12]{8x^8 y^4}}{xy}$

69. $2x^2 y^{-3} x^4 = 2x^6 y^{-3} = \dfrac{2x^6}{y^3}$

71. $\sqrt{\sqrt[3]{t^4}} = \sqrt{t^{4/3}} = (t^{4/3})^{1/2} = t^{4/6} = t^{2/3}$

73. $\dfrac{2^0}{(2^{-2}x^{1/2}y^{-2})^3} = \dfrac{1}{2^{-6}x^{3/2}y^{-6}} = \dfrac{2^6 y^6}{x^{3/2}}$
$= \dfrac{64 y^6 \cdot x^{1/2}}{x^{3/2} \cdot x^{1/2}} = \dfrac{64 y^6 x^{1/2}}{x^2}$

75. $\sqrt[3]{x^2 y z^3}\sqrt[3]{xy^2} = \sqrt[3]{(x^2 y z^3)(xy^2)} = \sqrt[3]{x^3 y^3 z^3}$
$= xyz$

77. $3^2(27)^{-4/3} = 3^2(3^3)^{-4/3} = 3^2(3^{-4}) = 3^{-2}$
$= \dfrac{1}{3^2} = \dfrac{1}{9}$

79. $(2x^{-1}y^2)^2 = 2^2 x^{-2} y^4 = \dfrac{4y^4}{x^2}$

81. $\sqrt{x}\sqrt{x^2 y^3}\sqrt{xy^2} = x^{1/2}(x^2 y^3)^{1/2}(xy^2)^{1/2}$
$= x^{1/2}(xy^{3/2})(x^{1/2}y) = x^2 y^{5/2}$

3

83. $\dfrac{(x^2 y^{-1} z)^{-2}}{(xy^2)^{-4}} = \dfrac{x^{-4} y^2 z^{-2}}{x^{-4} y^{-8}} = \dfrac{y^{10}}{z^2}$

85. $\dfrac{(x^2)^3}{x^4} \div \left[\dfrac{x^3}{(x^3)^2}\right]^2 = \dfrac{x^6}{x^4} \div \dfrac{(x^3)^2}{(x^6)^2}$

$= x^2 \div \dfrac{x^6}{x^{12}} = x^2 \div x^{6-12} = x^2 \div x^{-6}$

$= x^2 \div \dfrac{1}{x^6} = x^2 \cdot x^6 = x^8$

87. $-\dfrac{8s^{-2}}{2s^3} = -\dfrac{4}{s^3 s^2} = -\dfrac{4}{s^5}$

89. $\left(\dfrac{2x^2 y}{3y^3 z^{-2}}\right)^2 = \left(\dfrac{2x^2 z^2}{3y^2}\right)^2 = \dfrac{2^2 (x^2)^2 (z^2)^2}{3^2 (y^2)^2}$

$= \dfrac{4x^4 z^4}{9y^4}$

Exercise 0.6

1. $8x - 4y + 2 + 3x + 2y - 5 = 11x - 2y - 3$

3. $8t^2 - 6s^2 + 4s^2 - 2t^2 + 6 = 6t^2 - 2s^2 + 6$

5. $\sqrt{x} + \sqrt{2y} + \sqrt{x} + \sqrt{3z} = 2\sqrt{x} + \sqrt{2y} + \sqrt{3z}$

7. $6x^2 - 10xy + \sqrt{2} - 2z + xy - 4$
$= 6x^2 - 9xy - 2z + \sqrt{2} - 4$

9. $\sqrt{x} + \sqrt{2y} - \sqrt{x} - \sqrt{3z} = \sqrt{2y} - \sqrt{3z}$

11. $9x + 6y - 15 - 16x + 8y - 4 = -7x + 14y - 19$

13. $3(x^2 + y^2) - x(y + 2x) + 2y(x + 3y)$
$= 3x^2 + 3y^2 - xy - 2x^2 + 2xy + 6y^2$
$= x^2 + 9y^2 + xy$

15. $2\{3[3x^2 + 6 - 2x^2 + 10]\} = 2\{3[x^2 + 16]\}$
$= 2\{3x^2 + 48\} = 6x^2 + 96$

17. $-3\{4x(x + 2) - 2[x^2 - (3 - x)]\}$
$= -3\{4x^2 + 8x - 2[x^2 - 3 + x]\}$
$= -3\{4x^2 + 8x - 2x^2 + 6 - 2x\}$
$= -3\{2x^2 + 6x + 6\}$
$= -6x^2 - 18x - 18$

19. $x^2 + (4 + 5)x + 4(5) = x^2 + 9x + 20$

21. $(x + 3)(x - 2) = x^2 + (3 - 2)x + 3(-2)$
$= x^2 + x - 6$

23. $(2x)(5x) + [(2)(2) + (3)(5)]x + 3(2)$
$= 10x^2 + 19x + 6$

25. $(x + 3)^2 = x^2 + 2(3)(x) + 3^2 = x^2 + 6x + 9$

27. $x^2 - 2(5)x + 5^2 = x^2 - 10x + 25$

29. $\left(\sqrt{2y} + 3\right)^2 = \left(\sqrt{2y}\right)^2 + 2\left(\sqrt{2y}\right)(3) + 3^2$
$= 2y + 6\sqrt{2y} + 9$

31. $(2s)^2 - 1^2 = 4s^2 - 1$

33. $(x^2 - 3)(x + 4) = x^2(x + 4) - 3(x + 4)$
$= x^3 + 4x^2 - 3x - 12$

35. $x^2(2x^2 + 2x - 3) - 1(2x^2 + 2x - 3)$
$= 2x^4 + 2x^3 - 3x^2 - 2x^2 - 2x + 3$
$= 2x^4 + 2x^3 - 5x^2 - 2x + 3$

37. $x\{3(x - 1)(x - 2) + 2[x(x + 7)]\}$
$= x\{3(x^2 - 3x + 2) + 2[x^2 + 7x]\}$
$= x\{3x^2 - 9x + 6 + 2x^2 + 14x\}$
$= x\{5x^2 + 5x + 6\}$
$= 5x^3 + 5x^2 + 6x$

39. $x(3x + 2y - 4) + y(3x + 2y - 4) + 2(3x + 2y - 4)$
$$= 3x^2 + 2xy - 4x + 3xy + 2y^2 - 4y + 6x + 4y - 8$$
$$= 3x^2 + 2y^2 + 5xy + 2x - 8$$

41. $(x + 5)^3 = x^3 + 3x^2(5) + 3x(5)^2 + 5^3$
$$= x^3 + 15x^2 + 75x + 125$$

43. $(2x)^3 - 3(2x)^2(3) + 3(2x)(3)^2 - 3^3$
$$= 8x^3 - 36x^2 + 54x - 27$$

45. $\dfrac{z^2 - 4z}{z} = \dfrac{z^2}{z} - \dfrac{4z}{z} = z - 4$

47. $\dfrac{6x^5}{2x^2} + \dfrac{4x^3}{2x^2} - \dfrac{1}{2x^2} = 3x^3 + 2x - \dfrac{1}{2x^2}$

49.
$$
\begin{array}{r}
x \\
x + 3 \overline{) x^2 + 3x - 1} \\
\underline{x^2 + 3x} \\
-1
\end{array}
$$
Answer: $x + \dfrac{-1}{x + 3}$

51.
$$
\begin{array}{r}
3x^2 - 8x + 17 \\
x + 2 \overline{) 3x^3 - 2x^2 + x - 3} \\
\underline{3x^3 + 6x^2} \\
-8x^2 + x \\
\underline{-8x^2 - 16x} \\
17x - 3 \\
\underline{17x + 34} \\
-37
\end{array}
$$
Answer: $3x^2 - 8x + 17 + \dfrac{-37}{x + 2}$

53.
$$
\begin{array}{r}
t + 8 \\
t - 8 \overline{) t^2 + 0t + 0} \\
\underline{t^2 - 8t} \\
8t + 0 \\
\underline{8t - 64} \\
64
\end{array}
$$
Answer: $t + 8 + \dfrac{64}{t - 8}$

55.
$$
\begin{array}{r}
x - 2 \\
3x + 2 \overline{) 3x^2 - 4x + 3} \\
\underline{3x^2 + 2x} \\
-6x + 3 \\
\underline{-6x - 4} \\
7
\end{array}
$$
Answer: $x - 2 + \dfrac{7}{3x + 2}$

Exercise 0.7

1. $6x + 4 = 2(3x + 2)$

3. $5x(2y + z)$

5. $8a^3bc - 12ab^3cd + 4b^4c^2d^2$
$$= 4bc(2a^3 - 3ab^2d + b^3cd^2)$$

7. $x^2 - 5^2 = (x + 5)(x - 5)$

9. $p^2 + 4p + 3 = (p + 3)(p + 1)$

11. $(4x)^2 - 3^2 = (4x + 3)(4x - 3)$

13. $z^2 + 6z + 8 = (z + 4)(z + 2)$

15. $x^2 + 2(3)(x) + 3^2 = (x + 3)^2$

17. $2x^2 + 12x + 16 = 2(x^2 + 6x + 8)$
$$= 2(x + 4)(x + 2)$$

19. $3(x^2 - 1^2) = 3(x+1)(x-1)$

21. $6y^2 + 13y + 2 = (6y+1)(y+2)$

23. $2s(6s^2 + 5s - 4) = 2s(3s+4)(2s-1)$

25. $x^{2/3}y - 4x^{8/3}y^2 = x^{2/3}y(1 - 4x^2y)$
$= x^{2/3}y[1^2 - (2xy)^2]$
$= x^{2/3}y(1 + 2xy)(1 - 2xy)$

27. $2x(x^2 + x - 6) = 2x(x+3)(x-2)$

29. $(4x+2)^2 = [2(2x+1)]^2 = 2^2(2x+1)^2$
$= 4(2x+1)^2$

31. $x(x^2y^2 - 10xy + 25)$
$= x[(xy)^2 - 2(xy)(5) + 5^2]$
$= x(xy - 5)^2$

33. $(x^3 - 4x) + (8 - 2x^2)$
$= x(x^2 - 4) + 2(4 - x^2)$
$= x(x^2 - 4) - 2(x^2 - 4)$
$= (x^2 - 4)(x - 2)$
$= (x+2)(x-2)(x-2)$
$= (x-2)^2(x+2)$

35. $y^2(y^2 + 8y + 16) - (y^2 + 8y + 16)$
$= (y^2 + 8y + 16)(y^2 - 1)$
$= (y+4)^2(y+1)(y-1)$

37. $x^3 + 8 = x^3 + 2^3 = (x+2)(x^2 - 2x + 4)$

39. $(x^3)^2 - 1^2 = (x^3 + 1)(x^3 - 1)$
$= (x+1)(x^2 - x + 1)(x-1)(x^2 + x + 1)$

41. $(x+3)^3(x-1) + (x+3)^2(x-1)^2$
$= (x+3)^2(x-1)[(x+3) + (x-1)]$
$= (x+3)^2(x-1)[2x+2]$
$= (x+3)^2(x-1)[2(x+1)]$
$= 2(x+3)^2(x-1)(x+1)$

43. $[P(1+r)] + [P(1+r)]r = [P(1+r)](1+r)$
$= P(1+r)^2$

45. $x^4 - 16 = (x^2)^2 - 4^2 = (x^2 + 4)(x^2 - 4)$
$= (x^2 + 4)(x+2)(x-2)$

47. $(y^4)^2 - 1^2 = (y^4 + 1)(y^4 - 1)$
$= (y^4 + 1)(y^2 + 1)(y^2 - 1)$
$= (y^4 + 1)(y^2 + 1)(y+1)(y-1)$

49. $x^4 + x^2 - 2 = (x^2 + 2)(x^2 - 1)$
$= (x^2 + 2)(x+1)(x-1)$

51. $x(x^4 - 2x^2 + 1) = x(x^2 - 1)^2$
$= x[(x+1)(x-1)]^2$
$= x(x+1)^2(x-1)^2$

Exercise 0.8

1. $\dfrac{x^2 - 4}{x^2 - 2x} = \dfrac{(x+2)(x-2)}{x(x-2)} = \dfrac{x+2}{x}$

3. $\dfrac{x^2 - 9x + 20}{x^2 + x - 20} = \dfrac{(x-5)(x-4)}{(x+5)(x-4)} = \dfrac{x-5}{x+5}$

5. $\dfrac{6x^2 + x - 2}{2x^2 + 3x - 2} = \dfrac{(3x+2)(2x-1)}{(x+2)(2x-1)} = \dfrac{3x+2}{x+2}$

7. $\dfrac{y^2(-1)}{(y-3)(y+2)} = -\dfrac{y^2}{(y-3)(y+2)}$

9. $\dfrac{(2x-3)(2-x)}{(x-2)(2x+3)} = \dfrac{(2x-3)(-1)(x-2)}{(x-2)(2x+3)}$
$= \dfrac{(2x-3)(-1)}{2x+3} = \dfrac{3-2x}{2x+3}$

11. $\dfrac{2(x-1)}{(x-4)(x+2)} \cdot \dfrac{(x+4)(x+1)}{(x+1)(x-1)}$
$= \dfrac{2(x-1)(x+4)(x+1)}{(x-4)(x+2)(x+1)(x-1)}$
$= \dfrac{2(x+4)}{(x-4)(x+2)}$

13. $\dfrac{x^2}{6} \div \dfrac{x}{3} = \dfrac{x^2}{6} \cdot \dfrac{3}{x} = \dfrac{3x^2}{6x} = \dfrac{x}{2}$

15. $\dfrac{2m}{n^3} \cdot \dfrac{n^2}{4m} = \dfrac{2mn^2}{4mn^3} = \dfrac{1}{2n}$

17. $\dfrac{4x}{3} \div 2x = \dfrac{4x}{3} \cdot \dfrac{1}{2x} = \dfrac{4x}{6x} = \dfrac{2}{3}$

19. $\dfrac{-9x^3}{1} \cdot \dfrac{3}{x} = \dfrac{-27x^3}{x} = -27x^2$

21. $\dfrac{x-5}{\dfrac{x^2-7x+10}{x-2}} = (x-5) \cdot \dfrac{x-2}{x^2-7x+10}$

$= (x-5) \cdot \dfrac{x-2}{(x-5)(x-2)} = (x-5) \cdot \dfrac{1}{x-5} = 1$

23. $\dfrac{10x^3}{(x+1)(x-1)} \cdot \dfrac{x+1}{5x} = \dfrac{10x^3(x+1)}{5x(x+1)(x-1)}$

$= \dfrac{2x^2}{x-1}$

25. $\dfrac{x^2+7x+10}{x^2-2x-8} \div \dfrac{x^2+6x+5}{x^2-3x-4}$

$= \dfrac{x^2+7x+10}{x^2-2x-8} \cdot \dfrac{x^2-3x-4}{x^2+6x+5}$

$= \dfrac{(x+5)(x+2)}{(x-4)(x+2)} \cdot \dfrac{(x-4)(x+1)}{(x+5)(x+1)} = 1$

27. $\dfrac{(2x+3)(2x-3)}{(x+4)(x-1)} \cdot \dfrac{(1+x)(1-x)}{2x-3}$

$= \dfrac{(2x+3)(1+x)(1-x)}{(x+4)(x-1)}$

$= \dfrac{(2x+3)(1+x)(-1)(x-1)}{(x+4)(x-1)}$

$= -\dfrac{(2x+3)(1+x)}{x+4}$

29. $\dfrac{x^2}{x+3} + \dfrac{5x+6}{x+3} = \dfrac{x^2+(5x+6)}{x+3}$

$= \dfrac{(x+3)(x+2)}{x+3} = x+2$

31. LCD $= 3t$, so $\dfrac{1}{t} + \dfrac{2}{3t} = \dfrac{3}{3t} + \dfrac{2}{3t} = \dfrac{3+2}{3t} = \dfrac{5}{3t}$.

33. LCD $= p^2 - 1$

$1 - \dfrac{p^2}{p^2-1} = \dfrac{p^2-1}{p^2-1} - \dfrac{p^2}{p^2-1}$

$= \dfrac{p^2-1-p^2}{p^2-1} = \dfrac{-1}{p^2-1} = \dfrac{1}{1-p^2}$

35. LCD $= (2x-1)(x+3)$

$\dfrac{4(x+3)}{(2x-1)(x+3)} + \dfrac{x(2x-1)}{(x+3)(2x-1)}$

$= \dfrac{4(x+3)+x(2x-1)}{(2x-1)(x+3)} = \dfrac{2x^2+3x+12}{(2x-1)(x+3)}$

37. $x^2 - x - 2 = (x-2)(x+1)$ and $x^2 - 1 = (x+1)(x-1)$, so
LCD $= (x-2)(x+1)(x-1)$.

$\dfrac{1}{(x-2)(x+1)} + \dfrac{1}{(x+1)(x-1)}$

$= \dfrac{x-1}{(x-2)(x+1)(x-1)} + \dfrac{x-2}{(x+1)(x-1)(x-2)}$

$= \dfrac{(x-1)+(x-2)}{(x-2)(x+1)(x-1)} = \dfrac{2x-3}{(x-2)(x+1)(x-1)}$

39. $\text{LCD} = (x-1)(x+5)$

$$\frac{4(x+5)}{(x-1)(x+5)} - \frac{3(x-1)(x+5)}{(x-1)(x+5)} + \frac{3x^2}{(x-1)(x+5)}$$

$$= \frac{4x+20-3(x^2+4x-5)+3x^2}{(x-1)(x+5)}$$

$$= \frac{35-8x}{(x-1)(x+5)}$$

41. $(1+x^{-1})^2 = \left(1+\frac{1}{x}\right)^2 = \left(\frac{x}{x}+\frac{1}{x}\right)^2$

$$= \left(\frac{x+1}{x}\right)^2$$

$$= \frac{(x+1)^2}{x^2} = \frac{x^2+2x+1}{x^2}$$

43. $\left(\frac{1}{x}-y\right)^{-1} = \left(\frac{1}{x}-\frac{xy}{x}\right)^{-1} = \left(\frac{1-xy}{x}\right)^{-1}$

$$= \frac{x}{1-xy}$$

45. Multiplying the numerator and denominator of the given fraction by x gives

$$\frac{1+\frac{1}{x}}{3} = \frac{\left(1+\frac{1}{x}\right)x}{3x} = \frac{x+1}{3x}.$$

47. Multiplying numerator and denominator by $2x(x+2)$ gives

$$\frac{3(2x)(x+2)-1(x+2)}{x(2x)(x+2)+x(2x)} = \frac{(x+2)[3(2x)-1]}{2x^2[(x+2)+1]}$$

$$= \frac{(x+2)(6x-1)}{2x^2(x+3)}$$

49. $\text{LCD} = \sqrt{x+h}\cdot\sqrt{x}$

$$\frac{2}{\sqrt{x+h}} - \frac{2}{\sqrt{x}} = \frac{2\sqrt{x}}{\sqrt{x+h}\sqrt{x}} - \frac{2\sqrt{x+h}}{\sqrt{x}\sqrt{x+h}}$$

$$= \frac{2\sqrt{x}-2\sqrt{x+h}}{\sqrt{x}\sqrt{x+h}}$$

51. $\dfrac{1}{2+\sqrt{3}}\cdot\dfrac{2-\sqrt{3}}{2-\sqrt{3}} = \dfrac{2-\sqrt{3}}{4-3} = 2-\sqrt{3}$

53. $\dfrac{\sqrt{2}}{\sqrt{3}-\sqrt{6}} = \dfrac{\sqrt{2}}{\sqrt{3}-\sqrt{6}}\cdot\dfrac{\sqrt{3}+\sqrt{6}}{\sqrt{3}+\sqrt{6}}$

$$= \frac{\sqrt{2}\left(\sqrt{3}+\sqrt{6}\right)}{3-6} = \frac{\sqrt{6}+\sqrt{12}}{-3} = -\frac{\sqrt{6}+2\sqrt{3}}{3}$$

55. $\dfrac{2\sqrt{2}}{\sqrt{2}-\sqrt{3}}\cdot\dfrac{\sqrt{2}+\sqrt{3}}{\sqrt{2}+\sqrt{3}} = \dfrac{2\sqrt{2}\left(\sqrt{2}+\sqrt{3}\right)}{2-3}$

$$= \frac{4+2\sqrt{6}}{-1} = -4-2\sqrt{6}$$

57. $\dfrac{1}{x+\sqrt{5}} = \dfrac{1}{x+\sqrt{5}}\cdot\dfrac{x-\sqrt{5}}{x-\sqrt{5}} = \dfrac{x-\sqrt{5}}{x^2-5}$

59. $\dfrac{5\left(1-\sqrt{3}\right)}{\left(1+\sqrt{3}\right)\left(1-\sqrt{3}\right)} - \dfrac{4\left(2+\sqrt{2}\right)}{\left(2-\sqrt{2}\right)\left(2+\sqrt{2}\right)}$

$$= \frac{5\left(1-\sqrt{3}\right)}{1-3} - \frac{4\left(2+\sqrt{2}\right)}{4-2}$$

$$= \frac{5\left(1-\sqrt{3}\right)}{-2} - \frac{4\left(2+\sqrt{2}\right)}{2}$$

$$= \frac{5\left(\sqrt{3}-1\right)-4\left(2+\sqrt{2}\right)}{2} = \frac{5\sqrt{3}-4\sqrt{2}-13}{2}$$

Chapter 1

Principles in Practice 1.1

1. The amount of fencing material needed is the same as the perimeter of the rectangular garden, P.
   Let w = the width of the garden. Then $w + 2$ = the length, l, of the garden.
   $P = 2l + 2w$
   $P = 2(w + 2) + 2w$
   $P = 2w + 4 + 2w$
   $P = 4w + 4$
   $(4w + 4)$ feet of fencing are needed.

2. Revenues equal costs when $2.25x = 0.75x + 300$.
   $2.25x = 0.75x + 300$
   $1.5x = 300$
   $x = 200$
   The coffee house needs to sell 200 specialty coffees each day.

3. Let x = the number of weeks. After x weeks, Monica will have saved $40x - 125$. Pedro has already saved $3(\$35) = \$105$. After x weeks, Pedro will have saved $35x + 105$.
   $40x - 125 = 35x + 105$
   $5x = 230$
   $x = 46$
   $40(46) - 125 = 1840 - 125 = 1715$
   Monica and Pedro will pool their savings in 46 weeks. Each will have saved $1715.

4. $d = rt$
   $\dfrac{d}{t} = r$
   The rate is $r = \dfrac{d}{t}$.

5. The box must have sides of length equal to the diameter of the sphere.
   $4\pi\left(\dfrac{d}{2}\right)^2 = S$
   $\left(\dfrac{d}{2}\right)^2 = \dfrac{S}{4\pi}$
   $\dfrac{d}{2} = \sqrt{\dfrac{S}{4\pi}} = \dfrac{1}{2}\sqrt{\dfrac{S}{\pi}}$
   $d = \sqrt{\dfrac{S}{\pi}}$

   The box must have sides of length $\sqrt{\dfrac{S}{\pi}}$.

Exercise 1.1

1. $9x - x^2 = 0$
   Set $x = 1$:
   $9(1) - (1)^2 \overset{?}{=} 0$
   $9 - 1 \overset{?}{=} 0$
   $8 \neq 0$
   Set $x = 0$:
   $9(0) - (0)^2 \overset{?}{=} 0$
   $0 - 0 \overset{?}{=} 0$
   $0 = 0$
   Thus, 0 satisfies the equation, but 1 does not.

3. $y + 2(y - 3) = 4$
   Set $x = \dfrac{10}{3}$:
   $\dfrac{10}{3} + 2\left(\dfrac{10}{3} - 3\right) \overset{?}{=} 4$
   $\dfrac{10}{3} + \dfrac{20}{3} - 6 \overset{?}{=} 4$
   $4 = 4$
   Set $x = 1$:
   $1 + 2(1 - 3) \overset{?}{=} 4$
   $1 - 4 \overset{?}{=} 4$
   $-3 \neq 4$
   Thus, $\dfrac{10}{3}$ satisfies the equation but 1 does not.

5. $x(7 + x) - 2(x + 1) - 3x = -2$
Set $x = -3$:
$(-3)(7 - 3) - 2(-3 + 1) - 3(-3) \stackrel{?}{=} -2$
$-3(4) - 2(-2) + 9 \stackrel{?}{=} -2$
$-12 + 4 + 9 \stackrel{?}{=} -2$
$1 \neq -2$
Set $x = 0$:
$0(7) - 2(1) - 3(0) \stackrel{?}{=} -2$
$-2 = -2$
Thus, 0 satisfies the equation but -3 does not.

7. Adding 5 to both sides; equivalence guaranteed

9. Squaring both sides; equivalence not guaranteed

11. Dividing both sides by x; equivalence not guaranteed

13. Multiplying both sides by $x - 1$; equivalence not guaranteed

15. Multiplying both sides by $\dfrac{x-5}{x}$;
equivalence not guaranteed

17. $4x = 10$
Dividing both sides by 4 gives $x = \dfrac{10}{4} = \dfrac{5}{2}$.

19. $3y = 0$
Dividing both sides by 3 gives $y = \dfrac{0}{3} = 0$.

21. $-5x = 10 - 15$
$-5x = -5$
Dividing both sides by -5 gives $x = \dfrac{-5}{-5} = 1$.

23. $5x - 3 = 9$
$5x = 12$
$x = \dfrac{12}{5}$

25. $7x + 7 = 2(x + 1)$
$7x + 7 = 2x + 2$
$5x + 7 = 2$
$5x = -5$
$x = \dfrac{-5}{5} = -1$

27. $2(p - 1) - 3(p - 4) = 4p$
$2p - 2 - 3p + 12 = 4p$
$-p + 10 = 4p$
$10 = 5p$
$p = 2$

29. $\dfrac{x}{5} = 2x - 6$
$x = 5(2x - 6)$
$x = 10x - 30$
$30 = 9x$
$x = \dfrac{30}{9} = \dfrac{10}{3}$

31. $5 + \dfrac{4x}{9} = \dfrac{x}{2}$
Multiplying both sides by $9 \cdot 2$ gives
$9 \cdot 2 \cdot 5 + 2(4x) = 9(x)$
$90 + 8x = 9x$
$x = 90$

33. $q = \dfrac{3}{2}q - 4$
Multiplying both sides by 2 gives
$2q = 3q - 8$
$-q = -8$
$q = 8$

35. $3x + \dfrac{x}{5} - 5 = \dfrac{1}{5} + 5x$
Multiplying both sides by 5 gives
$15x + x - 25 = 1 + 25x$
$16x - 25 = 1 + 25x$
$-9x = 26$
$x = -\dfrac{26}{9}$

37. $\dfrac{2y-3}{4} = \dfrac{6y+7}{3}$

Multiplying both sides by 12 gives
$3(2y - 3) = 4(6y + 7)$
$6y - 9 = 24y + 28$
$-18y = 37$
$y = -\dfrac{37}{18}$

39. $w + \dfrac{w}{2} - \dfrac{w}{3} + \dfrac{w}{4} = 5$

Multiplying both sides by 12 gives
$12w + 6w - 4w + 3w = 60$
$17w = 60$
$w = \dfrac{60}{17}$

41. $\dfrac{x+2}{3} - \dfrac{2-x}{6} = x - 2$

Multiplying both sides by 6 gives
$2(x + 2) - (2 - x) = 6(x - 2)$
$2x + 4 - 2 + x = 6x - 12$
$3x + 2 = 6x - 12$
$2 = 3x - 12$
$14 = 3x$
$x = \dfrac{14}{3}$

43. $\dfrac{9}{5}(3 - x) = \dfrac{3}{4}(x - 3)$

Multiplying both sides by 20 gives
$36(3 - x) = 15(x - 3)$
$108 - 36x = 15x - 45$
$153 = 51x$
$x = 3$

45. $\dfrac{3}{2}(4x - 3) = 2[x - (4x - 3)]$

$3(4x - 3) = 4[x - 4x + 3]$
$12x - 9 = -12x + 12$
$24x = 21$
$x = \dfrac{21}{24} = \dfrac{7}{8}$

47. $I = Prt$
$I = P(rt)$
$P = \dfrac{I}{rt}$

49. $p = 8q - 1$
$p + 1 = 8q$
$q = \dfrac{p+1}{8}$

51. $S = P(1 + rt)$
$S = P + Prt$
$S - P = r(Pt)$
$r = \dfrac{S - P}{Pt}$

53. $S = \dfrac{n}{2}(a_1 + a_n)$
$2S = n(a_1 + a_n)$
$2S = na_1 + na_n$
$2S - na_n = na_1$
$a_1 = \dfrac{2S - na_n}{n}$

55. $P = 2l + 2w$
$960 = 2(360) + 2w$
$960 = 720 + 2w$
$240 = 2w$
$w = 120 \text{ m}$

57. $c = x + 0.0825x = 1.0825x$

59. $V = C\left(1 - \dfrac{n}{N}\right)$
$1000 = 1600\left(1 - \dfrac{n}{8}\right)$
$1000 = 1600 - 200n$
$200n = 600$
$n = 3$

61. Paula's weekly salary for working h hours is $22h + 8$. Sam's weekly salary for working h hours is $26h$.

$\dfrac{1}{4}(22h + 8 + 26h) = 350$
$48h + 8 = 1400$
$48h = 1392$
$h = 29$

They must each work 29 hours each week.

63. $I = I_0[1 + \alpha(T - T_0)]$

$1.001 = 1[1 + \alpha(100 - 0)]$

$1.001 = 1 + 100\alpha$

$0.001 = 100\alpha$

$\alpha = \dfrac{0.001}{100} = 0.00001$

65. $\dfrac{1}{8}, -\dfrac{1}{14}$

67. $\dfrac{14}{61}$

Principles in Practice 1.2

1. $d = rt$ where d = distance, r = rate, and t = time. The times for the two boats are the same. For the first boat, $d = 10$ and the rate is $r + 2$. For the second boat, $d = 6$ and the rate is $r - 2$.

$t = \dfrac{d}{r}$

$\dfrac{10}{r+2} = \dfrac{6}{r-2}$

$(r+2)(r-2)\dfrac{10}{r+2} = (r+2)(r-2)\dfrac{6}{r-2}$

$10r - 20 = 6r + 12$

$4r = 32$

$r = 8$

The boats are going 8 miles per hour.

2. $t = \dfrac{d}{r+w}$

$t(r + w) = d$

$tr + tw = d$

$tw = d - tr$

$w = \dfrac{d - tr}{t} = \dfrac{d}{t} - r$

3. Let x = the horizontal distance that the ramp covers. By the Pythagorean theorem, the length of the ramp is $\sqrt{x^2 + v^2}$ where v is the vertical distance the ramp covers.

$\sqrt{x^2 + v^2} - x = 2$

$\sqrt{x^2 + 16} - x = 2$

$\sqrt{x^2 + 16} = x + 2$

$x^2 + 16 = (x + 2)^2$

$x^2 + 16 = x^2 + 4x + 4$

$12 = 4x$

$3 = x$

$\sqrt{x^2 + v^2} = \sqrt{3^2 + 16} = \sqrt{9 + 16} = \sqrt{25} = 5$

The length of the ramp is 5 feet.

Exercise 1.2

1. $\dfrac{5}{x} = 25$

Multiplying both sides by x gives

$5 = 25x$

$x = \dfrac{5}{25}$

$x = \dfrac{1}{5}$

3. Multiplying both sides by $7 - x$ gives $3 = 0$, which is **false**. Thus there is no solution, so the **solution set** is $\varnothing$.

5. $\dfrac{4}{8 - x} = \dfrac{3}{4}$

$4(4) = 3(8 - x)$

$16 = 24 - 3x$

$3x = 8$

$x = \dfrac{8}{3}$

7. $\dfrac{q}{3q - 4} = 3$

$q = 3(3q - 4)$

$q = 9q - 12$

$12 = 8q$

$q = \dfrac{3}{2}$

9. $\dfrac{1}{p - 1} = \dfrac{2}{p - 2}$

$p - 2 = 2(p - 1)$

$p - 2 = 2p - 2$

$p = 0$

11. $\dfrac{1}{x}+\dfrac{1}{5}=\dfrac{4}{5}$

$\dfrac{1}{x}=\dfrac{3}{5}$

$5x\left(\dfrac{1}{x}\right)=5x\left(\dfrac{3}{5}\right)$

$5=3x$

$x=\dfrac{5}{3}$

13. $\dfrac{3x-2}{2x+3}=\dfrac{3x-1}{2x+1}$

$(3x-2)(2x+1)=(3x-1)(2x+3)$

$6x^2-x-2=6x^2+7x-3$

$1=8x$

$x=\dfrac{1}{8}$

15. $\dfrac{y-6}{y}-\dfrac{6}{y}=\dfrac{y+6}{y-6}$

$y(y-6)\left[\dfrac{y-6}{y}-\dfrac{6}{y}\right]=y(y-6)\left[\dfrac{y+6}{y-6}\right]$

$(y-6)^2-6(y-6)=y(y+6)$

$y^2-12y+36-6y+36=y^2+6y$

$y^2-18y+72=y^2+6y$

$72=24y$

$y=3$

17. $\dfrac{-4}{x-1}=\dfrac{7}{2-x}+\dfrac{3}{x+1}$

Multiplying both sides by
$(x-1)(2-x)(x+1)$ gives
$-4(2-x)(x+1)$
$=7(x-1)(x+1)+3(x-1)(2-x)$
$-4(-x^2+x+2)=7(x^2-1)+3(-x^2+3x-2)$

$4x^2-4x-8=4x^2+9x-13$

$-13x=-5$

$x=\dfrac{5}{13}$

19. $\dfrac{9}{x-3}=\dfrac{3x}{x-3}$

$9=3x$

$x=3$

But the given equation is not defined for
$x=3$, so there is no solution. The solution
set is $\varnothing$.

21. $\sqrt{x+6}=3$

$\left(\sqrt{x+6}\right)^2=3^2$

$x+6=9$

$x=3$

23. $\sqrt{5x-6}-16=0$

$\sqrt{5x-6}=16$

$\left(\sqrt{5x-6}\right)^2=16^2$

$5x-6=256$

$5x=262$

$x=\dfrac{262}{5}$

25. $\sqrt{\dfrac{x}{2}+1}=\dfrac{2}{3}$

Squaring both sides:

$\dfrac{x}{2}+1=\dfrac{4}{9}$

$\dfrac{x}{2}=-\dfrac{5}{9}$

$x=2\left(-\dfrac{5}{9}\right)=-\dfrac{10}{9}$

27. $\sqrt{4x-6}=\sqrt{x}$

$\left(\sqrt{4x-6}\right)^2=\left(\sqrt{x}\right)^2$

$4x-6=x$

$3x=6$

$x=2$

29. $(x-3)^{3/2}=8$

$[(x-3)^{3/2}]^{2/3}=8^{2/3}$

$x-3=4$

$x=7$

31. $\sqrt{y} + \sqrt{y+2} = 3$

$\sqrt{y+2} = 3 - \sqrt{y}$

$\left(\sqrt{y+2}\right)^2 = \left(3 - \sqrt{y}\right)^2$

$y + 2 = 9 - 6\sqrt{y} + y$

$6\sqrt{y} = 7$

$\left(6\sqrt{y}\right)^2 = 7^2$

$36y = 49$

$y = \dfrac{49}{36}$

33. $\sqrt{z^2 + 2z} = 3 + z$

Squaring both sides gives

$z^2 + 2z = (3+z)^2$

$z^2 + 2z = 9 + 6z + z^2$

$-9 = 4z$

$z = -\dfrac{9}{4}$

35. $r = \dfrac{d}{1 - dt}$

$r(1 - dt) = d$

$r - rdt = d$

$r = d + rdt$

$r = d(1 + rt)$

$d = \dfrac{r}{1 + rt}$

37. $r = \dfrac{2ml}{B(n+1)}$

Multiplying both sides by $n + 1$ gives

$r(n+1) = \dfrac{2ml}{B}$

$n + 1 = \dfrac{2ml}{rB}$

$n = \dfrac{2ml}{rB} - 1$

39. $y = \dfrac{10x}{1 + 0.1x}$

With $y = 50$ the equation is $50 = \dfrac{10x}{1 + 0.1x}$.

Multiplying both sides by $1 + 0.1x$ gives

$50(1 + 0.1x) = 10x$

$50 + 5x = 10x$

$50 = 5x$

$x = 10$

The prey density should be 10.

41. $t = \dfrac{d}{r - c}$

$t(r - c) = d$

$tr - tc = d$

$tr = d + tc$

$r = \dfrac{d + tc}{t} = \dfrac{d}{t} + c$

43. Let $x =$ Jill's height above the surface of Earth. Jill can see $0.85\sqrt{x}$ miles to the horizon. Jack's height above the surface of Earth is $x + 85$, and he can see $0.85\sqrt{x + 85}$ miles.

$0.85\sqrt{x + 85} = 0.85\sqrt{x} + 4.25$

$\sqrt{x + 85} = \sqrt{x} + 5$

$x + 85 = \left(\sqrt{x} + 5\right)^2$

$x + 85 = x + 10\sqrt{x} + 25$

$60 = 10\sqrt{x}$

$6 = \sqrt{x}$

$36 = x$

Jill is 36 feet above the surface, Jack is $36 + 85 = 121$ feet above the surface.

Principles in Practice 1.3

1. Let $x =$ the number.

$x^2 = x + 30$

$x^2 - x - 30 = 0$

$(x - 6)(x + 5) = 0$

$x - 6 = 0 \qquad$ or $\quad x + 5$

$x = 6 \qquad\qquad$ or $\quad x = -5$

The number is -5 or 6.

2. Let $l =$ the length of the mural. The width is $l - 10$.

$l(l - 10) = 3000$

$l^2 - 10l = 3000$

$l^2 - 10l - 3000 = 0$

$(l - 60)(l + 50) = 0$

$$l - 60 = 0 \qquad \text{or} \quad l + 50 = 0$$
$$l = 60 \qquad \text{or} \quad l = -50$$
Since a length cannot be negative, $l = 60$ and the width is $60 - 10 = 50$.
The dimensions are 50 feet by 60 feet.

3. Let $w =$ the width of the prism. Then the height is $5w$ and its volume is
$$w \cdot w(5w) = 5w^3.$$
$$5w^3 = 5w$$
$$w^3 = w$$
$$w^3 - w = 0$$
$$w(w^2 - 1) = 0$$
$$w(w + 1)(w - 1) = 0$$
$$w = 0 \quad \text{or} \quad w + 1 = 0 \quad \text{or} \quad w - 1 = 0$$
$$w = 0 \quad \text{or} \quad w = -1 \qquad \text{or} \quad w = 1$$
Since the width must be positive, $w = 1$. The dimensions are 1 by 1 by 5.

4. $x^2 = 225$
$$x^2 - 225 = 0$$
$$(x - 15)(x + 15) = 0$$
$$x - 15 = 0 \qquad \text{or} \quad x + 15 = 0$$
$$x = 15 \qquad \text{or} \quad x = -15$$
Since you cannot sell a negative number of items, $x = 15$. You sold 15 items for \$15 each.

5. $h = 160t - 16t^2$
$$300 = 160t - 16t^2$$
$$16t^2 - 160t + 300 = 0$$
$$4t^2 - 40t + 75 = 0$$
$$t = \frac{40 \pm \sqrt{(-40)^2 - 4(4)(75)}}{2(4)}$$
$$= \frac{40 \pm \sqrt{1600 - 1200}}{8}$$
$$= \frac{40 \pm \sqrt{400}}{8}$$
$$= \frac{40 \pm 20}{8}$$
$$t = \frac{40 + 20}{8} = \frac{15}{2} \quad \text{or} \quad t = \frac{40 - 20}{8} = \frac{5}{2}$$
The fireworks will be 300 feet off the ground when $t = \dfrac{5}{2}$ s and when $t = \dfrac{15}{2}$ s.

6. $20,000 = -2p^2 + 400p$
$$2p^2 - 400p + 20,000 = 0$$
$$p^2 - 200p + 10,000 = 0$$
$$p = \frac{200 \pm \sqrt{(-200)^2 - 4(1)(10,000)}}{2(1)}$$
$$= \frac{200 \pm \sqrt{0}}{2}$$
$$= 100$$
The price is \$100.

7. $500 = 160t - 16t^2$
$$16t^2 - 160t + 500 = 0$$
$$4t^2 - 40t + 125 = 0$$
$$t = \frac{40 \pm \sqrt{(-40)^2 - 4(4)(125)}}{2(4)}$$
$$= \frac{40 \pm \sqrt{-400}}{8}$$
Since no real number exists whose square is -400, the equation has no real roots.
The fireworks are never 500 feet off the ground.

Exercise 1.3

1. $x^2 - 4x + 4 = 0$
$$(x - 2)^2 = 0$$
$$x - 2 = 0$$
$$x = 2$$

3. $(y - 4)(y - 3) = 0$
$$y - 4 = 0 \qquad \text{or} \quad y - 3 = 0$$
$$y = 4 \qquad \text{or} \quad y = 3$$

5. $(x - 3)(x + 1) = 0$
$$x - 3 = 0 \qquad \text{or} \quad x + 1 = 0$$
$$x = 3 \qquad \text{or} \quad x = -1$$

7. $x^2 - 12x + 36 = 0$
$$(x - 6)^2 = 0$$
$$x - 6 = 0$$
$$x = 6$$

9. $(x - 2)(x + 2) = 0$
$$x - 2 = 0 \qquad \text{or} \quad x + 2 = 0$$
$$x = 2 \qquad \text{or} \quad x = -2$$

11. $z^2 - 8z = 0$
$z(z-8) = 0$
$z = 0$ or $z - 8 = 0$
$z = 0$ or $z = 8$

13. $4x^2 + 1 = 4x$
$4x^2 - 4x + 1 = 0$
$(2x-1)^2 = 0$
$2x - 1 = 0$
$2x = 1$
$x = \dfrac{1}{2}$

15. $y(2y+3) = 5$
$2y^2 + 3y - 5 = 0$
$(y-1)(2y+5) = 0$
$y - 1 = 0$ or $2y + 5 = 0$
$y = 1$ or $y = -\dfrac{5}{2}$

17. $-x^2 + 3x + 10 = 0$
$x^2 - 3x - 10 = 0$
$(x-5)(x+2) = 0$
$x - 5 = 0$ or $x + 2 = 0$
$x = 5$ or $x = -2$

19. $2p^2 - 3p = 0$
$p(2p-3) = 0$
$p = 0$ or $2p - 3 = 0$
$p = 0$ or $p = \dfrac{3}{2}$

21. $x(x-1)(x+2) = 0$
$x = 0$ or $x - 1 = 0$ or $x + 2 = 0$
$x = 0$ or $x = 1$ or $x = -2$

23. $x(x^2 - 64) = 0$
$x(x-8)(x+8) = 0$
$x = 0$ or $x - 8 = 0$ or $x + 8 = 0$
$x = 0$ or $x = 8$ or $x = -8$

25. $6x^3 + 5x^2 - 4x = 0$
$x(6x^2 + 5x - 4) = 0$
$x(2x-1)(3x+4) = 0$

$x = 0$ or $2x - 1 = 0$ or $3x + 4 = 0$
$x = 0$ or $x = \dfrac{1}{2}$ or $x = -\dfrac{4}{3}$

27. $(x+3)(x+1)(x-2) = 0$
$x + 3 = 0$ or $x + 1 = 0$ or $x - 2 = 0$
$x = -3$ or $x = -1$ or $x = 2$

29. $p(p-3)^2 - 4(p-3)^3 = 0$
Factoring out $(p-3)^2$ gives
$(p-3)^2[p - 4(p-3)] = 0$
$(p-3)^2(12 - 3p) = 0$
$3(p-3)^2(4-p) = 0$
$p - 3 = 0$ or $4 - p = 0$
$p = 3$ or $p = 4$

31. $x^2 + 2x - 24 = 0$
$a = 1, \, b = 2, \, c = -24$
$x = \dfrac{-b \pm \sqrt{b^2 - 4ac}}{2a}$
$= \dfrac{-2 \pm \sqrt{4 - 4(1)(-24)}}{2(1)}$
$= \dfrac{-2 \pm \sqrt{100}}{2}$
$= \dfrac{-2 \pm 10}{2}$
$x = \dfrac{-2 + 10}{2} = 4$ or $x = \dfrac{-2 - 10}{2} = -6$

33. $4x^2 - 12x + 9 = 0$
$a = 4, \, b = -12, \, c = 9$
$x = \dfrac{-b \pm \sqrt{b^2 - 4ac}}{2a}$
$= \dfrac{-(-12) \pm \sqrt{144 - 4(4)(9)}}{2(4)}$
$= \dfrac{12 \pm \sqrt{0}}{8}$
$= \dfrac{12 \pm 0}{8}$
$= \dfrac{3}{2}$

35. $p^2 - 5p + 3 = 0$

$a = 1, \, b = -5, \, c = 3$

$$p = \frac{-b \pm \sqrt{b^2 - 4ac}}{2a}$$

$$= \frac{-(-5) \pm \sqrt{25 - 4(1)(3)}}{2(1)}$$

$$= \frac{5 \pm \sqrt{13}}{2}$$

$$p = \frac{5 + \sqrt{13}}{2} \qquad \text{or} \qquad p = \frac{5 - \sqrt{13}}{2}$$

37. $4 - 2n + n^2 = 0$

$n^2 - 2n + 4 = 0$

$a = 1, \, b = -2, \, c = 4$

$$n = \frac{-b \pm \sqrt{b^2 - 4ac}}{2a}$$

$$= \frac{-(-2) \pm \sqrt{4 - 4(1)(4)}}{2(1)}$$

$$= \frac{2 \pm \sqrt{-12}}{2}$$

no real roots

39. $6x^2 + 7x - 5 = 0$

$a = 6, \, b = 7, \, c = -5$

$$x = \frac{-b \pm \sqrt{b^2 - 4ac}}{2a}$$

$$= \frac{-7 \pm \sqrt{49 - 4(6)(-5)}}{2(6)}$$

$$= \frac{-7 \pm \sqrt{169}}{12}$$

$$= \frac{-7 \pm 13}{12}$$

$$x = \frac{-7 + 13}{12} = \frac{1}{2} \text{ or } x = \frac{-7 - 13}{12} = -\frac{5}{3}$$

41. $2x^2 - 3x = 20$

$2x^2 - 3x - 20 = 0$

$a = 2, \, b = -3, \, c = -20$

$$x = \frac{-b \pm \sqrt{b^2 - 4ac}}{2a}$$

$$= \frac{-(-3) \pm \sqrt{9 - 4(2)(-20)}}{2(2)}$$

$$= \frac{3 \pm \sqrt{169}}{4}$$

$$= \frac{3 \pm 13}{4}$$

$$x = \frac{3 + 13}{4} = \frac{16}{4} = 4 \text{ or}$$

$$x = \frac{3 - 13}{4} = \frac{-10}{4} = -\frac{5}{2}$$

43. $2x^2 + 4x - 5 = 0$

$a = 2, \, b = 4, \, c = -5$

$$x = \frac{-b \pm \sqrt{b^2 - 4ac}}{2a}$$

$$= \frac{-4 \pm \sqrt{16 - 4(2)(-5)}}{2(2)}$$

$$= \frac{-4 \pm \sqrt{56}}{4}$$

$$= \frac{-4 \pm 2\sqrt{14}}{4}$$

$$= \frac{-2 \pm \sqrt{14}}{2}$$

$$x = \frac{-2 + \sqrt{14}}{2} \text{ or } x = \frac{-2 - \sqrt{14}}{2}$$

45. $(x^2)^2 - 5(x^2) + 6 = 0$

Let $w = x^2$. Then

$w^2 - 5w + 6 = 0$

$(w - 3)(w - 2) = 0$

Thus, $w = 3, 2$.

Hence $x^2 = 3$ or $x^2 = 2$, so

$x = \pm\sqrt{3}, \, \pm\sqrt{2}$.

47. $2\left(\dfrac{1}{x}\right)^2 + 3\left(\dfrac{1}{x}\right) - 2 = 0$

Let $w = \dfrac{1}{x}$. Then

$2w^2 + 3w - 2 = 0$

$(2w - 1)(w + 2) = 0,$

so $w = \dfrac{1}{2}, -2$. Thus, $x = 2, -\dfrac{1}{2}$.

49. $(x^{-2})^2 - 9(x^{-2}) + 14 = 0$

Set $w = x^{-2}$.

$w^2 - 9w + 14 = 0$

$(w - 7)(w - 2) = 0,$

$w = 7, 2$

Thus, $\dfrac{1}{x^2} = 7$ or $\dfrac{1}{x^2} = 2$, so $x^2 = \dfrac{1}{7}$ or

$x^2 = \dfrac{1}{2}$. $x = \pm\dfrac{\sqrt{7}}{7}, \pm\dfrac{\sqrt{2}}{2}$.

51. $(x - 3)^2 + 9(x - 3) + 14 = 0$

Let $w = x - 3$. Then

$w^2 + 9w + 14 = 0$

$(w + 7)(w + 2) = 0$

$w = -7, -2$

If $x - 3 = -7$, then $x = -4$, and if $x - 3 = -2$,

then $x = 1$. Thus, $x = -4, 1$.

53. If $w = \dfrac{1}{x - 2}$, then

$w^2 - 12w + 35 = 0$

$(w - 7)(w - 5) = 0$

$w = 7, 5$

Thus, $\dfrac{1}{x - 2} = 7$ or $\dfrac{1}{x - 2} = 5$.

$x = \dfrac{15}{7}, \dfrac{11}{5}$.

55. $x^2 = \dfrac{x + 3}{2}$

$2x^2 = x + 3$

$2x^2 - x - 3 = 0$

$(2x - 3)(x + 1) = 0$

$2x - 3 = 0 \qquad\qquad$ or $\quad x + 1 = 0$

$x = \dfrac{3}{2} \qquad\qquad\quad$ or $\quad x = -1$

57. $\dfrac{3}{x - 4} + \dfrac{x - 3}{x} = 2$

Multiplying both sides by the LCD, $x(x - 4)$,
gives

$3x + (x - 3)(x - 4) = 2x(x - 4)$

$3x + x^2 - 7x + 12 = 2x^2 - 8x$

$x^2 - 4x + 12 = 2x^2 - 8x$

$0 = x^2 - 4x - 12$

$0 = (x - 6)(x + 2)$

Thus, $x = 6, -2$.

59. $\dfrac{6x + 7}{2x + 1} - \dfrac{6x + 1}{2x} = 1$

Multiplying both sides by the LCD,
$2x(2x + 1)$, gives

$2x(6x + 7) - (2x + 1)(6x + 1) = 1(2x)(2x + 1)$

$12x^2 + 14x - (12x^2 + 8x + 1) = 4x^2 + 2x$

$6x - 1 = 4x^2 + 2x$

$0 = 4x^2 - 4x + 1$

$0 = (2x - 1)^2$

$2x - 1 = 0$

$2x = 1$

$x = \dfrac{1}{2}$

61. $\dfrac{2}{r - 2} - \dfrac{r + 1}{r + 4} = 0$

Multiplying both sides by the LCD,
$(r - 2)(r + 4)$, gives

$2(r + 4) - (r - 2)(r + 1) = 0$

$2r + 8 - (r^2 - r - 2) = 0$

$-r^2 + 3r + 10 = 0$

$r^2 - 3r - 10 = 0$

$(r - 5)(r + 2) = 0$

Thus, $r = 5, -2$.

63. $\dfrac{y + 1}{y + 3} + \dfrac{y + 5}{y - 2} = \dfrac{14y + 7}{(y + 3)(y - 2)}$

Multiplying both sides by the LCD,
$(y + 3)(y - 2)$, gives

$(y + 1)(y - 2) + (y + 5)(y + 3) = 14y + 7$

$y^2 - y - 2 + y^2 + 8y + 15 = 14y + 7$

$2y^2 + 7y + 13 = 14y + 7$

$2y^2 - 7y + 6 = 0$

$(2y - 3)(y - 2) = 0$

$y = \dfrac{3}{2}$ or $y = 2$

But $y = 2$ does not check. The solution is

$y = \dfrac{3}{2}$.

65. $\dfrac{2}{x^2 - 1} - \dfrac{1}{x(x-1)} = \dfrac{2}{x^2}$

Multiplying both sides by the LCD,
$x^2(x+1)(x-1)$, gives

$2x^2 - x(x+1) = 2(x+1)(x-1)$

$2x^2 - x^2 - x = 2x^2 - 2$

$x^2 - x = 2x^2 - 2$

$0 = x^2 + x - 2 = (x+2)(x-1)$

$x = -2$ or $x = 1$

But $x = 1$ does not check. The solution is -2.

67. $\left(\sqrt{x+2}\right)^2 = (x-4)^2$

$x + 2 = x^2 - 8x + 16$

$0 = x^2 - 9x + 14$

$0 = (x-7)(x-2)$

$x = 7$ or $x = 2$

69. $(q+2)^2 = \left(2\sqrt{4q-7}\right)^2$

$q^2 + 4q + 4 = 16q - 28$

$q^2 - 12q + 32 = 0$

$(q-4)(q-8) = 0$

Thus, $q = 4, 8$.

71. $\sqrt{x+7} = 1 + \sqrt{2x}$

$\left(\sqrt{x+7}\right)^2 = \left(1 + \sqrt{2x}\right)^2$

$x + 7 = 1 + 2\sqrt{2x} + 2x$

$6 - x = 2\sqrt{2x}$

Squaring both sides again gives

$(6-x)^2 = 4(2x)$

$36 - 12x + x^2 = 8x$

$x^2 - 20x + 36 = 0$

$(x-18)(x-2) = 0$

$x = 18$ or $x = 2$

Only $x = 2$ checks.

73. $\sqrt{x} + 1 = \sqrt{2x+1}$

$\left(\sqrt{x} + 1\right)^2 = \left(\sqrt{2x+1}\right)^2$

$x + 2\sqrt{x} + 1 = 2x + 1$

$2\sqrt{x} = x$

$\left(2\sqrt{x}\right)^2 = x^2$

$4x = x^2$

$0 = x^2 - 4x$

$0 = x(x-4)$

Thus, $x = 0, 4$.

75. $\sqrt{x+5} + 1 = 2\sqrt{x}$

$\left(\sqrt{x+5} + 1\right)^2 = \left(2\sqrt{x}\right)^2$

$x + 5 + 2\sqrt{x+5} + 1 = 4x$

$2\sqrt{x+5} = 3x - 6$

$\left(2\sqrt{x+5}\right)^2 = (3x-6)^2$

$4(x+5) = 9x^2 - 36x + 36$

$0 = 9x^2 - 40x + 16$

$0 = (9x-4)(x-4)$

$x = \dfrac{4}{9}$ or $x = 4$

Only $x = 4$ checks.

77. $x = \dfrac{-(-4.7) \pm \sqrt{(-4.7)^2 - 4(0.02)(8.6)}}{2(0.02)}$

≈ 233.16 or 1.84

79. Let $l =$ the length of the picture, then its width is $l - 2$.

$l(l-2) = 48$

$l^2 - 2l - 48 = 0$

$(l-8)(l+6) = 0$

$l - 8 = 0$ or $l + 6 = 0$

$l = 8$ or $l = -6$

Since length cannot be negative, $l = 8$. The width of the picture is

$l - 2 = 8 - 2 = 6$ inches.

The dimensions of the picture are 6 inches by 8 inches.

81. $\overline{M} = \dfrac{Q(Q+10)}{44}$

$44\overline{M} = Q^2 + 10Q$

$0 = Q^2 + 10Q - 44\overline{M}$

From the quadratic formula with $a = 1$,
$b = 10$, $c = -44\overline{M}$,

$Q = \dfrac{-10 \pm \sqrt{100 - 4(1)(-44\overline{M})}}{2(1)}$

$= \dfrac{-10 + 2\sqrt{25 + 44\overline{M}}}{2}$

$= -5 \pm \sqrt{25 + 44\overline{M}}$

Thus, $-5 + \sqrt{25 + 44\overline{M}}$ is a root.

83. $\dfrac{A}{A+12}d = \dfrac{A+1}{24}d.$

Dividing both sides by d and then
multiplying both sides by $24(A + 12)$ gives
$24A = (A + 12)(A + 1)$

$24A = A^2 + 13A + 12$

$0 = A^2 - 11A + 12$

From the quadratic formula,

$A = \dfrac{11 \pm \sqrt{121 - 48}}{2} = \dfrac{11 \pm \sqrt{73}}{2}.$

$A = \dfrac{11 + \sqrt{73}}{2} \approx 10$ or $A = \dfrac{11 - \sqrt{73}}{2} \approx 1.$

The doses are the same at 1 year and 10
years.

85. $\dfrac{1}{p} + \dfrac{1}{120 - p} = \dfrac{1}{24}$

Multiplying both sides by $24p(120 - p)$
gives
$24(120 - p) + 24p = p(120 - p)$

$2880 - 24p + 24p = 120p - p^2$

$p^2 - 120p + 2880 = 0$

By the quadratic formula,

$p = \dfrac{-(-120) \pm \sqrt{(-120)^2 - 4(1)(2880)}}{2}$

$= \dfrac{120 \pm \sqrt{2880}}{2}$

≈ 86.8 cm or 33.2 cm

87. a. When the object strikes the ground, h
must be 0, so
$0 = 44.1t - 4.9t^2 = t(44.1 - 4.9t)$
$t = 0$ or $t = 9$
The object will strike the ground 9 s
after being thrown.

b. Setting $h = 88.2$ gives
$88.2 = 44.1t - 4.9t^2$
$4.9t^2 - 44.1t + 88.2 = 0$

$t = \dfrac{44.1 \pm \sqrt{(-44.1)^2 - 4(4.9)(88.2)}}{2(4.9)}$

$= \dfrac{44.1 \pm 14.7}{9.8}$

$t = 3$ s or $t = 6$ s

89. By a program, roots are 1.5 and 0.75.
Algebraically:
$8x^2 - 18x + 9 = 0$
$(2x - 3)(4x - 3) = 0$
Thus, $2x - 3 = 0$ or $4x - 3 = 0$.

So $x = \dfrac{3}{2} = 1.5$ or $x = \dfrac{3}{4} = 0.75$.

91. No real root

93. $(\pi t - 4)^2 = 4.1t - 3$
$\pi^2 t^2 - 8\pi t + 16 = 4.1t - 3$
$\pi^2 t^2 + (-8\pi - 4.1)t + 19 = 0$
Roots: 1.999, 0.963

Chapter 1 Review Problems

1. $4 - 3x = 2 + 5x$
$2 = 8x$
$x = \dfrac{2}{8} = \dfrac{1}{4}$

3. $3[2 - 4(1 + x)] = 5 - 3(3 - x)$
$3[2 - 4 - 4x] = 5 - 9 + 3x$
$-6 - 12x = -4 + 3x$
$-2 = 15x$
$x = -\dfrac{2}{15}$

5. $2 - w = 3 + w$

$-2w = 1$

$w = -\dfrac{1}{2}$

7. $x = 2x - (7 + x)$

$x = x - 7$

$0 = -7$

No solution

9. $2\left(4 - \dfrac{3}{5}p\right) = 5$

$8 - \dfrac{6}{5}p = 5$

$-\dfrac{6}{5}p = -3$

$-6p = -15$

$p = \dfrac{5}{2}$

11. $\dfrac{3x-1}{x+4} = 0$

$3x - 1 = 0$

$3x = 1$

$x = \dfrac{1}{3}$

13. $\dfrac{2x}{x-3} - \dfrac{x+1}{x+2} = 1$

Multiplying both sides by the LCD,
$(x-3)(x+2)$, gives

$(x-3)(x+2)\left[\dfrac{2x}{x-3} - \dfrac{x+1}{x+2}\right] = (x-3)(x+2)[1]$

$2x(x+2) - (x-3)(x+1) = (x-3)(x+2)$

$2x^2 + 4x - (x^2 - 2x - 3) = x^2 - x - 6$

$2x^2 + 4x - x^2 + 2x + 3 = x^2 - x - 6$

$x^2 + 6x + 3 = x^2 - x - 6$

$7x = -9$

$x = -\dfrac{9}{7}$

15. $(3x + 5)(x - 1) = 0$

$3x + 5 = 0$ or $x - 1 = 0$

$x = -\dfrac{5}{3}$ or $x = 1$

17. $5q^2 = 7q$

$5q^2 - 7q = 0$

$q(5q - 7) = 0$

$q = 0$ or $5q - 7 = 0$

$q = 0$ or $q = \dfrac{7}{5}$

19. $(x - 5)^2 = 0$

$x - 5 = 0$

$x = 5$

21. $3x^2 - 5 = 0$

$3x^2 = 5$

$x^2 = \dfrac{5}{3}$

$x = \pm\sqrt{\dfrac{5}{3}} = \pm\dfrac{\sqrt{15}}{3}$

23. $(8t - 5)(2t + 6) = 0$

$8t - 5 = 0$ or $2t + 6 = 0$

$t = \dfrac{5}{8}$ or $t = -3$

25. $-3x^2 + 5x - 1 = 0$

$3x^2 - 5x + 1 = 0$

Using the quadratic formula with $a = 3$,
$b = -5$ and $c = 1$ gives

$x = \dfrac{-b \pm \sqrt{b^2 - 4ac}}{2a}$

$= \dfrac{-(-5) \pm \sqrt{25 - 4(3)(1)}}{2(3)}$

$= \dfrac{5 \pm \sqrt{13}}{6}$

27. $x(x^2 - 9) - 4(x^2 - 9) = 0$

$(x^2 - 9)(x - 4) = 0$

$(x + 3)(x - 3)(x - 4) = 0$

Setting each factor equal to 0 gives

$x = \pm 3, 4.$

29. $\dfrac{6w+7}{2w+1} - \dfrac{6w+1}{2w} = 1$

Multiplying both sides by the LCD,
$(2w + 1)(2w)$, gives

$2w(6w + 7) - (2w + 1)(6w + 1)$
$\qquad = (2w + 1)(2w)$
$12w^2 + 14w - (12w^2 + 8w + 1) = 4w^2 + 2w$
$6w - 1 = 4w^2 + 2w$
$0 = 4w^2 - 4w + 1$
$0 = (2w - 1)^2$
$2w - 1 = 0$
$2w = 1$
$w = \dfrac{1}{2}$

31. Multiplying both sides by the LCD, $(x + 3)(x - 3)$, gives
$2 - 3x(x - 3) = 1(x + 3)$
$2 - 3x^2 + 9x = x + 3$
$0 = 3x^2 - 8x + 1$
$x = \dfrac{-b \pm \sqrt{b^2 - 4ac}}{2a} = \dfrac{-(-8) \pm \sqrt{64 - 4(3)(1)}}{2(3)}$
$= \dfrac{8 \pm \sqrt{52}}{6} = \dfrac{8 \pm 2\sqrt{13}}{6} = \dfrac{4 \pm \sqrt{13}}{3}$

33. $\sqrt{2x + 5} = 5$
$\left(\sqrt{2x + 5}\right)^2 = 5^2$
$2x + 5 = 25$
$2x = 20$
$x = 10$

35. $\left(\sqrt[3]{11x + 9}\right)^3 = 4^3$
$11x + 9 = 64$
$11x = 55$
$x = 5$

37. $\sqrt{y} + 6 = 5$

$\sqrt{y} = -1$, which has no solution because the square root of a real number cannot be negative.

39. $\left(\sqrt{x - 1}\right)^2 = \left(7 - \sqrt{x + 6}\right)^2$
$x - 1 = 49 - 14\sqrt{x + 6} + x + 6$
$14\sqrt{x + 6} = 56$
$\sqrt{x + 6} = 4$
$x + 6 = 16$
$x = 10$

41. $x + 2 = 2\sqrt{4x - 7}$
$(x + 2)^2 = \left(2\sqrt{4x - 7}\right)^2$
$x^2 + 4x + 4 = 4(4x - 7)$
$x^2 + 4x + 4 = 16x - 28$
$x^2 - 12x + 32 = 0$
$(x - 4)(x - 8) = 0$
$x = 4 \text{ or } x = 8$

43. Set $w = y^{1/3}$.
$w^2 + w - 2 = 0$
$(w + 2)(w - 1) = 0$
$w = -2 \text{ or } w = 1$
Thus, $y^{1/3} = -2 \text{ or } y^{1/3} = 1$
$\qquad y = -8 \quad \text{ or } \quad y = 1$

45. $E = \dfrac{4\pi kQ}{A}$
$EA = (4\pi k)Q$
$Q = \dfrac{EA}{4\pi k}$

47. $n - 1 = C + \dfrac{C'}{\lambda^2}$
$n - 1 - C = \dfrac{C'}{\lambda^2}$
$C' = \lambda^2(n - 1 - C)$

49. $T^2 = 4\pi^2\left(\dfrac{L}{g}\right)$
$T = \pm\sqrt{4\pi^2\left(\dfrac{L}{g}\right)} = \pm 2\pi\sqrt{\dfrac{L}{g}}$

51. $mgh = \dfrac{1}{2}mv^2 + \dfrac{1}{2}I\omega^2$
$2mgh = mv^2 + I\omega^2$
$mgh - mv^2 = I\omega^2$
$\omega^2 = \dfrac{2mgh - mv^2}{I}$
$\omega = \pm\sqrt{\dfrac{2mgh - mv^2}{I}}$

53. $S^2 + \dfrac{R}{L}S + \dfrac{1}{LC} = 0$

By the quadratic formula,

$$S = \frac{-\left(\frac{R}{L}\right) \pm \sqrt{\left(\frac{R}{L}\right)^2 - 4(1)\left[\frac{1}{(LC)}\right]}}{2(1)}$$

$$= -\frac{R}{2L} \pm \frac{\sqrt{\left(\frac{R}{L}\right)^2 - \frac{4}{LC}}}{2}$$

Introducing the denominator 2 into the radical gives

$$S = -\frac{R}{2L} \pm \sqrt{\frac{\left(\frac{R}{L}\right)^2 - \frac{4}{LC}}{4}}.$$

$$= -\frac{R}{2L} \pm \sqrt{\left(\frac{R}{2L}\right)^2 - \frac{1}{LC}}$$

55. $6, \dfrac{5}{4}$

57. $4.6 - 7.2x - 19.3x^2$
$a = -19.3,\ b = -7.2,\ c = 4.6$
Roots: $-0.709,\ 0.336$

Mathematical Snapshot Chapter 1

1. a. $\$100 + \$100(0.114) = \$111.40$

   b. $\$1 + \$1(0.135) \approx \$1.14$

   c. $\$100 \cdot \dfrac{1\ \text{lb}}{\$1} = 100\ \text{lb}$

   d. $\$111.40 \cdot \dfrac{1\ \text{lb}}{\$1.135} \approx 98.15\ \text{lb}$

   e. $g = \dfrac{98.15 - 100}{100} = -0.0185 = -1.85\%$
   (a loss of 1.85%)

   f. $g = \dfrac{y - i}{1 + i} = \dfrac{0.114 - 0.135}{1 + 0.135} \approx -0.0185$
   $= -1.85\%$

Chapter 2

Exercise 2.1

1. Let w be the width and $2w$ be the length of the plot.

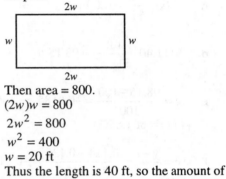

Then area = 800.

$$(2w)w = 800$$
$$2w^2 = 800$$
$$w^2 = 400$$
$$w = 20 \text{ ft}$$

Thus the length is 40 ft, so the amount of fencing needed is $2(40) + 2(20) = 120$ ft.

3. Let n = number of ounces in each part. Then we have

$$3n + 5n = 128$$
$$8n = 128$$
$$n = 16$$

Thus there should be $3(16) = 48$ ounces of A and $5(16) = 80$ ounces of B.

5. Let n = number of ounces in each part. Then we have

$$2n + 1n = 16$$
$$3n = 16$$
$$n = \frac{16}{3}$$

Thus the turpentine needed is

$$(1)n = \frac{16}{3} = 5\frac{1}{3} \text{ ounces.}$$

7. Let w = width (in meters) of pavement. The remaining plot for flowers has dimensions $8 - 2w$ by $4 - 2w$.

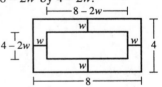

Thus

$$(8 - 2w)(4 - 2w) = 12$$
$$32 - 24w + 4w^2 = 12$$
$$4w^2 - 24w + 20 = 0$$
$$w^2 - 6w + 5 = 0$$
$$(w - 1)(w - 5) = 0$$

Hence $w = 1, 5$. But $w = 5$ is impossible since one dimension of the original plot is 4 m. Thus the width of the pavement should be 1 m.

9. Let q = number of units for \$50,000 profit.

Profit = Total Revenue – Total Cost

$$50,000 = 3q - (2.20q + 95,000)$$
$$50,000 = 0.80q - 95,000$$
$$145,000 = 0.8q$$
$$\frac{145,000}{0.8} = q$$
$$q = 181,250 \text{ units}$$

11. Let x = amount at 6% and

$$20,000 - x = \text{amount at } 7\frac{1}{2}\%.$$

$$x(0.06) + (20,000 - x)(0.075) = 1440$$
$$-0.015x + 1500 = 1440$$
$$-0.015x = -60$$
$$x = 4000, \text{ so } 20,000 - x = 16,000.$$ Thus the investment consisted of \$4000 at 6% and

\$16,000 at $7\frac{1}{2}\%$.

13. Let p = selling price. Then profit = $0.2p$.

selling price = cost + profit

$$p = 3.40 + 0.2p$$
$$0.8p = 3.40$$
$$p = \frac{3.40}{0.8} = \$4.25$$

15. Following the procedure in Example 6 we obtain

$$2,000,000(1 + r)^2 = 2,163,200$$
$$(1 + r)^2 = \frac{676}{625}$$
$$(1 + r) = \pm\frac{26}{25}$$

$$r = -1 \pm \frac{26}{25}$$

We choose $r = \frac{1}{25} = 0.04 = 4\%$.

17. Let n = number of room applications sent out.
$$0.95n = 76$$
$$n = \frac{76}{0.95} = 80$$

19. Let s = monthly salary of deputy sheriff.
$$0.30s = 200$$
$$s = \frac{200}{0.30}$$
Yearly salary $= 12s = 12\left(\frac{200}{0.30}\right) = \$8000$

21. Let q = number of cartridges sold to break even.
total revenue = total cost
$$19.95q = 14.95q + 8000$$
$$5q = 8000$$
$$q = 1600$$

23. Let v = total annual vision-care expenses (in dollars) covered by program. Then
$$35 + 0.80(v - 35) = 100$$
$$0.80v + 7 = 100$$
$$0.80v = 93$$
$$v = \$116.25$$

25. Revenue
= (number of units sold)(price per unit)
Thus
$$400 = q\left[\frac{80 - q}{4}\right]$$
$$1600 = 80q - q^2$$
$$q^2 - 80q + 1600 = 0$$
$$(q - 40)^2 = 0$$
$$q = 40 \text{ units}$$

27. Let q = required number of units. We equate incomes under both proposals.
$$2000 + 0.50q = 25,000$$
$$0.50q = 23,000$$
$$q = 46,000 \text{ units}$$

29. Let n = number of $20 increases. Then at the rental charge of $400 + 20n$ dollars per unit, the number of units that can be rented is $50 - 2n$. The total of all monthly rents is $(400 + 20n)(50 - 2n)$, which must equal 20,240.
$$20,240 = (400 + 20n)(50 - 2n)$$
$$20,240 = 20,000 + 200n - 40n^2$$
$$40n^2 - 200n + 240 = 0$$
$$n^2 - 5n + 6 = 0$$
$$(n - 2)(n - 3) = 0$$
$$n = 2, 3$$
Thus the rent should be either
$400 + 2(\$20) = \$440$ or $400 + 3(\$20) = \$460$.

31. $$10,000 = 800p - 7p^2$$
$$7p^2 - 800p + 10,000 = 0$$
$$p = \frac{800 \pm \sqrt{640,000 - 280,000}}{14}$$
$$= \frac{800 \pm \sqrt{360,000}}{14} = \frac{800 \pm 600}{14}$$
For $p > 50$ we choose
$$p = \frac{(800 + 600)}{14} = \$100.$$

33. To have supply = demand,
$$2p - 8 = 300 - 2p$$
$$4p = 308$$
$$p = 77$$

35. Let w = width (in ft) of enclosed area. Then length of enclosed area is
$$300 - w - w = 300 - 2w.$$

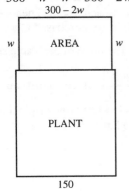

25

Thus
$$w(300 - 2w) = 11,200$$
$$2w(150 - w) = 11,200$$
$$w(150 - w) = 5600$$
$$0 = w^2 - 150w + 5600$$
$$0 = (w - 80)(w - 70)$$
Hence $w = 80, 70$. If $w = 70$, then length is $300 - 2w = 300 - 2(70) = 160$. Since building has length of only 150 ft, we reject $w = 70$. If $w = 80$, then length is $300 - 2w = 300 - 2(80) = 140$. Thus the dimensions are 80 ft by 140 ft.

37. Original volume $= (10)(5)(2) = 100 \text{ cm}^3$
Volume cut from bar $= 0.28(100) = 28 \text{ cm}^3$
Volume of new bar $= 100 - 28 = 72 \text{ cm}^3$
Let $x =$ number of centimeters that the length and width are each reduced. Then
$$(10 - x)(5 - x)2 = 72$$
$$(10 - x)(5 - x) = 36$$
$$x^2 - 15x + 50 = 36$$
$$x^2 - 15x + 14 = 0$$
$$(x - 1)(x - 14) = 0$$
$$x = 1 \text{ or } 14$$
Because of the length and width of the original bar, we reject $x = 14$ and choose $x = 1$. The new bar has length $10 - x = 10 - 1 = 9$ cm and width is $5 - x = 5 - 1 = 4$ cm.

39. Let $x =$ amount of loan. Then the funds actually received are $x - 0.15x$. Hence,
$$x - 0.15x = 95,000$$
$$0.85x = 95,000$$
$$x = \$112,000 \text{ (to the nearest thousand)}$$

41. Let $n =$ number of acres sold. Then $n + 20$ acres were originally purchased at a cost of $\dfrac{7200}{n + 20}$ each. The price of each acre sold was $30 + \left[\dfrac{7200}{n + 20}\right]$. Since the revenue from selling n acres is \$7200 (the original cost of the parcel), we have

$$n\left[30 + \frac{7200}{n + 20}\right] = 7200$$
$$n\left[\frac{30n + 600 + 7200}{n + 20}\right] = 7200$$
$$n(30n + 600 + 7200) = 7200(n + 20)$$
$$30n^2 + 7800n = 7200n + 144,000$$
$$n^2 + 20n - 4800 = 0$$
$$(n + 80)(n - 60) = 0$$
$$n = 60 \text{ acres (since } n > 0)$$

43. Let $q =$ number of units of B and $q + 25 =$ number of units of A.
Each unit of B costs $\dfrac{1000}{q}$, and each unit of A costs $\dfrac{1500}{q + 25}$. Therefore,
$$\frac{1500}{q + 25} = \frac{1000}{q} + 2$$
$$1500q = 1000(q + 25) + 2(q)(q + 25)$$
$$0 = 2q^2 - 450q + 25,000$$
$$0 = q^2 - 225q + 12,500$$
$$0 = (q - 100)(q - 125)$$
$$q = 100 \text{ or } q = 125$$
If $q = 100$, then $q + 25 = 125$; if $q = 125$, $q + 25 = 150$. Thus the company produces either 125 units of A and 100 units of B, or 150 units of A and 125 units of B.

Principles in Practice 2.2

1. $200 + 0.8S \geq 4500$
$0.8S \geq 4300$
$S \geq 5375$
He must sell at least 5375 products per month.

2. Since $x_1 \geq 0$, $x_2 \geq 0$, $x_3 \geq 0$, and $x_4 \geq 0$, we have the inequalities
$$150 - x_4 \geq 0$$
$$3x_4 - 210 \geq 0$$
$$x_4 + 60 \geq 0$$
$$x_4 \geq 0$$

Exercise 2.2

1. $3x > 12$

$x > \dfrac{12}{3}$

$x > 4$

$(4, \infty)$

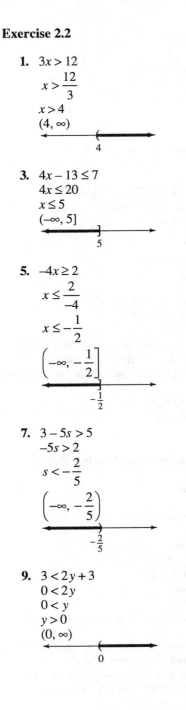

3. $4x - 13 \le 7$

$4x \le 20$

$x \le 5$

$(-\infty, 5]$

5. $-4x \ge 2$

$x \le \dfrac{2}{-4}$

$x \le -\dfrac{1}{2}$

$\left(-\infty, -\dfrac{1}{2}\right]$

7. $3 - 5s > 5$

$-5s > 2$

$s < -\dfrac{2}{5}$

$\left(-\infty, -\dfrac{2}{5}\right)$

9. $3 < 2y + 3$

$0 < 2y$

$0 < y$

$y > 0$

$(0, \infty)$

11. $2x - 3 \le 4 + 7x$

$-5x \le 7$

$x \ge -\dfrac{7}{5}$

$\left[-\dfrac{7}{5}, \infty\right)$

13. $3(2 - 3x) > 4(1 - 4x)$

$6 - 9x > 4 - 16x$

$7x > -2$

$x > -\dfrac{2}{7}$

$\left(-\dfrac{2}{7}, \infty\right)$

15. $2(3x - 2) > 3(2x - 1)$

$6x - 4 > 6x - 3$

$0 > 1$, which is false for all x. Thus the solution set is $\varnothing$.

17. $x + 2 < \sqrt{3} - x$

$2x < \sqrt{3} - 2$

$x < \dfrac{\sqrt{3} - 2}{2}$

$\left(-\infty, \dfrac{\sqrt{3} - 2}{2}\right)$

19. $\dfrac{5}{3}x < 10$

$5x < 30$

$x < 6$

$(-\infty, 6)$

21. $\dfrac{9y+1}{4} \le 2y-1$

$9y+1 \le 8y-4$

$y \le -5$

$(-\infty, -5]$

-5

23. $4x-1 \ge 4(x-2)+7$

$4x-1 \ge 4x-1$

$0 \ge 0$, which is true for all x. The solution is

$-\infty < x < \infty$.

$(-\infty, \infty)$

25. $\dfrac{1-t}{2} < \dfrac{3t-7}{3}$

$3-3t < 6t-14$

$-9t < -17$

$t > \dfrac{17}{9}$

$\left(\dfrac{17}{9}, \infty\right)$

$\dfrac{17}{9}$

27. $2x+3 \ge \dfrac{1}{2}x-4$

$4x+6 \ge x-8$

$3x \ge -14$

$x \ge -\dfrac{14}{3}$

$\left[-\dfrac{14}{3}, \infty\right)$

$-\dfrac{14}{3}$

29. $\dfrac{2}{3}r < \dfrac{5}{6}r$

$4r < 5r$

$0 < r$

$r > 0$

$(0, \infty)$

0

31. $\dfrac{y}{2}+\dfrac{y}{3} > y+\dfrac{y}{5}$

$15y+10y > 30y+6y$

$25y > 36y$

$0 > 11y$

$0 > y$

$y < 0$

$(-\infty, 0)$

0

33. $0.1(0.03x+4) \ge 0.02x+0.434$

$0.003x+0.4 \ge 0.02x+0.434$

$-0.017x \ge 0.034$

$x \le -2$

$(-\infty, -2]$

-2

35. $12(37{,}000) < S < 12(53{,}000)$

$444{,}000 < S < 636{,}000$

37. The measures of the acute angles of a right triangle sum to 90°. If x is the measure of one acute angle, the other angle has measure $90-x$.

$x < 3(90-x)+10$

$x < 270-3x+10$

$4x < 280$

$x < 70$

The measure of the angle is less than 70°.

Exercise 2.3

1. Let q = number of units sold.

Profit > 0

Total revenue − Total cost > 0

$20q-(15q+600{,}000) > 0$

$5q-600{,}000 > 0$

$5q > 600{,}000$

$q > 120{,}000$

Thus at least 120,001 units must be sold.

3. Let x = number of miles driven per year. If auto is rented, the annual cost is $12(400)+0.10x$. If auto is purchased, the annual cost is $3000+0.18x$. We want Rental cost ≤ Purchase cost.

$12(400) + 0.10x \le 3000 + 0.18x$

$4800 + 0.10x \le 3000 + 0.18x$

$1800 \le 0.08x$

$22{,}500 \le x$

The least number of miles driven per year must be 22,500.

5. Let q be the required number of magazines. Then cost of publication is $q(0.65)$. Revenue from dealers is $0.60q$ and from advertising is $0.10(q - 10{,}000)(0.60)$. Thus

Profit ≥ 0

Total Revenue – Total Cost ≥ 0

$0.60q + 0.10(q - 10{,}000)(0.60) - 0.65q \ge 0$

$0.01q - 600 \ge 0$

$0.01q \ge 600$

$q \ge 60{,}000$

At least 60,000 magazines are required.

7. Let x = amount at $6\frac{3}{4}\%$ and

$30{,}000 - x$ = amount at 5%. Then

interest at $6\frac{3}{4}\%$ + interest at 5%

$\ge$ interest at $6\frac{1}{2}\%$

$x(0.0675) + (30{,}000 - x)(0.05) \ge$
$(0.065)(30{,}000)$

$0.0175x + 1500 \ge 1950$

$0.0175x \ge 450$

$x \ge 25{,}714.29$

Thus at least \$25,714.29 must be invested at $6\frac{3}{4}\%$.

9. Let q be the number of units sold this month at \$4.00 each. Then $2500 - q$ will be sold at \$4.50 each. Then

Total revenue $\ge 10{,}750$

$4q + 4.5(2500 - q) \ge 10{,}750$

$-0.5q + 11{,}250 \ge 10{,}750$

$500 \ge 0.5q$

$1000 \ge q$

The maximum number of units that can be sold this month is 1000.

11. For $t < 40$, we want
income on hourly basis
> income on per-job basis

$8.50t > 300 + 3(40 - t)$

$8.50t > 420 - 3t$

$11.50t > 420$

$t > 36.5$ hr

13. Let c be the cost (in dollars) of a ticket.

$1000 + 0.40(800c) \le 2440$

$320c \le 1440$

$c \le 4.50$

Thus the dean could charge at most \$4.50 per ticket. With this charge, the amount left for expenses is

$800(4.50) - [1000 + 0.40(800)(4.50)]$
$= \$1160$.

Principles in Practice 2.4

1. $|w - 22| \le 0.3$

Exercise 2.4

1. $|-13| = 13$

3. $|8 - 2| = |6| = 6$

5. $\left| 3\left(-\dfrac{5}{3}\right) \right| = |-5| = 5$

7. $|x| < 3,\ -3 < x < 3$

9. Because $2 - \sqrt{5} < 0$,

   $\left| 2 - \sqrt{5} \right| = -\left(2 - \sqrt{5}\right) = \sqrt{5} - 2$.

11. **a.** $|x - 7| < 3$

    b. $|x - 2| < 3$

    c. $|x - 7| \le 5$

    d. $|x - 7| = 4$

    e. $|x + 4| < 2$

    f. $|x| < 3$

g. $|x| > 6$

h. $|x - 6| > 4$

i. $|x - 105| < 3$

j. $|x - 850| < 100$

13. $|p_1 - p_2| \le 2$

15. $|x| = 7$
$x = \pm 7$

17. $\left|\dfrac{x}{3}\right| = 2$

$\dfrac{x}{3} = \pm 2$

$x = \pm 6$

19. $|x - 5| = 8$
$x - 5 = \pm 8$
$x = 5 \pm 8$
$x = 13 \text{ or } x = -3$

21. $|5x - 2| = 0$
$5x - 2 = 0$
$x = \dfrac{2}{5}$

23. $|7 - 4x| = 5$
$7 - 4x = \pm 5$
$-4x = -7 \pm 5$
$-4x = -2 \text{ or } -12$
$x = \dfrac{1}{2} \text{ or } x = 3$

25. $|x| < 4$
$-4 < x < 4$
$(-4, 4)$

27. $\left|\dfrac{x}{4}\right| > 2$

$\dfrac{x}{4} < -2$ or $\dfrac{x}{4} > 2$

$x < -8$ or $x > 8,$
so the solution is $(-\infty, -8) \cup (8, \infty)$.

29. $|x + 7| < 2$
$-2 < x + 7 < 2$
$-9 < x < -5$
$(-9, -5)$

31. $\left|x - \dfrac{1}{2}\right| > \dfrac{1}{2}$

$x - \dfrac{1}{2} < -\dfrac{1}{2}$ or $x - \dfrac{1}{2} > \dfrac{1}{2}$

$x < 0$ or $x > 1$
$(-\infty, 0) \cup (1, \infty)$

33. $|5 - 2x| \le 1$
$-1 \le 5 - 2x \le 1$
$-6 \le -2x \le -4$
$3 \ge x \ge 2$, which may be rewritten as
$2 \le x \le 3$, or $[2, 3]$.

35. $\left|\dfrac{3x - 8}{2}\right| \ge 4$

$\dfrac{3x - 8}{2} \le -4$ or $\dfrac{3x - 8}{2} \ge 4$

$3x - 8 \le -8$ or $3x - 8 \ge 8$
$3x \le 0$ or $3x \ge 16$

$x \le 0$ or $x \ge \dfrac{16}{3}$

The solution is $(-\infty, 0] \cup \left[\dfrac{16}{3}, \infty\right)$.

37. $|d - 10| \le 1$ cm or $|d - 10| \le 0.01$ m

39. $|x - \mu| > h\sigma$
Either $x - \mu < -h\sigma$, or $x - \mu > h\sigma$. Thus
either $x < \mu - h\sigma$ or $x > \mu + h\sigma$, so the
solution is $(-\infty, \mu - h\sigma) \cup (\mu + h\sigma, \infty)$.

Chapter 2 Review Problems

1. $3x - 8 \ge 4(x - 2)$
$3x - 8 \ge 4x - 8$
$-x \ge 0$
$x \le 0$
$(-\infty, 0]$

3. $-(5x + 2) < -(2x + 4)$
$-5x - 2 < -2x - 4$
$-3x < -2$
$x > \dfrac{2}{3},$ or $\left(\dfrac{2}{3}, \infty \right)$

5. $3p(1 - p) > 3(2 + p) - 3p^2$
$3p - 3p^2 > 6 + 3p - 3p^2$
$0 > 6$, which is false for all x. The solution set is $\varnothing$.

7. Multiplying both sides by 6 gives
$2(x + 1) - 3(1) \le 6(2)$
$2x + 2 - 3 \le 12$
$2x \le 13$
$x \le \dfrac{13}{2}$
$\left(-\infty, \dfrac{13}{2} \right]$

9. Multiplying both sides by 8 gives
$2s - 24 \le 3 + 2s$
$0 \le 27$, which is true for all s. Thus
$-\infty < s < \infty$, or $(-\infty, \infty)$.

11. $|3 - 2x| = 7$
$3 - 2x = 7$ or $3 - 2x = -7$
$-2x = 4$ or $-2x = -10$
$x = -2$ or $x = 5$

13. $|4t - 1| < 1$
$-1 < 4t - 1 < 1$
$0 < 4t < 2$
$0 < t < \dfrac{1}{2}$
$\left(0, \dfrac{1}{2} \right)$

15. $|3 - 2x| \ge 4$
$3 - 2x \ge 4$ or $3 - 2x \le -4$
$-2x \ge 1$ or $-2x \le -7$
$x \le -\dfrac{1}{2}$ or $x \ge \dfrac{7}{2}$
The solution is $\left(-\infty, -\dfrac{1}{2} \right] \cup \left[\dfrac{7}{2}, \infty \right)$.

17. Let x be the number of issues with decline, and $x + 48$ be the number of issues with increase. Then
$x + (x + 48) = 1132$
$2x = 1084$
$x = 542$

19. Let q units be produced at A and $10,000 - q$ at B.
Cost at A + Cost at B $\le 117,000$
$[5q + 30,000] + [5.50(10,000 - q) + 35,000]$
$\qquad \le 117,000$
$-0.5q + 120,000 \le 117,000$
$-0.5q \le -3000$
$q \ge 6000$
Thus at least 6000 units must be produced at plant A.

Mathematical Snapshot Chapter 2

1. $t = 2l - 4 = 2\left(2\dfrac{1}{2} \right) - 4 = 1$ hour

3. $l = 2\dfrac{2}{3}$ hours. Thus
$t = \dfrac{3}{2}l - 3 = \dfrac{3}{2}\left(2\dfrac{2}{3} \right) - 3 = 1$ hour.

5. An appropriate formula for this situation is
$\dfrac{t}{4} + \dfrac{l - \frac{lc}{60} - t}{2} = 1$
$\dfrac{t}{4} + \dfrac{3 - \frac{3(8)}{60} - t}{2} = 1$
$t + 2\left(3 - \dfrac{2}{5} - t \right) = 4$
$-t + \dfrac{26}{5} = 4$
$t = \dfrac{6}{5}$ hr = 1 hr and 12 min

Chapter 3

Principles in Practice 3.1

1. a. The formula for the area of a circle is πr^2, where r is the radius.
$$a(r) = \pi r^2$$

b. The domain of $a(r)$ is all real numbers.

c. Since a radius cannot be negative or zero, the domain for the function, in context, is $r > 0$.

2. a. The formula relating distance, time, and speed is $d = rt$ where d is the distance, r is the speed, and t is the time. This can also be written as $t = \dfrac{d}{r}$. When $d = 300$, we have $t(r) = \dfrac{300}{r}$.

b. The domain of $t(r)$ is all real numbers except 0.

c. Since speed is not negative, the domain for the function, in context, is $r > 0$.

d. Replacing r by x: $t(x) = \dfrac{300}{x}$.

Replacing r by $\dfrac{x}{2}$: $t\left(\dfrac{x}{2}\right) = \dfrac{300}{\frac{x}{2}} = \dfrac{600}{x}$.

Replacing r by $\dfrac{x}{4}$:

$t\left(\dfrac{x}{4}\right) = \dfrac{300}{\frac{x}{4}} = \dfrac{1200}{x}$.

e. When the speed is reduced (divided) by a constant, the time is scaled (multiplied) by the same constant;
$$t\left(\frac{r}{c}\right) = \frac{300c}{r}.$$

3. a. If the price is \$18.50 per large pizza, $p = 18.5$.
$$18.5 = 26 - \frac{q}{40}$$
$$-7.5 = -\frac{q}{40}$$
$$300 = q$$
At a price of \$18.50 per large pizza, 300 pizzas are sold each week.

b. If 200 large pizzas are being sold each week, $q = 200$.
$$p = 26 - \frac{200}{40}$$
$$p = 26 - 5$$
$$p = 21$$
The price is \$21 per pizza if 200 large pizzas are being sold each week.

c. To double the number of large pizzas sold, use $q = 400$.
$$p = 26 - \frac{400}{40}$$
$$p = 26 - 10$$
$$p = 16$$
To sell 400 large pizzas each week, the price should be \$16 per pizza.

Exercise 3.1

1. The denominator is zero when $x = 0$. Any other real number can be used for x.
Answer: all real numbers except 0

3. For $\sqrt{x-3}$ to be real, $x - 3 \geq 0$, so $x \geq 3$.
Answer: all real numbers ≥ 3

5. Any real number can be used for t.
Answer: all real numbers

7. We exclude values of x where
    $$2x + 5 = 0$$
    $$2x = -5$$
    $$x = -\frac{5}{2}$$
    Answer: all real numbers except $-\frac{5}{2}$

9. We exclude values of y for which
    $$y^2 - y = 0$$
    $$y(y - 1) = 0$$
    $$y = 0 \text{ or } 1$$
    Answer: all real numbers except 0 and 1

11. We exclude all values of s for which
    $$2s^2 - 7s - 4 = 0$$
    $$(s - 4)(2s + 1) = 0$$
    $$s = 4, -\frac{1}{2}$$
    Answer: all real numbers except 4 and $-\frac{1}{2}$

13. $f(x) = 2x + 1$
    $f(0) = 2(0) + 1 = 1$
    $f(3) = 2(3) + 1 = 7$
    $f(-4) = 2(-4) + 1 = -7$

15. $G(x) = 2 - x^2$
    $G(-8) = 2 - (-8)^2 = 2 - 64 = -62$
    $G(u) = 2 - u^2$
    $G(u^2) = 2 - (u^2)^2 = 2 - u^4$

17. $g(u) = u^2 + u$
    $g(-2) = (-2)^2 + (-2) = 4 - 2 = 2$
    $g(2v) = (2v)^2 + (2v) = 4v^2 + 2v$
    $g(-x^2) = (-x^2)^2 + (-x^2) = x^4 - x^2$

19. $f(x) = x^2 + 2x + 1$
    $f(1) = 1^2 + 2(1) + 1 = 1 + 2 + 1 = 4$
    $f(-1) = (-1)^2 + 2(-1) + 1 = 1 - 2 + 1 = 0$
    $f(x + h) = (x + h)^2 + 2(x + h) + 1$
    $\qquad = x^2 + 2xh + h^2 + 2x + 2h + 1$

21. $g(x) = \dfrac{x - 5}{x^2 + 4}$
    $g(5) = \dfrac{5 - 5}{5^2 + 4} = 0$
    $g(3x) = \dfrac{3x - 5}{(3x)^2 + 4} = \dfrac{3x - 5}{9x^2 + 4}$
    $g(x + h) = \dfrac{(x + h) - 5}{(x + h)^2 + 4} = \dfrac{x + h - 5}{x^2 + 2xh + h^2 + 4}$

23. $f(x) = x^{4/3}$
    $f(0) = 0^{4/3} = 0$
    $f(64) = 64^{4/3} = \left(\sqrt[3]{64}\right)^4 = (4)^4 = 256$
    $f\left(\dfrac{1}{8}\right) = \left(\dfrac{1}{8}\right)^{4/3} = \left(\sqrt[3]{\dfrac{1}{8}}\right)^4 = \left(\dfrac{1}{2}\right)^4 = \dfrac{1}{16}$

25. $f(x) = 4x - 5$

    a. $f(x + h) = 4(x + h) - 5$
        $\qquad = 4x + 4h - 5$

    b. $\dfrac{f(x + h) - f(x)}{h}$
        $= \dfrac{(4x + 4h - 5) - (4x - 5)}{h}$
        $= \dfrac{4h}{h} = 4$

27. $f(x) = x^2 + 2x$

    a. $f(x + h) = (x + h)^2 + 2(x + h)$

           $= x^2 + 2xh + h^2 + 2x + 2h$

    b. $\dfrac{f(x + h) - f(x)}{h}$

        $= \dfrac{(x^2 + 2xh + h^2 + 2x + 2h) - (x^2 + 2x)}{h}$

        $= \dfrac{2xh + h^2 + 2h}{h} = 2x + h + 2$

29. $f(x) = 2 - 4x - 3x^2$

    a. $f(x + h) = 2 - 4(x + h) - 3(x + h)^2$

           $= 2 - 4x - 4h - 3(x^2 + 2xh + h^2)$

           $= 2 - 4x - 4h - 3x^2 - 6xh - 3h^2$

    b. $\dfrac{f(x + h) - f(x)}{h} = \dfrac{2 - 4x - 4h - 3x^2 - 6xh - 3h^2 - (2 - 4x - 3x^2)}{h}$

        $= \dfrac{-4h - 6xh - 3h^2}{h} = \dfrac{h(-4 - 6x - 3h)}{h} = -4 - 6x - 3h$

31. $f(x) = \dfrac{1}{x}$

    a. $f(x + h) = \dfrac{1}{x + h}$

    b. $\dfrac{f(x + h) - f(x)}{h} = \dfrac{\frac{1}{x+h} - \frac{1}{x}}{h}$

        $= \dfrac{\frac{x-(x+h)}{x(x+h)}}{h} = \dfrac{-h}{x(x+h)h} = -\dfrac{1}{x(x+h)}$

33. $f(x) = 9x + 7$

    $\dfrac{f(2 + h) - f(2)}{h} = \dfrac{9(2 + h) + 7 - [9(2) + 7]}{h}$

    $= \dfrac{25 + 9h - [25]}{h} = \dfrac{9h}{h} = 9$

35. $y - 3x - 4 = 0$

The equivalent form $y = 3x + 4$ shows that for each input x there is exactly one output, $3x - 4$. Thus y is a function of x. Solving for x gives $x = \dfrac{y - 4}{3}$. This shows that for each input y there is exactly one output, $\dfrac{y - 4}{3}$. Thus x is a function of y.

37. $y = 7x^2$

For each input x, there is exactly one output $7x^2$. Thus y is a function of x. Solving for x gives $x = \pm\sqrt{\dfrac{y}{7}}$. If, for example, $y = 7$, then $x = \pm 1$, so x is not a function of y.

39. Yes, because corresponding to each input r there is exactly one output, πr^2.

41. Weekly excess of income over expenses is $2000 - 1600 = 400$.
After t weeks the excess accumulates to $400t$. Thus the value of V of the business at the end of t weeks is given by
$V = f(t) = 10,000 + 400t$.

43. Yes; for each input q there corresponds exactly one output, $1.25q$, so P is a function of q. The dependent variable is P and the independent variable is q.

45. The function can be written as $q = 50p$. At \$8.00 per pound, the coffee house will supply $q = 50(8) = 400$ pounds per week. At \$20.00 per pound, the coffee house will supply $q = 50(20) = 1000$ pounds per week. The amount the coffee house supplies increases as the price increases.

47. a. $f(1000) = \dfrac{\left(\sqrt[3]{1000}\right)^4}{2500} = \dfrac{10^4}{2500}$
$= \dfrac{10,000}{2500} = 4$

   b. $f(2000) = \dfrac{\left[\sqrt[3]{1000(2)}\right]^4}{2500} = \dfrac{\left(10\sqrt[3]{2}\right)^4}{2500}$
$= \dfrac{10,000\sqrt[3]{2^4}}{2500} = 4\sqrt[3]{2^3 \cdot 2} = 8\sqrt[3]{2}$

   c. $f(2I_0) = \dfrac{(2I_0)^{4/3}}{2500} = \dfrac{2^{4/3} I_0^{4/3}}{2500}$
$= 2\sqrt[3]{2}\left[\dfrac{I_0^{4/3}}{2500}\right] = 2\sqrt[3]{2} f(I_0)$
Thus $f(2I_0) = 2\sqrt[3]{2} f(I_0)$, which means that doubling the intensity increases the response by a factor of $2\sqrt[3]{2}$.

49. a. Domain: 3000, 2900, 2300, 2000
$f(2900) = 12, f(3000) = 10$

   b. Domain: 10, 12, 17, 20
$g(10) = 3000, g(17) = 2300$

51. a. -5.13

   b. 2.64

   c. -17.43

53. a. 11.33

   b. 50.62

   c. 2.29

Principles in Practice 3.2

1. a. Let n = the number of visits and $p(n)$ be the premium amount.
$p(n) = 125$

   b. The premiums do not change regardless of the number of doctor visits.

   c. This is a constant function.

2. a. $d(t) = 3t^2$ is a quadratic function.

   b. The degree of $d(t) = 3t^2$ is 2.

   c. The leading coefficient of $d(t) = 3t^2$ is 3.

3. The price for n pairs of socks is given by
$$c(n) = \begin{cases} 3.5n & 0 \le n \le 5 \\ 3n & 5 < n \le 10 \\ 2.75n & 10 < n \end{cases}$$

4. Think of the bookshelf having 7 slots, from left to right. You have a choice of 7 books for the first slot. Once a book has been put in the first slot, you have 6 choices for which book to put in the second slot, etc. The number of arrangements is
$7 \cdot 6 \cdot 5 \cdot 4 \cdot 3 \cdot 2 \cdot 1 = 7! = 5040$.

Exercise 3.2

1. yes

3. no

5. yes

7. yes

9. all real numbers

11. all real numbers

13. **a.** 3

    b. 7

15. **a.** 4

    b. −3

17. $f(x) = 8$
    $f(2) = 8$
    $f(t + 8) = 8$
    $f\left(-\sqrt{17}\right) = 8$

19. $F(10) = 1$
    $F\left(-\sqrt{3}\right) = -1$
    $F(0) = 0$
    $F\left(-\dfrac{18}{5}\right) = -1$

21. $G(8) = 8$
    $G(3) = 3$
    $G(-1) = 2 - (-1) = 3$
    $G(1) = 2 - 1 = 1$

23. $6! = 6 \cdot 5 \cdot 4 \cdot 3 \cdot 2 \cdot 1 = 720$

25. $(4 - 2)! = 2! = 2 \cdot 1 = 2$

27. $\dfrac{5!}{4!} = \dfrac{5 \cdot 4 \cdot 3 \cdot 2 \cdot 1}{4 \cdot 3 \cdot 2 \cdot 1} = 5$

29. Let i = the passenger's income and
    $c(i)$ = the cost for the ticket.
    $c(i) = 3.5$
    This is a constant function.

31. **a.** $C = 850 + 3q$

    b. $1600 = 850 + 3q$
    $750 = 3q$
    $q = 250$

33. The cost for buying n tickets is
    $c(n) = \begin{cases} 7.5n & 0 \leq n < 10 \\ 7n & 10 \leq n \end{cases}$

35. $P(2) = \dfrac{3!\left(\frac{1}{4}\right)^2\left(\frac{3}{4}\right)^1}{2!(1!)} = \dfrac{6\left(\frac{1}{16}\right)\left(\frac{3}{4}\right)}{2(1)} = \dfrac{9}{64}$

37. **a.** all T such that $30 \leq T \leq 39$

    b. $f(30) = \dfrac{1}{24}(30) + \dfrac{11}{4} = \dfrac{5}{4} + \dfrac{11}{4} = \dfrac{16}{4} = 4$

    $f(36) = \dfrac{1}{24}(36) + \dfrac{11}{4} = \dfrac{6}{4} + \dfrac{11}{4} = \dfrac{17}{4}$

    $f(39) = \dfrac{4}{3}(39) - \dfrac{175}{4} = 52 - \dfrac{175}{4} = \dfrac{33}{4}$

39. **a.** 237,077.34

    b. −434.97

    c. 52.19

41. **a.** 2.21

    b. 9.98

    c. −14.52

Principles in Practice 3.3

1. The customer's price is
   $(c \circ s)(x) = c(s(x)) = c(x + 3) = 2(x + 3)$
   $= 2x + 6$

2. $g(x) = (x + 3)^2$ can be written as
   $g(x) = a(l(x)) = (a \circ l)(x)$ where $a(x) = x^2$
   and $l(x) = x + 3$. Then $l(x)$ represents the
   length of the sides of the square, while $a(x)$
   is the area of a square with side of length x.

Exercise 3.3

1. $f(x) = x + 3$, $g(x) = x + 5$

   a. $(f + g)(x) = f(x) + g(x) = (x + 3) + (x + 5)$
   $= 2x + 8$

   b. $(f + g)(0) = 2(0) + 8 = 8$

   c. $(f - g)(x) = f(x) - g(x) = (x + 3) - (x + 5)$
   $= -2$

d. $(fg)(x) = f(x)g(x) = (x+3)(x+5)$
$$= x^2 + 8x + 15$$

e. $(fg)(-2) = (-2)^2 + 8(-2) + 15 = 3$

f. $\dfrac{f}{g}(x) = \dfrac{f(x)}{g(x)} = \dfrac{x+3}{x+5}$

g. $(f \circ g)(x) = f(g(x)) = f(x+5)$
$$= (x+5) + 3$$
$$= x + 8$$

h. $(f \circ g)(3) = 3 + 8 = 11$

i. $(g \circ f)(x) = g(f(x)) = g(x+3)$
$$= (x+3) + 5$$
$$= x + 8$$

3. $f(x) = x^2$, $g(x) = x^2 + x$

a. $(f+g)(x) = f(x) + g(x)$
$$= x^2 + (x^2 + x) = 2x^2 + x$$

b. $(f-g)(x) = f(x) - g(x) = x^2 - (x^2 + x)$
$$= -x$$

c. $(f-g)\left(-\dfrac{1}{2}\right) = -\left(-\dfrac{1}{2}\right) = \dfrac{1}{2}$

d. $(fg)(x) = f(x)g(x)$
$$= x^2(x^2 + x) = x^4 + x^3$$

e. $\dfrac{f}{g}(x) = \dfrac{f(x)}{g(x)} = \dfrac{x^2}{x^2 + x}$
$$= \dfrac{x}{x+1} \text{ (for } x \neq 0)$$

f. $\dfrac{f}{g}\left(-\dfrac{1}{2}\right) = \dfrac{-\frac{1}{2}}{(-\frac{1}{2})+1} = \dfrac{-\frac{1}{2}}{\frac{1}{2}} = -1$

g. $(f \circ g)(x) = f(g(x)) = f(x^2 + x)$
$$= (x^2 + x)^2 = x^4 + 2x^3 + x^2$$

h. $(g \circ f)(x) = g(f(x)) = g(x^2)$
$$= (x^2)^2 + x^2 = x^4 + x^2$$

i. $(g \circ f)(-3) = (-3)^4 + (-3)^2$
$$= 81 + 9 = 90$$

5. $f(g(2)) = f(4-4) = f(0) = 0 + 6 = 6$
$g(f(2)) = g(12+6) = g(18) = 4 - 36 = -32$

7. $(F \circ G)(t) = F(G(t))$
$$= F\left(\left(\dfrac{2}{t-1}\right)^2 + 3\left(\dfrac{2}{t-1}\right) + 1\right)$$
$$= \dfrac{4}{(t-1)^2} + \dfrac{6}{t-1} + 1$$
$(G \circ F)(t) = G(F(t)) = G(t^2 + 3t + 1)$
$$= \dfrac{2}{(t^2 + 3t + 1) - 1} = \dfrac{2}{t^2 + 3t}$$

9. $(f \circ g)(v) = f(g(v)) = f\left(\sqrt{v+2}\right)$
$$= \dfrac{2}{\left(\sqrt{v+2}\right)^2 + 1}$$
$$= \dfrac{1}{v+2+1} = \dfrac{1}{v+3}$$
$(g \circ f)(w) = g(f(w)) = g\left(\dfrac{1}{w^2 + 1}\right)$
$$= \sqrt{\dfrac{1}{w^2 + 1} + 2}$$
$$= \sqrt{\dfrac{1 + 2(w^2 + 1)}{w^2 + 1}} = \sqrt{\dfrac{2w^2 + 3}{w^2 + 1}}$$

11. Let $g(x) = 4x - 3$ and $f(x) = x^5$. Then
$h(x) = (4x - 3)^5 = [g(x)]^5 = f(g(x))$

13. Let $g(x) = x^2 - 2$ and $f(x) = \dfrac{1}{x}$. Then
$$h(x) = \dfrac{1}{x^2 - 2} = \dfrac{1}{g(x)} = f(g(x))$$

15. Let $g(x) = \dfrac{x+1}{3}$ and $f(x) = \sqrt[5]{x}$. Then
$$h(x) = \sqrt[5]{g(x)} = f(g(x))$$

17. a. The revenue is \$9.75 per pound of coffee sold, so $r(x) = 9.75x$.

b. The expenses are $e(x) = 4500 + 4.25x$.

c. Profit = revenue − expenses.
$(r - e)(x) = 9.75x - (4500 + 4.25x)$
$= 5.5x - 4500$.

19. $(g \circ f)(m) = g(f(m)) = g\left(\dfrac{40m - m^2}{4}\right)$

$= 40\left(\dfrac{40m - m^2}{4}\right)$

$= 10(40m - m^2) = 400m - 10m^2$.

This represents the total revenue received when the total output of m employees is sold.

21. a. 1.52

b. 1747.24

23. a. 345.03

b. −1.94

Principles in Practice 3.4

1. Let y = the amount of money in the account. Then, after one month,
$y = 7250 - (1 \cdot 600) = \$6650$, and after two months $y = 7250 - (2 \cdot 600) = \$6050$. Thus, in general, if we let x = the number of months during which Rachel spends from this account,
$y = 7250 - 600x$. To identify the x-intercept, we set $y = 0$ and solve for x.
$y = 7250 - 600\ x$
$0 = 7250 - 600x$
$600x = 7250$

$x = 12\dfrac{1}{12}$

The x-intercept is $\left(12\dfrac{1}{12}, 0\right)$.

Therefore, after 12 months and approximately 2.5 days Rachel will deplete her savings. To identify the y-intercept, we set $x = 0$ and solve for y.

$y = 7250 - 600x$
$y = 7250 - 600(0)$
$y = 7250$
The y-intercept is (0, 7250).
Therefore, before any months have gone by, Rachel has \$7250 in her account.

2. Let y = the cost to the customer and let x = the number of rides he or she takes. Since the cost does not change, regardless of the number of rides taken, the equation $y = 24.95$ represents this situation. The graph of $y = 24.95$ is a horizontal line whose y-intercept is (0, 24.95). Since the line parallels the x-axis, there is no x-intercept.

3. The formula relating distance, time, and speed is $d = rt$, where d is the distance, r is the speed, and t is the time. Let x = the time spent biking (in hours). Then, $12x$ = the distance traveled. Brett bikes $12 \cdot 2.5 = 30$ miles and then turns around and bikes the same distance back to the rental shop. Therefore, we can represent the distance from the turn-around point at any time x as $|30 - 12x|$. Similarly, the distance from the rental shop at any time x can be represented by the function $y = 30 - |30 - 12x|$.

x	0	1	2	2.5	3	4	5
y	0	12	24	30	24	12	0

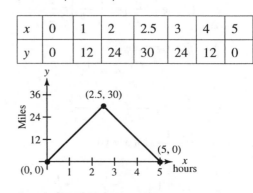

4. The monthly cost of x therms of gas is
$$y = \begin{cases} 0.53x, & \text{if } 0 \le x \le 70 \\ 0.53(70) + 0.74(x - 70), & \text{if } x > 70 \end{cases}$$
or
$$y = \begin{cases} 0.53x, & \text{if } 0 \le x \le 70 \\ 0.74x - 14.7, & \text{if } x > 70. \end{cases}$$

x	0	10	30	50	70	80	90	100
y	0	5.3	15.9	26.5	37.1	44.5	51.9	59.3

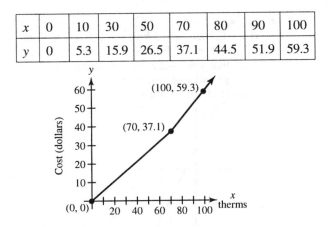

Exercise 3.4

1.

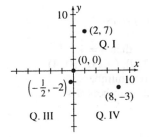

3. a. $f(0) = 1$
$f(2) = 2$
$f(4) = 3$
$f(-2) = 0$

   b. Domain: all real numbers

   c. Range: all real numbers

   d. $f(x) = 0$ for $x = -2$. So real zero is -2.

5. a. $f(0) = 0$
$f(1) = -1$
$f(-1) = -1$

   b. Domain: all real numbers

   c. Range: all nonpositive real numbers

   d. $f(x) = 0$ for $x = 0$. So real zero is 0.

7. $y = x$
If $y = 0$, then $x = 0$. If $x = 0$, then $y = 0$.
Intercept: $(0, 0)$

y is a function of x.
Domain: all real numbers
Range: all real numbers

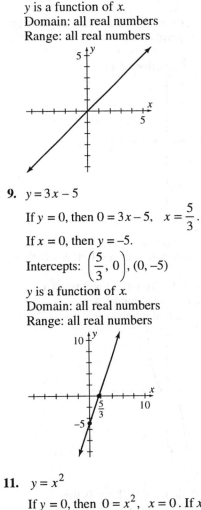

9. $y = 3x - 5$
If $y = 0$, then $0 = 3x - 5$, $x = \dfrac{5}{3}$.
If $x = 0$, then $y = -5$.
Intercepts: $\left(\dfrac{5}{3}, 0\right)$, $(0, -5)$
y is a function of x.
Domain: all real numbers
Range: all real numbers

11. $y = x^2$
If $y = 0$, then $0 = x^2$, $x = 0$. If $x = 0$, then $y = 0$. Intercept: $(0, 0)$
y is a function of x. Domain: all real numbers
Range: all real numbers ≥ 0

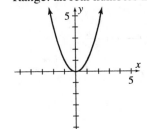

39

13. $x = 0$

If $y = 0$, then $x = 0$. If $x = 0$, then y can be any real number. Intercepts: every point on y-axis

y is not a function of x.

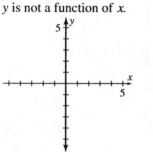

15. $y = x^3$

If $y = 0$, then $0 = x^3$, $x = 0$. If $x = 0$, then $y = 0$.

Intercept: $(0, 0)$. y is a function of x.

Domain: all real numbers

Range: all real numbers

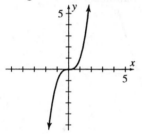

17. $x = -3y^2$

If $y = 0$, then $x = 0$. If $x = 0$, then $0 = -3y^2$, $y = 0$. Intercept: $(0, 0)$

y is not a function of x.

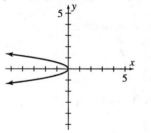

19. $2x + y - 2 = 0$

If $y = 0$, then $2x - 2 = 0$, $x = 1$. If $x = 0$, then $y - 2 = 0$, $y = 2$. Intercepts: $(1, 0)$, $(0, 2)$

Note that $y = 2 - 2x$. y is a function of x.

Domain: all real numbers

Range: all real numbers

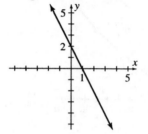

21. $s = f(t) = 4 - t^2$

If $s = 0$, then $0 = 4 - t^2$

$0 = (2 + t)(2 - t)$

$t = \pm 2$. If $t = 0$, then $s = 4$.

Intercepts: $(2, 0)$, $(-2, 0)$, $(0, 4)$

Domain: all real numbers

Range: all real numbers ≤ 4

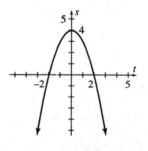

23. $y = g(x) = 2$

Because y cannot be 0, there is no x-intercept. If $x = 0$, then $y = 2$.

Intercept: $(0, 2)$

Domain: all real numbers

Range: 2

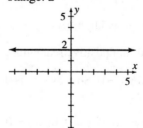

25. $y = h(x) = x^2 - 4x + 1$

If $y = 0$, then $0 = x^2 - 4x + 1$, and by the

quadratic formula, $x = \dfrac{4 \pm \sqrt{12}}{2} = 2 \pm \sqrt{3}$. If

$x = 0$, then $y = 1$. Intercepts:

$(2 \pm \sqrt{3}, 0), (0, 1)$

Domain: all real numbers

Range: all real numbers ≥ -3

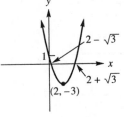

27. $f(t) = -t^3$

If $f(t) = 0$, then $0 = -t^3$, $t = 0$.

If $t = 0$, then $f(t) = 0$. Intercept: $(0, 0)$

Domain: all real numbers

Range: all real number

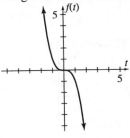

29. $s = F(r) = \sqrt{r - 5}$

Note that for $\sqrt{r - 5}$ to be a real number,

$r - 5 \geq 0$, or $r \geq 5$. If $s = 0$, then $0 = \sqrt{r - 5}$,

$0 = r - 5$, or $r = 5$. Because $r \geq 5$, we know

$r \neq 0$, so no s-intercept exists.

Intercept: $(5, 0)$

Domain, all real numbers ≥ 5

Range: all real numbers ≥ 0

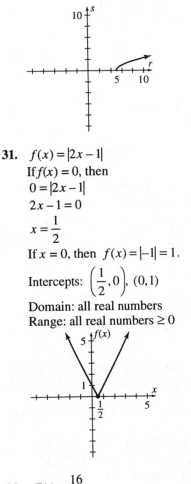

31. $f(x) = |2x - 1|$

If $f(x) = 0$, then

$0 = |2x - 1|$

$2x - 1 = 0$

$x = \dfrac{1}{2}$

If $x = 0$, then $f(x) = |-1| = 1$.

Intercepts: $\left(\dfrac{1}{2}, 0\right)$, $(0, 1)$

Domain: all real numbers

Range: all real numbers ≥ 0

33. $F(t) = \dfrac{16}{t^2}$

If $F(t) = 0$, then $0 = \dfrac{16}{t^2}$, which has no

solution. Because $t \neq 0$, there is no vertical-

axis intercept. No intercepts

Domain: all nonzero real numbers

Range: all positive real numbers

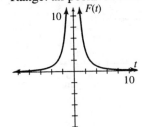

35. Domain: all real numbers ≥ 0
Range: all real c such that $0 \leq c \leq 2$

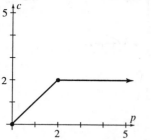

37. Domain: all real numbers
Range: all real numbers ≥ 0

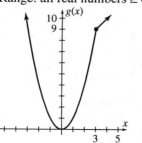

39. From the vertical-line test, the graphs that represent functions of x are (a), (b), and (d).

41. The cost of an item as a function of the time of day, x is

$$y = \begin{cases} 9, & \text{if } 10{:}30 \text{ A.M.} \leq x < 2{:}30 \text{ P.M.} \\ 8, & \text{if } 2{:}30 \text{ P.M.} \leq x < 4{:}30 \text{ P.M.} \\ 13, & \text{if } 4{:}30 \text{ P.M.} \leq x < 6{:}00 \text{ P.M.} \\ 18, & \text{if } 6{:}00 \text{ P.M.} \leq x < 8{:}00 \text{ P.M.} \\ 13, & \text{if } 8{:}00 \text{ P.M.} \leq x \leq 10{:}00 \text{ P.M.} \end{cases}$$

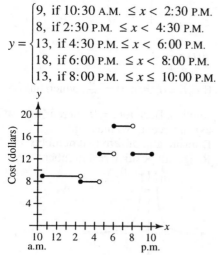

43. As price decreases, quantity increases; p is a function of q.

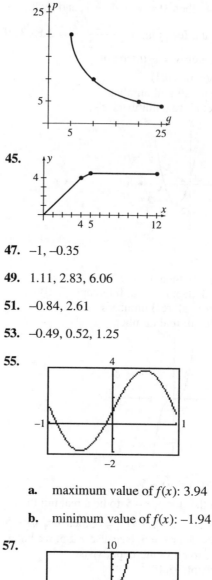

45.

47. $-1, -0.35$

49. $1.11, 2.83, 6.06$

51. $-0.84, 2.61$

53. $-0.49, 0.52, 1.25$

55.

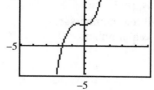

   a. maximum value of $f(x)$: 3.94

   b. minimum value of $f(x)$: -1.94

57.

   a. range: $(-\infty, \infty)$

b. intercepts: $(-1.73, 0)$, $(0, 4)$

59.

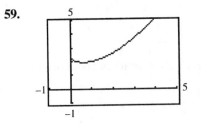

a. minimum value of $f(x)$: 1.93

b. range: $[1.93, \infty)$

c. intercept: $(0, 2.48)$

d. no real zero

Exercise 3.5

1. $y = 5x$

Intercepts: If $y = 0$, then $5x = 0$, or $x = 0$; if $x = 0$, then $y = 5 \cdot 0 = 0$. Testing for symmetry gives:

x-axis: $-y = 5x$
                 $y = -5x$
y-axis: $y = 5(-x) = -5x$
origin: $-y = 5(-x)$
                 $y = 5x$

Since equivalent equation is obtained in the third case only, the graph only has symmetry about the origin.
Answer: $(0, 0)$; symmetry about origin

3. $2x^2 + y^2 x^4 = 8 - y$

Intercepts: If $y = 0$, then

$2x^2 = 8$
$x^2 = 4$
$x = \pm 2$

If $x = 0$, then $0 = 8 - y$, so $y = 8$. Testing for symmetry gives:

x-axis: $2x^2 + (-y)^2 x^4 = 8 - (-y)$
             $2x^2 + y^2 x^4 = 8 + y$
y-axis: $2(-x)^2 + y^2(-x)^4 = 8 - y$
             $2x^2 + y^2 x^4 = 8 - y$

origin: $2(-x)^2 + (-y)^2(-x)^4 = 8 - (-y)$
            $2x^2 + y^2 x^4 = 8 + y$

Answer: $(\pm 2, 0)$, $(0, 8)$; symmetry about y-axis

5. $4x^2 - 9y^2 = 36$

Intercepts: If $y = 0$, then

$4x^2 = 36$
$x^2 = 9$
$x = \pm 3$; if $x = 0$, then
$-9y^2 = 36$
$y^2 = -4$, which has no real root. Testing for symmetry gives:

x-axis: $4x^2 - 9(-y)^2 = 36$
              $4x^2 - 9y^2 = 36$
y-axis: $4(-x)^2 - 9y^2 = 36$
              $4x^2 - 9y^2 = 36$
origin: Since the graph has symmetry about x- and y-axes, there is also symmetry about origin.

Answer: $(\pm 3, 0)$; symmetry about x-axis, y-axis, origin

7. $x = -2$

Intercepts: If $y = 0$, then $x = -2$; because $x \neq 0$, there is no y-intercept.
Symmetry:

x-axis: $x = -2$
y-axis: $-x = -2$
            $x = 2$
origin: $-x = -2$
            $x = 2$

Answer: $(-2, 0)$; symmetry about x-axis

9. $x = -y^{-4}$

Intercepts: Because $y \neq 0$, there is no x–intercept; if $x = 0$, then $0 = -\dfrac{1}{y^4}$, which has no solution. Symmetry:

x-axis: $x = -(-y)^{-4}$
            $x = -y^{-4}$
y-axis: $-x = -y^{-4}$
            $x = y^{-4}$

origin: $\qquad -x = -(-y)^{-4}$

$\qquad\qquad x = y^{-4}$

Answer: no intercepts; symmetry about x-axis

11. $x - 4y - y^2 + 21 = 0$

Intercepts: If $y = 0$, then

$x + 21 = 0$

$x = -21$

If $x = 0$, then

$-4y - y^2 + 21 = 0$

$y^2 + 4y - 21 = 0$

$(y + 7)(y - 3) = 0$

$y = -7$ or $y = 3$

Symmetry:

x-axis: $\qquad x - 4(-y) - (-y)^2 + 21 = 0$

$\qquad\qquad x + 4y - y^2 + 21 = 0$

y-axis: $\qquad (-x) - 4y - y^2 + 21 = 0$

$\qquad\qquad -x - 4y - y^2 + 21 = 0$

origin: $\qquad (-x) - 4(-y) - (-y)^2 + 21 = 0$

$\qquad\qquad -x + 4y - y^2 + 21 = 0$.

Answer: $(-21, 0)$, $(0, -7)$, $(0, 3)$; no symmetry of the given types

13. $y = f(x) = \dfrac{x^3}{x^2 + 5}$

Intercepts: If $y = 0$, then

$\dfrac{x^3}{x^2 + 5} = 0$

$x = 0$

If $x = 0$, then $y = 0$. Symmetry:

x-axis: $\quad$ Because f is not the zero function, there is no x-axis symmetry;

y-axis: $\qquad y = \dfrac{(-x)^3}{(-x)^2 + 5}$

$\qquad\qquad y = -\dfrac{x^3}{x^2 + 5}$

origin: $\qquad -y = \dfrac{(-x)^3}{(-x)^2 + 5}$

$\qquad\qquad y = \dfrac{x^3}{x^2 + 5}$

Answer: $(0, 0)$; symmetry about origin

15. $y = \dfrac{1}{x^3 + 1}$

Intercepts: If $y = 0$, then $\dfrac{1}{x^3 + 1} = 0$, which

has no solution; if $x = 0$, then $y = 1$.

Symmetry:

x-axis: $\qquad -y = \dfrac{1}{x^3 + 1}$

$\qquad\qquad y = -\dfrac{1}{x^3 + 1}$

y-axis: $\qquad y = \dfrac{1}{(-x)^3 + 1}$

$\qquad\qquad y = \dfrac{1}{-x^3 + 1}$

origin: $\qquad -y = \dfrac{1}{(-x)^3 + 1}$

$\qquad\qquad -y = \dfrac{1}{-x^3 + 1}$

$\qquad\qquad y = \dfrac{1}{x^3 - 1}$

Answer: $(0, 1)$; no symmetry of the given types

17. $2x + y^2 = 4$

Intercepts: If $y = 0$, then

$2x = 4$

$x = 2$

if $x = 0$, then

$y^2 = 4$

$y = \pm 2$.

Symmetry:

x-axis: $\qquad 2x + (-y)^2 = 4$

$\qquad\qquad 2x + y^2 = 4$

y-axis: $\qquad 2(-x) + y^2 = 4$

$\qquad\qquad -2x + y^2 = 4$

origin: $2(-x) + (-y)^2 = 4$
$-2x + y^2 = 4$

Answer: (2, 0), (0, ±2); symmetry about x-axis

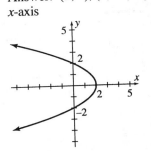

19. $y = f(x) = x^3 - 4x$

Intercepts: If $y = 0$, then

$x^3 - 4x = 0$
$x(x + 2)(x - 2) = 0$
$x = 0$ or $x = \pm 2$.
If $x = 0$, then $y = 0$.

Symmetry:

x-axis: Because f is not the zero unction, there is no x-axis symmetry.

y-axis: $y = (-x)^3 - 4(-x)$
$y = -x^3 + 4x$

origin: $-y = (-x)^3 - 4(-x)$
$y = x^3 - 4x$

Answer: (0, 0), (±2, 0); symmetry about origin.

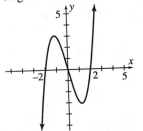

21. $|x| - |y| = 0$

Intercepts: If $y = 0$, then
$|x| = 0$
$x = 0$

If $x = 0$, then
$-|y| = 0$
$y = 0$

Symmetry:

x-axis: $|x| - |-y| = 0$
$|x| - |y| = 0$

y-axis: $|-x| - |y| = 0$
$|x| - |y| = 0$

origin: Since there is symmetry about x- and y-axes, symmetry about origin exists.

Answer: (0, 0); symmetry about x-axis, y-axis, origin.

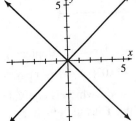

23. $4x^2 + y^2 = 16$

Intercepts: If $y = 0$, then
$4x^2 = 16$
$x^2 = 4$
$x = \pm 2$
If $x = 0$, then
$y^2 = 16$
$y = \pm 4$

Symmetry:

x-axis: $4x^2 + (-y)^2 = 16$
$4x^2 + y^2 = 16$

y-axis: $4(-x)^2 + y^2 = 16$
$4x^2 + y^2 = 16$

origin: Since there is symmetry about x- and y-axes, symmetry about origin exists.

Answer: (±2, 0), (0, ±4); symmetry about x-axis, y-axis, origin

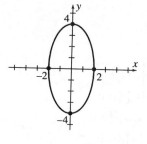

3.

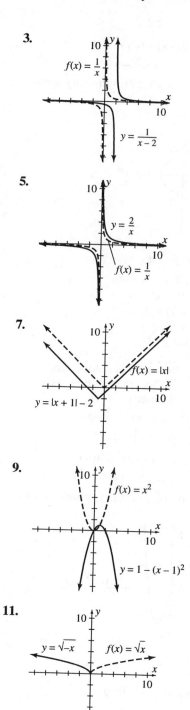

25.

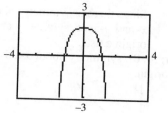

$y = f(x) = 2 - 0.03x^2 - x^4$. Replacing x by $-x$ gives $y = 2 - 0.03(-x)^2 - (-x)^4$ or $y = 2 - 0.03x^2 - x^4$, which is equivalent to original equation. Thus the graph is symmetric about y-axis.

a. Intercepts: $(\pm 1.18, 0)$, $(0, 2)$

b. Maximum value of $f(x)$: 2

c. Range: $(-\infty, 2]$

Exercise 3.6

1.

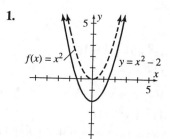

5.

7.

9.

11.

13. Translate 4 units to the right and 3 units upward.

15. Reflect about the *y*-axis and translate 3 units upward.

17.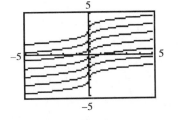

Compared to the graph for $k = 0$, the graphs for $k = 1, 2,$ and 3 are vertical shifts upward of 1, 2, and 3 units, respectively. The graphs for $k = -1, -2,$ and -3 are vertical shifts downward of 1, 2, and 3 units, respectively.

19.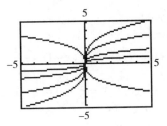

Compared to the graph for $k = 1$, the graphs for $k = 2$ and 3 are vertical stretches away from the *x*-axis by factors of 2 and 3, respectively. The graph for $k = \dfrac{1}{2}$ is a vertical shrinking toward the *x*-axis.

Chapter 3 Review Problems

1. Denominator is 0 when
$$x^2 - 3x + 2 = 0$$
$$(x - 1)(x - 2) = 0$$
$$x = 1, 2$$
Domain: all real numbers except 1 and 2.

3. all real numbers

5. For $\sqrt{x}$ to be real, *x* must be nonnegative. For the denominator $x - 1$ to be different from 0, *x* cannot be 1. Both conditions are satisfied by all nonnegative numbers except 1.
Domain: all nonnegative real numbers except 1.

7. $f(x) = 3x^2 - 4x + 7$
$$f(0) = 3(0)^2 - 4(0) + 7 = 7$$
$$f(-3) = 3(-3)^2 - 4(-3) + 7$$
$$= 27 + 12 + 7 = 46$$
$$f(5) = 3(5)^2 - 4(5) + 7 = 75 - 20 + 7 = 62$$
$$f(t) = 3t^2 - 4t + 7$$

9. $G(x) = \sqrt{x - 1}$
$$G(1) = \sqrt{1 - 1} = \sqrt{0} = 0$$
$$G(1) = \sqrt{10 - 1} = \sqrt{9} = 3$$
$$G(t + 1) = \sqrt{(t + 1) - 1} = \sqrt{t}$$
$$G(x^2) = \sqrt{x^2 - 1}$$

11. $h(u) = \dfrac{\sqrt{u + 4}}{u}$
$$h(5) = \frac{\sqrt{5 + 4}}{5} = \frac{\sqrt{9}}{5} = \frac{3}{5}$$
$$h(-4) = \frac{\sqrt{-4 + 4}}{-4} = \frac{0}{-4} = 0$$
$$h(x) = \frac{\sqrt{x + 4}}{x}$$
$$h(u - 4) = \frac{\sqrt{(u - 4) + 4}}{u - 4} = \frac{\sqrt{u}}{u - 4}$$

13. $f(4) = 8 - 4^2 = 8 - 16 = -8$
$$f(-2) = 4$$
$$f(0) = 4$$
$$f(10) = 8 - 10^2 = 8 - 100 = -92$$

15. a. $f(x + h) = 3 - 7(x + h) = 3 - 7x - 7h$

b. $\dfrac{f(x+h)-f(x)}{h}$

$= \dfrac{(3-7x-7h)-(3-7x)}{h}$

$= \dfrac{-7h}{h} = -7$

17. a. $f(x+h) = 4(x+h)^2 + 2(x+h) - 5$

$= 4x^2 + 8xh + 4h^2 + 2x + 2h - 5$

b. $\dfrac{f(x+h)-f(x)}{h} = \dfrac{(4x^2 + 8xh + 4h^2 + 2x + 2h - 5) - (4x^2 + 2x - 5)}{h}$

$= \dfrac{8xh + 4h^2 + 2h}{h} = \dfrac{h(8x+4h+2)}{h} = 8x + 4h + 2$

19. $f(x) = 3x - 1, g(x) = 2x + 3$

a. $(f+g)(x) = f(x) + g(x)$
$= (3x-1) + (2x+3)$
$= 5x + 2$

b. $(f+g)(4) = 5(4) + 2 = 22$

c. $(f-g)(x) = f(x) - g(x)$
$= (3x-1) - (2x+3)$
$= x - 4$

d. $(fg)(x) = f(x)g(x) = (3x-1)(2x+3)$
$= 6x^2 + 7x - 3$

e. $(fg)(1) = 6(1)^2 + 7(1) - 3 = 10$

f. $\dfrac{f}{g}(x) = \dfrac{f(x)}{g(x)} = \dfrac{3x-1}{2x+3}$

g. $(f \circ g)(x) = f(g(x)) = f(2x+3)$
$= 3(2x+3) - 1 = 6x + 8$

h. $(f \circ g)(5) = 6(5) + 8 = 38$

i. $(g \circ f)(x) = g(f(x)) = g(3x-1)$
$= 2(3x-1) + 3 = 6x + 1$

21. $f(x) = \dfrac{1}{x}$

$g(x) = x - 1$

$(f \circ g)(x) = f(g(x)) = f(x-1) = \dfrac{1}{x-1}$

$(g \circ f)(x) = g(f(x)) = g\left(\dfrac{1}{x}\right) = \dfrac{1}{x} - 1 = \dfrac{1-x}{x}$

23. $f(x) = x + 2$

$g(x) = x^3$

$(f \circ g)(x) = f(g(x)) = f(x^3) = x^3 + 2$

$(g \circ f)(x) = g(f(x)) = g(x+2) = (x+2)^3$

25. $y = 2x - 3x^3$

Intercepts: If $y = 0$, then

$0 = 2x - 3x^3$

$0 = 3x\left(\dfrac{2}{3} - x^2\right)$

$x = 0$ or $x = \pm\sqrt{\dfrac{2}{3}}$

If $x = 0$, then $y = 0$. Testing for symmetry gives:

x-axis: $\quad -y = 2x - 3x^3$

$y = -2x + 3x^3$, which is not the original equation.

y-axis: $y = 2(-x) - 3(-x)^3$

            $y = -2x + 3x^3$, which is not the original equation.

origin: $-y = 2(-x) - 3(-x)^3$

            $y = 2x - 3x^3$, which is the original equation.

Answer: $(0, 0)$, $\left(\pm\sqrt{\dfrac{2}{3}}, 0\right)$; symmetry about origin

27. $y = 9 - x^2$

Intercepts: If $y = 0$, then

$0 = 9 - x^2 = (3 + x)(3 - x)$, or $x = \pm 3$

If $x = 0$, then $y = 9$. Testing for symmetry gives:

x-axis: $-y = 9 - x^2$

           $y = -9 + x^2$, which is not the original equation.

y-axis: $y = 9 - (-x)^2$

           $y = 9 - x^2$, which is the original equation.

origin: There is y-axis symmetry but there is no x-axis symmetry. So there can be no symmetry about origin.

Answer: $(0, 9)$, $(\pm 3, 0)$; symmetry about y-axis.

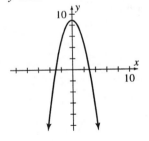

29. $G(u) = \sqrt{u + 4}$

If $G(u) = 0$, then $0 = \sqrt{u + 4}$.

$0 = u + 4,$

$u = -4$

If $u = 0$, then $G(u) = \sqrt{4} = 2$.

Intercepts: $(0, 2)$, $(-4, 0)$

Domain: all real numbers u such that $u \geq -4$

Range: all real numbers ≥ 0

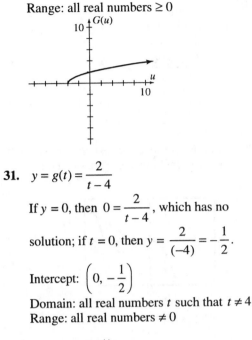

31. $y = g(t) = \dfrac{2}{t - 4}$

If $y = 0$, then $0 = \dfrac{2}{t - 4}$, which has no

solution; if $t = 0$, then $y = \dfrac{2}{(-4)} = -\dfrac{1}{2}$.

Intercept: $\left(0, -\dfrac{1}{2}\right)$

Domain: all real numbers t such that $t \neq 4$

Range: all real numbers $\neq 0$

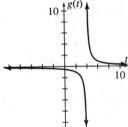
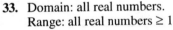

33. Domain: all real numbers.

Range: all real numbers ≥ 1

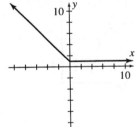

35.

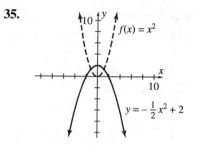

37. From the vertical-line test, the graphs that represent functions of x are (a) and (c).

39.

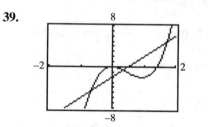

$-0.67; 0.34, 1.73$

41.

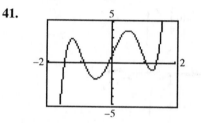

$-1.50, -0.88, -0.11, 1.09, 1.40$

43.

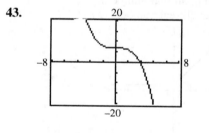

a. $(-\infty, \infty)$

b. $(1.92, 0), (0, 7)$

45. $k = 0, 2, 4$

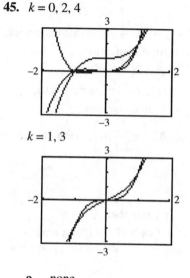

$k = 1, 3$

a. none

b. $1, 3$

Mathematical Snapshot Chapter 3

1. $f(100,000)$
$= 22,532 + 0.31(100,000 - 99,600)$
$= 22,656$
Answer: $22,656

3. $f(280,000)$
$= 81,646.50 + 0.396(280,000 - 271,050)$
$= 85,190.70$
Answer: $85,190.70

Chapter 4

Principles in Practice 4.1

1. Let x = the time (in years) and let y = the selling price. Then,

   In 1991: $x_1 = 1991$ and $y_1 = 32,000$

   In 1994: $x_2 = 1994$ and $y_2 = 26,000$

   The slope is

   $$m = \frac{y_2 - y_1}{x_2 - x_1}$$

   $$= \frac{26,000 - 32,000}{1994 - 1991}$$

   $$= \frac{-6000}{3}$$

   $$= -2000$$

   The car depreciated by \$2000 per year.

   ```
   y (price)
   ```
   (price in thousands of dollars graph with points at 1991≈32 and 1994≈26, Year on x-axis 1990 1991 1992 1993 1994, Price in thousands of dollars on y-axis 10 20 30 40)

2. An equation relating the growth in enrollment to the number of years can be found by using the point-slope form of an equation of a line. If
   S = the number of students enrolled, and
   T = the number of years, then the point-slope form can be written as

   $$S - S_1 = m(T - T_1)$$

   Let $m = 14$, $S_1 = 50$, and $T_1 = 3$.

   $$S - 50 = 14(T - 3)$$
   $$S - 50 = 14T - 42$$
   $$S = 14T + 8$$

3. A linear function relating Fahrenheit temperature to Celsius temperature can be found by using the point-slope form of an equation of a line.

   $$m = \frac{F_2 - F_1}{C_2 - C_1} = \frac{77 - 41}{25 - 5} = \frac{36}{20} = \frac{9}{5}$$

   $$F - F_1 = m(C - C_1)$$
   $$F - 41 = \frac{9}{5}(C - 5)$$
   $$F - 41 = \frac{9}{5}C - 9$$
   $$F = \frac{9}{5}C + 32$$

4. To find the slope and y-intercept, let $a = 1000$, then write the equation in slope-intercept form.

   $$y = \frac{1}{24}(t+1)a$$
   $$y = \frac{1}{24}(t+1)1000$$
   $$y = \frac{1000}{24}t + \frac{1000}{24}$$
   $$y = \frac{125}{3}t + \frac{125}{3}$$

   Thus the slope, m, is $\frac{125}{3}$ and the y-intercept, b, is $\frac{125}{3}$.

5. $F = \frac{9}{5}C + 32$

   $$5(F) = 5\left(\frac{9}{5}C + 32\right)$$
   $$5F = 9C + 160$$
   $$0 = 9C - 5F + 160$$

   Thus, $9C - 5F + 160 = 0$ is a general linear form of $F = \frac{9}{5}C + 32$.

6.

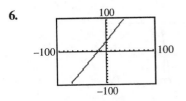

   To convert Celsius to Fahrenheit, locate the Celsius temperature on the horizontal axis, move vertically to the line, then move horizontally to read the Fahrenheit temperature of the vertical axis.

7. Right angles are formed by perpendicular lines. The slopes of the sides of the triangle are:

$$\overline{AB}\left\{m = \frac{0-0}{6-0} = \frac{0}{6} = 0\right.$$

$$\overline{BC}\left\{m = \frac{7-0}{7-6} = \frac{7}{1} = 7\right.$$

$$\overline{AC}\left\{m = \frac{7-0}{7-0} = \frac{7}{7} = 1\right.$$

Since none of the slopes are negative reciprocals of each other, there are no perpendicular lines. Therefore, the points do not define a right triangle.

Exercise 4.1

1. $m = \frac{10-1}{7-4} = \frac{9}{3} = 3$

3. $m = \frac{3-(-2)}{-6-4} = \frac{5}{-10} = -\frac{1}{2}$

5. The difference in the x-coordinates is $5 - 5 = 0$, so the slope is undefined.

7. $m = \frac{-2-(-2)}{4-5} = \frac{0}{-1} = 0$

9. $y - 8 = 6(x - 2)$
$y - 8 = 6x - 12$
$6x - y - 4 = 0$

11. $y - 5 = -\frac{1}{4}[x - (-2)]$
$4(y - 5) = -(x + 2)$
$4y - 20 = -x - 2$
$x + 4y - 18 = 0$

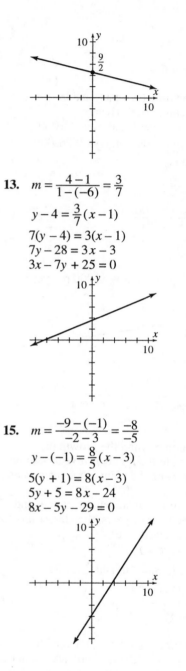

13. $m = \frac{4-1}{1-(-6)} = \frac{3}{7}$

$y - 4 = \frac{3}{7}(x - 1)$

$7(y - 4) = 3(x - 1)$
$7y - 28 = 3x - 3$
$3x - 7y + 25 = 0$

15. $m = \frac{-9-(-1)}{-2-3} = \frac{-8}{-5}$

$y - (-1) = \frac{8}{5}(x - 3)$

$5(y + 1) = 8(x - 3)$
$5y + 5 = 8x - 24$
$8x - 5y - 29 = 0$

17. $y = 2x + 4$
$2x - y + 4 = 0$

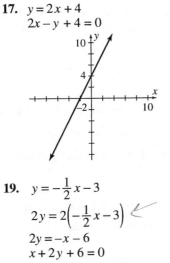

19. $y = -\dfrac{1}{2}x - 3$

$2y = 2\left(-\dfrac{1}{2}x - 3\right)$

$2y = -x - 6$
$x + 2y + 6 = 0$

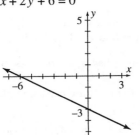

21. A horizontal line has the form $y = b$. Thus $y = -2$, or $y + 2 = 0$.

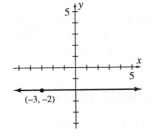

23. Line passes through $(2, -3)$ and is vertical. Thus $x = 2$, or $x - 2 = 0$.

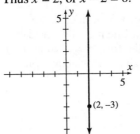

25. $y = 2x - 1$ has the form $y = mx + b$, where $m = 2$ and $b = -1$.

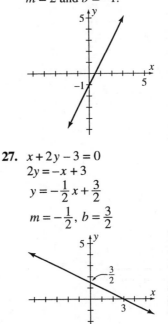

27. $x + 2y - 3 = 0$
$2y = -x + 3$
$y = -\dfrac{1}{2}x + \dfrac{3}{2}$
$m = -\dfrac{1}{2},\ b = \dfrac{3}{2}$

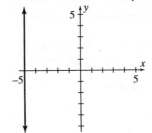

29. $x = -5$ is a vertical line. Thus the slope is undefined. There is no y-intercept.

31. $y = 3x$
$y = 3x + 0$
$m = 3, \ b = 0$

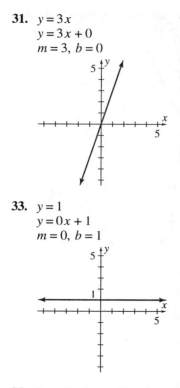

33. $y = 1$
$y = 0x + 1$
$m = 0, \ b = 1$

35. $2x = 5 - 3y$, or $2x + 3y - 5 = 0$
(general form)
$3y = -2x + 5$, or $y = -\dfrac{2}{3}x + \dfrac{5}{3}$
(slope-intercept form)

37. $4x + 9y - 5 = 0$ is a general form.
$9y = -4x + 5$, or $y = -\dfrac{4}{9}x + \dfrac{5}{9}$
(slope-intercept form)

39. $\dfrac{x}{2} - \dfrac{y}{3} = -4$
$6\left(\dfrac{x}{2} - \dfrac{y}{3}\right) = 6(-4)$
$3x - 2y = -24$
$3x - 2y + 24 = 0$ (general form)
$-2y = -3x - 24$
$y = \dfrac{3}{2}x + 12$ (slope-intercept form)

41. The lines $y = 7x + 2$ and $y = 7x - 3$ have the same slope, 7. Thus they are parallel.

43. The lines $y = 5x + 2$ and $-5x + y - 3 = 0$ (or $y = 5x + 3$) have the same slope, 5. Thus they are parallel.

45. The line $x + 2y + 1 = 0$ $\left(\text{or } y = -\dfrac{1}{2}x - \dfrac{1}{2}\right)$ has slope $m_1 = -\dfrac{1}{2}$ and the line $y = -2x$ has slope $m_2 = -2$. Since $m_1 \ne m_2$ and $m_1 \ne -\dfrac{1}{m_2}$, the lines are neither parallel nor perpendicular.

47. The line $y = 3$ is horizontal and the line $x = -\dfrac{1}{3}$ is vertical, so the lines are perpendicular.

49. The line $3x + y = 4$ (or $y = -3x + 4$) has slope $m = -3$, and the line $x - 3y + 1 = 0$ $\left(\text{or } y = \dfrac{1}{3}x + \dfrac{1}{3}\right)$ has slope $m_2 = \dfrac{1}{3}$. Since $m_2 = -\dfrac{1}{m_2}$, the lines are perpendicular.

51. The slope of $y = 4x - 5$ is 4, so the slope of a line parallel to it must also be 4. An equation of the desired line is $y - 3 = 4[x - (-1)]$, or $y = 4x + 7$.

53. $y = 2$ is a horizontal line. A line parallel to it has the form $y = b$. Since the line must pass through $(2, 1)$ its equation is $y = 1$.

55. $y = 3x - 5$ has slope $3 \Rightarrow$ perpendicular line has slope $-\dfrac{1}{3}$ and its equation is
$y - 4 = -\dfrac{1}{3}(x - 3)$
$y = -\dfrac{1}{3}x + 5$

57. $y = -4$ is a horizontal line, so the perpendicular line must be vertical with equation of the form $x = a$. Since that line passes through $(7, 4)$, its equation is $x = 7$.

59. $2x + 3y + 6 = 0 \left(\text{or } y = -\dfrac{2}{3}x - 2 \right)$ has slope

$-\dfrac{2}{3}$. Parallel line has $m = -\dfrac{2}{3}$. Equation is

$y - (-5) = -\dfrac{2}{3}[x - (-7)]$

$y = -\dfrac{2}{3}x - \dfrac{29}{3}$

61. $(1, 2), (-3, 8)$

$m = \dfrac{8 - 2}{-3 - 1} = \dfrac{6}{-4} = -\dfrac{3}{2}$

Point-slope form: $y - 2 = -\dfrac{3}{2}(x - 1)$. If first

coordinate is 5, then $x = 5$ and

$y - 2 = -\dfrac{3}{2}(5 - 1)$

$y - 2 = -\dfrac{3}{2}(4)$

$y - 2 = -6$

$y = -4$

Thus the point is $(5, -4)$.

63. Let $x =$ the time (in years) and
$y =$ the price per share. Then,
In 1986: $x_1 = 1986$ and $y_1 = 30$
In 1996: $x_2 = 1996$ and $y_2 = 10$
The slope is

$m = \dfrac{10 - 30}{1996 - 1986} = \dfrac{-20}{10} = -2$

The stock price dropped an average of $2
per year.

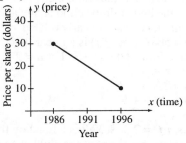

65. The number of home runs hit increased as a
function of time (in months). The given
points are $(x_1, y_1) = (3, 14)$ and

$(x_2, y_2) = (5, 20)$.

$m = \dfrac{y_2 - y_1}{x_2 - x_1} = \dfrac{20 - 14}{5 - 3} = \dfrac{6}{2} = 3$

Using the point-slope form with $m = 3$ and

$(x_1, y_1) = (3, 14)$ gives

$y - y_1 = m(x - x_1)$

$y - 14 = 3(x - 3)$

$y - 14 = 3x - 9$

$y = 3x + 5$

67. Solve the equation for t.
$L = 1.53t - 6.7$
$L + 6.7 = 1.53t$

$\dfrac{(L + 6.7)}{1.53} = t$

$0.65L + 4.38 = t$
The slope is approximately 0.65 and the
y-intercept is approximately 4.38.

69. a. Using the points $(0.5, 0)$ and $(3.5, -1)$

gives a slope of $m = \dfrac{-1 - 0}{3.5 - 0.5} = -\dfrac{1}{3}$.

And an equation is

$y - 0 = -\dfrac{1}{3}(x - 0.5)$, or $y = -\dfrac{1}{3}x + \dfrac{1}{6}$.

b. Using the points $(0.5, 0)$ and $(-1, -4.5)$

gives a slope of $\dfrac{-4.5 - 0}{-1 - 0.5} = 3$, so an

equation is
$y - 0 = 3(x - 0.5)$

$y = 3x - \dfrac{3}{2}$

The paths are perpendicular to each other

because the slope of the line in Part (a), $-\dfrac{1}{3}$,

is the negative reciprocal of the slope in Part
(b), 3.

71. Let $x =$ the distance traveled and let
$y =$ the altitude. The path of descent is a
straight line with a slope of -1 and
y-intercept of 3300. Therefore, using the
slope-intercept form with $m = -1$ and
$b = 3300$ gives
$y = mx + b$
$y = (-1)x + 3300$
$y = -x + 3300$

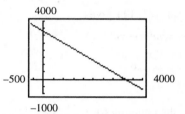

If the airport was located 4000 feet from where the plane begins its descent, the plane will crash 700 feet short of the airport.

73. The line has slope 50,000 and passes through (5, 330,000). Thus
$R - 330,000 = 50,000(T - 5)$ or
$R = 50,000T + 80,000$.

75. The lines are parallel, which is expected because they have the same slope, 1.5.

77. The slope of the first line is
$m_1 = \dfrac{0.1875}{0.3} = 0.625$, and the slope of the second line is $m_2 = -\dfrac{0.32}{0.2} = -1.6$. Since
$m_1 = -\dfrac{1}{m_2}$, the lines are mutually perpendicular.

Principles in Practice 4.2

1. Let x = the number of skis that are produced and let y = the number of boots that are produced. Then, the equation
$8x + 14y = 1000$ describes all possible production levels of the two products.

2. The quantity and price are linearly related such that $p = 575$ when $q = 1200$, and $p = 725$ when $q = 800$. Thus $(q_1,\ p_1) = (1200,\ 575)$ and $(q_2,\ p_2) = (800,\ 725)$. The slope is
$m = \dfrac{725 - 575}{800 - 1200} = -\dfrac{3}{8}$.

An equation of the line is
$$p - p_1 = m(q - q_1)$$
$$p - 575 = -\frac{3}{8}(q - 1200)$$
$$p - 575 = -\frac{3}{8}q + 450$$
$$p = -\frac{3}{8}q + 1025$$

3. Answers may vary, but two possible points are (0, 60) and (2, 140).
$f(x) = 40x + 60$

x	$f(x)$
0	60
2	140

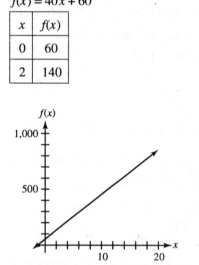

4. If t = the age of the child, then
$f(t)$ = the height of the child at any age t. The height and age are linearly related such that $f(8) = 50.6$. Since $f(t)$ is a linear function it has the form $f(t) = at + b$. Let $a = 2.3$. Then,
$f(t) = at + b$
$f(8) = 2.3(8) + b$
$50.6 = 18.4 + b$
$32.2 = b$
Thus, $f(t) = 2.3t + 32.2$ is a function that describes the height of the child at age t.

5. Let $y = f(x)$ = a linear function that describes the value of the necklace after x years. The problem states that $f(3) = 360$ and $f(7) = 640$. Thus, we set
$(x_1,\ y_1) = (3,\ 360) = (x_2,\ y_2) = (7,\ 640)$.

The slope is

$$m = \frac{y_2 - y_1}{x_2 - x_1} = \frac{640 - 360}{7 - 3} = \frac{280}{4} = 70$$

Using the point-slope form with $m = 70$ and $(x_1, y_1) = (3, 360)$ gives

$$y - y_1 = m(x - x_1)$$
$$y - 360 = 70(x - 3)$$
$$y = f(x) = 70x + 150$$

Exercise 4.2

1. $y = f(x) = -4x = -4x + 0$ has the form $f(x) = ax + b$ with $a = -4$ and $b = 0$. Thus the slope is -4 and the vertical-axis intercept is 0.

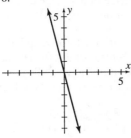

3. $g(t) = 2t - 4$ has the form $g(t) = at + b$ with $a = 2$ (the slope) and $b = -4$ (the vertical-axis intercept).

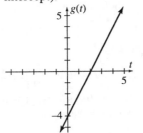

5. $h(q) = \frac{7 - q}{2} = \frac{7}{2} - \frac{1}{2}q$ has the form $h(q) = aq + b$ where $a = -\frac{1}{2}$ (the slope) and $b = \frac{7}{2}$ (the vertical-axis intercept).

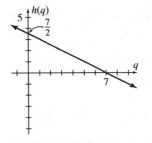

7. $f(x) = ax + b = 4x + b$. Since $f(2) = 8$, $8 = 4(2) + b$, $8 = 8 + b$, $b = 0 \Rightarrow f(x) = 4x$.

9. Let $y = f(x)$. The points $(1, 2)$ and $(-2, 8)$ lie on the graph of f. $m = \frac{8 - 2}{-2 - 1} = -2$. Thus
$$y - 2 = -2(x - 1), \text{ so}$$
$$y = -2x + 4 \Rightarrow f(x) = -2x + 4.$$

11. $f(x) = ax + b = -\frac{1}{2}x + b$. Since $f\left(-\frac{1}{2}\right) = 4$, we have
$$4 = -\frac{1}{2}\left(-\frac{1}{2}\right) + b$$
$$b = 4 - \frac{1}{4} = \frac{15}{4},$$
so $f(x) = -\frac{1}{2}x + \frac{15}{4}$.

13. Let $y = f(x)$. The point $(-2, -1)$ and $(-4, -3)$ lie on the graph of f. $m = \frac{-3 + 1}{-4 + 2} = 1$. Thus $y + 1 = 1(x + 2)$, so $y = x + 1 \Rightarrow f(x) = x + 1$.

15. The points $(40, 12)$ and $(25, 18)$ lie on the graph of the equation, which is a line. $m = \frac{18 - 12}{25 - 40} = -\frac{2}{5}$. Hence an equation of the line is $p - 12 = \frac{-2}{5}(q - 40)$, which can be written $p = \frac{-2}{5}q + 28$. When $q = 30$, then $p = \frac{-2}{5}(30) + 28 = -12 + 28 = \$16$.

17. The line passes through $(300, 840)$ and $(220, 640)$, so $m = \frac{640 - 840}{220 - 300} = 2.5$. Then $p - 640 = 2.5(q - 220)$ or $p = 2.5q + 90$.

19. The line passing through (10, 40) and (20, 70) has slope $\frac{70-40}{20-10} = 3$, so an equation for the line is

$c - 40 = 3(q - 10)$
$c = 3q + 10$
If $q = 35$, then
$c = 3(35) + 10 = 105 + 10 = \$115$.

21. If x = the number of kilowatt hours used in a month, then $f(x)$ = the total monthly charges for x kilowatt hours of electricity. If $f(x)$ is a linear function it has the form $f(x) = ax + b$. The problem states that $f(380) = 51.65$. Let $a = 0.115$.

$f(x) = ax + b$
$51.65 = 0.115(380) + b$
$51.65 = 43.7 + b$
$7.95 = b$
Hence, $f(x) = 0.115x + 7.95$ is a linear function that describes the total monthly charges for any number of kilowatt hours x.

23. Each year the value decreases by $0.10(8000)$. After t years the total decrease is $0.10(8000)t$. Thus

$v = 8000 - 0.10(8000)t$
$v = -800t + 8000$
The slope is -800.

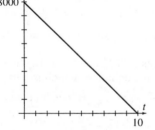

25. The line has slope 40,000 and passes through (5, 760,000). Thus
$y - 760,000 = 40,000(x - 5)$ or
$y = f(x) = 40,000x + 560,000$.

27. If x = the number of hours of service, then $f(x)$ = the price of x hours of service. Since $f(x)$ is a linear function, it has the form $f(x) = ax + b$. The problem states that $f(1) = 150$ and $f(3) = 280$. Thus, after 1 hour of service

$f(x) = ax + b$
$150 = a(1) + b$
$150 = a + b$
and after 3 hours of service
$f(x) = ax + b$
$280 = a(3) + b$
$280 = 3a + b$
To find the slope a and the y-intercept b we subtract
$280 = 3a + b$
$150 = a + b$
$130 = 2a$
$65 = a$
Since $a = 65$, $b = 150 - 65 = 85$. Hence, $f(x) = 65x + 85$ is a linear function that describes the price of a service call where x is the number of hours of service.

29. At $200/ton, x tons cost $200x$, and at $2000/acre, y acres cost $2000y$. Hence the required equation is $200x + 2000y = 20,000$, which can be written as $x + 10y = 100$.

31. a. $m = \frac{100-80}{100-56} = \frac{20}{44} = \frac{5}{11}$

$y - 100 = \frac{5}{11}(x - 100)$

$y = \frac{5}{11}x - \frac{500}{11} + 100$

$y = \frac{5}{11}x + \frac{600}{11}$

b. $60 = \frac{5}{11}x + \frac{600}{11}$

$\frac{5}{11}x = 60 - \frac{600}{11} = \frac{660}{11} - \frac{600}{11} = \frac{60}{11}$

$x = 12$, which is the lowest passing score on original scale.

33. $p = f(t) = at + b$, $f(5) = 0.32$, a = slope = 0.059.

a. $p = f(t) = 0.059t + b$. Since $f(5) = 0.32$, $0.32 = 0.059(5) + b$, $0.32 = 0.295 + b$, so $b = 0.025$. Thus $p = 0.059t + 0.025$.

b. When $t = 9$, then $p = 0.059(9) + 0.025 = 0.556$.

35. a. $m = \dfrac{t_2 - t_1}{c_2 - c_1} = \dfrac{80 - 68}{172 - 124} = \dfrac{12}{48} = \dfrac{1}{4}$.

$t - 68 = \dfrac{1}{4}(c - 124)$, $t - 68 = \dfrac{1}{4}c - 31$,

or $t = \dfrac{1}{4}c + 37$.

b. Since c is the number of chirps per minute, then $\dfrac{1}{4}c$ is the number of chirps in $\dfrac{1}{4}$ minute or 15 seconds. Thus from part (a), to estimate temperature add 37 to the number of chirps in 15 seconds.

37. $m = \dfrac{P_2 - P_1}{T_2 - T_1} = \dfrac{100 - 90}{80 - 40} = \dfrac{1}{4}$, so an equation is given by

$P - 100 = \dfrac{1}{4}(T - 80)$

$P - 100 = \dfrac{1}{4}T - 20$

$P = \dfrac{T}{4} + 80$

39. a. Yes: $Q = \left(1.8704b^2\right)x + \left(3.340b^3\right)$, where b is a constant, is the equation of a straight line in slope-intercept form. The slope is $1.8704b^2$ and the Q-intercept is $3.340b^3$.

b. If $b = 1$, the slope is $1.8704\left(1^2\right) = 1.8704$.

Principles in Practice 4.3

1. In the quadratic function

$y = P(x) = -x^2 + 2x + 399$, $a = -1$, $b = 2$, $c = 399$. Since $a < 0$, the parabola opens downward. The x-coordinate of the vertex is

$-\dfrac{b}{2a} = -\dfrac{2}{2(-1)} = 1$.

The y-coordinate of the vertex is

$P(1) = -\left(1^2\right) + 2(1) + 399 = 400$. Thus, the vertex is (1, 400). Since $c = 399$, the y-intercept is (0, 399). To find the x-intercepts we set

$y = p(x) = 0$.

$0 = -x^2 + 2x + 399$

$0 = -\left(x^2 - 2x - 399\right)$

$0 = -(x + 19)(x - 21)$

Thus, the x-intercepts are $(-19, 0)$ and $(21, 0)$.

2. In the quadratic function

$h(t) = -16t^2 + 32t + 8$,

$a = -16$, $b = 32$, and $c = 8$. Since $a < 0$, the parabola opens downward. The x-coordinate of the vertex is $-\dfrac{b}{2a} = -\dfrac{32}{2(-16)} = 1$. The y-coordinate of the vertex is

$h(1) = -16\left(1^2\right) + 32(1) + 8 = 24$. Thus, the vertex is (1, 24). Since $c = 8$, the y-intercept is (0, 8). To find the x-intercepts we set $y = h(t) = 0$.

$0 = -16t^2 + 32t + 8$

$t = \dfrac{-b \pm \sqrt{b^2 - 4ac}}{2a}$

$= \dfrac{-32 \pm \sqrt{32^2 - 4(-16)(8)}}{2(-16)}$

$= \dfrac{-32 \pm \sqrt{1536}}{-32} = \dfrac{-32 \pm 16\sqrt{6}}{-32} = 1 \pm \dfrac{\sqrt{6}}{2}$

Thus, the x-intercepts are $\left(1 + \dfrac{\sqrt{6}}{2},\, 0\right)$ and

$\left(1 - \dfrac{\sqrt{6}}{2},\, 0\right)$.

3. If we express the revenue r as a function of the quantity produced q, we obtain
$$r = pq$$
$$r = (6 - 0.003q)q$$
$$r = 6q - 0.003q^2$$
We note that this is a quadratic function with $a = -0.003$, $b = 6$, and $c = 0$. Since $a < 0$, the graph of the function is a parabola that opens downward, and r is maximum at the vertex (q, r).
$$q = -\frac{b}{2a} = -\frac{6}{2(-0.003)} = 1000$$
$$r = 6(1000) - 0.003(1000)^2 = 3000$$
Thus, the maximum revenue that the manufacturer can receive is $3000, which occurs at a production level of 1000 units.

Exercise 4.3

1. $f(x) = 5x^2$ has the form
$f(x) = ax^2 + bx + c$ where $a = 5$, $b = 0$, and $c = 0 \Rightarrow$ quadratic.

3. $g(x) = 7 - 6x$ cannot be put in the form
$g(x) = ax^2 + bx + c$ where
$a \neq 0 \Rightarrow$ not quadratic.

5. $h(q) = (q + 4)^2 = q^2 + 8q + 16$ has form
$h(q) = aq^2 + bq + c$ where $a = 1$, $b = 8$, and
$c = 16 \Rightarrow$ quadratic.

7. $f(s) = \frac{s^2 - 4}{2} = \frac{1}{2}s^2 - 2$ has the form
$f(s) = as^2 + bs + c$ where $a = \frac{1}{2}$, $b = 0$, and
$c = -2 \Rightarrow$ quadratic.

9. $y = f(x) = -4x^2 + 8x + 7$
$a = -4$, $b = 8$, $c = 7$
   a. Vertex occurs when
   $$x = -\frac{b}{2a} = -\frac{8}{2(-4)} = 1. \text{ When } x = 1,$$
   then $y = f(1) = -4(1)^2 + 8(1) + 7 = 11$.
   Vertex: (1, 11)

   b. $a = -4 < 0$, so the vertex corresponds to the highest point.

11. $y = f(x) = x^2 + 2x - 8$
$a = 1$, $b = 2$, $c = -8$
    a. $c = -8$. Thus the y-intercept is -8.

    b. $x^2 + 2x - 8 = (x + 4)(x - 2) = 0$, so
    $x = -4, 2$. x-intercepts: -4, 2

    c. $\frac{-b}{2a} = \frac{-2}{2 \cdot 1} = -1$
    $f(-1) = (-1)^2 + 2(-1) - 8 = -9$
    Vertex: $(-1, -9)$

13. $y = f(x) = x^2 - 6x + 5$
$a = 1$, $b = -6$, $c = 5$
Vertex: $-\frac{b}{2a} = -\frac{-6}{2 \cdot 1} = 3$
$f(3) = 3^2 - 6(3) + 5 = -4$
Vertex $= (3, -4)$
y-intercept: $c = 5$
x-intercepts:
$x^2 - 6x + 5 = (x - 1)(x - 5) = 0$, so $x = 1, 5$.
Range: all $y \geq -4$

15. $y = g(x) = -2x^2 - 6x$

$a = -2,\ b = -6,\ c = 0$

Vertex: $-\dfrac{b}{2a} = \dfrac{-(-6)}{2(-2)} = \dfrac{6}{-4} = -\dfrac{3}{2}$

$f\left(\dfrac{-3}{2}\right) = -2\left(\dfrac{-3}{2}\right)^2 - 6\left(\dfrac{-3}{2}\right) = \dfrac{-9}{2} + 9 = \dfrac{9}{2}$

Vertex $= \left(\dfrac{-3}{2}, \dfrac{9}{2}\right)$

y-intercept: $c = 0$

x-intercepts: $-2x^2 - 6x = -2x(x + 3) = 0$,

so $x = 0, -3$.

Range: all $y \le \dfrac{9}{2}$

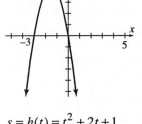

17. $s = h(t) = t^2 + 2t + 1$

$a = 1,\ b = 2,\ c = 1$

Vertex: $-\dfrac{b}{2a} = -\dfrac{2}{2 \cdot 1} = -1$

$h(-1) = (-1)^2 + 2(-1) + 1 = 0$

Vertex $= (-1, 0)$

s-intercept: $c = 1$

t-intercepts: $t^2 + 2t + 1 = (t + 1)^2 = 0$, so

$t = -1$.

Range: all $s \ge 0$

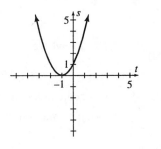

19. $y = f(x) = -9 + 8x - 2x^2$

$a = -2,\ b = 8,\ c = -9$

Vertex: $-\dfrac{b}{2a} = -\dfrac{8}{2(-2)} = 2$

$f(2) = -9 + 8(2) - 2(2)^2 = -1$

Vertex $= (2, -1)$

y-intercept: $c = -9$

x-intercepts: Because the parabola opens downward ($a < 0$) and the vertex is below the x-axis, there is no x-intercept.

Range: $y \le -1$

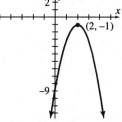

21. $t = f(s) = s^2 - 8s + 13$

$a = 1,\ b = -8,\ c = 13$

Vertex: $-\dfrac{b}{2a} = -\dfrac{-8}{2 \cdot 1} = 4$

$f(4) = 4^2 - 8(4) + 13 = -3$

Vertex $= (4, -3)$

t-intercept: $c = 13$

s-intercepts: Solving $s^2 - 8s + 13 = 0$ by the quadratic formula:

$s = \dfrac{-(-8) \pm \sqrt{(-8)^2 - 4(1)(13)}}{2(1)}$

$= \dfrac{8 \pm \sqrt{12}}{2} = \dfrac{8 \pm 2\sqrt{3}}{2} = 4 \pm \sqrt{3}$

Range: all $t \ge -3$

23. $f(x) = 100x^2 - 20x + 25$

Since $a = 100 > 0$, the parabola opens upward and $f(x)$ has a minimum value that occurs at the vertex where

$x = -\dfrac{b}{2a} = -\dfrac{-20}{2 \cdot 100} = \dfrac{1}{10}$. The minimum value is

$f\left(\dfrac{1}{10}\right) = 100\left(\dfrac{1}{10}\right)^2 - 20\left(\dfrac{1}{10}\right) + 25 = 24$.

25. $f(x) = 4x - 50 - 0.1x^2$

Since $a = -0.1 < 0$, the parabola opens downward and $f(x)$ has a maximum value that occurs when

$x = -\dfrac{b}{2a} = -\dfrac{4}{2(-0.1)} = 20$. The maximum value is

$f(20) = 4(20) - 50 - 0.1(20)^2 = -10$.

27. If we express the revenue r as a function of the quantity produced q, we obtain

$r = pq$

$r = (1200 - 3q)q$

$r = 1200q - 3q^2$

This is a quadratic function with $a = -3$, $b = 1200$, and $c = 0$. Since $a < 0$, the graph of the function is a parabola that opens downward, and r is maximum at the vertex (q, r).

$q = -\dfrac{b}{2a} - \dfrac{1200}{2(-3)} = 200$

$r = 1200(200) - 3(200)^2 = 120,000$

Thus, the maximum revenue that the manufacturer can receive is $120,000, which occurs at a production level of 200 units.

29. If we express the revenue r as a function of the quantity produced q, we obtain

$r = pq$

$r = (2400 - 6q)q$

$r = 2400q - 6q^2$

This is a quadratic function with $a = -6$, $b = 2400$, and $c = 0$. Since $a < 0$, the graph of the function is a parabola that opens downward, and r is maximum at the vertex (q, r).

$q = -\dfrac{b}{2a} = -\dfrac{2400}{2(-6)} = 200$

$r = 2400(200) - 6(200)^2 = 240,000$

Thus, the maximum revenue that the manufacturer can receive is $240,000, which occurs at a production level of 200 units.

31. In the quadratic function

$P(x) = -x^2 + 18x + 144$,

$a = -1$, $b = 18$, and $c = 144$. Since $a < 0$, the graph of the function is a parabola that opens downward. The x-coordinate of the vertex

is $-\dfrac{b}{2a} = -\dfrac{18}{2(-1)} = 9$. The y-coordinate of the vertex is

$P(9) = -\left(9^2\right) + 18(9) + 144 = 225$. Thus, the vertex is $(9, 225)$. Since $c = 144$, the y-intercept is $(0, 144)$. To find the x-intercepts, let $y = P(x) = 0$.

$0 = -x^2 + 18x + 144$

$0 = -\left(x^2 - 18x - 144\right)$

$0 = -(x - 24)(x + 6)$

Thus, the x-intercepts are $(24, 0)$ and $(-6, 0)$.

33. $f(P) = -\dfrac{1}{50}P^2 + 2P + 20$, where

$0 \le P \le 100$. Because $a = -\dfrac{1}{50} < 0$, $f(P)$ has a maximum value that occurs at the vertex.

$-\dfrac{b}{2a} = -\dfrac{2}{2\left(-\frac{1}{50}\right)} = 50$. The maximum value of $f(P)$ is

$f(50) = \dfrac{-1}{50}(50)^2 + 2(50) + 20 = 70$ grams.

35. $h(t) = -16t^2 + 64t + 32$

Since $a = -16 < 0$, $h(t)$ has a maximum value that occurs at the vertex where

$$t = -\frac{b}{2a} = -\frac{64}{2(-16)} = 2 \text{ sec. When } t = 2,$$

then, $h(t) = -16(2)^2 + 64(2) + 32 = 96$ feet.

37. In the quadratic function
$h(t) = -16t^2 + 80t + 16$, $a = -16$, $b = 80$, and $c = 16$. Since $a < 0$, the graph of the function is a parabola that opens downward. The x-coordinate of the vertex is

$$-\frac{b}{2a} = -\frac{80}{2(-16)} = \frac{5}{2}.$$

The y-coordinate of the vertex is

$$h\left(\frac{5}{2}\right) = -16\left(\frac{5}{2}\right)^2 + 80\left(\frac{5}{2}\right) + 16 = 116$$

Thus, the vertex is $\left(\frac{5}{2}, 116\right)$.

Since $c = 16$, the y-intercept is $(0, 16)$. To find the x-intercepts, we let $y = h(t) = 0$.

$$0 = -16t^2 + 80t + 16$$

$$t = \frac{-b \pm \sqrt{b^2 - 4ac}}{2a}$$

$$= \frac{-80 \pm \sqrt{80^2 - 4(-16)(16)}}{2(-16)}$$

$$= \frac{-80 \pm \sqrt{7424}}{-32} = \frac{5 \pm \sqrt{29}}{2}$$

Thus, the x-intercepts are $\left(\frac{5 + \sqrt{29}}{2}, 0\right)$ and $\left(\frac{5 - \sqrt{29}}{2}, 0\right)$.

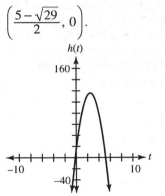

39. $s = 3.2t^2 - 16t + 28.7$ (quadratic with $a = 3.2 > 0$).

a. s is minimum when

$$t = -\frac{b}{2a} = -\frac{-16}{2(3.2)} = 2.50 \text{ s}$$

b. $t = 2.50 \Rightarrow s = 3.2(2.50)^2$
$-16(2.50) + 28.7 = 8.70$ m

41. $M = \frac{w < x}{2} - \frac{wx^2}{2}$, which is quadratic (in x) with $a = -\frac{w}{2} < 0$.

a. M is a maximum when

$$x = -\frac{b}{2a} = -\frac{\frac{w\ell}{2}}{2\left(-\frac{w}{2}\right)} = \frac{\ell}{2}$$

b. If $x = \frac{\ell}{2}$, then

$$M = \frac{w\ell}{2}\left(\frac{\ell}{2}\right) - \frac{w}{2}\left(\frac{\ell}{2}\right)^2 = \frac{w\ell^2}{4} - \frac{w\ell^2}{8}$$

$$= \frac{w\ell^2}{8}$$

c. $0 = \frac{w\ell x}{2} - \frac{wx^2}{2} = \frac{wx}{2}(\ell - x) \Rightarrow x = 0$
or $x = \ell$.

43. Since the total length of fencing is 200, the side opposite the stream has length $200 - 2x$. The area A is given by

$A = x(200 - 2x) = 200x - 2x^2$, which is quadratic with $a = -2 < 0$. Thus A is

maximum when $x = -\frac{200}{2(-2)} = 50$. Then the

side opposite the stream is
$200 - 2x = 200 - 2(50) = 100$. Thus the
dimensions are 50 ft by 100 ft.

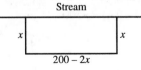

45. $(1.11, 2.88)$

47. a. none

b. one

c. two

49. 6.89

Principles in Practice 4.4

1. Let x = the number invested at 9% and let y = the amount invested at 8%. Then, the problem states
$$\begin{cases} x + y = 200,000, \\ 0.09x + 0.08y = 17,200. \end{cases}$$
We eliminate x by multiplying the first equation by –0.09 and then adding
$$\begin{cases} -0.09x - 0.09y = -18,000, \\ 0.09x + 0.08y = 17,200. \end{cases}$$
$$-0.01y = -800,$$
$$y = 80,000.$$
Therefore,
$$\begin{cases} x = 120,000, \\ y = 80,000. \end{cases}$$
Thus, \$120,000 is invested at 9% and \$80,000 is invested at 8%.

2. Let A = the number of deer of species A, and let B = the number of deer of species B. Then, the number of pounds of food pellets that will be consumed is $4A + 2B = 4000$. The number of pounds of hay that will be consumed is $5A + 7B = 9500$. Then, we have
$$\begin{cases} 4A + 2B = 4000, \\ 5A + 7B = 9500. \end{cases}$$
If we solve the first equation for B, we obtain
$$\begin{cases} B = 2000 - 2A, \\ 5A + 7B = 9500. \end{cases}$$
Substituting $2000 - 2A$ for B in the second equation gives
$$5A + 7(2000 - 2A) = 9500$$
$$A = 500$$

Thus
$$\begin{cases} B = 2000 - 2A, \\ A = 500. \end{cases}$$
and
$$\begin{cases} B = 1000, \\ A = 500. \end{cases}$$
The food will support 500 of species A and 1000 of species B.

3. Let A = the number of fish of species A, and let B = the number of fish of species B. Then, the number of milligrams of the first supplement that will be consumed is $15A + 20B = 100,000$. The number of milligrams of the second supplement that will be consumed is $30A + 40B = 200,000$.
$$\begin{cases} 15A + 20B = 100,000, \\ 30A + 40B = 200,000. \end{cases}$$
We multiply the second equation by $-\frac{1}{2}$ and then add.
$$\begin{cases} 15A + 20B = 100,000, \\ -15A - 20B = -1000, \\ 0 = 0 \end{cases}$$
Thus, there are infinitely many solutions of the form $A = \dfrac{20,000}{3} - \dfrac{4}{3}r$, $B = r$, where $0 \le r \le 5000$.

4. Let A = the amount of type A used, let B = the amount of type B used, and let C = the amount of type C used. If the final blend will sell for \$8.50 per pound, then $12A + 9B + 7C = 8.50$, and $A + B + C = 1$. Furthermore, since the amount of type B is to be twice the amount of type A, $B = 2A$. Thus, the system of equations is
$$\begin{cases} 12A + 9B + 7C = 8.50, \\ A + B + C = 1, \\ B = 2A. \end{cases}$$
Simplifying gives
$$\begin{cases} 30A + 7C = 8.50, \\ 3A + C = 1, \\ B = 2A. \end{cases}$$

$$\begin{cases} A = \frac{1}{6}, \\ C = \frac{1}{2}, \\ B = \frac{1}{3}. \end{cases}$$

Thus, the final mixture will consist of $\frac{1}{6}$ lb of A, $\frac{1}{3}$ lb of B, and $\frac{1}{2}$ lb of C.

Exercise 4.4

1. $\begin{cases} x + 4y = 3, & (1) \\ 3x - 2y = -5. & (2) \end{cases}$

From Eq. (1), $x = 3 - 4y$. Substituting in Eq. (2) gives
$3(3 - 4y) - 2y = -5$
$9 - 12y - 2y = -5$
$-14y = -14,$
or $y = 1 \Rightarrow x = 3 - 4y = 3 - 4(1) = -1.$
Thus $x = -1$, $y = 1$.

3. $\begin{cases} 3x - 4y = 13, & (1) \\ 2x + 3y = 3. & (2) \end{cases}$

Multiplying Eq. (1) by 3 and Eq. (2) by 4 gives
$\begin{cases} 9x - 12y = 39, \\ 8x + 12y = 12. \end{cases}$
Adding gives
$17x = 51$
$x = 3$
From Eq. (2) we have
$2(3) + 3y = 3$
$3y = -3$
$y = -1$
Thus $x = 3$, $y = -1$.

5. $\begin{cases} 5v + 2w = 36, & (1) \\ 8v - 3w = -54. & (2) \end{cases}$

Multiplying Eq. (1) by 3 and Eq. (2) by 2 gives
$\begin{cases} 15v + 6w = 108, \\ 16v - 6w = -108. \end{cases}$

Adding gives $31v = 0 \Rightarrow v = 0$. From Eq. (1) we have
$5(0) + 2w = 36$
$w = 18$
Therefore, $v = 0$, $w = 18$.

7. $\begin{cases} x - 2y = 8, & (1) \\ 5x + 3y = 1. & (2) \end{cases}$

From Eq. (1), $x = 2y + 8$. Substituting in Eq. (2) gives
$5(2y + 8) + 3y = 1$
$13y = -39$
$y = -3 \Rightarrow x = 2y + 8 = 2(-3) + 8 = 2.$
Thus $x = 2$, $y = -3$.

9. $\begin{cases} 4x - 3y - 2 = 3x - 7y, \\ x + 5y - 2 = y + 4. \end{cases}$

Simplifying, we have
$\begin{cases} x + 4y = 2, \\ x + 4y = 6. \end{cases}$
Subtracting the second equation from the first gives $0 = -4$, which is never true. Thus there is no solution.

11. $\begin{cases} \frac{2}{3}x + \frac{1}{2}y = 2, \\ \frac{3}{8}x + \frac{5}{6}y = -\frac{11}{2}. \end{cases}$

Clearing fractions gives the system
$\begin{cases} 4x + 3y = 12, \\ 9x + 20y = -132. \end{cases}$
Multiplying the first equation by 9 and the second equation by -4 gives
$\begin{cases} 36x + 27y = 108, \\ -36x - 80y = 528. \end{cases}$
Adding gives
$-53y = 636$
$y = -12$
From $4x + 3y = 12$, we have
$4x + 3(-12) = 12$
$4x = 48 \Rightarrow x = 12.$ Thus $x = 12$, $y = -12$.

13. $4p + 12q = 6,$ (1)

$2p + 6q = 3.$ (2)

Multiplying Eq. (2) by –2 gives

$$\begin{cases} 4p + 12q = 6, \\ -4p - 12q = -6. \end{cases}$$

Adding gives $0 = 0$, which implies that both equations represent the same line,

$4p + 12q = 6$

$p = \dfrac{3}{2} - 3q$

There are infinitely many solutions, given parametrically by

$p = \dfrac{3}{2} - 3r$

$q = r,$

where r is any real number.

15. $\begin{cases} 2x + y + 6z = 3, & (1) \\ x - y + 4z = 1, & (2) \\ 3x + 2y - 2z = 2. & (3) \end{cases}$

Adding Eq. (1) and (2), and adding 2 times Eq. (2) to Eq. (3) give

$$\begin{cases} 3x + 10z = 4, \\ 5x + 6z = 4. \end{cases}$$

Multiplying the first equation by 5 and the second equation by –3 gives

$$\begin{cases} 15x + 50z = 20, \\ -15x - 18z = -12. \end{cases}$$

Adding $\Rightarrow 32z = 8$, or $z = \dfrac{1}{4}$. From

$3x + 10z = 4$, we have

$3x + 10\left(\dfrac{1}{4}\right) = 4$

$3x = \dfrac{3}{2}$

$x = \dfrac{1}{2}$

From $2x + y + 6z = 3$, we have

$2\left(\dfrac{1}{2}\right) + y + 6\left(\dfrac{1}{4}\right) = 3$

$y = \dfrac{1}{2}$

Therefore $x = \dfrac{1}{2}$, $y = \dfrac{1}{2}$, $z = \dfrac{1}{4}$.

17. $\begin{cases} 5x - 7y + 4z = 2, & (1) \\ 3x + 2y - 2z = 3, & (2) \\ 2x - y + 3z = 4. & (3) \end{cases}$

From Eq. (3), $y = 2x + 3z - 4$. Substituting in Eqs. (1) and (2) gives

$$\begin{cases} 5x - 7(2x + 3z - 4) + 4z = 2, \\ 3x + 2(2x + 3z - 4) - 2z = 3, \end{cases}$$

or

$$\begin{cases} -9x - 17z = -26, \\ 7x + 4z = 11. \end{cases}$$

Multiplying the first equation by 7 and the second by 9 give

$$\begin{cases} -63x - 119z = -182, \\ 63x + 36z = 99. \end{cases}$$

By adding we have

$-83z = -83$

$z = 1$

From $7x + 4z = 11$, we have

$7x + 4(1) = 11$

$7x = 7$

$x = 1$

From $2x - y + 3z = 4$ we get

$2(1) - y + 3(1) = 4$

$-y = -1$

$y = 1$

Therefore $x = 1$, $y = 1$, $z = 1$.

19. $\begin{cases} x - 2z = 1, & (1) \\ y + z = 3. & (2) \end{cases}$

From Eq. (1), $x = 1 + 2z$; from Eq. (2), $y = 3 - z$. Setting $z = r$ gives the parametric solution $x = 1 + 2r$, $y = 3 - r$, $z = r$, where r is any real number.

21. $\begin{cases} x - y + 2z = 0, & (1) \\ 2x + y - z = 0 & (2) \\ x + 2y - 3z = 0 & (3) \end{cases}$

Adding Eq. (1) to Eq. (3) gives

$$\begin{cases} x - y + 2z = 0, \\ 2x + y - z = 0 \\ 2x + y - z = 0 \end{cases}$$

We can ignore the third equation because the second equation can be used to reduce it to $0 = 0$. We have

$$\begin{cases} x - y + 2z = 0, \\ 2x + y - z = 0. \end{cases}$$

Adding the first equation to the second gives

$$3x + z = 0$$

$$x = -\frac{1}{3}z$$

Substituting in the first equation we have

$$-\frac{1}{3}z - y + 2z = 0$$

$$y = \frac{5}{3}z$$

Letting $z = r$ gives the parametric solution $x = -\frac{1}{3}r$, $y = \frac{5}{3}r$, $z = r$, where r is any real number.

23. $\begin{cases} 2x + 2y - z = 3, & (1) \\ 4x + 4y - 2z = 6. & (2) \end{cases}$

Multiplying Eq. (2) by $-\frac{1}{2}$ gives

$$\begin{cases} 2x + 2y - z = 3, \\ -2x - 2y + z = -3. \end{cases}$$

Adding the first equation to the second equation gives

$$\begin{cases} 2x + 2y - z = 3, \\ 0 = 0. \end{cases}$$

Solving the first equation for x, we have $x = \frac{3}{2} - y + \frac{1}{2}z$. Letting $y = r$ and $z = s$ gives the parametric solution $x = \frac{3}{2} - r + \frac{1}{2}s$, $y = r$, $z = s$, where r and s are any real numbers.

25. Let $x =$ number of gallons of 20% solution and
$y =$ number of gallons of 30% solution. Then

$$\begin{cases} x + y = 700, & (1) \\ 0.20x + 0.30y = 0.24(700). & (2) \end{cases}$$

From Eq. (1), $y = 700 - x$. Substituting in Eq. (2) gives

$$0.20x + 0.30(700 - x) = 0.24(700)$$
$$-0.10x + 210 = 168$$
$$-0.10x = -42$$
$$x = 420$$

$y = 700 - x = 700 - 420 = 280$. Thus 420 gal of 20% solution and 280 gal of 30% solution must be mixed.

27. Let $C =$ the number of pounds of cotton, let $P =$ the number of pounds of polyester, and let $N =$ the number of pounds of nylon. If the final blend will cost \$3.25 per pound to make, then $4C + 3P + 2N = 3.25$. Furthermore, if we use the same amount of nylon as polyester to prepare, say, 1 pound of fabric, then $N = P$ and $C + P + N = 1$. Thus, the system of equations is

$$\begin{cases} 4C + 3P + 2N = 3.25, \\ C + P + N = 1, \\ N = P. \end{cases}$$

Simplifying gives

$$\begin{cases} 4C + 5N = 3.25, \\ C + 2N = 1, \\ N = P. \end{cases}$$

$$\begin{cases} N = 0.25, \\ C = 0.5, \\ P = 0.25. \end{cases}$$

Thus, the final fabric will contain 0.25 lb each of nylon and polyester, and 0.5 lb of cotton.

29. Let $p =$ plane speed and $w =$ wind speed. Now solve the system

$$\begin{cases} p + w = \dfrac{900}{3} \\ p - w = \dfrac{900}{3.6}, \end{cases}$$

which has solution

$$\begin{cases} p = 275, \\ w = 25. \end{cases}$$

Plane speed in still air = 275 mph and wind speed = 25 mph.

31. Let $x =$ number of Early American units and $y =$ number of Contemporary units. The fact that 20% more of Early American styles are sold than Contemporary styles means that

$$x = y + 0.20y$$
$$x = 1.20y$$

An analysis of profit gives
$250x + 350y = 130,000$. Thus we have the system
$$\begin{cases} x = 1.20y, & (1) \\ 250x + 350y = 130,000. & (2) \end{cases}$$
Substituting $1.20y$ for x in Eq. (2) gives
$250(1.20y) + 350y = 130,000$
$300y + 350y = 130,000$
$650y = 130,000$
$y = 200$
Thus $x = 1.20y = 1.20(200) = 240$. Therefore 240 units of Early American and 200 units of Contemporary must be sold.

33. Let x = number of calculators produced at Exton, and y = number of calculators produced at Whyton. The total cost of Exton is $7.50x + 7000$, and the total cost at Whyton is $6.00y + 8800$. Thus
$7.50x + 7000 = 6.00y + 8800$. Also, $x + y = 1500$. This gives the system
$$\begin{cases} x + y = 1500, & (1) \\ 7.50x + 7000 = 6.00y + 8800. & (2) \end{cases}$$
From Eq. (1), $y = 1500 - x$. Substituting in Eq. (2) gives
$7.50x + 7000 = 6.00(1500 - x) + 8800$
$7.50x + 7000 = 9000 - 6x + 8800$
$13.5x = 10,800$
$x = 800$
Thus $y = 1500 - x = 1500 - 800 = 700$. Therefore 800 calculators must be made at the Exton plant and 700 calculators at the Whyton plant.

35. Let x = rate on first \$100,000 and y = rate on sales over \$100,000. Then
$$\begin{cases} 100,000x + 75,000y = 8500, & (1) \\ 100,000x + 180,000y = 14,800. & (2) \end{cases}$$
Subtracting Eq. (1) from Eq. (2) gives
$105,000y = 6300$
$y = 0.06$

Substituting in Eq. (1) gives
$100,000x + 75,000(0.06) = 8500$
$100,000x + 4500 = 8500$, $100,000x = 4000$,
or $x = 0.04$. Thus the rates are 4% on the first \$100,000 and 6% on the remainder.

37. Let x = number of units of Argon I and y = number of units of Argon II that the company can make. These require $6x + 10y$ doodles and $3x + 8y$ skeeters. Thus
$$\begin{cases} 6x + 10y = 760, & (1) \\ 3x + 8y = 500. & (2) \end{cases}$$
Multiplying Eq. (2) by -2 gives
$$\begin{cases} 6x + 10y = 760, \\ -6x - 16y = -1000. \end{cases}$$
Adding gives
$-6y = -240$
$y = 40$
From Eq. (1),
$6x + 10(40) = 760$
$6x = 360$
$x = 60$
Thus 60 units of Argon I and 40 units of Argon II can be made.

39. Let c = number of chairs company makes, r = number of rockers, and L = number of chaise lounges.
Wood used: $(1)c + (1)r + (1)L = 400$
Plastic used: $(1)c + (1)r + (2)L = 600$
Aluminum used: $(2)c + (3)r + (5)L = 1500$
Thus we have the system
$$\begin{cases} c + r + L = 400, & (1) \\ c + r + 2L = 600, & (2) \\ 2c + 3r + 5L = 1500. & (3) \end{cases}$$
Subtracting Eq. (1) from Eq. (2) gives $L = 200$. Adding -2 times Eq. (1) to Eq. (3) gives
$r + 3L = 700$, from which
$r + 3(200) = 700$,
$r = 100$
From Eq. (1) we have $c + 100 + 200 = 400$, or $c = 100$. Thus 100 chairs, 100 rockers and 200 chaise lounges should be made.

41. Let x = number of skilled workers employed,
y = number of semiskilled workers employed,
z = number of shipping clerks employed.
Then we have the system

$$\begin{cases} \text{number of workers:} & x + y + z = 70, \quad (1) \\ \text{wages:} & 15x + 9y + 10z = 760, \quad (2) \\ \text{semiskilled:} & y = 2x. \quad (3) \end{cases}$$

From Eq. (3), $y = 2x$. Substituting in Eqs. (1) and (2) gives

$$\begin{cases} x + (2x) + z = 70, \\ 15x + 9(2x) + 10z = 760, \end{cases} \text{ or}$$

$$\begin{cases} 3x + z = 70, \\ 33x + 10z = 760. \end{cases}$$

Adding -10 times the first equation to the second gives
$3x = 60$
$x = 20$,
so $y = 2x = 2(20) = 40$. From
$x + y + z = 70$ we get
$20 + 40 + z = 70$
$z = 10$
The company should hire 40 semiskilled workers, 20 skilled workers, and 10 shipping clerks.

45. $x = 4$, $y = 2$

47. $x = 8.3$, $y = 14.0$

Exercise 4.5

In the following solutions, any reference to Eq. (1) or Eq. (2) refers to the first or second equation, respectively, in the given system.

1. From Eq. (2), $y = -3x$. Substituting in Eq. (1) gives
$-3x = 4 - x^2$
$x^2 - 3x - 4 = 0$
$(x - 4)(x + 1) = 0$
Thus $x = 4, -1$. From $y = -3x$, if $x = 4$, then
$y = -3(4) = -12$; if $x = -1$, then
$y = -3(-1) = 3$. Thus there are two solutions:
$x = 4$, $y = -12$; $x = -1$, $y = 3$.

3. From Eq. (2), $q = p - 2$. Substituting in Eq. (1) gives
$p^2 = 4 - (p - 2)$
$p^2 + p - 6 = 0$
$(p + 3)(p - 2) = 0$
Thus $p = -3, 2$. From $q = p - 2$, if $p = -3$, we have $q = -3 - 2 = -5$; if $p = 2$, then
$q = 2 - 2 = 0$. There are two solutions:
$p = -3$, $q = -5$; $p = 2$, $q = 0$.

5. Substituting $y = x^2$ into $x = y^2$ gives
$x = x^4$, $x^4 - x = 0$
$x\left(x^3 - 1\right) = 0$
Thus $x = 0, 1$. From $y = x^2$, if $x = 0$, then
$y = 0^2 = 0$; $x = 1$, then $y = 1^2 = 1$. There are two solutions: $x = 0$, $y = 0$; $x = 1$, $y = 1$.

7. Substituting $y = x^2 - 2x$ in Eq. (1) $\Rightarrow$
$x^2 - 2x = 4x - x^2 + 8$
$2x^2 - 6x - 8 = 0$
$x^2 - 3x - 4 = 0$
$(x - 4)(x + 1) = 0$
Thus $x = 4, -1$. From $y = x^2 - 2x$, if $x = 4$, then we have $y = 4^2 - 2(4) = 8$; if $x = -1$, then $y = (-1)^2 - 2(-1) = 3$. There are two solutions: $x = 4$, $y = 8$, $x = -1$, $y = 3$.

9. Substituting $p = \sqrt{q}$ in Eq. (2) gives

$\sqrt{q} = q^2$. Squaring both sides gives

$q = q^4$

$q^4 - q = 0$

$q\left(q^3 - 1\right) = 0$

Thus $q = 0, 1$. From $p = \sqrt{q}$, if $q = 0$, then

$p = \sqrt{0} = 0$; if $q = 1$, then $p = \sqrt{1} = 1$. There are two solutions: $p = 0, q = 0$; $p = 1, q = 1$.

11. Replacing x^2 by $y^2 + 14$ in Eq. (2) gives

$y = \left(y^2 + 14\right) - 16$

$y^2 - y - 2 = 0$

$(y - 2)(y + 1) = 0$

Thus $y = 2, -1$. If $y = 2$, then

$x^2 = y^2 + 14 = 2^2 + 14 = 18$, so

$x = \pm\sqrt{18} = \pm 3\sqrt{2}$. If $y = -1$, then

$x^2 = y^2 + 14 = (-1)^2 + 14 = 15$, so

$x = \pm\sqrt{15}$. Therefore, the system has four solutions: $x = 3\sqrt{2}, y = 2$; $x = -3\sqrt{2}, y = 2$; $x = \sqrt{15}, y = -1$; $x = -\sqrt{15}, y = -1$.

13. Substituting $x = y + 6$ in Eq. (2) gives

$y = 3\sqrt{(y + 6) + 4} = 3\sqrt{y + 10}$. Squaring, we have

$y^2 = 9(y + 10)$

$y^2 - 9y - 90 = 0$

$(y - 15)(y + 6) = 0$

Thus $y = 15, -6$. But $y = -6$ does not satisfy Eq. (2) [a negative number does not equal a nonnegative number]. If $y = 15$, then $x = y + 6 = 15 + 6 = 21$. These values of x and y satisfy the system. Thus the only solution is $x = 21, y = 15$.

15. We can write the following system of equations.

$\begin{cases} y = 0.01x^2 + 0.01x + 7, \\ y = 0.01x + 8.0. \end{cases}$

By substituting $0.01x + 8.0$ for y in the first equation and simplifying, we obtain

$0.01x + 8.0 = 0.01x^2 + 0.01x + 7$

$0 = 0.01x^2 - 1$

$0 = (0.1x + 1)(0.1x - 1)$

$x = -10$ or $x = 10$

Hence, if $x = -10$ then $y = 7.9$, and if $x = 10$ then $y = 8.1$. The rope touches the streamer twice, 10 feet away from center on each side at $(-10, 7.9)$ and $(10, 8.1)$.

17. Three

19. $x = -1.3, y = 5.1$

21. $x = 1.76$

23. $x = -1.46$

Exercise 4.6

1. Equating p-values gives

$\frac{3}{100}q + 2 = -\frac{7}{100}q + 12$, from which

$\frac{1}{10}q = 10$, or $q = 100$. If $q = 100$, then

$p = \frac{3}{100}q + 2 = \frac{3}{100}(100) + 2 = 5$. The equilibrium point is $(100, 5)$.

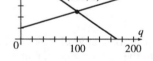

3. $\begin{cases} 35q - 2p + 250 = 0, & (1) \\ 65q + p - 537.5 = 0. & (2) \end{cases}$

Multiplying Eq. (2) by 2 and adding equations gives

$165q - 825 = 0$

$q = 5$

From Eq. (2),

$65(5) + p - 537.5 = 0$

$p = 212.50$

Thus the equilibrium point is $(5, 212.50)$.

5. Equating p-values:

$2q + 20 = 200 - 2q^2$

$2q^2 + 2q - 180 = 0$

$q^2 + q - 90 = 0$

$(q + 10)(q - 9) = 0$

Thus $q = -10, 9$. Since $q \geq 0$, choose $q = 9$. Then $p = 2q + 20 = 2(9) + 20 = 38$. The equilibrium point is (9, 38).

7. Equating p-values gives $20 - q = \sqrt{q + 10}$. Squaring both sides gives

$400 - 40q + q^2 = q + 10$

$q^2 - 41q + 390 = 0$

$(q - 26)(q - 15) = 0$

Thus $q = 26, 15$. If $q = 26$, then $p = 20 - q = 20 - 26 = -6$. But p cannot be negative. If $q = 15$, then $p = 20 - q = 20 - 15 = 5$. The equilibrium point is (15, 5).

9. Letting $y_{TR} = y_{TC}$ gives $3q = 2q + 4500$, or $q = 4500$ units.

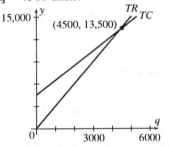

11. Letting $y_{TR} = y_{TC}$ gives

$0.05q = 0.85q + 600$

$-0.80q = 600$

$q = -750$, which is negative. Thus one cannot break even at any level of production.

13. Letting $y_{TR} = y_{TC}$ gives

$100 - \dfrac{1000}{q + 10} = q + 40$. Multiplying both

sides by $q + 10$ gives

$100(q + 10) - 1000 = (q + 10)(q + 40)$

$q^2 - 50q + 400 = 0$

$(q - 10)(q - 40) = 0$

Thus $q = 10$ or 40 units.

15.
$$\begin{cases} 3q - 200p + 1800 = 0, & (1) \\ 3q + 100p - 1800 = 0. & (2) \end{cases}$$

a. Subtracting Eq. (2) from Eq. (1) gives

$-300p + 3600 = 0$

$p = \$12$

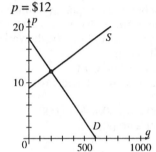

b. Before the tax the supply equation is

$3q - 200p + 1800 = 0$

$-200p = -3q - 1800$

$p = \dfrac{3}{200}q + 9$

After the tax the supply equation is

$p = \dfrac{3}{200}q + 9 + 0.27$

$p = \dfrac{3}{200}q + 9.27$

This equation can be written $-3q + 200p - 1854 = 0$, and the new system to solve is

$$\begin{cases} -3q + 200p - 1854 = 0, \\ 3q + 100p - 1800 = 0. \end{cases}$$

Adding gives

$300p - 3654 = 0 \Rightarrow$

$p = \dfrac{3654}{300} = \$12.18$.

17. Since profit = total revenue – total cost, then $4600 = 8.35q - (2116 + 7.20q)$. Solving gives $4600 = 1.15q - 2116$

$1.15q = 6716$

$q = \dfrac{6716}{1.15} = 5840$ units

For a loss (negative profit) of \$1150, we solve $-1150 = 8.35q - (2116 + 7.20q)$. Thus

$-1150 = 1.15q - 2116$

$1.15q = 966$

$q = 840$ units

To break even, we have $y_{TR} = y_{TC}$, or
$$8.35q = 2116 + 7.20q$$
$$1.15q = 2116$$
$$q = 1840 \text{ units}$$

19. Let $q =$ break-even quantity. Since total revenue is $5q$, we have $5q = 200{,}000$, which yields $q = 40{,}000$. Let c be the variable cost per unit. Then
    Tot. Rev. = Tot. Cost
    = Variable Cost + Fixed Cost.
    Thus
    $$200{,}000 = 40{,}000c + 40{,}000$$
    $$160{,}000 = 40{,}000c$$
    $$c = \$4.$$

21. $y_{TC} = 2q + 1050$: $y_{TR} = 50\sqrt{q}$. Letting $y_{TR} = y_{TC}$ gives
    $$50\sqrt{q} = 2q + 1050$$
    $$25\sqrt{q} = q + 525$$
    Squaring gives
    $$625q = q^2 + 1050q + (525)^2$$
    $$q^2 + 425q + (525)^2 = 0$$
    Using quad. formula,
    $$q = \frac{-425 \pm \sqrt{(425)^2 - 4(1)(525)^2}}{2}, \text{ which is}$$
    not real. Thus total cost always exceeds total revenue $\Rightarrow$ no break-even point.

23. After the subsidy the supply equation is
    $$p = \left[\frac{8}{100}q + 50\right] - 1.50$$
    $$p = \frac{8}{100}q + 48.50$$
    The system to consider is
    $$\begin{cases} p = \dfrac{8}{100}q + 48.50, \\ p = -\dfrac{7}{100}q + 65. \end{cases}$$
    Equating p-values gives
    $$\frac{8}{100}q + 48.50 = -\frac{7}{100}q + 65$$
    $$\frac{15}{100}q = 16.5$$
    $$q = 110$$

When $q = 110$, then
$$p = \frac{8}{100}q + 48.50 = \frac{8}{100}(110) + 48.50$$
$$= 8.8 + 48.50 = 57.30.$$
Thus the original equilibrium price decreases by $0.70.

25. Equating q_A-values gives
    $$8 - p_A + p_B = -2 + 5p_A - p_B$$
    $$10 = 6p_A - 2p_B$$
    $$5 = 3p_A - p_B$$
    Equating q_B-values gives
    $$26 + p_A - p_B = -4 - p_A + 3p_B$$
    $$30 = -2p_A + 4p_B$$
    $$15 = -p_A + 2p_B.$$
    Now we solve
    $$\begin{cases} 3p_A - p_B = 5 \\ -p_A + 2p_B = 15 \end{cases}$$
    Adding 2 times the first equation to the second gives
    $$5p_A = 25$$
    $$p_A = 5$$
    From $3p_A - p_B = 5$, $3(5) - p_B = 5$, or $p_B = 10$. Thus $p_A = 5$ and $p_B = 10$.

27. 2.4 and 11.3

Chapter 4 Review Problems

1. Solving $\dfrac{k-5}{3-2} = 4$ gives $k - 5 = 4$, $k = 9$.

3. $(3, -2)$ and $(0, 1)$ lie on the line, so
   $$m = \frac{1 - (-2)}{0 - 3} = -1. \text{ Slope-intercept form:}$$
   $y = mx + b \Rightarrow y = -x + 1$. A general form:
   $x + y - 1 = 0$.

5. $y - 4 = \dfrac{1}{2}(x - 10)$
   $$y - 4 = \frac{1}{2}x - 5$$
   $$y = \frac{1}{2}x - 1, \text{ which is slope-intercept form.}$$

Clearing fractions, we have

$$2y = 2\left(\frac{1}{2}x - 1\right)$$
$$2y = x - 2$$
$x - 2y - 2 = 0$, which is a general form.

7. Slope of a horizontal line is 0. Thus
$$y - 4 = 0[x - (-2)]$$
$$y - 4 = 0,$$
so slope-intercept form is $y = 4$. A general form is $y - 4 = 0$.

9. $y + 3x = 2$ (or $y = -3x + 2$) has slope -3, so the line perpendicular to it has slope $\frac{1}{3}$.
Since the y-intercept is 2, the equation is
$$y = \frac{1}{3}x + 2.$$ A general form is
$$x - 3y + 6 = 0.$$

In Problems 11–15, m_1 = slope of first line, and m_2 = slope of second line.

11. $x + 4y + 2 = 0 \left(\text{or } y = -\frac{1}{4}x - \frac{1}{2}\right)$ has slope
$m_1 = -\frac{1}{4}$ and $8x - 2y - 2 = 0$ (or $y = 4x - 1$)
has slope $m_2 = 4$. Since $m_1 = -\frac{1}{m_2}$, the lines are perpendicular to each other.

13. $x - 3 = 2(y + 4) \left(\text{or } y = \frac{1}{2}x - \frac{11}{2}\right)$ has slope
$m_1 = \frac{1}{2}$, and $y = 4x + 2$ has slope $m_2 = 4$.
Since $m_1 \neq m_2$ and $m_1 \neq -\frac{1}{m_2}$, the lines are neither parallel nor perpendicular to each other.

15. $y = \frac{1}{2}x + 5$ has slope $\frac{1}{2}$, and $2x = 4y - 3$
$\left(\text{or } y = \frac{1}{2}x + \frac{3}{4}\right)$ has slope $\frac{1}{2}$. Since
$m_1 = m_2$, the lines are parallel.

17. $3x - 2y = 4$
$$-2y = -3x + 4$$
$$y = \frac{3}{2}x - 2$$
$$m = \frac{3}{2}$$

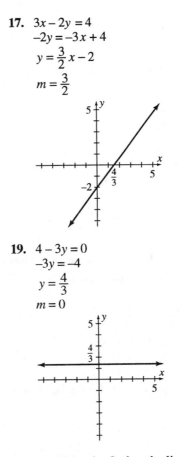

19. $4 - 3y = 0$
$$-3y = -4$$
$$y = \frac{4}{3}$$
$$m = 0$$

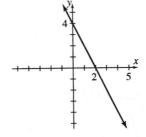

21. $y = f(x) = 4 - 2x$ has the linear form $f(x) = ax + b$, where $a = -2$ and $b = 4$. Slope $= -2$; y-intercept $(0, 4)$.

23. $y = f(x) = 9 - x^2$ has the quadratic form
$f(x) = ax^2 + bx + c$, where $a = -1$, $b = 0$ and
$c = 9$.
Vertex: $-\frac{b}{2a} = -\frac{0}{2(-1)} = 0$

$f(0) = 9 - 0^2 = 9$
$\Rightarrow$ Vertex = (0, 9)
y-intercept: $c = 9$
x-intercepts: $9 - x^2 = (3 - x)(3 + x) = 0$, so
$x = 3, -3$.

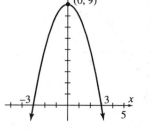

25. $y = h(t) = t^2 - 4t - 5$ has the quadratic form
$h(t) = at^2 + bt + c$, where $a = 1$, $b = -4$, and
$c = -5$.
Vertex: $-\dfrac{b}{2a} = -\dfrac{-4}{2 \cdot 1} = 2$
$h(2) = 2^2 - 4(2) - 5 = -9$
$\Rightarrow$ Vertex = (2, -9)
y-intercept: $c = -5$
t-intercepts: $t^2 - 4t - 5 = (t - 5)(t + 1) = 0$
$\Rightarrow t = 5, -1$

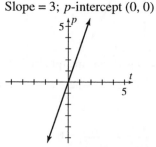

27. $p = g(t) = 3t$ has the linear form $g(t) = at + b$,
where $a = 3$ and $b = 0$.
Slope = 3; p-intercept (0, 0)

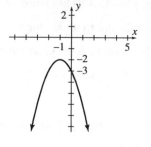

29. $y = F(x) = -\left(x^2 + 2x + 3\right) = -x^2 - 2x - 3$

has the quadratic form $F(x) = ax^2 + bx + c$,
where $a = -1$, $b = -2$, and $c = -3$
Vertex: $-\dfrac{b}{2a} = -\dfrac{-2}{2(-1)} = -1$

$F(-1) = -\left[(-1)^2 + 2(-1) + 3\right] = -2$
$\Rightarrow$ Vertex = (-1, -2)
y-intercept: $c = -3$
x-intercepts: Because the parabola opens
downward $(a < 0)$ and the vertex is below
the x-axis, there is no x-intercept.

31. $\begin{cases} 2x - y = 6, & (1) \\ 3x + 2y = 5. & (2) \end{cases}$

From Eq. (1), $y = 2x - 6$. Substituting in Eq.
(2) gives
$3x + 2(2x - 6) = 5$
$7x - 12 = 5$, $7x = 17$
$x = \dfrac{17}{7} \Rightarrow y = 2x - 6 = 2 \cdot \dfrac{17}{7} - 6 = -\dfrac{8}{7}$.
Thus $x = \dfrac{17}{7}$, $y = -\dfrac{8}{7}$.

33. $\begin{cases} 4x + 5y = 3, & (1) \\ 3x + 4y = 2. & (2) \end{cases}$

Multiplying Eq. (1) by 3 and Eq. (2) by -4
gives $\begin{cases} 12x + 15y = 9, \\ -12x - 16y = -8. \end{cases}$
Adding gives $-y = 1$, or $y = -1$. From Eq.
(1),
$4x + 5(-1) = 3$
$4x = 8$
$x = 2$
Thus $x = 2$, $y = -1$.

35. $\begin{cases} \frac{1}{4}x - \frac{3}{2}y = -4, & (1) \\ \frac{3}{4}x + \frac{1}{2}y = 8. & (2) \end{cases}$

Multiplying Eq. (2) by 3 gives

$\begin{cases} \frac{1}{4}x - \frac{3}{2}y = -4, \\ \frac{9}{4}x + \frac{3}{2}y = 24. \end{cases}$

Adding the first equation to the second gives

$\frac{5}{2}x = 20$

$x = 8$

From Eq. (1),

$\frac{1}{4}(8) - \frac{3}{2}y = -4$

$-\frac{3}{2}y = -6$

$y = 4$

Thus

$x = 8, y = 4$.

37. $\begin{cases} 3x - 2y + z = -2, & (1) \\ 2x + y + z = 1, & (2) \\ x + 3y - z = 3. & (3) \end{cases}$

Subtracting Eq. (2) from Eq. (1) and adding
Eq. (2) to Eq. (3) give

$\begin{cases} x - 3y = -3, \\ 3x + 4y = 4. \end{cases}$

Multiplying the first equation by –3 gives

$\begin{cases} -3x + 9y = 9, \\ 3x + 4y = 4. \end{cases}$

Adding the first equation to the second gives

$13y = 13$

$y = 1$

From the equation $x - 3y = -3$ we get

$x - 3(1) = -3$

$x = 0$

From

$3x - 2y + z = -2$

$3(0) - 2(1) + z = -2$

$z = 0$

Thus $x = 0, y = 1, z = 0$.

39. $\begin{cases} x^2 - y + 2x = 7, & (1) \\ x^2 + y = 5. & (2) \end{cases}$

From Eq. (2), $y = 5 - x^2$. Substituting in
Eq. (1) gives

$x^2 - \left(5 - x^2\right) + 2x = 7$

$2x^2 + 2x - 12 = 0$

$x^2 + x - 6 = 0$

$(x + 3)(x - 2) = 0$

Thus $x = -3, 2$. Since $y = 5 - x^2$, if $x = -3$,

then $y = 5 - (-3)^2 = -4$; if $x = 2$, then

$y = 5 - 2^2 = 1$. Thus the two solutions are

$x = -3, y = -4$, and $x = 2, y = 1$.

41. $\begin{cases} x + 2z = -2, & (1) \\ x + y + z = 5. & (2) \end{cases}$

From Eq. (1) we have $x = -2 - 2z$.
Substituting in Eq. (2) gives
$-2 - 2z + y + z = 5$, so $y = 7 + z$. Letting $z = r$
gives the parametric solution $x = -2 - 2r$,
$y = 7 + r, z = r$, where r is any real number.

43. $\begin{cases} x - y - z = 0, & (1) \\ 2x - 2y + 3z = 0. & (2) \end{cases}$

Multiplying Eq. (1) by –2 gives

$\begin{cases} -2x + 2y + 2z = 0, \\ 2x - 2y + 3z = 0. \end{cases}$

Adding Eq. (1) to Eq. (2) gives

$\begin{cases} -2x + 2y + 2z = 0, \\ 5z = 0. \end{cases}$

From the second equation, $z = 0$.
Substituting in Eq. (1) gives $x - y - 0 = 0$, so
$x = y$. Letting $y = r$ gives the parametric
solution $x = r, y = r, z = 0$, where r is any
real number.

45. $a = 1$ when $b = 2$; $a = 2$ when $b = 1$, so

$m = \dfrac{a_2 - a_1}{b_2 - b_1} = \dfrac{2 - 1}{1 - 2} = \dfrac{1}{-1} = -1$. Thus an

equation relating a and b is

$a - 1 = -1(b - 2)$
$a - 1 = -b + 2$
$a + b - 3 = 0$
When $b = 3$, then $a = -b + 3 = -(3) + 3 = 0$.

47. Slope is $\frac{-4}{3} \Rightarrow f(x) = ax + b = \frac{-4}{3}x + b$.
Since $f(1) = 5$,
$5 = -\frac{4}{3}(1) + b$
$b = \frac{19}{3}$
Thus $f(x) = -\frac{4}{3}x + \frac{19}{3}$.

49. $r = pq = (200 - 2q)q = 200q - 2q^2$, which
is a quadratic function with $a = -2$, $b = 200$,
$c = 0$. Since $a < 0$, r has a maximum value
when $q = -\frac{b}{2a} = -\frac{200}{-4} = 50$ units. If
$q = 50$, then $r = [200 - 2(50)](50) = \$5000$.

51. $\begin{cases} 125p - q - 250 = 0, \\ 100p + q - 1100 = 0. \end{cases}$

Adding gives $225p - 1350 = 0$, or
$p = \frac{1350}{225} = 6$.

53. a. $R = aL + b$. If $L = 0$, then $R = 1310$.
Thus we have $1310 = 0 \cdot L + b$, or
$b = 1310$. So $R = aL + 1310$. Since
$R = 1460$ when $L = 2$,
$1460 = a(2) + 1310$
$150 = 2a$
$a = 75$
Thus $R = 75L + 1310$.

b. If $L = 1$, then $R = 75(1) + 1310 = 1385$
milliseconds.

c. Since $R = 75L + 1310$, the slope is 75.
The slope gives the change in R for each
1-unit increase in L. Thus the time
necessary to travel from one level to the
next level is 75 milliseconds.

55. Considering cost we get
$5x + 3(2y) = 3000 \Rightarrow y = \frac{3000 - 5x}{6}$.

Stream

Area $= A = xy$, so
$A = x\left(\frac{3000 - 5x}{6}\right)$
$A = 500x - \frac{5}{6}x^2$,
which is quadratic with $a < 0$. Thus A has a
maximum value when $x = -\frac{500}{2\left(-\frac{5}{6}\right)} = 300$,

which gives $y = \frac{3000 - 5(300)}{6} = 250$. Thus
the dimensions are 300 ft by 250 ft.

57. $x = 230$, $y = -130$

59. $x = 0.75$, $y = 1.43$

Mathematical Snapshot Chapter 4

1. $m = 16$, $h = 1$, $t = 45$, $c = 4$

a. $z = \left[\frac{(m - c)(60h + t)}{30c} + 1.5\right]$
$= \left[\frac{(16 - 4)(60 \cdot 1 + 45)}{30 \cdot 4} + 1.5\right]$
$= \left[\frac{12(105)}{120} + 1.5\right] = [10.5 + 1.5]$
$= [12] = 12$

b.

$$F(x) = \begin{cases} \left[\frac{12}{11}c + 0.5\right], & \text{if } x = 2, \\ \left[\frac{16}{11}c + 0.5\right], & \text{if } x = 3, \\ \left[\frac{m-c}{z-1}(x-1) + c + 0.5\right], & \text{otherwise} \end{cases}$$

$$= \begin{cases} \left[\frac{12}{11}(4) + 0.5\right], & \text{if } x = 2, \\ \left[\frac{16}{11}(4) + 0.5\right], & \text{if } x = 3, \\ \left[\frac{16-4}{12-1}(x-1) + 4 + 0.5\right], & \text{otherwise} \end{cases}$$

$$= \begin{cases} [4.864], & \text{if } x = 2, \\ [6.318], & \text{if } x = 3, \\ \left[\frac{12}{11}(x-1) + 4.5\right], & \text{otherwise} \end{cases}$$

$$= \begin{cases} 4, & \text{if } x = 2, \\ 6, & \text{if } x = 3, \\ \left[\frac{12}{11}(x-1) + 4.5\right], & \text{otherwise} \end{cases}$$

c. $F(1) = [0 + 4.5] = [4.5] = 4,$

$F(2) = 4,$

$F(3) = 6,$

$F(4) = \left[\frac{12}{11}(3) + 4.5\right] = [7.773] = 7,$

$F(5) = \left[\frac{12}{11}(4) + 4.5\right] = [8.864] = 8,$

$F(6) = \left[\frac{12}{11}(5) + 4.5\right] = [9.955] = 9,$

$F(7) = \left[\frac{12}{11}(6) + 4.5\right] = [11.045] = 11,$

$F(8) = \left[\frac{12}{11}(7) + 4.5\right] = [12.136] = 12,$

$F(9) = \left[\frac{12}{11}(8) = 4.5\right] = [13.227] = 13,$

$F(10) = \left[\frac{12}{11}(9) + 4.5\right] = [14.318] = 14,$

$F(11) = \left[\frac{12}{11}(10) + 4.5\right] = [15.409] = 15,$

$F(12) = \left[\frac{12}{11}(11) + 4.5\right] = [16.5] = 16.$

Chapter 5

Principles in Practice 5.1

1. The shapes of the graphs are the same. The value of A scales the value of any point by A.

2. If P = the amount of money invested and r = the annual rate at which P increases, then after 1 year, the investment has grown from P to $P + Pr = P(1 + r)$. Since $r = 0.10$, the factor by which P increases for the first year is $1 + r = 1 + 0.1 = 1.1$. Similarly, during the second year the investment grows from $P(1 + r)$ to

$P(1+r) + r[P(1+r)] = P(1+r)^2$. Again, since $r = 0.10$, the multiplicative increase for the second year is

$(1 + 0.10)^2 = (1.1)^2 = 1.21$. This pattern will continue as shown in the table.

Year	Multiplicative Increase	Expression
0	1	1.1^0
1	1.1	1.1^1
2	1.21	1.1^2
3	1.33	1.1^3
4	1.46	1.1^4

Thus, the growth of the initial investment is exponential with a base of
$1 + r = 1 + 0.1 = 1.1$.
If we graph the multiplicative increase as a function of years we obtain the following.

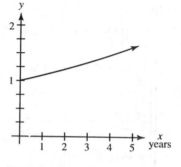

3. If V = the value of the car and r = the annual rate at which V depreciates, then after 1 year the value of the car is $V - rV = V(1 - r)$. Since $r = 0.15$, the factor by which V decreases for the first year is $1 - r = 1 - 0.15 = 0.85$. Similarly, after the second year the value of the car is

$V(1 - r) - r[V(1 - r)] = V(1 - r)^2$. Again, since $r = 0.15$, the multiplicative decrease for the second year is

$(1 - r)^2 = (1 - 0.15)^2 = 0.72$. This pattern will continue as shown in the table.

Year	Multiplicative Decrease	Expression
0	1	0.85^0
1	0.85	0.85^1
2	0.72	0.85^2
3	0.61	0.85^3

Thus, the depreciation is exponential with a base of $1 - r = 1 - 0.15 = 0.85$. If we graph the multiplicative decrease as a function of years, we obtain the following.

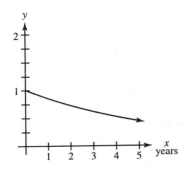

4. Let t = the time at which George's sister began saving, then since George is 3 years behind, $t - 3$ = the time when George began saving. Therefore, if $y = 1.08^t$ represents the multiplicative increase in George's sister's account $y = 1.08^{t-3}$ represents the multiplicative increase in George's account. A graph showing the projected increase in George's money will have the same shape as the graph of the projected increase in his sister's account, but will be shifted 3 units to the right.

5. $S = P(1 + r)^n$

$S = 2000(1 + 0.13)^5 = 2000(1.13)^5$

≈ 3684.87

The value of the investment after 5 years will be \$3684.87. The interest earned over the first 5 years is

$3684.87 - 2000 = \$1684.87$.

6. Let $P = 2000$. With two interest periods per year, there will be a total of $n = 5(2) = 10$ interest periods. The periodic rate r is $\dfrac{0.065}{2} = 0.0325$.

$S = P(1 + r)^n$

$S = 2000(1 + 0.0325)^{10} = 2000(1.0325)^{10}$

≈ 2753.79

The value of the investment after 5 years is \$2753.79. The interest earned over the first 5 years is $2753.79 - 2000 = \$753.79$.

7. Let $N(t)$ = the number of employees at time t, where t is in years. Then,

$N(4) = 5(1 + 1.2)^4 = 5(2.2)^4 = 117.128$

Thus, there will be 117 employees at the end of 4 years.

8. $P = e^{-0.06t} = \left(\dfrac{1}{e}\right)^{0.06t}$

Since $0 < \dfrac{1}{e} < 1$, the graph is that of an exponential function falling from left to right.

x	y
0	1
2	0.89
4	0.79
6	0.70
8	0.62
10	0.55

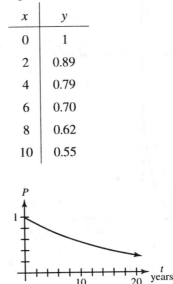

Exercise 5.1

1.

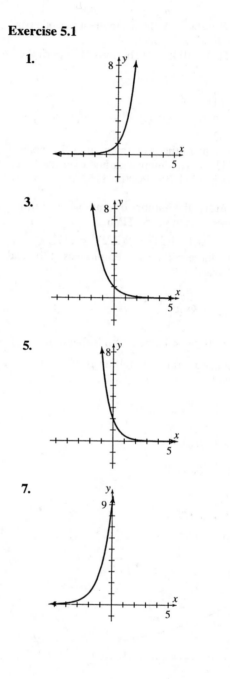

3.

5.

7.

9.

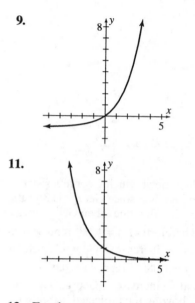

11.

13. For the curves, the bases involved are 0.4, 2, and 5. For base 5, the curve rises from left to right, and in the first quadrant it rises faster than the curve for base 2. Thus the graph of $y = 5^x$ is *B*.

15. For 2015 we have $t = 20$, so
$$P = 125,000(1.12)^{\frac{20}{20}} = 125,000(1.12)^1$$
$$= 140,000.$$

17. $P = 1 - \frac{1}{2}(1-c)^0 = 1 - \frac{1}{2}(1) = \frac{1}{2}$

19. a. $4000(1.06)^7 \approx \$6014.52$

     b. $6014.52 - 4000 = \$2014.52$

21. a. $700(1.035)^{30} \approx \$1964.76$

     b. $1964.76 - 700 = \$1264.76$

23. a. $4000\left(1 + \frac{0.085}{4}\right)^{60} \approx \$14,124.86$

     b. $14,124.86 - 4000 = \$10,124.86$

25. a. $5000(1.0075)^{30} \approx \$6256.36$

     b. $6256.36 - 5000 = \$1256.36$

27. a. $8000\left(1+\dfrac{0.0625}{365}\right)^{3(365)} \approx \$9649.69$

   b. $9649.69 - 8000 = \$1649.69$

29. $6000(1.02)^{28} \approx \$10,446.15$

31. a. $N = 400(1.05)^{t}$

   b.   When $t = 1$, then
       $N = 400(1.05)^{1} = 420$.

   c.   When $t = 4$, then
       $N = 400(1.05)^{4} \approx 486$.

33. Let $P =$ the amount of plastic recycled and
let $r =$ the rate at which P increases each
year. Then after the first year, the amount of
plastic recycled, increases from P to
$P + rP = P(1 + r)$, since $r = 0.3$, the factor by
which P increases for the first year, is
$1 + r = 1 + 0.3 = 1.3$. Similarly, during the
second year, the amount of plastic recycled
increases from $P(1 + r)$ to
$P(1 + r) + r[P(1+r)] = P(1+r)^{2}$. Again,
since $r = 0.3$, the multiplicative increase for
the second year is
$(1 + r)^{2} = (1 + 0.3)^{2} = (1.3)^{2} = 1.69$. This
pattern will continue as shown in the table.

Year	Multiplicative Increase	Expression
0	1	1.3^{0}
1	1.3	1.3^{1}
2	1.69	1.3^{2}
3	2.20	1.3^{3}

Thus, the increase in recycling is
exponential with a base $= 1 + r = 1 + 0.3$
$= 1.3$. If we graph the multiplicative increase
as function of years, we obtaining the
following.

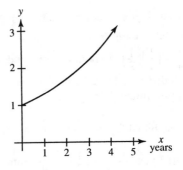

35. $P = 100,000(1 - 0.01)^{t} = 100,000(0.99)^{t}$,
where P is the population after t years.
When $t = 3$, $P = 100,000(0.99)^{3} \approx 97,030$.

37.   4.4817

39.   0.6703

41.

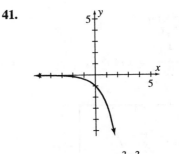

43. For $x = 3$, $P = \dfrac{e^{-3}3^{3}}{3!} \approx 0.2240$

45. $e^{kt} = \left(e^{k}\right)^{t} = b^{t}$, where $b = e^{k}$

47. a.   When $t = 0$,
       $N = 10e^{-0.028(0)} = 10 \cdot 1 = 10$.

   b.   When $t = 10$,
       $N = 10e^{-0.028(10)} = 10e^{-0.28} \approx 7.6$.

   c.   When $t = 50$, $N = 10e^{-0.028(50)} \approx 2.5$.

d. After 50 hours, approximately $\frac{1}{4}$ of the initial amount remains. Because $\frac{1}{4} = \left(\frac{1}{2}\right)\left(\frac{1}{2}\right)$, 50 hours corresponds to 2 half-lives. Thus the half-life is approximately 25 hours.

49. After one half-life, $\frac{1}{2}$ gram remains. After two half-lives, $\frac{1}{2} \cdot \frac{1}{2} = \left(\frac{1}{2}\right)^2 = \frac{1}{4}$ gram remains. Continuing in this manner, after n half-lives, $\left(\frac{1}{2}\right)^n$ gram remains. Because $\frac{1}{16} = \left(\frac{1}{2}\right)^4$, after 4 half-lives, $\frac{1}{16}$ gram remains. This corresponds to $4 \cdot 8 = 32$ years.

51. $f(x) = \dfrac{e^{-4} 4^x}{x!}$

$f(2) = \dfrac{e^{-4} 4^2}{2!} \approx 0.1465$

53.

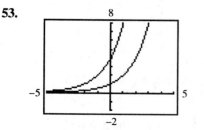

$y = 4 \cdot 2^x = 2^2 \cdot 2^x = 2^{x+2}$

If $f(x) = 2^x$, then

$y = 4 \cdot 2^x = 2^{x+2} = f(x+2)$. This implies that the graph of $y = 4 \cdot 2^x$ is the graph of $y = 2^x$ shifted two units to the left.

55. 1.58

57. $300\left(\dfrac{4}{3}\right)^{4.1} \approx 976$

$300\left(\dfrac{4}{3}\right)^{4.2} \approx 1004$

4.2 minutes

59. The first integer t for which the graph of $P = 1000(1.05)^t$ lies on or above the horizontal line $P = 2000$ is 15.

Principles in Practice 5.2

1. If $16 = 2^t$ is the exponential form then $t = \log_2 16$ is the logarithmic form, where t represents the number of times the bacteria have doubled.

2. If $8.3 = \log_{10}\left(\dfrac{I}{I_0}\right)$ is the logarithmic form, then $\dfrac{I}{I_0} = 10^{8.3}$ is the exponential form.

3. Let $R =$ the amount of material recycled every year. If the amount being recycled increases by 50% every year, then the amount recycled at the end of y years is $R(1 + r)^y = R(1 + 0.5)^y = R(1.5)^y$ Thus, the multiplicative increase in recycling at the end of y years is $(1.5)^y$. If we let $x =$ the multiplicative increase, then $x = (1.5)^y$ and, in logarithmic form, $\log_{1.5} x = y$.

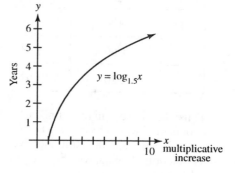

4. Let V = the value of the boat. If the value depreciates by 20% every year, then at the end of y years the value of the boat is $V(1-r)^y = V(1.02)^y = V(0.8)^y$. Thus, the multiplicative decrease in value at the end of y years is $(0.8)^y$. If we let x = the multiplicative decrease, then $x = (0.8)^y$ and, in logarithmic form, $\log_{0.8} x = y$

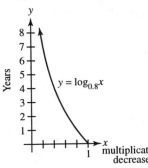

5. The equation $t(r) = \dfrac{\ln 4}{r}$ can be rewritten as

$r = \dfrac{\ln 4}{t(r)}$. When this equation is graphed we find that the annual rate r needed to quadruple the investment in 10 years is approximately 13.9%. Alternatively, we can solve for r by setting $t(r) = 10$.

$r = \dfrac{\ln(4)}{t(r)}$

$r = \dfrac{\ln(4)}{10} \approx 0.139$ or $\approx 13.9\%$

6. Since $m = e^{rt}$, then $\ln m = rt$.

$\ln m = rt$

$\dfrac{\ln m}{t} = r$

Let $m = 3$ and $t = 12$.

$\dfrac{\ln 3}{12} = r$

$0.092 = r$

Thus, to triple your investment in 12 years, invest at an annual percentage rate of 9.2%.

Exercise 5.2

1. $\log 10{,}000 = 4$

3. $2^6 = 64$

5. $\ln 7.3891 = 2$

7. $e^{1.09861} = 3$

9.

11.

13.

15.

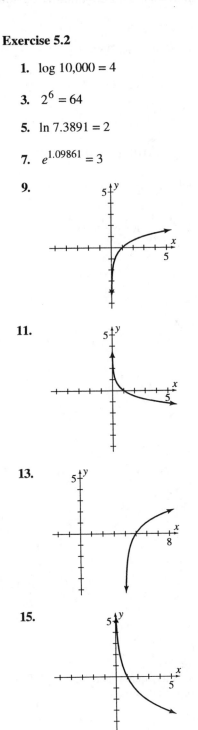

17. Because $6^2 = 36$, $\log_6 36 = 2$

19. Because $3^3 = 27$, $\log_3 27 = 3$

21. Because $7^1 = 7$, $\log_7 7 = 1$

23. Because $10^{-2} = 0.01$, $\log 0.01 = -2$

25. Because $5^0 = 1$, $\log_5 1 = 0$

27. Because $2^{-3} = \dfrac{1}{8}$, $\log_2 \dfrac{1}{8} = -3$

29. $3^2 = x$
$x = 9$

31. $5^3 = x$
$x = 125$

33. $10^{-1} = x$
$x = \dfrac{1}{10}$

35. $e^2 = x$

37. $x^3 = 8$
$x = 2$

39. $x^{-1} = \dfrac{1}{6}$
$x = 6$

41. $3^{-4} = x$
$x = \dfrac{1}{81}$

43. $x^2 = 6 - x$
$x^2 + x - 6 = 0$
$(x + 3)(x - 2) = 0$
The roots of this equation are -3 and 2. But since $x > 0$, we choose $x = 2$.

45. $2 + \log_2 4 = 3x - 1$
$2 + 2 = 3x - 1$
$5 = 3x$
$x = \dfrac{5}{3}$

47. $x^2 = 2x + 8$
$x^2 - 2x - 8 = 0$
$(x - 4)(x + 2) = 0$
The roots of this equation are 4 and -2. But since $x > 0$, we choose $x = 4$.

49. $e^{3x} = 2$
$3x = \ln 2$
$x = \dfrac{\ln 2}{3}$

51. $e^{2x-5} + 1 = 4$
$e^{2x-5} = 3$
$2x - 5 = \ln 3$
$x = \dfrac{5 + \ln 3}{2}$

53. 1.60944

55. 2.00013

57. If $5.5 = \log \dfrac{1}{h}$ then $10^{5.5} = \dfrac{1}{h}$.

59. $c = (12 \ln 6) + 20 \approx 41.50$

61. $1.5M = \log\left(\dfrac{E}{2.5 \times 10^{11}}\right)$
$10^{1.5M} = \dfrac{E}{2.5 \times 10^{11}}$
$E = \left(2.5 \times 10^{11}\right)\left(10^{1.5M}\right)$
$E = 2.5 \times 10^{11+1.5M}$

63. a. $p = 760e^{-0.125(7.3)} \approx 305.2$ mm of mercury

b. $400 = 760e^{-0.125h}$

$\dfrac{400}{760} = e^{-0.125h}$

$\ln\dfrac{400}{760} = -0.125h$

$h = \dfrac{\ln\frac{400}{760}}{-0.125} \approx 5.13$ km

65. $u_0 = A\ln(x_1) + \dfrac{x_2^2}{2}$

$u_0 - \dfrac{x_2^2}{2} = A\ln(x_1)$

$\ln(x_1) = \dfrac{u_0 - \frac{x_2^2}{2}}{A}$

$x_1 = e^{\frac{u_0 - (x_2^2/2)}{A}}$

67. $T = \dfrac{\ln 2}{0.03194} \approx 21.7$ years

69. $x + 2e^{3y} - 10 = 0$

$2e^{3y} = 10 - x$

$e^{3y} = \dfrac{10 - x}{2}$

$3y = \ln\dfrac{10 - x}{2}$

$y = \dfrac{1}{3}\ln\dfrac{10 - x}{2}$

71.

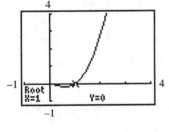

(1, 0)

73. For $y = \ln x$, when $y = 2$, then $2 = \ln x$ or $x = e^2$.

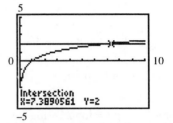

From the graph of $y = \ln x$, when $y = 2$, then $x = e^2 \approx 7.39$.

Principles in Practice 5.3

1. The magnitude (Richter Scale) of an earthquake is given by $R = \log\left(\dfrac{I}{I_0}\right)$ where I is the intensity of the earthquake and I_0 is the intensity of a zero-level reference earthquake. $\dfrac{I}{I_0} =$ how many times greater the earthquake is than a zero-level earthquake. Thus, when $\dfrac{I}{I_0} = 900,000$,

$R_1 = \log(900,000)$ When $\dfrac{I}{I_0} = 9000$

$R_2 = \log(9000)$

$R_1 - R_2 = \log(900,000) - \log 9000$

$= \log\dfrac{900,000}{9000} = \log 100 = \log 10^2$

$= 2\log 10 = 2$

Thus, the two earthquakes differ by 2 on the Richter scale.

2. The magnitude (Richter Scale) of an earthquake is given by $R = \log\left(\dfrac{I}{I_0}\right)$ where I is the intensity of the earthquake and I_0 is the intensity of a zero-level reference earthquake. $\dfrac{I}{I_0} =$ how many times greater the earthquake is than a zero-level earthquake. Thus, if $\dfrac{I}{I_0} = 10,000$, then

$R = \log 10,000 = \log 10^4 = 4\log 10 = 4$

The earthquake measures 4 on the Richter scale.

Exercise 5.3

1. $\log 15 = \log(3 \cdot 5) = \log 3 + \log 5 = b + c$

3. $\log \frac{2}{3} = \log 2 - \log 3 = a - b$

5. $\log \frac{8}{3} = \log 8 - \log 3 = \log 2^3 - \log 3$
   $= 3 \log 2 - \log 3 = 3a - b$

7. $\log 36 = \log(2 \cdot 3)^2 = 2\log(2 \cdot 3)$
   $= 2(\log 2 + \log 3) = 2(a + b)$

9. $\log_2 3 = \frac{\log_{10} 3}{\log_{10} 2} = \frac{\log 3}{\log 2} = \frac{b}{a}$

11. $\log_7 7^{48} = 48$

13. $\log 0.0001 = \log 10^{-4} = -4$

15. $\ln e^{5.01} = \log_e e^{5.01} = 5.01$

17. $\ln \frac{1}{e} = -\ln e = -\log_e e = -1$

19. $\log 10 + \ln e^3 = \log_{10} 10 + \log_e e^3$
   $= 1 + 3 = 4$

21. $\ln\left[x(x+1)^2\right] = \ln x + \ln(x+1)^2$
   $= \ln x + 2\ln(x+1)$

23. $\ln \frac{x^2}{(x+1)^3} = \ln x^2 - \ln(x+1)^3$
   $= 2\ln x - 3\ln(x+1)$

25. $\ln\left(\frac{x}{x+1}\right)^3 = 3\ln \frac{x}{x+1} = 3[\ln x - \ln(x+1)]$

27. $\ln \frac{x}{(x+1)(x+2)} = \ln x - \ln[(x+1)(x+2)] =$
   $\ln x - [\ln(x+1) + \ln(x+2)]$
   $= \ln x - \ln(x+1) - \ln(x+2)$

29. $\ln \frac{\sqrt{x}}{(x+1)^2(x+2)^3}$
   $= \ln x^{\frac{1}{2}} - \ln\left[(x+1)^2(x+2)^3\right]$
   $= \frac{1}{2}\ln x - \left[\ln(x+1)^2 + \ln(x+2)^3\right]$
   $= \frac{1}{2}\ln x - [2\ln(x+1) + 3\ln(x+2)]$
   $= \frac{1}{2}\ln x - 2\ln(x+1) - 3\ln(x+2)$

31. $\ln\left[\frac{1}{x+2}\sqrt[5]{\frac{x^2}{x+1}}\right] = \ln\left[\frac{1}{x+2}\left(\frac{x^2}{x+1}\right)^{\frac{1}{5}}\right]$
   $= \ln \frac{x^{\frac{2}{5}}}{(x+2)(x+1)^{\frac{1}{5}}}$
   $= \ln x^{\frac{2}{5}} - \ln\left[(x+2)(x+1)^{\frac{1}{5}}\right]$
   $= \frac{2}{5}\ln x - \left[\ln(x+2) + \ln(x+1)^{\frac{1}{5}}\right]$
   $= \frac{2}{5}\ln x - \ln(x+2) - \frac{1}{5}\ln(x+1)$

33. $\log(7 \cdot 4) = \log 28$

35. $\log_2 \frac{2x}{x+1}$

37. $\log 7^9 + \log 23^5 = \log\left[7^9(23)^5\right]$

39. $2 + 10\log(1.05) = \log 100 + \log(1.05)^{10}$
   $= \log\left[100(1.05)^{10}\right]$

41. $e^{4\ln 3 - 3\ln 4} = e^{\ln 3^4 - \ln 4^3} = e^{\ln\left(\frac{3^4}{4^3}\right)}$
   $= \frac{3^4}{4^3} = \frac{81}{64}$

43. $\log_6 54 - \log_6 9 = \log_6 \frac{54}{9} = \log_6 6 = 1$

45. $e^{\ln(2x)} = 5$
   $2x = 5$
   $x = \frac{5}{2}$

47. $10^{\log x^2} = 4$

$x^2 = 4$

$x = \pm 2$

49. From the change of base formula with
$b = 10$,
$m = x + 8$, and $a = e$, we have
$$\log(x+8) = \frac{\log_e(x+8)}{\log_e 10} = \frac{\ln(x+8)}{\ln 10}.$$

51. From the change of base formula with $b = 3$,
$m = x^2 + 1$, and $a = e$, we have
$$\log_3\left(x^2 + 1\right) = \frac{\log_e\left(x^2 + 1\right)}{\log_e 3} = \frac{\ln\left(x^2 + 1\right)}{\ln 3}.$$

53. $e^{\ln z} = 7e^y$

$z = 7e^y$

$\frac{z}{7} = e^y$

$y = \ln \frac{z}{7}$

55. $C = B + E$

$C = B\left(1 + \frac{E}{B}\right)$

$\ln C = \ln\left[B\left(1 + \frac{E}{B}\right)\right]$

$\ln C = \ln B + \ln\left(1 + \frac{E}{B}\right)$

57. $M = \log(A) + 3$

a. $M = \log(1) + 3 = 0 + 3 = 3$

b. Given $M_1 = \log(A_1) + 3$, let

$M = \log(100 A_1) + 3$

$M = \log 100 + \log(A_1) + 3$

$M = 2 + \left[\log(A_1) + 3\right]$

$M = 2 + M_1$

59. $\text{pH} = -\log\left(3 \times 10^{-4}\right) = -\left[\log 3 + \log 10^{-4}\right]$

$= -[\log(3) - 4] = 4 - \log 3 \approx 3.5229$

61. $\left[\text{H}^+\right] \cdot \left(3 \times 10^{-2}\right) = 10^{-14}, \left[\text{H}^+\right] = \frac{1}{3} \times 10^{-12}$

$\text{pH} = -\log\left(\frac{1}{3} \times 10^{-12}\right)$

$= -\left[\log\frac{1}{3} + \log 10^{-12}\right]$

$= -[-\log(3) - 12] = 12 + \log 3 \approx 12.4771$

63. $y = \log_4(x+2) = \frac{\ln(x+2)}{\ln 4}$

65.

$y = \ln(4x) = \ln 4 + \ln x$. If $f(x) = \ln x$, then
$y = \ln(4x) = f(x) + \ln 4$. Thus the graph of
$y = \ln(4x)$ is the graph of $y = \ln x$ shifted
$\ln 4$ units upward.

Principles in Practice 5.4

1. Let $x =$ the number and let
$y =$ the unknown exponent. Then
$x \cdot 32^y = x \cdot 4^{(3y-9)}$
$32^y = 4^{(3y-9)}$
$\log 32^y = \log 4^{(3y-9)}$
$y \log 32 = (3y - 9) \log 4$
$y \log 32 = 3y \log 4 - 9 \log 4$
$y(\log 32 - 3 \log 4) = -9 \log 4$
$y = \dfrac{-9 \log 4}{\log \frac{32}{4^3}}$
$y = 18$
Thus, Greg used 32 to the power of 18.

2. Let $S = 450$.

$$S = 800\left(\frac{4}{3}\right)^{-0.1d}$$

$$450 = 800\left(\frac{4}{3}\right)^{-0.1d}$$

$$\frac{450}{800} = \left(\frac{4}{3}\right)^{-0.1d}$$

$$\log\frac{450}{800} = -0.1d\log\left(\frac{4}{3}\right)$$

$$\frac{\log\frac{450}{800}}{-0.1\log\left(\frac{4}{3}\right)} = d$$

$$20 = d$$

Thus, he should start the new campaign 20 days after the last one ends.

3. The magnitude (Richter Scale) of an earthquake is given by $R = \log\left(\frac{I}{I_0}\right)$ where I is the intensity of the earthquake and I_0 is the intensity of a zero-level reference earthquake. $\frac{I}{I_0} =$ how many times greater the earthquake is than a zero-level earthquake.

$$R_1 = \log(675,000)$$

$$R_2 = \log\left(\frac{I}{I_0}\right)$$

Since $R_1 - 4 = R_2$

$$\log(675,000) - 4 = \log\left(\frac{I}{I_0}\right)$$

$$\log\left(6.75 \times 10^5\right) - 4 = \log\left(\frac{I}{I_0}\right)$$

$$\log 6.75 + 5\log 10 - 4 = \log\left(\frac{I}{I_0}\right)$$

$$1.83 = \log\left(\frac{I}{I_0}\right)$$

$$10^{1.83} = \frac{I}{I_0}$$

$$67.5 = \frac{I}{I_0}$$

Thus, the other earthquake is 67.5 times as intense as a zero-level earthquake.

Exercise 5.4

1. $\log(2x + 1) = \log(x + 6)$
$2x + 1 = x + 6$
$x = 5.000$

3. $\log x - \log(x - 1) = \log 4$

$\log\frac{x}{x-1} = \log 4$

$\frac{x}{x-1} = 4$

$x = 4x - 4$

$4 = 3x$

$x = \frac{4}{3} \approx 1.333$

5. $\ln(-x) = \ln\left(x^2 - 6\right)$

$-x = x^2 - 6$

$x^2 + x - 6 = 0$

$(x + 3)(x - 2) = 0$

$x = -3$ or $x = 2$

However, $x = -3$ is the only value that satisfies the original equation.

Answer: -3.000

7. $e^{2x}e^{5x} = e^{14}$

$e^{7x} = e^{14}$

$7x = 14$

$x = 2.000$

9. $(16)^{3x} = 2$

$\left(2^4\right)^{3x} = 2$

$2^{12x} = 2^1$

$12x = 1$

$x = \frac{1}{12} \approx 0.083$

11. $e^{2x} = 5$

$2x = \ln 5$

$x = \frac{\ln 5}{2} \approx 0.805$

13. $3e^{3x+1} = 15$

$e^{3x+1} = 5$

$3x + 1 = \ln 5$

$x = \frac{\ln(5) - 1}{3} \approx 0.203$

15. $10^{\frac{4}{x}} = 6$

$\dfrac{4}{x} = \log 6$

$x = \dfrac{4}{\log 6} \approx 5.140$

17. $\dfrac{5}{10^{2x}} = 7$

$10^{2x} = \dfrac{5}{7}$

$2x = \log \dfrac{5}{7}$

$x = \dfrac{\log\left(\frac{5}{7}\right)}{2} \approx -0.073$

19. $2^x = 5$

$\ln 2^x = \ln 5$

$x \ln 2 = \ln 5$

$x = \dfrac{\ln 5}{\ln 2} \approx 2.322$

21. $5^{2x-5} = 9$

$\ln 5^{2x-5} = \ln 9$

$(2x - 5)\ln 5 = \ln 9$

$2x - 5 = \dfrac{\ln 9}{\ln 5}$

$2x = \dfrac{\ln 9}{\ln 5} + 5$

$x = \dfrac{\frac{\ln 9}{\ln 5} + 5}{2} \approx 3.183$

23. $2^{-\frac{2x}{3}} = \dfrac{4}{5}$

$\ln 2^{-\frac{2x}{3}} = \ln \dfrac{4}{5}$

$-\dfrac{2x}{3} \ln 2 = \ln \dfrac{4}{5}$

$-\dfrac{2x}{3} = \dfrac{\ln\left(\frac{4}{5}\right)}{\ln 2}$

$x = -\dfrac{3\ln\left(\frac{4}{5}\right)}{2\ln 2} \approx 0.483$

25. $(4)5^{3-x} - 7 = 2$

$5^{3-x} = \dfrac{9}{4}$

$\ln 5^{3-x} = \ln \dfrac{9}{4}$

$(3 - x)\ln 5 = \ln \dfrac{9}{4}$

$3 - x = \dfrac{\ln\left(\frac{9}{4}\right)}{\ln 5}$

$x = 3 - \dfrac{\ln\left(\frac{9}{4}\right)}{\ln 5} \approx 2.496$

27. $\log(x - 3) = 3$

$10^3 = x - 3$

$x = 10^3 + 3 = 1003.000$

29. $\log_4(3x - 4) = 2$

$4^2 = 3x - 4$

$3x = 4^2 + 4$

$x = \dfrac{4^2 + 4}{3} = \dfrac{20}{3} = 6.667$

31. $\log(3x - 1) - \log(x - 3) = 2$

$\log \dfrac{3x - 1}{x - 3} = 2$

$10^2 = \dfrac{3x - 1}{x - 3}$

$100(x - 3) = 3x - 1$

$97x = 299$

$x = \dfrac{299}{97} \approx 3.082$

33. $\log_3(2x + 3) = 4 - \log_3(x + 6)$

$\log_3(2x + 3) + \log_3(x + 6) = 4$

$\log_3[(2x + 3)(x + 6)] = 4$

$3^4 = (2x + 3)(x + 6)$

$2x^2 + 15x + 18 = 81$

$2x^2 + 15x - 63 = 0$

$(2x + 21)(x - 3) = 0$

$x = -\dfrac{21}{2}$ or $x = 3$

However, $x = 3$ is the only value that satisfies the original equation.

Answer: 3.000

35. $\log_2\left(\dfrac{2}{x}\right) = 3 + \log_2 x$

   $\log_2\left(\dfrac{2}{x}\right) - \log_2 x = 3$

   $\log_2 \dfrac{\frac{2}{x}}{x} = 3$

   $\log_2 \dfrac{2}{x^2} = 3$

   $2^3 = \dfrac{2}{x^2}$

   $x^2 = \dfrac{1}{4}$

   $x = \pm\dfrac{1}{2}$

   However, $x = \dfrac{1}{2}$ is the only value that satisfies the original equation.
   Answer: 0.500

37. $\log S = \log 12.4 + 0.26 \log A$

   $\log S = \log 12.4 + \log A^{0.26}$

   $\log S = \log\left[12.4 A^{0.26}\right]$

   $S = 12.4 A^{0.26}$

39. a. When $t = 0$,

   $Q = 100 e^{-0.035(0)} = 100 e^0$
   $= 100 \cdot 1 = 100$

   b. If $Q = 20$, then $20 = 100 e^{-0.035t}$.
   Solving for t gives

   $\dfrac{20}{100} = e^{-0.035t}$

   $\dfrac{1}{5} = e^{-0.035t}$

   $\ln\dfrac{1}{5} = -0.035t$

   $-\ln 5 = -0.035t$

   $t = \dfrac{\ln 5}{0.035} \approx 46$

41. If $P = 1{,}500{,}000$, then
   $1{,}500{,}000 = 1{,}000{,}000(1.02)^t$.
   Solving for t gives

   $\dfrac{1{,}500{,}000}{1{,}000{,}000} = (1.02)^t$

   $1.5 = (1.02)^t$

   $\ln 1.5 = \ln(1.02)^t$

   $\ln 1.5 = t \ln 1.02$

   $t = \dfrac{\ln 1.5}{\ln 1.02} \approx 20.5$.

43. $q = 80 - 2^p$

   $2^p = 80 - q$

   $\log 2^p = \log(80 - q)$

   $p \log 2 = \log(80 - q)$

   $p = \dfrac{\log(80 - q)}{\log 2}$

   When $q = 60$, then $p = \dfrac{\log 20}{\log 2} \approx 4.32$.

45. Let I be the original intensity. the intensity of light passes through 1 sheet of $0.9I$. The intensity of light passing through 2 sheets is $0.9[(0.9)I] = (0.9)^2 I$. Continuing in this manner, the light passing through n sheets is $(0.9)^n I$. The equation to solve is $(0.9)^n I = 0.5I$ or, more simply, $(0.9)^n = 0.5$. Solving gives

   $\ln(0.9)^n = \ln 0.5$

   $n \ln 0.9 = \ln 0.5$

   $n = \dfrac{\ln 0.5}{\ln 0.9} \approx 7$

47. $q = 500\left(1 - e^{-0.2t}\right)$

   a. If $t = 1$, then $q = 500\left(1 - e^{-0.2}\right) \approx 91$.

   b. If $t = 10$, then $q = 500\left(1 - e^{-2}\right) \approx 432$.

c. We solve the equation

$$400 = 500\left(1 - e^{-0.2t}\right)$$

$$\frac{4}{5} = 1 - e^{-0.2t}$$

$$e^{-0.2t} = \frac{1}{5}$$

$$-0.2t = \ln\frac{1}{5} = -\ln 5$$

$$t = \frac{\ln 5}{0.2} \approx 8$$

49.

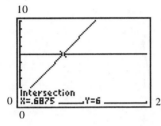

0.69

51. $4x + (3)4^y = 1$

$$(3)4^y = 1 - 4x$$

$$4^y = \frac{1 - 4x}{3}$$

$$\ln 4^y = \ln\left(\frac{1 - 4x}{3}\right)$$

$$y\ln 4 = \ln\left(\frac{1 - 4x}{3}\right)$$

$$y = \frac{\ln\left(\frac{1-4x}{3}\right)}{\ln 4}$$

Graph of the original equation is the graph

of $y = \frac{\ln\left(\frac{1-4x}{3}\right)}{\ln 4}$.

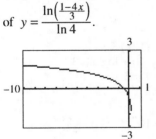

Chapter 5 Review Problems

1. $\log_3 243 = 5$

3. $16^{\frac{1}{4}} = 2$

5. $\ln 54.598 = 4$

7. Because $5^3 = 125$, $\log_5 125 = 3$

9. Because $2^{-4} = \frac{1}{16}$, $\log_2 \frac{1}{16} = -4$

11. Because $\left(\frac{1}{3}\right)^{-2} = 3^2 = 9$, $\log_{\frac{1}{3}} 9 = -2$

13. $5^x = 125$
    $x = 3$

15. $10^{-2} = x$
    $x = \frac{1}{10^2} = \frac{1}{100}$

17. $\log_x(2x+3) = 2$
    $x^2 = 2x + 3$
    $x^2 - 2x - 3 = 0$
    $(x - 3)(x + 1) = 0$
    $x = 3$ or $x = -1$
    However, $x = 3$ is the only value that
    satisfies original equation.
    Answer: 3

19. $\log 8000 = \log(2 \cdot 10)^3 = 3\log(2 \cdot 10)$
    $= 3(\log 2 + \log 10) = 3(a + 1)$

21. $2\log 5 - 3\log 3 = \log 5^2 - \log 3^3 = \log\frac{5^2}{3^3}$
    $= \log\frac{25}{27}$

23. $2\ln x + \ln y - 3\ln z = \ln x^2 + \ln y - \ln z^3$
    $= \ln x^2 y - \ln z^3 = \ln\frac{x^2 y}{z^3}$

25. $\dfrac{1}{2}\log_2 x + 2\log_2 x^2 - 3\log_2(x+1) - 4\log_2(x+2)$

$= \log_2 x^{\frac{1}{2}} + \log_2\left(x^2\right)^2 - \left[\log_2(x+1)^3 + \log_2(x+2)^4\right]$

$= \log_2\left(x^{\frac{1}{2}}x^4\right) - \log_2\left[(x+1)^3(x+2)^4\right]$

$= \log_2 \dfrac{x^{\frac{9}{2}}}{(x+1)^3(x+2)^4}$

27. $\ln\dfrac{x^2 y}{z^3} = \ln x^2 y - \ln z^3 = \ln x^2 + \ln y - \ln z^3$

$= 2\ln x + \ln y - 3\ln z$

29. $\ln\sqrt[3]{xyz} = \ln(xyz)^{\frac{1}{3}} = \dfrac{1}{3}\ln(xyz)$

$= \dfrac{1}{3}(\ln x + \ln y + \ln z)$

31. $\ln\left[\dfrac{1}{x}\sqrt{\dfrac{y}{z}}\right] = \ln\dfrac{\left(\frac{y}{z}\right)^{1/2}}{x} = \ln\left(\dfrac{y}{z}\right)^{\frac{1}{2}} - \ln x$

$= \dfrac{1}{2}\ln\dfrac{y}{z} - \ln x = \dfrac{1}{2}(\ln y - \ln z) - \ln x$

33. $\log_3(x+5) = \dfrac{\log_e(x+5)}{\log_e 3} = \dfrac{\ln(x+5)}{\ln 3}$

35. $\log_5 19 = \dfrac{\log_2 19}{\log_2 5} = \dfrac{4.2479}{2.3219} \approx 1.8295$

37. $\ln\left(16\sqrt{3}\right) = \ln 4^2 + \ln\sqrt{3} = 2\ln 2 + \dfrac{1}{2}\ln 3$

$= 2y + \dfrac{1}{2}x$

39. $e^{\ln x} + \ln e^x + \ln 1 = x + x + 0 = 2x$

41. In exponential form, $y = e^{x^2+2}$.

43.

45. $4x + 1 = x + 2$
$3x = 1$
$x = \dfrac{1}{3}$

47. $3^{4x} = 9^{x+1}$
$3^{4x} = \left(3^2\right)^{x+1}$
$3^{4x} = 3^{2(x+1)}$
$4x = 2(x+1)$
$4x = 2x + 2$
$2x = 2$
$x = 1$

49. $\log x + \log(10x) = 3$
$\log x + \log 10 + \log x = 3$
$2\log(x) + 1 = 3$
$2\log(x) = 2$
$\log x = 1$
$x = 10^1 = 10$

51. $\ln(\log_x 2) = -1$

$\log_x 2 = e^{-1}$

$x^{e^{-1}} = 2$

$\left(x^{e^{-1}}\right)^e = 2^e$

$x^{e^{-1}e} = 2^e$

$x^1 = 2^e$

$x = 2^e$

53. $e^{3x} = 2$

$3x = \ln 2$

$x = \dfrac{\ln 2}{3} \approx 0.231$

55. $3\left(10^{x+4} - 3\right) = 9$

$10^{x+4} - 3 = 3$

$10^{x+4} = 6$

$x + 4 = \log 6$

$x = \log(6) - 4 \approx -3.222$

57. $4^{x+3} = 7$

$\ln 4^{x+3} = \ln 7$

$(x + 3)\ln 4 = \ln 7$

$x + 3 = \dfrac{\ln 7}{\ln 4}$

$x = \dfrac{\ln 7}{\ln 4} - 3 \approx -1.596$

59. Quarterly rate $= \dfrac{0.06}{4} = 0.015$

$6\frac{1}{2}$ yrs = 26 quarters

    a. $2600(1.015)^{26} \approx \$3829.04$

    b. $3829.04 - 2600 = \$1229.04$

61. Monthly rate $= \dfrac{0.11}{12}$

5 yrs = 60 mos.

$4000\left(1 + \dfrac{0.11}{12}\right)^{60} \approx \$6915.66$

63. **a.** $P = 8000(1 + 0.02)^t$ or

        $P = 8000(1.02)^t$

    b. When $t = 2$, then

        $P = 8000(1.02)^2 \approx 8323$

65. $N = 10e^{-0.41t}$

    a. When $t = 0$, then

        $N = 10e^0 = 10 \cdot 1 = 10$ mg

    b. When $t = 2$, then

        $N = 10e^{-0.82} \approx 4.4$ mg

    c. When $t = 10$, then

        $N = 10e^{-4.1} \approx 0.2$ mg

    d. $\dfrac{\ln 2}{0.41} \approx 1.7$

    e. If $N = 1$, then $1 = 10e^{-0.41t}$. Solving for t gives

        $\dfrac{1}{10} = e^{-0.41t}$

        $-0.41t = \ln\dfrac{1}{10} = -\ln 10$

        $t = \dfrac{\ln 10}{0.41} \approx 5.6$

67. $R = 10e^{-\frac{t}{40}}$

    a. If $t = 20$, $R = 10e^{-\frac{20}{40}} = 10e^{-\frac{1}{2}} \approx 6$.

    b. $5 = 10e^{-\frac{t}{40}}$, $\dfrac{1}{2} = e^{-\frac{t}{40}}$. Thus

        $-\dfrac{t}{40} = \ln\dfrac{1}{2} = -\ln 2$

        $t = 40\ln 2 \approx 28$.

69. $T_t - T_e = \left(T_t - T_e\right)_o e^{-at}$

$e^{-at} = \dfrac{T_t - T_e}{\left(T_t - T_e\right)_o}$

$-at = \ln\dfrac{T_t - T_e}{\left(T_t - T_e\right)_o}$

$a = -\dfrac{1}{t}\ln\dfrac{T_t - T_e}{\left(T_t - T_e\right)_o}$

$a = \dfrac{1}{t}\ln\dfrac{\left(T_t - T_e\right)_o}{T_t - T_e}$

71.

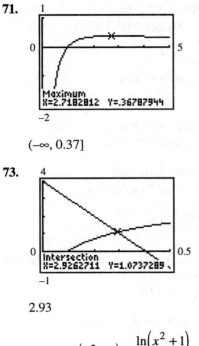

$(-\infty, 0.37]$

73.

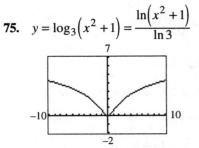

2.93

75. $y = \log_3\left(x^2 + 1\right) = \dfrac{\ln\left(x^2 + 1\right)}{\ln 3}$

Mathematical Snapshot Chapter 5

1. $T = \dfrac{P\left(1 - e^{-dkI}\right)}{e^{kI} - 1}$

   a. $T\left(e^{kI} - 1\right) = P\left(1 - e^{-dkI}\right)$

      $\dfrac{T\left(e^{kI} - 1\right)}{1 - e^{-dkI}} = P$ or $P = \dfrac{T\left(e^{kI} - 1\right)}{1 - e^{-dkI}}$

   b. $T\left(e^{kI} - 1\right) = P - Pe^{-dkI}$,

      $Pe^{-dkI} = P - T\left(e^{kI} - 1\right)$,

      $e^{-dkI} = \dfrac{P - T\left(e^{kI} - 1\right)}{P}$,

$-dkI = \ln\left[\dfrac{P - T\left(e^{kI} - 1\right)}{P}\right]$,

$d = -\dfrac{1}{kI}\ln\left[\dfrac{P - T\left(e^{kI} - 1\right)}{P}\right]$,

$d = \dfrac{1}{kI}\ln\left[\dfrac{P}{P - T\left(e^{kI} - 1\right)}\right]$

3. $P = 100,\ I = 4,\ d = 3,\ H = 8,\ k = \dfrac{\ln 2}{H} = \dfrac{\ln 2}{8}$

   a. $T = \dfrac{P\left(1 - e^{-dkI}\right)}{e^{kI} - 1} = \dfrac{100\left(1 - e^{-3 \cdot \frac{\ln 2}{8} \cdot 4}\right)}{e^{\frac{\ln 2}{8} \cdot 4} - 1}$

      $= \dfrac{100\left(1 - \left[e^{\ln 2}\right]^{-\frac{3}{2}}\right)}{\left[e^{\ln 2}\right]^{\frac{1}{2}} - 1}$

      $= \dfrac{100\left(1 - 2^{-\frac{3}{2}}\right)}{2^{\frac{1}{2}} - 1} \approx 156$

   b. $R = P\left(1 - e^{-dkI}\right)$. From part (a),

      $P\left(1 - e^{-dkI}\right) = 100\left(1 - 2^{-\frac{3}{2}}\right)$. Thus

      $R = 100\left(1 - 2^{-\frac{3}{2}}\right) \approx 65.$

94

Chapter 6

Principles in Practice 6.1

1. There are 3 rows, one for each source. There are two columns, one for each raw material. Thus, the order of the matrix is 3×2.

2. The first column consists of 1's each representing the 1 hour needed for each phase of project 1. The second column consists of 2's for each phase of project 2 and so on. In general the nth column will consist of 2^n's, each representing the 2^n hours needed for each phase of project n. The time-analysis matrix is as follows.

$$\begin{bmatrix} 1 & 2 & 4 & 8 & 16 \\ 1 & 2 & 4 & 8 & 16 \\ 1 & 2 & 4 & 8 & 16 \end{bmatrix}$$

Exercise 6.1

1. a. The order is the number of rows by the columns. Thus **A** is 2×3, **B** is 3×3, **C** is 3×2, **D** is 2×2, **E** is 4×4, **F** is 1×2, **G** is 3×1, **H** is 3×3, **J** is 1×1.

   b. A square matrix has the same number of rows as columns. Thus the square matrices are **B**, **D**, **E**, **H**, and **J**.

   c. An upper triangular matrix is a square matrix where all entries below the main diagonal are zeros. Thus **H** and **J** are upper triangular. A lower triangular matrix is a square matrix where all entries above the main diagonal are zeros. Thus **D** and **J** are lower triangular.

   d. A row vector (or row matrix) has only one row. Thus **F** and **J** are row vectors.

   e. A column vector (or column matrix) has only one column. Thus **G** and **J** are column vectors.

3. a_{43} is the entry in the 4th row and 3rd column, namely 2.

5. a_{32} is the entry in the 3rd row and 2nd column, namely 4.

7. a_{14} is the entry in the 1st row and 4th column, namely 6.

9. The main diagonal entries are the entries on the diagonal extending from the upper left corner to the lower right corner. Thus the main diagonal entries are 7, 2, 1, 0.

11. $$\begin{bmatrix} 2 \cdot 1 + 3 \cdot 1 & 2 \cdot 1 + 3 \cdot 2 & 2 \cdot 1 + 3 \cdot 3 & 2 \cdot 1 + 3 \cdot 4 \\ 2 \cdot 2 + 3 \cdot 1 & 2 \cdot 2 + 3 \cdot 2 & 2 \cdot 2 + 3 \cdot 3 & 2 \cdot 2 + 3 \cdot 4 \\ 2 \cdot 3 + 3 \cdot 1 & 2 \cdot 3 + 3 \cdot 2 & 2 \cdot 3 + 3 \cdot 3 & 2 \cdot 3 + 3 \cdot 4 \end{bmatrix} = \begin{bmatrix} 5 & 8 & 11 & 14 \\ 7 & 10 & 13 & 16 \\ 9 & 12 & 15 & 18 \end{bmatrix}$$

13. $12 \cdot 10 = 120$, so **A** has 120 entries. For a_{33}, $i = 3 = j$, so $a_{33} = 1$. Since $5 \neq 2$, $a_{52} = 0$. For $a_{10, 10}$, $i = 10 = j$, so $a_{10, 10} = 1$. Since $12 \neq 10$, $a_{12, 10} = 0$.

15. A zero matrix is a matrix in which all entries are zeros.

a.
$$\begin{bmatrix} 0 & 0 & 0 & 0 \\ 0 & 0 & 0 & 0 \\ 0 & 0 & 0 & 0 \\ 0 & 0 & 0 & 0 \end{bmatrix}$$

b.
$$\begin{bmatrix} 0 & 0 & 0 & 0 & 0 & 0 \\ 0 & 0 & 0 & 0 & 0 & 0 \\ 0 & 0 & 0 & 0 & 0 & 0 \\ 0 & 0 & 0 & 0 & 0 & 0 \\ 0 & 0 & 0 & 0 & 0 & 0 \\ 0 & 0 & 0 & 0 & 0 & 0 \end{bmatrix}$$

17. $\mathbf{A}^T = \begin{bmatrix} 6 & -3 \\ 2 & 4 \end{bmatrix}^T = \begin{bmatrix} 6 & 2 \\ -3 & 4 \end{bmatrix}$

19. $\mathbf{A}^T = \begin{bmatrix} 1 & 3 & 2 & 3 \\ 3 & 2 & -2 & 0 \\ -4 & 2 & 0 & 1 \end{bmatrix}^T = \begin{bmatrix} 1 & 3 & -4 \\ 3 & 2 & 2 \\ 2 & -2 & 0 \\ 3 & 0 & 1 \end{bmatrix}$

21. a. A and C are diagonal matrices.

b. All are them are triangular matrices.

23. $\mathbf{A}^T = \begin{bmatrix} 1 & 2 & 3 \\ 4 & 5 & 6 \\ 7 & 8 & 9 \end{bmatrix}^T = \begin{bmatrix} 1 & 4 & 7 \\ 2 & 5 & 8 \\ 3 & 6 & 9 \end{bmatrix}$

$\left(\mathbf{A}^T\right)^T = \begin{bmatrix} 1 & 4 & 7 \\ 2 & 5 & 8 \\ 3 & 6 & 9 \end{bmatrix}^T = \begin{bmatrix} 1 & 2 & 3 \\ 4 & 5 & 6 \\ 7 & 8 & 9 \end{bmatrix} = \mathbf{A}$

25. Equating corresponding entries gives $6 = 6$, $2 = 2$, $x = 6$, $7 = 7$, $3y = 2$, and $2z = 7$. Thus $x = 6$, $y = \dfrac{2}{3}$, $z = \dfrac{7}{2}$.

27. Equating corresponding entries gives $2x = y$, $7 = 7$, $7 = 7$, and $2y = y$. Now $2y = y$ yields $y = 0$. Thus from $2x = y$ we get $2x = 0$, so $x = 0$. The solution is $x = 0$, $y = 0$.

29. a. From **J**, the entry in row 3 (super-duper) and column 2 (white) is 7. Thus in January, 7 white super-duper models were sold.

b. From **F**, the entry in row 2 (deluxe) and column 3 (blue) is 3. Thus in February, 3 blue deluxe models were sold.

c. The entries in row 1 (regular) and column 4 (purple) give the number of purple regular models sold. For **J** the entry is 2 and for **F** the entry is 4. Thus more purple regular models were sold in February.

d. In both January and February, the deluxe blue models (row 2, column 3) sold the same number of units (3).

e. In January a total of $0 + 1 + 3 + 5 = 9$ deluxe models were sold. In February a total of $2 + 3 + 3 + 2 = 10$ deluxe models were sold. Thus more deluxe models were sold in February.

f. In January a total of $2 + 0 + 2 = 4$ red widgets were sold, while in February a total of $0 + 2 + 4 = 6$ red widgets were sold. Thus more red widgets were sold in February.

g. Adding all entries in matrix **J** yields that a total of 35 widgets were sold in January.

31. By equating entries we find that x must satisfy $x^2 + 1993x = 1994$ and $\sqrt{x^2} = -x$. The second equation implies that $x < 0$. From the first equation,
$x^2 + 1993x - 1994 = 0$,
$(x + 1994)(x - 1) = 0$, so $x = -1994$.

33. $\begin{bmatrix} 3 & 1 & 1 \\ 1 & 7 & 4 \\ 4 & 3 & 1 \\ 2 & 6 & 2 \end{bmatrix}$

Principles in Practice 6.2

1. $\mathbf{T} = \mathbf{J} + \mathbf{F} = \begin{bmatrix} 120 & 80 \\ 105 & 130 \end{bmatrix} + \begin{bmatrix} 110 & 140 \\ 85 & 125 \end{bmatrix}$

   $= \begin{bmatrix} 120+110 & 80+140 \\ 105+85 & 130+125 \end{bmatrix} = \begin{bmatrix} 230 & 220 \\ 190 & 155 \end{bmatrix}$

2. $0.8 \begin{bmatrix} x_1 \\ x_2 \\ x_3 \end{bmatrix} - \begin{bmatrix} 40 \\ 30 \\ 60 \end{bmatrix} = 2 \begin{bmatrix} 248 \\ 319 \\ 532 \end{bmatrix}$

   $\begin{bmatrix} 0.8x_1 \\ 0.8x_2 \\ 0.8x_3 \end{bmatrix} - \begin{bmatrix} 40 \\ 30 \\ 60 \end{bmatrix} = \begin{bmatrix} 496 \\ 638 \\ 1064 \end{bmatrix}$

   $\begin{bmatrix} 0.8x_1 - 40 \\ 0.8x_2 - 30 \\ 0.8x_3 - 60 \end{bmatrix} = \begin{bmatrix} 496 \\ 638 \\ 1064 \end{bmatrix}$

   Solve $0.8x_1 - 40 = 496$ to get $x_1 = 670$.
   Solve $0.8x_2 - 30 = 638$ to get $x_2 = 835$.
   Solve $0.8x_3 - 60 = 1064$ to get $x_3 = 1405$

Exercise 6.2

1. $\begin{bmatrix} 2 & 0 & -3 \\ -1 & 4 & 0 \\ 1 & -6 & 5 \end{bmatrix} + \begin{bmatrix} 2 & -3 & 4 \\ -1 & 6 & 5 \\ 9 & 11 & -2 \end{bmatrix} = \begin{bmatrix} 2+2 & 0+(-3) & -3+4 \\ -1+(-1) & 4+6 & 0+5 \\ 1+9 & -6+11 & 5+(-2) \end{bmatrix} = \begin{bmatrix} 4 & -3 & 1 \\ -2 & 10 & 5 \\ 10 & 5 & 3 \end{bmatrix}$

3. $\begin{bmatrix} 1 & 4 \\ -2 & 7 \\ 6 & 9 \end{bmatrix} - \begin{bmatrix} 6 & -1 \\ 7 & 2 \\ 1 & 0 \end{bmatrix} = \begin{bmatrix} 1-6 & 4-(-1) \\ -2-7 & 7-2 \\ 6-1 & 9-0 \end{bmatrix} = \begin{bmatrix} -5 & 5 \\ -9 & 5 \\ 5 & 9 \end{bmatrix}$

5. $3\begin{bmatrix} 1 & -3 & 1 \end{bmatrix} + 2\begin{bmatrix} -6 & 1 & 4 \end{bmatrix} - 0\begin{bmatrix} -2 & 7 & 4 \end{bmatrix}$

   $= \begin{bmatrix} 3 & -9 & 3 \end{bmatrix} + \begin{bmatrix} -12 & 2 & 8 \end{bmatrix} - \begin{bmatrix} 0 & 0 & 0 \end{bmatrix}$

   $= \begin{bmatrix} 3-12-0 & -9+2-0 & 3+8-0 \end{bmatrix} = \begin{bmatrix} -9 & -7 & 11 \end{bmatrix}$

7. $\begin{bmatrix} 1 & 2 \\ 3 & 4 \end{bmatrix}$ has order 2×2, and $\begin{bmatrix} 5 \\ 6 \end{bmatrix}$ has order 2×1. Thus the sum is not defined.

9. $-6 \begin{bmatrix} 2 & -6 & 7 & 1 \\ 7 & 1 & 6 & -2 \end{bmatrix} = \begin{bmatrix} -6 \cdot 2 & -6(-6) & -6 \cdot 7 & -6 \cdot 1 \\ -6 \cdot 7 & -6 \cdot 1 & -6 \cdot 6 & -6(-2) \end{bmatrix} = \begin{bmatrix} -12 & 36 & -42 & -6 \\ -42 & -6 & -36 & 12 \end{bmatrix}$

11. $\begin{bmatrix} 2 & -4 & 0 \\ 0 & 6 & -2 \\ -4 & 0 & 10 \end{bmatrix} + \frac{1}{3}\begin{bmatrix} 9 & 0 & 3 \\ 0 & 3 & 0 \\ 3 & 9 & 9 \end{bmatrix} = \begin{bmatrix} 2 & -4 & 0 \\ 0 & 6 & -2 \\ -4 & 0 & 10 \end{bmatrix} + \begin{bmatrix} 3 & 0 & 1 \\ 0 & 1 & 0 \\ 1 & 3 & 3 \end{bmatrix} = \begin{bmatrix} 5 & -4 & 1 \\ 0 & 7 & -2 \\ -3 & 3 & 13 \end{bmatrix}$

13. $-\mathbf{B} = -\begin{bmatrix} -6 & -5 \\ 2 & -3 \end{bmatrix} = (-1)\begin{bmatrix} -6 & -5 \\ 2 & -3 \end{bmatrix} = \begin{bmatrix} -1(-6) & -1(-5) \\ -1(2) & -1(-3) \end{bmatrix} = \begin{bmatrix} 6 & 5 \\ -2 & 3 \end{bmatrix}$

15. $2\mathbf{O} = 2\begin{bmatrix} 0 & 0 \\ 0 & 0 \end{bmatrix} = \begin{bmatrix} 2\cdot 0 & 2\cdot 0 \\ 2\cdot 0 & 2\cdot 0 \end{bmatrix} = \begin{bmatrix} 0 & 0 \\ 0 & 0 \end{bmatrix} = \mathbf{O}$

17. $2(\mathbf{A} - 2\mathbf{B}) = 2\left\{ \begin{bmatrix} 2 & 1 \\ 3 & -3 \end{bmatrix} - 2\begin{bmatrix} -6 & -5 \\ 2 & -3 \end{bmatrix} \right\}$

$= 2\left\{ \begin{bmatrix} 2 & 1 \\ 3 & -3 \end{bmatrix} - \begin{bmatrix} -12 & -10 \\ 4 & -6 \end{bmatrix} \right\} = 2\begin{bmatrix} 14 & 11 \\ -1 & 3 \end{bmatrix} = \begin{bmatrix} 28 & 22 \\ -2 & 6 \end{bmatrix}$

19. $3(\mathbf{A} - \mathbf{C})$ is a 2×2 matrix and 6 is a number. Therefore $3(\mathbf{A} - \mathbf{C}) + 6$ is not defined.

21. $2\mathbf{B} - 3\mathbf{A} + 2\mathbf{C} = 2\begin{bmatrix} -6 & -5 \\ 2 & -3 \end{bmatrix} - 3\begin{bmatrix} 2 & 1 \\ 3 & -3 \end{bmatrix} + 2\begin{bmatrix} -2 & -1 \\ -3 & 3 \end{bmatrix}$

$= \begin{bmatrix} -12 & -10 \\ 4 & -6 \end{bmatrix} - \begin{bmatrix} 6 & 3 \\ 9 & -9 \end{bmatrix} + \begin{bmatrix} -4 & -2 \\ -6 & 6 \end{bmatrix}$

$= \begin{bmatrix} -18 & -13 \\ -5 & 3 \end{bmatrix} + \begin{bmatrix} -4 & -2 \\ -6 & 6 \end{bmatrix} = \begin{bmatrix} -22 & -15 \\ -11 & 9 \end{bmatrix}$

23. $\frac{1}{2}\mathbf{A} - 2(\mathbf{B} + 2\mathbf{C}) = \frac{1}{2}\begin{bmatrix} 2 & 1 \\ 3 & -3 \end{bmatrix} - 2\left\{ \begin{bmatrix} -6 & -5 \\ 2 & -3 \end{bmatrix} + 2\begin{bmatrix} -2 & -1 \\ -3 & 3 \end{bmatrix} \right\}$

$= \begin{bmatrix} 1 & \frac{1}{2} \\ \frac{3}{2} & -\frac{3}{2} \end{bmatrix} - 2\left\{ \begin{bmatrix} -6 & -5 \\ 2 & -3 \end{bmatrix} + \begin{bmatrix} -4 & -2 \\ -6 & 6 \end{bmatrix} \right\}$

$= \begin{bmatrix} 1 & \frac{1}{2} \\ \frac{3}{2} & -\frac{3}{2} \end{bmatrix} - 2\begin{bmatrix} -10 & -7 \\ -4 & 3 \end{bmatrix} = \begin{bmatrix} 1 & \frac{1}{2} \\ \frac{3}{2} & -\frac{3}{2} \end{bmatrix} - \begin{bmatrix} -20 & -14 \\ -8 & 6 \end{bmatrix} = \begin{bmatrix} 21 & \frac{29}{2} \\ \frac{19}{2} & -\frac{15}{2} \end{bmatrix}$

25. $3(\mathbf{A} + \mathbf{B}) = 3\begin{bmatrix} -4 & -4 \\ 5 & -6 \end{bmatrix} = \begin{bmatrix} -12 & -12 \\ 15 & -18 \end{bmatrix}$

$3\mathbf{A} + 3\mathbf{B} = \begin{bmatrix} 6 & 3 \\ 9 & -9 \end{bmatrix} + \begin{bmatrix} -18 & -15 \\ 6 & -9 \end{bmatrix} = \begin{bmatrix} -12 & -12 \\ 15 & -18 \end{bmatrix}$

Thus $3(\mathbf{A} + \mathbf{B}) = 3\mathbf{A} + 3\mathbf{B}$.

27. $k_1(k_2\mathbf{A}) = k_1\begin{bmatrix} 2k_2 & k_2 \\ 3k_2 & -3k_2 \end{bmatrix} = \begin{bmatrix} 2k_1k_2 & k_1k_2 \\ 3k_1k_2 & -3k_1k_2 \end{bmatrix}$

$(k_1k_2)\mathbf{A} = \begin{bmatrix} 2k_1k_2 & k_1k_2 \\ 3k_1k_2 & -3k_1k_2 \end{bmatrix}$.

Thus $k_1(k_2\mathbf{A}) = (k_1k_2)\mathbf{A}$.

29. $3\mathbf{A}^T + \mathbf{D} = 3\begin{bmatrix} 1 & 0 & 2 \\ 2 & -1 & 0 \end{bmatrix} + \begin{bmatrix} 1 & 2 & -1 \\ 1 & 0 & 2 \end{bmatrix} = \begin{bmatrix} 3 & 0 & 6 \\ 6 & -3 & 0 \end{bmatrix} + \begin{bmatrix} 1 & 2 & -1 \\ 1 & 0 & 2 \end{bmatrix} = \begin{bmatrix} 4 & 2 & 5 \\ 7 & -3 & 2 \end{bmatrix}$

31. $2\mathbf{B}^T - 3\mathbf{C}^T = 2\begin{bmatrix} 1 & 4 \\ 3 & -1 \end{bmatrix} - 3\begin{bmatrix} 1 & 1 \\ 0 & 2 \end{bmatrix} = \begin{bmatrix} 2 & 8 \\ 6 & -2 \end{bmatrix} - \begin{bmatrix} 3 & 3 \\ 0 & 6 \end{bmatrix} = \begin{bmatrix} -1 & 5 \\ 6 & -8 \end{bmatrix}$

33. $\mathbf{C}^T - \mathbf{D} = \begin{bmatrix} 1 & 0 \\ 1 & 2 \end{bmatrix}^T - \begin{bmatrix} 1 & 2 & -1 \\ 1 & 0 & 2 \end{bmatrix}$ is impossible because $\mathbf{C}^T$ and $\mathbf{D}$ are not of the same size.

35. $x\begin{bmatrix} 2 \\ 1 \end{bmatrix} - y\begin{bmatrix} -3 \\ 5 \end{bmatrix} = 2\begin{bmatrix} 8 \\ 11 \end{bmatrix}$

$\begin{bmatrix} 2x \\ x \end{bmatrix} - \begin{bmatrix} -3y \\ 5y \end{bmatrix} = \begin{bmatrix} 16 \\ 22 \end{bmatrix}$

$\begin{bmatrix} 2x + 3y \\ x - 5y \end{bmatrix} = \begin{bmatrix} 16 \\ 22 \end{bmatrix}$

Equating corresponding entries gives
$\begin{cases} 2x + 3y = 16 \\ x - 5y = 22 \end{cases}$.

From the second equation, $x = 22 + 5y$.
Substituting in the first equation gives
$2(22 + 5y) + 3y = 16$, $13y = -28$, or

$y = -\dfrac{28}{13}$. Therefore

$x = 22 + 5y = 22 + 5\left(-\dfrac{28}{13}\right) = \dfrac{146}{13}$. The

solution is $x = \dfrac{146}{13}$, $y = -\dfrac{28}{13}$.

37. $3\begin{bmatrix} x \\ y \end{bmatrix} - 3\begin{bmatrix} -2 \\ 4 \end{bmatrix} = 4\begin{bmatrix} 6 \\ -2 \end{bmatrix}$

$\begin{bmatrix} 3x + 6 \\ 3y - 12 \end{bmatrix} = \begin{bmatrix} 24 \\ -8 \end{bmatrix}$

$3x + 6 = 24$, $3x = 18$, or $x = 6$.

$3y - 12 = -8$, $3y = 4$, or $y = \dfrac{4}{3}$.

Thus $x = 6$, $y = \dfrac{4}{3}$.

39. $\begin{bmatrix} 2 \\ 4 \\ 6 \end{bmatrix} + 2\begin{bmatrix} x \\ y \\ 4z \end{bmatrix} = \begin{bmatrix} -10 \\ -24 \\ 14 \end{bmatrix}$

$\begin{bmatrix} 2 + 2x \\ 4 + 2y \\ 6 + 8z \end{bmatrix} = \begin{bmatrix} -10 \\ -24 \\ 14 \end{bmatrix}$

$2 + 2x = -10$, $2x = -12$, or $x = -6$.
$4 + 2y = -24$, $2y = -28$, or $y = -14$.
$6 + 8z = 14$, $8z = 8$, or $z = 1$.
Thus $x = -6$, $y = -14$, $z = 1$.
$2x - 2 = 8$, $2x = 10$, or $x = 5$.
$2y = 4$, or $y = 2$.
$3x + 12 - 3y = 3x + 12 - 3y$, or $0 = 0$, which
is true for all values of x and y. Thus $x = 5$,
$y = 2$.

41. $X + Y = \begin{bmatrix} 20 & 40 \\ 45 & 30 \\ 15 & 10 \end{bmatrix} + \begin{bmatrix} 15 & 25 \\ 30 & 25 \\ 10 & 5 \end{bmatrix} = \begin{bmatrix} 20+15 & 40+25 \\ 45+30 & 30+25 \\ 15+10 & 10+5 \end{bmatrix}$

$= \begin{bmatrix} 35 & 65 \\ 75 & 55 \\ 25 & 15 \end{bmatrix}$

43. $P + 0.1P = [p_1 \quad p_2 \quad p_3] + [0.1p_1 \quad 0.1p_2 \quad 0.1p_3] = [1.1p_1 \quad 1.1p_2 \quad 1.1p_3] = 1.1P$
Thus P must be multiplied by 1.1.

45. $\begin{bmatrix} 15 & -4 & 26 \\ 4 & 7 & 30 \end{bmatrix}$

47. $\begin{bmatrix} -10 & 22 & 12 \\ 24 & 36 & -44 \end{bmatrix}$

Principles in Practice 6.3

1. Represent the value of each book by $[28 \quad 22 \quad 16]$ and the number of each book by

$\begin{bmatrix} 100 \\ 70 \\ 90 \end{bmatrix}$.

The total value is given by the following matrix product.

$[28 \quad 22 \quad 16] \begin{bmatrix} 100 \\ 70 \\ 90 \end{bmatrix} = [2800 + 1540 + 1440] = [5780]$

The total value is $5780.

2. The total cost is given by the matrix product PQ.

$PQ = [26.25 \quad 34.75 \quad 28.50] \begin{bmatrix} 250 \\ 325 \\ 175 \end{bmatrix}$

$= [6562.5 \quad 11,293.75 \quad 4987.5] = 22,843.75$

The total cost is $22,843.75.

3. First, write the equations with the variable terms on the left-hand side.

$\begin{cases} y + \dfrac{8}{5}x = \dfrac{8}{5} \\ y + \dfrac{1}{3}x = \dfrac{5}{3} \end{cases}$

Let $\mathbf{A} = \begin{bmatrix} 1 & \frac{8}{5} \\ 1 & \frac{1}{3} \end{bmatrix}$, $\mathbf{X} = \begin{bmatrix} y \\ x \end{bmatrix}$, and $\mathbf{B} = \begin{bmatrix} \frac{8}{5} \\ \frac{5}{3} \end{bmatrix}$.

Then the pair of lines is equivalent to the matrix equation $\mathbf{AX} = \mathbf{B}$ or $\begin{bmatrix} 1 & \frac{8}{5} \\ 1 & \frac{1}{3} \end{bmatrix} \begin{bmatrix} y \\ x \end{bmatrix} = \begin{bmatrix} \frac{8}{5} \\ \frac{5}{3} \end{bmatrix}$.

Exercise 6.3

1. $c_{11} = 1(0) + 3(-2) + (-2)(3) = -12$

3. $c_{32} = 0(-2) + 4(4) + 3(1) = 19$

5. $c_{22} = -2(-2) + 1(4) + (-1)(1) = 7$

7. **A** is 2×3 and **E** is 3×2, so **AE** is 2×2;
   $2 \cdot 2 = 4$ entries

9. **E** is 3×2 and **C** is 2×5, so **EC** is 3×5;
   $3 \cdot 5 = 15$ entries

11. **F** is 2×3 and **B** is 3×1, so **FB** is 2×1;
    $2 \cdot 1 = 2$ entries

13. **E** is 3×2 and **A** is 2×3, so **EA** is 3×3;
    $3 \cdot 3 = 9$ entries

15. **E** is 3×2. **F** is 2×3 and **B** is 3×1, so **FB** is 2×1.
    Thus **E(FB)** is 3×1; $3 \cdot 1 = 3$ entries.

17. An identity matrix is a square matrix (in this case 4×4) with 1's on the main diagonal and all other entries 0's.

$$\mathbf{T}_4 = \begin{bmatrix} 1 & 0 & 0 & 0 \\ 0 & 1 & 0 & 0 \\ 0 & 0 & 1 & 0 \\ 0 & 0 & 0 & 1 \end{bmatrix}$$

19. $\begin{bmatrix} 2 & -4 \\ 3 & 2 \end{bmatrix} \begin{bmatrix} 3 & 0 \\ -1 & 4 \end{bmatrix} = \begin{bmatrix} 2(3) + (-4)(-1) & 2(0) + (-4)(4) \\ 3(3) + 2(-1) & 3(0) + 2(4) \end{bmatrix} = \begin{bmatrix} 10 & -16 \\ 7 & 8 \end{bmatrix}$

21. $\begin{bmatrix} 2 & 0 & 3 \\ -1 & 4 & 5 \end{bmatrix} \begin{bmatrix} 1 \\ 4 \\ 7 \end{bmatrix} = \begin{bmatrix} 2(1) + 0(4) + 3(7) \\ -1(1) + 4(4) + 5(7) \end{bmatrix} = \begin{bmatrix} 23 \\ 50 \end{bmatrix}$

23. $\begin{bmatrix} 1 & 4 & -1 \\ 0 & 0 & 2 \\ -2 & 1 & 1 \end{bmatrix}\begin{bmatrix} -2 & 1 & 0 \\ 0 & 1 & 1 \\ 1 & 1 & 2 \end{bmatrix}$

$= \begin{bmatrix} 1(-2)+4(0)+(-1)1 & 1(1)+4(1)+(-1)(1) & 1(0)+4(1)+(-1)(2) \\ 0(-2)+0(0)+2(1) & 0(1)+0(1)+2(1) & 0(0)+0(1)+2(2) \\ -2(-2)+1(0)+1(1) & -2(1)+1(1)+1(1) & -2(0)+1(1)+1(2) \end{bmatrix} = \begin{bmatrix} -3 & 4 & 2 \\ 2 & 2 & 4 \\ 5 & 0 & 3 \end{bmatrix}$

25. $\begin{bmatrix} -1 & 2 & 3 \end{bmatrix}\begin{bmatrix} 3 & 1 & -1 & 2 \\ 0 & 4 & 3 & 1 \\ -1 & 3 & 1 & -2 \end{bmatrix}$

$= \begin{bmatrix} -3+0-3 & -1+8+9 & 1+6+3 & -2+2-6 \end{bmatrix} = \begin{bmatrix} -6 & 16 & 10 & -6 \end{bmatrix}$

27. $\begin{bmatrix} 2 \\ 3 \\ -4 \\ 1 \end{bmatrix}\begin{bmatrix} 2 & 3 & -2 & 3 \end{bmatrix} = \begin{bmatrix} 2(2) & 2(3) & 2(-2) & 2(3) \\ 3(2) & 3(3) & 3(-2) & 3(3) \\ -4(2) & -4(3) & -4(-2) & -4(3) \\ 1(2) & 1(3) & 1(-2) & 1(3) \end{bmatrix} = \begin{bmatrix} 4 & 6 & -4 & 6 \\ 6 & 9 & -6 & 9 \\ -8 & -12 & 8 & -12 \\ 2 & 3 & -2 & 3 \end{bmatrix}$

29. $3\left\{\begin{bmatrix} -2 & 0 & 2 \\ 3 & -1 & 1 \end{bmatrix} + 2\begin{bmatrix} -1 & 0 & 2 \\ 1 & 1 & -2 \end{bmatrix}\right\}\begin{bmatrix} 1 & 2 \\ 3 & 4 \\ 5 & 6 \end{bmatrix}$

$= 3\left\{\begin{bmatrix} -2 & 0 & 2 \\ 3 & -1 & 1 \end{bmatrix} + \begin{bmatrix} -2 & 0 & 4 \\ 2 & 2 & -4 \end{bmatrix}\right\}\begin{bmatrix} 1 & 2 \\ 3 & 4 \\ 5 & 6 \end{bmatrix}$

$= 3\left\{\begin{bmatrix} -4 & 0 & 6 \\ 5 & 1 & -3 \end{bmatrix}\right\}\begin{bmatrix} 1 & 2 \\ 3 & 4 \\ 5 & 6 \end{bmatrix} = \begin{bmatrix} -12 & 0 & 18 \\ 15 & 3 & -9 \end{bmatrix}\begin{bmatrix} 1 & 2 \\ 3 & 4 \\ 5 & 6 \end{bmatrix}$

$= \begin{bmatrix} -12(1)+0(3)+18(5) & -12(2)+0(4)+18(6) \\ 15(1)+3(3)+(-9)(5) & 15(2)+3(4)+(-9)(6) \end{bmatrix} = \begin{bmatrix} 78 & 84 \\ -21 & -12 \end{bmatrix}$

31. $\begin{bmatrix} 1 & 2 \\ 3 & 4 \end{bmatrix}\left\{\begin{bmatrix} 2 & 0 & 1 \\ 1 & 0 & -2 \end{bmatrix}\begin{bmatrix} 1 & -2 \\ 2 & 1 \\ 3 & 0 \end{bmatrix}\right\} = \begin{bmatrix} 1 & 2 \\ 3 & 4 \end{bmatrix}\left\{\begin{bmatrix} 2+0+3 & -4+0+0 \\ 1+0-6 & -2+0+0 \end{bmatrix}\right\}$

$= \begin{bmatrix} 1 & 2 \\ 3 & 4 \end{bmatrix}\begin{bmatrix} 5 & -4 \\ -5 & -2 \end{bmatrix} = \begin{bmatrix} 5-10 & -4-4 \\ 15-20 & -12-8 \end{bmatrix} = \begin{bmatrix} -5 & -8 \\ -5 & -20 \end{bmatrix}$

33. $\begin{bmatrix} 1 & 0 & 0 \\ 0 & 1 & 0 \\ 0 & 0 & 1 \end{bmatrix}\begin{bmatrix} x \\ y \\ z \end{bmatrix} = \mathbf{I}\begin{bmatrix} x \\ y \\ z \end{bmatrix} = \begin{bmatrix} x \\ y \\ z \end{bmatrix}$

35. $\begin{bmatrix} 2 & 1 & 3 \\ 4 & 9 & 7 \end{bmatrix} \begin{bmatrix} x_1 \\ x_2 \\ x_3 \end{bmatrix} = \begin{bmatrix} 2x_1 + x_2 + 3x_3 \\ 4x_1 + 9x_2 + 7x_3 \end{bmatrix}$

37. $\mathbf{DI} - \frac{1}{3}\mathbf{E} = \mathbf{D} - \frac{1}{3}\mathbf{E} = \begin{bmatrix} 1 & 0 & 0 \\ 0 & 1 & 1 \\ 1 & 2 & 1 \end{bmatrix} - \frac{1}{3}\begin{bmatrix} 3 & 0 & 0 \\ 0 & 6 & 0 \\ 0 & 0 & 3 \end{bmatrix}$

$= \begin{bmatrix} 1 & 0 & 0 \\ 0 & 1 & 1 \\ 1 & 2 & 1 \end{bmatrix} - \begin{bmatrix} 1 & 0 & 0 \\ 0 & 2 & 0 \\ 0 & 0 & 1 \end{bmatrix}$

$= \begin{bmatrix} 0 & 0 & 0 \\ 0 & -1 & 1 \\ 1 & 2 & 0 \end{bmatrix}$

39. $3\mathbf{A} - 2\mathbf{BC} = 3\begin{bmatrix} 1 & -2 \\ 0 & 3 \end{bmatrix} - 2\begin{bmatrix} -2 & 3 & 0 \\ 1 & -4 & 1 \end{bmatrix}\begin{bmatrix} -1 & 1 \\ 0 & 3 \\ 2 & 4 \end{bmatrix}$

$= \begin{bmatrix} 3 & -6 \\ 0 & 9 \end{bmatrix} - 2\begin{bmatrix} 2+0+0 & -2+9+0 \\ -1+0+2 & 1-12+4 \end{bmatrix}$

$= \begin{bmatrix} 3 & -6 \\ 0 & 9 \end{bmatrix} - \begin{bmatrix} 4 & 14 \\ 2 & -14 \end{bmatrix} = \begin{bmatrix} -1 & -20 \\ -2 & 23 \end{bmatrix}$

41. $2\mathbf{I} - \frac{1}{2}\mathbf{EF} = 2\mathbf{I} - \frac{1}{2}\begin{bmatrix} 3 & 0 & 0 \\ 0 & 6 & 0 \\ 0 & 0 & 3 \end{bmatrix}\begin{bmatrix} \frac{1}{3} & 0 & 0 \\ 0 & \frac{1}{6} & 0 \\ 0 & 0 & \frac{1}{3} \end{bmatrix}$

$= 2\mathbf{I} - \begin{bmatrix} \frac{3}{2} & 0 & 0 \\ 0 & 3 & 0 \\ 0 & 0 & \frac{3}{2} \end{bmatrix}\begin{bmatrix} \frac{1}{3} & 0 & 0 \\ 0 & \frac{1}{6} & 0 \\ 0 & 0 & \frac{1}{3} \end{bmatrix}$

$= 2\mathbf{I} - \begin{bmatrix} \frac{1}{2}+0+0 & 0+0+0 & 0+0+0 \\ 0+0+0 & 0+\frac{1}{2}+0 & 0+0+0 \\ 0+0+0 & 0+0+0 & 0+0+\frac{1}{2} \end{bmatrix}$

$= \begin{bmatrix} 2 & 0 & 0 \\ 0 & 2 & 0 \\ 0 & 0 & 2 \end{bmatrix} - \begin{bmatrix} \frac{1}{2} & 0 & 0 \\ 0 & \frac{1}{2} & 0 \\ 0 & 0 & \frac{1}{2} \end{bmatrix} = \begin{bmatrix} \frac{3}{2} & 0 & 0 \\ 0 & \frac{3}{2} & 0 \\ 0 & 0 & \frac{3}{2} \end{bmatrix}$

43. $(\mathbf{DC})\mathbf{A} = \left\{ \begin{bmatrix} 1 & 0 & 0 \\ 0 & 1 & 1 \\ 1 & 2 & 1 \end{bmatrix} \begin{bmatrix} -1 & 1 \\ 0 & 3 \\ 2 & 4 \end{bmatrix} \right\} \mathbf{A} = \begin{bmatrix} -1+0+0 & 1+0+0 \\ 0+0+2 & 0+3+4 \\ -1+0+2 & 1+6+4 \end{bmatrix} \mathbf{A}$

$$= \begin{bmatrix} -1 & 1 \\ 2 & 7 \\ 1 & 11 \end{bmatrix} \begin{bmatrix} 1 & -2 \\ 0 & 3 \end{bmatrix} = \begin{bmatrix} -1+0 & 2+3 \\ 2+0 & -4+21 \\ 1+0 & -2+33 \end{bmatrix} = \begin{bmatrix} -1 & 5 \\ 2 & 17 \\ 1 & 31 \end{bmatrix}$$

45. Impossible: $\mathbf{A}$ is not a square matrix, so $\mathbf{A}^2$ is not defined.

47. $\mathbf{B}^3 = \left(\mathbf{B}^2 \right) \mathbf{B} = \begin{bmatrix} 0 & 0 & -1 \\ 2 & -1 & 0 \\ 0 & 0 & 2 \end{bmatrix}^2 \mathbf{B} = \begin{bmatrix} 0 & 0 & -1 \\ 2 & -1 & 0 \\ 0 & 0 & 2 \end{bmatrix} \begin{bmatrix} 0 & 0 & -1 \\ 2 & -1 & 0 \\ 0 & 0 & 2 \end{bmatrix} \mathbf{B}$

$$= \begin{bmatrix} 0 & 0 & -2 \\ -2 & 1 & -2 \\ 0 & 0 & 4 \end{bmatrix} \begin{bmatrix} 0 & 0 & -1 \\ 2 & -1 & 0 \\ 0 & 0 & 2 \end{bmatrix} = \begin{bmatrix} 0 & 0 & -4 \\ 2 & -1 & -2 \\ 0 & 0 & 8 \end{bmatrix}$$

49. $(\mathbf{AC})^2 = \left\{ \begin{bmatrix} 1 & -1 & 0 \\ 0 & 1 & 1 \end{bmatrix} \begin{bmatrix} 1 & 0 \\ 2 & -1 \\ 0 & 1 \end{bmatrix} \right\}^2 = \begin{bmatrix} -1 & 1 \\ 2 & 0 \end{bmatrix}^2 = \begin{bmatrix} -1 & 1 \\ 2 & 0 \end{bmatrix} \begin{bmatrix} -1 & 1 \\ 2 & 0 \end{bmatrix} = \begin{bmatrix} 3 & -1 \\ -2 & 2 \end{bmatrix}$

51. $\left(\mathbf{BA}^{\mathrm{T}} \right)^{\mathrm{T}} = \left\{ \begin{bmatrix} 0 & 0 & -1 \\ 2 & -1 & 0 \\ 0 & 0 & 2 \end{bmatrix} \begin{bmatrix} 1 & 0 \\ -1 & 1 \\ 0 & 1 \end{bmatrix} \right\}^{\mathrm{T}} = \begin{bmatrix} 0 & -1 \\ 3 & -1 \\ 0 & 2 \end{bmatrix}^{\mathrm{T}} = \begin{bmatrix} 0 & 3 & 0 \\ -1 & -1 & 2 \end{bmatrix}$

53. $(2\mathbf{I})^2 - 2\mathbf{I}^2 = (2\mathbf{I})^2 - 2\mathbf{I} = \begin{bmatrix} 2 & 0 & 0 \\ 0 & 2 & 0 \\ 0 & 0 & 2 \end{bmatrix}^2 - \begin{bmatrix} 2 & 0 & 0 \\ 0 & 2 & 0 \\ 0 & 0 & 2 \end{bmatrix}$

$$= \begin{bmatrix} 2 & 0 & 0 \\ 0 & 2 & 0 \\ 0 & 0 & 2 \end{bmatrix} \begin{bmatrix} 2 & 0 & 0 \\ 0 & 2 & 0 \\ 0 & 0 & 2 \end{bmatrix} - \begin{bmatrix} 2 & 0 & 0 \\ 0 & 2 & 0 \\ 0 & 0 & 2 \end{bmatrix} = \begin{bmatrix} 4 & 0 & 0 \\ 0 & 4 & 0 \\ 0 & 0 & 4 \end{bmatrix} - \begin{bmatrix} 2 & 0 & 0 \\ 0 & 2 & 0 \\ 0 & 0 & 2 \end{bmatrix} = \begin{bmatrix} 2 & 0 & 0 \\ 0 & 2 & 0 \\ 0 & 0 & 2 \end{bmatrix}$$

55. $\mathbf{A}(\mathbf{I} - \mathbf{O}) = \mathbf{A}(\mathbf{I}) = \mathbf{AI}$. Since $\mathbf{I}$ is 3×3 and $\mathbf{A}$ has three columns, $\mathbf{AI} = \mathbf{A}$. Thus

$$\mathbf{A}(\mathbf{I} - \mathbf{O}) = \mathbf{A} = \begin{bmatrix} 1 & -1 & 0 \\ 0 & 1 & 1 \end{bmatrix}.$$

57. $(AB)(AB)^T = \begin{bmatrix} 1 & -1 & 0 \\ 0 & 1 & 1 \end{bmatrix} \begin{bmatrix} 0 & 0 & -1 \\ 2 & -1 & 0 \\ 0 & 0 & 2 \end{bmatrix} (AB)^T = \begin{bmatrix} -2 & 1 & -1 \\ 2 & -1 & 2 \end{bmatrix} (AB)^T$

$= \begin{bmatrix} -2 & 1 & -1 \\ 2 & -1 & 2 \end{bmatrix} \begin{bmatrix} -2 & 2 \\ 1 & -1 \\ -1 & 2 \end{bmatrix} = \begin{bmatrix} 6 & -7 \\ -7 & 9 \end{bmatrix}$

59. $AX = B$

$A = \begin{bmatrix} 3 & 1 \\ 7 & -2 \end{bmatrix}$

$X = \begin{bmatrix} x \\ y \end{bmatrix}$

$B = \begin{bmatrix} 6 \\ 5 \end{bmatrix}$

The system is represented by $\begin{bmatrix} 3 & 1 \\ 7 & -2 \end{bmatrix} \begin{bmatrix} x \\ y \end{bmatrix} = \begin{bmatrix} 6 \\ 5 \end{bmatrix}$.

61. $AX = B$

$A = \begin{bmatrix} 4 & -1 & 3 \\ 3 & 0 & -1 \\ 0 & 3 & 2 \end{bmatrix}$

$X = \begin{bmatrix} r \\ s \\ t \end{bmatrix}$

$B = \begin{bmatrix} 9 \\ 7 \\ 15 \end{bmatrix}$

The system is represented by

$\begin{bmatrix} 4 & -1 & 3 \\ 3 & 0 & -1 \\ 0 & 3 & 2 \end{bmatrix} \begin{bmatrix} r \\ s \\ t \end{bmatrix} = \begin{bmatrix} 9 \\ 7 \\ 15 \end{bmatrix}$

63. $\begin{bmatrix} 6 & 10 & 7 \end{bmatrix} \begin{bmatrix} 55 \\ 150 \\ 35 \end{bmatrix} = [6 \cdot 55 + 10 \cdot 150 + 7 \cdot 35]$

$= [330 + 1500 + 245]$
$= [2075]$

The value of the inventory is $2075.

65. $\mathbf{Q} = \begin{bmatrix} 7 & 3 & 5 \end{bmatrix}$

$$\mathbf{R} = \begin{bmatrix} 5 & 20 & 16 & 7 & 17 \\ 7 & 18 & 12 & 9 & 21 \\ 6 & 25 & 8 & 5 & 13 \end{bmatrix}$$

$$\mathbf{C} = \begin{bmatrix} 1500 \\ 800 \\ 500 \\ 100 \\ 1000 \end{bmatrix}$$

$$\mathbf{QRC} = \mathbf{Q(RC)} = \mathbf{Q} \begin{bmatrix} 5 \cdot 1500 + 20 \cdot 800 + 16 \cdot 500 + 7 \cdot 100 + 17 \cdot 1000 \\ 7 \cdot 1500 + 18 \cdot 800 + 12 \cdot 500 + 9 \cdot 100 + 21 \cdot 1000 \\ 6 \cdot 1500 + 25 \cdot 800 + 8 \cdot 500 + 5 \cdot 100 + 13 \cdot 1000 \end{bmatrix}$$

$$= \begin{bmatrix} 7 & 3 & 5 \end{bmatrix} \begin{bmatrix} 49,200 \\ 52,800 \\ 46,500 \end{bmatrix} = [7 \cdot 49,200 + 3 \cdot 52,800 + 5 \cdot 46,500]$$

$$= [735,300]$$

The total cost of raw materials is \$735,300.

67. a. Amount spent on goods:

coal industry: $\mathbf{D_C P} = \begin{bmatrix} 0 & 1 & 4 \end{bmatrix} \begin{bmatrix} 10,000 \\ 20,000 \\ 40,000 \end{bmatrix} = [180,000]$

elec. industry: $\mathbf{D_E P} = \begin{bmatrix} 20 & 0 & 8 \end{bmatrix} \begin{bmatrix} 10,000 \\ 20,000 \\ 40,000 \end{bmatrix} = [520,000]$

steel industry: $\mathbf{D_S P} = \begin{bmatrix} 30 & 5 & 0 \end{bmatrix} \begin{bmatrix} 10,000 \\ 20,000 \\ 40,000 \end{bmatrix} = [400,000]$

The coal industry spends \$180,000, the electric industry spends \$520,000, and the steel industry spends \$400,000.

consumer 1: $\mathbf{D_1 P} = \begin{bmatrix} 3 & 2 & 5 \end{bmatrix} \begin{bmatrix} 10,000 \\ 20,000 \\ 40,000 \end{bmatrix} = [270,000]$

consumer 2: $\mathbf{D_2 P} = \begin{bmatrix} 0 & 17 & 1 \end{bmatrix} \begin{bmatrix} 10,000 \\ 20,000 \\ 40,000 \end{bmatrix} = [380,000]$

$$\text{consumer 3: } \mathbf{D_3P} = \begin{bmatrix} 4 & 6 & 12 \end{bmatrix} \begin{bmatrix} 10,000 \\ 20,000 \\ 40,000 \end{bmatrix} = \begin{bmatrix} 640,000 \end{bmatrix}$$

Consumer 1 pays \$270,000, consumer 2 pays \$380,000 and consumer 3 pays \$640,000.

b. From Example 3 of Sec. 6.2, the number of units sold of coal, electricity, and steel are 57, 31, and 30, respectively. Thus profit for coal is $10,000(57) - 180,000 = \$390,000$, the profit for elec. is $20,000(31) - 520,000 = \$100,000$, and the profit for steel is $40,000(30) - 400,000 = \$800,000$.

c. From (a), the total amount of money that is paid by all the industries and consumers is
$180,000 + 520,000 + 400,000 + 270,000 + 380,000 + 640,000 = \$2,390,000$.

d. The proportion of the total amount in (c) paid out by the industries is
$$\frac{180,000 + 520,000 + 400,000}{2,390,000} = \frac{110}{239}$$
Proportion of total amount in (c) paid by consumers is
$$\frac{270,000 + 380,000 + 640,000}{2,390,000} = \frac{129}{239}$$

69. $\begin{bmatrix} 1 & 2 \\ 1 & 2 \end{bmatrix}\begin{bmatrix} 2 & -3 \\ -1 & \frac{3}{2} \end{bmatrix} = \begin{bmatrix} 1(2)+(2)(-1) & 1(-3)+2\left(\frac{3}{2}\right) \\ 1(2)+2(-1) & 1(-3)+2\left(\frac{3}{2}\right) \end{bmatrix} = \begin{bmatrix} 0 & 0 \\ 0 & 0 \end{bmatrix}$

71. $\begin{bmatrix} 72.82 & -9.8 \\ 51.32 & -36.32 \end{bmatrix}$

73. $\begin{bmatrix} 15.606 & 64.08 \\ -739.428 & 373.056 \end{bmatrix}$

Principles in Practice 6.4

1. The corresponding system is
$$\begin{cases} 6A + B + 3C = 35, \\ 3A + 2B + 3C = 22, \\ A + 5B + 3C = 18. \end{cases}$$
Reduce the augmented coefficient matrix of the system.
$$\begin{bmatrix} 6 & 1 & 3 & | & 35 \\ 3 & 2 & 3 & | & 22 \\ 1 & 5 & 3 & | & 18 \end{bmatrix}$$
$$\xrightarrow{R_1 \leftrightarrow R_3} \begin{bmatrix} 1 & 5 & 3 & | & 18 \\ 3 & 2 & 3 & | & 22 \\ 6 & 1 & 3 & | & 35 \end{bmatrix}$$

$$\xrightarrow[-6R_1+R_3]{-3R_1+R_2} \begin{bmatrix} 1 & 5 & 3 & | & 18 \\ 0 & -13 & -6 & | & -32 \\ 0 & -29 & -15 & | & -73 \end{bmatrix}$$

$$\xrightarrow{-\frac{1}{13}R_2} \begin{bmatrix} 1 & 5 & 3 & | & 18 \\ 0 & 1 & \frac{6}{13} & | & \frac{32}{13} \\ 0 & -29 & -15 & | & -73 \end{bmatrix}$$

$$\xrightarrow[29R_2+R_3]{-5R_2+R_1} \begin{bmatrix} 1 & 0 & \frac{9}{13} & | & \frac{74}{13} \\ 0 & 1 & \frac{6}{13} & | & \frac{32}{13} \\ 0 & 0 & -\frac{21}{13} & | & -\frac{21}{13} \end{bmatrix}$$

$$\xrightarrow{-\frac{13}{21}R_3} \begin{bmatrix} 1 & 0 & \frac{9}{13} & | & \frac{74}{13} \\ 0 & 1 & \frac{6}{13} & | & \frac{32}{13} \\ 0 & 0 & 1 & | & 1 \end{bmatrix}$$

$$\xrightarrow[-\frac{6}{13}R_3+R_2]{-\frac{9}{13}R_3+R_1} \begin{bmatrix} 1 & 0 & 0 & | & 5 \\ 0 & 1 & 0 & | & 2 \\ 0 & 0 & 1 & | & 1 \end{bmatrix}$$

Thus there should be 5 blocks of A, 2 blocks of B, and 1 block of C suggested.

2. Let x be the number of tablets of X, y be the number of tablet of Y, and z be the number of tablets Z. The system is
$$40x + 10y + 10z = 180$$
$$20x + 10y + 50z = 200$$
$$10x + 30y + 20z = 190$$
Reduce the augmented coefficient matrix of the system.

$$\begin{bmatrix} 40 & 10 & 10 & | & 180 \\ 20 & 10 & 50 & | & 200 \\ 10 & 30 & 20 & | & 190 \end{bmatrix}$$

$\xrightarrow{R_1 \leftrightarrow R_3} \begin{bmatrix} 10 & 30 & 20 & | & 190 \\ 20 & 10 & 50 & | & 200 \\ 40 & 10 & 10 & | & 180 \end{bmatrix}$

$\xrightarrow[\frac{1}{10}R_3]{\substack{\frac{1}{10}R_1 \\ \frac{1}{10}R_2}} \begin{bmatrix} 1 & 3 & 2 & | & 19 \\ 2 & 1 & 5 & | & 20 \\ 4 & 1 & 1 & | & 18 \end{bmatrix}$

$\xrightarrow[-4R_1+R_3]{-2R_1+R_2} \begin{bmatrix} 1 & 3 & 2 & | & 19 \\ 0 & -5 & 1 & | & -18 \\ 0 & -11 & -7 & | & -58 \end{bmatrix}$

$\xrightarrow{-\frac{1}{5}R_2} \begin{bmatrix} 1 & 3 & 2 & | & 19 \\ 0 & 1 & -\frac{1}{5} & | & \frac{18}{5} \\ 0 & -11 & -7 & | & -58 \end{bmatrix}$

$\xrightarrow[11R_2+R_3]{-3R_2+R_1} \begin{bmatrix} 1 & 0 & \frac{13}{5} & | & \frac{41}{5} \\ 0 & 1 & -\frac{1}{5} & | & \frac{18}{5} \\ 0 & 0 & -\frac{46}{5} & | & -\frac{92}{5} \end{bmatrix}$

$\xrightarrow{-\frac{5}{46}R_3} \begin{bmatrix} 1 & 0 & \frac{13}{5} & | & \frac{41}{5} \\ 0 & 1 & -\frac{1}{5} & | & \frac{18}{5} \\ 0 & 0 & 1 & | & 2 \end{bmatrix}$

$\xrightarrow[\frac{1}{5}R_3+R_2]{-\frac{13}{5}R_3+R_1} \begin{bmatrix} 1 & 0 & 0 & | & 3 \\ 0 & 1 & 0 & | & 4 \\ 0 & 0 & 1 & | & 2 \end{bmatrix}$

She should take 3 tables of X, 4 tablets of Y, and 2 tablets of Z.

3. Let $a, b, c,$ and d be the number of bags of foods A, B, C, and D, respectively. The corresponding system is

$$\begin{cases} 5a + 5b + 10c + 5d = 10,000, \\ 10a + 5b + 30c + 10d = 20,000, \\ 5a + 15b + 10c + 25d = 20,000. \end{cases}$$

Reduce the augmented coefficient matrix of the system.

$$\begin{bmatrix} 5 & 5 & 10 & 5 & | & 10,000 \\ 10 & 5 & 30 & 10 & | & 20,000 \\ 5 & 15 & 10 & 25 & | & 20,000 \end{bmatrix}$$

$\xrightarrow{\frac{1}{5}R_1} \begin{bmatrix} 1 & 1 & 2 & 1 & | & 2000 \\ 10 & 5 & 30 & 10 & | & 20,000 \\ 5 & 15 & 10 & 25 & | & 20,000 \end{bmatrix}$

$\xrightarrow[-5R_1+R_3]{-10R_1+R_2} \begin{bmatrix} 1 & 1 & 2 & 1 & | & 2000 \\ 0 & -5 & 10 & 0 & | & 0 \\ 0 & 10 & 0 & 20 & | & 10,000 \end{bmatrix}$

$\xrightarrow{-\frac{1}{5}R_2} \begin{bmatrix} 1 & 1 & 2 & 1 & | & 2000 \\ 0 & 1 & -2 & 0 & | & 0 \\ 0 & 10 & 0 & 20 & | & 10,000 \end{bmatrix}$

$\xrightarrow[-10R_2+R_3]{-R_2+R_1} \begin{bmatrix} 1 & 0 & 4 & 1 & | & 2000 \\ 0 & 1 & -2 & 0 & | & 0 \\ 0 & 0 & 20 & 20 & | & 10,000 \end{bmatrix}$

$\xrightarrow{\frac{1}{20}R_3} \begin{bmatrix} 0 & 0 & 4 & 0 & | & 2000 \\ 0 & 1 & -2 & 0 & | & 0 \\ 0 & 0 & 1 & 1 & | & 500 \end{bmatrix}$

$\xrightarrow[2R_3+R_2]{-4R_3+R_1} \begin{bmatrix} 1 & 0 & 0 & -3 & | & 0 \\ 0 & 1 & 0 & 2 & | & 1000 \\ 0 & 0 & 1 & 1 & | & 500 \end{bmatrix}$

This reduced matrix corresponds to the system $\begin{cases} a - 3d = 0, \\ b + 2d = 1000, \\ c + d = 500. \end{cases}$

Letting $d = r$, we get the general solution of the system:
$a = 3r,$
$b = -2r + 1000,$
$c = -r + 500.$
$d = r$
Note that $a, b, c,$ and d cannot be negative, given the context, hence $0 \le r \le 50$. One specific solution is when $r = 250$, then $a = 750, b = 500,$
$c = 250,$ and $d = 250$.

Exercise 6.4

1. The first nonzero entry in row 2 is not to the right of the first nonzero entry in row 1, hence not reduced.

3. Reduced.

5. The first row consists entirely of zeros and is not below each row containing a nonzero entry, hence not reduced.

7. $\begin{bmatrix} 1 & 3 \\ 4 & 0 \end{bmatrix} \xrightarrow{-4R_1 + R_2} \begin{bmatrix} 1 & 3 \\ 0 & -12 \end{bmatrix} \xrightarrow{-\frac{1}{12}R_2} \begin{bmatrix} 1 & 3 \\ 0 & 1 \end{bmatrix} \xrightarrow{-3R_2 + R_1} \begin{bmatrix} 1 & 0 \\ 0 & 1 \end{bmatrix}$

9. $\begin{bmatrix} 2 & 4 & 6 \\ 1 & 2 & 3 \\ 1 & 2 & 3 \end{bmatrix} \xrightarrow{R_1 \leftrightarrow R_3} \begin{bmatrix} 1 & 2 & 3 \\ 1 & 2 & 3 \\ 2 & 4 & 6 \end{bmatrix} \xrightarrow[-2R_1 + R_3]{R_1 + R_2} \begin{bmatrix} 1 & 2 & 3 \\ 0 & 0 & 0 \\ 0 & 0 & 0 \end{bmatrix}$

11. $\begin{bmatrix} 2 & 0 & 3 & 1 \\ 1 & 4 & 2 & 2 \\ -1 & 3 & 1 & 4 \\ 0 & 2 & 1 & 0 \end{bmatrix} \xrightarrow{R_1 \leftrightarrow R_2} \begin{bmatrix} 1 & 4 & 2 & 2 \\ 2 & 0 & 3 & 1 \\ -1 & 3 & 1 & 4 \\ 0 & 2 & 1 & 0 \end{bmatrix}$

$\xrightarrow[R_1 + R_3]{-2R_1 + R_2} \begin{bmatrix} 1 & 4 & 2 & 2 \\ 0 & -8 & -1 & -3 \\ 0 & 7 & 3 & 6 \\ 0 & 2 & 1 & 0 \end{bmatrix} \xrightarrow{-\frac{1}{8}R_2} \begin{bmatrix} 1 & 4 & 2 & 2 \\ 0 & 1 & \frac{1}{8} & \frac{3}{8} \\ 0 & 7 & 3 & 6 \\ 0 & 2 & 1 & 0 \end{bmatrix}$

$\xrightarrow[\substack{-7R_2 + R_3 \\ -2R_2 + R_4}]{-4R_2 + R_1} \begin{bmatrix} 1 & 0 & \frac{3}{2} & \frac{1}{2} \\ 0 & 1 & \frac{1}{8} & \frac{3}{8} \\ 0 & 0 & \frac{17}{8} & \frac{27}{8} \\ 0 & 0 & \frac{3}{4} & -\frac{3}{4} \end{bmatrix} \xrightarrow{\frac{8}{17}R_3} \begin{bmatrix} 1 & 0 & \frac{3}{2} & \frac{1}{2} \\ 0 & 1 & \frac{1}{8} & \frac{3}{8} \\ 0 & 0 & 1 & \frac{27}{17} \\ 0 & 0 & \frac{3}{4} & -\frac{3}{4} \end{bmatrix}$

$\xrightarrow[\substack{-\frac{1}{8}R_3 + R_2 \\ -\frac{3}{4}R_3 + R_4}]{-\frac{3}{2}R_3 + R_1} \begin{bmatrix} 1 & 0 & 0 & -\frac{32}{17} \\ 0 & 1 & 0 & \frac{3}{17} \\ 0 & 0 & 1 & \frac{27}{17} \\ 0 & 0 & 0 & -\frac{33}{17} \end{bmatrix}$

$\xrightarrow{-\frac{17}{33}R_4} \begin{bmatrix} 1 & 0 & 0 & -\frac{32}{17} \\ 0 & 1 & 0 & \frac{3}{17} \\ 0 & 0 & 1 & \frac{27}{17} \\ 0 & 0 & 0 & 1 \end{bmatrix} \xrightarrow[\substack{-\frac{3}{17}R_4 + R_2 \\ -\frac{27}{17}R_4 + R_3}]{\frac{32}{17}R_4 + R_1} \begin{bmatrix} 1 & 0 & 0 & 0 \\ 0 & 1 & 0 & 0 \\ 0 & 0 & 1 & 0 \\ 0 & 0 & 0 & 1 \end{bmatrix}$

13. $\begin{bmatrix} 2 & 3 & | & 5 \\ 1 & -2 & | & -1 \end{bmatrix} \rightarrow \begin{bmatrix} 1 & -2 & | & -1 \\ 2 & 3 & | & 5 \end{bmatrix} \rightarrow \begin{bmatrix} 1 & -2 & | & -1 \\ 0 & 7 & | & 7 \end{bmatrix} \rightarrow \begin{bmatrix} 1 & -2 & | & -1 \\ 0 & 1 & | & 1 \end{bmatrix} \rightarrow \begin{bmatrix} 1 & 0 & | & 1 \\ 0 & 1 & | & 1 \end{bmatrix}$

Thus $x = 1$, $y = 1$.

15. $\begin{bmatrix} 3 & 1 & | & 4 \\ 12 & 4 & | & 2 \end{bmatrix} \rightarrow \begin{bmatrix} 3 & 1 & | & 4 \\ 0 & 0 & | & -14 \end{bmatrix} \rightarrow \begin{bmatrix} 1 & \frac{1}{3} & | & \frac{4}{3} \\ 0 & 0 & | & -14 \end{bmatrix} \rightarrow \begin{bmatrix} 1 & \frac{1}{3} & | & \frac{4}{3} \\ 0 & 0 & | & 1 \end{bmatrix} \rightarrow \begin{bmatrix} 1 & \frac{1}{3} & | & 0 \\ 0 & 0 & | & 1 \end{bmatrix}$

The last row indicates $0 = 1$, which is never true, so there is no solution.

17. $\begin{bmatrix} 1 & 2 & 1 & | & 4 \\ 3 & 0 & 2 & | & 5 \end{bmatrix} \rightarrow \begin{bmatrix} 1 & 2 & 1 & | & 4 \\ 0 & -6 & -1 & | & -7 \end{bmatrix} \rightarrow \begin{bmatrix} 1 & 2 & 1 & | & 4 \\ 0 & 1 & \frac{1}{6} & | & \frac{7}{6} \end{bmatrix} \rightarrow \begin{bmatrix} 1 & 0 & \frac{2}{3} & | & \frac{5}{3} \\ 0 & 1 & \frac{1}{6} & | & \frac{7}{6} \end{bmatrix},$

which gives $\begin{cases} x + \frac{2}{3}z = \frac{5}{3} \\ y + \frac{1}{6}z = \frac{7}{6} \end{cases}.$

Thus, $x = -\frac{2}{3}r + \frac{5}{3}$, $y = -\frac{1}{6}r + \frac{7}{6}$, $z = r$, where r is any real number.

19. $\begin{bmatrix} 1 & -3 & | & 0 \\ 2 & 2 & | & 3 \\ 5 & -1 & | & 1 \end{bmatrix} \rightarrow \begin{bmatrix} 1 & -3 & | & 0 \\ 0 & 8 & | & 3 \\ 0 & 14 & | & 1 \end{bmatrix} \rightarrow \begin{bmatrix} 1 & -3 & | & 0 \\ 0 & 1 & | & \frac{3}{8} \\ 0 & 14 & | & 1 \end{bmatrix} \rightarrow \begin{bmatrix} 1 & 0 & | & \frac{9}{8} \\ 0 & 1 & | & \frac{3}{8} \\ 0 & 0 & | & -\frac{17}{4} \end{bmatrix}$

From third row, $0 = -\frac{17}{4}$, which is never true, so there is no solution.

21. $\begin{bmatrix} 1 & -1 & -3 & | & -4 \\ 2 & -1 & -4 & | & -7 \\ 1 & 1 & -1 & | & -2 \end{bmatrix} \rightarrow \begin{bmatrix} 1 & -1 & -3 & | & -4 \\ 0 & 1 & 2 & | & 1 \\ 0 & 2 & 2 & | & 2 \end{bmatrix} \rightarrow \begin{bmatrix} 1 & 0 & -1 & | & -3 \\ 0 & 1 & 2 & | & 1 \\ 0 & 0 & -2 & | & 0 \end{bmatrix}$

$\rightarrow \begin{bmatrix} 1 & 0 & -1 & | & -3 \\ 0 & 1 & 2 & | & 1 \\ 0 & 0 & 1 & | & 0 \end{bmatrix} \rightarrow \begin{bmatrix} 1 & 0 & 0 & | & -3 \\ 0 & 1 & 0 & | & 1 \\ 0 & 0 & 1 & | & 0 \end{bmatrix}$

Thus, $x = -3$, $y = 1$, $z = 0$.

23. $\begin{bmatrix} 2 & 0 & -4 & | & 8 \\ 1 & -2 & -2 & | & 14 \\ 1 & 1 & -2 & | & -1 \\ 3 & 1 & 1 & | & 0 \end{bmatrix} \rightarrow \begin{bmatrix} 1 & 0 & -2 & | & 4 \\ 1 & -2 & -2 & | & 14 \\ 1 & 1 & -2 & | & -1 \\ 3 & 1 & 1 & | & 0 \end{bmatrix} \rightarrow \begin{bmatrix} 1 & 0 & -2 & | & 4 \\ 0 & -2 & 0 & | & 10 \\ 0 & 1 & 0 & | & -5 \\ 0 & 1 & 7 & | & -12 \end{bmatrix}$

$\rightarrow \begin{bmatrix} 1 & 0 & -2 & | & 4 \\ 0 & 1 & 0 & | & -5 \\ 0 & -2 & 0 & | & 10 \\ 0 & 1 & 7 & | & -12 \end{bmatrix} \rightarrow \begin{bmatrix} 1 & 0 & -2 & | & 4 \\ 0 & 1 & 0 & | & -5 \\ 0 & 0 & 0 & | & 0 \\ 0 & 0 & 7 & | & -7 \end{bmatrix} \rightarrow \begin{bmatrix} 1 & 0 & -2 & | & 4 \\ 0 & 1 & 0 & | & -5 \\ 0 & 0 & 1 & | & -1 \\ 0 & 0 & 0 & | & 0 \end{bmatrix} \rightarrow \begin{bmatrix} 1 & 0 & 0 & | & 2 \\ 0 & 1 & 0 & | & -5 \\ 0 & 0 & 1 & | & -1 \\ 0 & 0 & 0 & | & 0 \end{bmatrix}$

Thus $x = 2$, $y = -5$, $z = -1$.

25.
$$\begin{bmatrix} 1 & 1 & -1 & 1 & 1 & | & 0 \\ 1 & 1 & 1 & -1 & 1 & | & 0 \\ 1 & -1 & -1 & 1 & -1 & | & 0 \\ 1 & 1 & -1 & -1 & -1 & | & 0 \end{bmatrix} \rightarrow \begin{bmatrix} 1 & 1 & -1 & 1 & 1 & | & 0 \\ 0 & 0 & 2 & -2 & 0 & | & 0 \\ 0 & -2 & 0 & 0 & -2 & | & 0 \\ 0 & 0 & 0 & -2 & -2 & | & 0 \end{bmatrix}$$

$$\rightarrow \begin{bmatrix} 1 & 1 & -1 & 1 & 1 & | & 0 \\ 0 & -2 & 0 & 0 & -2 & | & 0 \\ 0 & 0 & 2 & -2 & 0 & | & 0 \\ 0 & 0 & 0 & -2 & -2 & | & 0 \end{bmatrix} \rightarrow \begin{bmatrix} 1 & 1 & -1 & 1 & 1 & | & 0 \\ 0 & 1 & 0 & 0 & 1 & | & 0 \\ 0 & 0 & 1 & -1 & 0 & | & 0 \\ 0 & 0 & 0 & 1 & 1 & | & 0 \end{bmatrix}$$

$$\rightarrow \begin{bmatrix} 1 & 0 & -1 & 1 & 0 & | & 0 \\ 0 & 1 & 0 & 0 & 1 & | & 0 \\ 0 & 0 & 1 & -1 & 0 & | & 0 \\ 0 & 0 & 0 & 1 & 1 & | & 0 \end{bmatrix} \rightarrow \begin{bmatrix} 1 & 0 & 0 & 0 & 0 & | & 0 \\ 0 & 1 & 0 & 0 & 1 & | & 0 \\ 0 & 0 & 1 & -1 & 0 & | & 0 \\ 0 & 0 & 0 & 1 & 1 & | & 0 \end{bmatrix} \rightarrow \begin{bmatrix} 1 & 0 & 0 & 0 & 0 & | & 0 \\ 0 & 1 & 0 & 0 & 1 & | & 0 \\ 0 & 0 & 1 & 0 & 1 & | & 0 \\ 0 & 0 & 0 & 1 & 1 & | & 0 \end{bmatrix}$$

Thus, $x_1 = 0$, $x_2 = -r$, $x_3 = -r$, $x_4 = -r$, $x_5 = r$, where r is any real number.

27. Let x = federal tax and y = state tax. Then $x = 0.25(312,000 - y)$ and $y = 0.10(312,000 - x)$. Equivalently,
$$\begin{cases} x + 0.25y = 78,000 \\ 0.10x + y = 31,200. \end{cases}$$
$$\begin{bmatrix} 1 & 0.25 & | & 78,000 \\ 0.10 & 1 & | & 31,200 \end{bmatrix} \rightarrow \begin{bmatrix} 1 & 0.25 & | & 78,000 \\ 0 & 0.975 & | & 23,400 \end{bmatrix} \rightarrow \begin{bmatrix} 1 & 0.25 & | & 78,000 \\ 0 & 1 & | & 24,000 \end{bmatrix} \rightarrow \begin{bmatrix} 1 & 0 & | & 72,000 \\ 0 & 1 & | & 24,000 \end{bmatrix}.$$
Thus $x = 72,000$ and $y = 24,000$, so the federal tax is \$72,000 and the state tax is \$24,000.

29. Let x = number of units of A produced, y = number of units of B produced, and z = number of units of C produced. Then
no. of units: $x + y + z = 11,000$
total cost: $4x + 5y + 7z + 17,000 = 80,000$
total profit: $x + 2y + 3z = 25,000$
Equivalently,
$$\begin{cases} x + y + z = 11,000 \\ 4x + 5y + 7z = 63,000 \\ x + 2y + 3z = 25,000 \end{cases}$$
$$\begin{bmatrix} 1 & 1 & 1 & | & 11,000 \\ 4 & 5 & 7 & | & 63,000 \\ 1 & 2 & 3 & | & 25,000 \end{bmatrix} \rightarrow \begin{bmatrix} 1 & 1 & 1 & | & 11,000 \\ 0 & 1 & 3 & | & 19,000 \\ 0 & 1 & 2 & | & 14,000 \end{bmatrix}$$
$$\rightarrow \begin{bmatrix} 1 & 0 & -2 & | & -8,000 \\ 0 & 1 & 3 & | & 19,000 \\ 0 & 0 & -1 & | & -5,000 \end{bmatrix} \rightarrow \begin{bmatrix} 1 & 0 & -2 & | & -8,000 \\ 0 & 1 & 3 & | & 19,000 \\ 0 & 0 & 1 & | & 5,000 \end{bmatrix} \rightarrow \begin{bmatrix} 1 & 0 & 0 & | & 2000 \\ 0 & 1 & 0 & | & 4000 \\ 0 & 0 & 1 & | & 5000 \end{bmatrix}$$
Thus $x = 2000$, $y = 4000$, and $z = 5000$, so 2000 units of A, 4000 units of B and 5000 units of C should be produced.

31. Let x = number of brand X pills, y = number of brand Y pills, and z = number of brand Z pills. Considering the unit requirements gives the system

$$\begin{cases} 2x + 1y + 1z = 10 & \text{(vitamin A)} \\ 3x + 3y + 0z = 9 & \text{(vitamin D)} \\ 5x + 4y + 1z = 19 & \text{(vitamin E)} \end{cases}$$

$$\begin{bmatrix} 2 & 1 & 1 & | & 10 \\ 3 & 3 & 0 & | & 9 \\ 5 & 4 & 1 & | & 19 \end{bmatrix} \rightarrow \begin{bmatrix} 1 & \frac{1}{2} & \frac{1}{2} & | & 5 \\ 3 & 3 & 0 & | & 9 \\ 5 & 4 & 1 & | & 19 \end{bmatrix} \rightarrow \begin{bmatrix} 1 & \frac{1}{2} & \frac{1}{2} & | & 5 \\ 0 & \frac{3}{2} & -\frac{3}{2} & | & -6 \\ 0 & \frac{3}{2} & -\frac{3}{2} & | & -6 \end{bmatrix}$$

$$\rightarrow \begin{bmatrix} 1 & \frac{1}{2} & \frac{1}{2} & | & 5 \\ 0 & 1 & -1 & | & -4 \\ 0 & 0 & 0 & | & 0 \end{bmatrix} \rightarrow \begin{bmatrix} 1 & 0 & 1 & | & 7 \\ 0 & 1 & -1 & | & -4 \\ 0 & 0 & 0 & | & 0 \end{bmatrix}$$

Thus $\begin{cases} x = 7 - r \\ y = r - 4 \\ z = r \end{cases}$ where $r = 4, 5, 6, 7$.

The only solutions for the problem are $z = 4$, $x = 3$, and $y = 0$; $z = 5$, $x = 2$, and $y = 1$; $z = 6$, $x = 1$, and $y = 2$; $z = 7$, $x = 0$, and $y = 3$. Their respective costs (in cents) are 15, 23, 31, and 39.

a. The possible combinations are 3 of X, 4 of Z; 2 of X, 1 of Y, 5 of Z; 1 of X, 2 of Y, 6 of Z; 3 of Y, 7 of Z.

b. The combination 3 of X, 4 of Z costs 15 cents a day.

c. The least expensive combination is 3 of X, 4 of Z; the most expensive is 3 of Y, 7 of Z.

33. a. Let s, d, and g represent the number of units of S, D, and G, respectively. Then

$$\begin{cases} 12s + 20g + 32d = 220 & \text{(stock A)} \\ 16s + 12g + 28d = 176 & \text{(stock B)} \\ 8s + 28g + 36d = 264 & \text{(stock C)} \end{cases}$$

$$\begin{bmatrix} 12 & 20 & 32 & | & 220 \\ 16 & 12 & 28 & | & 176 \\ 8 & 28 & 36 & | & 264 \end{bmatrix} \begin{array}{l} \left(\frac{1}{4}\right)R_1 \\ \xrightarrow{\left(\frac{1}{4}\right)R_2} \\ \left(\frac{1}{8}\right)R_3 \end{array} \begin{bmatrix} 3 & 5 & 8 & | & 55 \\ 4 & 3 & 7 & | & 44 \\ 1 & \frac{7}{2} & \frac{9}{2} & | & 33 \end{bmatrix}$$

$$\xrightarrow{R_1 \leftrightarrow R_3} \begin{bmatrix} 1 & \frac{7}{2} & \frac{9}{2} & | & 33 \\ 4 & 3 & 7 & | & 44 \\ 3 & 5 & 8 & | & 55 \end{bmatrix}$$

$$\xrightarrow[-3R_1 + R_3]{-4R_1 + R_2} \begin{bmatrix} 1 & \frac{7}{2} & \frac{9}{2} & | & 33 \\ 0 & -11 & -11 & | & -88 \\ 0 & -\frac{11}{2} & -\frac{11}{2} & | & -44 \end{bmatrix}$$

$$\xrightarrow{-\frac{1}{11}R_2} \begin{bmatrix} 1 & \frac{7}{2} & \frac{9}{2} & 33 \\ 0 & 1 & 1 & 8 \\ 0 & -\frac{11}{2} & -\frac{11}{2} & -44 \end{bmatrix}$$

$$\xrightarrow[\frac{11}{2}R_2+R_3]{-\frac{7}{2}R_2+R_1} \begin{bmatrix} 1 & 0 & 1 & 5 \\ 0 & 1 & 1 & 8 \\ 0 & 0 & 0 & 0 \end{bmatrix}$$

Thus $s = 5 - r$, $d = 8 - r$, and $g = r$, where $r = 0, 1, 2, 3, 4, 5$.
The six possible combinations are given by

COMBINATION

r	0	1	2	3	4	5
S	5	4	3	2	1	0
D	8	7	6	5	4	3
G	0	1	2	3	4	5

b. Computing the cost of each combination, we find that they are 4700, 4600, 4500, 4400, 4300, and 4200 dollars, respectively. Buying 3 units of Deluxe and 5 units of Gold Star ($s = 0$, $d = 3$, $g = 5$) minimizes the cost.

Principles in Practice 6.5

1. Write the coefficients matrix and reduce.

$$\begin{bmatrix} 5 & 3 & 4 \\ 6 & 8 & 7 \\ 3 & 1 & 2 \end{bmatrix} \xrightarrow{\frac{1}{5}R_1} \begin{bmatrix} 1 & \frac{3}{5} & \frac{4}{5} \\ 6 & 8 & 7 \\ 3 & 1 & 2 \end{bmatrix} \xrightarrow[-3R_1+R_3]{-6R_1+R_2} \begin{bmatrix} 1 & \frac{3}{5} & \frac{4}{5} \\ 0 & \frac{22}{5} & \frac{11}{5} \\ 0 & -\frac{4}{5} & -\frac{2}{5} \end{bmatrix}$$

$$\xrightarrow{\frac{5}{22}R_2} \begin{bmatrix} 1 & \frac{3}{5} & \frac{4}{5} \\ 0 & 1 & \frac{1}{2} \\ 0 & -\frac{4}{5} & -\frac{2}{5} \end{bmatrix} \xrightarrow[\frac{4}{5}R_2+R_3]{-\frac{3}{5}R_2+R_1} \begin{bmatrix} 1 & 0 & \frac{1}{2} \\ 0 & 1 & \frac{1}{2} \\ 0 & 0 & 0 \end{bmatrix}$$

The system has infinitely many solutions since there are two nonzero rows in the reduced coefficient matrix.

$$x + \frac{1}{2}z = 0$$

$$y + \frac{1}{2}z = 0$$

Let $z = r$, so $x = -\frac{1}{2}r$ and $y = -\frac{1}{2}r$, where r is any real number.

Exercise 6.5

1. $\begin{bmatrix} 1 & -1 & -1 & 4 & | & 5 \\ 2 & -3 & -4 & 9 & | & 13 \\ 2 & 1 & 4 & 5 & | & 1 \end{bmatrix} \rightarrow \begin{bmatrix} 1 & -1 & -1 & 4 & | & 5 \\ 0 & -1 & -2 & 1 & | & 3 \\ 0 & 3 & 6 & -3 & | & -9 \end{bmatrix}$

$\rightarrow \begin{bmatrix} 1 & -1 & -1 & 4 & | & 5 \\ 0 & 1 & 2 & -1 & | & -3 \\ 0 & 3 & 6 & -3 & | & -9 \end{bmatrix} \rightarrow \begin{bmatrix} 1 & 0 & 1 & 3 & | & 2 \\ 0 & 1 & 2 & -1 & | & -3 \\ 0 & 0 & 0 & 0 & | & 0 \end{bmatrix}$

Thus $w = -r - 3s + 2$, $x = -2r + s - 3$, $y = r$, $z = s$ (where r and s are any real numbers).

3. $\begin{bmatrix} 3 & -1 & -3 & -1 & | & -2 \\ 2 & -2 & -6 & -6 & | & -4 \\ 2 & -1 & -3 & -2 & | & -2 \\ 3 & 1 & 3 & 7 & | & 2 \end{bmatrix} \rightarrow \begin{bmatrix} 1 & -\frac{1}{3} & -1 & -\frac{1}{3} & | & -\frac{2}{3} \\ 2 & -2 & -6 & -6 & | & -4 \\ 2 & -1 & -3 & -2 & | & -2 \\ 3 & 1 & 3 & 7 & | & 2 \end{bmatrix}$

$\rightarrow \begin{bmatrix} 1 & -\frac{1}{3} & -1 & -\frac{1}{3} & | & -\frac{2}{3} \\ 0 & -\frac{4}{3} & -4 & -\frac{16}{3} & | & -\frac{8}{3} \\ 0 & -\frac{1}{3} & -1 & -\frac{4}{3} & | & -\frac{2}{3} \\ 0 & 2 & 6 & 8 & | & 4 \end{bmatrix} \rightarrow \begin{bmatrix} 1 & -\frac{1}{3} & -1 & -\frac{1}{3} & | & -\frac{2}{3} \\ 0 & 1 & 3 & 4 & | & 2 \\ 0 & -\frac{1}{3} & -1 & -\frac{4}{3} & | & -\frac{2}{3} \\ 0 & 2 & 6 & 8 & | & 4 \end{bmatrix} \rightarrow \begin{bmatrix} 1 & 0 & 0 & 1 & | & 0 \\ 0 & 1 & 3 & 4 & | & 2 \\ 0 & 0 & 0 & 0 & | & 0 \\ 0 & 0 & 0 & 0 & | & 0 \end{bmatrix}$

Thus, $w = -s$, $x = -3r - 4s + 2$, $y = r$, $z = s$ (where r and s are any real numbers).

5. $\begin{bmatrix} 1 & 1 & 3 & -1 & | & 2 \\ 2 & 1 & 5 & -2 & | & 0 \\ 2 & -1 & 3 & -2 & | & -8 \\ 3 & 2 & 8 & -3 & | & 2 \\ 1 & 0 & 2 & -1 & | & -2 \end{bmatrix} \rightarrow \begin{bmatrix} 1 & 1 & 3 & -1 & | & 2 \\ 0 & -1 & -1 & 0 & | & -4 \\ 0 & -3 & -3 & 0 & | & -12 \\ 0 & -1 & -1 & 0 & | & -4 \\ 0 & -1 & -1 & 0 & | & -4 \end{bmatrix}$

$\rightarrow \begin{bmatrix} 1 & 1 & 3 & -1 & | & 2 \\ 0 & 1 & 1 & 0 & | & 4 \\ 0 & -3 & -3 & 0 & | & -12 \\ 0 & -1 & -1 & 0 & | & -4 \\ 0 & -1 & -1 & 0 & | & -4 \end{bmatrix} \rightarrow \begin{bmatrix} 1 & 0 & 2 & -1 & | & -2 \\ 0 & 1 & 1 & 0 & | & 4 \\ 0 & 0 & 0 & 0 & | & 0 \\ 0 & 0 & 0 & 0 & | & 0 \\ 0 & 0 & 0 & 0 & | & 0 \end{bmatrix}$

Thus, $w = -2r + s - 2$, $x = -r + 4$, $y = r$, $z = s$ (where r and s are any real numbers).

7. $\begin{bmatrix} 4 & -3 & 5 & -10 & 11 & | & -8 \\ 2 & 1 & 5 & 0 & 3 & | & 6 \end{bmatrix} \rightarrow \begin{bmatrix} 0 & -5 & -5 & -10 & 5 & | & -20 \\ 2 & 1 & 5 & 0 & 3 & | & 6 \end{bmatrix}$

$\rightarrow \begin{bmatrix} 2 & 1 & 5 & 0 & 3 & | & 6 \\ 0 & -5 & -5 & -10 & 5 & | & -20 \end{bmatrix} \rightarrow \begin{bmatrix} 2 & 1 & 5 & 0 & 3 & | & 6 \\ 0 & 1 & 1 & 2 & -1 & | & 4 \end{bmatrix}$

$\rightarrow \begin{bmatrix} 2 & 0 & 4 & -2 & 4 & | & 2 \\ 0 & 1 & 1 & 2 & -1 & | & 4 \end{bmatrix} \rightarrow \begin{bmatrix} 1 & 0 & 2 & -1 & 2 & | & 1 \\ 0 & 1 & 1 & 2 & -1 & | & 4 \end{bmatrix}$

Thus, $x_1 = -2r + s - 2t + 1$, $x_2 = -r - 2s + t + 4$, $x_3 = r$, $x_4 = s$, $x_5 = t$ (where r, s and t are any real numbers).

114

9. The system is homogeneous with fewer equations than unknowns ($2 < 3$), so there are infinitely many solutions.

11. $\begin{bmatrix} 3 & -4 \\ 1 & 5 \\ 4 & -1 \end{bmatrix} \rightarrow \begin{bmatrix} 1 & 5 \\ 3 & -4 \\ 4 & -1 \end{bmatrix} \rightarrow \begin{bmatrix} 1 & 5 \\ 0 & -19 \\ 0 & -21 \end{bmatrix} \rightarrow \begin{bmatrix} 1 & 5 \\ 0 & 1 \\ 0 & -21 \end{bmatrix} \rightarrow \begin{bmatrix} 1 & 0 \\ 0 & 1 \\ 0 & 0 \end{bmatrix} = \mathbf{A}$

A has $k = 2$ nonzero rows. Number of unknowns is $n = 2$. Thus $k = n$, so the system has the trivial solution only.

13. $\begin{bmatrix} 1 & 1 & 1 \\ 1 & 0 & -1 \\ 1 & -2 & -5 \end{bmatrix} \rightarrow \begin{bmatrix} 1 & 1 & 1 \\ 0 & -1 & -2 \\ 0 & -3 & -6 \end{bmatrix} \rightarrow \begin{bmatrix} 1 & 1 & 1 \\ 0 & 1 & 2 \\ 0 & -3 & -6 \end{bmatrix} \rightarrow \begin{bmatrix} 1 & 0 & -1 \\ 0 & 1 & 2 \\ 0 & 0 & 0 \end{bmatrix} = \mathbf{A}$

A has $k = 2$ nonzero rows. Number of unknowns is $n = 3$. Thus $k < n$, so the system has infinitely many solutions.

15. $\begin{bmatrix} 1 & 1 \\ 3 & -4 \end{bmatrix} \rightarrow \begin{bmatrix} 1 & 1 \\ 0 & -7 \end{bmatrix} \rightarrow \begin{bmatrix} 1 & 1 \\ 0 & 1 \end{bmatrix} \rightarrow \begin{bmatrix} 1 & 0 \\ 0 & 1 \end{bmatrix}$

The solution is $x = 0$, $y = 0$.

17. $\begin{bmatrix} 1 & 6 & -2 \\ 2 & -3 & 4 \end{bmatrix} \rightarrow \begin{bmatrix} 1 & 6 & -2 \\ 0 & -15 & 8 \end{bmatrix} \rightarrow \begin{bmatrix} 1 & 6 & -2 \\ 0 & 1 & -\frac{8}{15} \end{bmatrix} \rightarrow \begin{bmatrix} 1 & 0 & \frac{6}{5} \\ 0 & 1 & -\frac{8}{15} \end{bmatrix}$

The solution is $x = -\dfrac{6}{5}r$, $y = \dfrac{8}{15}r$, $z = r$.

19. $\begin{bmatrix} 1 & 1 \\ 3 & -4 \\ 5 & -8 \end{bmatrix} \rightarrow \begin{bmatrix} 1 & 1 \\ 0 & -7 \\ 0 & -13 \end{bmatrix} \rightarrow \begin{bmatrix} 1 & 1 \\ 0 & 1 \\ 0 & -13 \end{bmatrix} \rightarrow \begin{bmatrix} 1 & 0 \\ 0 & 1 \\ 0 & 0 \end{bmatrix}$

The solution is $x = 0$, $y = 0$.

21. $\begin{bmatrix} 1 & 1 & 1 \\ 5 & -2 & -9 \\ 3 & 1 & -1 \\ 3 & -2 & -7 \end{bmatrix} \rightarrow \begin{bmatrix} 1 & 1 & 1 \\ 0 & -7 & -14 \\ 0 & -2 & -4 \\ 0 & -5 & -10 \end{bmatrix} \rightarrow \begin{bmatrix} 1 & 1 & 1 \\ 0 & 1 & 2 \\ 0 & -2 & -4 \\ 0 & -5 & -10 \end{bmatrix} \rightarrow \begin{bmatrix} 1 & 0 & -1 \\ 0 & 1 & 2 \\ 0 & 0 & 0 \\ 0 & 0 & 0 \end{bmatrix}$

The solution is $x = r$, $y = -2r$, $z = r$.

23. $\begin{bmatrix} 1 & 1 & 1 & 4 \\ 1 & 1 & 0 & 5 \\ 2 & 1 & 3 & 4 \\ 1 & -3 & 2 & -9 \end{bmatrix} \rightarrow \begin{bmatrix} 1 & 1 & 1 & 4 \\ 0 & 0 & -1 & 1 \\ 0 & -1 & 1 & -4 \\ 0 & -4 & 1 & -13 \end{bmatrix} \rightarrow \begin{bmatrix} 1 & 1 & 1 & 4 \\ 0 & -1 & 1 & -4 \\ 0 & 0 & -1 & 1 \\ 0 & -4 & 1 & -13 \end{bmatrix}$

$\rightarrow \begin{bmatrix} 1 & 1 & 1 & 4 \\ 0 & 1 & -1 & 4 \\ 0 & 0 & -1 & 1 \\ 0 & -4 & 1 & -13 \end{bmatrix} \rightarrow \begin{bmatrix} 1 & 0 & 2 & 0 \\ 0 & 1 & -1 & 4 \\ 0 & 0 & -1 & 1 \\ 0 & 0 & -3 & 3 \end{bmatrix} \rightarrow \begin{bmatrix} 1 & 0 & 2 & 0 \\ 0 & 1 & -1 & 4 \\ 0 & 0 & 1 & -1 \\ 0 & 0 & -3 & 3 \end{bmatrix} \rightarrow \begin{bmatrix} 1 & 0 & 0 & 2 \\ 0 & 1 & 0 & 3 \\ 0 & 0 & 1 & -1 \\ 0 & 0 & 0 & 0 \end{bmatrix}$

The solution is $w = -2r, x = -3r, y = r, z = r$.

Principles in Practice 6.6

1. $\begin{bmatrix} 1 & 3 \\ 2 & 4 \end{bmatrix} \begin{bmatrix} -2 & 1.5 \\ 1 & -0.5 \end{bmatrix} = \begin{bmatrix} 1 & 0 \\ 0 & 1 \end{bmatrix}$

Yes, they are inverses.

2. $\begin{bmatrix} -2 & 1.5 \\ 1 & -0.5 \end{bmatrix} \begin{bmatrix} 28 \\ 46 \end{bmatrix} = \begin{bmatrix} 13 \\ 5 \end{bmatrix} = \begin{bmatrix} M \\ E \end{bmatrix}$

$\begin{bmatrix} -2 & 1.5 \\ 1 & -0.5 \end{bmatrix} \begin{bmatrix} 65 \\ 90 \end{bmatrix} = \begin{bmatrix} 5 \\ 20 \end{bmatrix} = \begin{bmatrix} E \\ T \end{bmatrix}$

$\begin{bmatrix} -2 & 1.5 \\ 1 & -0.5 \end{bmatrix} \begin{bmatrix} 61 \\ 82 \end{bmatrix} = \begin{bmatrix} 1 \\ 20 \end{bmatrix} = \begin{bmatrix} A \\ T \end{bmatrix}$

$\begin{bmatrix} -2 & 1.5 \\ 1 & -0.5 \end{bmatrix} \begin{bmatrix} 59 \\ 88 \end{bmatrix} = \begin{bmatrix} 14 \\ 15 \end{bmatrix} = \begin{bmatrix} N \\ O \end{bmatrix}$

$\begin{bmatrix} -2 & 1.5 \\ 1 & -0.5 \end{bmatrix} \begin{bmatrix} 57 \\ 86 \end{bmatrix} = \begin{bmatrix} 15 \\ 14 \end{bmatrix} = \begin{bmatrix} O \\ N \end{bmatrix}$

$\begin{bmatrix} -2 & 1.5 \\ 1 & -0.5 \end{bmatrix} \begin{bmatrix} 60 \\ 84 \end{bmatrix} = \begin{bmatrix} 6 \\ 18 \end{bmatrix} = \begin{bmatrix} F \\ R \end{bmatrix}$

$\begin{bmatrix} -2 & 1.5 \\ 1 & -0.5 \end{bmatrix} \begin{bmatrix} 21 \\ 34 \end{bmatrix} = \begin{bmatrix} 9 \\ 4 \end{bmatrix} = \begin{bmatrix} I \\ D \end{bmatrix}$

$\begin{bmatrix} -2 & 1.5 \\ 1 & -0.5 \end{bmatrix} \begin{bmatrix} 76 \\ 102 \end{bmatrix} = \begin{bmatrix} 1 \\ 25 \end{bmatrix} = \begin{bmatrix} A \\ Y \end{bmatrix}$

The message is "MEET AT NOON FRIDAY."

3. $[\mathbf{E} \,|\, \mathbf{I}] = \begin{bmatrix} 3 & 1 & 2 & | & 1 & 0 & 0 \\ 2 & 2 & 2 & | & 0 & 1 & 0 \\ 2 & 1 & 3 & | & 0 & 0 & 1 \end{bmatrix}$

$\xrightarrow{R_1 \leftrightarrow R_2} \begin{bmatrix} 2 & 2 & 2 & | & 0 & 1 & 0 \\ 3 & 1 & 2 & | & 1 & 0 & 0 \\ 2 & 1 & 3 & | & 0 & 0 & 1 \end{bmatrix}$

$\xrightarrow{\frac{1}{2}R_1} \begin{bmatrix} 1 & 1 & 1 & | & 0 & \frac{1}{2} & 0 \\ 3 & 1 & 2 & | & 1 & 0 & 0 \\ 2 & 1 & 3 & | & 0 & 0 & 1 \end{bmatrix}$

$\xrightarrow[-2R_1 + R_3]{-3R_1 + R_2} \begin{bmatrix} 1 & 1 & 1 & | & 0 & \frac{1}{2} & 0 \\ 0 & -2 & -1 & | & 1 & -\frac{3}{2} & 0 \\ 0 & -1 & 1 & | & 0 & -1 & 1 \end{bmatrix}$

$\xrightarrow{R_2 \leftrightarrow R_3} \begin{bmatrix} 1 & 1 & 1 & | & 0 & \frac{1}{2} & 0 \\ 0 & -1 & 1 & | & 0 & -1 & 1 \\ 0 & -2 & -1 & | & 1 & -\frac{3}{2} & 0 \end{bmatrix}$

$\xrightarrow{-R_2} \begin{bmatrix} 1 & 1 & 1 & | & 0 & \frac{1}{2} & 0 \\ 0 & 1 & -1 & | & 0 & 1 & -1 \\ 0 & -2 & -1 & | & 1 & -\frac{3}{2} & 0 \end{bmatrix}$

$\xrightarrow[2R_2 + R_3]{-R_2 + R_1} \begin{bmatrix} 1 & 0 & 2 & | & 0 & -\frac{1}{2} & 1 \\ 0 & 1 & -1 & | & 0 & 1 & -1 \\ 0 & 0 & -3 & | & 1 & \frac{1}{2} & -2 \end{bmatrix}$

$\xrightarrow{-\frac{1}{3}R_3} \begin{bmatrix} 1 & 0 & 2 & | & 0 & -\frac{1}{2} & 1 \\ 0 & 1 & -1 & | & 0 & 1 & -1 \\ 0 & 0 & 1 & | & -\frac{1}{3} & -\frac{1}{6} & \frac{2}{3} \end{bmatrix}$

$\xrightarrow[R_3 + R_2]{-2R_3 + R_1} \begin{bmatrix} 1 & 0 & 0 & | & \frac{2}{3} & -\frac{1}{6} & -\frac{1}{3} \\ 0 & 1 & 0 & | & -\frac{1}{3} & \frac{5}{6} & -\frac{1}{3} \\ 0 & 0 & 1 & | & -\frac{1}{3} & -\frac{1}{6} & \frac{2}{3} \end{bmatrix}$

$\mathbf{E}^{-1} = \begin{bmatrix} \frac{2}{3} & -\frac{1}{6} & -\frac{1}{3} \\ -\frac{1}{3} & \frac{5}{6} & -\frac{1}{3} \\ -\frac{1}{3} & -\frac{1}{6} & \frac{2}{3} \end{bmatrix}$

$[\mathbf{E} \,|\, \mathbf{I}] = \begin{bmatrix} 2 & 1 & 2 & | & 1 & 0 & 0 \\ 3 & 2 & 3 & | & 0 & 1 & 0 \\ 4 & 3 & 4 & | & 0 & 0 & 1 \end{bmatrix}$

$$\xrightarrow{\frac{1}{2}R_1} \begin{bmatrix} 1 & \frac{1}{2} & 1 & \frac{1}{2} & 0 & 0 \\ 3 & 2 & 3 & 0 & 1 & 0 \\ 4 & 3 & 4 & 0 & 0 & 1 \end{bmatrix}$$

$$\xrightarrow[-4R_1+R_3]{-3R_1+R_2} \begin{bmatrix} 1 & \frac{1}{2} & 1 & \frac{1}{2} & 0 & 0 \\ 0 & \frac{1}{2} & 0 & -\frac{3}{2} & 1 & 0 \\ 0 & 1 & 0 & -2 & 0 & 1 \end{bmatrix}$$

$$\xrightarrow{2R_2} \begin{bmatrix} 1 & \frac{1}{2} & 1 & \frac{1}{2} & 0 & 0 \\ 0 & 1 & 0 & -3 & 2 & 0 \\ 0 & 1 & 0 & -2 & 0 & 1 \end{bmatrix}$$

$$\xrightarrow[-R_2+R_3]{-\frac{1}{2}R_2+R_1} \begin{bmatrix} 1 & 0 & 1 & 2 & -1 & 0 \\ 0 & 1 & 0 & -3 & 2 & 0 \\ 0 & 0 & 0 & 1 & -2 & 1 \end{bmatrix}$$

$\mathbf{F}$ does not reduce to $\mathbf{I}$ so $\mathbf{F}$ is not invertible.

4. Let x be the number of shares of A, y be the number of shares of B, and z be the number of shares of C. We got the following equations from the given conditions.

$50x + 20y + 80z = 500{,}000$

$x = 2z$

$0.13(50x) + 0.15(20y) + 0.10(80z)$

$= 0.12(50x + 20y + 80z)$

Simplify the first equation.

$5x + 2y + 8z = 50{,}000$

Simplify the second equation.

$x - 2z = 0$

Simplify the third equation.

$6.5x + 3y + 8z = 6x + 2.4y + 9.6z$

$0.5x + 0.6y - 1.6z = 0$

$5x + 6y - 16z = 0$

Thus, we solve the following system of equations.

$x - 2z = 0$

$5x + 6y - 16z = 0$

$5x + 2y + 8z = 50{,}000$

The coefficient matrix is $\mathbf{A} = \begin{bmatrix} 1 & 0 & -2 \\ 5 & 6 & -16 \\ 5 & 2 & 8 \end{bmatrix}$.

$$[\mathbf{A}\,|\,\mathbf{I}] = \begin{bmatrix} 1 & 0 & -2 & 1 & 0 & 0 \\ 5 & 6 & -16 & 0 & 1 & 0 \\ 5 & 2 & 8 & 0 & 0 & 1 \end{bmatrix}$$

$$\xrightarrow[-5R_1+R_3]{-5R_1+R_2} \begin{bmatrix} 1 & 0 & -2 & 1 & 0 & 0 \\ 0 & 6 & -6 & -5 & 1 & 0 \\ 0 & 2 & 18 & -5 & 0 & 1 \end{bmatrix}$$

$$\xrightarrow{\frac{1}{6}R_2} \begin{bmatrix} 1 & 0 & -2 & | & 1 & 0 & 0 \\ 0 & 1 & -1 & | & -\frac{5}{6} & \frac{1}{6} & 0 \\ 0 & 2 & 18 & | & -5 & 0 & 1 \end{bmatrix}$$

$$\xrightarrow{-2R_2+R_3} \begin{bmatrix} 1 & 0 & -2 & | & 1 & 0 & 0 \\ 0 & 1 & -1 & | & -\frac{5}{6} & \frac{1}{6} & 0 \\ 0 & 0 & 20 & | & -\frac{10}{3} & -\frac{1}{3} & 1 \end{bmatrix}$$

$$\xrightarrow{\frac{1}{20}R_3} \begin{bmatrix} 1 & 0 & -2 & | & 1 & 0 & 0 \\ 0 & 1 & -1 & | & -\frac{5}{6} & \frac{1}{6} & 0 \\ 0 & 0 & 1 & | & -\frac{1}{6} & -\frac{1}{60} & \frac{1}{20} \end{bmatrix}$$

$$\xrightarrow[R_3+R_2]{2R_3+R_1} \begin{bmatrix} 1 & 0 & 0 & | & \frac{2}{3} & -\frac{1}{30} & \frac{1}{10} \\ 0 & 1 & 0 & | & -1 & \frac{3}{20} & \frac{1}{20} \\ 0 & 0 & 1 & | & -\frac{1}{6} & -\frac{1}{60} & \frac{1}{20} \end{bmatrix}$$

$$\mathbf{A}^{-1} = \begin{bmatrix} \frac{2}{3} & -\frac{1}{30} & \frac{1}{10} \\ -1 & \frac{3}{20} & \frac{1}{20} \\ -\frac{1}{6} & -\frac{1}{60} & \frac{1}{20} \end{bmatrix}$$

$$\begin{bmatrix} x \\ y \\ z \end{bmatrix} = \begin{bmatrix} \frac{2}{3} & -\frac{1}{30} & \frac{1}{10} \\ -1 & \frac{3}{20} & \frac{1}{20} \\ -\frac{1}{6} & -\frac{1}{60} & \frac{1}{20} \end{bmatrix} \begin{bmatrix} 0 \\ 0 \\ 50,000 \end{bmatrix} = \begin{bmatrix} 5000 \\ 2500 \\ 2500 \end{bmatrix}$$

They should buy 5000 shares of Company A, 2500 shares of Company B, and 2500 shares of Company C.

Exercise 6.6

1. $\begin{bmatrix} 6 & 1 & | & 1 & 0 \\ 5 & 1 & | & 0 & 1 \end{bmatrix} \rightarrow \begin{bmatrix} 1 & \frac{1}{6} & | & \frac{1}{6} & 0 \\ 5 & 1 & | & 0 & 1 \end{bmatrix} \rightarrow \begin{bmatrix} 1 & \frac{1}{6} & | & \frac{1}{6} & 0 \\ 0 & \frac{1}{6} & | & -\frac{5}{6} & 1 \end{bmatrix}$

   $\rightarrow \begin{bmatrix} 1 & 0 & | & 1 & -1 \\ 0 & \frac{1}{6} & | & -\frac{5}{6} & 1 \end{bmatrix} \rightarrow \begin{bmatrix} 1 & 0 & | & 1 & -1 \\ 0 & 1 & | & -5 & 6 \end{bmatrix}$

   The inverse is $\begin{bmatrix} 1 & -1 \\ -5 & 6 \end{bmatrix}$.

3. $\begin{bmatrix} 1 & 1 & | & 1 & 0 \\ 1 & 1 & | & 0 & 1 \end{bmatrix} \rightarrow \begin{bmatrix} 1 & 1 & | & 1 & 0 \\ 0 & 0 & | & -1 & 1 \end{bmatrix}$

   The given matrix is not invertible.

5. $\begin{bmatrix} 1 & 0 & 0 & | & 1 & 0 & 0 \\ 0 & -3 & 0 & | & 0 & 1 & 0 \\ 0 & 0 & 4 & | & 0 & 0 & 1 \end{bmatrix} \rightarrow \begin{bmatrix} 1 & 0 & 0 & | & 1 & 0 & 0 \\ 0 & 1 & 0 & | & 0 & -\frac{1}{3} & 0 \\ 0 & 0 & 1 & | & 0 & 0 & \frac{1}{4} \end{bmatrix}$

The inverse is $\begin{bmatrix} 1 & 0 & 0 \\ 0 & -\frac{1}{3} & 0 \\ 0 & 0 & \frac{1}{4} \end{bmatrix}$.

7. $\begin{bmatrix} 1 & 2 & 3 & | & 1 & 0 & 0 \\ 0 & 0 & 4 & | & 0 & 1 & 0 \\ 0 & 0 & 5 & | & 0 & 0 & 1 \end{bmatrix} \rightarrow \begin{bmatrix} 1 & 2 & 3 & | & 1 & 0 & 0 \\ 0 & 0 & 1 & | & 0 & \frac{1}{4} & 0 \\ 0 & 0 & 5 & | & 0 & 0 & 1 \end{bmatrix}$

$\rightarrow \begin{bmatrix} 1 & 2 & 0 & | & 1 & -\frac{3}{4} & 0 \\ 0 & 0 & 1 & | & 0 & \frac{1}{4} & 0 \\ 0 & 0 & 0 & | & 0 & -\frac{5}{4} & 1 \end{bmatrix}$

The given matrix is not invertible.

9. The matrix is not square, so it is not invertible.

11. $\begin{bmatrix} 1 & 1 & 1 & | & 1 & 0 & 0 \\ 0 & 1 & 1 & | & 0 & 1 & 0 \\ 0 & 0 & 1 & | & 0 & 0 & 1 \end{bmatrix} \rightarrow \begin{bmatrix} 1 & 0 & 0 & | & 1 & -1 & 0 \\ 0 & 1 & 1 & | & 0 & 1 & 0 \\ 0 & 0 & 1 & | & 0 & 0 & 1 \end{bmatrix} \rightarrow \begin{bmatrix} 1 & 0 & 0 & | & 1 & -1 & 0 \\ 0 & 1 & 0 & | & 0 & 1 & -1 \\ 0 & 0 & 1 & | & 0 & 0 & 1 \end{bmatrix}$

The inverse is $\begin{bmatrix} 1 & -1 & 0 \\ 0 & 1 & -1 \\ 0 & 0 & 1 \end{bmatrix}$.

13. $\begin{bmatrix} 7 & 0 & -2 & | & 1 & 0 & 0 \\ 0 & 1 & 0 & | & 0 & 1 & 0 \\ -3 & 0 & 1 & | & 0 & 0 & 1 \end{bmatrix} \rightarrow \begin{bmatrix} 1 & 0 & -\frac{2}{7} & | & \frac{1}{7} & 0 & 0 \\ 0 & 1 & 0 & | & 0 & 1 & 0 \\ -3 & 0 & 1 & | & 0 & 0 & 1 \end{bmatrix}$

$\rightarrow \begin{bmatrix} 1 & 0 & -\frac{2}{7} & | & \frac{1}{7} & 0 & 0 \\ 0 & 1 & 0 & | & 0 & 1 & 0 \\ 0 & 0 & \frac{1}{7} & | & \frac{3}{7} & 0 & 1 \end{bmatrix} \rightarrow \begin{bmatrix} 1 & 0 & 0 & | & 1 & 0 & 2 \\ 0 & 1 & 0 & | & 0 & 1 & 0 \\ 0 & 0 & \frac{1}{7} & | & \frac{3}{7} & 0 & 1 \end{bmatrix} \rightarrow \begin{bmatrix} 1 & 0 & 0 & | & 1 & 0 & 2 \\ 0 & 1 & 0 & | & 0 & 1 & 0 \\ 0 & 0 & 1 & | & 3 & 0 & 7 \end{bmatrix}$

The inverse is $\begin{bmatrix} 1 & 0 & 2 \\ 0 & 1 & 0 \\ 3 & 0 & 7 \end{bmatrix}$.

15. $\begin{bmatrix} 2 & 1 & 0 & | & 1 & 0 & 0 \\ 4 & -1 & 5 & | & 0 & 1 & 0 \\ 1 & -1 & 2 & | & 0 & 0 & 1 \end{bmatrix} \rightarrow \begin{bmatrix} 1 & -1 & 2 & | & 0 & 0 & 1 \\ 4 & -1 & 5 & | & 0 & 1 & 0 \\ 2 & 1 & 0 & | & 1 & 0 & 0 \end{bmatrix}$

$\rightarrow \begin{bmatrix} 1 & -1 & 2 & | & 0 & 0 & 1 \\ 0 & 3 & -3 & | & 0 & 1 & -4 \\ 0 & 3 & -4 & | & 1 & 0 & -2 \end{bmatrix} \rightarrow \begin{bmatrix} 1 & -1 & 2 & | & 0 & 0 & 1 \\ 0 & 1 & -1 & | & 0 & \frac{1}{3} & -\frac{4}{3} \\ 0 & 3 & -4 & | & 1 & 0 & -2 \end{bmatrix}$

$\rightarrow \begin{bmatrix} 1 & 0 & 1 & | & 0 & \frac{1}{3} & -\frac{1}{3} \\ 0 & 1 & -1 & | & 0 & \frac{1}{3} & -\frac{4}{3} \\ 0 & 0 & -1 & | & 1 & -1 & 2 \end{bmatrix} \rightarrow \begin{bmatrix} 1 & 0 & 1 & | & 0 & \frac{1}{3} & -\frac{1}{3} \\ 0 & 1 & -1 & | & 0 & \frac{1}{3} & -\frac{4}{3} \\ 0 & 0 & 1 & | & -1 & 1 & -2 \end{bmatrix}$

$\rightarrow \begin{bmatrix} 1 & 0 & 0 & | & 1 & -\frac{2}{3} & \frac{5}{3} \\ 0 & 1 & 0 & | & -1 & \frac{4}{3} & -\frac{10}{3} \\ 0 & 0 & 1 & | & -1 & 1 & -2 \end{bmatrix}.$

The inverse is $\begin{bmatrix} 1 & -\frac{2}{3} & \frac{5}{3} \\ -1 & \frac{4}{3} & -\frac{10}{3} \\ -1 & 1 & -2 \end{bmatrix}.$

17. $\begin{bmatrix} 1 & 2 & 3 & | & 1 & 0 & 0 \\ 1 & 3 & 5 & | & 0 & 1 & 0 \\ 1 & 5 & 12 & | & 0 & 0 & 1 \end{bmatrix} \rightarrow \begin{bmatrix} 1 & 2 & 3 & | & 1 & 0 & 0 \\ 0 & 1 & 2 & | & -1 & 1 & 0 \\ 0 & 3 & 9 & | & -1 & 0 & 1 \end{bmatrix}$

$\rightarrow \begin{bmatrix} 1 & 0 & -1 & | & 3 & -2 & 0 \\ 0 & 1 & 2 & | & -1 & 1 & 0 \\ 0 & 0 & 3 & | & 2 & -3 & 1 \end{bmatrix} \rightarrow \begin{bmatrix} 1 & 0 & -1 & | & 3 & -2 & 0 \\ 0 & 1 & 2 & | & -1 & 1 & 0 \\ 0 & 0 & 1 & | & \frac{2}{3} & -1 & \frac{1}{3} \end{bmatrix}$

$\rightarrow \begin{bmatrix} 1 & 0 & 0 & | & \frac{11}{3} & -3 & \frac{1}{3} \\ 0 & 1 & 0 & | & -\frac{7}{3} & 3 & -\frac{2}{3} \\ 0 & 0 & 1 & | & \frac{2}{3} & -1 & \frac{1}{3} \end{bmatrix}$

The inverse is $\begin{bmatrix} \frac{11}{3} & -3 & \frac{1}{3} \\ -\frac{7}{3} & 3 & -\frac{2}{3} \\ \frac{2}{3} & -1 & \frac{1}{3} \end{bmatrix}.$

19. $\mathbf{X} = \begin{bmatrix} x_1 \\ x_2 \end{bmatrix} = \mathbf{A}^{-1}\mathbf{B} = \begin{bmatrix} 1 & 2 \\ 1 & 1 \end{bmatrix}\begin{bmatrix} 2 \\ 4 \end{bmatrix} = \begin{bmatrix} 10 \\ 6 \end{bmatrix} \Rightarrow x_1 = 10,\ x_2 = 6$

21. $\begin{bmatrix} 6 & 5 & | & 1 & 0 \\ 1 & 1 & | & 0 & 1 \end{bmatrix} \rightarrow \begin{bmatrix} 1 & 1 & | & 0 & 1 \\ 6 & 5 & | & 1 & 0 \end{bmatrix} \rightarrow \begin{bmatrix} 1 & 1 & | & 0 & 1 \\ 0 & -1 & | & 1 & -6 \end{bmatrix}$

$\rightarrow \begin{bmatrix} 1 & 1 & | & 0 & 1 \\ 0 & 1 & | & -1 & 6 \end{bmatrix} \rightarrow \begin{bmatrix} 1 & 0 & | & 1 & -5 \\ 0 & 1 & | & -1 & 6 \end{bmatrix}$

$\begin{bmatrix} x \\ y \end{bmatrix} = A^{-1}B = \begin{bmatrix} 1 & -5 \\ -1 & 6 \end{bmatrix} \begin{bmatrix} 2 \\ -3 \end{bmatrix} = \begin{bmatrix} 17 \\ -20 \end{bmatrix} \Rightarrow x = 17, \ y = -20$

23. $\begin{bmatrix} 2 & 1 & | & 1 & 0 \\ 3 & -1 & | & 0 & 1 \end{bmatrix} \rightarrow \begin{bmatrix} 1 & \frac{1}{2} & | & \frac{1}{2} & 0 \\ 3 & -1 & | & 0 & 1 \end{bmatrix} \rightarrow \begin{bmatrix} 1 & \frac{1}{2} & | & \frac{1}{2} & 0 \\ 0 & -\frac{5}{2} & | & -\frac{3}{2} & 1 \end{bmatrix}$

$\rightarrow \begin{bmatrix} 1 & \frac{1}{2} & | & \frac{1}{2} & 0 \\ 0 & 1 & | & \frac{3}{5} & -\frac{2}{5} \end{bmatrix} \rightarrow \begin{bmatrix} 1 & 0 & | & \frac{1}{5} & \frac{1}{5} \\ 0 & 1 & | & \frac{3}{5} & -\frac{2}{5} \end{bmatrix}$

$\begin{bmatrix} x \\ y \end{bmatrix} = A^{-1}B = \begin{bmatrix} \frac{1}{5} & \frac{1}{5} \\ \frac{3}{5} & -\frac{2}{5} \end{bmatrix} \begin{bmatrix} 5 \\ 0 \end{bmatrix} = \begin{bmatrix} 1 \\ 3 \end{bmatrix} \Rightarrow x = 1, \ y = 3$

25. The coefficient matrix is not invertible. The method of reduction yields
$\begin{bmatrix} 2 & 6 & | & 2 \\ 3 & 9 & | & 3 \end{bmatrix} \rightarrow \begin{bmatrix} 1 & 3 & | & 1 \\ 3 & 9 & | & 3 \end{bmatrix} \rightarrow \begin{bmatrix} 1 & 3 & | & 1 \\ 0 & 0 & | & 0 \end{bmatrix}$.
Thus $x = -3r + 1$, $y = r$.

27. $\begin{bmatrix} 1 & 2 & 1 & | & 1 & 0 & 0 \\ 3 & 0 & 1 & | & 0 & 1 & 0 \\ 1 & -1 & 1 & | & 0 & 0 & 1 \end{bmatrix} \rightarrow \begin{bmatrix} 1 & 2 & 1 & | & 1 & 0 & 0 \\ 0 & -6 & -2 & | & -3 & 1 & 0 \\ 0 & -3 & 0 & | & -1 & 0 & 1 \end{bmatrix}$

$\rightarrow \begin{bmatrix} 1 & 2 & 1 & | & 1 & 0 & 0 \\ 0 & 1 & \frac{1}{3} & | & \frac{1}{2} & -\frac{1}{6} & 0 \\ 0 & -3 & 0 & | & -1 & 0 & 1 \end{bmatrix} \rightarrow \begin{bmatrix} 1 & 0 & \frac{1}{3} & | & 0 & \frac{1}{3} & 0 \\ 0 & 1 & \frac{1}{3} & | & \frac{1}{2} & -\frac{1}{6} & 0 \\ 0 & 0 & 1 & | & \frac{1}{2} & -\frac{1}{2} & 1 \end{bmatrix}$

$\rightarrow \begin{bmatrix} 1 & 0 & 0 & | & -\frac{1}{6} & \frac{1}{2} & -\frac{1}{3} \\ 0 & 1 & 0 & | & \frac{1}{3} & 0 & -\frac{1}{3} \\ 0 & 0 & 1 & | & \frac{1}{2} & -\frac{1}{2} & 1 \end{bmatrix}$

$\begin{bmatrix} x \\ y \\ z \end{bmatrix} = A^{-1}B = \begin{bmatrix} -\frac{1}{6} & \frac{1}{2} & -\frac{1}{3} \\ \frac{1}{3} & 0 & -\frac{1}{3} \\ \frac{1}{2} & -\frac{1}{2} & 1 \end{bmatrix} \begin{bmatrix} 4 \\ 2 \\ 1 \end{bmatrix} = \begin{bmatrix} 0 \\ 1 \\ 2 \end{bmatrix}$

Thus, $x = 0$, $y = 1$, $z = 2$.

29. $\begin{bmatrix} 1 & 1 & 1 & | & 1 & 0 & 0 \\ 1 & -1 & 1 & | & 0 & 1 & 0 \\ 1 & -1 & -1 & | & 0 & 0 & 1 \end{bmatrix} \rightarrow \begin{bmatrix} 1 & 1 & 1 & | & 1 & 0 & 0 \\ 0 & -2 & 0 & | & -1 & 1 & 0 \\ 0 & -2 & -2 & | & -1 & 0 & 1 \end{bmatrix}$

$\rightarrow \begin{bmatrix} 1 & 1 & 1 & | & 1 & 0 & 0 \\ 0 & 1 & 0 & | & \frac{1}{2} & -\frac{1}{2} & 0 \\ 0 & -2 & -2 & | & -1 & 0 & 1 \end{bmatrix} \rightarrow \begin{bmatrix} 1 & 0 & 1 & | & \frac{1}{2} & \frac{1}{2} & 0 \\ 0 & 1 & 0 & | & \frac{1}{2} & -\frac{1}{2} & 0 \\ 0 & 0 & -2 & | & 0 & -1 & 1 \end{bmatrix}$

$\rightarrow \begin{bmatrix} 1 & 0 & 1 & | & \frac{1}{2} & \frac{1}{2} & 0 \\ 0 & 1 & 0 & | & \frac{1}{2} & -\frac{1}{2} & 0 \\ 0 & 0 & 1 & | & 0 & \frac{1}{2} & -\frac{1}{2} \end{bmatrix} \rightarrow \begin{bmatrix} 1 & 0 & 0 & | & \frac{1}{2} & 0 & \frac{1}{2} \\ 0 & 1 & 0 & | & \frac{1}{2} & -\frac{1}{2} & 0 \\ 0 & 0 & 1 & | & 0 & \frac{1}{2} & -\frac{1}{2} \end{bmatrix}$

$\begin{bmatrix} x \\ y \\ z \end{bmatrix} = \mathbf{A}^{-1}\mathbf{B} = \begin{bmatrix} \frac{1}{2} & 0 & \frac{1}{2} \\ \frac{1}{2} & -\frac{1}{2} & 0 \\ 0 & \frac{1}{2} & -\frac{1}{2} \end{bmatrix}\begin{bmatrix} 2 \\ 1 \\ 0 \end{bmatrix} = \begin{bmatrix} 1 \\ \frac{1}{2} \\ \frac{1}{2} \end{bmatrix}$

Thus, $x = 1$, $y = \frac{1}{2}$, $z = \frac{1}{2}$.

31. The coefficient matrix is not invertible. The method of reduction yields

$\begin{bmatrix} 1 & 3 & 3 & | & 7 \\ 2 & 1 & 1 & | & 4 \\ 1 & 1 & 1 & | & 4 \end{bmatrix} \rightarrow \begin{bmatrix} 1 & 3 & 3 & | & 7 \\ 0 & -5 & -5 & | & -10 \\ 0 & -2 & -2 & | & -3 \end{bmatrix} \rightarrow \begin{bmatrix} 1 & 3 & 3 & | & 7 \\ 0 & 1 & 1 & | & 2 \\ 0 & -2 & -2 & | & -3 \end{bmatrix} \rightarrow \begin{bmatrix} 1 & 0 & 0 & | & 1 \\ 0 & 1 & 1 & | & 2 \\ 0 & 0 & 0 & | & 1 \end{bmatrix}.$

The third row indicates that $0 = 1$, which is never true, so there is no solution.

33. $\begin{bmatrix} 1 & 0 & 2 & 1 & | & 1 & 0 & 0 & 0 \\ 1 & -1 & 0 & 2 & | & 0 & 1 & 0 & 0 \\ 2 & 1 & 0 & 1 & | & 0 & 0 & 1 & 0 \\ 1 & 2 & 1 & 1 & | & 0 & 0 & 0 & 1 \end{bmatrix} \rightarrow \begin{bmatrix} 1 & 0 & 2 & 1 & | & 1 & 0 & 0 & 0 \\ 0 & -1 & -2 & 1 & | & -1 & 1 & 0 & 0 \\ 0 & 1 & -4 & -1 & | & -2 & 0 & 1 & 0 \\ 0 & 2 & -1 & 0 & | & -1 & 0 & 0 & 1 \end{bmatrix}$

$\rightarrow \begin{bmatrix} 1 & 0 & 2 & 1 & | & 1 & 0 & 0 & 0 \\ 0 & 1 & 2 & -1 & | & 1 & -1 & 0 & 0 \\ 0 & 0 & -6 & 0 & | & -3 & 1 & 1 & 0 \\ 0 & 0 & -5 & 2 & | & -3 & 2 & 0 & 1 \end{bmatrix} \rightarrow \begin{bmatrix} 1 & 0 & 2 & 1 & | & 1 & 0 & 0 & 0 \\ 0 & 1 & 2 & -1 & | & 1 & -1 & 0 & 0 \\ 0 & 0 & 1 & 0 & | & \frac{1}{2} & -\frac{1}{6} & -\frac{1}{6} & 0 \\ 0 & 0 & -5 & 2 & | & -3 & 2 & 0 & 1 \end{bmatrix}$

$\rightarrow \begin{bmatrix} 1 & 0 & 0 & 1 & | & 0 & \frac{1}{3} & \frac{1}{3} & 0 \\ 0 & 1 & 0 & -1 & | & 0 & -\frac{2}{3} & \frac{1}{3} & 0 \\ 0 & 0 & 1 & 0 & | & \frac{1}{2} & -\frac{1}{6} & -\frac{1}{6} & 0 \\ 0 & 0 & 0 & 2 & | & -\frac{1}{2} & \frac{7}{6} & -\frac{5}{6} & 1 \end{bmatrix} \rightarrow \begin{bmatrix} 1 & 0 & 0 & 1 & | & 0 & \frac{1}{3} & \frac{1}{3} & 0 \\ 0 & 1 & 0 & -1 & | & 0 & -\frac{2}{3} & \frac{1}{3} & 0 \\ 0 & 0 & 1 & 0 & | & \frac{1}{2} & -\frac{1}{6} & -\frac{1}{6} & 0 \\ 0 & 0 & 0 & 1 & | & -\frac{1}{4} & \frac{7}{12} & -\frac{5}{12} & \frac{1}{2} \end{bmatrix}$

$\rightarrow \begin{bmatrix} 1 & 0 & 0 & 0 & | & \frac{1}{4} & -\frac{1}{4} & \frac{3}{4} & -\frac{1}{2} \\ 0 & 1 & 0 & 0 & | & -\frac{1}{4} & -\frac{1}{12} & -\frac{1}{12} & \frac{1}{2} \\ 0 & 0 & 1 & 0 & | & \frac{1}{2} & -\frac{1}{6} & -\frac{1}{6} & 0 \\ 0 & 0 & 0 & 1 & | & -\frac{1}{4} & \frac{7}{12} & -\frac{5}{12} & \frac{1}{2} \end{bmatrix}$

$$\begin{bmatrix} w \\ x \\ y \\ z \end{bmatrix} = \mathbf{A}^{-1}\mathbf{B} = \begin{bmatrix} \frac{1}{4} & -\frac{1}{4} & \frac{3}{4} & -\frac{1}{2} \\ -\frac{1}{4} & -\frac{1}{12} & -\frac{1}{12} & \frac{1}{2} \\ \frac{1}{2} & -\frac{1}{6} & -\frac{1}{6} & 0 \\ -\frac{1}{4} & \frac{7}{12} & -\frac{5}{12} & \frac{1}{2} \end{bmatrix}\begin{bmatrix} 4 \\ 12 \\ 12 \\ 12 \end{bmatrix} = \begin{bmatrix} 1 \\ 3 \\ -2 \\ 7 \end{bmatrix}$$

Thus, $w = 1, x = 3, y = -2, z = 7$.

35. $\mathbf{I} - \mathbf{A} = \begin{bmatrix} 1 & 0 \\ 0 & 1 \end{bmatrix} - \begin{bmatrix} 2 & -1 \\ 1 & 3 \end{bmatrix} = \begin{bmatrix} -1 & 1 \\ -1 & -2 \end{bmatrix}$

$$\begin{bmatrix} -1 & 1 & | & 1 & 0 \\ -1 & -2 & | & 0 & 1 \end{bmatrix} \rightarrow \begin{bmatrix} 1 & -1 & | & -1 & 0 \\ -1 & -2 & | & 0 & 1 \end{bmatrix} \rightarrow \begin{bmatrix} 1 & -1 & | & -1 & 0 \\ 0 & -3 & | & -1 & 1 \end{bmatrix}$$

$$\rightarrow \begin{bmatrix} 1 & -1 & | & -1 & 0 \\ 0 & 1 & | & \frac{1}{3} & -\frac{1}{3} \end{bmatrix} \rightarrow \begin{bmatrix} 1 & 0 & | & -\frac{2}{3} & -\frac{1}{3} \\ 0 & 1 & | & \frac{1}{3} & -\frac{1}{3} \end{bmatrix}$$

Thus $(\mathbf{I} - \mathbf{A})^{-1} = \begin{bmatrix} -\frac{2}{3} & -\frac{1}{3} \\ \frac{1}{3} & -\frac{1}{3} \end{bmatrix}$.

37. Let x = number of model A and y = number of model B.

a. The system is
$$\begin{cases} x + y = 100 & \text{(painting)} \\ \frac{1}{2}x + y = 80 & \text{(polishing)} \end{cases}$$

Let $\mathbf{A} = \begin{bmatrix} 1 & 1 \\ \frac{1}{2} & 1 \end{bmatrix}$

$$\begin{bmatrix} 1 & 1 & | & 1 & 0 \\ \frac{1}{2} & 1 & | & 0 & 1 \end{bmatrix} \rightarrow \begin{bmatrix} 1 & 1 & | & 1 & 0 \\ 0 & \frac{1}{2} & | & -\frac{1}{2} & 1 \end{bmatrix} \rightarrow \begin{bmatrix} 1 & 1 & | & 1 & 0 \\ 0 & 1 & | & -1 & 2 \end{bmatrix} \rightarrow \begin{bmatrix} 1 & 0 & | & 2 & -2 \\ 0 & 1 & | & -1 & 2 \end{bmatrix}$$

$$\begin{bmatrix} x \\ y \end{bmatrix} = \mathbf{A}^{-1}\begin{bmatrix} 100 \\ 80 \end{bmatrix} = \begin{bmatrix} 2 & -2 \\ -1 & 2 \end{bmatrix}\begin{bmatrix} 100 \\ 80 \end{bmatrix} = \begin{bmatrix} 40 \\ 60 \end{bmatrix}$$

Thus 40 of model A and 60 of model B can be produced.

b. The system is
$$\begin{cases} 10x + 7y = 800 & \text{(widgets)} \\ 14x + 10y = 1130 & \text{(shims)} \end{cases}$$

Let $\mathbf{A} = \begin{bmatrix} 10 & 7 \\ 14 & 10 \end{bmatrix}$.

$$\begin{bmatrix} 10 & 7 & | & 1 & 0 \\ 14 & 10 & | & 0 & 1 \end{bmatrix} \rightarrow \begin{bmatrix} 1 & \frac{7}{10} & | & \frac{1}{10} & 0 \\ 14 & 10 & | & 0 & 1 \end{bmatrix}$$

$$\rightarrow \begin{bmatrix} 1 & \frac{7}{10} & | & \frac{1}{10} & 0 \\ 0 & \frac{1}{5} & | & -\frac{7}{5} & 1 \end{bmatrix} \rightarrow \begin{bmatrix} 1 & \frac{7}{10} & | & \frac{1}{10} & 0 \\ 0 & 1 & | & -7 & 5 \end{bmatrix} \rightarrow \begin{bmatrix} 1 & 0 & | & 5 & -\frac{7}{2} \\ 0 & 1 & | & -7 & 5 \end{bmatrix}$$

$$\begin{bmatrix} x \\ y \end{bmatrix} = \mathbf{A}^{-1} \begin{bmatrix} 800 \\ 1130 \end{bmatrix} = \begin{bmatrix} 5 & -\frac{7}{2} \\ -7 & 5 \end{bmatrix} \begin{bmatrix} 800 \\ 1130 \end{bmatrix} = \begin{bmatrix} 45 \\ 50 \end{bmatrix}$$

Thus 45 of model A and 50 of model B can be produced.

39. a. $\left(\mathbf{B}^{-1} \mathbf{A}^{-1} \right)(\mathbf{AB}) = \mathbf{B}^{-1} \left(\mathbf{A}^{-1} \mathbf{A} \right) \mathbf{B} = \mathbf{B}^{-1} \mathbf{IB} = \mathbf{B}^{-1} \mathbf{B} = \mathbf{I}$

Since an invertible matrix has exactly one inverse, $\mathbf{B}^{-1} \mathbf{A}^{-1}$ is the inverse of $\mathbf{AB}$.

b. From Part (a),

$$(\mathbf{AB})^{-1} = \mathbf{B}^{-1} \mathbf{A}^{-1} = \begin{bmatrix} 1 & 1 \\ 1 & 2 \end{bmatrix} \begin{bmatrix} 1 & 2 \\ 3 & 4 \end{bmatrix} = \begin{bmatrix} 4 & 6 \\ 7 & 10 \end{bmatrix}$$

41. $\mathbf{P}^{\mathrm{T}} \mathbf{P} = \begin{bmatrix} \frac{3}{5} & \frac{4}{5} \\ -\frac{4}{5} & \frac{3}{5} \end{bmatrix} \begin{bmatrix} \frac{3}{5} & -\frac{4}{5} \\ \frac{4}{5} & \frac{3}{5} \end{bmatrix} = \begin{bmatrix} 1 & 0 \\ 0 & 1 \end{bmatrix} = \mathbf{I}$, so $\mathbf{P}^{\mathrm{T}} = \mathbf{P}^{-1}$. Yes, $\mathbf{P}$ is orthogonal.

43. Let x be the number of shares of D, y be the number of shares of E, and z be the number of shares of F. We get the following conditions.

$60x + 80y + 30z = 500{,}000$

$0.16(60x) + 0.12(80y) + 0.09(30z) = 0.1368(60x + 80y + 30z)$

$z = 4y$

Simplify the first equation.

$6x + 8y + 3z = 50{,}000$

Simplify the second equation.

$9.6x + 9.6y + 2.7z = 8.208x + 10.944y + 4.104z$

$1.392x - 1.344y - 1.404z = 0$

$1392x - 1344y - 1404z = 0$

$116x - 112y - 117z = 0$

Simplify the third equation.

$4y - z = 0$

Thus we solve the following system of equations.

$6x + 8y + 3z = 50{,}000$

$116x - 112y - 117z = 0$

$4y - z = 0$

The coefficient matrix is $\mathbf{A} = \begin{bmatrix} 6 & 8 & 3 \\ 116 & -112 & -117 \\ 0 & 4 & -1 \end{bmatrix}$.

$$[\mathbf{A} \,|\, \mathbf{I}] = \begin{bmatrix} 6 & 8 & 3 & | & 1 & 0 & 0 \\ 116 & -112 & -117 & | & 0 & 1 & 0 \\ 0 & 4 & -1 & | & 0 & 0 & 1 \end{bmatrix}$$

$$\xrightarrow{\frac{1}{6} R_1} \begin{bmatrix} 1 & \frac{4}{3} & \frac{1}{2} & | & \frac{1}{6} & 0 & 0 \\ 116 & -112 & -117 & | & 0 & 1 & 0 \\ 0 & 4 & -1 & | & 0 & 0 & 1 \end{bmatrix}$$

$$\xrightarrow{-116R_1 + R_2} \begin{bmatrix} 1 & \frac{4}{3} & \frac{1}{2} & \frac{1}{6} & 0 & 0 \\ 0 & -\frac{800}{3} & -175 & -\frac{58}{3} & 1 & 0 \\ 0 & 4 & -1 & 0 & 0 & 1 \end{bmatrix}$$

$$\xrightarrow[-\frac{1}{4}R_3]{-\frac{3}{800}R_2} \begin{bmatrix} 1 & \frac{4}{3} & \frac{1}{2} & \frac{1}{6} & 0 & 0 \\ 0 & 1 & \frac{21}{32} & \frac{29}{400} & -\frac{3}{800} & 0 \\ 0 & -1 & \frac{1}{4} & 0 & 0 & -\frac{1}{4} \end{bmatrix}$$

$$\xrightarrow{R_2 + R_3} \begin{bmatrix} 1 & \frac{4}{3} & \frac{1}{2} & \frac{1}{6} & 0 & 0 \\ 0 & 1 & \frac{21}{32} & \frac{29}{400} & -\frac{3}{800} & 0 \\ 0 & 0 & \frac{29}{32} & \frac{29}{400} & -\frac{3}{800} & -\frac{1}{4} \end{bmatrix}$$

$$\xrightarrow{\frac{32}{29}R_3} \begin{bmatrix} 1 & \frac{4}{3} & \frac{1}{2} & \frac{1}{6} & 0 & 0 \\ 0 & 1 & \frac{21}{32} & \frac{29}{400} & -\frac{3}{800} & 0 \\ 0 & 0 & 1 & \frac{2}{25} & -\frac{3}{725} & -\frac{8}{29} \end{bmatrix}$$

$$\xrightarrow[-\frac{21}{32}R_3 + R_2]{-\frac{1}{2}R_3 + R_1} \begin{bmatrix} 1 & \frac{4}{3} & 0 & \frac{19}{150} & \frac{3}{1450} & \frac{4}{29} \\ 0 & 1 & 0 & \frac{1}{50} & -\frac{3}{2900} & \frac{21}{116} \\ 0 & 0 & 1 & \frac{2}{25} & -\frac{3}{725} & -\frac{8}{29} \end{bmatrix}$$

$$\xrightarrow{-\frac{4}{3}R_2 + R_1} \begin{bmatrix} 1 & 0 & 0 & \frac{1}{10} & \frac{1}{290} & -\frac{3}{29} \\ 0 & 1 & 0 & \frac{1}{50} & -\frac{3}{2900} & \frac{21}{116} \\ 0 & 0 & 1 & \frac{2}{25} & -\frac{3}{725} & -\frac{8}{29} \end{bmatrix}$$

$$\begin{bmatrix} x \\ y \\ z \end{bmatrix} = \begin{bmatrix} \frac{1}{10} & \frac{1}{290} & -\frac{3}{29} \\ \frac{1}{50} & -\frac{3}{2900} & \frac{21}{116} \\ \frac{2}{25} & -\frac{3}{725} & -\frac{8}{29} \end{bmatrix} \begin{bmatrix} 50,000 \\ 0 \\ 0 \end{bmatrix} = \begin{bmatrix} 5000 \\ 1000 \\ 4000 \end{bmatrix}$$

They should buy 5000 shares of company D, 1000 shares of company E, and 4000 shares of company F.

45. a. $\begin{bmatrix} 1.46 & 0.56 \\ 0.51 & 1.35 \end{bmatrix}$

b. $\begin{bmatrix} \frac{130}{89} & \frac{50}{89} \\ \frac{45}{89} & \frac{120}{89} \end{bmatrix}$

47. $\begin{bmatrix} 1.80 & 1.10 & -0.46 \\ 0.35 & 1.31 & -0.17 \\ 0.44 & 0.42 & 0.59 \end{bmatrix}$

49. $\begin{bmatrix} w \\ x \\ y \\ z \end{bmatrix} = \begin{bmatrix} \frac{2}{5} & 4 & \frac{1}{2} & -\frac{3}{7} \\ \frac{5}{9} & -\frac{2}{3} & -4 & -1 \\ 0 & 1 & -\frac{4}{9} & \frac{5}{6} \\ \frac{1}{2} & 0 & 4 & -\frac{1}{3} \end{bmatrix}^{-1} \begin{bmatrix} \frac{14}{13} \\ \frac{7}{8} \\ 9 \\ \frac{4}{7} \end{bmatrix}$

$$= \begin{bmatrix} 14.44 \\ 0.03 \\ -0.80 \\ 10.33 \end{bmatrix}$$

$w = 14.44$, $x = 0.03$, $y = -0.80$, $z = 10.33$

Principles in Practice 6.7

1. Expand along the first row.

$$\begin{vmatrix} 1 & 1 & 2 \\ 3 & 4 & 10 \\ 4 & 2 & 6 \end{vmatrix}$$

$$= (1)(-1)^2 \begin{vmatrix} 4 & 10 \\ 2 & 6 \end{vmatrix} - (1)(-1)^3 \begin{vmatrix} 3 & 10 \\ 4 & 6 \end{vmatrix} + (2)(-1)^4 \begin{vmatrix} 3 & 4 \\ 4 & 2 \end{vmatrix} = (1)(4) + (-1)(-22) + 2(-10) = 6$$

Exercise 6.7

1. $2(2) - 1(3) = 4 - 3 = 1$

3. $(-2)(-6) - (-3)(-4) = 12 - 12 = 0$

5. $1(y) - x(0) = y$

7. $\dfrac{1(4) - 2(3)}{2(6) - 1(5)} = \dfrac{-2}{7} = -\dfrac{2}{7}$

9. $2(k) - 3(4) = 12,\ 2k - 12 = 12,\ 2k = 24,\ k = 12$

11. $\begin{vmatrix} 1 & 3 \\ 7 & 9 \end{vmatrix} = 1(9) - 3(7) = -12$

13. $(-1)^{3+2} \begin{vmatrix} 1 & 3 \\ 4 & 6 \end{vmatrix} = -[1(6) - 3(4)] = -[-6] = 6$

15. $\begin{vmatrix} a_{11} & a_{13} & a_{14} \\ a_{21} & a_{23} & a_{24} \\ a_{41} & a_{43} & a_{44} \end{vmatrix}$

17. $(-1)^{1+3} \begin{vmatrix} a_{21} & a_{22} & a_{24} \\ a_{31} & a_{32} & a_{34} \\ a_{41} & a_{42} & a_{44} \end{vmatrix} = (-1)^4 \cdot \begin{vmatrix} a_{21} & a_{22} & a_{24} \\ a_{31} & a_{32} & a_{34} \\ a_{41} & a_{42} & a_{44} \end{vmatrix}$

$$= \begin{vmatrix} a_{21} & a_{22} & a_{24} \\ a_{31} & a_{32} & a_{34} \\ a_{41} & a_{42} & a_{44} \end{vmatrix}$$

19. Expanding along column 2 gives

$$1(-1)^3 \begin{vmatrix} 2 & 1 \\ -4 & 6 \end{vmatrix} + 0 + 0 = 1(-1)[12 - (-4)] = -16$$

21. Expanding along row 1 gives

$$1(-1)^2 \begin{vmatrix} 5 & 4 \\ -2 & 1 \end{vmatrix} + 2(-1)^3 \begin{vmatrix} 4 & 4 \\ 3 & 1 \end{vmatrix} - 3(-1)^4 \begin{vmatrix} 4 & 5 \\ 3 & -2 \end{vmatrix}$$
$$= 1(1)[5 - (-8)] + 2(-1)[4 - 12] - 3(1)[-8 - 15]$$
$$= 13 + 16 + 69 = 98$$

23. Expanding along row 3 gives

$$0 + 6(-1)^5 \begin{vmatrix} 2 & 5 \\ -3 & -1 \end{vmatrix} - 1(-1)^6 \begin{vmatrix} 2 & 1 \\ -3 & 4 \end{vmatrix}$$
$$= 6(-1)[-2 - (-15)] - 1(1)[8 - (-3)]$$
$$= -78 - 11 = -89.$$

25. Expanding along row 1 gives

$$2(-1)^2 \begin{vmatrix} 1 & -1 \\ 2 & -3 \end{vmatrix} - 1(-1)^3 \begin{vmatrix} 1 & -1 \\ 1 & -3 \end{vmatrix} + 3(-1)^4 \begin{vmatrix} 1 & 1 \\ 1 & 2 \end{vmatrix}$$
$$= 2(1)[-3 - (-2)] - 1(-1)[-3 - (-1)] + 3(1)[2 - 1]$$
$$= -2 - 2 + 3 = -1.$$

27. Expanding along row 1 gives

$$\frac{1}{2}(-1)^2 \begin{vmatrix} \frac{1}{3} & \frac{2}{3} \\ -4 & 1 \end{vmatrix} + \frac{2}{3}(-1)^3 \begin{vmatrix} -1 & \frac{2}{3} \\ 3 & 1 \end{vmatrix} - \frac{1}{2}(-1)^4 \begin{vmatrix} -1 & \frac{1}{3} \\ 3 & -4 \end{vmatrix}$$
$$= \frac{1}{2}(1)\left[\frac{1}{3} - \left(-\frac{8}{3}\right)\right] + \frac{2}{3}(-1)[-1 - 2] - \frac{1}{2}(1)[4 - 1]$$
$$= \frac{3}{2} + 2 - \frac{3}{2} = 2$$

29. Expanding along column 3 gives

$$3(-1)^4 \begin{vmatrix} 4 & -1 & 1 \\ 2 & 1 & 3 \\ -1 & 2 & -1 \end{vmatrix} + 0 + 0 + 3(-1)^7 \begin{vmatrix} 1 & 0 & 2 \\ 4 & -1 & 1 \\ 2 & 1 & 3 \end{vmatrix}$$
$$= 3\left\{4(-1)^2 \begin{vmatrix} 1 & 3 \\ 2 & -1 \end{vmatrix} - 1(-1)^3 \begin{vmatrix} 2 & 3 \\ -1 & -1 \end{vmatrix} + 1(-1)^4 \begin{vmatrix} 2 & 1 \\ -1 & 2 \end{vmatrix}\right\} - 3\left\{1(-1)^2 \begin{vmatrix} -1 & 1 \\ 1 & 3 \end{vmatrix} + 0 + 2(-1)^4 \begin{vmatrix} 4 & -1 \\ 2 & 1 \end{vmatrix}\right\}$$
$$= 3\{4(1)[-1 - 6] - 1(-1)[-2 - (-3)] + 1(1)[4 - (-1)]\} - 3\{1(1)[-3 - 1] + 2(1)[4 - (-2)]\}$$
$$= 3\{-28 + 1 + 5\} - 3\{-4 + 12\} = -66 - 24 = -90.$$

31. Since all entries below the main diagonal are zeros, the determinant is $(1)(1)(1)(1) = 1$.

33. Since all entries below (as well as above) main diagonal are zeros, the determinant is $(1)(-2)(4)(-3) = 24$.

35. $$\begin{vmatrix} 1 & -1 & 2 & -1 \\ 2 & 3 & -1 & 2 \\ 1 & 4 & -3 & 3 \\ 4 & 1 & 3 & 0 \end{vmatrix} \xrightarrow{R_3 + R_1} \begin{vmatrix} 2 & 3 & -1 & 2 \\ 2 & 3 & -1 & 2 \\ 1 & 4 & -3 & 3 \\ 4 & 1 & 3 & 0 \end{vmatrix} = 0, \text{ since row 1 and row two are identical}$$

37. Multiplying column 2 by 2 and adding the result to column 5 gives all zeros in column 5. Thus the determinant is 0.

39. $\begin{vmatrix} x & -2 \\ 7 & 7-x \end{vmatrix} = 26$

$x(7-x) - (-2)(7) = 26$

$7x - x^2 + 14 = 26$

$x^2 - 7x + 12 = 0$

$(x-3)(x-4) = 0$ so $x = 3$ or $x = 4$

41. Multiplying each entry of $\mathbf{A}$ by 2 gives $2\mathbf{A}$. Since A has order 4, property 7 gives

$|2\mathbf{A}| = 2^4|\mathbf{A}| = 16(12) = 192$.

43. a. Since $\mathbf{A}^{-1}\mathbf{A} = \mathbf{I}$, we have

$\left|\mathbf{A}^{-1}\mathbf{A}\right| = |\mathbf{I}|$ so $\left|\mathbf{A}^{-1}\right||\mathbf{A}| = 1$.

Thus $\left|\mathbf{A}^{-1}\right| = \dfrac{1}{|\mathbf{A}|}$.

b. From part (a), if $|\mathbf{A}| = 3$, then

$\left|\mathbf{A}^{-1}\right| = \dfrac{1}{|\mathbf{A}|} = \dfrac{1}{3}$.

45. The given system is equivalent to the system

$\begin{cases} x + 3y + 2z = 0 \\ x + cy + 4z = 0 \\ 2y + cz = 0 \end{cases}$

For the system to have infinitely many solutions, the coefficient matrix must not be invertible; that is, its determinant must be zero.

$\begin{vmatrix} 1 & 3 & 2 \\ 1 & c & 4 \\ 0 & 2 & c \end{vmatrix} = 0$

$\left(c^2 + 4 + 0\right) - (0 + 8 + 3c) = 0$

$c^2 - 3c - 4 = 0$

$(c+1)(c-4) = 0$

$c = -1$ or $c = 4$

47. -1630

49. -3864

Exercise 6.8

1. $\Delta = \begin{vmatrix} 2 & -1 \\ 3 & 1 \end{vmatrix} = 5$

$\Delta_x = \begin{vmatrix} 4 & -1 \\ 5 & 1 \end{vmatrix} = 9$

$\Delta_y = \begin{vmatrix} 2 & 4 \\ 3 & 5 \end{vmatrix} = -2$

$x = \dfrac{\Delta_x}{\Delta} = \dfrac{9}{5}$

$y = \dfrac{\Delta_y}{\Delta} = -\dfrac{2}{5}$

3. $\begin{cases} -2x = 4 - 3y \\ y = 6x - 1 \end{cases}$ is equivalent to

$\begin{cases} -2x + 3y = 4 \\ -6x + y = -1 \end{cases}$

$\Delta = \begin{vmatrix} -2 & 3 \\ -6 & 1 \end{vmatrix} = 16$

$\Delta_x = \begin{vmatrix} 4 & 3 \\ -1 & 1 \end{vmatrix} = 7$

$\Delta_y = \begin{vmatrix} -2 & 4 \\ -6 & -1 \end{vmatrix} = 26$

$x = \dfrac{\Delta_x}{\Delta} = \dfrac{7}{16}$

$y = \dfrac{\Delta_y}{\Delta} = \dfrac{26}{16} = \dfrac{13}{8}$

5. $\begin{cases} 3(x+2) = 5 \\ 6(x+y) = -8 \end{cases}$ is equivalent to

$\begin{cases} 3x = -1 \\ 6x + 6y = -8 \end{cases}$

$\Delta = \begin{vmatrix} 3 & 0 \\ 6 & 6 \end{vmatrix} = 18$

$\Delta_x = \begin{vmatrix} -1 & 0 \\ -8 & 6 \end{vmatrix} = -6$

$\Delta_y = \begin{vmatrix} 3 & -1 \\ 6 & -8 \end{vmatrix} = -18$

$$x = \frac{\Delta_x}{\Delta} = -\frac{6}{18} = -\frac{1}{3}$$

$$y = \frac{\Delta_y}{\Delta} = -\frac{18}{18} = -1$$

7. $\Delta = \begin{vmatrix} \frac{3}{2} & -\frac{1}{4} \\ \frac{1}{3} & \frac{1}{2} \end{vmatrix} = \frac{5}{6}$

$\Delta_x = \begin{vmatrix} 1 & -\frac{1}{4} \\ 2 & \frac{1}{2} \end{vmatrix} = 1$

$\Delta_z = \begin{vmatrix} \frac{3}{2} & 1 \\ \frac{1}{3} & 2 \end{vmatrix} = \frac{8}{3}$

$x = \frac{\Delta_x}{\Delta} = \frac{1}{\frac{5}{6}} = \frac{6}{5}$

$z = \frac{\Delta_z}{\Delta} = \frac{\frac{8}{3}}{\frac{5}{6}} = \frac{16}{5}$

9. $\Delta = \begin{vmatrix} 1 & 1 & 1 \\ 1 & -1 & 1 \\ 2 & -1 & 3 \end{vmatrix} = -2$

$\Delta_x = \begin{vmatrix} 6 & 1 & 1 \\ 2 & -1 & 1 \\ 6 & -1 & 3 \end{vmatrix} = -8$

$\Delta_y = \begin{vmatrix} 1 & 6 & 1 \\ 1 & 2 & 1 \\ 2 & 6 & 3 \end{vmatrix} = -4$

$\Delta_z = \begin{vmatrix} 1 & 1 & 6 \\ 1 & -1 & 2 \\ 2 & -1 & 6 \end{vmatrix} = 0$

$$x = \frac{\Delta_x}{\Delta} = \frac{-8}{-2} = 4$$

$$y = \frac{\Delta_y}{\Delta} = \frac{-4}{-2} = 2$$

$$z = \frac{\Delta_z}{\Delta} = \frac{0}{-2} = 0$$

11. $\Delta = \begin{vmatrix} 2 & -3 & 4 \\ 1 & 1 & -3 \\ 3 & 2 & -1 \end{vmatrix} = 30$

$\Delta_x = \begin{vmatrix} 0 & -3 & 4 \\ 4 & 1 & -3 \\ 0 & 2 & -1 \end{vmatrix} = 20$

$\Delta_y = \begin{vmatrix} 2 & 0 & 4 \\ 1 & 4 & -3 \\ 3 & 0 & -1 \end{vmatrix} = -56$

$\Delta_z = \begin{vmatrix} 2 & -3 & 0 \\ 1 & 1 & 4 \\ 3 & 2 & 0 \end{vmatrix} = -52$

$x = \frac{\Delta_x}{\Delta} = \frac{20}{30} = \frac{2}{3}$

$y = \frac{\Delta_y}{\Delta} = \frac{-56}{30} = -\frac{28}{15}$

$z = \frac{\Delta_z}{\Delta} = \frac{-52}{30} = -\frac{26}{15}$

13. $\Delta = \begin{vmatrix} 1 & -2 & 1 \\ 2 & 1 & 2 \\ 1 & 8 & 1 \end{vmatrix} = 0$, so Cramer's rule does not apply. We solve the system by matrix reduction.

$$\begin{bmatrix} 1 & -2 & 1 & | & 3 \\ 2 & 1 & 2 & | & 6 \\ 1 & 8 & 1 & | & 3 \end{bmatrix} \rightarrow \begin{bmatrix} 1 & -2 & 1 & | & 3 \\ 0 & 5 & 0 & | & 0 \\ 0 & 10 & 0 & | & 0 \end{bmatrix} \rightarrow \begin{bmatrix} 1 & -2 & 1 & | & 3 \\ 0 & 1 & 0 & | & 0 \\ 0 & 0 & 0 & | & 0 \end{bmatrix} \rightarrow \begin{bmatrix} 1 & 0 & 1 & | & 3 \\ 0 & 1 & 0 & | & 0 \\ 0 & 0 & 0 & | & 0 \end{bmatrix}$$

Thus $x = 3 - r$, $y = 0$, $z = r$.

15. $\Delta = \begin{vmatrix} 2 & -3 & 1 \\ 1 & -6 & 3 \\ 3 & 3 & -2 \end{vmatrix} = -6$

$\Delta_x = \begin{vmatrix} -2 & -3 & 1 \\ -2 & -6 & 3 \\ 2 & 3 & -2 \end{vmatrix} = -6$

$\Delta_y = \begin{vmatrix} 2 & -2 & 1 \\ 1 & -2 & 3 \\ 3 & 2 & -2 \end{vmatrix} = -18$

$\Delta_z = \begin{vmatrix} 2 & -3 & -2 \\ 1 & -6 & -2 \\ 3 & 3 & 2 \end{vmatrix} = -30$

$x = \dfrac{\Delta_x}{\Delta} = \dfrac{-6}{-6} = 1$

$y = \dfrac{\Delta_y}{\Delta} = \dfrac{-18}{-6} = 3$

$z = \dfrac{\Delta_z}{\Delta} = \dfrac{-30}{-6} = 5$

17. $\Delta = \begin{vmatrix} 1 & -1 & 3 & 1 \\ 1 & 2 & 0 & -3 \\ 2 & 3 & 6 & 1 \\ 1 & 1 & 1 & 1 \end{vmatrix}$

$= 1(-1)^3 \begin{vmatrix} -1 & 3 & 1 \\ 3 & 6 & 1 \\ 1 & 1 & 1 \end{vmatrix} + 2(-1)^4 \begin{vmatrix} 1 & 3 & 1 \\ 2 & 6 & 1 \\ 1 & 1 & 1 \end{vmatrix} + 0 - 3(-1)^6 \begin{vmatrix} 1 & -1 & 3 \\ 2 & 3 & 6 \\ 1 & 1 & 1 \end{vmatrix}$

$= 1(-1)(-14) + 2(1)(-2) - 3(1)(-10) = 14 - 4 + 30 = 40$

$\Delta_y = \begin{vmatrix} 1 & -14 & 3 & 1 \\ 1 & 12 & 0 & -3 \\ 2 & 1 & 6 & 1 \\ 1 & 6 & 1 & 1 \end{vmatrix}$

$= 3(-1)^4 \begin{vmatrix} 1 & 12 & -3 \\ 2 & 1 & 1 \\ 1 & 6 & 1 \end{vmatrix} + 0 + 6(-1)^6 \begin{vmatrix} 1 & -14 & 1 \\ 1 & 12 & -3 \\ 1 & 6 & 1 \end{vmatrix} + 1(-1)^7 \begin{vmatrix} 1 & -14 & 1 \\ 1 & 12 & -3 \\ 2 & 1 & 1 \end{vmatrix}$

$= 3(1)(-50) + 6(1)(80) + 1(-1)(90) = -150 + 480 - 90 = 240$

$$\Delta_w = \begin{vmatrix} 1 & -1 & 3 & -14 \\ 1 & 2 & 0 & 12 \\ 2 & 3 & 6 & 1 \\ 1 & 1 & 1 & 6 \end{vmatrix}$$

$$= 1(-1)^3 \begin{vmatrix} -1 & 3 & -14 \\ 3 & 6 & 1 \\ 1 & 1 & 6 \end{vmatrix} + 2(-1)^4 \begin{vmatrix} 1 & 3 & -14 \\ 2 & 6 & 1 \\ 1 & 1 & 6 \end{vmatrix} + 0 + 12(-1)^6 \begin{vmatrix} 1 & -1 & 3 \\ 2 & 3 & 6 \\ 1 & 1 & 1 \end{vmatrix}$$

$$= 1(-1)(-44) + 2(1)(58) + 12(1)(-10) = 44 + 116 - 120 = 40$$

Thus $y = \dfrac{\Delta_y}{\Delta} = \dfrac{240}{40} = 6$, $w = \dfrac{\Delta_w}{\Delta} = \dfrac{40}{40} = 1$

19. $\begin{cases} 2 - y = x \\ 3 + x = -y \end{cases}$ is equivalent to $\begin{cases} x + y = 2 \\ x + y = -3 \end{cases}$

Since $\Delta = \begin{vmatrix} 1 & 1 \\ 1 & 1 \end{vmatrix} = 0$, Cramer's rule does

not apply. However, the equations represent distinct parallel lines, so no solutions exists.

21. Let c, h, t denote the number of concerts, hockey games, and theater productions she should attend, respectively. Then we are given that

$c + h + t = 24$, $c = 2h$, and $c = \dfrac{h+t}{2}$.

Simplifying gives the system
$c + h + t = 24$
$c - 2h = 0$
$2c - h - t = 0$

$$\Delta = \begin{vmatrix} 1 & 1 & 1 \\ 1 & -2 & 0 \\ 2 & -1 & -1 \end{vmatrix} = 6$$

$$\Delta_h = \begin{vmatrix} 1 & 24 & 1 \\ 1 & 0 & 0 \\ 2 & 0 & -1 \end{vmatrix} = 24$$

$h = \dfrac{\Delta_h}{\Delta} = \dfrac{24}{6} = 4$ hockey games

23. $\Delta = \begin{vmatrix} \frac{4}{7} & -\frac{7}{3} & \frac{2}{5} \\ -8 & \frac{5}{8} & -6 \\ 2 & \frac{3}{5} & \frac{4}{3} \end{vmatrix}$

$$x = \frac{\Delta_x}{\Delta} = \frac{\begin{vmatrix} \frac{14}{9} & -\frac{7}{3} & \frac{2}{5} \\ \frac{13}{9} & \frac{5}{8} & -6 \\ \frac{10}{3} & \frac{3}{5} & \frac{4}{3} \end{vmatrix}}{\Delta} \approx 17.85$$

$$y = \frac{\Delta_y}{\Delta} = \frac{\begin{vmatrix} \frac{4}{7} & \frac{14}{9} & \frac{2}{5} \\ -8 & \frac{13}{9} & -6 \\ 2 & \frac{10}{3} & \frac{4}{3} \end{vmatrix}}{\Delta} \approx -0.42$$

$$z = \frac{\Delta_z}{\Delta} = \frac{\begin{vmatrix} \frac{4}{7} & -\frac{7}{3} & \frac{14}{9} \\ -8 & \frac{5}{8} & \frac{13}{9} \\ 2 & \frac{3}{5} & \frac{10}{3} \end{vmatrix}}{\Delta} \approx -24.09$$

Exercise 6.9

1. $A = \begin{bmatrix} \frac{200}{1200} & \frac{500}{1500} \\ \frac{400}{1200} & \frac{200}{1500} \end{bmatrix}$

    $C = \begin{bmatrix} 600 \\ 805 \end{bmatrix}$

    $X = (I - A)^{-1} C = \begin{bmatrix} 1290 \\ 1425 \end{bmatrix}$

The total value of other production costs is

$$P_A + P_B = \frac{600}{1200}(1290) + \frac{800}{1500}(1425)$$
$$= 1405$$

3. $A = \begin{bmatrix} \frac{18}{108} & \frac{30}{120} & \frac{45}{180} \\ \frac{27}{108} & \frac{30}{120} & \frac{60}{180} \\ \frac{54}{108} & \frac{40}{120} & \frac{60}{180} \end{bmatrix}$

  a. $C = \begin{bmatrix} 50 \\ 40 \\ 30 \end{bmatrix}$

       $X = (I - A)^{-1} C = \begin{bmatrix} 297.80 \\ 349.54 \\ 443.12 \end{bmatrix}$

  b. $C = \begin{bmatrix} 10 \\ 10 \\ 24 \end{bmatrix}$

       $X = (I - A)^{-1} C = \begin{bmatrix} 102.17 \\ 125.28 \\ 175.27 \end{bmatrix}$

5. $A = \begin{bmatrix} \frac{400}{1000} & \frac{200}{1000} & \frac{200}{1000} \\ \frac{200}{1000} & \frac{400}{1000} & \frac{100}{1000} \\ \frac{200}{1000} & \frac{100}{1000} & \frac{300}{1000} \end{bmatrix}$

    $C = \begin{bmatrix} 300 \\ 350 \\ 450 \end{bmatrix}$

    $(I - A)^{-1} C = \begin{bmatrix} 1301 \\ 1215 \\ 1188 \end{bmatrix}$

7. $A = \begin{bmatrix} \frac{400}{1000} & \frac{200}{1000} & \frac{200}{1000} \\ \frac{200}{1000} & \frac{400}{1000} & \frac{100}{1000} \\ \frac{200}{1000} & \frac{100}{1000} & \frac{300}{1000} \end{bmatrix}$

    $C = \begin{bmatrix} 250 \\ 300 \\ 350 \end{bmatrix}$

    $(I - A)^{-1} C = \begin{bmatrix} 1073 \\ 1016 \\ 952 \end{bmatrix}$

Chapter 6 Review Problems

1. $3\begin{bmatrix} 3 & 4 \\ -5 & 1 \end{bmatrix} - 2\begin{bmatrix} 1 & 0 \\ 2 & 4 \end{bmatrix} = \begin{bmatrix} 9 & 12 \\ -15 & 3 \end{bmatrix} - \begin{bmatrix} 2 & 0 \\ 4 & 8 \end{bmatrix} = \begin{bmatrix} 7 & 12 \\ -19 & -5 \end{bmatrix}$

3. $\begin{bmatrix} 1 & 7 \\ 2 & -3 \\ 1 & 0 \end{bmatrix}\begin{bmatrix} 1 & 0 & -2 \\ 0 & 5 & 1 \end{bmatrix} = \begin{bmatrix} 1+0 & 0+35 & -2+7 \\ 2+0 & 0-15 & -4-3 \\ 1+0 & 0+0 & -2+0 \end{bmatrix} = \begin{bmatrix} 1 & 35 & 5 \\ 2 & -15 & -7 \\ 1 & 0 & -2 \end{bmatrix}$

5. $\begin{bmatrix} 1 & 0 \\ -1 & 4 \end{bmatrix} \left\{ \begin{bmatrix} 1 & 4 \\ 6 & 5 \end{bmatrix} - \begin{bmatrix} 2 & 6 \\ 5 & 0 \end{bmatrix} \right\} = \begin{bmatrix} 1 & 0 \\ -1 & 4 \end{bmatrix} \begin{bmatrix} -1 & -2 \\ 1 & 5 \end{bmatrix}$

$= \begin{bmatrix} -1+0 & -2+0 \\ 1+4 & 2+20 \end{bmatrix} = \begin{bmatrix} -1 & -2 \\ 5 & 22 \end{bmatrix}$

7. $2\begin{bmatrix} 1 & -2 \\ 3 & 1 \end{bmatrix}^2 [1 \;\; -2]^T = 2\begin{bmatrix} -5 & -4 \\ 6 & -5 \end{bmatrix}\begin{bmatrix} 1 \\ -2 \end{bmatrix} = 2\begin{bmatrix} 3 \\ 16 \end{bmatrix} = \begin{bmatrix} 6 \\ 32 \end{bmatrix}$

9. $(2\mathbf{A})^T - 3\mathbf{I}^2 = 2\mathbf{A}^T - 3\mathbf{I} = 2\begin{bmatrix} 1 & -1 \\ 1 & 2 \end{bmatrix} - \begin{bmatrix} 3 & 0 \\ 0 & 3 \end{bmatrix}$

$= \begin{bmatrix} 2 & -2 \\ 2 & 4 \end{bmatrix} - \begin{bmatrix} 3 & 0 \\ 0 & 3 \end{bmatrix} = \begin{bmatrix} -1 & -2 \\ 2 & 1 \end{bmatrix}$

11. $\mathbf{B}^4 + \mathbf{I}^4 = \begin{bmatrix} 1 & 0 \\ 0 & 2 \end{bmatrix}^4 + \begin{bmatrix} 1 & 0 \\ 0 & 1 \end{bmatrix}^4 = \begin{bmatrix} 1 & 0 \\ 0 & 16 \end{bmatrix} + \begin{bmatrix} 1 & 0 \\ 0 & 1 \end{bmatrix} = \begin{bmatrix} 2 & 0 \\ 0 & 17 \end{bmatrix}$

13. $\begin{bmatrix} 5x \\ 2x \end{bmatrix} = \begin{bmatrix} 15 \\ y \end{bmatrix}$

$5x = 15$, or $x = 3$

$2x = y$, $2 \cdot 3 = y$, or $y = 6$

15. $\begin{bmatrix} 1 & 4 \\ 5 & 8 \end{bmatrix} \rightarrow \begin{bmatrix} 1 & 4 \\ 0 & -12 \end{bmatrix} \rightarrow \begin{bmatrix} 1 & 4 \\ 0 & 1 \end{bmatrix} \rightarrow \begin{bmatrix} 1 & 0 \\ 0 & 1 \end{bmatrix}$

17. $\begin{bmatrix} 2 & 4 & 3 \\ 1 & 2 & 3 \\ 4 & 8 & 6 \end{bmatrix} \rightarrow \begin{bmatrix} 1 & 2 & 3 \\ 2 & 4 & 3 \\ 4 & 8 & 6 \end{bmatrix} \rightarrow \begin{bmatrix} 1 & 2 & 3 \\ 0 & 0 & -3 \\ 0 & 0 & -6 \end{bmatrix} \rightarrow \begin{bmatrix} 1 & 2 & 3 \\ 0 & 0 & 1 \\ 0 & 0 & -6 \end{bmatrix} \rightarrow \begin{bmatrix} 1 & 2 & 0 \\ 0 & 0 & 1 \\ 0 & 0 & 0 \end{bmatrix}$

19. $\left[\begin{array}{cc|c} 2 & -5 & 0 \\ 4 & 3 & 0 \end{array}\right] \rightarrow \left[\begin{array}{cc|c} 2 & -5 & 0 \\ 0 & 13 & 0 \end{array}\right] \rightarrow \left[\begin{array}{cc|c} 1 & -\frac{1}{2} & 0 \\ 0 & 1 & 0 \end{array}\right] \rightarrow \left[\begin{array}{cc|c} 1 & 0 & 0 \\ 0 & 1 & 0 \end{array}\right]$

Thus $x = 0$, $y = 0$.

21. $\left[\begin{array}{ccc|c} 1 & 1 & 2 & 1 \\ 3 & -2 & -4 & -7 \\ 2 & -1 & -2 & 2 \end{array}\right] \rightarrow \left[\begin{array}{ccc|c} 1 & 1 & 2 & 1 \\ 0 & -5 & -10 & -10 \\ 0 & -3 & -6 & 0 \end{array}\right] \rightarrow \left[\begin{array}{ccc|c} 1 & 1 & 2 & 1 \\ 0 & 1 & 2 & 2 \\ 0 & -3 & -6 & 0 \end{array}\right] \rightarrow \left[\begin{array}{ccc|c} 1 & 0 & 0 & -1 \\ 0 & 1 & 2 & 2 \\ 0 & 0 & 0 & 6 \end{array}\right]$

Row three indicates that $0 = 6$, which is never true, so there is no solution.

23. $\begin{bmatrix} 1 & 5 & | & 1 & 0 \\ 3 & 9 & | & 0 & 1 \end{bmatrix} \rightarrow \begin{bmatrix} 1 & 5 & | & 1 & 0 \\ 0 & -6 & | & -3 & 1 \end{bmatrix} \rightarrow \begin{bmatrix} 1 & 5 & | & 1 & 0 \\ 0 & 1 & | & \frac{1}{2} & -\frac{1}{6} \end{bmatrix}$

$\rightarrow \begin{bmatrix} 1 & 0 & | & -\frac{3}{2} & \frac{5}{6} \\ 0 & 1 & | & \frac{1}{2} & -\frac{1}{6} \end{bmatrix} \Rightarrow \mathbf{A}^{-1} = \begin{bmatrix} -\frac{3}{2} & \frac{5}{6} \\ \frac{1}{2} & -\frac{1}{6} \end{bmatrix}$

25. $\begin{bmatrix} 1 & 3 & -2 & | & 1 & 0 & 0 \\ 4 & 1 & 0 & | & 0 & 1 & 0 \\ 3 & -2 & 2 & | & 0 & 0 & 1 \end{bmatrix} \rightarrow \begin{bmatrix} 1 & 3 & -2 & | & 1 & 0 & 0 \\ 0 & -11 & 8 & | & -4 & 1 & 0 \\ 0 & -11 & 8 & | & -3 & 0 & 0 \end{bmatrix}$

$\begin{bmatrix} 1 & 3 & -2 & | & 1 & 0 & 0 \\ 0 & -11 & 8 & | & -4 & 1 & 0 \\ 0 & 0 & 0 & | & 1 & -1 & 0 \end{bmatrix} \rightarrow \begin{bmatrix} 1 & 3 & -2 & | & 1 & 0 & 0 \\ 0 & 1 & -\frac{8}{11} & | & \frac{4}{11} & -\frac{1}{11} & 0 \\ 0 & 0 & 0 & | & 1 & -1 & 0 \end{bmatrix}$

$\rightarrow \begin{bmatrix} 1 & 0 & \frac{2}{11} & | & -\frac{1}{11} & \frac{3}{11} & 0 \\ 0 & 1 & -\frac{8}{11} & | & \frac{4}{11} & -\frac{1}{11} & 0 \\ 0 & 0 & 0 & | & 1 & 0 & 0 \end{bmatrix} \Rightarrow$ no inverse exists

27. $\begin{bmatrix} 3 & 1 & 4 & | & 1 & 0 & 0 \\ 1 & 0 & 1 & | & 0 & 1 & 0 \\ 0 & 2 & 1 & | & 0 & 0 & 1 \end{bmatrix} \rightarrow \begin{bmatrix} 1 & 0 & 1 & | & 0 & 1 & 0 \\ 3 & 1 & 4 & | & 1 & 0 & 0 \\ 0 & 2 & 1 & | & 0 & 0 & 1 \end{bmatrix}$

$\rightarrow \begin{bmatrix} 1 & 0 & 1 & | & 0 & 1 & 0 \\ 0 & 1 & 1 & | & 1 & -3 & 0 \\ 0 & 2 & 1 & | & 0 & 0 & 1 \end{bmatrix} \rightarrow \begin{bmatrix} 1 & 0 & 1 & | & 0 & 1 & 0 \\ 0 & 1 & 1 & | & 1 & -3 & 0 \\ 0 & 0 & -1 & | & -2 & 6 & 1 \end{bmatrix}$

$\rightarrow \begin{bmatrix} 1 & 0 & 1 & | & 0 & 1 & 0 \\ 0 & 1 & 1 & | & 1 & -3 & 0 \\ 0 & 0 & 1 & | & 2 & -6 & -1 \end{bmatrix} \rightarrow \begin{bmatrix} 1 & 0 & 0 & | & -2 & 7 & 1 \\ 0 & 1 & 0 & | & -1 & 3 & 1 \\ 0 & 0 & 1 & | & 2 & -6 & -1 \end{bmatrix}$

$\begin{bmatrix} x \\ y \\ z \end{bmatrix} = \mathbf{A}^{-1}\mathbf{B} = \begin{bmatrix} -2 & 7 & 1 \\ -1 & 3 & 1 \\ 2 & -6 & -1 \end{bmatrix} \begin{bmatrix} 1 \\ 0 \\ 2 \end{bmatrix} = \begin{bmatrix} 0 \\ 1 \\ 0 \end{bmatrix}$

Thus $x = 0$, $y = 1$, $z = 0$.

29. $2(7) - (-1)4 = 18$

31. Expanding along row 2 gives

$0 + 1(-1)^4 \begin{vmatrix} 1 & -1 \\ 1 & 2 \end{vmatrix} + 4(-1)^5 \begin{vmatrix} 1 & 2 \\ 1 & 2 \end{vmatrix}$

$= 1(1)[2 - (-1)] + 4(-1)[2 - 2] = 3 + 0 = 3$

33. Since all entries below the main diagonal are zeros, the determinant is $(r)(i)(c)(h) = $ *rich*.

35. $\Delta = \begin{vmatrix} 3 & -1 \\ 2 & 3 \end{vmatrix} = 11$

$\Delta_x = \begin{vmatrix} 1 & -1 \\ 8 & 3 \end{vmatrix} = 11$

$\Delta_y = \begin{vmatrix} 3 & 1 \\ 2 & 8 \end{vmatrix} = 22$

$$x = \frac{\Delta_x}{\Delta} = \frac{11}{11} = 1$$

$$y = \frac{\Delta_y}{\Delta} = \frac{22}{11} = 2$$

37. $\left| \mathbf{A}^{-1} \mathbf{B}^{\mathsf{T}} \right| = \left| \mathbf{A}^{-1} \right| \left| \mathbf{B}^{\mathsf{T}} \right| = \frac{1}{|\mathbf{A}|} \cdot |\mathbf{B}| = \frac{1}{-2} \cdot 4 = -2$

39. $\mathbf{A}^2 = \mathbf{A}\mathbf{A} = \begin{bmatrix} 0 & 0 & 1 \\ 0 & 1 & 0 \\ 1 & 0 & 0 \end{bmatrix} \begin{bmatrix} 0 & 0 & 1 \\ 0 & 1 & 0 \\ 1 & 0 & 0 \end{bmatrix} = \begin{bmatrix} 1 & 0 & 0 \\ 0 & 1 & 0 \\ 0 & 0 & 1 \end{bmatrix} = \mathbf{I}_3$

From above, $\mathbf{A}\mathbf{A} = \mathbf{I}$. Since $\mathbf{A}^{-1}$ is unique, $\mathbf{A}^{-1} = \mathbf{A}$.

$\mathbf{A}^{1994} = \left(\mathbf{A}^2 \right)^{997} = \mathbf{I}^{997} = \mathbf{I}_3$

41. $\Delta = \begin{vmatrix} a & 0 & c \\ b & b & 0 \\ a & a & c \end{vmatrix} = (abc + abc + 0) - (abc + 0 + 0) = abc$

$\Delta_x = \begin{vmatrix} a & 0 & c \\ b & b & 0 \\ c & a & c \end{vmatrix} = (abc + abc + 0) - \left(bc^2 + 0 + 0\right) = 2abc - bc^2$

$\Delta_y = \begin{vmatrix} a & a & c \\ b & b & 0 \\ a & c & c \end{vmatrix} = \left(abc + bc^2 + 0\right) - (abc + 0 + abc) = bc^2 - abc$

$\Delta_z = \begin{vmatrix} a & 0 & a \\ b & b & b \\ a & a & c \end{vmatrix} = \left(abc + a^2 b + 0\right) - \left(a^2 b + a^2 b + 0\right) = abc - a^2 b$

Thus $x = \frac{\Delta_x}{\Delta} = \frac{2abc - bc^2}{abc} = 2 - \frac{c}{a}$

$y = \frac{\Delta_y}{\Delta} = \frac{bc^2 - abc}{abc} = \frac{c}{a} - 1$

$z = \frac{\Delta_y}{\Delta} = \frac{abc - a^2 b}{abc} = 1 - \frac{a}{c}$

43. **a.** Let $x, y,$ and z represent the weekly doses of capsules of brand I, II, and III, respectively. Then

$$\begin{cases} x + y + 4z = 13 & \text{(vitamin A)} \\ x + 2y + 7z = 22 & \text{(vitamin B)} \\ x + 3y + 10z = 31 & \text{(vitamin C)} \end{cases}$$

$$\begin{bmatrix} 1 & 1 & 4 & | & 13 \\ 1 & 2 & 7 & | & 22 \\ 1 & 3 & 10 & | & 31 \end{bmatrix} \begin{array}{c} -1R_1 + R_2 \\ \xrightarrow{\hspace{1cm}} \\ -1R_1 + R_3 \end{array} \begin{bmatrix} 1 & 1 & 4 & | & 13 \\ 0 & 1 & 3 & | & 9 \\ 0 & 2 & 6 & | & 18 \end{bmatrix}$$

$$\frac{(-1)R_2 + R_1}{(-2)R_2 + R_3} \Rightarrow \begin{bmatrix} 1 & 0 & 1 & 4 \\ 0 & 1 & 3 & 9 \\ 0 & 0 & 0 & 0 \end{bmatrix}$$

Thus $x = 4 - r$, $y = 9 - 3r$, and $z = r$, where $r = 0, 1, 2, 3$.
The four possible combinations are

Combination	x	y	z
1	4	9	0
2	3	6	1
3	2	3	2
4	1	0	3

    b. Computing the cost of each combination, we find that they are 83, 77, 71, and 65 cents, respectively. Thus combination 4, namely $x = 1$, $y = 0$, $z = 3$, minimizes weekly cost.

45. $\begin{bmatrix} 215 & 87 \\ 89 & 141 \end{bmatrix}$

47. $\mathbf{A} = \begin{bmatrix} \frac{10}{34} & \frac{20}{39} \\ \frac{15}{34} & \frac{14}{39} \end{bmatrix}$

$\mathbf{C} = \begin{bmatrix} 8 \\ 8 \end{bmatrix}$

$\mathbf{X} = (\mathbf{I} - \mathbf{A})^{-1}\mathbf{C} = \begin{bmatrix} 40.8 \\ 40.56 \end{bmatrix}$

Mathematical Snapshot Chapter 6

1. $\mathbf{A} = \begin{bmatrix} 20 & 40 & 30 & 10 \\ 30 & 0 & 10 & 10 \\ 10 & 0 & 30 & 50 \end{bmatrix}$

$\mathbf{T} = \begin{bmatrix} 7 \\ 10 \\ 7 \\ 5 \end{bmatrix}$

$\mathbf{C} = \begin{bmatrix} 9 \\ 8 \\ 10 \end{bmatrix}$

$$\mathbf{C}^T(\mathbf{AT}) = \mathbf{C}^T \left\{ \begin{bmatrix} 20 & 40 & 30 & 10 \\ 30 & 0 & 10 & 10 \\ 10 & 0 & 30 & 50 \end{bmatrix} \begin{bmatrix} 7 \\ 10 \\ 7 \\ 5 \end{bmatrix} \right\} = \mathbf{C}^T \begin{bmatrix} 800 \\ 330 \\ 530 \end{bmatrix}$$

$$= \begin{bmatrix} 9 & 8 & 10 \end{bmatrix} \begin{bmatrix} 800 \\ 330 \\ 530 \end{bmatrix} = [15,140]$$

The cost is $151.40.

Chapter 7

Principles in Practice 7.1

1. Let x = the number of type A magnets and y = the number of type B magnets.
The cost for producing x type A magnets and y type B magnets is $50 + 0.90x + 0.70y$. The revenue for selling x type A magnets and y type B magnets is $2.00x + 1.50y$.
Revenue is greater than cost when
$2x + 1.5y > 50 + 0.9x + 0.7y$.
$0.8y > -1.1x + 50$
$y > -1.375x + 62.5$
Sketch the dashed line $y = -1.375x + 62.5$ and shade the half plane above the line. In order to make a profit, the number of magnets of types A and B must correspond to an ordered pair in the shaded region. Also, to take reality into account, both x and y must be positive (negative numbers of magnets are not feasible).

2. Since negative numbers of cameras cannot be sold, $x \geq 0$ and $y \geq 0$. Selling at least 50 cameras per week corresponds to $x + y \geq 50$. Selling twice as many of type I as of type II corresponds to $x \geq 2y$. The system of inequalities is
$$\begin{cases} x + y \geq 50, \\ x \geq 2y, \\ x \geq 0, \\ y \geq 0. \end{cases}$$
The region consists of points on or above the x-axis and on or to the right of the y-axis. In addition, the points must be on or above the line $x + y = 50$ and on or below the line $x = 2y$.

Exercise 7.1

1.

3.

5.

7.

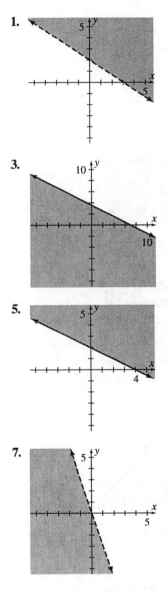

139

9.

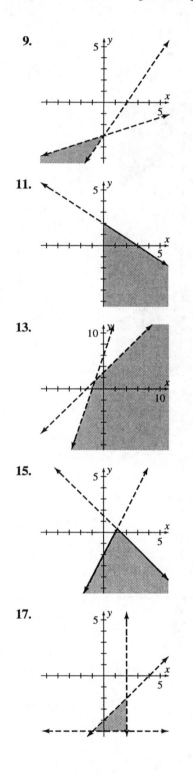

11.

13.

15.

17.

19.

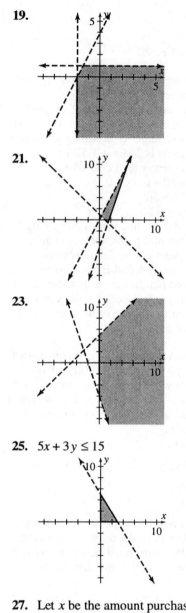

21.

23.

25. $5x + 3y \leq 15$

27. Let x be the amount purchased from supplier A, and y the amount purchased from B. The system of inequalities is
$x + y \leq 100$,
$x \geq 0$,
$y \geq 0$.

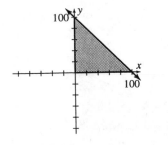

29. Since negative numbers of chairs cannot be produced, $x \geq 0$ and $y \geq 0$. The inequality for assembly time is $3x + 2y \leq 24$. The inequality for painting time is $\frac{1}{2}x + y \leq 8$.

    The system of inequalities is

    $$\begin{cases} 3x + 2y \leq 24, \\ \dfrac{1}{2}x + y \leq 8, \\ \qquad x \geq 0, \\ \qquad y \geq 0. \end{cases}$$

    The region consists of points on or above the x-axis and on or to the right of the y-axis. In addition, the points must be on or below the line $3x + 2y = 24$ and on or below the line $\frac{1}{2}x + y = 8$ (or, equivalently $x + 2y = 16$).

Exercise 7.2

1. The feasible region appears below. The corner points are $(0, 0)$, $(60, 0)$ and $(40, 20)$. Using the method of evaluating the objective function at each corner point, we have $P(0, 0) = 0$, $P(60, 0) = 600$, and $P(40, 20) = 640$. Thus P has a maximum value of 640 at $(40, 20)$ That is, P has a maximum value of 640 when $x = 40$ and $y = 20$. [Alternatively, the indicated dashed line is the member of the family of lines

    $$P = 10x + 12y \left(\text{or } y = -\frac{5}{6}x + \frac{P}{12}\right) \text{ that}$$

    gives a maximum value of P and that has at least one point in common with the feasible region. It is clear that the line contains corner point $(40, 20)$.]

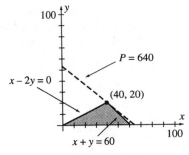

3. The feasible region appears below. The corner points are $(2, 3)$, $(0, 5)$, $(0, 7)$ and $\left(\frac{10}{3}, 7\right)$.

    Evaluating Z at each point, we find that Z has a maximum value of -10 when $x = 2$ and $y = 3$.

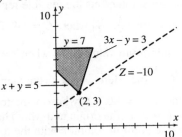

5. The feasible region is empty, so there is no optimum solution.

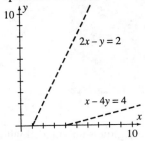

7. The feasible region is a line segment. The corner points are $(0, 1)$ and $(4, 5)$. Z has a minimum value of 3 when $x = 0$ and $y = 1$.

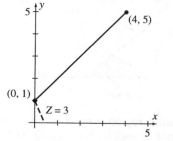

9. The feasible region is unbounded with 4 corner points. The member (see dashed line) of the family of lines $C = 2x + y$ which gives a minimum value of C, subject to the constraints, intersects the feasible region at corner point $\left(\frac{3}{5}, \frac{6}{5}\right)$ where $C = 2.4$. Thus C has a minimum value of 2.4 when $x = \frac{3}{5}$ and $y = \frac{6}{5}$. [Note: Here we chose the member of the family $y = -2x + C$ whose y-intercept was *closest* to the origin and which had at least one point in common with the feasible region.]

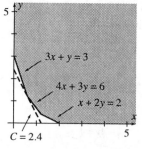

11. The feasible region is unbounded with 2 corner points. The family of lines given by $Z = 10x + 2y$ has members (see dashed lines for two sample members) that have arbitrarily large values of Z and that also intersect the feasible region. Thus no optimum solution exists.

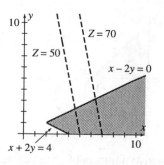

13. Let x and y be the numbers of widgets and wadgits made per week, respectively. Then we are to maximize $P = 4x + 6y$ subject to
$$\begin{cases} x \geq 0, \\ y \geq 0, \\ 2x + y \leq 70 \text{ (for machine A)}, \\ x + y \leq 40 \text{ (for machine B)}, \\ x + 3y \leq 90 \text{ (for finishing)}. \end{cases}$$

The feasible region appears below. The corner points are $(0, 0)$, $(0, 30)$, $(15, 25)$, $(30, 10)$ and $(35, 0)$. By evaluating P at each corner point, we find that P is maximized at corner point $(15, 25)$, where its value is 210. Thus 15 widgets and 25 wadgets should be made each week to give a maximum profit of \$210.

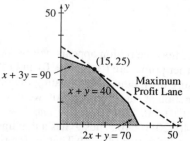

15. Let x and y be the numbers of units of Food A and Food B, respectively, that are purchased. Then we are to minimize $C = 1.20x + 0.80y$, where
$$\begin{cases} x \geq 0, \\ y \geq 0, \\ 2x + 2y \geq 16 \text{ (for carbohydrates)}, \\ 4x + y \geq 20 \text{ (for protein)}. \end{cases}$$
The feasible region is unbounded. The corner points are $(8, 0)$, $(4, 4)$ and $(0, 20)$. C is minimized at corner point $(4, 4)$ where $C = 8$ (see the minimum cost line). Thus 4 units of Food A and 4 units of Food B gives

a minimum cost of $8.

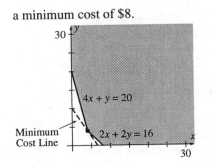

17. Let x and y be the numbers of tons of ores I and II, respectively, that are processed. Then we are to minimize $C = 50x + 60y$, where

$$\begin{cases} x \geq 0, \\ y \geq 0, \\ 100x + 200y \geq 3000 \text{ (for mineral A)}, \\ 200x + 50y \geq 2500 \text{ (for mineral B)}. \end{cases}$$

The feasible region is unbounded with 3 corner points. C is minimized at the corner point $(10, 10)$ where $C = 1100$ (see the minimum cost line). Thus 10 tons of ore I and 10 tons of ore II give a minimum cost of $1100.

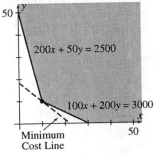

19. Let x and y be the number of chambers of type A and B, respectively. Then we are to minimize $C = 600,000x + 300,000y$, where

$$\begin{cases} x \geq 4, \\ y \geq 4, \\ 10x + 4y \geq 100 \text{ (for polymer P}_1), \\ 20x + 30y \geq 420 \text{ (for polymer P}_2). \end{cases}$$

The feasible region is unbounded with 3 corner points. Evaluating C at each corner point, we find C is minimized at corner point $(6, 10)$ where $C = 6,600,000$. Thus the solution is 6 chambers of type A and 10 chambers of type B.

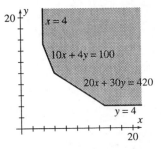

21. a. A builds x km of highway and y km of expressway, so B builds $(200 - x)$ km of highway and $(100 - y)$ km of expressway. Thus

$$D = 1x + 6y + 2(200 - x) + 5(100 - y)$$
$$= 900 - x + y.$$

b. The first constraint is company A's construction limit. The second constraint is company B's construction limit, which arises as follows:

$$(200 - x) + (100 - y) \leq 150,$$
$$300 - x - y \leq 150,$$
$$-x - y \leq -150,$$
$$x + y \geq 150.$$

The third constraint is the minimum contract for A. The fourth constraint is the minimum contract for B, which arises as follows:

$$1(200 - x) + 5(100 - y) \geq 250,$$
$$700 - x - 5y \geq 250,$$
$$-x - 5y \geq -450,$$
$$x + 5y \leq 450.$$

c. The feasible region (see below) is bounded. The corner points are $(75, 75)$, $(125, 25)$, $(187.5, 12.5)$ and $(137.5, 62.5)$. Evaluating D at each corner point, we find that D is maximized at point $(75, 75)$, where $D = 900$. That is, D is maximized if $x = y = 75$.

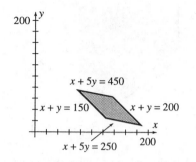

23. $Z = 15.54$ when $x = 2.56$, $y = 6.74$

25. $Z = -75.98$ when $x = 9.48$, $y = 16.67$

Principles in Practice 7.3

1. Using the hint, the cost of shipping the TV sets is
$$Z = 18x + 24(25 - x) + 9y + 15(30 - y)$$
$$= 1050 - 6x - 6y.$$
Since negative numbers of TV sets cannot be shipped, $x \geq 0$, $y \geq 0$, $25 - x \geq 0$, and $30 - y \geq 0$. Since warehouse C has only 45 TV sets, $x + y \leq 45$. Similarly, since warehouse D has only 40 TV sets, $25 - x + 30 - y \leq 45$ or $x + y \geq 10$.
We need to minimize $Z = 1050 - 6x - 6y$ subject to the constraints
$$x + y \leq 45,$$
$$x + y \geq 10,$$
$$x \leq 25,$$
$$y \leq 30,$$
$$x \geq 0, \quad y \geq 0.$$

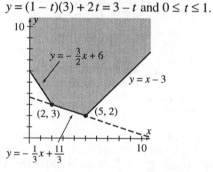

The feasible region shown has corners $A = (0, 10)$, $B = (0, 30)$, $C = (15, 30)$, $D = (25, 20)$, $E = (25, 0)$, and $F = (10, 0)$. Evaluating the cost function at the corners gives

$Z(A) = 1050 - 6(0) - 6(10) = 990$
$Z(B) = 1050 - 6(0) - 6(30) = 870$
$Z(C) = 1050 - 6(15) - 6(30) = 780$
$Z(D) = 1050 - 6(25) - 6(20) = 780$
$Z(E) = 1050 - 6(25) - 6(0) = 900$
$Z(F) = 1050 - 6(10) - 6(0) = 990$
The minimum value of Z is 780 which occurs at all points on the line segment joining C and D.
This is $x = (1 - t)(15) + t(25) = 15 + 10t$ and $y = (1 - t)(30) + t(20) = 30 - 10t$ for $0 \leq t \leq 1$.
Thus, ship $10t + 15$ TV sets from C to A, $-10t + 30$ TV sets from C to B, $25 - (10t + 15) = -10t + 10$ TV sets from D to A, and $30 - (-10t + 30) = 10t$ TV sets from D to B, for $0 \leq t \leq 1$. The minimum cost is \$780.

Exercise 7.3

1. The feasible region is unbounded. Z is minimized at corner points $(2, 3)$ and $(5, 2)$, where its value is 33. Z is also minimized at all points on the line segment joining $(2, 3)$ and $(5, 2)$, so the solution is $Z = 33$ when
$$x = (1 - t)(2) + 5t = 2 + 3t$$
$$y = (1 - t)(3) + 2t = 3 - t \text{ and } 0 \leq t \leq 1.$$

3. The feasible region appears below. The corner points are $(0, 0)$, $(0, 4)$, $(3, 2)$ and $(4, 0)$. Z is maximized at $(3, 2)$ and $(4, 0)$, where its value is 72. Thus Z is also maximized at all points on the line segment joining $(3, 2)$ and $(4, 0)$. The solution is
$$Z = 72 \text{ when } x = (1 - t)(3) + 4t = 3 + t$$
$$y = (1 - t)(2) + 0t = 2 - 2t \text{ and } 0 \leq t \leq 1$$

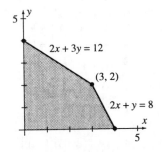

Principles in Practice 7.4

In these problems, the pivot entry is underlined.

1. Let x_1, x_2, and x_3 be the numbers of Type 1, Type 2, and Type 3 gadgets, respectively, that the company produces. The situation is to maximize the profit $P = 150x_1 + 250x_2 + 200x_3$, subject to the constraints

$$300x_1 + 300x_2 + 400x_3 \le 30,000,$$
$$15x_1 + 15x_2 + 10x_3 \le 1200,$$
$$2x_1 + 2x_2 + 3x_3 \le 180 \text{ , and}$$
$$x_1, \ x_2, \ x_3 \ge 0.$$

The constraint inequalities can be simplified by dividing by the greatest common factor of the numbers involved. Thus, we will use

$$3x_1 + 3x_2 + 4x_3 \le 300,$$
$$3x_1 + 3x_2 + 2x_3 \le 240,$$
$$2x_1 + 2x_2 + 3x_3 \le 180 \text{ , and}$$
$$x_1, \ x_2, \ x_3 \ge 0.$$

	x_1	x_2	x_3	s_1	s_2	s_3	P	b
s_1	3	3	4	1	0	0	0	300
s_2	3	$\underline{3}$	2	0	1	0	0	240
s_3	2	2	3	0	0	1	0	180
P	−150	−250	−200	0	0	0	1	0

	x_1	x_2	x_3	s_1	s_2	s_3	P	b
s_1	0	0	2	1	−1	0	0	60
x_2	1	1	$\frac{2}{3}$	0	$\frac{1}{3}$	0	0	80
s_3	0	0	$\underline{\frac{5}{3}}$	0	$-\frac{2}{3}$	1	0	20
P	100	0	$-\frac{100}{3}$	0	$\frac{250}{3}$	0	1	20,000

	x_1	x_2	x_3	s_1	s_2	s_3	P	b
s_1	0	0	0	1	$-\frac{1}{5}$	$-\frac{6}{5}$	0	36
x_2	1	1	0	0	$\frac{3}{5}$	$-\frac{2}{5}$	0	72
x_3	0	0	1	0	$-\frac{2}{5}$	$\frac{3}{5}$	0	12
P	100	0	0	0	70	20	1	20,400

The maximum value of P is 20,400 when $x_1 = 0$, $x_2 = 72$, and $x_3 = 12$. The maximum profit is \$20,400 when 72 Type 2 gadgets and 12 Type 3 gadgets are produced and sold.

Exercise 7.4

1.

$$\begin{array}{c} \\ s_1 \\ s_2 \\ Z \end{array} \begin{array}{ccccc} x_1 & x_2 & s_1 & s_2 & Z \\ \left[\begin{array}{ccccc|c} 2 & 1 & 1 & 0 & 0 & 8 \\ 2 & \underline{3} & 0 & 1 & 0 & 12 \\ \hline -1 & -2 & 0 & 0 & 1 & 0 \end{array}\right] \begin{array}{c} 8 \\ 4 \\ \\ \end{array} \end{array}$$

$$\begin{array}{c} \\ s_1 \\ x_2 \\ Z \end{array} \begin{array}{ccccc} x_1 & x_2 & s_1 & s_2 & Z \\ \left[\begin{array}{ccccc|c} \frac{4}{3} & 0 & 1 & -\frac{1}{3} & 0 & 4 \\ \frac{2}{3} & 1 & 0 & \frac{1}{3} & 0 & 4 \\ \hline \frac{1}{3} & 0 & 0 & \frac{2}{3} & 1 & 8 \end{array}\right] \end{array}$$

The solution is $Z = 8$ when $x_1 = 0$, $x_2 = 4$.

3.

$$\begin{array}{c} \\ s_1 \\ s_2 \\ Z \end{array} \begin{array}{ccccc} x_1 & x_2 & s_1 & s_2 & Z \\ \left[\begin{array}{ccccc|c} 1 & 1 & 1 & 0 & 0 & 6 \\ -1 & \underline{1} & 0 & 1 & 0 & 4 \\ \hline 1 & -3 & 0 & 0 & 1 & 0 \end{array}\right] \begin{array}{c} 6 \\ 4 \\ \\ \end{array} \end{array}$$

$$\begin{array}{c} \\ s_1 \\ x_2 \\ Z \end{array} \begin{array}{ccccc} x_1 & x_2 & s_1 & s_2 & Z \\ \left[\begin{array}{ccccc|c} \underline{2} & 0 & 1 & -1 & 0 & 2 \\ -1 & 1 & 0 & 1 & 0 & 4 \\ \hline -2 & 0 & 0 & 3 & 1 & 12 \end{array}\right] \begin{array}{c} 1 \\ \\ \\ \end{array} \end{array}$$

$$\begin{array}{c} \\ x_1 \\ x_2 \\ Z \end{array} \begin{array}{ccccc} x_1 & x_2 & s_1 & s_2 & Z \\ \left[\begin{array}{ccccc|c} 1 & 0 & \frac{1}{2} & -\frac{1}{2} & 0 & 1 \\ 0 & 1 & \frac{1}{2} & \frac{1}{2} & 0 & 5 \\ \hline 0 & 0 & 1 & 2 & 1 & 14 \end{array}\right] \end{array}$$

The solution is $Z = 14$ when $x_1 = 1$, $x_2 = 5$.

5.

$$\begin{array}{c} \\ s_1 \\ s_2 \\ s_3 \\ Z \end{array} \begin{array}{cccccc} x_1 & x_2 & s_1 & s_2 & s_3 & Z \\ \left[\begin{array}{cccccc|c} \underline{1} & -1 & 1 & 0 & 0 & 0 & 1 \\ 1 & 2 & 0 & 1 & 0 & 0 & 8 \\ 1 & 1 & 0 & 0 & 1 & 0 & 5 \\ \hline -8 & -2 & 0 & 0 & 0 & 1 & 0 \end{array}\right] \begin{array}{c} 1 \\ 8 \\ 5 \\ \\ \end{array} \end{array}$$

$$\begin{array}{c} \\ x_1 \\ s_2 \\ s_3 \\ Z \end{array} \begin{array}{cccccc} x_1 & x_2 & s_1 & s_2 & s_3 & Z \\ \left[\begin{array}{cccccc|c} 1 & -1 & 1 & 0 & 0 & 0 & 1 \\ 0 & 3 & -1 & 1 & 0 & 0 & 7 \\ 0 & \underline{2} & -1 & 0 & 1 & 0 & 4 \\ \hline 0 & -10 & 8 & 0 & 0 & 1 & 8 \end{array}\right] \begin{array}{c} \\ \frac{7}{3} \\ 2 \\ \\ \end{array} \end{array}$$

$$\begin{array}{c} \\ x_1 \\ s_2 \\ x_2 \\ Z \end{array} \begin{array}{cccccc} x_1 & x_2 & s_1 & s_2 & s_3 & Z \\ \left[\begin{array}{cccccc|c} 1 & 0 & \frac{1}{2} & 0 & \frac{1}{2} & 0 & 3 \\ 0 & 0 & \frac{1}{2} & 1 & -\frac{3}{2} & 0 & 1 \\ 0 & 1 & -\frac{1}{2} & 0 & \frac{1}{2} & 0 & 2 \\ \hline 0 & 0 & 3 & 0 & 5 & 1 & 28 \end{array}\right] \end{array}$$

The solution is $Z = 28$ when $x_1 = 3$, $x_2 = 2$.

7.

$$\begin{array}{c} \\ s_1 \\ s_2 \\ Z \end{array} \begin{array}{cccccc} x_1 & x_2 & x_3 & s_1 & s_2 & Z \\ \left[\begin{array}{cccccc|c} 1 & 2 & 0 & 1 & 0 & 0 & 10 \\ 2 & \underline{2} & 1 & 0 & 1 & 0 & 10 \\ \hline -3 & -4 & -\frac{3}{2} & 0 & 0 & 1 & 0 \end{array}\right] \begin{array}{c} 5 \\ 5 \\ \\ \end{array} \end{array}$$

choosing s_2 as departing variable

$$\begin{array}{c} \\ s_1 \\ x_2 \\ Z \end{array} \begin{array}{cccccc} x_1 & x_2 & x_3 & s_1 & s_2 & Z \\ \left[\begin{array}{cccccc|c} -1 & 0 & -1 & 1 & 0 & 0 & 4 \\ 1 & 1 & \frac{1}{2} & 0 & \frac{1}{2} & 0 & 5 \\ \hline 1 & 0 & \frac{1}{2} & 0 & 2 & 1 & 20 \end{array}\right] \end{array}$$

The solution is $Z = 20$ when
$x_1 = 0$, $x_2 = 5$, $x_3 = 0$

$$\begin{array}{c} \\ x_1 \\ s_2 \\ Z \end{array} \begin{array}{cccccc} x_1 & x_2 & x_3 & s_1 & s_2 & Z \\ \left[\begin{array}{cccccc|c} 1 & \frac{1}{2} & -\frac{1}{2} & \frac{1}{2} & 0 & 0 & 2 \\ 0 & \frac{1}{2} & \frac{3}{2} & -\frac{1}{2} & 1 & 0 & 0 \\ \hline 0 & 2 & -2 & 1 & 0 & 1 & 4 \end{array}\right] \begin{array}{c} \\ 0 \\ \\ \end{array} \end{array}$$

$$\begin{array}{c} \\ x_1 \\ x_3 \\ Z \end{array} \begin{array}{cccccc} x_1 & x_2 & x_3 & s_1 & s_2 & Z \\ \left[\begin{array}{cccccc|c} 1 & \frac{2}{3} & 0 & \frac{1}{3} & \frac{1}{3} & 0 & 2 \\ 0 & \frac{1}{3} & 1 & -\frac{1}{3} & \frac{2}{3} & 0 & 0 \\ \hline 0 & \frac{8}{3} & 0 & \frac{1}{3} & \frac{4}{3} & 1 & 4 \end{array}\right] \end{array}$$

The solution is $Z = 4$ when
$x_1 = 2$, $x_2 = 0$, $x_3 = 0$.

9. To obtain a standard linear programming problem, we write the second constraint as $-x_1 + 2x_2 + x_3 \le 2$.

$$
\begin{array}{c}
\begin{array}{cccccc} x_1 & x_2 & x_3 & s_1 & s_2 & Z \end{array} \\
\begin{array}{c} s_1 \\ s_2 \\ Z \end{array}
\left[\begin{array}{cccccc|c}
1 & 1 & 0 & 1 & 0 & 0 & 1 \\
-1 & 2 & 1 & 0 & 1 & 0 & 2 \\
\hline
-2 & -1 & 1 & 0 & 0 & 1 & 0
\end{array}\right]
\begin{array}{c} 1 \\ \\ \\ \end{array}
\end{array}
$$

$$
\begin{array}{c}
\begin{array}{cccccc} x_1 & x_2 & x_3 & s_1 & s_2 & Z \end{array} \\
\begin{array}{c} x_1 \\ s_2 \\ Z \end{array}
\left[\begin{array}{cccccc|c}
1 & 1 & 0 & 1 & 0 & 0 & 1 \\
0 & 3 & 1 & 1 & 1 & 0 & 3 \\
\hline
0 & 1 & 1 & 2 & 0 & 1 & 2
\end{array}\right]
\end{array}
$$

The solution is $Z = 2$ when $x_1 = 1$, $x_2 = 0$, $x_3 = 0$.

11.

$$
\begin{array}{c}
\begin{array}{ccccccc} x_1 & x_2 & s_1 & s_2 & s_3 & s_4 & Z \end{array} \\
\begin{array}{c} s_1 \\ s_2 \\ s_3 \\ s_4 \\ Z \end{array}
\left[\begin{array}{ccccccc|c}
1 & -1 & 1 & 0 & 0 & 0 & 0 & 4 \\
-1 & 1 & 0 & 1 & 0 & 0 & 0 & 4 \\
8 & 5 & 0 & 0 & 1 & 0 & 0 & 40 \\
2 & 1 & 0 & 0 & 0 & 1 & 0 & 6 \\
\hline
-1 & -1 & 0 & 0 & 0 & 0 & 1 & 0
\end{array}\right]
\begin{array}{c} 4 \\ \\ 5 \\ 3 \\ \\ \end{array}
\end{array}
$$

choosing x_1 as departing variable

$$
\begin{array}{c}
\begin{array}{ccccccc} x_1 & x_2 & s_1 & s_2 & s_3 & s_4 & Z \end{array} \\
\begin{array}{c} s_1 \\ s_2 \\ s_3 \\ x_1 \\ Z \end{array}
\left[\begin{array}{ccccccc|c}
0 & -\frac{3}{2} & 1 & 0 & 0 & -\frac{1}{2} & 0 & 1 \\
0 & \frac{3}{2} & 0 & 1 & 0 & \frac{1}{2} & 0 & 7 \\
0 & 1 & 0 & 0 & 1 & -4 & 0 & 16 \\
1 & \frac{1}{2} & 0 & 0 & 0 & \frac{1}{2} & 0 & 3 \\
\hline
0 & -\frac{1}{2} & 0 & 0 & 0 & \frac{1}{2} & 1 & 3
\end{array}\right]
\begin{array}{c} \\ \frac{14}{3} \\ 16 \\ 6 \\ \\ \end{array}
\end{array}
$$

$$
\begin{array}{c}
\begin{array}{ccccccc} x_1 & x_2 & s_1 & s_2 & s_3 & s_4 & Z \end{array} \\
\begin{array}{c} s_1 \\ x_2 \\ s_3 \\ x_1 \\ Z \end{array}
\left[\begin{array}{ccccccc|c}
0 & 0 & 1 & 1 & 0 & 0 & 0 & 8 \\
0 & 1 & 0 & \frac{2}{3} & 0 & \frac{1}{3} & 0 & \frac{14}{3} \\
0 & 0 & 0 & -\frac{2}{3} & 1 & -\frac{13}{3} & 0 & \frac{34}{3} \\
1 & 0 & 0 & -\frac{1}{3} & 0 & \frac{1}{3} & 0 & \frac{2}{3} \\
\hline
0 & 0 & 0 & \frac{1}{3} & 0 & \frac{2}{3} & 1 & \frac{16}{3}
\end{array}\right]
\end{array}
$$

Thus the maximum value of Z is $\dfrac{16}{3}$, when $x_1 = \dfrac{2}{3}$, $x_2 = \dfrac{14}{3}$. If we choose x_2 as the entering variable, then we have:

$$
\begin{array}{c}
\begin{array}{ccccccc} x_1 & x_2 & s_1 & s_2 & s_3 & s_4 & Z \end{array} \\
\begin{array}{c} s_1 \\ s_2 \\ s_3 \\ s_4 \\ Z \end{array}
\left[\begin{array}{ccccccc|c}
1 & -1 & 1 & 0 & 0 & 0 & 0 & 4 \\
-1 & 1 & 0 & 1 & 0 & 0 & 0 & 4 \\
8 & 5 & 0 & 0 & 1 & 0 & 0 & 40 \\
2 & 1 & 0 & 0 & 0 & 1 & 0 & 6 \\
\hline
-1 & -1 & 0 & 0 & 0 & 0 & 1 & 0
\end{array}\right]
\begin{array}{c} \\ 4 \\ 8 \\ 6 \\ \\ \end{array}
\end{array}
$$

$$
\begin{array}{c}
\begin{array}{ccccccc} x_1 & x_2 & s_1 & s_2 & s_3 & s_4 & Z \end{array} \\
\begin{array}{c} s_1 \\ x_2 \\ s_3 \\ s_4 \\ Z \end{array}
\left[\begin{array}{ccccccc|c}
0 & 0 & 1 & 1 & 0 & 0 & 0 & 8 \\
-1 & 1 & 0 & 1 & 0 & 0 & 0 & 4 \\
13 & 0 & 0 & -5 & 1 & 0 & 0 & 20 \\
3 & 0 & 0 & -1 & 0 & 1 & 0 & 2 \\
\hline
-2 & 0 & 0 & 1 & 0 & 0 & 1 & 4
\end{array}\right]
\begin{array}{c} \\ \\ \frac{20}{13} \\ \frac{2}{3} \\ \\ \end{array}
\end{array}
$$

$$
\begin{array}{c}
\begin{array}{ccccccc} x_1 & x_2 & s_1 & s_2 & s_3 & s_4 & Z \end{array} \\
\begin{array}{c} s_1 \\ x_2 \\ s_3 \\ x_1 \\ Z \end{array}
\left[\begin{array}{ccccccc|c}
0 & 0 & 1 & 1 & 0 & 0 & 0 & 8 \\
0 & 1 & 0 & \frac{2}{3} & 0 & \frac{1}{3} & 0 & \frac{14}{3} \\
0 & 0 & 0 & -\frac{2}{3} & 1 & -\frac{13}{3} & 0 & \frac{34}{3} \\
1 & 0 & 0 & -\frac{1}{3} & 0 & \frac{1}{3} & 0 & \frac{2}{3} \\
\hline
0 & 0 & 0 & \frac{1}{3} & 0 & \frac{2}{3} & 1 & \frac{16}{3}
\end{array}\right]
\end{array}
$$

The solution is $Z = \dfrac{16}{3}$ when $x_1 = \dfrac{2}{3}$, $x_2 = \dfrac{14}{3}$.

13. To obtain a standard linear programming problem, we write the second constraint as $-x_1 - x_2 + x_3 \le 2$ and the third constraint as $x_1 - x_2 - x_3 \le 1$.

$$
\begin{array}{c}
\begin{array}{ccccccc} x_1 & x_2 & x_3 & s_1 & s_2 & s_3 & W \end{array} \\
\begin{array}{c} s_1 \\ s_2 \\ s_3 \\ W \end{array}
\left[\begin{array}{ccccccc|c}
4 & 3 & -1 & 1 & 0 & 0 & 0 & 1 \\
-1 & -1 & 1 & 0 & 1 & 0 & 0 & 2 \\
1 & -1 & -1 & 0 & 0 & 1 & 0 & 1 \\
\hline
-1 & 12 & -4 & 0 & 0 & 0 & 1 & 0
\end{array}\right]
\begin{array}{c} \\ 2 \\ \\ \\ \end{array}
\end{array}
$$

$$
\begin{array}{c}
\begin{array}{ccccccc} x_1 & x_2 & x_3 & s_1 & s_2 & s_3 & W \end{array} \\
\begin{array}{c} s_1 \\ x_3 \\ s_3 \\ W \end{array}
\left[\begin{array}{ccccccc|c}
3 & 2 & 0 & 1 & 1 & 0 & 0 & 3 \\
-1 & -1 & 1 & 0 & 1 & 0 & 0 & 2 \\
0 & -2 & 0 & 0 & 1 & 1 & 0 & 3 \\
\hline
-5 & 8 & 0 & 0 & 4 & 0 & 1 & 8
\end{array}\right]
\begin{array}{c} 1 \\ \\ \\ \\ \end{array}
\end{array}
$$

$$\begin{array}{c}
\begin{array}{ccccccc} x_1 & x_2 & x_3 & s_1 & s_2 & s_3 & W \end{array}\\
\begin{array}{c} x_1 \\ x_3 \\ s_3 \\ \\ W \end{array}
\left[\begin{array}{ccccccc|c}
1 & \frac{2}{3} & 0 & \frac{1}{3} & \frac{1}{3} & 0 & 0 & 1 \\
0 & -\frac{1}{3} & 1 & \frac{1}{3} & \frac{4}{3} & 0 & 0 & 3 \\
0 & -2 & 0 & 0 & 1 & 1 & 0 & 3 \\
\hline
0 & \frac{34}{3} & 0 & \frac{5}{3} & \frac{17}{3} & 0 & 1 & 13
\end{array}\right]
\end{array}$$

The solution is $W = 13$ when $x_1 = 1$, $x_2 = 0$, $x_3 = 3$.

15.

$$\begin{array}{c}
\begin{array}{cccccccccc} x_1 & x_2 & x_3 & x_4 & s_1 & s_2 & s_3 & s_4 & Z \end{array}\\
\begin{array}{c} s_1 \\ s_2 \\ s_3 \\ s_4 \\ \\ Z \end{array}
\left[\begin{array}{ccccccccc|cc}
1 & -2 & 0 & 0 & 1 & 0 & 0 & 0 & 0 & 2 & \\
1 & 1 & 0 & 0 & 0 & 1 & 0 & 0 & 0 & 5 & \\
0 & 0 & \underline{1} & 1 & 0 & 0 & 1 & 0 & 0 & 4 & 4 \\
0 & 0 & 1 & -2 & 0 & 0 & 0 & 1 & 0 & 7 & 7 \\
\hline
-60 & 0 & -90 & 0 & 0 & 0 & 0 & 0 & 1 & 0 &
\end{array}\right]
\end{array}$$

$$\begin{array}{c}
\begin{array}{cccccccccc} x_1 & x_2 & x_3 & x_4 & s_1 & s_2 & s_3 & s_4 & Z \end{array}\\
\begin{array}{c} s_1 \\ s_2 \\ x_3 \\ s_4 \\ \\ Z \end{array}
\left[\begin{array}{ccccccccc|cc}
\underline{1} & -2 & 0 & 0 & 1 & 0 & 0 & 0 & 0 & 2 & 2 \\
1 & 1 & 0 & 0 & 0 & 1 & 0 & 0 & 0 & 5 & 5 \\
0 & 0 & 1 & 1 & 0 & 0 & 1 & 0 & 0 & 4 & \\
0 & 0 & 0 & -3 & 0 & 0 & -1 & 1 & 0 & 3 & \\
\hline
-60 & 0 & 0 & 90 & 0 & 0 & 90 & 0 & 1 & 360 &
\end{array}\right]
\end{array}$$

$$\begin{array}{c}
\begin{array}{cccccccccc} x_1 & x_2 & x_3 & x_4 & s_1 & s_2 & s_3 & s_4 & Z \end{array}\\
\begin{array}{c} x_1 \\ s_2 \\ x_3 \\ s_4 \\ \\ Z \end{array}
\left[\begin{array}{ccccccccc|cc}
1 & -2 & 0 & 0 & 1 & 0 & 0 & 0 & 0 & 2 & \\
0 & \underline{3} & 0 & 0 & -1 & 1 & 0 & 0 & 0 & 3 & 1 \\
0 & 0 & 1 & 1 & 0 & 0 & 1 & 0 & 0 & 4 & \\
0 & 0 & 0 & -3 & 0 & 0 & -1 & 1 & 0 & 3 & \\
\hline
0 & -120 & 0 & 90 & 60 & 0 & 90 & 0 & 1 & 480 &
\end{array}\right]
\end{array}$$

$$\begin{array}{c}
\begin{array}{cccccccccc} x_1 & x_2 & x_3 & x_4 & s_1 & s_2 & s_3 & s_4 & Z \end{array}\\
\begin{array}{c} x_1 \\ x_2 \\ x_3 \\ s_4 \\ \\ Z \end{array}
\left[\begin{array}{ccccccccc|c}
1 & 0 & 0 & 0 & \frac{1}{3} & \frac{2}{3} & 0 & 0 & 0 & 4 \\
0 & 1 & 0 & 0 & -\frac{1}{3} & \frac{1}{3} & 0 & 0 & 0 & 1 \\
0 & 0 & 1 & 1 & 0 & 0 & 1 & 0 & 0 & 4 \\
0 & 0 & 0 & -3 & 0 & 0 & -1 & 1 & 0 & 3 \\
\hline
0 & 0 & 0 & 90 & 20 & 40 & 90 & 0 & 1 & 600
\end{array}\right]
\end{array}$$

The solution is $Z = 600$ for $x_1 = 4$, $x_2 = 1$, $x_3 = 4$, $x_4 = 0$.

17. Let x_1 and x_2 denote the numbers of boxes transported from A and B, respectively. The revenue received is $R = 0.75x_1 + 0.50x_2$. We want to maximize R subject to

$$2x_1 + x_2 \le 2400 \ \text{(volume)},$$
$$3x_1 + 5x_2 \le 9200 \ \text{(weight)},$$
$$x_1,\ x_2 \ge 0.$$

$$
\begin{array}{c}
\begin{array}{ccccc} x_1 & x_2 & s_1 & s_2 & R \end{array} \\
\begin{array}{c} s_1 \\ s_2 \\ R \end{array}
\left[
\begin{array}{ccccc|c}
\underline{2} & 1 & 1 & 0 & 0 & 2400 \\
3 & 5 & 0 & 1 & 0 & 9200 \\
\hdashline
-\frac{3}{4} & -\frac{1}{2} & 0 & 0 & 1 & 0
\end{array}
\right]
\begin{array}{c} 1200 \\ 3066\frac{2}{3} \\ \end{array}
\end{array}
$$

$$
\begin{array}{c}
\begin{array}{ccccc} x_1 & x_2 & s_1 & s_2 & R \end{array} \\
\begin{array}{c} x_1 \\ s_2 \\ R \end{array}
\left[
\begin{array}{ccccc|c}
1 & \frac{1}{2} & \frac{1}{2} & 0 & 0 & 1200 \\
0 & \frac{7}{2} & -\frac{3}{2} & 1 & 0 & 5600 \\
\hdashline
0 & -\frac{1}{8} & \frac{3}{8} & 0 & 1 & 900
\end{array}
\right]
\begin{array}{c} 2400 \\ 1600 \\ \end{array}
\end{array}
$$

$$
\begin{array}{c}
\begin{array}{ccccc} x_1 & x_2 & s_1 & s_2 & R \end{array} \\
\begin{array}{c} x_1 \\ x_2 \\ R \end{array}
\left[
\begin{array}{ccccc|c}
1 & 0 & \frac{5}{7} & -\frac{1}{7} & 0 & 400 \\
0 & 1 & -\frac{3}{7} & \frac{2}{7} & 0 & 1600 \\
\hdashline
0 & 0 & \frac{9}{28} & \frac{1}{28} & 1 & 1100
\end{array}
\right]
\end{array}
$$

Thus 400 boxes from A and 1600 from B give a maximum revenue of $1100.

19. Let x_1, x_2, and x_3 denote the numbers of chairs, rockers, and chaise lounges produced, respectively. We want to maximize

$R = 7x_1 + 8x_2 + 12x_3$ subject to

$$
\begin{aligned}
x_1 + x_2 + x_3 &\le 400, \\
x_1 + x_2 + 2x_3 &\le 500, \\
2x_1 + 3x_2 + 5x_3 &\le 1450, \\
x_1,\ x_2,\ x_3 &\ge 0.
\end{aligned}
$$

$$
\begin{array}{c}
\begin{array}{ccccccc} x_1 & x_2 & x_3 & s_1 & s_2 & s_3 & R \end{array} \\
\begin{array}{c} s_1 \\ s_2 \\ s_3 \\ R \end{array}
\left[
\begin{array}{ccccccc|c}
1 & 1 & 1 & 1 & 0 & 0 & 0 & 400 \\
1 & 1 & \underline{2} & 0 & 1 & 0 & 0 & 500 \\
2 & 3 & 5 & 0 & 0 & 1 & 0 & 1450 \\
\hdashline
-7 & -8 & -12 & 0 & 0 & 0 & 1 & 0
\end{array}
\right]
\begin{array}{c} 400 \\ 250 \\ 290 \\ \end{array}
\end{array}
$$

$$
\begin{array}{c}
\begin{array}{ccccccc} x_1 & x_2 & x_3 & s_1 & s_2 & s_3 & R \end{array} \\
\begin{array}{c} s_1 \\ x_3 \\ s_3 \\ R \end{array}
\left[
\begin{array}{ccccccc|c}
\frac{1}{2} & \frac{1}{2} & 0 & 1 & -\frac{1}{2} & 0 & 0 & 150 \\
\frac{1}{2} & \frac{1}{2} & 1 & 0 & \frac{1}{2} & 0 & 0 & 250 \\
-\frac{1}{2} & \frac{1}{2} & 0 & 0 & -\frac{5}{2} & 1 & 0 & 200 \\
\hdashline
-1 & -2 & 0 & 0 & 6 & 0 & 1 & 3000
\end{array}
\right]
\begin{array}{c} 300 \\ 500 \\ 400 \\ \end{array}
\end{array}
$$

$$
\begin{array}{c}
\begin{array}{ccccccc} x_1 & x_2 & x_3 & s_1 & s_2 & s_3 & R \end{array} \\
\begin{array}{c} x_2 \\ x_3 \\ s_3 \\ R \end{array}
\left[
\begin{array}{ccccccc|c}
1 & 1 & 0 & 2 & -1 & 0 & 0 & 300 \\
0 & 0 & 1 & -1 & 1 & 0 & 0 & 100 \\
-1 & 0 & 0 & -1 & -2 & 1 & 0 & 50 \\
\hdashline
1 & 0 & 0 & 4 & 4 & 0 & 1 & 3600
\end{array}
\right]
\end{array}
$$

The production of 0 chairs, 300 rockers, and 100 chaise lounges gives the maximum revenue of $3600.

Principles in Practice 7.5

1. Let x_1, x_2, x_3 be the numbers of device 1, device 2, and device 3, respectively, that the company produces. The situation is to maximize the profit $P = 50x_1 + 50x_2 + 50x_3$ subject to the constraints
$$5.5x_1 + 5.5x_2 + 6.5x_3 \leq 190,$$
$$3.5x_1 + 6.5x_2 + 7.5x_3 \leq 180,$$
$$4.5x_1 + 6.0x_2 + 6.5x_3 \leq 165,$$
and x_1, x_2, $x_3 \geq 0$.

The matrices are shown rounded to 2 decimal places, although the exact values are used in the row operations. Since the indicators are equal, we choose the first column as the pivot column.

	x_1	x_2	x_3	s_1	s_2	s_3	P	b
s_1	5.5	5.5	6.5	1	0	0	0	190
s_2	3.5	6.5	7.5	0	1	0	0	180
s_3	4.5	6.0	6.5	0	0	1	0	165
P	−50	−50	−50	0	0	0	1	0

	x_1	x_2	x_2	s_1	s_2	s_3	P	b
x_1	1	1	1.18	0.18	0	0	0	34.55
s_2	0	3	3.36	−0.64	1	0	0	59.09
s_3	0	1.50	1.18	−0.82	0	1	0	9.55
P	0	0	9.09	9.09	0	0	1	1727.27

An optimum solution is $x_1 = 35$, $x_2 = 0$, $x_3 = 0$, and $P = 1727$. However, x_2 is a nonbasic variable and its indicator is 0, so we check for multiple solutions. Treating x_2 as an entering variable, the following tableau is obtained:

	x_1	x_2	x_3	s_1	s_2	s_3	P	b
x_1	1	0	0.39	0.73	0	−0.67	0	28.18
s_2	0	0	1.00	1.00	1	−2.00	0	40.00
x_2	0	1	0.79	−0.55	0	0.67	0	6.36
P	0	0	9.09	9.09	0	0	1	1727.27

Another optimum solution is $x_1 = 28$, $x_2 = 6$, $x_3 = 0$, and $P = 1727$.

Thus, the optimum solution is for the company to produce $(1 - t)35 + 28t = 35 - 7t$ of device 1, $(1 - t)0 + 6t = 6t$ of device 2, and none of device 3, for $0 \leq t \leq 1$.

Exercise 7.5

1. Yes; for the tableau, x_2 is the entering variable and the quotients $\dfrac{6}{2}$ and $\dfrac{3}{1}$ tie for being the smallest.

3.

	x_1	x_2	s_1	s_2	s_3	Z	
s_1	4	−3	1	0	0	0	4
s_2	3	−1	0	1	0	0	6
s_3	5	0	0	0	1	0	8
Z	−2	−7	0	0	0	1	0

The entering variable is x_2. Since no quotients exist, the problem has an unbounded solution. Thus, no optimum solution (unbounded).

5.

	x_1	x_2	s_1	s_2	s_3	Z		
s_1	1	–1	1	0	0	0	4	4
s_2	–1	1	0	1	0	0	4	
s_3	1	1	0	0	1	0	6	6
Z	–3	3	0	0	0	1	0	

	x_1	x_2	s_1	s_2	s_3	Z		
x_1	1	–1	1	0	0	0	4	
s_2	0	0	1	1	0	0	8	
s_3	0	2	–1	0	1	0	2	1
Z	0	0	3	0	0	1	12	

The maximum value of Z is 12, when $x_1 = 4$, $x_2 = 0$. Since x_2 is nonbasic for the last tableau and its indicator is 0, there may be multiple optimum solutions. Treating x_2 as an entering variable and continuing, we have

	x_1	x_2	s_1	s_2	s_3	Z	
x_1	1	0	$\frac{1}{2}$	0	$\frac{1}{2}$	0	5
s_2	0	0	1	1	0	0	8
x_2	0	1	$-\frac{1}{2}$	0	$\frac{1}{2}$	0	1
Z	0	0	3	0	0	1	12

Here $Z = 12$ when $x_1 = 5$, $x_2 = 1$. Thus multiple optimum solutions exist. Hence Z is maximum when $x_1 = (1-t)(4) + 5t = 4 + t$, $x_2 = (1-t)(0) + (1)t = t$, and $0 \le t \le 1$. For the last tableau, s_3 is nonbasic and its indicator is 0. If we continue the process for determining other optimum solutions, we return to the second tableau.

7.

	x_1	x_2	x_3	s_1	s_2	s_3	Z		
s_1	9	3	–2	1	0	0	0	5	$\frac{5}{3}$
s_2	4	2	–1	0	1	0	0	2	1
s_3	1	–4	1	0	0	1	0	3	
Z	–5	–6	–1	0	0	0	1	0	

	x_1	x_2	x_3	s_1	s_2	s_3	Z	
s_1	3	0	$-\frac{1}{2}$	1	$-\frac{3}{2}$	0	0	2
x_2	2	1	$-\frac{1}{2}$	0	$\frac{1}{2}$	0	0	1
s_3	9	0	–1	0	2	1	0	7
Z	7	0	–4	0	3	0	1	6

For the last tableau, x_3 is the entering variable. Since no quotients exist, the problem has an unbounded solution. Thus, no optimum solution (unbounded).

9. To obtain a standard linear programming problem, we write the second constraint as $4x_1 + x_2 \le 6$.

$$\begin{array}{c} \\ s_1 \\ s_2 \\ Z \end{array} \begin{array}{c} x_1 \quad x_2 \quad x_3 \quad s_1 \quad s_2 \quad Z \\ \left[\begin{array}{cccccc|c} 2 & 1 & 1 & 1 & 0 & 0 & 7 \\ 4 & 1 & 0 & 0 & 1 & 0 & 6 \\ \hline -6 & -2 & -1 & 0 & 0 & 1 & 0 \end{array} \right] \begin{array}{c} \frac{7}{2} \\ \frac{3}{2} \\ \end{array} \end{array}$$

$$\begin{array}{c} \\ s_1 \\ x_1 \\ Z \end{array} \begin{array}{c} x_1 \quad x_2 \quad x_3 \quad s_1 \quad s_2 \quad Z \\ \left[\begin{array}{cccccc|c} 0 & \frac{1}{2} & 1 & 1 & -\frac{1}{2} & 0 & 4 \\ 1 & \frac{1}{4} & 0 & 0 & \frac{1}{4} & 0 & \frac{3}{2} \\ \hline 0 & -\frac{1}{2} & -1 & 0 & \frac{3}{2} & 1 & 9 \end{array} \right] \begin{array}{c} 4 \\ \\ \end{array} \end{array}$$

$$\begin{array}{c} \\ x_3 \\ x_1 \\ Z \end{array} \begin{array}{c} x_1 \quad x_2 \quad x_3 \quad s_1 \quad s_2 \quad Z \\ \left[\begin{array}{cccccc|c} 0 & \frac{1}{2} & 1 & 1 & -\frac{1}{2} & 0 & 4 \\ 1 & \frac{1}{4} & 0 & 0 & \frac{1}{4} & 0 & \frac{3}{2} \\ \hline 0 & 0 & 0 & 1 & 1 & 1 & 13 \end{array} \right] \begin{array}{c} 8 \\ 6 \\ \end{array} \end{array}$$

Z has a maximum value of 13 when $x_1 = \frac{3}{2}$, $x_2 = 0$, $x_3 = 4$. Since x_2 is nonbasic for the last tableau and its indicator is 0, there may be multiple optimum solutions. Treating x_2 as an entering variable, we have

$$\begin{array}{c} \\ x_3 \\ x_2 \\ Z \end{array} \begin{array}{c} x_1 \quad x_2 \quad x_3 \quad s_1 \quad s_2 \quad Z \\ \left[\begin{array}{cccccc|c} -2 & 0 & 1 & 1 & -1 & 0 & 1 \\ 4 & 1 & 0 & 0 & 1 & 0 & 6 \\ \hline 0 & 0 & 0 & 1 & 1 & 1 & 13 \end{array} \right] \end{array}$$

Here $Z = 13$ when $x_1 = 0$, $x_2 = 6$, $x_3 = 1$. Thus multiple optimum solutions exist. Hence Z is maximum when

$$x_1 = (1-t)\left(\frac{3}{2}\right) + 0t = \frac{3}{2} - \frac{3}{2}t,$$
$$x_2 = (1-t)(0) + 6t = 6t,$$
$x_3 = (1-t)(4) + (1)t = 4 - 3t$, and $0 \le t \le 1$. For the last tableau, x_1 is nonbasic and its indicator is 0. If we continue the process for determining other optimum solutions, we return to the third tableau.

11. Let x_1, x_2, and x_3 denote the numbers of chairs, rockers, and chaise lounges produced, respectively. We want to maximize $R = 6x_1 + 8x_2 + 12x_3$ subject to
$x_1 + x_2 + x_3 \le 400$,
$x_1 + x_2 + 2x_3 \le 600$,
$2x_1 + 3x_2 + 5x_3 \le 1500$,
$x_1,\ x_2,\ x_3 \ge 0$.

$$\begin{array}{c} \\ s_1 \\ s_2 \\ s_3 \\ R \end{array} \begin{array}{c} x_1 \quad x_2 \quad x_3 \quad s_1 \quad s_2 \quad s_3 \quad R \\ \left[\begin{array}{ccccccc|c} 1 & 1 & 1 & 1 & 0 & 0 & 0 & 400 \\ 1 & 1 & 2 & 0 & 1 & 0 & 0 & 600 \\ 2 & 3 & 5 & 0 & 0 & 1 & 0 & 1500 \\ \hline -6 & -8 & -12 & 0 & 0 & 0 & 1 & 0 \end{array} \right] \begin{array}{c} 400 \\ 300 \\ 300 \\ \end{array} \end{array}$$

choosing s_3 as departing variable

	x_1	x_2	x_3	s_1	s_2	s_3	R		
s_1	$\frac{3}{5}$	$\frac{2}{5}$	0	1	0	$-\frac{1}{5}$	0	100	$\frac{500}{3}$
s_2	$\frac{1}{5}$	$-\frac{1}{5}$	0	0	1	$-\frac{2}{5}$	0	0	0
x_3	$\frac{2}{5}$	$\frac{3}{5}$	1	0	0	$\frac{1}{5}$	0	300	750
R	$-\frac{6}{5}$	$-\frac{4}{5}$	0	0	0	$\frac{12}{5}$	1	3600	

	x_1	x_2	x_3	s_1	s_2	s_3	R		
s_1	0	1	0	1	–3	1	0	100	100
x_1	1	–1	0	0	5	–2	0	0	0
x_3	0	1	1	0	–2	1	0	300	300
R	0	–2	0	0	6	0	1	3600	

	x_1	x_2	x_3	s_1	s_2	s_3	R		
x_2	0	1	0	1	–3	1	0	100	
x_1	1	0	0	1	2	–1	0	100	50
x_3	0	0	1	–1	1	0	0	200	200
R	0	0	0	2	0	2	1	3800	

The maximum value of R is 3800 when $x_1 = 100$, $x_2 = 100$, $x_3 = 200$. Since s_2 is nonbasic for the last tableau and its indicator is 0, there may be multiple optimum solutions. Treating s_2 as an entering variable, we have

	x_1	x_2	x_3	s_1	s_2	s_3	R	
x_2	$\frac{3}{2}$	1	0	$\frac{5}{2}$	0	$-\frac{1}{2}$	0	250
s_2	$\frac{1}{2}$	0	0	$\frac{1}{2}$	1	$-\frac{1}{2}$	0	50
x_3	$-\frac{1}{2}$	0	1	$-\frac{3}{2}$	0	$\frac{1}{2}$	0	150
R	0	0	0	2	0	2	1	3800

Here $R = 3800$ when $x_1 = 0$, $x_2 = 250$, $x_3 = 150$. Thus multiple optimum solutions exist. Hence R is maximum when

$x_1 = (1-t)(100) + 0t = 100 - 100t,$

$x_2 = (1-t)(100) + 250t = 100 + 150t$

$x_3 = (1-t)(200) + 150t = 200 - 50t,$ and

$0 \le t \le 1$. For the last tableau, x_1 is nonbasic and its indicator is 0. If we continue the process for determining other optimum solutions, we return to the fourth tableau. If we were to initially choose s_2 as the departing variable, then

	x_1	x_2	x_3	s_1	s_2	s_3	R		
s_1	1	1	1	1	0	0	0	400	400
s_2	1	1	2	0	1	0	0	600	300
s_3	2	3	5	0	0	1	0	1500	300
R	–6	–8	–12	0	0	0	1	0	

	x_1	x_2	x_3	s_1	s_2	s_3	R		
s_1	$\frac{1}{2}$	$\frac{1}{2}$	0	1	$-\frac{1}{2}$	0	0	100	200
x_3	$\frac{1}{2}$	$\frac{1}{2}$	1	0	$\frac{1}{2}$	0	0	300	600
s_3	$-\frac{1}{2}$	$\frac{1}{2}$	0	0	$-\frac{5}{2}$	1	0	0	0
R	0	-2	0	0	6	0	1	3600	

	x_1	x_2	x_3	s_1	s_2	s_3	R		
s_1	1	0	0	1	2	-1	0	100	50
x_3	1	0	1	0	3	-1	0	300	100
x_2	-1	1	0	0	-5	2	0	0	
R	-2	0	0	0	-4	4	1	3600	

	x_1	x_2	x_3	s_1	s_2	s_3	R		
s_2	$\frac{1}{2}$	0	0	$\frac{1}{2}$	1	$-\frac{1}{2}$	0	50	100
x_3	$-\frac{1}{2}$	0	1	$-\frac{3}{2}$	0	$\frac{1}{2}$	0	150	
x_2	$\frac{3}{2}$	1	0	$\frac{5}{2}$	0	$-\frac{1}{2}$	0	250	$\frac{500}{3}$
R	0	0	0	2	0	2	1	3800	

the maximum value of R is 3800 when $x_1 = 0$, $x_2 = 250$, $x_3 = 150$. For the last tableau, x_1 is nonbasic and its indicator is 0. Treating x_1 as an entering variable, we have

	x_1	x_2	x_3	s_1	s_2	s_3	R	
x_1	1	0	0	1	2	-1	0	100
x_3	0	0	1	-1	1	0	0	200
x_2	0	1	0	1	-3	1	0	100
R	0	0	0	2	0	2	1	3800

Here $R = 3800$ when $x_1 = 100$, $x_2 = 100$, $x_3 = 200$. For the last tableau, s_2 is nonbasic and its indicator is 0. If we continue the process of determining other optimum solutions, we return to the tableau corresponding to the solution $x_1 = 0$, $x_2 = 250$, $x_3 = 150$.

Thus, the maximum revenue is \$3800 when $x_1 = 100 - 100t$, $x_2 = 100 + 150t$, $x_3 = 200 - 50t$, and $0 \le t \le 1$

Principles in Practice 7.6

1. Using the hint, $1000 - x_1$ standard and $800 - x_2$ deluxe snowboards must be manufactured at plant II. The constraints for plant I are $x_1 + x_2 \le 1200$ and $x_2 - x_1 \le 200$. The constraints for plant II are $(1000 - x_1) + (800 - x_2) \le 1000$ or $x_1 + x_2 \ge 800$. The quantity to be maximized is the profit
$P = 40x_1 + 60x_2 + 45(1000 - x_1) + 50(800 - x_2)$
$= -5x_1 + 10x_2 + 85,000$ subject to the constraints
$x_1 + x_2 \le 1200,$
$-x_1 + x_2 \le 200,$
$x_1 + x_2 \ge 800,$
and $x_1,\ x_2 \ge 0$.
Note that maximizing $Z = -5x_1 + 10x_2$ also maximizes the profit. The corresponding equations are:

$$x_1 + x_2 + s_1 = 1200,$$
$$-x_1 + x_2 + s_2 = 200,$$
$$x_1 + x_2 - s_3 + t = 800.$$

The artificial objective equation is
$$W = -5x_1 + 10x_2 - Mt.$$

The augmented coefficient matrix is:

	x_1	x_2	s_1	s_2	s_3	t	w	
	1	1	1	0	0	0	0	1200
	−1	1	0	1	0	0	0	200
	1	1	0	0	−1	1	0	800
	5	−10	0	0	0	M	1	0

The simplex tableaux follow.

	x_1	x_2	s_1	s_2	t	W	
s_1	1	1	1	0	0	0	1200
s_2	−1	1	0	0	0	0	200
t_1	1	1	0	−1	1	0	800
W	$5 - M$	$-10 - M$	0	M	0	1	$-800M$

	x_1	x_2	s_1	s_2	t	W	
s_1	2	0	1	0	0	0	1000
x_2	−1	1	0	0	0	0	200
t_1	2	0	0	−1	1	0	600
W	$-5 - 2M$	0	0	M	0	1	$2000 - 600M$

	x_1	x_2	s_1	s_2	t	W	
s_1	0	0	1	1	−1	0	400
x_2	0	1	0	$-\frac{1}{2}$	$\frac{1}{2}$	0	500
x_1	1	0	0	$-\frac{1}{2}$	$\frac{1}{2}$	0	300
W	0	0	0	$-\frac{3}{2}$	$\frac{5}{2} + M$	1	3500

Delete the t-column since $t = 0$ and return to Z.

	x_1	x_2	s_1	s_2	Z	
s_2	0	0	1	1	0	400
x_2	0	1	$\frac{1}{2}$	0	0	700
x_1	1	0	$\frac{1}{2}$	0	0	500
Z	0	0	$\frac{5}{2}$	0	1	4500

Thus, $x_1 = 500$, $x_2 = 700$, and $Z = 4500$. Plant I should manufacture 500 standard and 700 deluxe snowboards. Plant II should manufacture
$1000 - 500 = 500$ standard and
$800 - 700 = 100$ deluxe snowboards. The maximum profit is
$P = -5(500) + 10(700) + 85,000 = \$89,500.$

Exercise 7.6

1.

$$
\begin{array}{c}
\begin{array}{cccccc} x_1 & x_2 & s_1 & s_2 & t_2 & W \end{array} \\
\left[\begin{array}{cccccc|c}
1 & 1 & 1 & 0 & 0 & 0 & 6 \\
-1 & 1 & 0 & -1 & 1 & 0 & 4 \\
\hline
-2 & -1 & 0 & 0 & M & 1 & 0
\end{array}\right]
\end{array}
$$

$$
\begin{array}{c}
\begin{array}{cccccc} x_1 & x_2 & s_1 & s_2 & t_2 & W \end{array} \\
\begin{array}{c} s_1 \\ t_2 \\ W \end{array}
\left[\begin{array}{cccccc|c}
1 & 1 & 1 & 0 & 0 & 0 & 6 \\
-1 & \underline{1} & 0 & -1 & 1 & 0 & 4 \\
\hline
-2+M & -1-M & 0 & M & 0 & 1 & -4M
\end{array}\right]
\begin{array}{c} 6 \\ 4 \\ \end{array}
\end{array}
$$

$$
\begin{array}{c}
\begin{array}{cccccc} x_1 & x_2 & s_1 & s_2 & t_2 & W \end{array} \\
\begin{array}{c} s_1 \\ x_2 \\ W \end{array}
\left[\begin{array}{cccccc|c}
\underline{2} & 0 & 1 & 1 & -1 & 0 & 2 \\
-1 & 1 & 0 & -1 & 1 & 0 & 4 \\
\hline
-3 & 0 & 0 & -1 & M+1 & 1 & 4
\end{array}\right]
\begin{array}{c} 1 \\ \\ \end{array}
\end{array}
$$

$$
\begin{array}{c}
\begin{array}{ccccc} x_1 & x_2 & s_1 & s_2 & Z \end{array} \\
\begin{array}{c} x_1 \\ x_2 \\ Z \end{array}
\left[\begin{array}{ccccc|c}
1 & 0 & \frac{1}{2} & \frac{1}{2} & 0 & 1 \\
0 & 1 & \frac{1}{2} & -\frac{1}{2} & 0 & 5 \\
\hline
0 & 0 & \frac{3}{2} & \frac{1}{2} & 1 & 7
\end{array}\right]
\end{array}
$$

The maximum is $Z = 7$ when $x_1 = 1$, $x_2 = 5$.

3.

$$
\begin{array}{c}
\begin{array}{ccccccc} x_1 & x_2 & x_3 & s_1 & s_2 & t_2 & W \end{array} \\
\left[\begin{array}{ccccccc|c}
1 & 2 & 1 & 1 & 0 & 0 & 0 & 5 \\
-1 & 1 & 1 & 0 & -1 & 1 & 0 & 1 \\
\hline
-2 & -1 & 1 & 0 & 0 & M & 1 & 0
\end{array}\right]
\end{array}
$$

$$
\begin{array}{c}
\begin{array}{ccccccc} x_1 & x_2 & x_3 & s_1 & s_2 & t_2 & W \end{array} \\
\begin{array}{c} s_1 \\ t_2 \\ W \end{array}
\left[\begin{array}{ccccccc|c}
1 & 2 & 1 & 1 & 0 & 0 & 0 & 5 \\
-1 & \underline{1} & 1 & 0 & -1 & 1 & 0 & 1 \\
\hline
-2+M & -1-M & 1-M & 0 & M & 0 & 1 & -M
\end{array}\right]
\begin{array}{c} \frac{5}{2} \\ 1 \\ \end{array}
\end{array}
$$

$$
\begin{array}{c}
\begin{array}{ccccccc} x_1 & x_2 & x_3 & s_1 & s_2 & t_2 & W \end{array} \\
\begin{array}{c} s_1 \\ x_2 \\ W \end{array}
\left[\begin{array}{ccccccc|c}
\underline{3} & 0 & -1 & 1 & 2 & -2 & 0 & 3 \\
-1 & 1 & 1 & 0 & -1 & 1 & 0 & 1 \\
\hline
-3 & 0 & 2 & 0 & -1 & 1+M & 1 & 1
\end{array}\right]
\begin{array}{c} 1 \\ \\ \end{array}
\end{array}
$$

$$\begin{array}{c} \\ x_1 \\ x_2 \\ Z \end{array} \begin{array}{cccccc} x_1 & x_2 & x_3 & s_1 & s_2 & Z \\ \left[\begin{array}{cccccc|c} 1 & 0 & -\frac{1}{3} & \frac{1}{3} & \frac{2}{3} & 0 & 1 \\ 0 & 1 & \frac{2}{3} & \frac{1}{3} & -\frac{1}{3} & 0 & 2 \\ \hline 0 & 0 & 1 & 1 & 1 & 1 & 4 \end{array}\right] \end{array}$$

The maximum is $Z = 4$ when $x_1 = 1$, $x_2 = 2$, $x_3 = 0$.

5.

$$\begin{array}{ccccccc} x_1 & x_2 & x_3 & s_1 & t_2 & W \\ \left[\begin{array}{cccccc|c} 2 & 1 & 3 & 1 & 0 & 0 & 10 \\ 1 & -1 & 1 & 0 & 1 & 0 & 4 \\ \hline -4 & -1 & -2 & 0 & M & 1 & 0 \end{array}\right] \end{array}$$

$$\begin{array}{c} \\ s_1 \\ t_2 \\ W \end{array} \begin{array}{cccccc} x_1 & x_2 & x_3 & s_1 & t_2 & W \\ \left[\begin{array}{cccccc|c} 2 & 1 & 3 & 1 & 0 & 0 & 10 \\ 1 & -1 & 1 & 0 & 1 & 0 & 4 \\ \hline -4-M & -1+M & -2-M & 0 & 0 & 1 & -4M \end{array}\right] \begin{array}{c} 5 \\ 4 \\ \end{array} \end{array}$$

$$\begin{array}{c} \\ s_1 \\ x_1 \\ W \end{array} \begin{array}{cccccc} x_1 & x_2 & x_3 & s_1 & t_2 & W \\ \left[\begin{array}{cccccc|c} 0 & \underline{3} & 1 & 1 & -2 & 0 & 2 \\ 1 & -1 & 1 & 0 & 1 & 0 & 4 \\ \hline 0 & -5 & 2 & 0 & 4+M & 1 & 16 \end{array}\right] \begin{array}{c} \frac{2}{3} \\ \\ \end{array} \end{array}$$

$$\begin{array}{c} \\ x_2 \\ x_1 \\ Z \end{array} \begin{array}{ccccc} x_1 & x_2 & x_3 & s_1 & Z \\ \left[\begin{array}{ccccc|c} 0 & 1 & \frac{1}{3} & \frac{1}{3} & 0 & \frac{2}{3} \\ 1 & 0 & \frac{4}{3} & \frac{1}{3} & 0 & \frac{14}{3} \\ \hline 0 & 0 & \frac{11}{3} & \frac{5}{3} & 1 & \frac{58}{3} \end{array}\right] \end{array}$$

The maximum is $Z = \dfrac{58}{3}$ when $x_1 = \dfrac{14}{3}$, $x_2 = \dfrac{2}{3}$, $x_3 = 0$.

7.

$$\begin{array}{ccccccc} x_1 & x_2 & s_1 & s_2 & s_3 & t_3 & W \\ \left[\begin{array}{ccccccc|c} 1 & -1 & 1 & 0 & 0 & 0 & 0 & 1 \\ 1 & 2 & 0 & 1 & 0 & 0 & 0 & 8 \\ 1 & 1 & 0 & 0 & -1 & 1 & 0 & 5 \\ \hline -1 & 10 & 0 & 0 & 0 & M & 1 & 0 \end{array}\right] \end{array}$$

$$
\begin{array}{c}
\begin{array}{c@{\quad}c@{\quad}c@{\ }c@{\ }c@{\ }c@{\ }c} & x_1 & x_2 & s_1 & s_2 & s_3 & t_3 & W \end{array}\\
\begin{array}{c}
s_1 \\ s_2 \\ t_3 \\ W
\end{array}
\left[
\begin{array}{ccccccc|c}
\underline{1} & -1 & 1 & 0 & 0 & 0 & 0 & 1 \\
1 & 2 & 0 & 1 & 0 & 0 & 0 & 8 \\
1 & 1 & 0 & 0 & -1 & 1 & 0 & 5 \\
\hdashline
-1-M & 10-M & 0 & 0 & M & 0 & 1 & -5M
\end{array}
\right]
\begin{array}{c} 1 \\ 8 \\ 5 \\ \\ \end{array}
\end{array}
$$

$$
\begin{array}{c}
\begin{array}{c@{\quad}c@{\quad}c@{\ }c@{\ }c@{\ }c@{\ }c} & x_1 & x_2 & s_1 & s_2 & s_3 & t_3 & W \end{array}\\
\begin{array}{c}
x_1 \\ s_2 \\ t_3 \\ W
\end{array}
\left[
\begin{array}{ccccccc|c}
1 & -1 & 1 & 0 & 0 & 0 & 0 & 1 \\
0 & 3 & -1 & 1 & 0 & 0 & 0 & 7 \\
0 & \underline{2} & -1 & 0 & -1 & 1 & 0 & 4 \\
\hdashline
0 & 9-2M & 1+M & 0 & M & 0 & 1 & 1-4M
\end{array}
\right]
\begin{array}{c} \frac{7}{3} \\ 2 \\ \\ \end{array}
\end{array}
$$

$$
\begin{array}{c}
\begin{array}{c@{\ }c@{\ }c@{\ }c@{\ }c@{\ }c@{\ }c} & x_1 & x_2 & s_1 & s_2 & s_3 & t_3 & W \end{array}\\
\begin{array}{c}
x_1 \\ s_2 \\ x_2 \\ W
\end{array}
\left[
\begin{array}{ccccccc|c}
1 & 0 & \frac{1}{2} & 0 & -\frac{1}{2} & \frac{1}{2} & 0 & 3 \\
0 & 0 & \frac{1}{2} & 1 & \frac{3}{2} & -\frac{3}{2} & 0 & 1 \\
0 & 1 & -\frac{1}{2} & 0 & -\frac{1}{2} & \frac{1}{2} & 0 & 2 \\
\hdashline
0 & 0 & \frac{11}{2} & 0 & \frac{9}{2} & -\frac{9}{2}+M & 1 & -17
\end{array}
\right]
\end{array}
$$

For the above tableau, $t_3 = 0$. Thus $W = Z$.

The maximum is $Z = -17$ when $x_1 = 3$, $x_2 = 2$.

9. We first write the third constraint as $-x_1 + x_2 + x_3 \geq 6$.

$$
\begin{array}{c}
\begin{array}{c@{\ }c@{\ }c@{\ }c@{\ }c@{\ }c@{\ }c@{\ }c@{\ }c} x_1 & x_2 & x_3 & s_1 & s_2 & s_3 & t_2 & t_3 & W \end{array}\\
\left[
\begin{array}{ccccccccc|c}
1 & 1 & 1 & 1 & 0 & 0 & 0 & 0 & 0 & 1 \\
1 & -1 & 1 & 0 & -1 & 0 & 1 & 0 & 0 & 2 \\
-1 & 1 & 1 & 0 & 0 & -1 & 0 & 1 & 0 & 6 \\
\hdashline
-3 & 2 & -1 & 0 & 0 & 0 & M & M & 1 & 0
\end{array}
\right]
\end{array}
$$

$$
\begin{array}{c}
\begin{array}{c@{\ }c@{\ }c@{\ }c@{\ }c@{\ }c@{\ }c@{\ }c@{\ }c} & x_1 & x_2 & x_3 & s_1 & s_2 & s_3 & t_2 & t_3 & W \end{array}\\
\begin{array}{c} s_1 \\ t_2 \\ t_3 \\ W \end{array}
\left[
\begin{array}{ccccccccc|c}
1 & 1 & \underline{1} & 1 & 0 & 0 & 0 & 0 & 0 & 1 \\
1 & -1 & 1 & 0 & -1 & 0 & 1 & 0 & 0 & 2 \\
-1 & 1 & 1 & 0 & 0 & -1 & 0 & 1 & 0 & 6 \\
\hdashline
-3 & 2 & -1-2M & 0 & M & M & 0 & 0 & 1 & -8M
\end{array}
\right]
\begin{array}{c} 1 \\ 2 \\ 6 \\ \\ \end{array}
\end{array}
$$

$$
\begin{array}{c}
\begin{array}{c@{\ }c@{\ }c@{\ }c@{\ }c@{\ }c@{\ }c@{\ }c@{\ }c} & x_1 & x_2 & x_3 & s_1 & s_2 & s_3 & t_2 & t_3 & W \end{array}\\
\begin{array}{c} x_3 \\ t_2 \\ t_3 \\ W \end{array}
\left[
\begin{array}{ccccccccc|c}
1 & 1 & 1 & 1 & 0 & 0 & 0 & 0 & 0 & 1 \\
0 & -2 & 0 & -1 & -1 & 0 & 1 & 0 & 0 & 1 \\
-2 & 0 & 0 & -1 & 0 & -1 & 0 & 1 & 0 & 5 \\
\hdashline
-2+2M & 3+2M & 0 & 1+2M & M & M & 0 & 0 & 1 & 1-6M
\end{array}
\right]
\end{array}
$$

There is no solution (empty feasible region).

11.

$$\begin{array}{ccccccc} x_1 & x_2 & s_1 & s_3 & t_2 & t_3 & W \\ \end{array}$$

$$\left[\begin{array}{ccccccc|c} 1 & -1 & 1 & 0 & 0 & 0 & 0 & 4 \\ -1 & 1 & 0 & 0 & 1 & 0 & 0 & 4 \\ 1 & 0 & 0 & -1 & 0 & 1 & 0 & 6 \\ \hline 3 & -2 & 0 & 0 & M & M & 1 & 0 \end{array}\right]$$

$$\begin{array}{cccccccc} & x_1 & x_2 & s_1 & s_3 & t_2 & t_3 & W \\ \end{array}$$

$$\begin{array}{c} s_1 \\ t_2 \\ t_3 \\ W \end{array}\left[\begin{array}{ccccccc|c} 1 & -1 & 1 & 0 & 0 & 0 & 0 & 4 \\ -1 & \underline{1} & 0 & 0 & 1 & 0 & 0 & 4 \\ 1 & 0 & 0 & -1 & 0 & 1 & 0 & 6 \\ \hline 3 & -2-M & 0 & M & 0 & 0 & 1 & -10M \end{array}\right]\begin{array}{c} \\ 4 \\ \\ \end{array}$$

$$\begin{array}{cccccccc} & x_1 & x_2 & s_1 & s_2 & s_3 & t_2 & t_3 & W \\ \end{array}$$

$$\begin{array}{c} s_1 \\ x_2 \\ t_3 \\ W \end{array}\left[\begin{array}{cccccccc|c} 0 & 0 & 1 & 0 & 1 & 0 & 0 & 8 \\ -1 & 1 & 0 & 0 & 1 & 0 & 0 & 4 \\ \underline{1} & 0 & 0 & -1 & 0 & 1 & 0 & 6 \\ \hline 1-M & 0 & 0 & M & 2+M & 0 & 1 & 8-6M \end{array}\right]\begin{array}{c} \\ \\ 6 \\ \end{array}$$

$$\begin{array}{cccccccc} & x_1 & x_2 & s_1 & s_2 & s_3 & t_2 & t_3 & W \\ \end{array}$$

$$\begin{array}{c} s_1 \\ x_2 \\ x_1 \\ W \end{array}\left[\begin{array}{cccccccc|c} 0 & 0 & 1 & 0 & 1 & 0 & 0 & 8 \\ 0 & 1 & 0 & -1 & 1 & 1 & 0 & 10 \\ 1 & 0 & 0 & -1 & 0 & 1 & 0 & 6 \\ \hline 0 & 0 & 0 & 1 & 2+M & -1+M & 1 & 2 \end{array}\right]$$

For the above tableau, $t_2 = t_3 = 0$. Thus $W = Z$.
The maximum is $Z = 2$ when $x_1 = 6$, $x_2 = 10$.

13. Let x_1 and x_2 denote the numbers of Standard and Executive bookcases produced, respectively, each week. We want to maximize the profit function $P = 10x_1 + 12x_2$ subject to

$$\begin{aligned} x_1 + 2x_2 &\le 400, \\ 2x_1 + 3x_2 &\le 510, \\ 2x_1 + 3x_2 &\ge 240, \\ x_1, \ x_2 &\ge 0. \end{aligned}$$

The artificial objective function is $W = P - Mt_3$.

$$\begin{array}{ccccccc} x_1 & x_2 & s_1 & s_2 & s_3 & t_3 & W \\ \end{array}$$

$$\left[\begin{array}{ccccccc|c} 1 & 2 & 1 & 0 & 0 & 0 & 0 & 400 \\ 2 & 3 & 0 & 1 & 0 & 0 & 0 & 510 \\ 2 & 3 & 0 & 0 & -1 & 1 & 0 & 240 \\ \hline -10 & -12 & 0 & 0 & 0 & M & 1 & 0 \end{array}\right]$$

$$
\begin{array}{c c}
\begin{array}{c}
s_1 \\
s_2 \\
t_3 \\
W
\end{array}
&
\begin{array}{c}
\begin{array}{ccccccc}
x_1 & x_2 & s_1 & s_2 & s_3 & t_3 & W
\end{array} \\
\left[
\begin{array}{ccccccc|c}
1 & 2 & 1 & 0 & 0 & 0 & 0 & 400 \\
2 & 3 & 0 & 1 & 0 & 0 & 0 & 510 \\
2 & 3 & 0 & 0 & -1 & 1 & 0 & 240 \\
\hline
-10-2M & -12-3M & 0 & 0 & M & 0 & 1 & -240M
\end{array}
\right]
\end{array}
&
\begin{array}{c}
200 \\
170 \\
80 \\
\;
\end{array}
\end{array}
$$

$$
\begin{array}{c c}
\begin{array}{c}
s_1 \\
s_2 \\
x_2 \\
W
\end{array}
&
\begin{array}{c}
\begin{array}{ccccccc}
x_1 & x_2 & s_1 & s_2 & s_3 & t_3 & W
\end{array} \\
\left[
\begin{array}{ccccccc|c}
-\frac{1}{3} & 0 & 1 & 0 & \frac{2}{3} & -\frac{2}{3} & 0 & 240 \\
0 & 0 & 0 & 1 & 1 & -1 & 0 & 270 \\
\frac{2}{3} & 1 & 0 & 0 & -\frac{1}{3} & \frac{1}{3} & 0 & 80 \\
\hline
-2 & 0 & 0 & 0 & -4 & 4+M & 1 & 960
\end{array}
\right]
\end{array}
&
\begin{array}{c}
360 \\
270 \\
\; \\
\;
\end{array}
\end{array}
$$

$$
\begin{array}{c c}
\begin{array}{c}
s_1 \\
s_3 \\
x_2 \\
P
\end{array}
&
\begin{array}{c}
\begin{array}{cccccc}
x_1 & x_2 & s_1 & s_2 & s_3 & P
\end{array} \\
\left[
\begin{array}{cccccc|c}
-\frac{1}{3} & 0 & 1 & -\frac{2}{3} & 0 & 0 & 60 \\
0 & 0 & 0 & 1 & 1 & 0 & 270 \\
\frac{2}{3} & 1 & 0 & \frac{1}{3} & 0 & 0 & 170 \\
\hline
-2 & 0 & 0 & 4 & 0 & 1 & 2040
\end{array}
\right]
\end{array}
&
\begin{array}{c}
\; \\
\; \\
255 \\
\;
\end{array}
\end{array}
$$

$$
\begin{array}{c}
\begin{array}{c}
s_1 \\
s_3 \\
x_1 \\
P
\end{array}
\begin{array}{c}
\begin{array}{cccccc}
x_1 & x_2 & s_1 & s_2 & s_3 & P
\end{array} \\
\left[
\begin{array}{cccccc|c}
0 & \frac{1}{2} & 1 & -\frac{1}{2} & 0 & 0 & 145 \\
0 & 0 & 0 & 1 & 1 & 0 & 270 \\
1 & \frac{3}{2} & 0 & \frac{1}{2} & 0 & 0 & 255 \\
\hline
0 & 3 & 0 & 5 & 0 & 1 & 2550
\end{array}
\right]
\end{array}
$$

To maximize profit, the company should produce 255 Standard and 0 Executive bookcases.

15. Suppose I is the total investment. Let x_1, x_2, and x_3 be the proportions invested in A, AA, and AAA bonds, respectively. If Z is the total annual yield expressed as a proportion of I, then
$ZI = 0.08x_1I + 0.07x_2I + 0.06x_3I$, or equivalently, $Z = 0.08x_1 + 0.07x_2 + 0.06x_3$. We want to maximize Z subject to
$$x_1 + x_2 + x_3 = 1,$$
$$x_2 + x_3 \geq 0.50,$$
$$x_1 + x_2 \leq 0.30,$$
$$x_1, \; x_2, \; x_3 \geq 0.$$
The artificial objective function is $W = Z - Mt_1 - Mt_2$.

$$
\begin{array}{c}
\begin{array}{ccccccccc}
x_1 & x_2 & x_3 & s_2 & s_3 & t_1 & t_2 & W
\end{array} \\
\left[
\begin{array}{cccccccc|c}
1 & 1 & 1 & 0 & 0 & 1 & 0 & 0 & 1 \\
0 & 1 & 1 & -1 & 0 & 0 & 1 & 0 & 0.5 \\
1 & 1 & 0 & 0 & 1 & 0 & 0 & 0 & 0.3 \\
\hline
-0.08 & -0.07 & -0.06 & 0 & 0 & M & M & 1 & 0
\end{array}
\right]
\end{array}
$$

	x_1	x_2	x_3	s_2	s_3	t_1	t_2	W		
t_1	1	1	1	0	0	1	0	0	1	1
t_2	0	1	1	-1	0	0	1	0	0.5	0.5
s_3	1	<u>1</u>	0	0	1	0	0	0	0.3	0.3
W	$-0.08-M$	$-0.07-2M$	$-0.06-2M$	M	0	0	0	1	$-1.5M$	

	x_1	x_2	x_3	s_2	s_3	t_1	t_2	W		
t_1	0	0	1	0	-1	1	0	0	0.7	0.7
t_2	-1	0	<u>1</u>	-1	-1	0	1	0	0.2	0.2
x_2	1	1	0	0	1	0	0	0	0.3	
W	$-0.01+M$	0	$-0.06-2M$	M	$0.07+2M$	0	0	1	$0.021-0.9M$	

	x_1	x_2	x_3	s_2	s_3	t_1	t_2	W		
t_1	1	0	0	1	0	1	-1	0	0.5	0.5
x_3	-1	0	1	-1	-1	0	1	0	0.2	
x_2	<u>1</u>	1	0	0	1	0	0	0	0.3	0.3
W	$-0.07-M$	0	0	$-0.06-M$	$.01$	0	$0.06+2M$	1	$0.033-0.5M$	

	x_1	x_2	x_3	s_2	s_3	t_1	t_2	W		
t_1	0	-1	0	<u>1</u>	-1	1	-1	0	0.2	0.2
x_3	0	1	1	-1	0	0	1	0	0.5	
x_1	1	1	0	0	1	0	0	0	0.3	
W	0	$0.07+M$	0	$-0.06-M$	$0.08+M$	0	$0.06+2M$	1	$0.054-0.2M$	

	x_1	x_2	x_3	s_2	s_3	t_1	t_2	W	
s_2	0	-1	0	1	-1	1	-1	0	0.2
x_3	0	0	1	0	-1	1	0	0	0.7
x_1	1	1	0	0	1	0	0	0	0.3
W	0	0.01	0	0	0.02	$0.06+M$	M	1	0.066

For the above tableau, $t_1 = t_2 = 0$. Thus $W = Z$.

The fund should put 30% in A bonds, 0% in AA, and 70% in AAA for a yield of 6.6%.

Exercise 7.7

1.

	x_1	x_2	s_1	s_2	t_1	t_2	W	
	-1	1	-1	0	1	0	0	6
	1	1	0	-1	0	1	0	10
	3	6	0	0	M	M	1	0

$$
\begin{array}{c}
\begin{array}{cccccccc} x_1 & x_2 & x_3 & s_2 & s_3 & t_1 & t_2 & W \end{array}\\
\begin{array}{c} t_1 \\ t_2 \\ W \end{array}
\left[\begin{array}{ccccccc|c}
-1 & \underline{1} & -1 & 0 & 1 & 0 & 0 & 6 \\
1 & 1 & 0 & -1 & 0 & 1 & 0 & 10 \\
\hline
3 & 6-2M & M & M & 0 & 0 & 1 & -16M
\end{array}\right]
\begin{array}{c} 6 \\ 10 \\ \; \end{array}
\end{array}
$$

$$
\begin{array}{c}
\begin{array}{cccccccc} x_1 & x_2 & x_3 & s_2 & s_3 & t_1 & t_2 & W \end{array}\\
\begin{array}{c} x_2 \\ t_2 \\ W \end{array}
\left[\begin{array}{ccccccc|c}
-1 & 1 & -1 & 0 & 1 & 0 & 0 & 6 \\
\underline{2} & 0 & 1 & -1 & -1 & 1 & 0 & 4 \\
\hline
9-2M & 0 & 6-M & M & -6+2M & 0 & 1 & -36-4M
\end{array}\right]
\begin{array}{c} \; \\ 2 \\ \; \end{array}
\end{array}
$$

$$
\begin{array}{c}
\begin{array}{cccccccc} x_1 & x_2 & x_3 & s_2 & s_3 & t_1 & t_2 & W \end{array}\\
\begin{array}{c} x_2 \\ x_1 \\ W \end{array}
\left[\begin{array}{ccccccc|c}
0 & 1 & -\frac{1}{2} & -\frac{1}{2} & \frac{1}{2} & \frac{1}{2} & 0 & 8 \\
1 & 0 & \frac{1}{2} & -\frac{1}{2} & -\frac{1}{2} & \frac{1}{2} & 0 & 2 \\
\hline
0 & 0 & \frac{3}{2} & \frac{9}{2} & -\frac{3}{2}+M & -\frac{9}{2}+M & 1 & -54
\end{array}\right]
\end{array}
$$

The minimum is $Z = 54$ when $x_1 = 2$, $x_2 = 8$.

3. $\begin{array}{cccccc} x_1 & x_2 & x_3 & s & t & W \end{array}$

$$
\left[\begin{array}{ccccc|c}
1 & -1 & -1 & -1 & 1 & 0 & 9 \\
\hline
4 & 2 & 1 & 0 & M & 1 & 0
\end{array}\right]
$$

$$
\begin{array}{c}
\begin{array}{cccccc} x_1 & x_2 & x_3 & s & t & W \end{array}\\
\begin{array}{c} t \\ W \end{array}
\left[\begin{array}{ccccc|c}
\underline{1} & -1 & -1 & -1 & 1 & 0 & 9 \\
\hline
4-M & 2+M & 1+M & M & 0 & 1 & -9M
\end{array}\right]
\begin{array}{c} 9 \\ \; \end{array}
\end{array}
$$

$$
\begin{array}{c}
\begin{array}{cccccc} x_1 & x_2 & x_3 & s & t & W \end{array}\\
\begin{array}{c} x_1 \\ W \end{array}
\left[\begin{array}{ccccc|c}
1 & -1 & -1 & -1 & 1 & 0 & 9 \\
\hline
0 & 6 & 5 & 4 & -4+M & 1 & -36
\end{array}\right]
\end{array}
$$

The minimum is $Z = 36$ when $x_1 = 9$, $x_2 = 0$, $x_3 = 0$.

5. We write the second constraint as $-x_1 + x_3 \geq 4$.

$$
\begin{array}{cccccccc} x_1 & x_2 & x_3 & s_1 & s_2 & s_3 & t_2 & W \end{array}
$$

$$
\left[\begin{array}{cccccccc|c}
1 & 1 & 1 & 1 & 0 & 0 & 0 & 0 & 6 \\
-1 & 0 & 1 & 0 & -1 & 0 & 1 & 0 & 4 \\
0 & 1 & 1 & 0 & 0 & 1 & 0 & 0 & 5 \\
\hline
2 & 3 & 1 & 0 & 0 & 0 & M & 1 & 0
\end{array}\right]
$$

$$
\begin{array}{c}
\begin{array}{cccccccc} x_1 & x_2 & x_3 & s_1 & s_2 & s_3 & t_2 & W \end{array}\\
\begin{array}{c} s_1 \\ t_2 \\ s_3 \\ W \end{array}
\left[\begin{array}{cccccccc|c}
1 & 1 & 1 & 1 & 0 & 0 & 0 & 0 & 6 \\
-1 & 0 & \underline{1} & 0 & -1 & 0 & 1 & 0 & 4 \\
0 & 1 & 1 & 0 & 0 & 1 & 0 & 0 & 5 \\
\hline
2+M & 3 & 1-M & 0 & M & 0 & 0 & 1 & -4M
\end{array}\right]
\begin{array}{c} 6 \\ 4 \\ 5 \\ \; \end{array}
\end{array}
$$

$$\begin{array}{c c} & \begin{array}{c c c c c c c c} x_1 & x_2 & x_3 & s_1 & s_2 & s_3 & t_2 & W \end{array} \\ \begin{array}{c} s_1 \\ x_3 \\ s_3 \\ W \end{array} & \left[\begin{array}{c c c c c c c c | c} 2 & 1 & 0 & 1 & 1 & 0 & -1 & 0 & 2 \\ -1 & 0 & 1 & 0 & -1 & 0 & 1 & 0 & 4 \\ 1 & 1 & 0 & 0 & 1 & 1 & -1 & 0 & 1 \\ \hline 3 & 3 & 0 & 0 & 1 & 0 & -1+M & 1 & -4 \end{array}\right] \end{array}$$

The minimum is $Z = 4$ when $x_1 = 0$, $x_2 = 0$, $x_3 = 4$.

7.

$$\begin{array}{c c} \begin{array}{c c c c c c c c} x_1 & x_2 & x_3 & s_3 & t_1 & t_2 & W \end{array} \\ \left[\begin{array}{c c c c c c c | c} 1 & 2 & 1 & 0 & 1 & 0 & 0 & 4 \\ 0 & 1 & 1 & 0 & 0 & 1 & 0 & 1 \\ 1 & 1 & 0 & 1 & 0 & 0 & 0 & 6 \\ \hline 1 & -1 & -3 & 0 & M & M & 1 & 0 \end{array}\right] \end{array}$$

$$\begin{array}{c c} & \begin{array}{c c c c c c c} x_1 & x_2 & x_3 & s_3 & t_1 & t_2 & W \end{array} \\ \begin{array}{c} t_1 \\ t_2 \\ s_3 \\ W \end{array} & \left[\begin{array}{c c c c c c c | c} 1 & 2 & 1 & 0 & 1 & 0 & 0 & 4 \\ 0 & \underline{1} & 1 & 0 & 0 & 1 & 0 & 1 \\ 1 & 1 & 0 & 1 & 0 & 0 & 0 & 6 \\ \hline 1-M & -1-3M & -3-2M & 0 & 0 & 0 & 1 & -5M \end{array}\right] \begin{array}{c} 2 \\ 1 \\ 6 \end{array} \end{array}$$

$$\begin{array}{c c} & \begin{array}{c c c c c c c} x_1 & x_2 & x_3 & s_3 & t_1 & t_2 & W \end{array} \\ \begin{array}{c} t_1 \\ x_2 \\ s_3 \\ W \end{array} & \left[\begin{array}{c c c c c c c | c} \underline{1} & 0 & -1 & 0 & 1 & -2 & 0 & 2 \\ 0 & 1 & 1 & 0 & 0 & 1 & 0 & 1 \\ 1 & 0 & -1 & 1 & 0 & -1 & 0 & 5 \\ \hline 1-M & 0 & -2+M & 0 & 0 & 1+3M & 1 & 1-2M \end{array}\right] \begin{array}{c} 2 \\ \\ 5 \end{array} \end{array}$$

$$\begin{array}{c c} & \begin{array}{c c c c c c c} x_1 & x_2 & x_3 & s_3 & t_1 & t_2 & W \end{array} \\ \begin{array}{c} x_1 \\ x_2 \\ s_3 \\ W \end{array} & \left[\begin{array}{c c c c c c c | c} 1 & 0 & -1 & 0 & 1 & -2 & 0 & 2 \\ 0 & 1 & \underline{1} & 0 & 0 & 1 & 0 & 1 \\ 0 & 0 & 0 & 1 & -1 & 1 & 0 & 3 \\ \hline 0 & 0 & -1 & 0 & -1+M & 3+M & 1 & -1 \end{array}\right] \begin{array}{c} \\ 1 \\ \end{array} \end{array}$$

$$\begin{array}{c c} & \begin{array}{c c c c c} x_1 & x_2 & x_3 & s_3 & -Z \end{array} \\ \begin{array}{c} x_1 \\ x_3 \\ s_3 \\ -Z \end{array} & \left[\begin{array}{c c c c c | c} 1 & 1 & 0 & 0 & 0 & 3 \\ 0 & 1 & 1 & 0 & 0 & 1 \\ 0 & 0 & 0 & 1 & 0 & 3 \\ \hline 0 & 1 & 0 & 0 & 1 & 0 \end{array}\right] \end{array}$$

The minimum is $Z = 0$ when $x_1 = 3$, $x_2 = 0$, $x_3 = 1$.

9.

	x_1	x_2	x_3	s_1	s_2	t_1	t_2	W	
	1	1	1	-1	0	1	0	0	8
	-1	2	1	0	-1	0	1	0	2
	1	8	5	0	0	M	M	1	0

	x_1	x_2	x_3	s_1	s_2	t_1	t_2	W		
t_1	1	1	1	-1	0	1	0	0	8	8
t_2	-1	2	1	0	-1	0	1	0	2	1
W	1	$8-3M$	$5-2M$	M	M	0	0	1	$-10M$	

	x_1	x_2	x_3	s_1	s_2	t_1	t_2	W		
t_1	$\frac{3}{2}$	0	$\frac{1}{2}$	-1	$\frac{1}{2}$	1	$-\frac{1}{2}$	0	7	$\frac{14}{3}$
x_2	$-\frac{1}{2}$	1	$\frac{1}{2}$	0	$-\frac{1}{2}$	0	$\frac{1}{2}$	0	1	
W	$5-\frac{3}{2}M$	0	$1-\frac{1}{2}M$	M	$4-\frac{1}{2}M$	0	$-4+\frac{3}{2}M$	1	$-8-7M$	

	x_1	x_2	x_3	s_1	s_2	t_1	t_2	W		
x_1	1	0	$\frac{1}{3}$	$-\frac{2}{3}$	$\frac{1}{3}$	$\frac{2}{3}$	$-\frac{1}{3}$	0	$\frac{14}{3}$	14
x_2	0	1	$\frac{2}{3}$	$-\frac{1}{3}$	$-\frac{1}{3}$	$\frac{1}{3}$	$\frac{1}{3}$	0	$\frac{10}{3}$	5
W	0	0	$-\frac{2}{3}$	$\frac{10}{3}$	$\frac{7}{3}$	$-\frac{10}{3}+M$	$-\frac{7}{3}+M$	1	$-\frac{94}{3}$	

	x_1	x_2	x_3	s_1	s_2	t_1	t_2	W	
x_1	1	$-\frac{1}{2}$	0	$-\frac{1}{2}$	$\frac{1}{2}$	$\frac{1}{2}$	$-\frac{1}{2}$	0	3
x_3	0	$\frac{3}{2}$	1	$-\frac{1}{2}$	$-\frac{1}{2}$	$\frac{1}{2}$	$\frac{1}{2}$	0	5
W	0	1	0	3	2	$-3+M$	$-2+M$	1	-28

The minimum is $Z = 28$ when $x_1 = 3$, $x_2 = 0$, $x_3 = 5$.

11. Let x_1, x_2, and x_3 denote the annual numbers of barrels of cement produced in kilns that use device A, device B, and no device, respectively. We want to minimize the annual emission control cost C (C in dollars) where

$C = \dfrac{1}{4}x_1 + \dfrac{2}{5}x_2 + 0x_3$ subject to

$x_1 + x_2 + x_3 = 3,300,000,$

$\dfrac{1}{2}x_1 + \dfrac{1}{4}x_2 + 2x_3 \le 1,000,000,$

$x_1,\ x_2,\ x_3 \ge 0.$

	x_1	x_2	x_3	s_2	t_1	W	
	1	1	1	0	1	0	3,300,000
	$\frac{1}{2}$	$\frac{1}{4}$	2	1	0	0	1,000,000
	$\frac{1}{4}$	$\frac{2}{5}$	0	0	M	1	0

	x_1	x_2	x_3	s_2	t_1	W		
t_1	1	1	1	0	1	0	3,300,000	3,300,000
s_2	$\frac{1}{2}$	$\frac{1}{4}$	2	1	0	0	1,000,000	500,000
W	$\frac{1}{4}-M$	$\frac{2}{5}-M$	$-M$	0	0	1	$-3,300,000M$	

	x_1	x_2	x_3	s_2	t_1	W		
t_1	$\frac{3}{4}$	$\frac{7}{8}$	0	$-\frac{1}{2}$	1	0	2,800,000	3,200,000
x_3	$\frac{1}{4}$	$\frac{1}{8}$	1	$\frac{1}{2}$	0	0	500,000	4,000,000
W	$\frac{1}{4}-\frac{3}{4}M$	$\frac{2}{5}-\frac{7}{8}M$	0	$\frac{1}{2}M$	0	1	$-2,800,000M$	

	x_1	x_2	x_3	s_2	t_1	W		
x_2	$\frac{6}{7}$	1	0	$-\frac{4}{7}$	$\frac{8}{7}$	0	3,200,000	$\frac{11,200,000}{3}$
x_3	$\frac{1}{7}$	0	1	$\frac{4}{7}$	$-\frac{1}{7}$	0	100,000	700,000
W	$-\frac{13}{140}$	0	0	$\frac{8}{35}$	$-\frac{16}{35}+M$	1	$-1,280,000$	

	x_1	x_2	x_3	s_2	$-C$		
x_2	0	1	-6	-4	0	2,600,000
x_1	1	0	7	4	0	700,000
$-C$	0	0	$\frac{13}{20}$	$\frac{3}{5}$	1	$-1,215,000$

Thus the minimum value of C is 1,215,000 when $x_1 = 700,000$, $x_2 = 2,600,000$, $x_3 = 0$.

The plant should install device A on kilns producing 700,000 barrels annually, and device B on kilns producing 2,600,000 barrels annually.

13. Let x_A = number of refrigerators shipped from A to Exton,

       x_B = number of refrigerators shipped from B to Exton,

       y_A = number of refrigerators shipped from A to Whyton,

       y_B = number of refrigerators shipped from B to Whyton.

We want to minimize $C = 15x_A + 11x_B + 13y_A + 12y_B$

subject to

$$x_A + x_B = 30,$$
$$y_A + y_B = 30,$$
$$x_A + y_A \le 50,$$
$$x_B + y_B \le 20,$$
$$x_A,\ x_B,\ y_A,\ y_B \ge 0.$$

x_A	x_B	y_A	y_B	s_3	s_4	t_1	t_2	W	
1	1	0	0	0	0	1	0	0	30
0	0	1	1	0	0	0	1	0	30
1	0	1	0	1	0	0	0	0	50
0	1	0	1	0	1	0	0	0	20
15	11	13	12	0	0	M	M	1	0

	x_A	x_B	y_A	y_B	s_3	s_4	t_1	t_2	W		
t_1	1	1	0	0	0	0	1	0	0	30	30
t_2	0	0	1	1	0	0	0	1	0	30	
s_3	1	0	1	0	1	0	0	0	0	50	
s_4	0	<u>1</u>	0	1	0	1	0	0	0	20	20
W	$15-M$	$11-M$	$13-M$	$12-M$	0	0	0	0	1	$-60M$	

	x_A	x_B	y_A	y_B	s_3	s_1	t_1	t_2	W		
t_1	1	0	0	-1	0	-1	1	0	0	10	
t_2	0	0	<u>1</u>	1	0	0	0	1	0	30	30
s_3	1	0	1	0	1	0	0	0	0	50	50
x_B	0	1	0	1	0	1	0	0	0	20	
W	$15-M$	0	$13-M$	1	0	$-11+M$	0	0	1	$-220-40M$	

	x_A	x_B	y_A	y_B	s_3	s_4	t_1	t_2	W		
t_1	<u>1</u>	0	0	-1	0	-1	1	0	0	10	10
y_A	0	0	1	1	0	0	0	1	0	30	
s_3	1	0	0	-1	1	0	0	-1	0	20	20
x_B	0	1	0	1	0	1	0	0	0	20	
W	$15-M$	0	0	$-12+M$	0	$-11+M$	0	$-13+M$	1	$-610-10M$	

	x_A	x_B	y_A	y_B	s_3	s_4	t_1	t_2	W	
x_A	1	0	0	-1	0	-1	1	0	0	10
y_A	0	0	1	1	0	0	0	1	0	30
s_3	0	0	0	0	1	1	-1	-1	0	10
x_B	0	1	0	1	0	1	0	0	0	20
W	0	0	0	3	0	4	$-15+M$	$-13+M$	1	-760

The retailer should ship as follows: to Exton, 10 from A and 20 from B; to Whyton, 30 from A. The transportation cost is $760

15. a. Roll width $\begin{cases} 15" \\ 10" \end{cases}$ $\begin{matrix} 3 & 2 & 1 & \underline{0} \\ 0 & 1 & \underline{3} & \underline{4} \end{matrix}$

Trim loss $3 \quad 8 \quad \underline{3} \quad \underline{8}$

b. We want to minimize $L\ 3x_1 + 8x_2 + 3x_3 + 8x_4$ subject to
$$3x_1 + 2x_2 + x_3 \geq 50,$$
$$x_2 + 3x_3 + 4x_4 \geq 60,$$
$$x_1,\ x_2,\ x_3,\ x_4 \geq 0.$$

$$
\begin{array}{c}
\begin{array}{ccccccccc} x_1 & x_2 & x_3 & x_4 & s_1 & s_2 & t_1 & t_2 & W \end{array} \\
\left[\begin{array}{ccccccccc|c}
3 & 2 & 1 & 0 & -1 & 0 & 1 & 0 & 0 & 50 \\
0 & 1 & 3 & 4 & 0 & -1 & 0 & 1 & 0 & 60 \\
\hline
3 & 8 & 3 & 8 & 0 & 0 & M & M & 1 & 0
\end{array}\right]
\end{array}
$$

	x_1	x_2	x_3	x_4	s_1	s_2	t_1	t_2	W		
t_1	3	2	1	0	-1	0	1	0	0	50	50
t_2	0	1	$\underline{3}$	4	0	-1	0	1	0	60	20
W	$3-3M$	$8-3M$	$3-4M$	$8-4M$	M	M	0	0	1	$-110M$	

	x_1	x_2	x_3	x_4	s_1	s_2	t_1	t_2	W		
t_1	3	$\frac{5}{3}$	0	$-\frac{4}{3}$	-1	$\frac{1}{3}$	1	$-\frac{1}{3}$	0	30	10
x_3	0	$\frac{1}{3}$	1	$\frac{4}{3}$	0	$-\frac{1}{3}$	0	$\frac{1}{3}$	0	20	
W	$3-3M$	$7-\frac{5}{3}M$	0	$4+\frac{4}{3}M$	M	$1-\frac{1}{3}M$	0	$-1+\frac{4}{3}M$	1	$-60-30M$	

	x_1	x_2	x_3	x_4	s_1	s_2	t_1	t_2	W	
x_1	1	$\frac{5}{9}$	0	$-\frac{4}{9}$	$-\frac{1}{3}$	$\frac{1}{9}$	$\frac{1}{3}$	$-\frac{1}{9}$	0	10
x_3	0	$\frac{1}{3}$	1	$\frac{4}{3}$	0	$-\frac{1}{3}$	0	$\frac{1}{3}$	0	20
W	0	$\frac{16}{3}$	0	$\frac{16}{3}$	1	$\frac{2}{3}$	$-1+M$	$-\frac{2}{3}+M$	1	-90

$x_1 = 10$, $x_2 = 0$, $x_3 = 20$, $x_4 = 0$.

(c) 90 in.

Principles in Practice 7.8

1. Let x_1, x_2, and x_3 be the numbers respectively, of Type 1, Type 2, and Type 3 gadgets produced. The original problem is to maximize $P = 300x_1 + 200x_2 + 200x_3$, subject to

   $300x_1 + 220x_2 + 180x_3 \le 60,000,$

   $\quad 20x_1 + 40x_2 + 20x_3 \le 2000,$

   $\qquad\quad 3x_1 + x_2 + 2x_3 \le 120,$

   $\qquad\quad$ and x_1, x_2, $x_3 \le 0$.

   The dual problem is to minimize $W = 60,000y_1 + 2000y_2 + 120y_3$, subject to

   $300y_1 + 20y_2 + 3y_3 \ge 300,$

   $220y_1 + 40y_2 + y_3 \ge 200,$

   $180y_1 + 20y_2 + 2y_3 \ge 200,$

   $\qquad$ and y_1, y_2, $y_3 \ge 0$.

2. Let x_1 and x_2 be the amounts, respectively of supplement 1 and supplement 2. The original problem is to minimize $C = 6x_1 + 2x_2$, subject to

   $20x_1 + 6x_2 \ge 98,$

   $8x_1 + 16x_2 \ge 80,$

   and x_1, $x_2 \ge 0$.

The dual problem is to maximize $W = 98y_1 + 80y_2$, subject to
$$20y_1 + 8y_2 \le 6,$$
$$6y_1 + 16y_2 \le 2,$$
and $y_1, \; y_2 \ge 0.$

3. Let x_1, x_2, and x_3 be the numbers, respectively, of devices 1, 2, and 3 produced.
The original problem is to maximize $P = 30x_1 + 20x_2 + 20x_3$, subject to
$$30x_1 + 15x_2 + 10x_3 \le 300, \quad 20x_1 + 30x_2 + 20x_3 \le 400, \quad 40x_1 + 30x_2 + 25x_3 \le 600, \text{ and } x_1, \; x_2, \; x_3 \ge 0.$$
The dual problem is to minimize $W = 300y_1 + 400y_2 + 600y_3$, subject to
$$30y_1 + 20y_2 + 40y_3 \ge 30, \quad 15y_1 + 30y_2 + 30y_3 \ge 20, \quad 10y_1 + 20y_2 + 25y_3 \ge 20,$$
and $y_1, \; y_2, \; y_3 \ge 0.$
The tableaux to maximize $Z = -W = -300y_1 - 400y_2 - 600y_3$ follow.

	y_1	y_2	y_3	s_1	s_2	s_3	t_1	t_2	t_3	Z	
	30	20	40	-1	0	0	1	0	0	0	30
	15	30	30	0	-1	0	0	1	0	0	20
	10	20	25	0	0	-1	0	0	1	0	20
	300	400	600	0	0	0	M	M	M	1	0

	y_1	y_2	y_3	s_1	s_2	s_3	t_1	t_2	t_3	Z	
t_1	30	20	40	-1	0	0	1	0	0	0	30
t_2	15	30	$\underline{30}$	0	-1	0	0	1	0	0	20
t_3	10	20	25	0	0	-1	0	0	1	0	20
Z	$300-55M$	$400-70M$	$600-95M$	M	M	M	0	0	0	1	$-70M$

	y_1	y_2	y_3	s_1	s_2	s_3	t_1	t_2	t_3	Z	
t_1	$\underline{10}$	-20	0	-1	$\frac{4}{3}$	0	1	$-\frac{4}{3}$	0	0	$\frac{10}{3}$
y_3	$\frac{1}{2}$	1	1	0	$-\frac{1}{30}$	0	0	$\frac{1}{30}$	0	0	$\frac{2}{3}$
t_3	$-\frac{5}{2}$	-5	0	0	$\frac{5}{6}$	-1	0	$-\frac{5}{6}$	1	0	$\frac{10}{3}$
Z	$-\frac{13}{2}M$	$-200+25M$	0	M	$20-\frac{13}{6}M$	M	0	$-20+\frac{19}{6}M$	0	1	$-400-\frac{20}{3}M$

	y_1	y_2	y_3	s_1	s_2	s_3	t_1	t_2	t_3	Z	
y_1	1	-2	0	$-\frac{1}{10}$	$\frac{2}{15}$	0	$\frac{1}{10}$	$-\frac{2}{15}$	0	0	$\frac{1}{3}$
y_3	0	2	1	$\frac{1}{20}$	$-\frac{1}{10}$	0	$-\frac{1}{20}$	$\frac{1}{10}$	0	0	$\frac{1}{2}$
t_3	0	-10	0	$-\frac{1}{4}$	$\frac{7}{6}$	-1	$\frac{1}{4}$	$-\frac{7}{6}$	1	0	$\frac{25}{6}$
Z	0	$-200+10M$	0	$\frac{1}{4}M$	$20-\frac{7}{6}M$	M	$\frac{3}{4}M$	$-20+\frac{13}{6}M$	0	1	$-400-\frac{25}{6}M$

	y_1	y_2	y_3	s_1	s_2	s_3	t_1	t_2	t_3	Z	
s_2	$\frac{15}{2}$	-15	0	$-\frac{3}{4}$	1	0	$\frac{3}{4}$	-1	0	0	$\frac{5}{2}$
y_3	$\frac{3}{4}$	$\frac{1}{2}$	1	$-\frac{1}{40}$	0	0	$\frac{1}{40}$	0	0	0	$\frac{3}{4}$
t_3	$-\frac{35}{4}$	$\frac{15}{2}$	0	$\frac{5}{8}$	0	-1	$-\frac{5}{8}$	0	1	0	$\frac{5}{4}$
Z	$-150+\frac{35}{4}M$	$100-\frac{15}{2}M$	0	$15-\frac{5}{8}M$	0	M	$-15+\frac{13}{8}M$	M	0	1	$-450-\frac{5}{4}M$

	y_1	y_2	y_3	s_1	s_2	s_3	t_1	t_2	t_3	Z	
s_2	-10	0	0	$\frac{1}{2}$	1	-2	$-\frac{1}{2}$	-1	2	0	5
y_3	$\frac{4}{3}$	0	1	$-\frac{1}{15}$	0	$\frac{1}{15}$	$\frac{1}{15}$	0	$-\frac{1}{15}$	0	$\frac{2}{3}$
y_2	$-\frac{7}{6}$	1	0	$\frac{1}{12}$	0	$-\frac{2}{15}$	$-\frac{1}{12}$	0	$\frac{2}{15}$	0	$\frac{1}{6}$
Z	$-\frac{100}{3}$	0	0	$\frac{20}{3}$	0	$\frac{40}{3}$	$-\frac{20}{3}+M$	M	$-\frac{40}{3}+M$	1	$-\frac{1400}{3}$

The t_1, t_2, and t_3 columns are no longer needed.

	y_1	y_2	y_3	s_1	s_2	s_3	Z	
s_2	0	0	$\frac{15}{2}$	0	1	$-\frac{3}{2}$	0	10
y_1	1	0	$\frac{3}{4}$	$-\frac{1}{20}$	0	$\frac{1}{20}$	0	$\frac{1}{2}$
y_2	0	1	$\frac{7}{8}$	$\frac{1}{40}$	0	$-\frac{3}{40}$	0	$\frac{3}{4}$
Z	0	0	25	5	0	15	1	-450

From this tableau, the maximum profit of \$450 corresponds to $x_1 = 5$, $x_2 = 0$, and $x_3 = 15$.

The company should produce 5 of device 1 per hour and 15 of device 3 per hour.

Exercise 7.8

1. Minimize $W = 6y_1 + 4y_2$ subject to
$$y_1 - y_2 \geq 2,$$
$$y_1 + y_2 \geq 3,$$
$$y_1,\ y_2 \geq 0.$$

3. Maximize $W = 8y_1 + 2y_2$ subject to
$$y_1 - y_2 \leq 1,$$
$$y_1 + 2y_2 \leq 8,$$
$$y_1 + y_2 \leq 5,$$
$$y_1,\ y_2 \geq 0.$$

5. The second and third constraints can be written as $x_1 - x_2 \leq -3$ and $-x_1 - x_2 \leq -11$.
Minimize $W = 13y_1 - 3y_2 - 11y_3$ subject to
$$-y_1 + y_2 - y_3 \geq 1,$$
$$2y_1 - y_2 - y_3 \geq -1,$$
$$y_1,\ y_2,\ y_3 \geq 0.$$

7. The first constraint can be written as $-x_1 + x_2 + x_3 \geq -3$. Maximize
$W = -3y_1 + 3y_2$ subject to
$$-y_1 + y_2 \leq 4,$$
$$y_1 - y_2 \leq 4,$$
$$y_1 + y_2 \leq 6,$$
$$y_1,\ y_2 \geq 0.$$

9. The dual is: Maximize $W = y_1 + 2y_2$ subject to
$$y_1 - y_2 \leq 4,$$
$$-y_1 + y_2 \leq 4,$$
$$y_1 + y_2 \leq 6,$$
$$y_1,\ y_2 \geq 0.$$

	y_1	y_2	s_1	s_2	s_3	W		
s_1	1	-1	1	0	0	0	4	
s_2	-1	1	0	1	0	0	4	4
s_3	1	1	0	0	1	0	6	6
W	-1	-2	0	0	0	1	0	

	y_1	y_2	s_1	s_2	s_3	W		
s_1	0	0	1	1	0	0	8	
y_2	-1	1	0	1	0	0	4	
s_3	2	0	0	-1	1	0	2	1
W	-3	0	0	2	0	1	8	

	y_1	y_2	s_1	s_2	s_3	W	
s_1	0	0	1	1	0	0	8
y_2	0	1	0	$\frac{1}{2}$	$\frac{1}{2}$	0	5
y_1	1	0	0	$-\frac{1}{2}$	$\frac{1}{2}$	0	1
W	0	0	0	$\frac{1}{2}$	$\frac{3}{2}$	1	11

The minimum is $Z = 11$ when
$$x_1 = 0,\ x_2 = \frac{1}{2},\ x_3 = \frac{3}{2}.$$

11. The dual is: Minimize $W = 8y_1 + 12y_2$ subject to

$$y_1 + y_2 \geq 3,$$
$$2y_1 + 6y_2 \geq 8,$$
$$y_1,\ y_2 \geq 0.$$

	y_1	y_2	s_1	s_2	t_1	t_2	U	
	1	1	−1	0	1	0	0	3
	2	6	0	−1	0	1	0	8
	8	12	0	0	M	M	1	0

	y_1	y_2	s_1	s_2	t_1	t_2	U		
t_1	1	1	−1	0	1	0	0	3	3
t_2	2	6	0	−1	0	1	0	8	$\frac{4}{3}$
U	$8-3M$	$12-7M$	M	M	0	0	1	$-11M$	

	y_1	y_2	s_1	s_2	t_1	t_2	U		
t_1	$\frac{2}{3}$	0	−1	$\frac{1}{6}$	1	$-\frac{1}{6}$	0	$\frac{5}{3}$	$\frac{5}{2}$
y_2	$\frac{1}{3}$	1	0	$-\frac{1}{6}$	0	$\frac{1}{6}$	0	$\frac{4}{3}$	4
U	$4-\frac{2}{3}M$	0	M	$2-\frac{1}{6}M$	0	$-2+\frac{7}{6}M$	1	$-16-\frac{5}{3}M$	

	y_1	y_2	s_1	s_2	t_1	t_2	U	
y_1	1	0	$-\frac{3}{2}$	$\frac{1}{4}$	$\frac{3}{2}$	$-\frac{1}{4}$	0	$\frac{5}{2}$
y_2	0	1	$\frac{1}{2}$	$-\frac{1}{4}$	$-\frac{1}{2}$	$\frac{1}{4}$	0	$\frac{1}{2}$
U	0	0	6	1	$-6+M$	$-1+M$	1	-26

The maximum is $Z = 26$ when $x_1 = 6$, $x_2 = 1$.

13. The first constraint can be written as $x_1 - x_2 \geq -1$. The dual is: Maximize $W = -y_1 + 3y_2$ subject to

$$y_1 + y_2 \leq 6,$$
$$-y_1 + y_2 \leq 4,$$
$$y_1,\ y_2 \geq 0.$$

	y_1	y_2	s_1	s_2	W		
s_1	1	1	1	0	0	6	6
s_2	−1	1	0	1	0	4	4
W	1	−3	0	0	1	0	

	y_1	y_2	s_1	s_2	W		
s_1	2	0	1	−1	0	2	1
y_2	−1	1	0	1	0	4	
W	−2	0	0	3	1	12	

$$
\begin{array}{c}
\begin{array}{cccccc} & y_1 & y_2 & s_1 & s_2 & W \end{array} \\
\begin{array}{c} y_1 \\ y_2 \\ W \end{array}
\left[
\begin{array}{ccccc|c}
1 & 0 & \frac{1}{2} & -\frac{1}{2} & 0 & 1 \\
0 & 1 & \frac{1}{2} & \frac{1}{2} & 0 & 5 \\
\hline
0 & 0 & 1 & 2 & 1 & 14
\end{array}
\right]
\end{array}
$$

The minimum is $Z = 14$ when $x_1 = 1$, $x_2 = 2$.

15. Let x_1 = amount spent on newspaper advertising,

x_2 = amount spent on radio advertising.

We want to minimize $C = x_1 + x_2$ subject to

$$40x_1 + 50x_2 \geq 8000,$$
$$100x_1 + 25x_2 \geq 6000,$$
$$x_1, \; x_2 \geq 0.$$

The dual is: Maximize $W = 8000y_1 + 6000y_2$ subject to

$$40y_1 + 100y_2 \leq 1,$$
$$50y_1 + 25y_2 \leq 1,$$
$$y_1, \; y_2 \geq 0.$$

$$
\begin{array}{c}
\begin{array}{cccccc} & y_1 & y_2 & s_1 & s_2 & W \end{array} \\
\begin{array}{c} s_1 \\ s_2 \\ W \end{array}
\left[
\begin{array}{ccccc|c}
40 & 100 & 1 & 0 & 0 & 1 \\
50 & 25 & 0 & 1 & 0 & 1 \\
\hline
-8000 & -6000 & 0 & 0 & 1 & 0
\end{array}
\right]
\begin{array}{c} \frac{1}{40} \\ \frac{1}{50} \\ \\ \end{array}
\end{array}
$$

$$
\begin{array}{c}
\begin{array}{cccccc} & y_1 & y_2 & s_1 & s_2 & W \end{array} \\
\begin{array}{c} s_1 \\ y_1 \\ W \end{array}
\left[
\begin{array}{ccccc|c}
0 & 80 & 1 & -\frac{4}{5} & 0 & \frac{1}{5} \\
1 & \frac{1}{2} & 0 & \frac{1}{50} & 0 & \frac{1}{50} \\
\hline
0 & -2000 & 0 & 160 & 1 & 160
\end{array}
\right]
\begin{array}{c} \frac{1}{400} \\ \frac{1}{25} \\ \\ \end{array}
\end{array}
$$

$$
\begin{array}{c}
\begin{array}{cccccc} & y_1 & y_2 & s_1 & s_2 & W \end{array} \\
\begin{array}{c} y_2 \\ y_1 \\ W \end{array}
\left[
\begin{array}{ccccc|c}
0 & 1 & \frac{1}{80} & -\frac{1}{100} & 0 & \frac{1}{400} \\
1 & 0 & -\frac{1}{160} & \frac{1}{40} & 0 & \frac{3}{160} \\
\hline
0 & 0 & 25 & 140 & 1 & 165
\end{array}
\right]
\end{array}
$$

The firm should spend \$25 on newspaper advertising and \$140 on radio advertising for a cost of \$165.

17. Let y_1 = number of shipping clerk apprentices,

y_2 = number of shipping clerks,

y_3 = number of semiskilled workers,

y_4 = number of skilled workers.

We want to minimize $W = 2y_1 + 5y_2 + 4y_3 + 7y_4$ subject to

$$y_1 + y_2 \geq 60,$$
$$-2y_1 + y_2 \geq 0,$$
$$y_3 + y_4 \geq 90,$$
$$y_3 - 2y_4 \geq 0,$$
$$y_1, \; y_2, \; y_3, \; y_4 \geq 0.$$

The dual is: Maximize $Z = 60x_1 + 0x_2 + 90x_3 + 0x_4$ subject to
$$x_1 - 2x_2 \le 2,$$
$$x_1 + x_2 \le 5,$$
$$x_3 + x_4 \le 4,$$
$$x_3 - 2x_4 \le 7,$$
$$x_1,\ x_2,\ x_3,\ x_4 \ge 0.$$

	x_1	x_2	x_3	x_4	s_1	s_2	s_3	s_4	Z		
s_1	1	-2	0	0	1	0	0	0	0	2	
s_2	1	1	0	0	0	1	0	0	0	5	
s_3	0	0	1	1	0	0	1	0	0	4	4
s_4	0	0	1	-2	0	0	0	1	0	7	7
Z	-60	0	-90	0	0	0	0	0	1	0	

	x_1	x_2	x_3	x_4	s_1	s_2	s_3	s_4	Z		
s_1	1	-2	0	0	1	0	0	0	0	2	2
s_2	1	1	0	0	0	1	0	0	0	5	5
x_3	0	0	1	1	0	0	1	0	0	4	
s_4	0	0	0	-3	0	0	-1	1	0	3	
Z	-60	0	0	90	0	0	90	0	1	360	

	x_1	x_2	x_3	x_4	s_1	s_2	s_3	s_4	Z		
x_1	1	-2	0	0	1	0	0	0	0	2	
s_2	0	3	0	0	-1	1	0	0	0	3	1
x_3	0	0	1	1	0	0	1	0	0	4	
s_4	0	0	0	-3	0	0	-1	1	0	3	
Z	0	-120	0	90	60	0	90	0	1	480	

	x_1	x_2	x_3	x_4	s_1	s_2	s_3	s_4	Z	
x_1	1	0	0	0	$\frac{1}{3}$	$\frac{2}{3}$	0	0	0	4
x_2	0	1	0	0	$-\frac{1}{3}$	$\frac{1}{3}$	0	0	0	1
x_3	0	0	1	1	0	0	1	0	0	4
s_4	0	0	0	-3	0	0	-1	1	0	3
Z	0	0	0	90	20	40	90	0	1	600

The company should employ 20 shipping clerk apprentices, 40 shipping clerks, 90 semiskilled workers, and 0 skilled workers for a total hourly wage of $600.

Chapter 7 Review Problems

1.

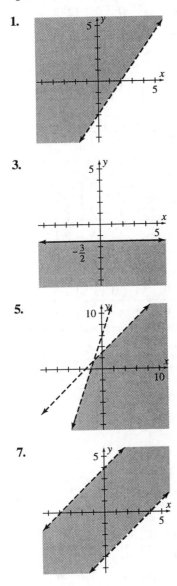

3.

5.

7.

9.

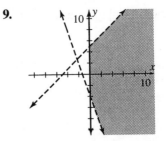

11. Feasible region follows. Corner points are
$(0, 0)$, $(0, 2)$, $(1, 3)$, $(3, 1)$, $(3, 0)$. Z is
maximized at
$(3, 0)$ where its value is 3.
Thus $Z = 3$ when $x = 3$ and $y = 0$.

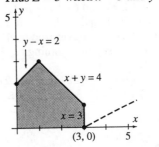

13. Feasible region is unbounded. Z is
minimized at the corner point $(0, 2)$ where
its value is -2. Thus $Z = -2$ when $x = 0$ and $y = 2$.

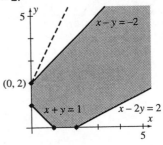

15. Feasible region is empty. Thus there is no optimum solution.

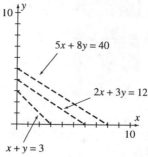

17. Feasible region follows. Corner points are $(0, 0)$, $(0, 4)$, $(2, 3)$, and $(4, 0)$. Z is maximized at $(2, 3)$ and $(4, 0)$ where its value is 36. Thus Z is maximized at all points on the line segment joining $(2, 3)$ and $(4, 0)$. The solution is
$Z = 36$ when $x = (1 - t)(2) + 4t = 2 + 2t$,
$y = (1 - t)(3) + 0t = 3 - 3t$, and $0 \le t \le 1$.

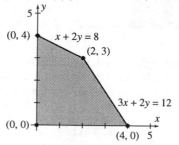

19.

$$
\begin{array}{c}
\begin{array}{ccccc} x_1 & x_2 & s_1 & s_2 & Z \end{array} \\
\begin{array}{c} s_1 \\ s_2 \\ Z \end{array}
\left[\begin{array}{ccccc|c}
1 & \underline{6} & 1 & 0 & 0 & 12 \\
1 & 2 & 0 & 1 & 0 & 8 \\
\hline
-4 & -5 & 0 & 0 & 1 & 0
\end{array}\right]
\begin{array}{c} 2 \\ 4 \\ \ \end{array}
\end{array}
$$

$$
\begin{array}{c}
\begin{array}{ccccc} x_1 & x_2 & s_1 & s_2 & Z \end{array} \\
\begin{array}{c} x_2 \\ s_2 \\ Z \end{array}
\left[\begin{array}{ccccc|c}
\frac{1}{6} & 1 & \frac{1}{6} & 0 & 0 & 2 \\
\frac{2}{3} & 0 & -\frac{1}{3} & 1 & 0 & 4 \\
\hline
-\frac{19}{6} & 0 & \frac{5}{6} & 0 & 1 & 10
\end{array}\right]
\begin{array}{c} 12 \\ 6 \\ \ \end{array}
\end{array}
$$

$$
\begin{array}{c}
\begin{array}{ccccc} x_1 & x_2 & s_1 & s_2 & Z \end{array} \\
\begin{array}{c} x_2 \\ x_1 \\ Z \end{array}
\left[\begin{array}{ccccc|c}
0 & 1 & \frac{1}{4} & -\frac{1}{4} & 0 & 1 \\
1 & 0 & -\frac{1}{2} & \frac{3}{2} & 0 & 6 \\
\hline
0 & 0 & -\frac{3}{4} & \frac{19}{4} & 1 & 29
\end{array}\right]
\begin{array}{c} 4 \\ \ \\ \ \end{array}
\end{array}
$$

$$
\begin{array}{c}
\begin{array}{ccccc} x_1 & x_2 & s_1 & s_2 & Z \end{array} \\
\begin{array}{c} s_1 \\ x_1 \\ Z \end{array}
\left[\begin{array}{ccccc|c}
0 & 4 & 1 & -1 & 0 & 4 \\
1 & 2 & 0 & 1 & 0 & 8 \\
\hline
0 & 3 & 0 & 4 & 1 & 32
\end{array}\right]
\end{array}
$$

Thus $Z = 32$ when $x_1 = 8$ and $x_2 = 0$.

21.

$$
\begin{array}{c}
\begin{array}{cccccc} x_1 & x_2 & x_3 & s & t & W \end{array} \\
\left[\begin{array}{cccccc|c}
1 & 2 & 3 & -1 & 1 & 0 & 6 \\
\hline
2 & 3 & 1 & 0 & M & 1 & 0
\end{array}\right]
\end{array}
$$

$$
\begin{array}{c}
\begin{array}{cccccc} x_1 & x_2 & x_3 & s & t & W \end{array} \\
\begin{array}{c} t \\ W \end{array}
\left[\begin{array}{cccccc|c}
1 & 2 & \underline{3} & -1 & 1 & 0 & 6 \\
\hline
2-M & 3-2M & 1-3M & M & 0 & 1 & -6M
\end{array}\right]
\begin{array}{c} 2 \\ \ \end{array}
\end{array}
$$

$$
\begin{array}{c}
\begin{array}{cccccc} x_1 & x_2 & x_3 & s & t & W \end{array} \\
\begin{array}{c} x_3 \\ W \end{array}
\left[\begin{array}{cccccc|c}
\frac{1}{3} & \frac{2}{3} & 1 & -\frac{1}{3} & \frac{1}{3} & 0 & 2 \\
\hline
\frac{5}{3} & \frac{7}{3} & 0 & \frac{1}{3} & -\frac{1}{3}+M & 1 & -2
\end{array}\right]
\end{array}
$$

Thus $Z = 2$ when $x_1 = 0$, $x_2 = 0$ and $x_3 = 2$.

23.

	x_1	x_2	s_1	s_2	s_3	t_2	W	
	1	1	1	0	0	0	0	12
	1	1	0	-1	0	1	0	5
	1	0	0	0	1	0	0	10
	-1	-2	0	0	0	M	1	0

	x_1	x_2	s_1	s_2	s_3	t_2	W		
s_1	1	1	1	0	0	0	0	12	12
t_2	1	$\underline{1}$	0	-1	0	1	0	5	5
s_3	1	0	0	0	1	0	0	10	
W	$-1-M$	$-2-M$	0	M	0	0	1	$-5M$	

	x_1	x_2	s_1	s_2	s_3	t_2	W		
s_1	0	0	1	$\underline{1}$	0	-1	0	7	7
x_2	1	1	0	-1	0	1	0	5	
s_3	1	0	0	0	1	0	0	10	
W	1	0	0	-2	0	$2+M$	1	10	

	x_1	x_2	s_1	s_2	s_3	Z	
s_2	0	0	1	1	0	0	7
x_2	1	1	1	0	0	0	12
s_3	1	0	0	0	1	0	10
Z	1	0	2	0	0	1	24

Thus $Z = 24$ when $x_1 = 0$ and $x_2 = 12$.

25. We write the first constraint as $-x_1 + x_2 + x_3 \geq 1$.

	x_1	x_2	x_3	s_1	t_1	t_2	W	
	-1	1	1	-1	1	0	0	1
	6	3	2	0	0	1	0	12
	1	2	1	0	M	M	1	0

	x_1	x_2	x_3	s_1	t_1	t_2	W		
t_1	-1	1	1	-1	1	0	0	1	
t_2	$\underline{6}$	3	2	0	0	1	0	12	2
W	$1-5M$	$2-4M$	$1-3M$	M	0	0	1	$-13M$	

	x_1	x_2	x_3	s_1	t_1	t_2	W		
t_1	0	$\dfrac{3}{2}$	$\dfrac{4}{3}$	-1	1	$\dfrac{1}{6}$	0	3	2
x_1	1	$\dfrac{1}{2}$	$\dfrac{1}{3}$	0	0	$\dfrac{1}{6}$	0	2	4
W	0	$\dfrac{3}{2}-\dfrac{3}{2}M$	$\dfrac{2}{3}-\dfrac{4}{3}M$	M	0	$-\dfrac{1}{6}+\dfrac{5}{6}M$	1	$-2-3M$	

$$
\begin{array}{c|cccccc|c}
 & x_1 & x_2 & x_3 & s_1 & t_1 & t_2 & W & \\
\hline
x_2 & 0 & 1 & \frac{8}{9} & -\frac{2}{3} & \frac{2}{3} & \frac{1}{9} & 0 & 2 \;\Big]^{\frac{9}{4}} \\
x_1 & 1 & 0 & -\frac{1}{9} & \frac{1}{3} & -\frac{1}{3} & \frac{1}{9} & 0 & 1 \\
\hline
W & 0 & 0 & -\frac{2}{3} & 1 & -1+M & -\frac{1}{3}+M & 1 & -5
\end{array}
$$

$$
\begin{array}{c|cccc|c}
 & x_1 & x_2 & x_3 & s_1 & -Z & \\
\hline
x_3 & 0 & \frac{9}{8} & 1 & -\frac{3}{4} & 0 & \frac{9}{4} \\
x_1 & 1 & \frac{1}{8} & 0 & \frac{1}{4} & 0 & \frac{5}{4} \\
\hline
-Z & 0 & \frac{3}{4} & 0 & \frac{1}{2} & 1 & -\frac{7}{2}
\end{array}
$$

Thus $Z = \dfrac{7}{2}$ when $x_1 = \dfrac{5}{4}$, $x_2 = 0$, and $x_3 = \dfrac{9}{4}$.

27.

$$
\begin{array}{c|cccccc|c}
 & x_1 & x_2 & x_3 & s_1 & s_2 & Z & \\
\hline
s_1 & 4 & -1 & 0 & 1 & 0 & 0 & 2 \\
s_2 & -10 & 1 & 3 & 0 & 1 & 0 & 1 \;\big]\,1 \\
\hline
Z & -1 & -4 & -2 & 0 & 0 & 1 & 0
\end{array}
$$

$$
\begin{array}{c|cccccc|c}
 & x_1 & x_2 & x_3 & s_1 & s_2 & Z & \\
\hline
x_2 & -6 & 0 & 3 & 1 & 1 & 0 & 3 \\
s_2 & -10 & 1 & 3 & 0 & 1 & 0 & 1 \\
\hline
Z & -41 & 0 & 10 & 0 & 4 & 1 & 4
\end{array}
$$

For the last tableau, x_1 is the entering variable. Since no quotients exist, the problem has an unbounded solution. That is, no optimum solution (unbounded).

29. The dual is: Maximize $W = 35y_1 + 25y_2$ subject to

$y_1 + y_2 \le 2,$
$2y_1 + y_2 \le 7,$
$3y_1 + y_2 \le 8,$
$y_1, \; y_2 \ge 0.$

$$
\begin{array}{c|cccccc|c}
 & y_1 & y_2 & s_1 & s_2 & s_3 & W & \\
\hline
s_1 & \underline{1} & 1 & 1 & 0 & 0 & 0 & 2 \;\big]\,2 \\
s_2 & 2 & 1 & 0 & 1 & 0 & 0 & 7 \;\big]\,\frac{7}{2} \\
s_3 & 3 & 1 & 0 & 0 & 1 & 0 & 8 \;\big]\,\frac{8}{3} \\
\hline
W & -35 & -25 & 0 & 0 & 0 & 1 & 0
\end{array}
$$

$$
\begin{array}{c|cccccc|c}
 & y_1 & y_2 & s_1 & s_2 & s_3 & W & \\
\hline
y_1 & 1 & 1 & 1 & 0 & 0 & 0 & 2 \\
s_2 & 0 & -1 & -2 & 1 & 0 & 0 & 3 \\
s_3 & 0 & -2 & -3 & 0 & 1 & 0 & 2 \\
\hline
W & 0 & 10 & 35 & 0 & 0 & 1 & 70
\end{array}
$$

Thus $Z = 70$ when $x_1 = 35$, $x_2 = 0$, and $x_3 = 0$.

31. Let x, y, and z denote the numbers of units of X, Y, and Z produced weekly, respectively. If P is the total profit obtained, we want to maximize $P = 10x + 15y + 22z$ subject to

$$x + 2y + 2z \leq 40,$$
$$x + y + 2z \leq 34,$$
$$x, \ y, \ z \geq 0.$$

	x	y	z	s_1	s_2	P		
s_1	1	2	2	1	0	0	40	20
s_2	1	1	2	0	1	0	34	17
P	−10	−15	−22	0	0	1	0	

	x	y	z	s_1	s_2	P		
s_1	0	1	0	1	−1	0	6	6
z	$\frac{1}{2}$	$\frac{1}{2}$	1	0	$\frac{1}{2}$	0	17	34
P	1	−4	0	0	11	1	374	

	x	y	z	s_1	s_2	P	
y	0	1	0	1	−1	0	6
z	$\frac{1}{2}$	0	1	$-\frac{1}{2}$	1	0	14
P	1	0	0	4	7	1	398

Thus 0 units of X , 6 units of Y, and 14 units of Z give a maximum profit of \$398.

33. Let x_{AC}, x_{AD}, x_{BC}, and x_{BD} denote the amounts (in hundreds of thousands of gallons) transported from A to C, A to D, B to C, and B to D, respectively. If C is the total transportation cost in thousands of dollars, we want to minimize $C = x_{AC} + 2x_{AD} + 2x_{BC} + 4x_{BD}$ subject to

$$x_{AC} + x_{AD} \leq 6,$$
$$x_{BC} + x_{BD} \leq 6,$$
$$x_{AC} + x_{BC} = 5,$$
$$x_{AD} + x_{BD} = 5,$$
$$x_{AC}, \ x_{AD}, \ x_{BC}, \ x_{BD} \geq 0.$$

x_{AC}	x_{AD}	x_{BC}	x_{BD}	s_1	s_2	t_3	t_4	W	
1	1	0	0	1	0	0	0	0	6
0	0	1	1	0	1	0	0	0	6
1	0	1	0	0	0	1	0	0	5
0	1	0	1	0	0	0	1	0	5
1	2	2	4	0	0	M	M	1	0

	x_{AC}	x_{AD}	x_{BC}	x_{BD}	s_1	s_2	t_3	t_4	W		
s_1	1	1	0	0	1	0	0	0	0	6	6
s_2	0	0	1	1	0	1	0	0	0	6	
t_3	1	0	1	0	0	0	1	0	0	5	5
t_4	0	1	0	1	0	0	0	1	0	5	
W	$1-M$	$2-M$	$2-M$	$4-M$	0	0	0	0	1	$-10M$	

	x_{AC}	x_{AD}	x_{BC}	x_{BD}	s_1	s_2	t_3	t_4	W		
s_1	0	1	−1	0	1	0	−1	0	0	1	1
s_2	0	0	1	1	0	1	0	0	0	6	
x_{AC}	1	0	1	0	0	0	1	0	0	5	
t_4	0	1	0	1	0	0	0	1	0	5	5
W	0	$2-M$	1	$4-M$	0	0	$-1+M$	0	1	$-5-5M$	

	x_{AC}	x_{AD}	x_{BC}	x_{BD}	s_1	s_2	t_3	t_4	W		
x_{AD}	0	1	−1	0	1	0	−1	0	0	1	
s_2	0	0	1	1	0	1	0	0	0	6	6
x_{AC}	1	0	1	0	0	0	1	0	0	5	5
t_4	0	0	1	1	−1	0	1	1	0	4	4
W	0	0	$3-M$	$4-M$	$-2+M$	0	1	0	1	$-7-4M$	

	x_{AC}	x_{AD}	x_{BC}	x_{BD}	s_1	s_2	t_3	t_4	W	
x_{AD}	0	1	0	1	0	0	0	1	0	5
s_2	0	0	0	0	1	1	−1	−1	0	2
x_{AC}	1	0	0	−1	1	0	0	−1	0	1
x_{BC}	0	0	1	1	−1	0	1	1	0	4
W	0	0	0	1	1	0	$-2+M$	$-3+M$	1	−19

The minimum value of C is 19, when $x_{AC} = 1$, $x_{AD} = 5$, $x_{BC} = 4$, and $x_{BD} = 0$. Thus 100,000 gal from A to C, 500,000 gal from A to D, and 400,000 gal from B to C give a minimum cost of $19,000.

35. Let x and y represent daily consumption of foods A and B in ounces. We want to minimize $C = 4x + 11y$ subject to the constraints

$$8x + 4y \geq 176,$$
$$16x + 32y \geq 1024,$$
$$2x + 5y \geq 200,$$
$$x \geq 0,$$
$$y \geq 0.$$

The feasible region is unbounded with corner points $(100, 0)$, $\left(\frac{5}{2}, \ 39\right)$ and $(0, 44)$. C has a minimum value at $(100, 0)$. Thus the animals should be fed 100 ounces of food A each day.

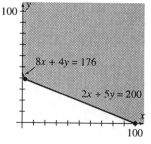

37.

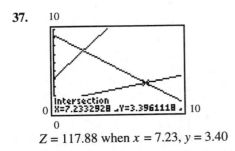

$Z = 117.88$ when $x = 7.23$, $y = 3.40$

Mathematical Snapshot Chapter 7

1.

	CURATIVE UNITS	TOXIC UNITS	RELATIVE DISCOMFORT
Drug (per ounce)	500	400	1
Radiation (per min)	1000	600	1
Requirement	≥ 2000	≤ 1400	

Let x_1 = number of ounces of drug and let x_2 = number of minutes of radiation. We want to minimize the discomfort D, where $D = x_1 + x_2$, subject to

$$500x_1 + 1000x_2 \geq 2000,$$
$$400x_1 + 600x_2 \leq 1400,$$

where x_1, $x_2 \geq 0$.

The corner points are $(0, 2)$, $\left(0, \dfrac{7}{3}\right)$, and $(2, 1)$.

At $(0, 2)$, $D = 0 + 2 = 2$;

at $\left(0, \dfrac{7}{3}\right)$, $D = 0 + \dfrac{7}{3} = \dfrac{7}{3}$;

at $(2, 1)$, $D = 2 + 1 = 3$.

Thus D is minimum at $(0, 2)$.

The patient should get 0 ounce of drug and 2 minutes of radiation.

Chapter 8

Principles in Practice 8.1

1. Let $P = 518$ and let $n = 3(365) = 1095$.

$$S = P(1+r)^n$$

$$S = 518\left(1+\frac{r}{365}\right)^{1095}$$

By graphing S as a function of the nominal rate r, we find that when $r = 0.049$, $S = 600$. Thus, at the nominal rate of 4.9% compounded daily, the initial amount of $518 will grow to $600 after 3 years.

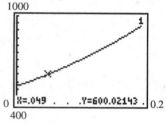

2. Let $P = 520$ and let $r = 0.052$.

$$S = P(1+r)^n$$

$$S = 520\left(1+\frac{0.052}{365}\right)^n$$

$$S = 520\left(\frac{365.052}{365}\right)^n$$

By graphing S as a function of n, we find that when $n = 2571$, $S = 750$. Thus, it will take $\frac{2571}{365} = 7.044$ years, or 7 years and 16 days for $520 to grow to $750 at the nominal rate of 5.2% compounded daily.

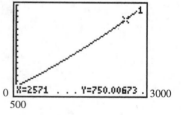

3. Let $n = 12$.

$$r_e = \left(1+\frac{r}{n}\right)^n - 1$$

$$r_e = \left(1+\frac{r}{12}\right)^{12} - 1$$

By graphing r_e as a function of r, we find that, when the nominal rate $r = 0.077208$ or 7.7208%, the effective rate $r_e = 0.08$ or 8%.

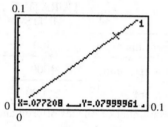

4. The respective effective rates of interest are found using the formula $r_e = \left(1+\frac{r}{n}\right)^n - 1$.

Let $n = 12$ when $r = 0.11$:

$r_e = \left(1+\frac{0.11}{12}\right)^{12} - 1 \approx 0.1157$. Hence, when the nominal rate $r = 11\%$ is compounded monthly, the effective rate $r_e = 11.57\%$. When $r = 0.1125$:

$r_e = \left(1+\frac{0.1125}{4}\right)^4 - 1 \approx 0.1173$. Hence in the second case when the nominal rate $r = 11.25\%$ is compounded quarterly, the effective rate $r_e = 11.73\%$. This is the better effective rate of interest. To find the better investment, compare the compound amounts, S at the end of n years. With $P = 10,000$ and $r_e = 0.1157$,

$S_1 = P(1+r)^n = 10,000(1+0.1157)^n$, and, in the second case, when $P = 9700$ and $r_e = 0.1173$

$S_2 = P(1+r)^n = 9700(1+0.1173)^n$.

$S_1(20) = 10,000(1.1157)^{20} \approx 89,319.99$

$S_2(20) = 9700(1.1173)^{20} \approx 89,159.52$

The $10,000 investment is slightly better over 20 years.

Exercise 8.1

1. **a.** $6000(1.08)^8 \approx \$11,105.58$

   b. $11,105.58 - 6000 = \$5105.58$

3. $\left(1 + \dfrac{0.08}{4}\right)^4 - 1 = (1.02)^4 - 1 \approx 0.08243$ or 8.243%

5. $\left(1 + \dfrac{0.08}{365}\right)^{365} - 1 \approx 0.08328$ or 8.328%

7. **a.** A nominal rate compounded yearly is the same as the effective rate, so the effective rate is 10%.

   b. $\left(1 + \dfrac{0.10}{2}\right)^2 - 1 = 0.1025$ or 10.25%

   c. $\left(1 + \dfrac{0.10}{4}\right)^4 - 1 \approx 0.10381$ or 10.381%

   d. $\left(1 + \dfrac{0.10}{12}\right)^{12} - 1 \approx 0.10471$ or 10.471%

   e. $\left(1 + \dfrac{0.10}{365}\right)^{365} - 1 \approx 0.10516$ or 10.516%

9. Let r_e be the effective rate. Then

   $2000(1 + r_e)^5 = 2950$

   $(1 + r_e)^5 = \dfrac{2950}{2000}$

   $1 + r_e = \sqrt[5]{\dfrac{2950}{2000}}$

   $r_e = \sqrt[5]{\dfrac{2950}{2000}} - 1$

   $r_e \approx 0.0808$ or 8.08%.

11. From Example 6, the number of years, n, is given by $n = \dfrac{\ln 2}{\ln(1.08)} \approx 9.0$ years.

13. $6000(1.08)^7 \approx \$10,282.95$

15. $18,500(1.06)^{10} \approx \$33,130.68$

17. **a.** $(0.015)(12) = 0.18$ or 18%

    b. $(1.015)^{12} - 1 \approx 0.1956$ or 19.56%

19. The compound amount after the first four years is $2000(1.06)^4$. After the next four years the compound amount is $\left[2000(1.06)^4\right](1.03)^8 \approx \$3198.54$.

21. 7.8% compounded semiannually is equivalent to an effective rate of $(1.039)^2 - 1 = 0.079521$ or 7.9521%. Thus 8% compounded annually, which is the effective rate, is the better rate.

23. **a.** $\left(1 + \dfrac{0.0525}{360}\right)^{365} - 1 \approx 0.0547$ or 5.47%

    b. $\left(1 + \dfrac{0.0525}{365}\right)^{365} - 1 \approx 0.0539$ or 5.39%

25. Let r_e = effective rate.

    $300,000 = 100,000(1 + r_e)^{10}$

    $(1 + r_e)^{10} = 3$

    $1 + r_e = \sqrt[10]{3}$

    $r_e = \sqrt[10]{3} - 1 \approx 0.1161$ or 11.61%.

27. Let r = the required nominal rate.

    $220\left(1 + \dfrac{r}{2}\right)^{28} = 1000$

    $\left(1 + \dfrac{r}{2}\right)^{28} = \dfrac{1000}{220} = \dfrac{50}{11}$

    $1 + \dfrac{r}{2} = \sqrt[28]{\dfrac{50}{11}}$

    $r = 2\left[\sqrt[28]{\dfrac{50}{11}} - 1\right] \approx 0.1111$ or 11.11%

Exercise 8.2

1. $6000(1.05)^{-20} \approx \$2261.34$

3. $4000(1.035)^{-24} \approx \$1751.83$

5. $8000\left(1+\dfrac{0.06}{4}\right)^{-30} \approx \$5118.10$

7. $8000\left(1+\dfrac{0.10}{12}\right)^{-60} \approx \$4862.31$

9. $10,000\left(1+\dfrac{0.095}{365}\right)^{-4(365)} \approx \$6838.95$

11. $10,000(1+0.01)^{-12} \approx \$8874.49$

13. $27,000(1.03)^{-22} \approx \$14,091.10$

15. Let x be the payment 2 years from now. The equation of value at year 2 is
    $x = 600(1.04)^{-2} + 800(1.04)^{-4}$, from which
    $x \approx \$1238.58$.

17. Let x be the payment at the end of 6 years. The equation of value at year 6 is
    $2000(1.07)^4 + 4000(1.07)^2 + x = 5000(1.07) + 5000(1.07)^{-4}$
    $x = 5000(1.07) + 5000(1.07)^{-4} - 2000(1.07)^4 - 4000(1.07)^2$
    $x \approx \$1963.28$.

19. **a.** $NPV = 8000(1.025)^{-6} + 10,000(1.025)^{-8} + 14,000(1.025)^{-12} - 25,000 \approx \$515.62$

    b. Since $NPV > 0$, the investment is profitable.

21. We consider the value of each investment at the end of eight years. The savings account has a value of
    $10,000(1.03)^{16} \approx \$16,047.06$.
    The business investment has a value of $16,000. Thus the better choice is the savings account.

23. $1000\left(1+\dfrac{0.115}{4}\right)^{-80} \approx \$103.56$

25. Let r be the nominal discount rate, compounded quarterly. Then
    $$4700 = 10,000\left(1+\frac{r}{4}\right)^{-32}$$
    $$4700 = \frac{10,000}{\left(1+\frac{r}{4}\right)^{32}}$$
    $$\left(1+\frac{r}{4}\right)^{32} = \frac{10,000}{4700} = \frac{100}{47}$$
    $$1+\frac{r}{4} = \sqrt[32]{\frac{100}{47}}$$
    $$r = 4\left[\sqrt[32]{\frac{100}{47}} - 1\right] \approx 0.0955 \text{ or } 9.55\%$$

Principles in Practice 8.3

1. Let $a = 64$ and let $r = \frac{3}{4}$. Then, the next five

   heights of the ball are $64\left(\frac{3}{4}\right)$, $64\left(\frac{3}{4}\right)^2$,

   $64\left(\frac{3}{4}\right)^3$, $64\left(\frac{3}{4}\right)^4$, $64\left(\frac{3}{4}\right)^5$, or 48 ft, 36 ft,

   27 ft, $20\frac{1}{4}$ ft, and $15\frac{3}{16}$ ft.

2. Let $a = 500$ and let $r = 1.5$. Then, the
   number of bacteria at the end of each minute
   for the first six minutes is $500(1.5)$,
   $500(1.5)^2$, $500(1.5)^3$, $500(1.5)^4$,
   $500(1.5)^5$, $500(1.5)^6$, or 750, 1125, 1688,
   2531, 3797, 5695.

3. The total vertical distance traveled in the air
   after n bounces is equal to 2 times the sum
   of heights. If $a = 6$ and $r = \frac{2}{3}$, then when the
   ball hits the ground for the twelfth time,
   $n = 12$ and the distance traveled in the air is

   $$2s = 2\left[\frac{a\left(1 - r^n\right)}{1 - r}\right] = 2\left[\frac{6\left(1 - \left(\frac{2}{3}\right)^{12}\right)}{1 - \frac{2}{3}}\right]$$

   ≈ 35.72 meters

4. The amount of profit earned in the first two
   years is the sum of the monthly profits. Let
   $a = 2000$,
   $r = 1.1$, and $n = 24$.
   $$s = \frac{2000\left(1 - (1.1)^{24}\right)}{1 - 1.1} \approx 176{,}994.65$$
   Thus, the company earned \$176,994.65 in
   the first two years.

5. Let $R = 500$ and let $n = 72$. Then, the present
   value A of the annuity is given by
   $$A = R\left(\frac{1 - (1 + r)^{-n}}{r}\right) = 500\left(\frac{1 - (1 + r)^{-72}}{r}\right)$$
   By graphing A as a function of r, we find
   that when $r \approx 0.005167$, $A = 30{,}000$. Thus,
   if the present value of the annuity is
   \$30,000, the monthly interest rate is

0.5167%, and the nominal rate is
$12(0.005167) = 0.062$ or 6.2%.

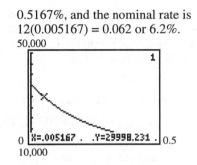

6. Since the man pays \$2000 for 6 years and
   \$3500 for 8 years, we can consider the
   payments to be an annuity of \$3500 for
   14 years minus an annuity of \$1500 for
   6 years so that the first 24 payments are
   \$2000 each. Thus, the present value is
   $3500a_{\overline{56}|0.015} - 1500a_{\overline{24}|0.015}$
   $\approx 3500(37.705879) - 1500(20.030405)$
   $= 101{,}924.97$
   Thus, the present value of the payments is
   \$101,925. Since the man made an initial
   down payment of \$20,000, list price was
   $101{,}925 + 20{,}000 = \$121{,}925$.

7. Let $r = \frac{0.048}{4} = 0.012$, and $n = 24$.
   $$A = R\left(\frac{1 - (1 + r)^{-n}}{r}\right)$$
   $$A = R\left(\frac{1 - (1 + 0.012)^{-24}}{0.012}\right)$$
   $$= R\left(\frac{1 - (1.012)^{-24}}{0.012}\right)$$
   By Graphing A as a function of R, we find
   that when $R = 723.03$, $A = 15{,}000$. Thus the
   monthly payment is \$723.03 if the present
   value of the annuity is \$15,000.

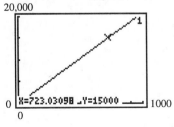

8. Find the annuity due. The man makes an initial payment of $1000 followed by an ordinary annuity of $1000 for 11 months. Thus, let $R = 1000$, $n = 11$, and $r = \frac{0.048}{12} = 0.004$.

The present value of the annuity due is

$1000\left(1 + a_{\overline{11}|0.009}\right) = 1000(1 + 10.740513)$

$= 11,740.51$

Thus, he should pay $11,740.51.

9. Let $R = 2000$ and let $r = 0.087$. Then, the value of the IRA at the end of 15 years, when $n = 15$, is given by

$$S = R\left(\frac{(1+r)^n - 1}{r}\right)$$

$$S = 2000\left(\frac{(1+0.087)^{15} - 1}{0.087}\right) \approx 57,355.58$$

Thus, at the end of 15 years the IRA will be worth $57,355.58.

10. Let $R = 2000$ and let $r = 0.087$. Since the deposits are made at the beginning of each year, the value of the IRA at the end of 15 years is given by

$$S = R\left(\frac{(1+r)^{n+1} - 1}{r}\right) - R.$$

Let $n = 15$.

$$S = 2000\left(\frac{(1+0.087)^{16} - 1}{0.087}\right) - 2000$$

$$\approx 62,345.51$$

Thus, the IRA is worth $62,345.51 at the end of 15 years.

Exercise 8.3

1. 64

$64\left(\frac{1}{2}\right) = 32$

$64\left(\frac{1}{2}\right)^2 = 16$

$64\left(\frac{1}{2}\right)^3 = 8$

$64\left(\frac{1}{2}\right)^4 = 4$

3. 100

$100(1.02) = 102$

$100(1.02)^2 = 104.04$

5. $s = \dfrac{\frac{2}{3}\left[1 - \left(\frac{2}{3}\right)^5\right]}{1 - \frac{2}{3}} = \dfrac{\frac{2}{3}\left[\frac{211}{243}\right]}{\frac{1}{3}} = \dfrac{422}{243}$

7. $s = \dfrac{1\left[1 - (0.1)^6\right]}{1 - 0.1} = 1.11111$

9. $a_{\overline{35}|0.04} \approx 18.664613$

11. $s_{\overline{8}|0.0075} \approx 8.213180$

13. $500a_{\overline{5}|0.07} \approx 500(4.100197) \approx \$2050.10$

15. $2000a_{\overline{18}|0.02} \approx 2000(14.992031)$

$\approx \$29,984.06$

17. $800 + 800a_{\overline{11}|0.035} \approx 800 + 800(9.001551)$

$\approx \$8001.24$

19. $2000s_{\overline{36}|0.0125} \approx 2000(45.115505)$

$= \$90,231.01$

21. $5000s_{\overline{20}|0.07} \approx 5000(40.995492)$

$= \$204,977.46$

23. $1200\left(s_{\overline{13}|0.08} - 1\right) \approx 1200(21.495297 - 1)$

$\approx \$24,594.36$

25. $75a_{\overline{30}|0.005} - 25a_{\overline{6}|0.005}$

$\approx 75(27.794054) - 25(5.896384)$

$\approx \$1937.14$

27. $R = \dfrac{5000}{a_{\overline{12}|0.015}} \approx \dfrac{5000}{10.907505} \approx \$458.40$

29. **a.** $\left(50s_{\overline{48}|0.005}\right)(1.005)^{24}$

$\approx 50(54.097832)(1.005)^{24}$

$\approx \$3048.85$

b. $3048.85 - 48(50) = \$648.85$

31. $R = \dfrac{48,000}{s_{\overline{10}|0.07}}$

      $\approx \dfrac{48,000}{13.816448}$

      $\approx \$3474.12$

33.   The original annual payment is $\dfrac{25,000}{s_{\overline{10}|0.06}}$.

      After six years the value of the fund is

      $\dfrac{25,000}{s_{\overline{10}|0.06}} s_{\overline{6}|0.06}$.

      This accumulates to

      $\left[\dfrac{25,000}{s_{\overline{10}|0.06}} s_{\overline{6}|0.06} \right] (1.07)^4$.

      Let x be the amount of the new payment.

      $x s_{\overline{4}|0.07}$

      $= 25,000 - \left[\dfrac{25,000}{s_{\overline{10}|0.06}} s_{\overline{6}|0.06} (1.07)^4 \right]$

      $x = \dfrac{25,000 - \left[\dfrac{25,000}{s_{\overline{10}|0.06}} s_{\overline{6}|0.06} (1.07)^4 \right]}{s_{\overline{4}|0.07}}$

      $x \approx \dfrac{25,000 - \left[\dfrac{25,000}{13.180795} (6.975319)(1.07)^4 \right]}{4.439943}$

      $x \approx \$1725$

35. $s_{\overline{60}|0.017} = \dfrac{(1.017)^{60} - 1}{0.017}$

      ≈ 102.91305

37. $700 a_{\overline{360}|0.0125} = 700 \left[\dfrac{1 - (1.0125)^{-360}}{0.0125} \right]$

      $\approx 55,360.30$

39. $R = \dfrac{3000}{s_{\overline{20}|0.01375}}$

      $= \dfrac{3000(0.01375)}{(1.01375)^{20} - 1}$

      $\approx \$131.34$

41. $50,000 + 50,000 a_{\overline{19}|0.12}$

      $= 50,000 + 50,000 \left[\dfrac{1 - (1.12)^{-19}}{0.12} \right]$

      $\approx \$418,288.84$

43.   For the first situation, the compound amount is

      $\left[2000 \left(s_{\overline{11}|0.07} - 1 \right) \right] (1.07)^{30}$

      $= 2000 \left[\dfrac{(1.07)^{11} - 1}{0.07} - 1 \right] (1.07)^{30}$

      $\approx \$225,073,$

      so the net earnings are
      $225,073 - 20,000 = \$205,073.$
      For the second situation, the compound amount is

      $2000 \left(s_{\overline{31}|0.07} - 1 \right)$

      $= 2000 \left[\dfrac{(1.07)^{31} - 1}{0.07} - 1 \right]$

      $\approx \$202,146,$

      so the net earnings are
      $202,146 - 60,000 = \$142,146.$

Exercise 8.4

1. $R = \dfrac{2000}{a_{\overline{36}|0.0125}} \approx \dfrac{2000}{28.847267} \approx \$69.33$

3. $R = \dfrac{8000}{a_{\overline{36}|0.01}} \approx \dfrac{8000}{30.107505} \approx \$265.71$

    Finance charge $= 36(265.71) - 8000 = \$1565.56$

5.   a. $R = \dfrac{7500}{a_{\overline{36}|0.01}} \approx \dfrac{7500}{30.107505} \approx \$249.11$

    b. $7500(0.01) = \$75$

    c. $249.11 - 75 = \$174.11$

7. $R = \dfrac{5000}{a_{\overline{4}|0.07}} \approx \dfrac{5000}{3.387211} \approx \$1476.14$

    The interest for the first period is $(0.07)(5000) = \$350$, so the principal repaid at the end of that period is $1476.14 - 350 = \$1126.14$. The principal outstanding at the beginning of period 2 is $5000 - 1126.14 = \$3873.86$. The interest for period 2 is $(0.07)(3873.86) = \$271.17$, so the principal repaid at the end of that period is $1476.14 - 271.17 = \$1204.97$. The principal outstanding at beginning of period 3 is $3873.86 - 1204.97 = \$2668.89$. Continuing in this manner, we construct the following amortization schedule.

Period	Prin. Outs. at Beginning	Int. for Period	Pmt. at End	Prin. Repaid at End
1	5000.00	350.00	1476.14	1126.14
2	3873.86	271.17	1476.14	1204.97
3	2668.89	186.82	1476.14	1289.32
4	1379.57	96.57	1476.14	1379.57
Total		904.56	5904.56	5000.00

9. $R = \dfrac{900}{a_{\overline{5}|0.025}} \approx \dfrac{900}{4.645828} \approx \$193.72$

    The interest for period 1 is $(0.025)(900) = \$22.50$, so the principal repaid at the end of that period is $193.72 - 22.50 = \$171.22$. The principal outstanding at the beginning of period 2 is $900 - 171.22 = \$728.78$. The interest for that period is $(0.025)(728.78) = \$18.22$, so the principal repaid at the end of that period is $193.72 - 18.22 = \$175.50$. The principal outstanding at the beginning of period 3 is $728.78 - 175.50 = \$553.28$. Continuing in this manner, we obtain the following amortization schedule. Note the adjustment in the final payment.

Period	Prin. Outs. at Beginning	Int. for Period	Pmt. at End	Prin. Repaid at End
1	900.00	22.50	193.72	171.22
2	728.78	18.22	193.72	175.50
3	553.28	13.83	193.72	179.89
4	373.39	9.33	193.72	184.39
5	189.00	4.73	193.73	189.00
Total		68.61	968.61	900.00

11. From Eq. (1),

$$n = \frac{\ln\left[\frac{100}{100-1000(0.02)}\right]}{\ln(1.02)} \approx 11.268.$$

Thus the number of full payments is 11.

13. Each of the original payments is $\dfrac{10,000}{a_{\overline{10}|0.04}}$.

After two years the value of the remaining

payments is $\left(\dfrac{10,000}{a_{\overline{10}|0.04}}\right)a_{\overline{6}|0.04}$. Thus the

new annual payment is

$$\frac{10,000a_{\overline{6}|0.04}}{a_{\overline{10}|0.04}} \cdot \frac{1}{a_{\overline{6}|0.05}}$$

$$\approx \frac{10,000(5.242137)}{8.110896} \cdot \frac{1}{5.075692} \approx \$1273.$$

15. a. Monthly interest rate is

$\dfrac{0.102}{12} = 0.0085$. Monthly payment is

$$\frac{45,000}{a_{\overline{300}|0.0085}} = 45,000\left[\frac{0.0085}{1-(1.0085)^{-300}}\right]$$

$$\approx \$415.28$$

b. $45,000(0.0085) = \$382.50$

c. $415.28 - 382.50 = \$32.78$

d. $300(415.28) - 45,000 = \$79,584$

17. $n = \dfrac{\ln\left[\frac{100}{100-2000(0.015)}\right]}{\ln 1.015} \approx 23.956$. Thus the

number of full payments is 23.

19. Present value of mortgage payments is

$$600a_{\overline{360}|\frac{0.126}{12}} = 600\left[\frac{1-\left(1+\frac{0.126}{12}\right)^{-360}}{\frac{0.126}{12}}\right]$$

$$\approx \$55,812.75$$

This amount is 75% of the purchase price x.

$0.75x = 55,812.75$

$x = \$74,417$

21. $\dfrac{25,000}{a_{\overline{60}|0.0125}} - \dfrac{25,000}{a_{\overline{60}|0.01}}$

$$= 25,000\left[\frac{1}{a_{\overline{60}|0.0125}} - \frac{1}{a_{\overline{60}|0.01}}\right]$$

$$= 25,000\left[\frac{0.0125}{1-(1.0125)^{-60}} - \frac{0.01}{1-(1.01)^{-60}}\right]$$

$$\approx \$38.64$$

Chapter 8 Review Problems

1. $s = 2 + 1 + \dfrac{1}{2} + \ldots + 2\left(\dfrac{1}{2}\right)^5 = \dfrac{2\left[1-\left(\frac{1}{2}\right)^6\right]}{1-\frac{1}{2}}$

$$= \frac{2\left[\frac{63}{64}\right]}{\frac{1}{2}} = \frac{63}{16}$$

3. 8.2% compounded semiannually corresponds to an effective rate of $(1.041)^2 - 1 = 0.083681$ or 8.37%. Thus the better choice is 8.5% compounded annually.

5. Let x be the payment at the end of 2 years. The equation of value at the end of year 2 is

$$1000(1.04)^4 + x = 1200(1.04)^{-4} + 1000(1.04)^{-8}$$
$$x = 1200(1.04)^{-4} + 1000(1.04)^{-8} - 1000(1.04)^4$$
$$\approx \$586.60$$

7. **a.** $A = 200a_{\overline{13}|0.04} \approx 200(9.985648)$

$$\approx \$1997.13$$

  b. $S = 200s_{\overline{13}|0.04} \approx 200(16.626838)$

$$\approx \$3325.37$$

9. $100s_{\overline{9}|0.035} - 100 \approx 100(10.368496) - 100$

$$\approx \$936.85$$

11. $\dfrac{5000}{s_{\overline{5}|0.06}} \approx \dfrac{5000}{5.637093} \approx \$886.98$

13. Let x be the first payment. The equation of value now is

$$x + 2x(1.07)^{-3} = 500(1.05)^{-3} + 500(1.03)^{-8}$$
$$x\left[1 + 2(1.07)^{-3}\right] = 500(1.05)^{-3} + 500(1.03)^{-8}$$
$$x = \frac{500(1.05)^{-3} + 500(1.03)^{-8}}{1 + 2(1.07)^{-3}}$$
$$x \approx \$314.00$$

15. $R = \dfrac{15,000}{a_{\overline{5}|0.0075}} \approx \dfrac{15,000}{4.889440} \approx \$3067.84$

  The interest for period 1 is $(0.0075)(15,000) = \$112.50$, so the principal repaid at the end of that period is $3067.84 - 112.50 = \$2955.34$. The principal outstanding at beginning of period 2 is $15,000 - 2955.34 = \$12,044.66$. The interest for period 2 is $0.0075(12,044.66) = \$90.33$, so the principal repaid at the end of that period is $3067.84 - 90.33 = \$2977.51$. Principal outstanding at the beginning of period 3 is $12,044.66 - 2977.51 = \$9067.15$. Continuing, we obtain the following amortization schedule. Note the adjustment in the final payment.

Period	Prin. Outs. at Beginning	Int. for Period	Pmt. at End	Prin. Repaid at End
1	15,000.00	112.50	3067.84	2955.34
2	12,044.66	90.33	3067.84	2977.51
3	9067.15	68.00	3067.84	2999.84
4	6067.31	45.50	3067.84	3022.34
5	3044.97	22.84	3067.81	3044.97
Total		339.17	15,339.17	15,000.00

17. The monthly payment is

$$\frac{11,000}{a_{\overline{48}|0.01125}} = 11,000\left[\frac{0.01125}{1-(1.01125)^{-48}}\right] \approx \$297.84$$

The finance charge is $48(297.84) - 11,000 = \$3296.32$

Mathematical Snapshot Chapter 8

1. $\dfrac{12+11+10+9}{78} \cdot 150 \approx \$80.77$

3. Monthly payment $= \dfrac{7500}{a_{\overline{36}|0.01}} \approx \dfrac{7500}{30.107505}$

$\approx \$249.11$

Finance charge $= 36(249.11) - 7500 = \$1467.96$

We have $1+2+\cdots+36 = \dfrac{36(37)}{2} = 666$, so the interest for the first month is $\dfrac{36}{666}(1467.96) \approx \$79.35$.

Thus the principal repaid is $249.11 - 79.35 = \$169.76$. The amount owed at the beginning of the second month is $7500 - 169.76 = \$7330.24$. The interest for the second month is $\dfrac{35}{666}(1467.96) = \$77.15$, so the principal repaid is $249.11 - 77.15 = \$171.96$. Thus the amount owed at the beginning of the second month is $7330.24 - 171.96 = \$7158.28$, which is the payoff amount.

Chapter 9

1.

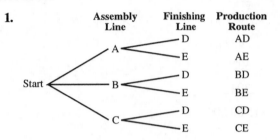

Assembly Line	Finishing Line	Production Route
A	D	AD
	E	AE
Start B	D	BD
	E	BE
C	D	CD
	E	CE

6 possible production routes

3.

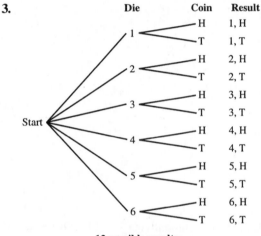

Die	Coin	Result
1	H	1, H
	T	1, T
2	H	2, H
	T	2, T
3	H	3, H
	T	3, T
Start 4	H	4, H
	T	4, T
5	H	5, H
	T	5, T
6	H	6, H
	T	6, T

12 possible results

5. There are 5 science courses and 4 humanities courses. By the basic counting principle, the number of selections is $5 \cdot 4 = 20$.

7. There are 2 appetizers, 4 entrees, 4 desserts, and 3 beverages. By the basic counting principle, the number of possible complete dinners is $2 \cdot 4 \cdot 4 \cdot 3 = 96$.

9. For each of the 10 questions, there are 2 choices. By the basic counting principle, the number of ways to answer the examination is $2 \cdot 2 \cdot \cdots \cdot 2 = 2^{10} = 1024$.

11. $_5P_2 = 5 \cdot 4 = 20$

13. $_6P_6 = \dfrac{6!}{(6-6)!} = \dfrac{6!}{0!} = \dfrac{6 \cdot 5 \cdot 4 \cdot 3 \cdot 2 \cdot 1}{1} = 720$

15. $_4P_2 \cdot _5P_3 = (4 \cdot 3)(5 \cdot 4 \cdot 3) = (12)(60) = 720$

17. $\dfrac{1000!}{999!} = \dfrac{1000 \cdot 999!}{999!} = 1000$

For most calculators, attempting to evaluate $\dfrac{1000!}{999!}$ results in an error message (because of the magnitude of the numbers involved).

19. A name for the firm is an ordered arrangement of the three last names. Thus the number of possible firm names is $_3P_3 = 3! = 3 \cdot 2 \cdot 1 = 6$.

21. The number of ways of selecting 3 of 8 contestants in an order is $_8P_3 = 8 \cdot 7 \cdot 6 = 336$.

23. On each roll of a die, there are 6 possible outcomes. By the basic counting principle, on 3 rolls the number of possible results is $6 \cdot 6 \cdot 6 = 6^3 = 216$.

25. The number of ways of selecting 3 of the 12 students in an order is $_{12}P_3 = 12 \cdot 11 \cdot 10 = 1320$.

27. The number of ways an employee can choose 3 of the 8 items in an order is $_8P_3 = 8 \cdot 7 \cdot 6 = 336$.

29. The number of ways to select six of the six different letters in the word **MEADOW** in an order is $_6P_6 = 6! = 6 \cdot 5 \cdot 4 \cdot 3 \cdot 2 \cdot 1 = 720$.

31. For an arrangement of books, order is important. The number of ways to arrange 5 of 7 books is $_7P_5 = 7 \cdot 6 \cdot 5 \cdot 4 \cdot 3 = 2520$.
All 7 books can be arranged in $_7P_7 = 7! = 5040$ ways.

33. After a "four of a kind" hand is dealt, the cards can be arranged so that the first four have the same face value, and order is not important, There are 13 possibilities for the first four cards (all 2's, all 3's, ..., all aces). The fifth card can be any one of the 48 cards that remain. By the basic counting principle, the number of "four of a kind" hands is $13 \cdot 48 = 624$.

35. The number of ways the waitress can place four of the four different sandwiches (and order is important) is
$$_4P_4 = 4! = 4 \cdot 3 \cdot 2 \cdot 1 = 24.$$

37. a. To fill the four offices by different people, 4 of 12 members must be selected, and order is important. This can be done in
$$_{12}P_4 = 12 \cdot 11 \cdot 10 \cdot 9 = 11,880 \text{ ways.}$$

   b. If the president and vice president must be different members, then there are 12 choices for president, 11 for vice president, 12 for secretary, and 12 for treasurer. By the basic counting principle, the offices can be filled in $12 \cdot 11 \cdot 12 \cdot 12 = 19,008$ ways.

39. There are 2 choices for the center position. After that choice is made, to fill the remaining four positions (and order is important), there are $_4P_4$ ways. By the basic counting principle, to assign positions to the five-member team there are $2 \cdot {}_4P_4 = 2(4!) = 2(24) = 48$ ways.

41. There are $_4P_4$ ways to select the first four batters (order is important) and there are $_5P_5$ ways to select the remaining batters. By the basic counting principle, the number of possible batting orders is
$$_4P_4 \cdot {}_5P_5 = 4! \cdot 5! = 24 \cdot 120 = 2880.$$

Exercise 9.2

1. $_6C_4 = \dfrac{6!}{4!(6-4)!} = \dfrac{6!}{4! \cdot 2!} = \dfrac{6 \cdot 5 \cdot 4!}{4!(2 \cdot 1)}$
$$= \dfrac{6 \cdot 5}{2 \cdot 1} = 15$$

3. $_{100}C_{100} = \dfrac{100!}{100!(100-100)!} = \dfrac{1}{0!} = \dfrac{1}{1} = 1$

5. $_3P_2 \cdot {}_3C_2 = (3 \cdot 2)\dfrac{3!}{2!(3-2)!}$
$$= (3 \cdot 2)\dfrac{3 \cdot 2!}{2! \cdot 1!} = (3 \cdot 2) \cdot 3 = 18$$

7. $_nC_r = \dfrac{n!}{r!(n-r)!}$

$_nC_{n-r} = \dfrac{n!}{(n-r)![n-(n-r)]!} = \dfrac{n!}{(n-r)!r!}.$
Thus $_nC_r = {}_nC_{n-r}.$

9. The number of ways of selecting 5 of 15 people so that order is not important is
$$_{15}C_5 = \dfrac{15!}{5!(15-5)!} = \dfrac{15!}{5! \cdot 10!}$$
$$= \dfrac{15 \cdot 14 \cdot 13 \cdot 12 \cdot 11 \cdot 10!}{5 \cdot 4 \cdot 3 \cdot 2 \cdot 1(10!)} = 3003$$

11. The number of ways of selecting 10 of 12 questions (without regard to order) is
$$_{12}C_{10} = \dfrac{12!}{10!(12-10)!} = \dfrac{12!}{10! \cdot 2!} = \dfrac{12 \cdot 11 \cdot 10!}{10! \cdot 2 \cdot 1}$$
$$= 66.$$

13. The order of selecting 10 of the 74 dresses is of no concern. Thus the number of possible samples $_{74}C_{10} = \dfrac{74!}{10! \cdot (74-10)!} = \dfrac{74!}{10! \cdot 64!}.$

15. To score 80, 90, or 100, exactly 8, 9, or 10 questions must be correct, respectively. The number of ways in which 8 of 10 questions can be correct is
$$_{10}C_8 = \dfrac{10!}{8!(10-8)!} = \dfrac{10!}{8! \cdot 2!} = \dfrac{10 \cdot 9 \cdot 8!}{8! \cdot 2 \cdot 1} = 45.$$
For 9 of 10 questions, the number of ways is

$$_{10}C_9 = \frac{10!}{9!(10-9)!} = \frac{10!}{9! \cdot 1!} = \frac{10 \cdot 9!}{9! \cdot 1} = 10,$$

and for 10 of 10 questions, it is

$$_{10}C_{10} = \frac{10!}{10!(10-10)!} = \frac{10!}{10! \cdot 0!} = 1.$$

Thus the number of ways to score 80 or better is $45 + 10 + 1 = 56$.

17. The word REMEMBER has 8 letters with repetition: two R's, three E's, two M's, and one B. Thus the number of distinguishable horizontal arrangements is

$$\frac{8!}{2! \cdot 3! \cdot 2! \cdot 1!} = \frac{8 \cdot 7 \cdot 6 \cdot 5 \cdot 4 \cdot 3!}{(2)3!(2)} = 1680.$$

19. The number of ways 4 heads and 2 tails can occur in 6 tosses of a coin is the same as the number of distinguishable permutations in the "word" HHHHTT, which is

$$\frac{6!}{4! \cdot 2!} = \frac{6 \cdot 5 \cdot 4!}{4!(2)} = 15.$$

21. Since the order in which the calls are made is important, the number of possible schedules for the 6 calls is $_6P_6 = 6! = 720$.

23. The number of ways to assign 9 scientists so 3 work on project A, 3 work on B, and 3 work on C is $\dfrac{9!}{3!3!3!} = 1680$.

25. A response to the true-false questions can be considered an ordered arrangement of 8 letters, 4 of which are T's and 4 of which are F's. The number of different responses is

$$\frac{8!}{4! \cdot 4!} = \frac{8 \cdot 7 \cdot 6 \cdot 5 \cdot 4!}{4!(4 \cdot 3 \cdot 2 \cdot 1)} = 70.$$

27. The number of ways to assign 15 clients to 3 caseworkers (cells) with 5 clients to each caseworker is $\dfrac{15!}{5! \cdot 5! \cdot 5!} = 756,756$.

29. **a.** Six flags must be arranged: two are red (type 1), two are green (type 2), and two are yellow (type 3). Thus the number of distinguishable arrangements (messages) is $\dfrac{6!}{2! \cdot 2! \cdot 2!} = 90$.

b. If exactly one yellow flag is used, then five flags are involved and the number of different messages is $\dfrac{5!}{2! \cdot 2! \cdot 1!} = 30$. If exactly two yellow flags are used, then six flags are involved and the number of different messages is $\dfrac{6!}{2! \cdot 2! \cdot 2!} = 90$. If all three yellow flags are used, then seven flags are involved and the number of different messages is $\dfrac{7!}{2! \cdot 2! \cdot 3!} = 210$. Thus if at least one yellow flag is used, the number of different messages is $30 + 90 + 210 = 330$.

31. The order in which the securities go into the portfolio is not important. The number of ways to select 8 of 12 stocks is $_{12}C_8$. The number of ways to select 4 of 7 bonds is $_7C_4$. By the basic counting principle, the number of ways to create the portfolio is

$$_{12}C_8 \cdot {}_7C_4 = \frac{12!}{8!(12-8)!} \cdot \frac{7!}{4!(7-4)!}$$

$$= \frac{12!}{8! \cdot 4!} \cdot \frac{7!}{4! \cdot 3!}$$

$$= \frac{12 \cdot 11 \cdot 10 \cdot 9 \cdot 8!}{8! \cdot 4 \cdot 3 \cdot 2 \cdot 1} \cdot \frac{7 \cdot 6 \cdot 5 \cdot 4!}{4! \cdot 3 \cdot 2 \cdot 1}$$

$$= 495 \cdot 35 = 17,325.$$

33. **a.** Selecting 3 of the 3 males can be done in only 1 way.

b. Selecting 4 of the 4 females can be done in only 1 way.

c. Selecting 2 males and 2 females can be considered as a two-stage process. In the first stage, 2 of the 3 males are selected (and order is not important), which can be done in $_3C_2$ ways. In the second stage, 2 of the 4 females are selected, which can be done in $_4C_2$ ways. By the basic counting principle, the ways of selecting the subcommittee is

$$_3C_2 \cdot _4C_2 = \frac{3!}{2!(3-2)!} \cdot \frac{4!}{2!(4-2)!}$$

$$= \frac{3!}{2! \cdot 1!} \cdot \frac{4!}{2! \cdot 2!} = 3 \cdot 6 = 18$$

35. There are 4 cards of a given denomination and the number of ways of selecting 3 cards of that denomination is $_4C_3$.

Since there are 13 denominations, the number of ways of selecting 3 cards of one denomination is $13 \cdot _4C_3$. After that selection is made, the 2 other cards must be of the same denomination (of which 12 denominations remain). Thus for the remaining 2 cards there are $12 \cdot _4C_2$ selections. By the basic counting principle, the number of possible full-house hands is

$$13 \cdot _4C_3 \cdot 12 \cdot _4C_2 = 13 \cdot \frac{4!}{3! \cdot 1!} \cdot 12 \cdot \frac{4!}{2! \cdot 2!}$$

$$= 13 \cdot 4 \cdot 12 \cdot 6 = 3744.$$

37. This situation can be considered as placing 18 tourists into 3 cells: 6 tourist go to the 6-passenger tram, 8 go to the 8-passenger tram, and 4 tourists remain at the bottom of the mountain. This can be done in

$$\frac{18!}{6! \cdot 8! \cdot 4!} = 9,189,180 \text{ ways.}$$

Principles in Practice 9.3

1. This is a combination problem because the order in which the videos are selected is not important. The number of possible choices is the number of ways 3 videos can be selected from 400 without regard to order.

$$_{400}C_3 = \frac{400!}{3!(400-3)!} = \frac{400!}{3! \, 397!}$$

$$= \frac{400 \cdot 399 \cdot 398 \cdot 397!}{3! \, 397!}$$

$$= \frac{400 \cdot 399 \cdot 398}{3 \cdot 2}$$

$$= 10,586,800$$

Exercise 9.3

1. {9D, 9H, 9C, 9S]

3. {1H, 1T, 2H, 2T, 3H, 3T, 4H, 4T, 5H, 5T, 6H, 6T}

5. {lo, lv, le, ov, oe, ve, ol, vl, el, vo, eo, ev}

7. a. {RR, RW, RB, WR, WW, WB, BR, BW};

    b. {RW, RB, WR, WB, BR, BW}

9. Sample space consists of ordered sets of six elements and each element is H or T. Since there are two possibilities for each toss (H or T), and there are six tosses, by he basic counting principle, the number of sample points is $2 \cdot 2 \cdot 2 \cdot 2 \cdot 2 \cdot 2 = 2^6 = 64$.

11. Sample space consists of ordered pairs where the first element indicates the card drawn (52 possibilities) and the second element indicates the number on the die (6 possibilities). By the basic counting principle, the number of sample points is $52 \cdot 6 = 312$.

13. Sample space consists of combinations of 52 cards taken 13 at a time. Thus the number of sample points is $_{52}C_{13}$.

15. The sample points that are either in E, or in F, or in both E and F are 1, 3, 5, 7, and 9. Thus $E \cup F = \{1, 3, 5, 7, 9\}$.

17. The sample points common to both E and F are 3 and 5. Thus $E \cap F = \{3, 5\}$.

19. The sample points in S that are not in F are 1, 2, 4, 6, 8, and 10. Thus $F' = \{1, 2, 4, 6, 8, 10\}$.

21. $(F \cap G)' = \varnothing' = S$

23. $E_1 \cap E_2 \neq \varnothing$; $E_1 \cap E_3 \neq \varnothing$; $E_1 \cap E_4 = \varnothing$; $E_2 \cap E_3 = \varnothing$; $E_2 \cap E_4 \neq \varnothing$; $E_3 \cap E_4 = \varnothing$. Thus E_1 and E_4, E_2 and E_3, and E_3 and E_4 are mutually exclusive.

25. $E \cap F \neq \varnothing$, $E \cap G \neq \varnothing$, $E \cap H = \varnothing$, $E \cap I \neq \varnothing$, $F \cap G \neq \varnothing$, $F \cap H \neq \varnothing$ $F \cap I \neq \varnothing$, $G \cap H = \varnothing$, $G \cap I \neq \varnothing$, $H \cap I = \varnothing$. Thus E and H, G and H, and H and I are mutually exclusive.

27. a. $S = \{$HHH, HHT, HTH, HTT, THH, THT, TTH, TTT$\}$

   b. $E_1 = \{$HHH, HHT, HTH, HTT, THH, THT, TTH$\}$

   c. $E_2 = \{$HHT, HTH, HTT, THH, THT, TTH, TTT$\}$

   d. $E_1 \cup E_2 = \{$HHH, HHT, HTH, HTT, THH, THT, TTH, TTT$\} = S$

   e. $E_1 \cap E_2 = \{$HHT, HTH, HTT, THH, THT, TTH$\}$

   f. $(E_1 \cup E_2)' = S' = \varnothing$

   g. $(E_1 \cap E_2)' = \{$HHT, HTH, HTT, THH, THT, TTH$\}' = \{$HHH, TTT$\}$

29. a. $\{$ABC, ACB, BAC, BCA, CAB, CBA$\}$

   b. $\{$ABC, ACB$\}$

   c. $\{$BAC, BCA, CAB, CBA$\}$

31. Using the properties in Table 9.1, we have
$(E \cap F) \cap (E \cap F')$
$= (E \cap F \cap E) \cap F'$ [property 15]
$= (E \cap E \cap F) \cap F'$ [property 11]
$= (E \cap E) \cap (F \cap F')$ [porperty 15]
$= E \cap \varnothing$ [property 5]
$= \varnothing$ [property 9]
Thus $(E \cap F) \cap (E \cap F') = \varnothing$, so $E \cap F$ and $E \cap F'$ are mutually exclusive.

Exercise 9.4

1. $2000 P(E) = 2000(0.3) = 600$

3. a. $P(E') = 1 - P(E) = 1 - 0.2 = 0.8$

   b. $P(E \cup F) = P(E) + P(F) - P(E \cap F)$
   $= 0.2 + 0.3 - 0.1 = 0.4$

5. If E and F are mutually exclusive, then $E \cap F = \varnothing$. Thus $P(E \cap F) = P(\varnothing) = 0$. Since it is given that $P(E \cap F) = 0.831 \neq 0$, E and F are not mutually exclusive.

7. a. $E_8 = \{(2, 6), (3, 5), (4, 4), (5, 3), (6, 2)\}$
   $P(E_8) = \dfrac{n(E_8)}{n(S)} = \dfrac{5}{36}$

   b. $E_{2 \text{ or } 3} = \{(1, 1), (1, 2), (2, 1)\}$
   $P(E_{2 \text{ or } 3}) = \dfrac{n(E_{2 \text{ or } 3})}{n(S)} = \dfrac{3}{36} = \dfrac{1}{12}$

   c. $E_{3, 4, \text{ or } 5} = \{(1, 2), (2, 1), (1, 3), (2, 2),$
   $(3, 1), (1, 4), (2, 3), (3, 2), (4, 1)\}$
   $P(E_{3, 4, \text{ or } 5}) = \dfrac{n(E_{3, 4, \text{ or } 5})}{n(S)} = \dfrac{9}{36} = \dfrac{1}{4}$

   d. $E_{12 \text{ or } 13} = E_{12}$, since E_{13} is an impossible event.
   $E_{12} = \{(6, 6)\}$
   $P(E_{12 \text{ or } 13}) = \dfrac{n(E_{12 \text{ or } 13})}{n(S)} = \dfrac{1}{36}$

e. $E_2 = \{(1,1)\}$

$E_4 = \{(1,3),(2,2),(3,1)\}$

$E_6 = \{(1,5),(2,4),(3,3,),(4,2),(5,1)\}$

$E_8 = \{(2,6),(3,5),(4,4),(5,3),(6,2)\}$

$E_{10} = \{(4,6),(5,5),(6,4)\}$

$E_{12} = \{(6,6)\}$

$P(E_{even}) = P(E_2) + P(E_4)$

$\quad + P(E_6) + P(E_8) + P(E_{10}) + P(E_{12})$

$= \dfrac{1}{36} + \dfrac{3}{36} + \dfrac{5}{36} + \dfrac{5}{36} + \dfrac{3}{36} + \dfrac{1}{36}$

$= \dfrac{18}{36} = \dfrac{1}{2}$

f. $P(E_{odd}) = 1 - P(E_{even}) = 1 - \dfrac{1}{2} = \dfrac{1}{2}$

g. $E'_{less\ than\ 10} = E_{10} \cup E_{11} \cup E_{12}$

$= \{(4,6),(5,5),(6,4)\} \cup \{(5,6),(6,5)\}$

$\quad \cup \{(6,6)\}$

$= \{(4,6),(5,5),(6,4),(5,6),(6,5),(6,6)\}$

$. P(E_{less\ than\ 10}) = 1 - P(E'_{less\ than\ 10})$

$= 1 - \dfrac{6}{36} = \dfrac{30}{36} = \dfrac{5}{6}.$

9. $n(S) = 52.$

a. $P(\text{king of hearts})$

$= \dfrac{n(E_{king\ of\ hearts})}{n(S)} = \dfrac{1}{52}$

b. $P(\text{diamond}) = \dfrac{n(E_{diamond})}{n(S)} = \dfrac{13}{52} = \dfrac{1}{4}$

c. $P(\text{jack}) = \dfrac{n(E_{jack})}{n(S)} = \dfrac{4}{52} = \dfrac{1}{13}$

d. $P(\text{red}) = \dfrac{n(E_{red})}{n(S)} = \dfrac{26}{52} = \dfrac{1}{2}$

e. Because a heart is not a club,

$E_{heart} \cap E_{club} = \varnothing.$

Thus

$P(E_{heart\ or\ club}) = P(E_{heart} \cup E_{club})$

$= P(E_{heart}) + P(E_{club})$

$= \dfrac{n(E_{heart})}{n(S)} + \dfrac{n(E_{club})}{n(S)} = \dfrac{13}{52} + \dfrac{13}{52}$

$= \dfrac{26}{52} = \dfrac{1}{2}$

f. $E_{club\ and\ 4} = \{4C\}$

$P(E_{club\ and\ 4}) = \dfrac{n(E_{club\ and\ 4})}{n(S)} = \dfrac{1}{52}$

g. $P(\text{club or 4})$

$= P(\text{club}) + P(4) - P(\text{club and 4})$

$= \dfrac{13}{52} + \dfrac{4}{52} - \dfrac{1}{52} = \dfrac{16}{52} = \dfrac{4}{13}$

h. $E_{red\ and\ king} = \{KH, KD\}$

$P(\text{red and king}) = \dfrac{n(E_{red\ and\ king})}{n(S)}$

$= \dfrac{2}{52} = \dfrac{1}{26}$

i. $E_{spade\ and\ heart} = \varnothing$

Thus $P(\text{spade and heart}) = 0$

11. $n(S) = 2 \cdot 6 \cdot 52 = 624$

a. $P(\text{tail, 3, queen of hearts})$

$= \dfrac{n(E_{T,3,QH})}{n(S)} = \dfrac{1 \cdot 1 \cdot 1}{624} = \dfrac{1}{624}$

b. $P(\text{tail, 3, queen})$

$= \dfrac{n(E_{T,3,Q})}{n(S)} = \dfrac{1 \cdot 1 \cdot 4}{624} = \dfrac{1}{156}$

c. $P(\text{head, 2 or 3, queen})$

$= \dfrac{n(E_{H,2\ or\ 3,Q})}{n(S)} = \dfrac{1 \cdot 2 \cdot 4}{624} = \dfrac{1}{78}$

d. $P(\text{head, even, diamond})$

$= \dfrac{n(E_{H,E,D})}{n(S)} = \dfrac{1 \cdot 3 \cdot 13}{624} = \dfrac{1}{16}$

13. $n(S) = 52 \cdot 51 = 2652$

a. $P(\text{both kings}) = \dfrac{n(E_{\text{both kings}})}{n(S)} = \dfrac{4 \cdot 3}{2652}$

$= \dfrac{1}{221}$

b. The number of ways that first card is a diamond and second card is a heart is $13 \cdot 13$; for first card a heart and second card a diamond, the number of ways is $13 \cdot 13$. Thus

$P(E_{\text{one card diamond \& other is heart}})$

$= \dfrac{13 \cdot 13 + 13 \cdot 13}{2652} = \dfrac{338}{2652} = \dfrac{13}{102}.$

15. $n(S) = 2 \cdot 2 \cdot 2 = 8$

a. $E_{3 \text{ girls}} = \{GGG\}$

$P(3 \text{ girls}) = \dfrac{n(E_{3 \text{ girls}})}{n(S)} = \dfrac{1}{8}$

b. $E_{1 \text{ boy}} = \{BGG, GBG, GGB\}$

$P(1 \text{ boy}) = \dfrac{n(E_{1 \text{ boy}})}{n(S)} = \dfrac{3}{8}$

c. $E_{\text{no girl}} = \{BBB\}$

$P(\text{no girl}) = \dfrac{n(E_{\text{no girl}})}{n(S)} = \dfrac{1}{8}$

d. $P(\text{at least 1 girl}) = 1 - P(\text{no girl})$

$= 1 - \dfrac{1}{8} = \dfrac{7}{8}$

17. The sample space consists of 60 stocks. Thus $n(S) = 60$.

a. $P(10\% \text{ or more}) = \dfrac{n(E_{10\% \text{ or more}})}{n(S)}$

$= \dfrac{48}{60} = \dfrac{4}{5}$

b. $P(\text{less than } 10\%) = 1 - P(10\% \text{ or more})$

$= 1 - \dfrac{4}{5} = \dfrac{1}{5}$

19. $n(S) = 40$

Of the 40 students, 4 received an A, 10 a B, 14 a C, 10 a D, and 2 an F.

a. $P(A) = \dfrac{n(E_A)}{n(S)} = \dfrac{4}{40} = \dfrac{1}{10} = 0.1$

b. $P(A \text{ or } B) = \dfrac{n(E_{A \text{ or } B})}{n(S)} = \dfrac{4 + 10}{40}$

$= \dfrac{14}{40} = 0.35$

c. $P(\text{neither D nor F}) = P(A, B, \text{ or } C)$

$= \dfrac{n(E_{A, B, \text{ or } C})}{n(S)} = \dfrac{4 + 10 + 14}{40}$

$= \dfrac{28}{40} = 0.7$

d. $P(\text{no F}) = 1 - P(F) = 1 - \dfrac{n(E_F)}{\cdot n(S)}$

$= 1 - \dfrac{2}{40} = \dfrac{38}{40} = 0.95$

e. Let $N = $ number of students. Then $n(S) = N$. Of the N students, $0.10N$ received an A, $0.25N$ a B, $0.35N$ a C, $0.25N$ a D, $0.05N$ an F.

$P(A) = \dfrac{0.10N}{N} = 0.1;$

$P(A \text{ or } B) = \dfrac{0.10N + 0.25N}{N}$

$= \dfrac{0.35N}{N} = 0.35$

$P(\text{neither D nor F}) = P(A, B, \text{ or } C)$

$= \dfrac{0.10N + 0.25N + 0.35N}{N}$

$\dfrac{0.70N}{N} = 0.7$

$P(\text{no F}) = 1 - P(F)$

$= 1 - \dfrac{0.05N}{N} = 1 - 0.05 = 0.95$

21. The sample space consists of combinations of 2 people selected from 5. Thus

$n(S) = {}_5C_2 = \dfrac{5!}{2! \cdot 3!} = \dfrac{5 \cdot 4}{2} = 10$. Because

there are only 2 women in the group, the number of possible 2 women committees is 1. Thus $P(2 \text{ women}) = \dfrac{n(E_{2 \text{ women}})}{n(S)} = \dfrac{1}{10}$.

23. Number of ways to answer exam is
$2^{10} = 1024 = n(S)$.

   a. There is only one way to achieve 100 points, namely to answer each question correctly. Thus

$$P(100 \text{ points}) = \frac{n(E_{100 \text{ points}})}{n(S)} = \frac{1}{1024}.$$

   b. Number of ways to score 90 points = number of ways that exactly one question is answered incorrectly = 10.
Thus
$P(90 \text{ or more points})$
$= P(90 \text{ points}) + P(100 \text{ points})$
$= \dfrac{10}{1024} + \dfrac{1}{1024} = \dfrac{11}{1024}.$

25. A poker hand is a 5 card deal from 52 cards. Thus $n(S) = {}_{52}C_5$. In 52 cards, there are 4 cards of a particular denomination. Thus, for a full house, the number of ways of selecting 3 of 4 cards of a particular denomination is ${}_4C_3$. Since there are 13 denominations, 3 cards of the same denomination can be dealt in $13 \cdot {}_4C_3$ ways. For the two remaining cards in the full house, there are 12 denominations that are possible, and for each denomination there are ${}_4C_2$ ways of dealing a pair. Thus
$P(\text{full house})$
$= \dfrac{n(E_{\text{full house}})}{n(S)} = \dfrac{13 \cdot {}_4C_3 \cdot 12 \cdot {}_4C_2}{{}_{52}C_5}$

27. $n(S) = {}_{100}C_3 = \dfrac{100!}{3! \cdot 97!} = 161{,}700$

   a. $n(E_{3 \text{ females}}) = {}_{35}C_3 = \dfrac{35!}{3! \cdot 32!} = 6545$

$$P(E_{3 \text{ females}}) = \frac{n(E_{3 \text{ females}})}{n(S)}$$

$$= \frac{6545}{161{,}700} \approx 0.040$$

   b. The number of ways of selecting one professor is 15; the number of ways of selecting two associate professors is ${}_{24}C_2$. Thus

$n(E_{1 \text{ professor \& 2 associate professors}})$

$= 15 \cdot \dfrac{24!}{2! \cdot 22!} = 15 \cdot 276 = 4140.$

Therefore,
$P(E_{1 \text{ professor \& 2 associate professers}})$

$= \dfrac{4140}{161{,}700} \approx 0.026.$

29. Let $p = P(1) = P(3) = P(5)$. Then
$2p = P(2) = P(4) = P(6)$. Since $P(S) = 1$,

then $3(p) + 3(2p) = 1, \; 9p = 1, \; p = p(1) = \dfrac{1}{9}$.

31. a. Of the 100 voters, 51 favor the tax increase. Thus

$$P(\text{favors tax increase}) = \frac{51}{100} = 0.51.$$

   b. Of the 100 voters, 44 oppose the tax increase. Thus

$$P(\text{opposes tax increase}) = \frac{44}{100} = 0.44.$$

   c. Of the 100 voters, 3 are Republican with no opinion. Thus
$P(\text{is a Republican with no opinion})$

$= \dfrac{3}{100}$
$= 0.03.$

33. $\dfrac{P(E)}{P(E')} = \dfrac{P(E)}{1-P(E)} = \dfrac{\frac{4}{5}}{1-\left(\frac{4}{5}\right)} = \dfrac{\frac{4}{5}}{\frac{1}{5}} = \dfrac{4}{1}$

The odds are 4:1.

35. $\dfrac{P(E)}{P(E')} = \dfrac{P(E)}{1-P(E)} = \dfrac{0.3}{1-0.3} = \dfrac{0.3}{0.7} = \dfrac{3}{7}$

The odds are 3:7.

37. $P(E) = \dfrac{5}{5+4} = \dfrac{5}{9}$

39. $P(E) = \dfrac{4}{4+10} = \dfrac{4}{14} = \dfrac{2}{7}$

41. $P(\text{rain}) = \dfrac{3}{3+1} = \dfrac{3}{4}$

Exercise 9.5

1. a. $P(E|F) = \dfrac{n(E \cap F)}{n(F)} = \dfrac{2}{5}$

   b. Using the result of part (a),

$P(E'|F) = 1 - P(E|F) = 1 - \dfrac{2}{5} = \dfrac{3}{5}$.

   c. $F' = \{3, 7, 8\}$

$P(E|F') = \dfrac{n(E \cap F')}{n(F')} = \dfrac{1}{3}$

   d. $P(F|E) = \dfrac{n(F \cap E)}{n(E)} = \dfrac{2}{3}$

   e. $F \cap G = \{2, 4, 5\}$

$P(E|(F \cap G)) = \dfrac{n(E \cap (F \cap G))}{n(F \cap G)} = \dfrac{1}{3}$

3. $P(E|E) = \dfrac{P(E \cap E)}{P(E)} = \dfrac{P(E)}{P(E)} = 1$

5. $P(E'|F) = 1 - P(E|F) = 1 - 0.63 = 0.37$

7. a. $P(E|F) = \dfrac{P(E \cap F)}{P(F)} = \dfrac{1/6}{1/3} = \dfrac{1}{2}$

   b. $P(F|E) = \dfrac{P(F \cap E)}{P(E)} = \dfrac{1/6}{1/4} = \dfrac{2}{3}$

9. a. $P(F|E) = \dfrac{P(F \cap E)}{P(E)} = \dfrac{1/5}{1/3} = \dfrac{3}{5}$

   b. $P(E \cup F) = P(E) + P(F) - P(E \cap F)$

$\dfrac{8}{15} = \dfrac{1}{3} + P(F) - \dfrac{1}{5}$

Thus $P(F) = \dfrac{8}{15} - \dfrac{1}{3} + \dfrac{1}{5} = \dfrac{2}{5}$.

   c. From part (b) $P(F) = \dfrac{2}{5}$.

Then $P(E|F) = \dfrac{P(E \cap F)}{P(F)} = \dfrac{1/5}{2/5} = \dfrac{1}{2}$.

   d. $P(E) = P(E \cap F) + P(E \cap F')$

$\dfrac{1}{3} = \dfrac{1}{5} + P(E \cap F')$

so $P(E \cap F') = \dfrac{1}{3} - \dfrac{1}{5} = \dfrac{2}{15}$.

Then $P(E|F') = \dfrac{P(E \cap F')}{P(F')}$

$= \dfrac{2/15}{1-(2/5)} = \dfrac{2/15}{3/5} = \dfrac{2}{9}$.

11. a. $P(F) = \dfrac{125}{200} = \dfrac{5}{8}$

   b. $P(F \mid \text{II}) = \dfrac{n(F \cap \text{II})}{n(\text{II})} = \dfrac{35}{58}$

   c. $P(O \mid \text{I}) = \dfrac{n(O \cap \text{I})}{n(\text{I})} = \dfrac{22}{78} = \dfrac{11}{39}$

   d. $P(\text{III}) = \dfrac{64}{200} = \dfrac{8}{25}$

   e. $P(\text{III} \mid O) = \dfrac{n(\text{III} \cap O)}{n(O)} = \dfrac{10}{47}$

f. $P(\text{II} \mid N') = \dfrac{n(\text{II} \cap N')}{n(N')}$

$\qquad = \dfrac{35 + 15}{125 + 47} = \dfrac{50}{172} = \dfrac{25}{86}$

13. a. $P(A \mid B) = \dfrac{P(A \cap B)}{P(B)} = \dfrac{0.20}{0.40} = \dfrac{1}{2}$

    b. $P(B \mid A) = \dfrac{P(B \cap A)}{P(A)} = \dfrac{0.20}{0.45} = \dfrac{4}{9}$

15. $S = \{BB, BG, GG, GB\}$
Let $E = \{\text{at least one girl}\} = \{BG, GG, GB\}$,
$F = \{\text{at least one boy}\} = \{BB, BG, GB\}$.
Thus $P(E \mid F) = \dfrac{n(E \cap F)}{n(F)} = \dfrac{2}{3}$.

17. $S = \{HHH, HHT, HTH, THH, THT, TTH,$
$TTT\}$.
Let $E = \{\text{exactly two tails}\}$
$= \{HTT, THT, TTH\}$,
$F = \{\text{second toss is a tail}\}$
$= \{HTH, HTT, TTH, TTT\}$,
$G = \{\text{second toss is a head}\}$
$= \{HHH, HHT, THH, THT\}$.

    a. $P(E \mid F) = \dfrac{n(E \cap F)}{n(F)} = \dfrac{2}{4} = \dfrac{1}{2}$

    b. $P(E \mid G) = \dfrac{n(E \cap G)}{n(G)} = \dfrac{1}{4}$

19. $P(< 4 \mid \text{odd}) = \dfrac{n(< 4 \cap \text{odd})}{n(\text{odd})}$

$\qquad = \dfrac{n(\{1, 3\})}{n(\{1, 3, 5\})} = \dfrac{2}{3}$

21.   *Method 1.* The usual sample space has 36
outcomes, where the event
"two 6's" is $\{(6, 6)\}$. Note that
$\{\text{at least one 6}\}' = \{\text{no 6' s}\}$, and the event
"no 6's" occurs in $5 \cdot 5 = 25$ ways. Thus

$P(\text{two 6's} \mid \text{at least one 6})$
$= \dfrac{n(\text{two 6' s} \cap \text{at least one 6})}{n(\text{at least one 6})}$
$= \dfrac{n(\{(6,6)\})}{36 - 25} = \dfrac{1}{11}$.

Method 2. From the usual sample space, we
find that the reduced sample space for "at
least one 6" (which has 11 outcomes) is
$\{(6, 1), (6, 2), (6, 3), (6, 4), (6, 5), (6, 6),$
$(1, 6), (2, 6), (3, 6), (4, 6), (5, 6)\}$.

Thus $P(\text{two 6's} \mid \text{at least one 6}) = \dfrac{1}{11}$.

23.   The usual sample space consists of ordered
pairs (R, G), where $R = $ no. on red die and
$G = $ no. on green die. Now,
$n(\text{green is even}) = 6 \cdot 3 = 18$, because the red
die can show any of six numbers and the
green any of three: 2, 4, or 6. Also,
$n(\text{total of } 7 \cap \text{green even})$
$= n(\{(5, 2), (3, 4), (1, 6)\}) = 3$.
Thus
    $P(\text{total of } 7 \mid \text{green even})$
$= \dfrac{n(\text{total of } 7 \cap \text{green even})}{n(\text{green even})}$
$= \dfrac{3}{18} = \dfrac{1}{6}$.

25.   The usual sample space consists of 36
ordered pairs.
Let $E = \{\text{total} > 5\}$ and $F = \{\text{first toss} < 4\}$.
Then $n(F) = 3 \cdot 6 = 18$, and
$n(E \cap F) = n(\{(1, 5), (1, 6), (2, 4), (2, 5),$
$(2, 6), (3, 3), (3, 4), (3, 5), (3, 6)\}) = 9$.
Thus $P(E \mid F) = \dfrac{n(E \cap F)}{n(F)} = \dfrac{9}{18} = \dfrac{1}{2}$.

27. $P(K \mid H) = \dfrac{n(K \cap H)}{n(H)} = \dfrac{1}{13}$

29.   Let $E = \{\text{second card is not a face card}\}$ and
$F = \{\text{first card is a face card}\}$.

$\qquad P(E \mid F) = \dfrac{n(E \cap F)}{n(F)} = \dfrac{12 \cdot \frac{51-11}{51}}{12} = \dfrac{40}{51}$

31. $P(K_1 \cap Q_2 \cap J_3) = P(K_1)P(Q_2 \mid K_1)P(J_3 \mid (K_1 \cap Q_2))$

$= \dfrac{4}{52} \cdot \dfrac{4}{51} \cdot \dfrac{4}{50} = \dfrac{8}{16,575}$

33. $P(D_1 \cap D_2 \cap D_3) = P(D_1)P(D_2 \mid D_1)P(D_3 \mid (D_1 \cap D_2))$

$= \dfrac{13}{52} \cdot \dfrac{12}{51} \cdot \dfrac{11}{50} = \dfrac{11}{850}$

35. Let $D = \{\text{two diamonds}\}$ and

$R = \{\text{first card red}\}$. We have $D \cap R = \{\text{two diamonds}\} = D$ and $P(D) = \dfrac{13}{52} \cdot \dfrac{12}{51}$.

Thus $P(D \mid R) = \dfrac{P(D \cap R)}{P(R)} = \dfrac{\frac{13}{52} \cdot \frac{12}{51}}{\frac{26}{52}} = \dfrac{2}{17}$.

37. a. $P(U) = P(F \cap U) + P(O \cap U) + P(N \cap U)$

$= P(F)P(U \mid F) + P(O)P(U \mid O) + P(N)P(U \mid N)$

$= (0.60)(0.45) + (0.30)(0.55) + (0.10)(0.35)$

$= 0.47 = \dfrac{47}{100}$

b. $P(F \mid U) = \dfrac{P(F \cap U)}{P(U)} = \dfrac{(0.60)(0.45)}{0.47} = \dfrac{27}{47}$

39. a. After the first draw, if the marble drawn is red, then 4 marbles remain, 3 of which are yellow.

$P(\text{second is yellow} \mid \text{first is red}) = \dfrac{3}{4}$

b. After red marble is replaced, 5 marbles remain, 3 of which are yellow.

$P(\text{second is yellow} \mid \text{first is red}) = \dfrac{3}{5}$

41. $P(W) = P(\text{Urn } 1 \cap W) + P(\text{Urn } 2 \cap W)$

$= P(\text{Urn } 1)P(W \mid \text{Urn } 1) + P(\text{Urn } 2)P(W \mid \text{Urn } 2)$

$= \dfrac{1}{2} \cdot \dfrac{2}{5} + \dfrac{1}{2} \cdot \dfrac{2}{4} = \dfrac{9}{20}$

43. $P(W_3) = P(U1 \cap G_2 \cap W_3) + P(U1 \cap R_2 \cap W_3) + P(U2 \cap W_2 \cap W_3)$

$= P(U1)P(G_2 \mid U1)P\big(W_3 \mid (G_2 \cap U1)\big) + P(U1)P(R_2 \mid U1)P\big(W_3 \mid (R_2 \cap U1)\big) + P(U2)P\big(W_2 \mid U2\big)P\big(W_3 \mid (W_2 \cap U2)\big)$

$= \dfrac{1}{2} \cdot \dfrac{1}{2} \cdot \dfrac{1}{3} + \dfrac{1}{2} \cdot \dfrac{1}{2} \cdot \dfrac{1}{3} + \dfrac{1}{2} \cdot \dfrac{1}{2} \cdot \dfrac{1}{3} = \dfrac{1}{4}$

45. $P(\text{Def}) = P(A \cap \text{Def}) + P(B \cap \text{Def})$

$= P(A)P(\text{Def} \mid A) + P(B)P(\text{Def} \mid B)$

$= \dfrac{200}{600} \cdot \dfrac{2}{100} + \dfrac{400}{600} \cdot \dfrac{5}{100} = \dfrac{1}{25}$

47. $P(\text{Def}) = P(A \cap \text{Def}) + P(B \cap \text{Def}) + P(C \cap \text{Def})$
$= P(A)P(\text{Def} \mid A) + P(B)P(\text{Def} \mid B) + P(C)P(\text{Def} \mid C)$
$= (0.10)(0.06) + (0.20)(0.04) + (0.70)(0.05) = 0.049$

49. a. $P(D \cap V) = P(D)P(V \mid D)$
$= (0.40)(0.15) = 0.06$

b. $P(V) = P(D \cap V) + P(R \cap V) + P(I \cap V)$
$= P(D)P(V \mid D) + P(R)P(V \mid R) + P(I)P(V \mid I)$
$= (0.40)(0.15) + (0.35)(0.20) + (0.25)(0.10)$
$= 0.155$

51. $P(3 \text{ Fem} \mid \text{at least one Fem})$
$= \dfrac{P(3\text{Fem} \cap \text{at least one Fem})}{P(\text{at least one Fem})}$

$\dfrac{P(3 \text{ Fem})}{1 - P(\text{no Fem})} = \dfrac{\frac{{}_5C_3}{{}_9C_3}}{1 - \frac{{}_4C_3}{{}_9C_3}} = \dfrac{\frac{5}{42}}{1 - \frac{1}{21}} = \dfrac{1}{8}$

Exercise 9.6

1. a. $P(E \cap F) = P(E)P(F) = \dfrac{1}{3} \cdot \dfrac{3}{4} = \dfrac{1}{4}$

b. $P(E \cup F) = P(E) + P(F) - P(E \cap F)$
$= \dfrac{1}{3} + \dfrac{3}{4} - \dfrac{1}{4} = \dfrac{5}{6}$

c. $P(E \mid F) = \dfrac{P(E \cap F)}{P(F)} = \dfrac{1/4}{3/4} = \dfrac{1}{3}$

d. $P(E' \mid F) = 1 - P(E \mid F) = 1 - \dfrac{1}{3} = \dfrac{2}{3}$

e. $P(E \cap F') = P(E)P(F') = \dfrac{1}{3} \cdot \dfrac{1}{4} = \dfrac{1}{12}$

f. $P(E \cup F') = P(E) + P(F') - P(E \cap F')$
$= \dfrac{1}{3} + \dfrac{1}{4} - \dfrac{1}{12} = \dfrac{1}{2}$

g. $P(E \mid F') = \dfrac{P(E \cap F')}{P(F')} = \dfrac{1/12}{1/4} = \dfrac{1}{3}$

3. $P(E \cap F) = P(E)P(F),$
$\dfrac{1}{3} = \dfrac{2}{5} \cdot P(F)$ so $P(F) = \dfrac{1}{3} \cdot \dfrac{5}{2} = \dfrac{5}{6}$

5. $P(E)P(F) = \dfrac{3}{4} \cdot \dfrac{8}{9} = \dfrac{2}{3} = P(E \cap F)$
Since $P(E)P(F) = P(E \cap F)$, events E and F are independent.

7. Let $F = \{\text{full service}\}$ and
$I = \{\text{increase in value}\}$.
$P(F) = \dfrac{400}{600} = \dfrac{2}{3}$
and $P(F \mid I) = \dfrac{n(F \cap I)}{n(I)} = \dfrac{320}{480} = \dfrac{2}{3}$
Since $P(F \mid I) = P(F)$, events F and I are independent.

9. Let S be the usual sample space consisting of ordered pairs of the form (R, G), where the first component of each pair represents the number showing on the red die. Then $n(S) = 6 \cdot 6 = 36$. For E, any of four numbers can occur on the red die, and any of six numbers can appear on the green die. Thus $n(E) = 4 \cdot 6 = 24$. For F we have $F = \{(1, 4), (2, 3), (3, 2), (4, 1)\}$, so $n(F) = 4$. Also, $E \cap F = \{(1,4),(2,3),(3,2)\}$ so, $n(E \cap F) = 3$. Thus
$P(E)P(F) = \dfrac{24}{36} \cdot \dfrac{4}{36} = \dfrac{2}{27}$ and
$P(E \cap F) = \dfrac{3}{36} = \dfrac{1}{12}.$
Since $P(E)P(F) \neq P(E \cap F)$, events E and F are dependent.

11. $S = \{HH, HT, TH, TT\}$,
    $E = \{HT, TH, TT\}$,
    $F = \{HT, TH\}$, and $E \cap F = \{HT, TH\}$.
    Thus $P(E) = \dfrac{3}{4}$
    $P(F) = \dfrac{2}{4} = \dfrac{1}{2}$, and
    $P(E \cap F) = \dfrac{2}{4} = \dfrac{1}{2}$. We have
    $P(E)P(F) = \dfrac{3}{4} \cdot \dfrac{1}{2} = \dfrac{3}{8} \neq P(E \cap F)$, so
    events E and F are dependent.

13. Let S be the set of ordered pairs those first
    (*second*) component represents the number
    on the first (*second*) chip. Then
    $n(S) = 6 \cdot 6 = 36$, $n(E) = 1 \cdot 6 = 6$, and
    $n(F) = 6 \cdot 1 = 6$. For G, if the first chip is 1,
    3, or 5, then the second chip must be 2, 4 or
    6; if the first chip is 2, 4 or 6, the second
    must be 1, 3 or 5. Thus
    $n(G) = 3 \cdot 3 + 3 \cdot 3 = 18$.

    a. $E \cap F = \{(3,3)\}$, so $P(E \cap F) = \dfrac{1}{36}$.
         Since
         $P(E)P(F) = \dfrac{6}{36} \cdot \dfrac{6}{36} = \dfrac{1}{36} = P(E \cap F)$,
         events E and F are independent.

    b. $E \cap G = \{(3,2),(3,4),(3,6)\}$,
         so $P(E \cap G) = \dfrac{3}{36} = \dfrac{1}{12}$. Since
         $P(E)P(G) = \dfrac{6}{36} \cdot \dfrac{18}{36} = \dfrac{1}{12} = P(E \cap G)$,
         events E and G are independent.

    c. $F \cap G = \{(2,3),(4,3),(6,3)\}$
         so $P(F \cap G) = \dfrac{3}{36} = \dfrac{1}{12}$.
         Since
         $P(F)P(G) = \dfrac{6}{36} \cdot \dfrac{18}{36} = \dfrac{1}{12} = P(F \cap G)$.
         Events F and G are independent.

    d. $E \cap F \cap G = \varnothing$, so $P(E \cap F \cap G) = 0$.
         However,
         $P(E)P(F)P(G) \neq 0 = P(E \cap F \cap G)$,
         so events E, F and G are not
         independent.

15. $P(E \cap F) = P(E)P(F \mid E)$, thus
    $P(E) = \dfrac{P(E \cap F)}{P(F \mid E)} = \dfrac{0.28}{0.4} = 0.7$
    Since $P(E) = 0.7 \neq 0.6 = P(E \mid F)$, E and F
    are dependent.

17. Let $E = \{\text{red } 4\}$ and $F = \{\text{green} > 4\}$.
    Assume E and F are independent.
    $P(E \cap F) = P(E)P(F) = \dfrac{1}{6} \cdot \dfrac{1}{3} = \dfrac{1}{18}$

19. Let $F = \{\text{first person attends regularly}\}$ and
    $S = \{\text{second person attends regularly}\}$.
    Then $P(F \cap S) = P(F)P(S) = \dfrac{1}{5} \cdot \dfrac{1}{5} = \dfrac{1}{25}$.

21. Because of replacement, assume the cards
    selected on the draws are independent
    events.
    $P(\text{ace, then face card, then spade}) = P(\text{ace}) \cdot$
    $P(\text{face card}) \cdot P(\text{spade})$
    $= \dfrac{4}{52} \cdot \dfrac{12}{52} \cdot \dfrac{13}{52} = \dfrac{3}{676}$

23. a. $P(\text{Bill gets A} \cap \text{Jim gets A} \cap \text{Linda gets A})$
         $= P(\text{Bill gets A}) \cdot P(\text{Jim gets A}) \cdot P(\text{Linda gets A})$
         $= \dfrac{3}{4} \cdot \dfrac{1}{2} \cdot \dfrac{4}{5} = \dfrac{3}{10}$.

b. $P(\text{Bill no A} \cap \text{Jim no A} \cap \text{Linda no A})$

$= P(\text{Bill no A}) \cdot P(\text{Jim no A}) \cdot P(\text{Linda no A})$

$= \dfrac{1}{4} \cdot \dfrac{1}{2} \cdot \dfrac{1}{5} = \dfrac{1}{40}$

c. $P(\text{Bill no A} \cap \text{Jim no A} \cap \text{Linda gets A})$

$= P(\text{Bill no A}) \cdot P(\text{Jim no A}) \cdot P(\text{Linda gets A})$

$= \dfrac{1}{4} \cdot \dfrac{1}{2} \cdot \dfrac{4}{5} = \dfrac{1}{10}$

25. Let $A = \{\text{A survives 15 more years}\}$,
$B = \{\text{B survives 15 more years}\}$.

    a. $P(A \cap B) = P(A)P(B) = \dfrac{2}{3} \cdot \dfrac{3}{5} = \dfrac{2}{5}$

    b. $P(A' \cap B) = P(A')P(B) = \dfrac{1}{3} \cdot \dfrac{3}{5} = \dfrac{1}{5}$

    c. $P[(A \cap B') \cup (A' \cap B)]$

      $= P(A)P(B') + P(A')P(B)$

      $(A \cap B'$ and $A' \cap B$ are mutually exclusive)

      $= \dfrac{2}{3} \cdot \dfrac{2}{5} + \dfrac{1}{3} \cdot \dfrac{3}{5} = \dfrac{7}{15}$

    d. From parts c and a,
      $P(\text{at least one survives})$
      $= P(\text{exactly one survives}) + P(\text{both survive})$

      $= \dfrac{7}{15} + \dfrac{2}{5} = \dfrac{13}{15}.$

    e. $P(\text{neither survives}) = 1 - P(\text{at least one survives})$

      $= 1 - \dfrac{13}{15} = \dfrac{2}{15}.$

27. Assume the colors selected on the draws are independent events.

    a. $P(W_1 \cap G_2) = P(W_1)P(G_2) = \dfrac{6}{15} \cdot \dfrac{5}{15} = \dfrac{2}{15}$

    b. $P[(W_1 \cap G_2) \cup (G_1 \cap W_2)] = P(W_1)P(G_2) + P(G_1)P(W_2)$

      $= \dfrac{6}{15} \cdot \dfrac{5}{15} + \dfrac{5}{15} \cdot \dfrac{6}{15} = \dfrac{4}{15}$

29. Assume that the selections are independent.

    $P(\text{both red} \cup \text{both white} \cup \text{both green}) = \dfrac{3}{18} \cdot \dfrac{3}{18} + \dfrac{6}{18} \cdot \dfrac{6}{18} + \dfrac{9}{18} \cdot \dfrac{9}{18} = \dfrac{7}{18}$

31. Assume that the draws are independent.

$P(\text{particular 1st ticket} \cap \text{particular 2nd ticket})$

$= \dfrac{1}{20} \cdot \dfrac{1}{20} = \dfrac{1}{400}$

$P(\text{sum is 35}) = P\{(20, 15), (19, 16), (18, 17), (17, 18), (16, 19), (15, 20)\}$

$= 6\left(\dfrac{1}{400}\right) = \dfrac{3}{200}$

33. a. $\dfrac{1}{12} \cdot \dfrac{1}{12} \cdot \dfrac{1}{12} = \dfrac{1}{1728}$

    b. To get exactly one even, there are $_3C_1 = 3$ ways.

$P(\text{one even and two odd}) = 3[P(\text{even 1st spin}) \cdot P(\text{odd 2nd spin}) \cdot P(\text{odd 3rd spin})]$

$= 3\left(\dfrac{6}{12} \cdot \dfrac{6}{12} \cdot \dfrac{6}{12}\right) = \dfrac{3}{8}.$

35. a. The number of ways of getting exactly four correct answers out of five is $_5C_4 = 5$. Each of these

ways has a probability of $\dfrac{1}{4} \cdot \dfrac{1}{4} \cdot \dfrac{1}{4} \cdot \dfrac{1}{4} \cdot \dfrac{3}{4} = \dfrac{3}{1024}$. Thus

$P(\text{exactly 4 correct}) = 5 \cdot \dfrac{3}{1024} = \dfrac{15}{1024}.$

    b. $P(\text{at least 4 correct}) = P(\text{exactly 4}) + P(\text{exactly 5})$

$= \dfrac{15}{1024} + \dfrac{1}{4} \cdot \dfrac{1}{4} \cdot \dfrac{1}{4} \cdot \dfrac{1}{4} \cdot \dfrac{1}{4} = \dfrac{1}{64}$

    c. The number of ways of getting exactly three correct answers out of five is

$_5C_3 = 10$. Each of these ways has a probability of $\dfrac{1}{4} \cdot \dfrac{1}{4} \cdot \dfrac{1}{4} \cdot \dfrac{3}{4} \cdot \dfrac{3}{4} = \dfrac{9}{1024}$, so

$P(\text{exactly 3 correct}) = 10 \cdot \dfrac{9}{1024} = \dfrac{45}{512}.$ Thus

$P(\text{3 or more correct}) = P(\text{exactly 3}) + P(\text{at least 4})$

$= \dfrac{45}{512} + \dfrac{1}{64} = \dfrac{53}{512}.$

37. A wrong majority decision can occur in one of two mutually exclusive ways: exactly two wrong
recommendations, or three wrong recommendations. Exactly two wrong recommendations can occur in
$_3C_2 = 3$ mutually exclusive ways. Thus

$P(\text{wrong majority decision})$

$= [(0.05)(0.05)(0.9) + (0.05)(0.95)(0.1) + (0.95)(0.05)(0.1)] + (0.05)(0.05)(0.1)$

$= 0.012.$

Exercise 9.7

1. $P(E|D) = \dfrac{P(E)P(D|E)}{P(E)P(D|E) + P(F)P(D|F)}$

$= \dfrac{\frac{2}{5} \cdot \frac{1}{10}}{\frac{2}{5} \cdot \frac{1}{10} + \frac{3}{5} \cdot \frac{1}{5}} = \dfrac{1}{4}$

For the second part, $P(D'|F) = 1 - P(D|F) = 1 - \dfrac{1}{5} = \dfrac{4}{5}$, and

$P(D'|E) = 1 - P(D|E) = 1 - \dfrac{1}{10} = \dfrac{9}{10}$. Then

$P(F|D') = \dfrac{P(F)P(D'|F)}{P(E)P(D'|E) + P(F)P(D'|F)}$

$= \dfrac{\frac{3}{5} \cdot \frac{4}{5}}{\frac{2}{5} \cdot \frac{9}{10} + \frac{3}{5} \cdot \frac{4}{5}} = \dfrac{4}{7}.$

3. $D = \{\text{is Democrat}\}$,
$R = \{\text{is Republican}\}$,
$I = \{\text{is Independent}\}$,
$V = \{\text{voted}\}$.

$P(D|V) = \dfrac{P(D)P(V|D)}{P(D)P(V|D) + P(R)P(V|R) + P(I)P(V|I)}$

$= \dfrac{(0.40)(0.15)}{(0.40)(0.15) + (0.35)(0.20) + (0.25)(0.10)}$

$= \dfrac{12}{31} \approx 0.387$

5. $D = \{\text{has the disease}\}$
$D' = \{\text{does not have the disease}\}$
$R = \{\text{positive reaction}\}$
$N = \{\text{negative reaction}\} = R'$

a. $P(D \mid R)$

$= \dfrac{P(D)P(R \mid D)}{P(D)P(R \mid D) + P(D')P(R \mid D')}$

$= \dfrac{(0.05)(0.98)}{(0.05)(0.98) + (0.95)(0.06)} = \dfrac{49}{106}$

≈ 0.462

b. $P(D \mid N)$

$= \dfrac{P(D)P(N \mid D)}{P(D)P(N \mid D) + P(D')P(N \mid D')}$

$= \dfrac{(0.05)(0.02)}{(0.05)(0.02) + (0.95)(0.94)} = \dfrac{1}{894}$

≈ 0.001

7. $U_1 = \{\text{first urn selected}\}$
$U_2 = \{\text{second urn selected}\}$
$R = \{\text{red marble drawn}\}$

$P(U_1) = P(U_2) = \dfrac{1}{2}.$

$$P(U_1 | R) = \frac{P(U_1)P(R|U_1)}{P(U_1)P(R|U_1) + P(U_2)P(R|U_2)}$$

$$= \frac{\frac{1}{2} \cdot \frac{4}{6}}{\frac{1}{2} \cdot \frac{4}{6} + \frac{1}{2} \cdot \frac{2}{5}} = \frac{5}{8}.$$

9. $A = \{\text{unit from line A}\}$
$B = \{\text{unit from line B}\}$
$D = \{\text{defective unit}\}$.

$$P(A) = \frac{200}{600} = \frac{1}{3}$$

$$P(B) = \frac{400}{600} = \frac{2}{3}$$

$$P(A|D) = \frac{P(A)P(D|A)}{P(A)P(D|A) + P(B)P(D|B)}$$

$$= \frac{\frac{1}{3} \cdot \frac{2}{100}}{\frac{1}{3} \cdot \frac{2}{100} + \frac{2}{3} \cdot \frac{5}{100}} = \frac{1}{6}$$

11. $C = \{\text{call made}\}$
$T = \{\text{on time for meeting}\}$

$$P(C|T) = \frac{P(C)P(T|C)}{P(C)P(T|C) + P(C')P(T|C')}$$

$$= \frac{(0.9)(0.9)}{(0.9)(0.9) + (0.1)(0.8)} = \frac{81}{89} \approx 0.910$$

13. $W = \{\text{walking reported}\}$
$B = \{\text{bicycling reported}\}$
$R = \{\text{running reported}\}$
$C = \{\text{completed requirement}\}$
$P(W | C)$

$$= \frac{P(W)P(C | W)}{P(W)P(C | W) + P(B)P(C | B) + P(R)P(C | R)}$$

$$= \frac{\frac{1}{2} \cdot \frac{9}{10}}{\frac{1}{2} \cdot \frac{9}{10} + \frac{1}{4} \cdot \frac{4}{5} + \frac{1}{4} \cdot \frac{2}{3}} = \frac{27}{49} \approx 0.551$$

55.1% would be expected to report walking.

15. $J = \{\text{had Japanese-made car}\}$
$E = \{\text{had European-made car}\}$
$A = \{\text{had American-made car}\}$
$B = \{\text{buy same make again}\}$
$P(J | B)$

$$= \frac{P(J)P(B | J)}{P(J)P(B | J) + P(E)P(B | E) + P(A)P(B | A)}$$

$$= \frac{\frac{3}{5} \cdot \frac{85}{100}}{\frac{3}{5} \cdot \frac{85}{100} + \frac{1}{10} \cdot \frac{50}{100} + \frac{3}{10} \cdot \frac{40}{100}} = \frac{3}{4}$$

17. $P = \{\text{pass the exam}\}$
$A = \{\text{answer every question}\}$

$$P(A|P) = \frac{P(A)P(P|A)}{P(A)P(P|A) + P(A')P(P|A')}$$

$$= \frac{(0.75)(0.8)}{(0.75)(0.8) + (0.25)(0.50)} = \frac{24}{29} \approx 0.828$$

19. $S = \{\text{signals sent}\}$
$D = \{\text{signals detected}\}$

$$P(S|D) = \frac{P(S)P(D|S)}{P(S)P(D|S) + P(S')P(D|S')}$$

$$= \frac{\frac{2}{5} \cdot \frac{3}{5}}{\frac{2}{5} \cdot \frac{3}{5} + \frac{3}{5} \cdot \frac{1}{10}} = \frac{4}{5}$$

21. $S = \{\text{movie is a success}\}$
$U = \{\text{"Two Thumbs Up"}\}$

$$P(S|U) = \frac{P(S)P(U|S)}{P(S)P(U|S) + P(S')P(U|S')}$$

$$= \frac{\frac{7}{10} \cdot \frac{80}{100}}{\frac{7}{10} \cdot \frac{80}{100} + \frac{3}{10} \cdot \frac{10}{100}} = \frac{56}{59} \approx 0.949$$

23. $S = \{\text{is substandard request}\}$
$C = \{\text{is considered substandard request by Risky}\}$

a. $P(C) = P(S)P(C | S) + P(S')P(C | S')$
$= (0.15)(0.8) + (0.85)(0.10) = 0.205 = \frac{41}{200}$

b. $P(S|C) = \frac{P(S)P(C|S)}{P(S)P(C|S) + P(S')P(C|S')}$

$$= \frac{(0.15)(0.8)}{0.205} = \frac{0.12}{0.205} = \frac{120}{205} = \frac{24}{41}$$
≈ 0.585

c. $P(\text{Error}) = P(C' \cap S) + P(C \cap S')$
$= P(S)(C' | S) + P(S')P(C | S')$
$= (0.15)(0.2) + (0.85)(0.10) = 0.115 = \frac{23}{200}$

25. a.

$$P(L|E) = \frac{P(L)P(E|L)}{P(L)P(E|L) + P(M)P(E|M) + P(H)P(E|H)}$$

$$= \frac{(0.25)(0.49)}{(0.25)(0.49) + (0.25)(0.64) + (0.5)(0.81)} \approx 0.18$$

b.

$$P(M|E) = \frac{P(M)P(E|M)}{P(L)P(E|L) + P(M)P(E|M) + P(H)P(E|H)}$$

$$= \frac{(0.25)(0.64)}{(0.25)(0.49) + (0.25)(0.64) + (0.5)(0.81)} \approx 0.23$$

c.

$$P(H|E) = \frac{P(H)P(E|H)}{P(L)P(E|L) + P(M)P(E|M) + P(H)P(E|H)}$$

$$= \frac{(0.5)(0.81)}{(0.25)(0.49) + (0.25)(0.64) + (0.5)(0.81)} \approx 0.59$$

d. High quality

27. $F = \{\text{fair weather}\}$
$I = \{\text{inclement weather}\}$
$W = \{\text{predict fair weather}\}.$

$$P(F|W) = \frac{P(F)P(W|F)}{P(F)P(W|F) + P(I)P(W|I)}$$

$$= \frac{(0.8)(0.7)}{(0.8)(0.7) + (0.2)(0.3)} = \frac{28}{31} \approx 0.90$$

Chapter 9 Review Problems

1. $_8P_3 = 8 \cdot 7 \cdot 6 = 336$

3. $_9C_7 = \dfrac{9!}{7!(9-7)!} = \dfrac{9!}{7! \cdot 2!} = \dfrac{9 \cdot 8 \cdot 7!}{7! \cdot 2 \cdot 1}$

$= \dfrac{9 \cdot 8}{2} = 36$

5. For each of the first two symbols there are 26 choices, for the third there are 9 choices, and for each of the last two symbols there are 10 choices. By the basic counting principle, the number of license plates that are possible is
$26 \cdot 26 \cdot 9 \cdot 10 \cdot 10 = 608,400.$

7. Each of the five switches has 2 possible positions. By the basic counting principle, the number of different codes is
$2 \cdot 2 \cdot 2 \cdot 2 \cdot 2 = 2^5 = 32$.

9. A possibility for first, second, and third place is a selection of three of the seven teams so that order is important. Thus the number of ways the season can end is
$_7P_3 = 7 \cdot 6 \cdot 5 = 210$.

11. A group is any five of the eight people, and the order of the five is not important. Thus the number of groups is
$_8C_5 = \dfrac{8!}{5! \cdot 3!} = \dfrac{8 \cdot 7 \cdot 6 \cdot 5!}{5! \cdot 3 \cdot 2 \cdot 1} = 56$.

13. a. Three bulbs are selected from 24, and the order of selection is not important. Thus the number of possible selections is ${}_{24}C_3 = \dfrac{24!}{3!(24-3)!} = \dfrac{24!}{3! \cdot 21!}$

$= \dfrac{24 \cdot 23 \cdot 22 \cdot 21!}{3 \cdot 2 \cdot 1 \cdot 21!} = \dfrac{24 \cdot 23 \cdot 22}{3 \cdot 2 \cdot 1} = 2024$.

b. Only one bulb is defective and that bulb must be included in the selection. The other two bulbs must be selected from the 23 remaining bulbs and there are ${}_{23}C_2$ such selections possible. Thus the number of ways of selecting three bulbs such that one is defective is

$1 \cdot {}_{23}C_2 = {}_{23}C_2 = \dfrac{23!}{2!(23-2)!} = \dfrac{23!}{2! \cdot 21!}$

$\dfrac{23 \cdot 22 \cdot 21!}{2 \cdot 1 \cdot 21!} = \dfrac{23 \cdot 22}{2 \cdot 1} = 253$.

15. In the word MISSISSIPPI, there are 11 letters with repetition: 1 M, 4 I's, 4 S's, and 2 P's. Thus the number of distinguishable horizontal arrangements is

$\dfrac{11!}{1! \cdot 4! \cdot 4! \cdot 2!} = 34,650$.

17. Of the eight nurses, three go to hospital A (Cell A), two go to hospital B (cell B), and three are not assigned (cell C). The number of possible assignments is $\dfrac{8!}{3! \cdot 2! \cdot 3!} = 560$.

19. a. $\{1, 2, 3, 4, 5, 6, 7\}$

b. $\{4, 5, 6\}$

c. $E_1' \cup E_2 = \{7, 8\} \cup \{4, 5, 6, 7\}$
$= \{4, 5, 6, 7, 8\}$

d. The intersection of any event and its complement is $\varnothing$.

e. $(E_1 \cap E_2')'$
$= (\{1, 2, 3, 4, 5, 6\} \cap \{1, 2, 3, 8\})'$
$= \{1, 2, 3\}' = \{4, 5, 6, 7, 8\}$

f. From (b), $E_1 \cap E_2 \neq \varnothing$, so E_1 and E_2 are not mutually exclusive.

21. a. $\{R_1R_2R_3, R_1R_2G_3, R_1G_2R_3, R_1G_2G_3,$
$G_1R_2R_3, G_1R_2G_3, G_1G_2R_3, G_1G_2G_3\}$

b. $\{R_1R_2G_3, R_1G_2R_3, G_1R_2R_3\}$

c. $\{R_1R_2R_3, G_1G_2G_3\}$

23. $n(S) = {}_{10}C_2 = \dfrac{10!}{2! \cdot 8!} = \dfrac{10 \cdot 9 \cdot 8!}{2 \cdot 1 \cdot 8!} = \dfrac{10 \cdot 9}{2 \cdot 1} = 45$

Let E be the event that box is rejected. If box is rejected, the one defective chip must be in the two-chip sample and there are nine possibilities for the other chip. Thus

$n(E) = 9$ and $P(E) = \dfrac{n(E)}{n(S)} = \dfrac{9}{45} = \dfrac{1}{5} = 0.2$.

25. Number of ways to answer exam is
$4^5 = 1024 = n(S)$. Let
$E = \{$exactly two questions are incorrect$\}$.
The number of ways of selecting two of the five questions that are incorrect is
${}_5C_2 = \dfrac{5!}{2! \cdot 3!} = 10$. However, there are three ways to answer a question incorrectly. Since two questions are incorrect
$n(E) = 10 \cdot 3 \cdot 3 = 90$. Thus
$P(E) = \dfrac{n(E)}{n(S)} = \dfrac{90}{1024} = \dfrac{45}{512}$.

27. a. There are 10 marbles in the urn.
$n(S) = 10 \cdot 10 = 100$
$n(E_{\text{both red}}) = 4 \cdot 4 = 16$
Thus

$P(E_{\text{both red}}) = \dfrac{n(E_{\text{both red}})}{n(S)} = \dfrac{16}{100} = \dfrac{4}{25}$.

b. $n(S) = 10 \cdot 9 = 90$
$n(E_{\text{both red}}) = 4 \cdot 3 = 12$

Thus $P(E_{\text{both red}}) = \dfrac{12}{90} = \dfrac{2}{15}$.

29. $n(S) = 52 \cdot 52$.

    a. There are 26 red cards in a deck. Thus $n(E_{\text{both red}}) = 26 \cdot 26$ and

$$P(E_{\text{both red}}) = \frac{26 \cdot 26}{52 \cdot 52} = \frac{1}{4}.$$

    b. There are 13 clubs in a deck, none of which are red. If E = event that one card is red and the other is a club, then E occurs if the first card is red and the second is a club, or vice versa. Thus $n(E) = 26 \cdot 13 + 13 \cdot 26 = 2 \cdot 26 \cdot 13$ and

$$P(E) = \frac{2 \cdot 26 \cdot 13}{52 \cdot 52} = \frac{1}{4}.$$

31. $\dfrac{P(E)}{P(E')} = \dfrac{\frac{3}{8}}{1 - \left(\frac{3}{8}\right)} = \dfrac{\frac{3}{8}}{\frac{5}{8}} = \dfrac{3}{5}$ or 3:5

33. $P(E) = \dfrac{6}{6+1} = \dfrac{6}{7}$

35. $P(F \mid H') = \dfrac{P(F \cap H')}{P(H')} = \dfrac{\frac{9}{52}}{\frac{39}{52}} = \dfrac{3}{13}$

37. $P(S \cap M) = P(S)P(M \mid S)$
$= (0.6)(0.7) = 0.42$

39. **a.** The reduced sample space consists of $(4, 1), (4, 2), (4, 3), (4, 4), (4, 5), (4, 6),$ $(1, 4), (2, 4), (3, 4), (5, 4), (6, 4).$ In two of these 11 points, the sum of the components is 7. Thus

$$P(\text{sum} = 7 \mid \text{a 4 shows}) = \frac{2}{11}.$$

    b. Out of 36 sample points, the event {getting a total of 7 and having a 4 show} is $\{(4, 3), (3, 4)\}$. Thus the probability of this event is $\dfrac{2}{36} = \dfrac{1}{18}.$

41. The second number must be a 5 or 6, so the reduced sample space has $6 \cdot 2 = 12$ sample points. Of these, the event {first number $\geq$ second number} consists of $(5,5), (6,5),$ and $(6,6)$. Thus the conditional probability is $\dfrac{3}{12} = \dfrac{1}{4}.$

43. **a.** $P(L' \mid F) = \dfrac{n(L' \cap F)}{n(F)} = \dfrac{160}{480} = \dfrac{1}{3}$

    b. $P(L) = \dfrac{400}{600} = \dfrac{2}{3}$ and

$$P(L \mid M) = \frac{n(L \cap M)}{n(M)} = \frac{80}{120} = \frac{2}{3}.$$

    Since $P(L \mid M) = P(L)$, events L and M are independent.

45. $P = \{\text{attend public college}\}$
$M = \{\text{from middle-class family}\}$
$$P(P) = \frac{125}{175} = \frac{5}{7}$$
$$P(P \mid M) = \frac{n(P \cap M)}{n(M)} = \frac{55}{80} = \frac{11}{16}$$
Since $P(P \mid M) \neq P(P)$, events P and M are dependent.

47. **a.** $P(\text{none takes root}) = (0.3)(0.3)(0.3)(0.3)$
$= 0.0081$

    b. The probability that a particular two shrubs take root and the remaining two do not is $(0.7)(0.7)(0.3)(0.3)$. The number of ways the two that take root can be chosen from the four shrubs is ${}_4C_2$. Thus
$P(\text{exactly two take root})$
$= {}_4C_2 (0.7)^2 (0.3)^2 = 0.2646.$

    c. For at most two shrubs to take root, either none does, exactly one does, or exactly two do.
    $P(\text{none}) + P(\text{exactly one}) + P(\text{exactly two})$

$$= 0.0081 + {}_4C_1(0.7)(0.3)^3 + 0.2646$$
$$= 0.0081 + 0.0756 + 0.2646$$
$$= 0.3483$$

49. $P(R_{II}) = P(G_I)P(R_{II} \mid G_I) + P(R_I)P(R_{II} \mid R_I)$

$$= \frac{3}{5} \cdot \frac{4}{9} + \frac{2}{5} \cdot \frac{5}{9} = \frac{22}{45}.$$

51. $P(G \mid A) = \dfrac{P(G \cap A)}{P(A)} = \dfrac{0.1}{0.4} = \dfrac{1}{4}$

53. a. $F = \{\text{produced by first shift}\}$
      $S = \{\text{produced by second shift}\}$
      $D = \{\text{defective}\}$
      $P(D) = P(F)P(D \mid F) + P(S)P(D \mid S)$

$$= \frac{300}{500} \cdot (0.01) + \frac{200}{500} \cdot (0.02)$$
$$= 0.006 + 0.008 = 0.014$$

  b. $P(S \mid D) = \dfrac{P(S)P(D \mid S)}{P(F)P(D \mid F) + P(S)P(D \mid S)}$

$$= \frac{0.008}{0.014} = \frac{4}{7} \approx 0.57$$

Chapter 10

1. $\mu = \sum_x x f(x) = 0(0.1) + 1(0.4) + 2(0.2) + 3(0.3) = 1.7$

   $$\begin{aligned} \text{Var}(X) &= \sum_x x^2 f(x) - \mu^2 \\ &= [0^2(0.1) + 1^2(0.4) + 2^2(0.2) + 3^2(0.3)] - (1.7)^2 \\ &= 1.01 \end{aligned}$$

   $\sigma = \sqrt{\text{Var}(X)} = \sqrt{1.01} \approx 1.00$

   See below for histogram.

3. $\mu = \sum_x x f(x) = 1\left(\dfrac{1}{4}\right) + 2\left(\dfrac{1}{4}\right) + 3\left(\dfrac{1}{2}\right) = \dfrac{9}{4} = 2.25$

   $\text{Var}(X) = \sum_x x^2 f(x) - \mu^2 = \left[1^2\left(\dfrac{1}{4}\right) + 2^2\left(\dfrac{1}{4}\right) + 3^2\left(\dfrac{1}{2}\right)\right] - \left(\dfrac{9}{4}\right)^2 = \dfrac{11}{16} = 0.6875$

   $\sigma = \sqrt{\dfrac{11}{16}} = \dfrac{\sqrt{11}}{4} \approx 0.83$

5. **a.** $P(X = 2) = 1 - [P(X = 4) + P(X = 7)] = 1 - [0.5 + 0.4] = 0.1.$

   b. $\mu = \sum_x x f(x) = 2(0.1) + 4(0.5) + 7(0.4) = 5$

   c. $\sigma^2 = \sum_x x^2 f(x) - \mu^2 = [2^2(0.1) + 4^2(0.5) + 7^2(0.4)] - 5^2 = 3$

7. Distribution of X:

   $f(0) = \dfrac{1}{8}, \ \ f(1) = \dfrac{3}{8}, \ \ f(2) = \dfrac{3}{8}, \ \ f(3) = \dfrac{1}{8}$

   $E(X) = \sum_x x f(x) = 0\left(\dfrac{1}{8}\right) + 1\left(\dfrac{3}{8}\right) + 2\left(\dfrac{3}{8}\right) + 3\left(\dfrac{1}{8}\right) = \dfrac{12}{8} = \dfrac{3}{2} = 1.5$

$$\sigma^2 = \mathrm{Var}(X) = \sum_x x^2 f(x) - [E(x)]^2$$

$$= \left[0^2 \left(\frac{1}{8} \right) + 1^2 \left(\frac{3}{8} \right) + 2^2 \left(\frac{3}{8} \right) + 3^2 \left(\frac{1}{8} \right) \right] - \left(\frac{3}{2} \right)^2$$

$$= \frac{24}{8} - \frac{9}{4} = \frac{6}{8} = \frac{3}{4} = 0.75$$

$$\sigma = \sqrt{\frac{3}{4}} = \frac{\sqrt{3}}{2} \approx 0.87$$

9. The number of outcomes in the sample space is $_5C_2 = 10$.

Distribution of X:

$$f(0) = \frac{_3C_2}{10} = \frac{3}{10}, \quad f(1) = \frac{_2C_1 \cdot _3C_1}{10} = \frac{3}{5},$$

$$f(2) = \frac{_2C_2}{10} = \frac{1}{10}$$

$$E(X) = \sum_x x f(x) = 0 \left(\frac{3}{10} \right) + 1 \left(\frac{3}{5} \right) + 2 \left(\frac{1}{10} \right)$$

$$= \frac{4}{5} = 0.8$$

$$\sigma^2 = \sum_x x^2 f(x) - [E(x)]^2$$

$$= \left[0^2 \left(\frac{3}{10} \right) + 1^2 \left(\frac{3}{5} \right) + 2^2 \left(\frac{1}{10} \right) \right] - \left(\frac{4}{5} \right)^2$$

$$= 1 - \frac{16}{25} = \frac{9}{25} = 0.36$$

$$\sigma = \sqrt{\frac{9}{25}} = \frac{3}{5} = 0.6$$

11. $f(0) = P(X = 0) = \dfrac{_2C_2}{_5C_2} = \dfrac{1}{10}$

$$f(1) = P(X = 1) = \frac{_3C_1 \cdot _2C_1}{_5C_2} = \frac{6}{10} = \frac{3}{5}$$

$$f(2) = P(X = 2) = \frac{_3C_2}{_5C_2} = \frac{3}{10}$$

13. a. If X is the gain (in dollars), then $X = -1$ or 8499.

Distribution of X:

$$f(-1) = \frac{9999}{10,000}, \quad f(8499) = \frac{1}{10,000}$$

$$E(X) = \sum_x x f(x)$$

$$= -1 \cdot \frac{9999}{10,000} + 8499 \cdot \frac{1}{10,000}$$

$$= -\frac{1500}{10,000} = -\$0.15 \text{ (a loss)}$$

b. Here $X = -2$ or 8498. Distribution of X:

$$f(-2) = \frac{9998}{10,000}, \quad f(8499) = \frac{2}{10,000}$$

$$E(X) = \sum_x x f(x)$$

$$= -2 \cdot \frac{9998}{10,000} + 8498 \cdot \frac{2}{10,000}$$

$$= -\$0.30 \text{ (a loss)}$$

15. Let X = daily earnings (in dollars). Distribution of X:

$$f(200) = \frac{4}{7}, \quad f(-30) = \frac{3}{7}$$

$$E(X) = \sum_x x f(x)$$

$$= 200 \cdot \frac{4}{7} + (-30) \cdot \frac{3}{7}$$

$$= \frac{710}{7} \approx \$101.43$$

17. The probability that a person in the group is not hospitalized is
$1 - (0.001 + 0.002 + 0.003 + 0.004 + 0.008) = 0.982$.
Let X = gain (in dollars) to the company from a policy.
Distribution of X:
$f(10) = 0.982, \quad f(-90) = 0.001, \quad f(-190) = 0.002, \quad f(-290) = 0.003$,
$f(-390) = 0.004, \quad f(-490) = 0.008$
$E(X) = 10(0.982) + (-90)(0.001) + (-190)(0.002) + (-290)(0.003) + (-390)(0.004) + (-490)(0.008)$
$= \$3.00$

19. Let p = the annual premium (in dollars) per policy. If X = gain (in dollars) to the company from a policy, then either $X = p$ or $X = -(80,000 - p)$. We set $E(X) = 50$:
$-(80,000 - p)(0.0002) + p(0.9998) = 50$
$-16 + 0.0002p + 0.9998p = 50$
$-16 + p = 50$
$p = \$66$

21. Let X = gain (in dollars) on a play.
If 0 heads show, then $X = 0 - 1.25 = -\dfrac{5}{4}$.
If exactly 1 head shows, then
$X = 1.00 - 1.25 = -\dfrac{1}{4}$.
If 2 heads show, then $X = 2.00 - 1.25 = \dfrac{3}{4}$.
Distribution of X:
$f\left(-\dfrac{5}{4}\right) = \dfrac{1}{4}, \quad f\left(-\dfrac{1}{4}\right) = \dfrac{1}{2}, \quad f\left(\dfrac{3}{4}\right) = \dfrac{1}{4}$
$E(X) = \left(-\dfrac{5}{4}\right)\left(\dfrac{1}{4}\right) + \left(-\dfrac{1}{4}\right)\left(\dfrac{1}{2}\right) + \left(\dfrac{3}{4}\right)\left(\dfrac{1}{4}\right)$
$= -\dfrac{1}{4} = -0.25$
Thus there is an expected loss of $0.25 on each play.
For a fair game, let
p = amount (in dollars) paid to play.
Distribution of X:
$f(-p) = \dfrac{1}{4}, \quad f(1-p) = \dfrac{1}{2}, \quad f(2-p) = \dfrac{1}{4}$

We set $E(X) = 0$:
$(-p)\dfrac{1}{4} + (1-p)\dfrac{1}{2} + (2-p)\dfrac{1}{4} = 0$
$-\dfrac{p}{4} + \dfrac{1}{2} - \dfrac{p}{2} + \dfrac{1}{2} - \dfrac{p}{4} = 0$
$1 - p = 0$
$p = 1$
Thus you should pay $1 for a fair game.

Principles in Practice 10.2

1. Here $p = 0.30$, $q = 1 - p = 0.70$, and $n = 4$.
$P(X = x) = {}_nC_x p^x q^{n-x}, \quad x = 0, 1, 2, 3, 4$
$P(X = 0) = {}_4C_0 (0.3)^0 (0.7)^4 = 0.2401$
$= \dfrac{2401}{10,000}$
$P(X = 1) = {}_4C_1 (0.3)^1 (0.7)^3 = 0.4116$
$= \dfrac{4116}{10,000}$
$P(X = 2) = {}_4C_2 (0.3)^2 (0.7)^2 = 0.2646$
$= \dfrac{2646}{10,000}$
$P(X = 3) = {}_4C_3 (0.3)^3 (0.7)^1 = 0.0756$
$= \dfrac{756}{10,000}$
$P(X = 4) = {}_4C_4 (0.3)^4 (0.7)^0 = 0.0081$
$= \dfrac{81}{10,000}$

Exercise 10.2

1. $f(0) = {}_2C_0\left(\dfrac{1}{4}\right)^0\left(\dfrac{3}{4}\right)^2 = \dfrac{2!}{0!\cdot2!}\cdot1\cdot\dfrac{9}{16}$

$= 1\cdot1\cdot\dfrac{9}{16} = \dfrac{9}{16}$

$f(1) = {}_2C_1\left(\dfrac{1}{4}\right)^1\left(\dfrac{3}{4}\right)^1 = \dfrac{2!}{1!\cdot1!}\cdot\dfrac{1}{4}\cdot\dfrac{3}{4}$

$= 2\cdot\dfrac{1}{4}\cdot\dfrac{3}{4} = \dfrac{3}{8}$

$f(2) = {}_2C_2\left(\dfrac{1}{4}\right)^2\left(\dfrac{3}{4}\right)^0 = \dfrac{2!}{2!\cdot0!}\cdot\dfrac{1}{16}\cdot1$

$= 1\cdot\dfrac{1}{16}\cdot1 = \dfrac{1}{16}.$

$\mu = np = 2\cdot\dfrac{1}{4} = \dfrac{1}{2};\ \sigma = \sqrt{npq} = \sqrt{2\cdot\dfrac{1}{4}\cdot\dfrac{3}{4}}$

$= \sqrt{\dfrac{6}{16}} = \dfrac{\sqrt{6}}{4}$

3. $f(0) = {}_3C_0\left(\dfrac{2}{3}\right)^0\left(\dfrac{1}{3}\right)^3 = 1\cdot1\cdot\dfrac{1}{27} = \dfrac{1}{27}$

$f(1) = {}_3C_1\left(\dfrac{2}{3}\right)^1\left(\dfrac{1}{3}\right)^2 = \dfrac{3!}{1!\cdot2!}\cdot\dfrac{2}{3}\cdot\dfrac{1}{9}$

$= 3\cdot\dfrac{2}{3}\cdot\dfrac{1}{9} = \dfrac{2}{9}$

$f(2) = {}_3C_2\left(\dfrac{2}{3}\right)^2\left(\dfrac{1}{3}\right)^1 = \dfrac{3!}{2!\cdot1!}\cdot\dfrac{4}{9}\cdot\dfrac{1}{3}$

$= 3\cdot\dfrac{4}{9}\cdot\dfrac{1}{3} = \dfrac{4}{9}$

$f(3) = {}_3C_3\left(\dfrac{2}{3}\right)^3\left(\dfrac{1}{3}\right)^0 = \dfrac{3!}{3!\cdot0!}\cdot\dfrac{8}{27}\cdot1$

$= 1\cdot\dfrac{8}{27}\cdot1 = \dfrac{8}{27}$

$\mu = np = 3\cdot\dfrac{2}{3} = 2;\ \sigma = \sqrt{npq} = \sqrt{3\cdot\dfrac{2}{3}\cdot\dfrac{1}{3}}$

$= \sqrt{\dfrac{2}{3}} = \dfrac{\sqrt{6}}{3}$

5. $P(X = 5) = {}_6C_5(0.2)^5(0.8)^1$
$= 6(0.00032)(0.8) = 0.001536$

7. $P(X = 2) = {}_4C_2\left(\dfrac{4}{5}\right)^2\left(\dfrac{1}{5}\right)^2 = 6\cdot\dfrac{16}{25}\cdot\dfrac{1}{25}$

$= \dfrac{96}{625} = 0.1536$

9. $P(X < 2) = P(X = 0) + P(X = 1)$

$= {}_5C_0\left(\dfrac{1}{2}\right)^0\left(\dfrac{1}{2}\right)^5 + {}_5C_1\left(\dfrac{1}{2}\right)^1\left(\dfrac{1}{2}\right)^4$

$= 1\cdot1\cdot\dfrac{1}{32} + 5\cdot\dfrac{1}{2}\cdot\dfrac{1}{16} = \dfrac{6}{32} = \dfrac{3}{16}$

11. Let X = number of heads that occurs.
$p = \dfrac{1}{2},\ n = 10$

$P(X = 8) = {}_{10}C_8\left(\dfrac{1}{2}\right)^8\left(\dfrac{1}{2}\right)^2 = 45\cdot\dfrac{1}{256}\cdot\dfrac{1}{4}$

$= \dfrac{45}{1024} \approx 0.044$

13. Let X = number of green marbles drawn. The probability of selecting a green marble on any draw is $\dfrac{6}{10} = \dfrac{3}{5}$. $n = 4$

$P(X = 1) = {}_4C_1\left(\dfrac{3}{5}\right)^1\left(\dfrac{2}{5}\right)^3 = 4\cdot\dfrac{3}{5}\cdot\dfrac{8}{125}$

$= \dfrac{96}{625} = 0.1536$

15. Let X = number of defective switches selected. The probability that a switch is defective is $p = 0.02$. $n = 4$.
$P(X = 2) = {}_4C_2(0.02)^2(0.98)^2$
$= 6(0.0004)(0.9604) \approx 0.002$

17. Let X = number of heads that occurs.
$p = \dfrac{1}{4},\ n = 3$

a. $P(X = 2) = {}_3C_2\left(\dfrac{1}{4}\right)^2\left(\dfrac{3}{4}\right)^1 = 3\cdot\dfrac{1}{16}\cdot\dfrac{3}{4}$

$= \dfrac{9}{64}$

b. $P(X = 3) = {}_3C_3\left(\dfrac{1}{4}\right)^3\left(\dfrac{3}{4}\right)^0 = 1 \cdot \dfrac{1}{64} \cdot 1$

$= \dfrac{1}{64}$

Thus

$P(X = 2) + P(X = 3) = \dfrac{9}{64} + \dfrac{1}{64}$

$= \dfrac{10}{64} = \dfrac{5}{32}$

19. Let X = number of defective in sample.

$p = \dfrac{1}{3},\ n = 4$

$P(X \le 1) = P(X = 0) + P(X = 1)$

$= {}_4C_0\left(\dfrac{1}{3}\right)^0\left(\dfrac{2}{3}\right)^4 + {}_4C_1\left(\dfrac{1}{3}\right)^1\left(\dfrac{2}{3}\right)^3$

$= 1 \cdot 1 \cdot \dfrac{16}{81} + 4 \cdot \dfrac{1}{3} \cdot \dfrac{8}{27} = \dfrac{48}{81}$

$= \dfrac{16}{27} \approx 0.593$

21. Let X = number of hits in four bats.

$p = 0.300,\ n = 4$

$P(X \ge 1) = 1 - P(X = 0)$

$= 1 - {}_4C_0(0.300)^0(0.700)^4$

$= 1 - 1 \cdot 1 \cdot (0.2401) = 0.7599$

23. Let X = number of girls. The probability that a child is a girl is $p = \dfrac{1}{2}$. Here $n = 5$. We must find

$P(X \ge 2) = 1 - P(X < 2)$

$= 1 - [P(X = 0) + P(X = 1)]$.

$P(X = 0) = {}_5C_0\left(\dfrac{1}{2}\right)^0\left(\dfrac{1}{2}\right)^5 = 1 \cdot 1 \cdot \dfrac{1}{32} = \dfrac{1}{32}$

$P(X = 1) = {}_5C_1\left(\dfrac{1}{2}\right)^1\left(\dfrac{1}{2}\right)^4 = 5 \cdot \dfrac{1}{2} \cdot \dfrac{1}{16} = \dfrac{5}{32}$

Thus,

$P(X \ge 2) = 1 - [P(X = 0) + P(X = 1)]$

$= 1 - \left[\dfrac{1}{32} + \dfrac{5}{32}\right] = 1 - \dfrac{3}{16} = \dfrac{13}{16}$

25. $\mu = 2,\ \sigma^2 = \dfrac{3}{2}$

Since $\mu = np$, then $np = 2$. Since $\sigma^2 = npq$,

then $(np)q = \dfrac{3}{2}$, or $2q = \dfrac{3}{2}$, so $q = \dfrac{3}{4}$.

Thus, $p = 1 - q = 1 - \dfrac{3}{4} = \dfrac{1}{4}$. Since $np = 2$,

then $n \cdot \dfrac{1}{4} = 2$, or $n = 8$. Thus

$P(X = 1) = {}_8C_1\left(\dfrac{1}{4}\right)^1\left(\dfrac{3}{4}\right)^7 = 8 \cdot \dfrac{3^7}{4^8} = \dfrac{2187}{8192}$

$\approx 0.267.$

Exercise 10.3

1. $\begin{bmatrix} \frac{1}{2} & 0 \\ \frac{2}{3} & \frac{1}{3} \end{bmatrix}$

No, since the sum of the entries in row 1 is not 1.

3. $\begin{bmatrix} \frac{1}{2} & -\frac{1}{4} & \frac{3}{4} \\ \frac{1}{8} & \frac{5}{8} & \frac{1}{4} \\ \frac{1}{3} & \frac{1}{3} & \frac{1}{3} \end{bmatrix}$

No, since there is a negative entry.

5. $\begin{bmatrix} 0.4 & 0.2 & 0.4 \\ 0 & 0.1 & 0.9 \\ 0.5 & 0.3 & 0.2 \end{bmatrix}$

Yes, since all entries are nonnegative and the sum of the entries in each row is 1.

7. $\begin{bmatrix} \frac{2}{3} & a \\ b & \frac{1}{4} \end{bmatrix}$

$\dfrac{2}{3} + a = 1$, so $a = \dfrac{1}{3}$. $b + \dfrac{1}{4} = 1$, so $b = \dfrac{3}{4}$.

9. $\begin{bmatrix} 0.4 & a & 0.2 \\ a & 0.1 & b \\ a & b & c \end{bmatrix}$

$0.4 + a + 0.2 = 1$, so $a = 0.4$.

$a + 0.1 + b = 1$, $0.4 + 0.1 + b = 1$, so $b = 0.5$.

$a + b + c = 1$, $0.4 + 0.5 + c = 1$, so $c = 0.1$.

215

11. [0.4, 0.6]
Yes, all entries are nonnegative and their sum is 1.

13. [0.2 0.7 0.5]
No, the sum of the entries is not 1.

15. $X_1 = X_0 T = \begin{bmatrix} \frac{1}{4} & \frac{3}{4} \end{bmatrix} \begin{bmatrix} \frac{2}{3} & \frac{1}{3} \\ 1 & 0 \end{bmatrix} = \begin{bmatrix} \frac{11}{12} & \frac{1}{12} \end{bmatrix}$

$X_2 = X_1 T = \begin{bmatrix} \frac{11}{12} & \frac{1}{12} \end{bmatrix} \begin{bmatrix} \frac{2}{3} & \frac{1}{3} \\ 1 & 0 \end{bmatrix} = \begin{bmatrix} \frac{25}{36} & \frac{11}{36} \end{bmatrix}$

$X_3 = X_2 T = \begin{bmatrix} \frac{25}{36} & \frac{11}{36} \end{bmatrix} \begin{bmatrix} \frac{2}{3} & \frac{1}{3} \\ 1 & 0 \end{bmatrix}$

$= \begin{bmatrix} \frac{83}{108} & \frac{25}{108} \end{bmatrix}$

17. $X_1 = X_0 T = \begin{bmatrix} 0.4 & 0.6 \end{bmatrix} \begin{bmatrix} 0.5 & 0.5 \\ 0.5 & 0.5 \end{bmatrix}$

$= \begin{bmatrix} 0.5 & 0.5 \end{bmatrix}$

$X_2 = X_1 T = \begin{bmatrix} 0.5 & 0.5 \end{bmatrix} \begin{bmatrix} 0.5 & 0.5 \\ 0.5 & 0.5 \end{bmatrix}$

$= \begin{bmatrix} 0.5 & 0.5 \end{bmatrix}$

$X_3 = X_2 T = \begin{bmatrix} 0.5 & 0.5 \end{bmatrix} \begin{bmatrix} 0.5 & 0.5 \\ 0.5 & 0.5 \end{bmatrix}$

$= \begin{bmatrix} 0.5 & 0.5 \end{bmatrix}$

19. $X_1 = X_0 T = \begin{bmatrix} 0.2 & 0 & 0.8 \end{bmatrix} \begin{bmatrix} 0.1 & 0.2 & 0.7 \\ 0 & 0.4 & 0.6 \\ 0.3 & 0.3 & 0.4 \end{bmatrix}$

$= \begin{bmatrix} 0.26 & 0.28 & 0.46 \end{bmatrix}$
$X_2 = X_1 T$

$= \begin{bmatrix} 0.26 & 0.28 & 0.46 \end{bmatrix} \begin{bmatrix} 0.1 & 0.2 & 0.7 \\ 0 & 0.4 & 0.6 \\ 0.3 & 0.3 & 0.4 \end{bmatrix}$

$= \begin{bmatrix} 0.164 & 0.302 & 0.534 \end{bmatrix};$
$X_3 = X_2 T$

$= \begin{bmatrix} 0.164 & 0.302 & 0.534 \end{bmatrix} \begin{bmatrix} 0.1 & 0.2 & 0.7 \\ 0 & 0.4 & 0.6 \\ 0.3 & 0.3 & 0.4 \end{bmatrix}$

$= \begin{bmatrix} 0.1766 & 0.3138 & 0.5096 \end{bmatrix}.$

21. a. $T^2 = \begin{bmatrix} \frac{1}{4} & \frac{3}{4} \\ \frac{3}{4} & \frac{1}{4} \end{bmatrix} \begin{bmatrix} \frac{1}{4} & \frac{3}{4} \\ \frac{3}{4} & \frac{1}{4} \end{bmatrix} = \begin{bmatrix} \frac{5}{8} & \frac{3}{8} \\ \frac{3}{8} & \frac{5}{8} \end{bmatrix}$

$T^3 = T^2 T = \begin{bmatrix} \frac{5}{8} & \frac{3}{8} \\ \frac{3}{8} & \frac{5}{8} \end{bmatrix} \begin{bmatrix} \frac{1}{4} & \frac{3}{4} \\ \frac{3}{4} & \frac{1}{4} \end{bmatrix}$

$= \begin{bmatrix} \frac{7}{16} & \frac{9}{16} \\ \frac{9}{16} & \frac{7}{16} \end{bmatrix}.$

b. Entry in row 1, column 2, of T^2 is $\frac{3}{8}$.

c. Entry in row 2, column 1 of T^3 is $\frac{9}{16}$.

23. a. T^2

$= \begin{bmatrix} 0 & 1 & 0 \\ 0.5 & 0.4 & 0.1 \\ 0.3 & 0.3 & 0.4 \end{bmatrix} \begin{bmatrix} 0 & 1 & 0 \\ 0.5 & 0.4 & 0.1 \\ 0.3 & 0.3 & 0.4 \end{bmatrix}$

$= \begin{bmatrix} 0.50 & 0.40 & 0.10 \\ 0.23 & 0.69 & 0.08 \\ 0.27 & 0.54 & 0.19 \end{bmatrix}$

$T^3 = T^2 T$

$= \begin{bmatrix} 0.50 & 0.40 & 0.10 \\ 0.23 & 0.69 & 0.08 \\ 0.27 & 0.54 & 0.19 \end{bmatrix} \begin{bmatrix} 0 & 1 & 0 \\ 0.5 & 0.4 & 0.1 \\ 0.3 & 0.3 & 0.4 \end{bmatrix}$

$= \begin{bmatrix} 0.230 & 0.690 & 0.080 \\ 0.369 & 0.530 & 0.101 \\ 0.327 & 0.543 & 0.130 \end{bmatrix}$

b. Entry in row 1, column 2, of T^2 is 0.40.

c. Entry in row 2, column 1 of T^3 is 0.369.

25. $\mathbf{T}^T - \mathbf{I} = \begin{bmatrix} \frac{1}{2} & \frac{3}{4} \\ \frac{1}{2} & \frac{1}{4} \end{bmatrix} - \begin{bmatrix} 1 & 0 \\ 0 & 1 \end{bmatrix} = \begin{bmatrix} -\frac{1}{2} & \frac{3}{4} \\ \frac{1}{2} & -\frac{3}{4} \end{bmatrix}$

$\begin{bmatrix} -\frac{1}{2} & \frac{3}{4} & \vdots & 0 \\ \frac{1}{2} & -\frac{3}{4} & \vdots & 0 \\ 1 & 1 & \vdots & 1 \end{bmatrix} \rightarrow \cdots \rightarrow \begin{bmatrix} 1 & 0 & \vdots & \frac{3}{5} \\ 0 & 1 & \vdots & \frac{2}{5} \\ 0 & 0 & \vdots & 0 \end{bmatrix}$

$\mathbf{Q} = \begin{bmatrix} \frac{3}{5} & \frac{2}{5} \end{bmatrix}$

27. $\mathbf{T}^T - \mathbf{I} = \begin{bmatrix} \frac{1}{5} & \frac{3}{5} \\ \frac{4}{5} & \frac{2}{5} \end{bmatrix} - \begin{bmatrix} 1 & 0 \\ 0 & 1 \end{bmatrix} = \begin{bmatrix} -\frac{4}{5} & \frac{3}{5} \\ \frac{4}{5} & -\frac{3}{5} \end{bmatrix}$

$\begin{bmatrix} -\frac{4}{5} & \frac{3}{5} & \vdots & 0 \\ \frac{4}{5} & -\frac{3}{5} & \vdots & 0 \\ 1 & 1 & \vdots & 1 \end{bmatrix} \rightarrow \cdots \rightarrow \begin{bmatrix} 1 & 0 & \vdots & \frac{3}{7} \\ 0 & 1 & \vdots & \frac{4}{7} \\ 0 & 0 & \vdots & 0 \end{bmatrix}$

$\mathbf{Q} = \begin{bmatrix} \frac{3}{7} & \frac{4}{7} \end{bmatrix}$

29. $\mathbf{T}^T - \mathbf{I} = \begin{bmatrix} 0.4 & 0.6 & 0.6 \\ 0.3 & 0.3 & 0.1 \\ 0.3 & 0.1 & 0.3 \end{bmatrix} - \begin{bmatrix} 1 & 0 & 0 \\ 0 & 1 & 0 \\ 0 & 0 & 1 \end{bmatrix} = \begin{bmatrix} -0.6 & 0.6 & 0.6 \\ 0.3 & -0.7 & 0.1 \\ 0.3 & 0.1 & -0.7 \end{bmatrix}$

$\begin{bmatrix} -0.6 & 0.6 & 0.6 & \vdots & 0 \\ 0.3 & -0.7 & 0.1 & \vdots & 0 \\ 0.3 & 0.1 & -0.7 & \vdots & 0 \\ 1 & 1 & 1 & \vdots & 1 \end{bmatrix} \rightarrow \cdots \rightarrow \begin{bmatrix} 1 & 0 & 0 & \vdots & 0.5 \\ 0 & 1 & 0 & \vdots & 0.25 \\ 0 & 0 & 1 & \vdots & 0.25 \\ 0 & 0 & 0 & \vdots & 0 \end{bmatrix}$

$\mathbf{Q} = \begin{bmatrix} 0.5 & 0.25 & 0.25 \end{bmatrix}$

31. a. $\mathbf{T} = \begin{matrix} \\ \text{Flu} \\ \text{No flu} \end{matrix} \begin{matrix} \text{Flu} \quad \text{No flu} \\ \begin{bmatrix} 0.1 & 0.9 \\ 0.2 & 0.8 \end{bmatrix} \end{matrix}$

b. $\mathbf{X_0} = \begin{bmatrix} \frac{120}{200} & \frac{80}{200} \end{bmatrix} = \begin{bmatrix} 0.6 & 0.4 \end{bmatrix}$.

If a period is 4 days, then 8 days corresponds to 2 periods, and 12 days corresponds to 3 periods. The state vector corresponding to 8 days from now is

$\mathbf{X_2} = \mathbf{X_0}\mathbf{T}^2 = \begin{bmatrix} 0.6 & 0.4 \end{bmatrix} \begin{bmatrix} 0.19 & 0.81 \\ 0.18 & 0.82 \end{bmatrix}$

$= \begin{bmatrix} 0.186 & 0.814 \end{bmatrix}$.

Thus $0.186(200) \approx 37$ students can be expected to have the flu 8 days from now.

The state vector corresponding to 12 days from now is

$\mathbf{X_3} = \mathbf{X_0}\mathbf{T}^3 = \begin{bmatrix} 0.6 & 0.4 \end{bmatrix} \begin{bmatrix} 0.181 & 0.819 \\ 0.182 & 0.818 \end{bmatrix}$

$= \begin{bmatrix} 0.1814 & 0.8186 \end{bmatrix}$.

Thus $0.1814(200) \approx 36$ students can be expected to have the flu 12 days from now.

33. **a.**
$$\mathbf{T} = \begin{array}{c} \\ \text{A} \\ \text{B} \end{array}\begin{array}{cc} \text{A} & \text{B} \\ \begin{bmatrix} 0.9 & 0.1 \\ 0.3 & 0.7 \end{bmatrix} \end{array}$$

b. Thursday corresponds to step 3.
$$\mathbf{T}^2 = \begin{bmatrix} 0.84 & 0.16 \\ 0.48 & 0.52 \end{bmatrix}$$
$$\mathbf{T}^3 = \begin{bmatrix} 0.804 & 0.196 \\ 0.588 & 0.412 \end{bmatrix}.$$
The probability is 0.804.

35. **a.**
$$\mathbf{T} = \begin{array}{c} \\ \text{D} \\ \text{R} \\ \text{O} \end{array}\begin{array}{ccc} \text{D} & \text{R} & \text{O} \\ \begin{bmatrix} 0.8 & 0.1 & 0.1 \\ 0.1 & 0.8 & 0.1 \\ 0.3 & 0.1 & 0.6 \end{bmatrix} \end{array}$$

b.
$$\mathbf{T}^2 = \begin{bmatrix} 0.68 & 0.17 & 0.15 \\ 0.19 & 0.66 & 0.15 \\ 0.43 & 0.17 & 0.40 \end{bmatrix}$$
The probability is 0.19.

c. $\mathbf{X_1} = \mathbf{X_0 T}$
$$= [0.40 \quad 0.40 \quad 0.20]\begin{bmatrix} 0.8 & 0.1 & 0.1 \\ 0.1 & 0.8 & 0.1 \\ 0.3 & 0.1 & 0.6 \end{bmatrix}$$
$$= [0.42 \quad 0.38 \quad 0.20]$$
38% will be Republican.

37. **a.**
$$\mathbf{T} = \begin{array}{c} \\ \text{A} \\ \text{Compet.} \end{array}\begin{array}{cc} \text{A} & \text{Compet.} \\ \begin{bmatrix} 0.8 & 0.2 \\ 0.3 & 0.7 \end{bmatrix} \end{array}$$

b. $\mathbf{X_1} = \mathbf{X_0 T} = [0.70 \quad 0.30]\begin{bmatrix} 0.8 & 0.2 \\ 0.3 & 0.7 \end{bmatrix} = [0.65 \quad 0.35]$

A is expected to control 65% of the market.

c. $\mathbf{T^T} - \mathbf{I} = \begin{bmatrix} 0.8 & 0.3 \\ 0.2 & 0.7 \end{bmatrix} - \begin{bmatrix} 1 & 0 \\ 0 & 1 \end{bmatrix} = \begin{bmatrix} -0.2 & 0.3 \\ 0.2 & -0.3 \end{bmatrix}$

$$\begin{bmatrix} -0.2 & 0.3 & | & 0 \\ 0.2 & -0.3 & | & 0 \\ 1 & 1 & | & 1 \end{bmatrix} \rightarrow \dots \rightarrow \begin{bmatrix} 1 & 0 & | & 0.6 \\ 0 & 1 & | & 0.4 \\ 0 & 0 & | & 0 \end{bmatrix}$$

$\mathbf{Q} = \begin{bmatrix} 0.6 & 0.4 \end{bmatrix}$

In the long run, A can expect to control 60% of the market.

39. **a.**
$$\mathbf{T} = \begin{array}{c} \\ 1 \\ 2 \end{array}\begin{array}{cc} 1 & 2 \\ \begin{bmatrix} \frac{5}{7} & \frac{2}{7} \\ \frac{3}{7} & \frac{4}{7} \end{bmatrix} \end{array}$$

b. $\mathbf{X_2} = \mathbf{X_0 T^2} = \begin{bmatrix} \frac{1}{2} & \frac{1}{2} \end{bmatrix}\begin{bmatrix} \frac{31}{49} & \frac{18}{49} \\ \frac{27}{49} & \frac{22}{49} \end{bmatrix} = \begin{bmatrix} \frac{29}{49} & \frac{20}{49} \end{bmatrix}$

$\approx [0.5918 \quad 0.4082]$

About 59.18% in compartment 1 and 40.82% in compartment 2.

c. $\mathbf{T^T - I} = \begin{bmatrix} \frac{5}{7} & \frac{3}{7} \\ \frac{2}{7} & \frac{4}{7} \end{bmatrix} - \begin{bmatrix} 1 & 0 \\ 0 & 1 \end{bmatrix} = \begin{bmatrix} -\frac{2}{7} & \frac{3}{7} \\ \frac{2}{7} & -\frac{3}{7} \end{bmatrix}$

$\left[\begin{array}{cc|c} -\frac{2}{7} & \frac{3}{7} & 0 \\ \frac{2}{7} & -\frac{3}{7} & 0 \\ 1 & 1 & 1 \end{array}\right] \rightarrow \dots \rightarrow \left[\begin{array}{cc|c} 1 & 0 & \frac{3}{5} \\ 0 & 1 & \frac{2}{5} \\ 0 & 0 & 0 \end{array}\right]$

$\mathbf{Q} = \begin{bmatrix} \frac{3}{5} & \frac{2}{5} \end{bmatrix} = [0.60 \quad 0.40]$

In the long run, there will be 60% in compartment 1 and 40% in compartment 2.

41. a. $\mathbf{T^T - I} = \begin{bmatrix} \frac{3}{4} & \frac{1}{2} \\ \frac{1}{4} & \frac{1}{2} \end{bmatrix} - \begin{bmatrix} 1 & 0 \\ 0 & 1 \end{bmatrix} = \begin{bmatrix} -\frac{1}{4} & \frac{1}{2} \\ \frac{1}{4} & -\frac{1}{2} \end{bmatrix}$

$\left[\begin{array}{cc|c} -\frac{1}{4} & \frac{1}{2} & 0 \\ \frac{1}{4} & -\frac{1}{2} & 0 \\ 1 & 1 & 1 \end{array}\right] \rightarrow \dots \rightarrow \left[\begin{array}{cc|c} 1 & 0 & \frac{2}{3} \\ 0 & 1 & \frac{1}{3} \\ 0 & 0 & 0 \end{array}\right]$

$\mathbf{Q} = \begin{bmatrix} \frac{2}{3} & \frac{1}{3} \end{bmatrix}$

b.   Presently, A accounts for 50% of sales and in long run A will account for $\frac{2}{3}$, or $66\frac{2}{3}\%$, of sales. Thus the percentage increase in sales above the present level is

$\dfrac{66\frac{2}{3} - 50}{50} \cdot 100\% = \dfrac{16\frac{2}{3}}{50} \cdot 100\% = 33\frac{1}{3}\%$.

43. $\mathbf{T}^2 = \mathbf{TT} = \begin{bmatrix} \frac{1}{2} & \frac{1}{2} \\ 1 & 0 \end{bmatrix}\begin{bmatrix} \frac{1}{2} & \frac{1}{2} \\ 1 & 0 \end{bmatrix} = \begin{bmatrix} \frac{3}{4} & \frac{1}{4} \\ \frac{1}{2} & \frac{1}{2} \end{bmatrix}$

Since all entries of $\mathbf{T}^2$ are positive, $\mathbf{T}$ is regular.

Chapter 10 Review Problems

1. $\mu = \displaystyle\sum_x xf(x) = 1 \cdot f(1) + 2 \cdot f(2) + 3 \cdot f(3)$

$= 1(0.7) + 2(0.1) + 3(0.2) = 1.5$

$\text{Var}(X) = \displaystyle\sum_x x^2 f(x) - \mu^2$

$= \left[1^2(0.7) + 2^2(0.1) + 3^2(0.2)\right] - (1.5)^2$

$= 0.65$

$$\sigma = \sqrt{\text{Var}(X)} = \sqrt{0.65} \approx 0.81$$

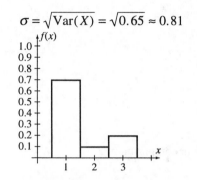

3. a. $n(S) = 2 \cdot 6 = 12$

$E_1 = \{T1\}, \quad E_2 = \{T2, H1\},$
$E_3 = \{T3, H2\}, \quad E_4 = \{T4, H3\},$
$E_5 = \{T5, H4\}, \quad E_6 = \{T6, H5\},$
$E_7 = \{H6\}$

$$f(1) = P(E_1) = \frac{n(E_1)}{n(S)} = \frac{1}{12}$$

$$f(2) = P(E_2) = \frac{n(E_2)}{n(S)} = \frac{2}{12} = \frac{1}{6}$$

Similarly, $f(3)$, $f(4)$, $f(5)$, and $f(6)$ equal $\frac{1}{6}$.

$$f(7) = P(E_7) = \frac{n(E_7)}{n(S)} = \frac{1}{12}$$

b. $E(X) = \displaystyle\sum_x xf(x)$

$$= 1 \cdot \frac{1}{12} + \frac{2+3+4+5+6}{6} + 7 \cdot \frac{1}{12}$$

$$= \frac{1}{12} + \frac{20}{6} + \frac{7}{12} = \frac{48}{12} = 4$$

5. Let X = gain (in dollars) on a play. If no 10 appears, then $X = 0 - \frac{1}{4} = -\frac{1}{4}$; if exactly one 10 appears, then $X = 1 - \frac{1}{4} = \frac{3}{4}$; if two 10's appear, then $X = 2 - \frac{1}{4} = \frac{7}{4}$.

$n(S) = 52 \cdot 52$. In a deck, there are 4 10's and 48 non 10's. Thus $n(E_{\text{no }10}) = 48 \cdot 48$. The event $E_{\text{one }10}$ occurs if the first card is a 10 and the second is a non-10, or vice versa. Thus $n(E_{\text{one }10}) = 4 \cdot 48 + 48 \cdot 4 = 2 \cdot 4 \cdot 48$.

$n(E_{\text{two }10's}) = 4 \cdot 4$.

Dist. of X:

$$f\left(-\frac{1}{4}\right) = \frac{48 \cdot 48}{52 \cdot 52} = \frac{144}{169},$$

$$f\left(\frac{3}{4}\right) = \frac{2 \cdot 4 \cdot 48}{52 \cdot 52} = \frac{24}{169},$$

$$f\left(\frac{7}{4}\right) = \frac{4 \cdot 4}{52 \cdot 52} = \frac{1}{169}.$$

$$E(X) = -\frac{1}{4} \cdot \frac{144}{169} + \frac{3}{4} \cdot \frac{24}{169} + \frac{7}{4} \cdot \frac{1}{169}$$

$$= \frac{-144 + 72 + 7}{4 \cdot 169} = -\frac{65}{676} = -\frac{5}{52} \approx -0.10$$

There is a loss of $0.10 per play.

7. a. Let X = gain (in dollars) on each unit shipped. Then $P(X = -100) = 0.08$ and $P(X = 200) = 1 - 0.08 = 0.92$.
$E(X) = -100f(-100) + 200f(200)$
$= -100(0.08) + 200(0.92)$
$= \$176$ per unit

b. Since the expected gain per unit is $176 and 4000 units are shipped per year, then expected annual profit is
$4000(176) = \$704,000$.

9. $f(0) = {}_3C_0(0.1)^0(0.9)^3 = \dfrac{3!}{0! \cdot 3!} \cdot 1(0.729)$

$= 1 \cdot 1(0.729) = 0.729$

$f(1) = {}_3C_1(0.1)^1(0.9)^2 = \dfrac{3!}{1! \cdot 2!}(0.1)(0.81)$

$= 3(0.1)(0.81) = 0.243$

$f(2) = {}_3C_2(0.1)^2(0.9)^1 = \dfrac{3!}{2! \cdot 1!}(0.01)(0.9)$

$= 3(0.01)(0.9) = 0.027$

$f(3) = {}_3C_3(0.1)^3(0.9)^0 = \dfrac{3!}{3! \cdot 0!}(0.001) \cdot 1$

$= 1 \cdot (0.001) \cdot 1 = 0.001$

$\mu = np = 3(0.1) = 0.3$

$\sigma = \sqrt{npq} = \sqrt{3(0.1)(0.9)} \approx 0.52$

11. $P(X \le 1) = P(X = 0) + P(X = 1)$

$= {}_5C_0\left(\dfrac{3}{4}\right)^0\left(\dfrac{1}{4}\right)^5 + {}_5C_1\left(\dfrac{3}{4}\right)^1\left(\dfrac{1}{4}\right)^4$

$= 1 \cdot 1 \cdot \dfrac{1}{1024} + 5 \cdot \dfrac{3}{4} \cdot \dfrac{1}{256} = \dfrac{16}{1024} = \dfrac{1}{64}$

13. The probability that a 2 or 3 results on one roll is $\dfrac{2}{6} = \dfrac{1}{3}$. Let X = number of 2's or 3's that appear on 4 rolls. Then X is binomial with $p = \dfrac{1}{3}$ and $n = 4$.

$$P(X = 3) = {}_4C_3\left(\frac{1}{3}\right)^3\left(\frac{2}{3}\right)^1 = 4 \cdot \frac{1}{27} \cdot \frac{2}{3} = \frac{8}{81}$$

15. Let X = number of heads that occur. Then X is binomial.

$$P(X = 0) = {}_4C_0\left(\frac{1}{3}\right)^0\left(\frac{2}{3}\right)^4 = \frac{4!}{0! \cdot 4!}(1)\left(\frac{16}{81}\right)$$

$$= 1(1)\left(\frac{16}{81}\right) = \frac{16}{81}$$

$$P(X = 1) = {}_4C_1\left(\frac{1}{3}\right)^1\left(\frac{2}{3}\right)^3 = \frac{4!}{1! \cdot 3!}\left(\frac{1}{3}\right)\left(\frac{8}{27}\right)$$

$$= 4\left(\frac{1}{3}\right)\left(\frac{8}{27}\right) = \frac{32}{81}$$

$$P(X \geq 2) = 1 - [P(X = 0) + P(X = 1)]$$

$$= 1 - \left[\frac{16}{81} + \frac{32}{81}\right] = 1 - \frac{48}{81} = \frac{11}{27}$$

17. From row 1, $0.1 + a + 0.6 = 1$, so $a = 0.3$.
From row 2, $2a + b + b = 1$, so $2b = 1 - 2a$,
or $b = \dfrac{1-2a}{2} = \dfrac{1-2(0.3)}{2} = 0.2$.
From row 3, $a + b + c = 1$, so $c = 1 - a - b$,
or $c = 1 - 0.3 - 0.2 = 0.5$.

19. $\mathbf{X_1} = \mathbf{X_0 T} = \begin{bmatrix} 0.5 & 0 & 0.5 \end{bmatrix}\begin{bmatrix} 0.1 & 0.2 & 0.7 \\ 0.3 & 0.4 & 0.3 \\ 0.1 & 0.1 & 0.8 \end{bmatrix}$

$= \begin{bmatrix} 0.10 & 0.15 & 0.75 \end{bmatrix}$

$\mathbf{X_2} = \mathbf{X_1 T}$

$= \begin{bmatrix} 0.10 & 0.15 & 0.75 \end{bmatrix}\begin{bmatrix} 0.1 & 0.2 & 0.7 \\ 0.3 & 0.4 & 0.3 \\ 0.1 & 0.1 & 0.8 \end{bmatrix}$

$= \begin{bmatrix} 0.130 & 0.155 & 0.715 \end{bmatrix}$

21. a. $\mathbf{T}^2 = \mathbf{TT} = \begin{bmatrix} \frac{1}{7} & \frac{6}{7} \\ \frac{3}{7} & \frac{4}{7} \end{bmatrix}\begin{bmatrix} \frac{1}{7} & \frac{6}{7} \\ \frac{3}{7} & \frac{4}{7} \end{bmatrix} = \begin{bmatrix} \frac{19}{49} & \frac{30}{49} \\ \frac{15}{49} & \frac{34}{49} \end{bmatrix}$

$\mathbf{T}^3 = \mathbf{T}^2\mathbf{T} = \begin{bmatrix} \frac{19}{49} & \frac{30}{49} \\ \frac{15}{49} & \frac{34}{49} \end{bmatrix}\begin{bmatrix} \frac{1}{7} & \frac{6}{7} \\ \frac{3}{7} & \frac{4}{7} \end{bmatrix}$

$= \begin{bmatrix} \frac{109}{343} & \frac{234}{343} \\ \frac{117}{343} & \frac{226}{343} \end{bmatrix}$

b. From $\mathbf{T}^2$, entry in row 1, column 2, is $\dfrac{30}{49}$.

c. From $\mathbf{T}^3$, entry in row 2, column 1, is $\dfrac{117}{343}$.

23. $\mathbf{T}^T - \mathbf{I} = \begin{bmatrix} \frac{1}{3} & \frac{2}{3} \\ \frac{2}{3} & \frac{1}{3} \end{bmatrix} - \begin{bmatrix} 1 & 0 \\ 0 & 1 \end{bmatrix} = \begin{bmatrix} -\frac{2}{3} & \frac{2}{3} \\ \frac{2}{3} & -\frac{2}{3} \end{bmatrix}$

$\begin{bmatrix} -\frac{2}{3} & \frac{2}{3} & | & 0 \\ \frac{2}{3} & -\frac{2}{3} & | & 0 \\ 1 & 1 & | & 1 \end{bmatrix} \to \ldots \to \begin{bmatrix} 1 & 0 & | & \frac{1}{2} \\ 0 & 1 & | & \frac{1}{2} \\ 0 & 0 & | & 0 \end{bmatrix}$

$\mathbf{Q} = \begin{bmatrix} \frac{1}{2} & \frac{1}{2} \end{bmatrix}$

25. $\mathbf{T} = \begin{matrix} \\ \text{Japanese} \\ \text{Non-Japanese} \end{matrix} \begin{matrix} \text{Japanese} \quad \text{Non-Japanese} \\ \begin{bmatrix} 0.8 & 0.2 \\ 0.6 & 0.4 \end{bmatrix} \end{matrix}$

a. $\mathbf{T}^2 = \begin{bmatrix} 0.8 & 0.2 \\ 0.6 & 0.4 \end{bmatrix}\begin{bmatrix} 0.8 & 0.2 \\ 0.6 & 0.4 \end{bmatrix}$

$= \begin{bmatrix} 0.76 & 0.24 \\ 0.72 & 0.28 \end{bmatrix}$

From row 1, column 1, the probability that a person who presently owns a Japanese car will buy a Japanese car two cars later is 0.76.

b. $X_2 = X_0 T^2 = [0.6 \quad 0.4]\begin{bmatrix} 0.76 & 0.24 \\ 0.72 & 0.28 \end{bmatrix}$

$= [0.744 \quad 0.256]$

In two years, we expect 74.4% Japanese, 25.6% non-Japanese.

c. $T^T - I = \begin{bmatrix} 0.8 & 0.6 \\ 0.2 & 0.4 \end{bmatrix} - \begin{bmatrix} 1 & 0 \\ 0 & 1 \end{bmatrix}$

$= \begin{bmatrix} -0.2 & 0.6 \\ 0.2 & -0.6 \end{bmatrix}$

$\begin{bmatrix} -0.2 & 0.6 & \vdots & 0 \\ 0.2 & -0.6 & \vdots & 0 \\ 1 & 1 & \vdots & 1 \end{bmatrix} \to \ldots$

$\to \begin{bmatrix} 1 & 0 & \vdots & 0.75 \\ 0 & 1 & \vdots & 0.25 \\ 0 & 0 & \vdots & 0 \end{bmatrix}$

$Q = [0.75 \quad 0.25]$

In the long run, 75% Japanese, 25% non-Japanese

Mathematical Snapshot Chapter 10

1. If X = number of correct predictions on first part of game, then X has a binomial distribution with $n = 3$ and $p = \dfrac{1}{2}$. Thus

   $E(X) = np = 3 \cdot \dfrac{1}{2} = \dfrac{3}{2}$. If $P(B)$ is the probability of selecting the shell with the ball under it, then

   $P(B) = \dfrac{\text{avg. no. of correct predictions}}{\text{no. of shells}}$

   $= \dfrac{\frac{3}{2}}{4} = \dfrac{3}{8}$.

Chapter 11

Principles in Practice 11.1

1. The graph of the greatest integer function is shown.

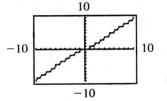

$$\lim_{x \to a} f(x)$$ does not exist when a is an integer since the limits are different depending on the side from which you approach the integer. $\lim_{x \to a} f(x)$ exists for all numbers which are not integers.

2. $\lim_{r \to 1} V(r) = \lim_{r \to 1} \frac{4}{3} \pi r^3 = \frac{4}{3} \pi \lim_{r \to 1} r^3$

$= \frac{4}{3} \pi (1)^3 = \frac{4}{3} \pi$

3. $\lim_{x \to 8} R(x) = \lim_{x \to 8} \left(500x - 6x^2 \right)$

$= \lim_{x \to 8} 500x - \lim_{x \to 8} 6x^2$

$= 500 \lim_{x \to 8} x - 6 \lim_{x \to 8} x^2 = 500(8) - 6(8)^2$

$= 4000 - 384 = 3616$

4. $\lim_{t \to 2} p = \lim_{t \to 2} \frac{50 \left(t^2 + 4t \right)}{t^2 + 3t + 20}$

$= \frac{\lim_{t \to 2} \left[50 \left(t^2 + 4t \right) \right]}{\lim_{t \to 2} \left(t^2 + 3t + 20 \right)}$

$= \frac{50 \left[2^2 + 4(2) \right]}{2^2 + 3(2) + 20} = \frac{600}{30} = 20$

5. As $h \to 0$, both the numerator and denominator approach 0. For $h \neq 0$,

$\lim_{h \to 0} \frac{125 + 2(x + h) - (125 + 2x)}{h}$

$= \lim_{h \to 0} \frac{125 + 2x + 2h - 125 - 2x}{h} = \lim_{h \to 0} \frac{2h}{h}$

$= \lim_{h \to 0} 2 = 2.$

Exercise 11.1

1. **a.** 1

   b. 0

   c. 1

3. **a.** 1

   b. does not exist

   c. 3

5. $f(0.9) = 2.8 \quad f(1.1) = 3.2$
   $f(0.99) = 2.98 \quad f(1.01) = 3.02$
   $f(0.999) = 2.998 \quad f(1.001) = 3.002$
   estimate of limit: 3

7. $f(-0.1) \approx 0.9516 \quad f(0.1) \approx 1.0517$
   $f(-0.01) \approx 0.9950 \quad f(0.01) \approx 1.0050$
   $f(-0.001) \approx 0.9995 \quad f(0.001) \approx 1.0005$
   estimate of limit: 1

9. $\lim_{x \to 2} 16 = 16$

11. $\lim_{t \to -5} \left(t^2 - 5 \right) = (-5)^2 - 5 = 25 - 5 = 20$

13. $\lim_{x \to -1} \left(x^3 - 3x^2 - 2x + 1 \right)$
    $= (-1)^3 - 3(-1)^2 - 2(-1) + 1$
    $= -1 - 3 + 2 + 1 = -1$

15. $\displaystyle\lim_{t \to -3} \frac{t-2}{t+5} = \frac{\displaystyle\lim_{t \to -3}(t-2)}{\displaystyle\lim_{t \to -3}(t+5)} = \frac{-3-2}{-3+5}$

$\displaystyle = \frac{-5}{2} = -\frac{5}{2}$

17. $\displaystyle\lim_{h \to 0} \frac{h}{h^2 - 7h + 1} = \frac{\displaystyle\lim_{h \to 0} h}{\displaystyle\lim_{h \to 0}\left(h^2 - 7h + 1\right)}$

$\displaystyle = \frac{0}{0^2 - 7(0) + 1} = 0$

19. $\displaystyle\lim_{p \to 4} \sqrt{p^2 + p + 5} = \sqrt{\lim_{p \to 4}\left(p^2 + p + 5\right)}$

$\displaystyle = \sqrt{4^2 + 4 + 5} = \sqrt{25} = 5$

21. $\displaystyle\lim_{x \to -2} \frac{x^2 + 2x}{x+2} = \lim_{x \to -2} \frac{x(x+2)}{x+2}$

$\displaystyle = \lim_{x \to -2} x = -2$

23. $\displaystyle\lim_{x \to 2} \frac{x^2 - x - 2}{x - 2} = \lim_{x \to 2} \frac{(x-2)(x+1)}{x-2}$

$\displaystyle = \lim_{x \to 2}(x+1) = 3$

25. $\displaystyle\lim_{x \to -1} \frac{x^2 + 2x + 1}{x+1} = \lim_{x \to -1} \frac{(x+1)^2}{x+1}$

$\displaystyle = \lim_{x \to -1}(x+1) = 0$

27. $\displaystyle\lim_{x \to 3} \frac{x-3}{x^2 - 9} = \lim_{x \to 3} \frac{x-3}{(x+3)(x-3)}$

$\displaystyle = \lim_{x \to 3} \frac{1}{x+3} = \frac{1}{6}$

29. $\displaystyle\lim_{x \to 4} \frac{x^2 - 9x + 20}{x^2 - 3x - 4} = \lim_{x \to 4} \frac{(x-4)(x-5)}{(x-4)(x+1)}$

$\displaystyle = \lim_{x \to 4} \frac{x-5}{x+1} = -\frac{1}{5}$

31. $\displaystyle\lim_{x \to 2} \frac{3x^2 - x - 10}{x^2 + 5x - 14} = \lim_{x \to 2} \frac{(3x+5)(x-2)}{(x+7)(x-2)}$

$\displaystyle = \lim_{x \to 2} \frac{3x+5}{x+7} = \frac{11}{9}$

33. $\displaystyle\lim_{h \to 0} \frac{(2+h)^2 - 2^2}{h} = \lim_{h \to 0} \frac{\left[4 + 4h + h^2\right] - 4}{h}$

$\displaystyle = \lim_{h \to 0} \frac{4h + h^2}{h} = \lim_{h \to 0} \frac{h(4+h)}{h}$

$\displaystyle = \lim_{h \to 0} 4 + h = 4$

35. $\displaystyle\lim_{h \to 0} \frac{(x+h)^2 - x^2}{h} = \lim_{h \to 0} \frac{2xh + h^2}{h}$

$\displaystyle = \lim_{h \to 0}(2x+h) = 2x$

37. $\displaystyle\lim_{h \to 0} \frac{f(x+h) - f(x)}{h}$

$\displaystyle = \lim_{h \to 0} \frac{[4 - (x+h)] - (4-x)}{h}$

$\displaystyle = \lim_{h \to 0} \frac{-h}{h} = \lim_{h \to 0} -1 = -1$

39. $\displaystyle\lim_{h \to 0} \frac{f(x+h) - f(x)}{h}$

$\displaystyle = \lim_{h \to 0} \frac{\left[(x+h)^2 - 3\right] - \left(x^2 - 3\right)}{h}$

$\displaystyle = \lim_{h \to 0} \frac{x^2 + 2xh + h^2 - 3 - \left(x^2 - 3\right)}{h}$

$\displaystyle = \lim_{h \to 0} \frac{2xh + h^2}{h} = \lim_{h \to 0}(2x+h) = 2x$

41. $\lim\limits_{h\to 0}\dfrac{f(x+h)-f(x)}{h}=\lim\limits_{h\to 0}\dfrac{\left[2(x+h)^2-3(x+h)\right]-\left(2x^2-3x\right)}{h}$

$=\lim\limits_{h\to 0}\dfrac{2x^2+4xh+2h^2-3x-3h-\left(2x^2-3x\right)}{h}=\lim\limits_{h\to 0}\dfrac{4xh+2h^2-3h}{h}$

$=\lim\limits_{h\to 0}\dfrac{h(4x+2h-3)}{h}=\lim\limits_{h\to 0}(4x+2h-3)=4x-3$

43. $\lim\limits_{x\to 6}\dfrac{\sqrt{x-2}-2}{x-6}=\lim\limits_{x\to 6}\dfrac{\left(\sqrt{x-2}-2\right)\left(\sqrt{x-2}+2\right)}{(x-6)\left(\sqrt{x-2}+2\right)}$

$=\lim\limits_{x\to 6}\dfrac{(x-2)-4}{(x-6)\left(\sqrt{x-2}+2\right)}=\lim\limits_{x\to 6}\dfrac{x-6}{(x-6)\left(\sqrt{x-2}+2\right)}$

$=\lim\limits_{x\to 6}\dfrac{1}{\sqrt{x-2}+2}=\dfrac{1}{4}$

45. a. $\lim\limits_{T_c\to 0}\dfrac{T_h-T_c}{T_h}=\dfrac{T_h-0}{T_h}=\dfrac{T_h}{T_h}=1$

b. $\lim\limits_{T_c\to T_h}\dfrac{T_h-T_c}{T_h}=\dfrac{T_h-T_h}{T_h}=\dfrac{0}{T_h}=0$

47.

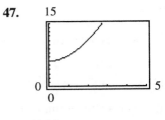

11.00

49.

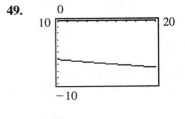

−7.00

51. The graph of $C(p)$ is shown. (Negative amounts of impurities and money are not reasonable, so only the first quadrant is shown.)

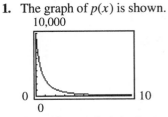

As p gets closer and closer to 0, the values of $C(p)$ increase without bound, so $\lim\limits_{p\to 0}C(p)$ does not exist.

Principles in Practice 11.2

1. The graph of $p(x)$ is shown.

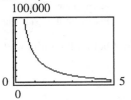

From the graph, it is apparent that $\lim\limits_{x\to\infty}p(x)=0$. The graph starts out high and quickly drops down toward zero. According to this function, a low price corresponds to a high demand and a high price corresponds to a low standard.

2. The graph of $y(x)$ is shown.

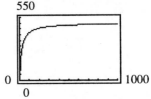

550

0 $\qquad$ 1000

0

From the graph, it is apparent that
$\lim\limits_{x\to\infty} y(x) = 500$. The greatest yearly sales
that the company can expect is $500,000,
even with unlimited spending on
advertising.

3. The graph of $C(x)$ is shown.

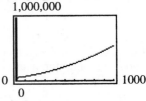

1,000,000

0 $\qquad$ 1000

0

From the graph it is apparent that
$\lim\limits_{x\to\infty} C(x) = \infty$. This indicates that the cost
increases without bound the more units that
you make.

Exercise 11.2

1. a. 2

b. 3

c. does not exist

d. $-\infty$

e. ∞

f. ∞

g. ∞

h. 0

i. 1

j. 1

k. 1

3. $\lim\limits_{x\to 3^+} (x-2)$
As $x \to 3^+$, then $x-2 \to 1$.

5. $\lim\limits_{x\to -\infty} 5x$
As x becomes very negative, so does $5x$.
Thus $\lim\limits_{x\to -\infty} 5x = -\infty$.

7. $\lim\limits_{x\to 0^-} \dfrac{6x}{x^4} = \lim\limits_{x\to 0^-} \dfrac{6}{x^3} = -\infty$ since x^3 is
negative and close to 0 for $x \to 0^-$.

9. $\lim\limits_{x\to -\infty} x^2 = \infty$ since x^2 is positive for
$x \to -\infty$.

11. $\lim\limits_{h\to 0^+} \sqrt{h}$
If h is positive and close to 0, then $\sqrt{h}$ is
close to 0.

13. $\lim\limits_{x\to 5^-} \dfrac{3}{x-5} = -\infty$

$\lim\limits_{x\to 5^+} \dfrac{3}{x-5} = \infty$

So $\lim\limits_{x\to 5} \dfrac{3}{x-5} = -\infty$ does not exist.

15. $\lim\limits_{x\to 1^+} \left(4\sqrt{x-1}\right)$. As $x \to 1^+$, then $x-1$
approaches 0 through positive values. So
$\sqrt{x-1} \to 0$. Thus
$\lim\limits_{x\to 1^+} \left(4\sqrt{x-1}\right) = 4 \cdot \lim\limits_{x\to 1^+} \sqrt{x-1} = 4 \cdot 0 = 0$.

17. $\lim\limits_{x\to\infty} \sqrt{x+10}$
As x becomes very large, so does $x + 10$.
Because square roots of very large numbers
are very large,
$\lim\limits_{x\to\infty} \sqrt{x+10} = \infty$.

19. $\lim\limits_{x\to\infty} \dfrac{3}{\sqrt{x}} = 3 \lim\limits_{x\to\infty} \dfrac{1}{x^{\frac{1}{2}}} = 3 \cdot 0 = 0$

21. $\displaystyle\lim_{x\to\infty}\frac{x+2}{x+3}=\lim_{x\to\infty}\frac{x}{x}=\lim_{x\to\infty}1=1$

23. $\displaystyle\lim_{x\to-\infty}\frac{x^2-1}{x^3+4x-3}=\lim_{x\to-\infty}\frac{x^2}{x^3}$

$\displaystyle=\lim_{x\to-\infty}\frac{1}{x}=0$

25. $\displaystyle\lim_{t\to\infty}\frac{5t^2+2t+1}{4t+7}=\lim_{t\to\infty}\frac{5t^2}{4t}=\lim_{t\to\infty}\frac{5t}{4}$

$\displaystyle=\lim_{t\to\infty}\left(\frac{5}{4}t\right)=\infty$

27. $\displaystyle\lim_{x\to\infty}\frac{7}{2x+1}=\lim_{x\to\infty}\frac{7}{2x}=\frac{7}{2}\cdot\lim_{x\to\infty}\frac{1}{x}$

$\displaystyle=\frac{7}{2}\cdot 0=0$

29. $\displaystyle\lim_{x\to\infty}\frac{3-4x-2x^3}{5x^3-8x+1}=\lim_{x\to\infty}\frac{-2x^3}{5x^3}$

$\displaystyle=\lim_{x\to\infty}\frac{-2}{5}=-\frac{2}{5}$

31. $\displaystyle\lim_{x\to3^-}\frac{x+2}{x^2-9}=\lim_{x\to3^-}\frac{x+3}{(x+3)(x-3)}$

$\displaystyle=\lim_{x\to3^-}\frac{1}{x-3}=-\infty$

33. $\displaystyle\lim_{w\to\infty}\frac{2w^2-3w+4}{5w^2+7w-1}=\lim_{w\to\infty}\frac{2w^2}{5w^2}$

$\displaystyle=\lim_{w\to\infty}\frac{2}{5}=\frac{2}{5}$

35. $\displaystyle\lim_{x\to\infty}\frac{6-4x^2+x^3}{4+5x-7x^2}=\lim_{x\to\infty}\frac{x^3}{-7x^2}$

$\displaystyle=\lim_{x\to\infty}\frac{x}{-7}=-\infty$

37. $\displaystyle\lim_{x\to-5}\frac{2x^2+9x-5}{x^2+5x}=\lim_{x\to-5}\frac{(2x-1)(x+5)}{x(x+5)}$

$\displaystyle=\lim_{x\to-5}\frac{2x-1}{x}=\frac{11}{5}$

39. $\displaystyle\lim_{x\to1}\frac{x^2-3x+1}{x^2+1}=\frac{\displaystyle\lim_{x\to1}\left(x^2-3x+1\right)}{\displaystyle\lim_{x\to1}\left(x^2+1\right)}$

$\displaystyle=\frac{-1}{2}=-\frac{1}{2}$

41. As $x\to1^+$, then $\dfrac{1}{x-1}\to\infty$. Thus

$\displaystyle\lim_{x\to1^+}\left[1+\frac{1}{x-1}\right]=\infty$

43. $\displaystyle\lim_{x\to-7^-}\frac{x^2+1}{\sqrt{x^2-49}}$. As $x\to-7^-$, then

$x^2+1\to50$ and $\sqrt{x^2-49}$
approaches 0 through positive values. Thus
$\dfrac{x^2+1}{\sqrt{x^2-49}}\to\infty$.

45. As $x\to0^+$, $x+x^2$ approaches 0 through
positive values. Thus $\dfrac{2}{x+x^2}\to\infty$.

47. $\displaystyle\lim_{x\to1^-}\frac{x}{x-1}=-\infty$

$\displaystyle\lim_{x\to1^+}\frac{x}{x-1}=\infty$

Answer: does not exist

49. As $x\to0^+$, $\dfrac{3}{x}\to\infty$. Thus $-\dfrac{3}{x}\to-\infty$.

Answer: $-\infty$

51. $\displaystyle\lim_{x\to0^+}|x|=\lim_{x\to0^+}x=0;\ \lim_{x\to0^-}|x|$

$\displaystyle=\lim_{x\to0^-}(-x)=0$

Thus $\displaystyle\lim_{x\to0}|x|=0$.

53. $\displaystyle\lim_{x\to-\infty}\frac{x+1}{x}=\lim_{x\to-\infty}\frac{x}{x}=\lim_{x\to-\infty}1=1$

55. $f(x)=\begin{cases}2 & \text{if }x\le2\\1 & \text{if }x>2\end{cases}$

a. $\displaystyle\lim_{x\to2^+}f(x)=\lim_{x\to2^+}1=1$

b. $\lim\limits_{x\to 2^-} f(x) = \lim\limits_{x\to 2^+} 2 = 2$

c. $\lim\limits_{x\to 2^+} f(x) \neq \lim\limits_{x\to 2^-} f(x),$ so $\lim\limits_{x\to 2} f(x)$
does not exist.

d. $\lim\limits_{x\to\infty} f(x) = \lim\limits_{x\to\infty} 1 = 1$

e. $\lim\limits_{x\to -\infty} f(x) = \lim\limits_{x\to -\infty} 2 = 2$

57. $g(x) = \begin{cases} x & \text{if } x < 0 \\ -x & \text{if } x > 0 \end{cases}$

a. $\lim\limits_{x\to 0^+} g(x) = \lim\limits_{x\to 0^+} -x = 0$

b. $\lim\limits_{x\to 0^-} g(x) = \lim\limits_{x\to 0^-} x = 0$

c. $\lim\limits_{x\to 0^+} g(x) = \lim\limits_{x\to 0^-} g(x) = 0,$ so
$\lim\limits_{x\to 0} g(x) = 0$

d. $\lim\limits_{x\to\infty} g(x) = \lim\limits_{x\to\infty} -x = -\infty$

e. $\lim\limits_{x\to -\infty} g(x) = \lim\limits_{x\to -\infty} x = -\infty$

59. $\lim\limits_{q\to -\infty} \bar{c} = \lim\limits_{q\to\infty} \left(\dfrac{5000}{q} + 6 \right)$
$= 0 + 6 = 6$

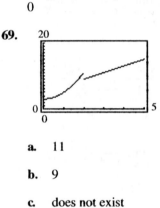

61. $\lim\limits_{t\to\infty} \left[20,000 + \dfrac{10,000}{(t+2)^2} \right] = 20,000 + 0$
$= 20,000$

63. $\lim\limits_{x\to\infty} y = \lim\limits_{x\to\infty} \dfrac{900x}{10 + 45x} = \lim\limits_{x\to\infty} \dfrac{900x}{45x}$
$= \lim\limits_{x\to\infty} 20 = 20$

65. 1, 0.5, 0.525, 0.631, 0.912, 0.986, 0.998;
conclude limit is 1.

67.
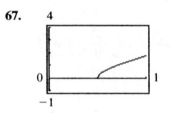

0

69.

a. 11

b. 9

c. does not exist

Exercise 11.3

1. $S = 4000e^{0.055(6)} \approx \$5563.87$
$5563.87 - 4000 = \$1563.87$

3. $P = 2500e^{-0.0675(8)} \approx \$1456.87$

5. $e^{0.04} - 1 \approx 0.0408$
Answer: 4.08%

7. $e^{0.10} - 1 \approx 0.1052$
Answer: 10.52%

9. $S = 100e^{0.055(2)} \approx \$111.63$

11. $P = 1,000,000e^{-0.08(5)} \approx \$670,320.05$

13. a. $10,000(1 + 0.1)^{20} \approx \$67,275$

b. $P = 67,275e^{-(0.12)(20)} \approx \$6103$

15. Effective rate $= e^r - 1$. Thus $0.05 = e^r - 1$,
$e^r = 1.05$, $r = \ln 1.05 \approx 0.0488$.
Answer: 4.88%

17. $100 \dfrac{1 - e^{-0.09(20)}}{0.09} \approx \$927$

19. $3P = Pe^{0.07t}$
$3 = e^{0.07t}$
$0.07t = \ln 3$
$t = \dfrac{\ln 3}{0.07} \approx 16$
Answer: 16 years

21. The accumulated amounts under each option are:

a. $1000e^{(0.1)(2)} \approx \$1221.40$

b. $1050(1.05)^4 \approx \$1276.28$

c. $500e^{(0.1)(2)} + 500(1.05)^4$
$\approx 610.70 + 607.75 = \$1218.45$

23. a. $9000(1.025)^4 \approx \$9934.32$

b. After one year the accumulated amount of the investment is
$10,000e^{0.11} \approx \$11,162.78$. The payoff for the loan (including interest) is
$1000 + 1000(0.16) = \$1160$. The net return is
$11,162.78 - 1160 = \$10,0002.78$.
Thus, this strategy is better by
$10,002.78 - 9934.32 = \$68.46$.

Exercise 11.4

1. $f(x) = x^3 - 5x; x = 2$

    (i) f is defined at $x = 2$: $f(2) = -2$

    (ii) $\lim\limits_{x \to 2} f(x) = \lim\limits_{x \to 2}\left(x^3 - 5x\right)$
            $= 2^3 - 5(2) = -2$
            which exists

    (iii) $\lim\limits_{x \to 2} f(x) = -2 = f(2)$
            Thus f is continuous at $x = 2$.

3. $g(x) = \sqrt{2 - 3x}; x = 0$

    (i) g is defined at $x = 0$; $g(0) = \sqrt{2}$.

    (ii) $\lim\limits_{x \to 0} g(x) = \lim\limits_{x \to 0} \sqrt{2 - 3x} = \sqrt{2}$, which exists

    (iii) $\lim\limits_{x \to 0} g(x) = \sqrt{2} = g(0)$
            Thus g is continuous at $x = 0$.

5. $h(x) = \dfrac{x - 4}{x + 4}; x = 4$

    (i) h is defined at $x = 4$, $h(4) = 0$.

    (ii) $\lim\limits_{x \to 4} h(x) = \lim\limits_{x \to 4} \dfrac{x - 4}{x + 4} = \dfrac{0}{8} = 0$, which exists.

    (iii) $\lim\limits_{x \to 4} h(x) = 0 = h(4)$
            Thus h is continuous at $x = 4$.

7. Continuous at -2 and 0 because f is a rational function and at neither point is the denominator zero.

9. Discontinuous at 3 and -3 because at both points the denominator of this rational function is zero.

11. $F(x) = \begin{cases} x + 2 & \text{if } x \geq 2 \\ x^2 & \text{if } x < 2 \end{cases}$
F is defined at $x = 2$ and $x = 0$; $F(2) = 4$,
$F(0) = 0$.
Because $\lim\limits_{x \to 2^+} F(x) = \lim\limits_{x \to 2^+} (x + 2) = 4$ and
$\lim\limits_{x \to 2^-} F(x) = \lim\limits_{x \to 2^-} x^2 = 4$, we have
$\lim\limits_{x \to 2} F(x) = 4$. In addition,
$\lim\limits_{x \to 0} F(x) = \lim\limits_{x \to 0} x^2 = 0$. Since

$\lim_{x \to 2} F(x) = 4 = F(2)$ and
$\lim_{x \to 0} F(x) = 0 = F(0)$, F is continuous at
both 2 and 0.
Answer: Continuous at 2 and 0.

13. f is a polynomial function.

15. f is a rational function and the denominator is never zero.

17. None, because f is a polynomial function.

19. The denominator of this rational function is zero only when $x = 4$. Thus f is discontinuous only for $x = 4$.

21. None, because g is a polynomial function.

23. $x^2 + 2x - 15 = 0$, $(x + 5)(x - 3) = 0$,
$x = -5$ or 3. Discontinuous at -5 and 3.

25. $x^3 - x = 0$, $x\left(x^2 - 1\right) = 0$,
$x(x + 1)(x - 1) = 0$, $x = 0, \pm 1$.
Discontinuous at $0, \pm 1$.

27. $x^2 + 1 = 0$ has no real roots, so no discontinuity exists.

29. $f(x) = \begin{cases} 1 & \text{if } x \geq 0 \\ -1 & \text{if } x < 0 \end{cases}$
For $x < 0$, $f(x) = -1$, which is a polynomial and hence continuous. For $x > 0$, $f(x) = 1$, which is a polynomial and hence continuous. Because
$\lim_{x \to 0^-} f(x) = \lim_{x \to 0^-} (-1) = -1$ and
$\lim_{x \to 0^+} f(x) = \lim_{x \to 0^+} 1 = 1$, $\lim_{x \to 0} f(x)$ does not exist. Thus f is discontinuous at $x = 0$.
Answer: 0

31. $f(x) = \begin{cases} 0 & \text{if } x \leq 1 \\ x - 1 & \text{if } x > 1 \end{cases}$
For $x < 1$, $f(x) = 0$, which is a polynomial and hence continuous. For $x > 1$,
$f(x) = x - 1$, which is a polynomial and hence continuous. For $x = 1$, f is defined

$[f(1) = 0]$. Because $\lim_{x \to 1^-} f(x) = \lim_{x \to 1^-} 0 = 0$
and $\lim_{x \to 1^+} f(x) = \lim_{x \to 1^+} (x - 1) = 0$, then
$\lim_{x \to 1} f(x) = 0$. Since $\lim_{x \to 1} f(x) = 0 = f(0)$, f
is continuous at $x = 1$.
Answer: none

33. $f(x) = \begin{cases} x^2 & \text{if } x > 2 \\ x - 1 & \text{if } x < 2 \end{cases}$
For $x < 2$, $f(x) = x - 1$, which is a polynomial and hence continuous. For $x > 2$, $f(x) = x^2$, which is a polynomial and hence continuous. Because f is not defined at $x = 2$, it is discontinuous there.
Answer: 2

35.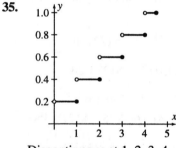
Discontinuous at 1, 2, 3, 4.

37.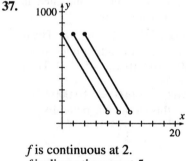
f is continuous at 2.
f is discontinuous at 5.
f is discontinuous at 10.
Ans. yes, no, no

Principles in Practice 11.5

1. We need to solve $V(x) > 0$. The zeros of $V(x)$ occur when $x = 0$, $8 - 2x = 0$, and $10 - 2x = 0$, or $x = 0$, 4, and 5. These zeros determine the intervals $(-\infty, 0)$ $(0, 4)$, $(4, 5)$, and $(5, \infty)$. Using $x = -1$, 1, 4.5, and 6 for test points, we find the sign of $V(x)$: $V(-1) = (-)(+)(+) = -$, so $V(x) < 0$ on $(-\infty, 0)$; $V(1) = (+)(+)(+) = +$, so $V(x) > 0$ on $(0, 4)$; $V(4.5) = (+)(-)(+) = -$, so $V(x) < 0$ on $(4, 5)$; $V(6) = (+)(-)(-) = +$, so $V(x) > 0$ on $(5, \infty)$. The volume is positive when $0 < x < 4$ or $5 < x$. However, $x > 5$ is unrealistic (as is $x < 0$) since the longest side of the piece of metal has length $2(5) = 10$ inches. Thus, the volume is positive when $0 < x < 4$.

Exercise 11.5

1. $x^2 - 3x - 4 > 0$

   $f(x) = x^2 - 3x - 4 = (x + 1)(x - 4)$ has zeros -1 and 4. By considering the intervals $(-\infty, -1)$, $(-1, 4)$, and $(4, \infty)$, we find $f(x) > 0$ on $(-\infty, -1)$ and $(4, \infty)$.
   Answer: $(-\infty, -1)$, $(4, \infty)$

3. $x^2 - 5x + 6 \le 0$

   $f(x) = x^2 - 5x + 6 = (x - 2)(x - 3)$ has zeros 2 and 3. By considering the intervals $(-\infty, 2)$, $(2, 3)$, and $(3, \infty)$, we find $f(x) < 0$ on $(2, 3)$.
   Answer: $[2, 3]$

5. $2x^2 + 11x + 14 < 0$

   $f(x) = 2x^2 + 11x + 14 = (2x + 7)(x + 2)$ has zeros $-\frac{7}{2}$ and -2. By considering the intervals $\left(-\infty, -\frac{7}{2}\right)$, $\left(-\frac{7}{2}, -2\right)$, and $(-2, \infty)$, we find $f(x) < 0$ on $\left(-\frac{7}{2}, -2\right)$.
   Answer: $\left(-\frac{7}{2}, -2\right)$

7. $x^2 + 4 < 0$. Since $x^2 + 4$ is always positive, the inequality $x^2 + 4 < 0$ has no solution.
   Answer: no solution

9. $(x + 2)(x - 3)(x + 6) \le 0$
   $f(x) = (x + 2)(x - 3)(x + 6)$ has zeros -2, 3, and -6. By considering the intervals $(-\infty, -6)$, $(-6, -2)$, $(-2, 3)$, and $(3, \infty)$, we find $f(x) < 0$ on $(-\infty, -6)$ and $(-2, 3)$.
   Answer: $(-\infty, -6]$, $[-2, 3]$

11. $-x(x - 5)(x + 4) > 0$, or equivalently, $x(x - 5)(x + 4) < 0$. $f(x) = x(x - 5)(x + 4)$ has zeros, 0, 5, and -4. By considering the intervals $(-\infty, -4)$, $(-4, 0)$, $(0, 5)$, and $(5, \infty)$, we find $f(x) < 0$ on $(-\infty, -4)$ and $(0, 5)$.
    Answer: $(-\infty, -4)$, $(0, 5)$

13. $x^3 + 4x \ge 0$

    $f(x) = x\left(x^2 + 4\right)$ has 0 as the only (real) zero. By considering the intervals $(-\infty, 0)$ and $(0, \infty)$, we find $f(x) > 0$ on $(0, \infty)$.
    Answer: $[0, \infty)$

15. $x^3 + 2x^2 - 3x > 0$
    $f(x) = x(x + 3)(x - 1)$ has zeros 0, -3, and 1. By considering the intervals $(-\infty, -3)$, $(-3, 0)$ $(0, 1)$, and $(1, \infty)$, we find $f(x) > 0$ on $(-3, 0)$ and $(1, \infty)$.
    Answer: $(-3, 0)$, $(1, \infty)$

17. $\dfrac{x}{x^2 - 1} < 0$

    $f(x) = \dfrac{x}{x^2 - 1}$ is discontinuous when $x = \pm 1$; f has 0 as a zero. By considering the intervals $(-\infty, -1)$, $(-1, 0)$, $(0, 1)$, and $(1, \infty)$, we find $f(x) < 0$ on $(-\infty, -1)$ and $(0, 1)$.
    Answer: $(-\infty, -1)$, $(0, 1)$

19. $\dfrac{4}{x - 1} \ge 0$

    $f(x) = \dfrac{4}{x - 1}$ is discontinuous when $x = 1$, and $f(x) = 0$ has no root. By considering the intervals $(-\infty, 1)$ and $(1, \infty)$, we find $f(x) > 0$ on $(1, \infty)$. Note also that $f(x) \ne 0$ for any x.
    Answer: $(1, \infty)$

21. $\dfrac{x^2 - x - 6}{x^2 + 4x - 5} \geq 0$

$f(x) = \dfrac{x^2 - x - 6}{x^2 + 4x - 5} = \dfrac{(x-3)(x+2)}{(x+5)(x-1)}$ is

discontinuous at $x = -5$ and $x = 1$; f has
zeros 3 and -2. By considering the intervals
$(-\infty, -5)$, $(-5, -2)$, $(-2, 1)$, $(1, 3)$, and $(3, \infty)$,
we find $f(x) > 0$ on $(-\infty, -5)$, $(-2, 1)$, and
$(3, \infty)$.
Answer: $(-\infty, -5)$, $[-2, 1)$, $[3, \infty)$

23. $\dfrac{3}{x^2 + 6x + 8} \leq 0$

$f(x) = \dfrac{3}{x^2 + 6x + 8} = \dfrac{3}{(x+4)(x+2)}$ is

never zero, but is discontinuous at $x = -4$
and $x = -2$. By considering the intervals
$(-\infty, -4)$, $(-4, -2)$, and $(-2, \infty)$, we find that
$f(x) < 0$ on $(-4, -2)$.
Answer: $(-4, -2)$

25. $x^2 + 2x \geq 2$, or equivalently,
$x^2 + 2x - 2 \geq 0$. $f(x) = x^2 + 2x - 2$ has
zeros $-1 \pm \sqrt{3}$. By considering the intervals
$\left(-\infty, -1-\sqrt{3}\right)$ $\left(-1-\sqrt{3}, -1+\sqrt{3}\right)$, and
$\left(-1+\sqrt{3}, \infty\right)$, we find $f(x) > 0$ on
$\left(-\infty, -1-\sqrt{3}\right)$ and $\left(-1+\sqrt{3}, \infty\right)$.
Answer: $\left(-\infty, -1-\sqrt{3}\right], \left[-1+\sqrt{3}, \infty\right)$

27. Revenue = (no. of units)(price per unit). We
want $q(20 - 0.1q) \geq 750$
$0.1q^2 - 20q + 750 \leq 0$
$q^2 - 200q + 7500 \leq 0$
$(q - 50)(q - 150) \leq 0$.
Solving gives $50 \leq q \leq 150$.
Answer: between 50 and 150 units, inclusive

29.

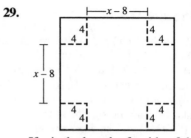

If x is the length of a side of the piece of
aluminum, then the box will be 4 by $x - 8$ by
$x - 8$.
$4(x - 8)^2 \geq 324$
$(x - 8)^2 \geq 81$
$x^2 - 16x - 17 \geq 0$
$(x - 17)(x + 1) \geq 0$
Solving $x \leq -1$ or $x \geq 17$. Since x must be
positive, we have $x \geq 17$.
Answer: 17 in. by 17 in.

31.

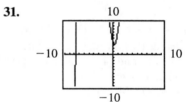

$(-\infty, -7.72]$

33.

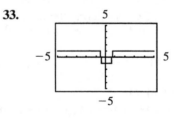

$(-\infty, -0.5)$, $(0.667, \infty)$

Chapter 11 Review Problems

1. $\lim\limits_{x \to -1} \left(2x^2 + 6x - 1\right) = 2(-1)^2 + 6(-1) - 1$
$= -5$

3. $\lim\limits_{x \to 3} \dfrac{x^2 - 9}{x^2 - 3x} = \lim\limits_{x \to 3} \dfrac{(x+3)(x-3)}{x(x-3)}$
$= \lim\limits_{x \to 3} \dfrac{x+3}{x} = \dfrac{6}{3} = 2$

5. $\lim\limits_{h \to 0} (x + h) = x + 0 = x$

7. $\lim\limits_{x \to -4} \dfrac{x^3 + 4x^2}{x^2 + 2x - 8} = \lim\limits_{x \to -4} \dfrac{x^2(x + 4)}{(x + 4)(x - 2)}$

$\lim\limits_{x \to -4} \dfrac{x^2}{x - 2} = \dfrac{16}{-6} = -\dfrac{8}{3}$

9. As $x \to \infty$, $x + 1 \to \infty$. Thus $\lim\limits_{x \to \infty} \dfrac{2}{x + 1} = 0$.

Answer: 0

11. $\lim\limits_{x \to \infty} \dfrac{3x - 2}{5x + 3} = \lim\limits_{x \to \infty} \dfrac{3x}{5x} = \lim\limits_{x \to \infty} \dfrac{3}{5} = \dfrac{3}{5}$

13. $\lim\limits_{t \to 3^-} \dfrac{2t - 3}{t - 3} = -\infty$ and $\lim\limits_{t \to 3^+} \dfrac{2t - 3}{t - 3} = \infty$. Thus $\lim\limits_{t \to 3} \dfrac{2t - 3}{t - 3}$ does not exist.

Answer: Limit does not exist

15. $\lim\limits_{x \to -\infty} \dfrac{x + 3}{1 - x} = \lim\limits_{x \to -\infty} \dfrac{x}{-x} = \lim\limits_{x \to -\infty} (-1) = -1$

17. $\lim\limits_{x \to \infty} \dfrac{x^2 - 1}{(3x + 2)^2} = \lim\limits_{x \to \infty} \dfrac{x^2 - 1}{9x^2 + 12x + 4}$

$= \lim\limits_{x \to \infty} \dfrac{x^2}{9x^2} = \lim\limits_{x \to \infty} \dfrac{1}{9} = \dfrac{1}{9}$

19. $\lim\limits_{x \to 3^-} \dfrac{x + 3}{x^2 - 9} = \lim\limits_{x \to 3^-} \dfrac{x + 3}{(x + 3)(x - 3)}$

$= \lim\limits_{x \to 3^-} \dfrac{1}{x - 3} = -\infty$

21. $\lim\limits_{x \to \infty} \sqrt{3x}$. As x becomes large, so does $3x$.
Because the square roots of large numbers are also large, $\lim\limits_{x \to \infty} \sqrt{3x} = \infty$.

Answer: ∞

23. $\lim\limits_{x \to \infty} \dfrac{x^{100} + \frac{1}{x^2}}{e - x^{98}} = \lim\limits_{x \to \infty} \dfrac{x^2\left(x^{100} + \frac{1}{x^2}\right)}{x^2\left(e - x^{98}\right)}$

$= \lim\limits_{x \to \infty} \dfrac{x^{102}}{ex^2 - x^{100}} = \lim\limits_{x \to \infty} \dfrac{x^{102}}{-x^{100}}$

$= \lim\limits_{x \to \infty} \left(-x^2\right) = -\infty$

25. $\lim\limits_{x \to 1^-} f(x) = \lim\limits_{x \to 1^-} x^2 = 1$

$\lim\limits_{x \to 1^+} f(x) = \lim\limits_{x \to 1^+} x = 1$

Thus $\lim\limits_{x \to 1} f(x) = 1$.

Answer: 1

27. $\lim\limits_{x \to 4^+} \dfrac{\sqrt{x^2 - 16}}{4 - x} = \lim\limits_{x \to 4^+} \dfrac{\sqrt{x - 4}\,\sqrt{x + 4}}{-(x - 4)}$

$= \lim\limits_{x \to 4^+} -\dfrac{\sqrt{x + 4}}{\sqrt{x - 4}}$

As $x \to 4^+$, $\sqrt{x - 4}$ approaches 0 through positive values and $\sqrt{x + 4} \to \sqrt{8}$. Thus

$-\dfrac{\sqrt{x + 4}}{\sqrt{x - 4}} \to -\infty$.

Answer: $-\infty$

29. $\lim\limits_{h \to 0} \dfrac{f(x + h) - f(x)}{h}$

$= \lim\limits_{h \to 0} \dfrac{[8(x + h) - 2] - [8x - 2]}{h}$

$= \lim\limits_{h \to 0} \dfrac{8h}{h} = \lim\limits_{h \to 0} 8 = 8$

31. $y = 11\left(1 - \dfrac{1}{1 + 2x}\right)$

Considering $\dfrac{1}{1 + 2x}$, we have

$\lim\limits_{x \to \infty} \dfrac{1}{1 + 2x} = \dfrac{1}{2} \cdot \lim\limits_{x \to \infty} \dfrac{1}{x} = \dfrac{1}{2} \cdot 0 = 0$. Thus

$\lim\limits_{x \to \infty} y = \lim\limits_{x \to \infty} \left[11\left(1 - \dfrac{1}{1 + 2x}\right)\right]$

$= 11(1 - 0) = 11$

Answer: 11

33. a. $S = 2500e^{0.07(14)} \approx \$6661.14$

b. $P = 2500e^{-0.07(14)} \approx \$938.28$

35. Effective rate $= e^{0.06} - 1 \approx 0.0618$
Answer: 6.18%

37. $S = Pe^{rt}$, $2P = Pe^{0.1t}$, $2 = e^{0.01t}$,
$0.1t = \ln 2$
$t = \dfrac{\ln 2}{0.1} = 10 \ln 2$
Answer: $10 \ln 2$

39. $f(x) = x + 5$; $x = 7$

(i) f is defined at $x = 7$; $f(7) = 12$

(ii) $\displaystyle\lim_{x \to 7} f(x) = \lim_{x \to 7} (x + 5) = 7 + 5 = 12$,
which exists

(iii) $\displaystyle\lim_{x \to 7} f(x) = 12 = f(7)$
Thus f is continuous at $x = 7$.

41. Since $f(x) = \frac{1}{4}x$ is polynomial function, it
is continuous everywhere.

43. $f(x) = \dfrac{x^2}{x + 3}$ is a rational function and the
denominator is zero at $x = -3$. Thus f is
discontinuous at $x = -3$.
Answer: $x = -3$

45. Since $f(x) = \dfrac{x - 1}{2x^2 + 3}$ is a rational function
whose denominator is never zero, f is
continuous everywhere.
Answer: none

47. $f(x) = \dfrac{4 - x^2}{x^2 + 3x - 4} = \dfrac{4 - x^2}{(x + 4)(x - 1)}$ is a
rational function and the denominator is zero
only when $x = -4$ or $x = 1$, so f is
discontinuous there.
Answer: $x = -4, 1$

49. $f(x) = \begin{cases} x + 4 & \text{if } x > -2 \\ 3x + 6 & \text{if } x \le -2 \end{cases}$
For $x < -2, f(x) = 3x + 6$, which is a
polynomial and hence continuous. For
$x > -2, f(x) = x + 4$, which is a polynomial
and hence continuous. Because
$\displaystyle\lim_{x \to -2^-} f(x) = \lim_{x \to -2^-} (3x + 6) = 0$ and
$\displaystyle\lim_{x \to -2^+} f(x) = \lim_{x \to -2^+} (x + 4) = 2$, $\displaystyle\lim_{x \to -2} f(x)$
does not exist. Thus f is discontinuous at $x = -2$.
Answer: $x = -2$

51. $x^2 + 4x - 12 > 0$
$f(x) = x^2 + 4x - 12 = (x + 6)(x - 2)$ has
zeros -6 and 2. By considering the intervals
$(-\infty, -6)$, $(-6, 2)$, and $(2, \infty)$, we find $f(x) > 0$
on $(-\infty, -6)$ and $(2, \infty)$.
Answer: $(-\infty, -6), (2, \infty)$

53. $x^3 \ge 2x^2$, $x^3 - 2x^2 \ge 0$
$f(x) = x^3 - 2x^2 = x^2(x - 2)$ has zeros 0
and 2. By considering the intervals $(-\infty, 0)$,
$(0, 2)$, and $(2, \infty)$, we find $f(x) > 0$ on $(2, \infty)$.
Answer: $[2, \infty)$, $x = 0$

55. $\dfrac{x + 5}{x^2 - 1} < 0$. $f(x) = \dfrac{x + 5}{(x + 1)(x - 1)}$ is
discontinuous when $x = \pm 1$, and f has -5 as a
zero. By considering the intervals $(-\infty, -5)$,
$(-5, -1)$, $(-1, 1)$, and $(1, \infty)$, we find $f(x) < 0$
on $(-\infty, -5)$ and $(-1, 1)$.
Answer: $(-\infty, -5), (-1, 1)$

57. $\dfrac{x^2 + 3x}{x^2 + 2x - 8} \ge 0$, or $\dfrac{x(x + 3)}{(x + 4)(x - 2)} \ge 0$. We
consider the intervals determined by
$x = 0, -3, -4$, and 2, namely $(-\infty, -4)$,
$(-4, -3)$, $(-3, 0)$, $(0, 2)$, and $(2, \infty)$. We find
$f(x) > 0$ on $(-\infty, -4)$, $(-3, 0)$, and $(2, \infty)$.
Answer: $(-\infty, -4), [-3, 0], (2, \infty)$

59.

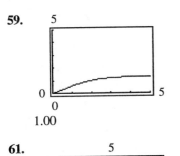

1.00

61.

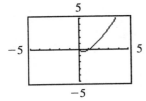

63.

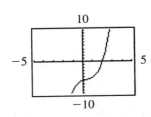

$[2.00, \infty)$

Mathematical Snapshot Chapter 11

1. $D = 5345e^{-rt}$
A year from now, $t = 1$ and $D = 4500$. Thus
$$4500 = 5345e^{-r}$$
$$e^{-r} = \frac{4500}{5345}$$
$$-r = \ln\frac{4500}{5345}$$
$$r = -\ln\frac{4500}{5345} \approx 0.17$$
The rate is 17%.

Chapter 12

Principles in Practice 12.1

1. $\dfrac{dH}{dt} = \dfrac{d}{dt}\left(6 + 40t - 16t^2\right)$

    $= \displaystyle\lim_{h \to 0} \dfrac{H(t+h) - H(t)}{h}$

    $= \displaystyle\lim_{h \to 0} \dfrac{\left[6 + 40(t+h) - 16(t+h)^2\right] - \left(6 + 40t - 16t^2\right)}{h}$

    $= \displaystyle\lim_{h \to 0} \dfrac{6 + 40t + 40h - 16t^2 - 32th - 16h^2 - 6 - 40t + 16t^2}{h}$

    $= \displaystyle\lim_{h \to 0} \dfrac{40h - 32th - 16h^2}{h} = \lim_{h \to 0} (40 - 32t - 16h)$

    $= 40 - 32t$

    $\dfrac{dH}{dt} = 40 - 32t$

Exercise 12.1

1. **a.** $f(x) = x^3 + 3$, $P = (2, 11)$

    To begin, if $x = 3$, then $m_{PQ} = \dfrac{\left(3^3 + 3\right) - 11}{3 - 2} = 19$. If $x = 2.5$, then $m_{PQ} = \dfrac{\left[(2.5)^3 + 3\right] - 11}{2.5 - 2} = 15.25$.

    Continuing in this manner, we complete the table:

x-value of Q	3	2.5	2.2	2.1	2.01	2.001
m_{PQ}	19	15.25	13.24	12.61	12.0601	12.0060

    b. We estimate that $m_{\tan}$ at P is 12.

3. $f(x) = x$

    $f'(x) = \displaystyle\lim_{h \to 0} \dfrac{f(x+h) - f(x)}{h}$

    $= \displaystyle\lim_{h \to 0} \dfrac{(x+h) - x}{h}$

    $= \displaystyle\lim_{h \to 0} \dfrac{h}{h} = \lim_{h \to 0} 1 = 1$

5. $y = 3x + 7$. Let $y = f(x)$.

    $\dfrac{dy}{dx} = \displaystyle\lim_{h \to 0} \dfrac{f(x+h) - f(x)}{h}$

    $= \displaystyle\lim_{h \to 0} \dfrac{[3(x+h) + 7] - [3x + 7]}{h}$

    $= \displaystyle\lim_{h \to 0} \dfrac{3x + 3h + 7 - 3x - 7}{h}$

    $= \displaystyle\lim_{h \to 0} \dfrac{3h}{h} = \lim_{h \to 0} 3 = 3$

7. Let $f(x) = 5 - 4x$.

    $\dfrac{d}{dx}(5 - 4x) = \displaystyle\lim_{h \to 0} \dfrac{f(x+h) - f(x)}{h}$

    $= \displaystyle\lim_{h \to 0} \dfrac{[5 - 4(x+h)] - [5 - 4x]}{h}$

    $= \displaystyle\lim_{h \to 0} \dfrac{-4h}{h} = \lim_{h \to 0} (-4) = -4$

9. $f(x) = 3$

$$f'(x) = \lim_{h \to 0} \frac{f(x+h) - f(x)}{h}$$

$$= \lim_{h \to 0} \frac{3 - 3}{h} = \lim_{h \to 0} \frac{0}{h} = \lim_{h \to 0} 0 = 0$$

11. $f(x) = x^2 + 4x - 8$

$$\frac{d}{dx}\left(x^2 + 4 - 8\right)$$

$$(x+h)^2 + 4(x+h) - 8$$

$$= \lim_{h \to 0} \frac{f(x+h) - f(x)}{h}$$

$$= \lim_{h \to 0} \frac{\left[(x+h)^2 + 4(x+h) - 8\right] - \left[x^2 + 4x - 8\right]}{h}$$

$$= \lim_{h \to 0} \frac{x^2 + 2xh + h^2 + 4x + 4h - 8 - x^2 - 4x + 8}{h}$$

$$= \lim_{h \to 0} \frac{2xh + h^2 + 4h}{h}$$

$$= \lim_{h \to 0} (2x + h + 4) = 2x + 0 + 4 = 2x + 4$$

13. $p = f(q) = 2q^2 + 5q - 1$

$$\frac{dp}{dq} = \lim_{h \to 0} \frac{f(q+h) - f(q)}{h}$$

$$= \lim_{h \to 0} \frac{\left[2(q+h)^2 + 5(q+h) - 1\right] - \left[2q^2 + 5q - 1\right]}{h}$$

$$= \lim_{h \to 0} \frac{4qh + 2h^2 + 5h}{h}$$

$$= \lim_{h \to 0} (4q + 2h + 5) = 4q + 0 + 5 = 4q + 5$$

15. $y = f(x) = \dfrac{1}{x}$

$$y' = \lim_{h \to 0} \frac{f(x+h) - f(x)}{h} = \lim_{h \to 0} \frac{\frac{1}{x+h} - \frac{1}{x}}{h}$$

Multiplying the numerator and denominator by $x(x+h)$ gives

$$y' = \lim_{h \to 0} \frac{x - (x+h)}{h(x)(x+h)} = \lim_{h \to 0} \frac{-h}{h(x)(x+h)}$$

$$= \lim_{h \to 0}\left[-\frac{1}{x(x+h)}\right] = -\frac{1}{x(x+0)} = -\frac{1}{x^2}$$

17. $f(x) = \sqrt{x+2}$

$$f'(x) = \lim_{h \to 0} \frac{f(x+h) - f(x)}{h}$$

$$= \lim_{h \to 0} \frac{\sqrt{x+h+2} - \sqrt{x+2}}{h}$$

Rationalizing the numerator gives

$$\frac{\sqrt{x+h+2}-\sqrt{x+2}}{h}$$

$$=\frac{\sqrt{x+h+2}-\sqrt{x+2}}{h}\cdot\frac{\sqrt{x+h+2}+\sqrt{x+2}}{\sqrt{x+h+2}+\sqrt{x+2}}$$

$$=\frac{(x+h+2)-(x+2)}{h\left(\sqrt{x+h+2}+\sqrt{x+2}\right)}$$

$$=\frac{1}{\sqrt{x+h+2}+\sqrt{x+2}}$$

Thus

$$f'(x)=\lim_{h\to0}\frac{1}{\sqrt{x+h+2}+\sqrt{x+2}}=\frac{1}{2\sqrt{x+2}}$$

19. $y=f(x)=x^2+4$

$$y'=\lim_{h\to0}\frac{f(x+h)-f(x)}{h}$$

$$=\lim_{h\to0}\frac{\left[(x+h)^2+4\right]-\left[x^2+4\right]}{h}$$

$$=\lim_{h\to0}\frac{2xh+h^2}{h}=\lim_{h\to0}(2x+h)$$

$$=2x+0=2x$$

The slope at $(-2, 8)$ is $y'(-2)=2(-2)=-4$.

21. $y=4x^2-5$

$$y'=\lim_{h\to0}\frac{\left[4(x+h)^2-5\right]-\left[4x^2-5\right]}{h}$$

$$=\lim_{h\to0}\frac{8xh+4h^2}{h}=\lim_{h\to0}(8x+4h)=8x$$

The slope when $x=0$ is $y'(0)=8(0)=0$.

23. $y=x+4$

$$y'=\lim_{h\to0}\frac{[(x+h)+4]-[x+4]}{h}=\lim_{h\to0}\frac{h}{h}=1$$

If $x=3$, then $y'=1$. The tangent line at the
point $(3, 7)$ is $y-7=1(x-3)$, or $y=x+4$.

25. $y=3x^2+3x-4$

y'

$$=\lim_{h\to0}\frac{\left[3(x+h)^2+3(x+h)-4\right]-\left[3x^2+3x-4\right]}{h}$$

$$=\lim_{h\to0}\frac{6xh+3h^2+3h}{h}$$

$$=\lim_{h\to0}(6x+3h+3)=6x+3$$

If $x=-1$, then $y'=6(-1)+3=-3$. The
tangent line at the point $(-1, -4)$ is
$y+4=-3(x+1)$, or $y=-3x-7$.

27. $y=\dfrac{3}{x+1}$

$$y'=\lim_{h\to0}\frac{\frac{3}{(x+h)+1}-\frac{3}{x+1}}{h}$$

$$=\lim_{h\to0}\frac{\frac{3(x+1)-3(x+h+1)}{(x+h+1)(x+1)}}{h}$$

$$=\lim_{h\to0}\frac{-3h}{h(x+h+1)(x+1)}$$

$$=\lim_{h\to0}\frac{-3}{(x+h+1)(x+1)}$$

$$=-\frac{3}{(x+1)^2}$$

If $x=2$, then $y'=-\dfrac{3}{9}=-\dfrac{1}{3}$. The tangent

line at $(2, 1)$ is $y-1=-\dfrac{1}{3}(x-2)$, or

$y=-\dfrac{1}{3}x+\dfrac{5}{3}$.

29. $r=\left(\dfrac{\eta}{1+\eta}\right)\left(r_L-\dfrac{dC}{dD}\right)$

$$(1+\eta)r=\eta\left(r_L-\frac{dC}{dD}\right)$$

$$r+\eta r=\eta\left(r_L-\frac{dC}{dD}\right)$$

$$r=\eta\left(r_L-\frac{dC}{dD}\right)-\eta r$$

$$r=\eta\left(r_L-\frac{dC}{dD}-r\right)$$

$$\eta=\frac{r}{r_L-r-\frac{dC}{dD}}$$

31. $-3.000,\ 13.445$

33. $-5.120,\ 0.038$

35.

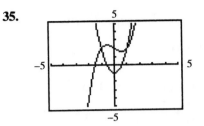

For the x-values of the points where the tangent to the graph of f is horizontal, the corresponding values of $f'(x)$ are 0. This is expected because the slope of a horizontal line is zero and the derivative gives the slope of the tangent line.

Principles in Practice 12.2

1. $r'(q) = \dfrac{d}{dq}(50q) - \dfrac{d}{dq}\left(0.3q^2\right)$

$= 50\dfrac{d}{dq}(q) - 0.3\dfrac{d}{dq}\left(q^2\right)$

$= 50(1) - 0.3(2q) = 50 - 0.6q$

The marginal revenue is $r'(q) = 50 - 0.6q$.

Exercise 12.2

1. $f(x) = 5$ is a constant function, so $f'(x) = 0$

3. $y = x^6$, $y' = 6x^{6-1} = 6x^5$

5. $y = x^{80}$, $\dfrac{dy}{dx} = 80x^{80-1} = 80x^{79}$

7. $f(x) = 9x^2$, $f'(x) = 9\left(2x^{2-1}\right) = 18x$

9. $g(w) = 4w^5$, $g'(w) = 4\left(5w^{5-1}\right) = 20w^4$

11. $y = \dfrac{2}{3}x^4$, $y' = \dfrac{2}{3}\left(4x^{3-1}\right) = \dfrac{8}{3}x^3$

13. $f(t) = \dfrac{1}{18}t^9$, $f'(t) = \dfrac{1}{18}\left(9t^{9-1}\right) = \dfrac{1}{2}t^8$

15. $f(x) = x + 3$, $f'(x) = 1 + 0 = 1$

17. $f'(x) = 3(2x) - 2(1) + 0 = 6x - 2$

19. $g'(p) = 4p^{4-1} - 3\left(3p^{3-1}\right) - 0 = 4p^3 - 9p^2$

21. $y' = -\left(8x^{8-1}\right) + 5x^{5-1} = -8x^7 + 5x^4$

23. $y' = -13\left(3x^2\right) + 14(2x) - 2(1) + 0$

$= -39x^2 + 28x - 2$

25. $f'(x) = 2\left(0 - 4x^3\right) = -8x^3$

27. $g(x) = \dfrac{1}{3}\left(13 - x^4\right)$,

$g'(x) = \dfrac{1}{3}\left(0 - 4x^3\right) = -\dfrac{4}{3}x^3$

29. $h(x) = 4x^4 + x^3 - \dfrac{9}{2}x^2 + 9x$

$h'(x) = 4\left(4x^3\right) + 3x^2 - \dfrac{9}{2}(2x) + 9(1)$

$= 16x^3 + 3x^2 - 9x + 9$

31. $f(x) = \dfrac{3}{2}x^4 + \dfrac{7}{3}x^3$

$f'(x) = \dfrac{3}{2}\left(4x^3\right) + \dfrac{7}{3}\left(3x^2\right) = 6x^3 + 7x^2$

33. $f'(x) = \dfrac{7}{2}x^{\left(\frac{7}{2}\right)-1} = \dfrac{7}{2}x^{\frac{5}{2}}$

35. $y' = \dfrac{3}{4}x^{\left(\frac{3}{4}\right)-1} + \dfrac{5}{3}x^{\left(\frac{5}{3}\right)-1} = \dfrac{3}{4}x^{-\frac{1}{4}} + \dfrac{5}{3}x^{\frac{2}{3}}$

37. $f(x) = \sqrt{x} = x^{\frac{1}{2}}$,

$f'(x) = \dfrac{1}{2}x^{\left(\frac{1}{2}\right)-1} = \dfrac{1}{2}x^{-\frac{1}{2}} = \dfrac{1}{2\sqrt{x}}$

39. $f(r) = 6r^{\frac{1}{3}}$, $f'(r) = 6\left(\dfrac{1}{3}r^{-\frac{2}{3}}\right) = 2r^{-\frac{2}{3}}$

41. $f'(x) = -4x^{-4-1} = -4x^{-5}$

43. $f'(x) = -3x^{-3-1} + \left(-5x^{-5-1}\right) - 2\left(-6x^{-6-1}\right)$

$= -3x^{-4} - 5x^{-6} + 12x^{-7}$

45. $y = \dfrac{1}{x} = x^{-1}$

$\dfrac{dy}{dx} = -1 \cdot x^{-1-1} = -x^{-2} = -\dfrac{1}{x^2}$

47. $y = \dfrac{3}{x^5} = 3x^{-5}$

$y' = 3\left(-5x^{-6}\right) = -15x^{-6}$

49. $g(x) = \dfrac{4}{3x^3} = \dfrac{4}{3}x^{-3}$

$g'(x) = \dfrac{4}{3}\left(-3x^{-4}\right) = -4x^{-4}$

51. $f(t) = \dfrac{1}{2}\left(\dfrac{1}{t}\right) = \dfrac{1}{2}t^{-1}$

$f'(t) = \dfrac{1}{2}\left(-1 \cdot t^{-2}\right) = -\dfrac{1}{2}t^{-2}$

53. $f(x) = \dfrac{1}{7}x + 7x^{-1}$

$f'(x) = \dfrac{1}{7}(1) + 7\left(-1x^{-2}\right) = \dfrac{1}{7} - 7x^{-2}$

55. $f'(x) = -9\left(\dfrac{1}{3}x^{-\frac{2}{3}}\right) + 5\left(-\dfrac{2}{5}x^{-\frac{7}{5}}\right)$

$= -3x^{-\frac{2}{3}} - 2x^{-\frac{7}{5}}$

57. $q(x) = \dfrac{1}{\sqrt[5]{x}} = \dfrac{1}{x^{\frac{1}{5}}} = x^{-\frac{1}{5}}$

$q'(x) = -\dfrac{1}{5}x^{-\frac{6}{5}}$

59. $y = \dfrac{2}{x^{\frac{1}{2}}} = 2x^{-\frac{1}{2}}$

$y' = 2\left(-\dfrac{1}{2}x^{-\frac{1}{2}}\right) = -x^{-\frac{3}{2}}$

61. $y = x^2\sqrt{x} = x^2\left(x^{\frac{1}{2}}\right) = x^{2+\left(\frac{1}{2}\right)} = x^{\frac{5}{2}}$

$y' = \dfrac{5}{2}x^{\frac{3}{2}}$

63. $f(x) = x\left(3x^2 - 7x + 7\right) = 3x^3 - 7x^2 + 7x$

$f'(x) = 9x^2 - 14x + 7$

65. $f(x) = x^3(3x)^2 = x^3\left(9x^2\right) = 9x^5$

$f'(x) = 45x^4$

67. $v(x) = x^{-\frac{2}{3}}(x + 5) = x^{\frac{1}{3}} + 5x^{-\frac{2}{3}}$

$v'(x) = \dfrac{1}{3}x^{-\frac{2}{3}} - \dfrac{10}{3}x^{-\frac{5}{3}} = \dfrac{1}{3}x^{-\frac{5}{3}}(x - 10)$

69. $f(q) = \dfrac{4q^3 + 7q - 4}{q} = \dfrac{4q^3}{q} + \dfrac{7q}{q} - \dfrac{4}{q}$

$= 4q^2 + 7 - 4q^{-1}$

$f'(q) = 8q + 4q^{-2} = 8q + \dfrac{4}{q^2}$

71. $f(x) = (x + 1)(x + 3) = x^2 + 4x + 3$

$f'(x) = 2x + 4 = 2(x + 2)$

73. $w(x) = \dfrac{x^2 + x^3}{x^2} = \dfrac{x^2}{x^2} + \dfrac{x^3}{x^2} = 1 + x$

$w'(x) = 0 + 1 = 1$

75. $y' = 6x + 4$

$y'\big|_{x=0} = 4$

$y'\big|_{x=2} = 16,\ y'\big|_{x=-3} = -14$

77. y is a constant, so $y' = 0$ for all x.

79. $y = 4x^2 + 5x + 2$

$y' = 8x + 5$

$y'\big|_{x=1} = 13$

An equation of the tangent line is
$y - 11 = 13(x - 1)$, or $y = 13x - 2$.

81. $y = \dfrac{2}{x^2} = 2x^{-2}$

$y' = 2\left(-2x^{-3}\right) = \dfrac{-4}{x^3}$

$y'\big|_{x=1} = -4$

An equation of the tangent line is
$y - 2 = -4(x - 1)$, or $y = -4x + 6$.

83. $y = 3 + x - 5x^2 + x^4$

$y' = 1 - 10x + 4x^3.$

When $x = 0$, then $y = 3$ and $y' = 1$. Thus an equation of the tangent line is
$y - 3 = 1(x - 0)$, or $y = x + 3$.

85. $y = \frac{1}{3}x^3 - x^2$

$y' = x^2 - 2x$

A horizontal tangent line has slope 0, so we set $x^2 - 2x = 0$. Then $x(x - 2) = 0$, $x = 0$ or $x = 2$. If $x = 0$, then $y = 0$. If $x = 2$, then $y = -\frac{4}{3}$. This gives the points $(0, 0)$ and $\left(2, -\frac{4}{3}\right)$.

87. $y = x^2 - 5x + 3$

$y' = 2x - 5$

Setting $2x - 5 = 1$ gives $2x = 6$, $x = 3$. When $x = 3$, then $y = -3$. This gives the point $(3, -3)$.

89. $f(x) = \sqrt{x} + \frac{1}{\sqrt{x}} = x^{\frac{1}{2}} + x^{-\frac{1}{2}}$

$f'(x) = \frac{1}{2}x^{-\frac{1}{2}} - \frac{1}{2}x^{-\frac{3}{2}} = \frac{1}{2\sqrt{x}} - \frac{1}{2x\sqrt{x}}$

$= \frac{x - 1}{2x\sqrt{x}}$

Thus $\frac{x - 1}{2x\sqrt{x}} - f'(x) = \frac{x - 1}{2x\sqrt{x}} - \frac{x - 1}{2x\sqrt{x}} = 0$.

91. $y = x^3 - 3x$

$y'(x) = 3x^2 - 3$

$y'|_{x=2} = 3(2^2) - 3 = 9$

The tangent line at (2, 2) is given by
$y - 2 = 9(x - 2)$, or $y = 9x - 16$.

Principles in Practice 12.3

1. Here $\frac{dP}{dp} = 5$ and $\Delta p = 25.5 - 25 = 0.5$.

$\Delta P \approx \frac{dP}{dp}\Delta p = 5(0.5) = 2.5$

The profit increases by 2.5 units when the price is changed from 25 to 25.5 per unit.

2. $\frac{dy}{dt} = \frac{d}{dt}\left(16t - 16t^2\right) = 16 - 16(2t)$
$= 16 - 32t$

$\left.\frac{dy}{dt}\right|_{t=0.5} = 16 - 32(0.5) = 16 - 16 = 0$

The graph of $y(t)$ is shown.

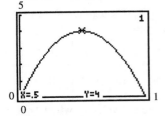

When $t = 0.5$, the object is at the peak of its flight.

3. $V'(r) = \frac{4}{3}\pi\left(3r^2\right) + 4\pi(2r) = 4\pi r^2 + 8\pi r$

When $r = 2$, $V'(r) = 4\pi(2)^2 + 8\pi(2) = 32\pi$
and

$V(r) = \frac{4}{3}\pi(2)^3 + 4\pi(2)^2$

$= \frac{32\pi}{3} + 16\pi = \frac{80}{3}\pi.$

The relative rate of change of the volume when $r = 2$ is $\frac{V'(2)}{V(2)} = \frac{32\pi}{\frac{80}{3}\pi} = \frac{6}{5} = 1.2$.

Multiplying 1.2 by 100 gives the percentage rate of change: $(1.2)(100) = 120\%$.

Exercise 12.3

1. $s = f(t) = t^3 + t$. If $\Delta t = 1$, then over $[1, 2]$ we have

    $$\frac{\Delta s}{\Delta t} = \frac{f(2) - f(1)}{\Delta t} = \frac{\left(2^3 + 2\right) - (1 + 1)}{1} = 8.$$

    If $\Delta t = 0.5$, then over $[1, 1.5]$ we have

    $$\frac{\Delta s}{\Delta t} = \frac{f(1.5) - f(1)}{\Delta t} = \frac{\left[(1.5)^3 + 1.5\right] - 2}{0.5}$$
    $$= 5.75.$$

    If $\Delta t = 0.2$, then over $[1, 1.2]$ we have

    $$\frac{\Delta s}{\Delta t} = \frac{f(1.2) - f(1)}{\Delta t} = \frac{\left[(1.2)^3 + 1.2\right] - 2}{0.2}$$
    $$= 4.64.$$

    Continuing in this way we obtain the following table:

Δt	1	0.5	0.2	0.1	0.01	0.001
$\dfrac{\Delta s}{\Delta t}$	8	5.75	4.64	4.31	4.0301	4.003001

    We estimate the velocity when $t = 1$ to be 4.0000 m/s. With differentiation we get

    $$v = \frac{ds}{dt} = 3t^2 + 1. \ \left.\frac{ds}{dt}\right|_{t=1} = 3\left(1^2\right) + 1 = 4 \text{ m/s}$$

3. $s = f(t) = t^2 - 3t$

    a. When $t = 4$, then $s = 4^2 - 3(4) = 4$ m.

    b. $$\frac{\Delta s}{\Delta t} = \frac{f(4.5) - f(4)}{0.5}$$
    $$= \frac{\left[(4.5)^2 - 3(4.5)\right] - 4}{0.5} = 5.5 \text{ m / s}$$

    c. $v = \dfrac{ds}{dt} = 2t - 3$. If $t = 4$, then
    $$v = 2(4) - 3 = 5 \text{ m/s}$$

5. $s = 2t^3 + 6$

    a. When $t = 1$, $s = 2(1)^3 + 6 = 8$ m.

    b. $$\frac{\Delta s}{\Delta t} = \frac{f(1.02) - f(1)}{0.02}$$
    $$= \frac{\left[2(1.02)^3 + 6\right] - 8}{0.02} = 6.1208 \text{ m/s}$$

    c. $v = \dfrac{ds}{dt} = 6t^2$. If $t = 1$, then
    $$v = 6(1)^2 = 6 \text{ m/s}$$

7. $s = t^4 - 2t^3 + t$

    a. When $t = 2$, $s = 2^4 - 2\left(2^3\right) + 2 = 2$ m.

    b. $$\frac{\Delta s}{\Delta t} = \frac{f(2.1) - f(2)}{0.1}$$
    $$= \frac{\left[(2.1)^4 - 2(2.1)^3 + 2.1\right] - 2}{0.1}$$
    $$= 10.261 \text{ m/s}$$

    c. $v = 4t^3 - 6t^2 + 1$
    $$v\big|_{t=2} = 4\left(2^3\right) - 6\left(2^2\right) + 1 = 9 \text{ m/s}$$

9. $i = \sqrt{P} = P^{\frac{1}{2}}$
    $$\frac{di}{dP} = \frac{1}{2} P^{-\frac{1}{2}} = \frac{1}{2\sqrt{P}}$$
    When $P = 4$, then $\dfrac{di}{dP} = \dfrac{1}{2\sqrt{4}} = \dfrac{1}{4}.$

11. $\dfrac{dy}{dx} = \dfrac{25}{2} x^{\frac{3}{2}}$. If $x = 9$,
    $$\frac{dy}{dx} = \frac{25}{2}(27) = 337.50.$$

13. $\dfrac{dT}{dT_e} = 0 + 0.27(1 - 0) = 0.27$

15. $c = 500 + 10q$, $\dfrac{dc}{dq} = 10$. When $q = 100$,
    $$\frac{dc}{dq} = 10.$$

17. $\dfrac{dc}{dq} = 0.3(2q) + 2 = 0.6q + 2$. When $q = 3$,
    $$\frac{dc}{dq} = 0.6(3) + 2 = 3.8.$$

19. $\dfrac{dc}{dq} = 2q + 50$. Evaluating when $q = 15$, 16 and 17 gives 80, 82 and 84, respectively.

21. $\bar{c} = 0.01q + 5 + \dfrac{500}{q}$

$c = \bar{c}q = 0.01q^2 + 5q + 500$

$\dfrac{dc}{dq} = 0.02q + 5$

$\dfrac{dc}{dq}\bigg|_{q=50} = 6$

$\dfrac{dc}{dq}\bigg|_{q=100} = 7$

23. $c = \bar{c}q$

$\quad = 0.00002q^3 - 0.01q^2 + 6q + 20,000$

$\dfrac{dc}{dq} = 0.00006q^2 - 0.02q + 6$

If $q = 100$, then $\dfrac{dc}{dq} = 4.6$. If $q = 500$, then

$\dfrac{dc}{dq} = 11$.

25. $\dfrac{dr}{dq} = 0.7$ for all q

27. $\dfrac{dr}{dq} = 250 + 90q - 3q^2$. Evaluating when $q = 5$, 10 and 25 gives 625, 850 and 625, respectively.

29. $\dfrac{dc}{dq} = 6.750 - 0.000328(2q)$

$\quad = 6.750 - 0.000656q$

$\dfrac{dc}{dq}\bigg|_{q=5000} = 6.750 - 0.000656(5000) = 3.47$

31. $PR^{0.93} = 5,000,000$

$\quad P = 5,000,000R^{-0.93}$

$\quad \dfrac{dP}{dR} = -4,650,000R^{-1.93}$

33. a. $\dfrac{dy}{dx} = -1.5 - x$

$\dfrac{dy}{dx}\bigg|_{x=6} = -1.5 - 6 = -7.5$

    b. Setting $-1.5 - x = -6$ gives $x = 4.5$.

35. a. $y' = 1$

    b. $\dfrac{y'}{y} = \dfrac{1}{x+4}$

    c. $y'(5) = 1$

    d. $\dfrac{1}{5+4} = \dfrac{1}{9} \approx 0.111$

    e. 11.1%

37. a. $y' = 6x$

    b. $\dfrac{y'}{y} = \dfrac{6x}{3x^2+6} = \dfrac{2x}{x^2+2}$

    c. $y'(2) = 6(2) = 12$

    d. $\dfrac{4}{4+2} = \dfrac{2}{3} \approx 0.667$

    e. 66.7%

39. a. $y' = -3x^2$

    b. $\dfrac{y'}{y} = \dfrac{-3x^2}{8-x^3}$

    c. $y'(1) = -3$

    d. $-\dfrac{3}{7} \approx -0.429$

    e. −42.9%

41. $c = 0.2q^2 + 1.2q + 4$

$\dfrac{dc}{dq} = 0.4q + 1.2$

If $q = 5$, then $\dfrac{dc}{dq} = 0.4(5) + 1.2 = 3.2$. If $q = 5$, then $c = 15$ and $\dfrac{\frac{dc}{dq}}{c}(100) = \dfrac{3.2}{15}(100) \approx 21.3\%$.

43. a. $\dfrac{dr}{dq} = 30 - 0.6q$

b. If $q = 10$, $\dfrac{r'}{r} = \dfrac{30-6}{300-30} = \dfrac{24}{270} = \dfrac{4}{45} \approx 0.09$.

c. 9%

45. $\dfrac{W'}{W} = \dfrac{0.864t^{-0.568}}{2t^{0.432}} = \dfrac{0.432}{t}$

47. The cost of $q = 20$ bikes is $q\bar{c} = 20(150) = \$3000$. The marginal cost, \$125, is the approximate cost of one additional bike. Thus the approximate cost of producing 21 bikes is $\$3000 + \$125 = \$3125$.

49. \$5.07 per unit

Principles in Practice 12.5

1. $\dfrac{dR}{dx} = (2 - 0.15x)\dfrac{d}{dx}(225 + 20x) + (225 + 20x)\dfrac{d}{dx}(2 - 0.15x)$

$= (2 - 0.15x)(20) + (225 + 20x)(-0.15)$

$= 40 - 3x - 33.75 - 3x = 6.25 - 6x$

$\dfrac{dR}{dx} = 6.25 - 6x$

2. $T(x) = x^2 - \dfrac{1}{3}x^3$

$T'(x) = 2x - x^2$

When the dosage is 1 milligram the sensitivity is $T'(1) = 2(1) - 1^2 = 1$.

Exercise 12.5

1. $f'(x) = (4x + 1)(6) + (6x + 3)(4)$

$= 24x + 6 + 24x + 12$

$= 48x + 18 = 6(8x + 3)$

3. $s'(t) = (8 - 7t)(2t) + (t^2 - 2)(-7)$

$= 16t - 14t^2 - 7t^2 + 14$

$= 14 + 16t - 21t^2$

5. $f'(r) = (3r^2 - 4)(2r - 5) + (r^2 - 5r + 1)(6r)$

$= 6r^3 - 15r^2 - 8r + 20 + 6r^3 - 30r^2 + 6r$

$= 12r^3 - 45r^2 - 2r + 20$

7. Without the product rule we have

$f(x) = x^2(x^2 - 5) = x^4 - 5x^2$

$f'(x) = 4x^3 - 10x$

9. $y' = \left(x^2 + 3x - 2\right)(4x - 1) + \left(2x^2 - x - 3\right)(2x + 3)$

   $= \left(4x^3 + 12x^2 - 8x - x^2 - 3x + 2\right) + \left(4x^3 - 2x^2 - 6x + 6x^2 - 3x - 9\right)$

   $= 8x^3 + 15x^2 - 20x - 7$

11. $f'(w) = \left(8w^2 + 2w - 3\right)\left(15w^2\right) + \left(5w^3 + 2\right)(16w + 2)$

    $= 120w^4 + 30w^3 - 45w^2 + 80w^4 + 10w^3 + 32w + 4$

    $= 200w^4 + 40w^3 - 45w^2 + 32w + 4$

13. $y' = \left(x^2 - 1\right)\left(9x^2 - 6\right) + \left(3x^3 - 6x + 5\right)(2x) - 4(8x + 2)$

    $= 15x^4 - 27x^2 - 22x - 2$

15. $f'(p) = \dfrac{3}{2}\left[\left(p^{\frac{1}{2}} - 4\right)(4) + (4p - 5)\left(\dfrac{1}{2}p^{-\frac{1}{2}}\right)\right]$

    $= \dfrac{3}{2}\left[4p^{\frac{1}{2}} - 16 + 2p^{\frac{1}{2}} - \dfrac{5}{2}p^{-\frac{1}{2}}\right]$

    $= \dfrac{3}{2}\left[6p^{\frac{1}{2}} - 16 - \dfrac{5}{2}p^{-\frac{1}{2}}\right]$

    $= \dfrac{3}{4}\left(12p^{\frac{1}{2}} - 5p^{-\frac{1}{2}} - 32\right)$

17. $y = 7 \cdot \dfrac{2}{3}$ is a constant function, so $y' = 0$.

19. $y = (2x - 1)(3x + 4)(x + 7)$

    $= [(2x - 1)(3x + 4)](x + 7)$

    $y' = [(2x - 1)(3x + 4)](1) + (x + 7)[(2x - 1)(3) + (3x + 4)(2)]$

    $= 6x^2 + 5x - 4 + (x + 7)[12x + 5]$

    $= 6x^2 + 5x - 4 + 12x^2 + 89x + 35$

    $= 18x^2 + 94x + 31$

    [handwritten: $6x - 3 + 6x + 8$ *]*

    [handwritten: $12x^2 + 84y + 5x + 35$ *]*

21. $f'(x) = \dfrac{(x - 1)(1) - (x)(1)}{(x - 1)^2} = -\dfrac{1}{(x - 1)^2}$

23. $f(x) = \dfrac{3}{2x^6} = \dfrac{3}{2}x^{-6}$

    $f'(x) = \dfrac{3}{2}\left(-6x^{-7}\right) = -\dfrac{9}{x^7}$

25. $y' = \dfrac{(x - 1)(1) - (x + 2)(1)}{(x - 1)^2}$

    $= \dfrac{x - 1 - x - 2}{(x - 1)^2}$

    $= -\dfrac{3}{(x - 1)^2}$

27. $h'(z) = \dfrac{\left(z^2 - 4\right)(-2) - (5 - 2z)(2z)}{\left(z^2 - 4\right)^2}$

$= \dfrac{-2z^2 + 8 - 10z + 4z^2}{\left(z^2 - 4\right)^2} = \dfrac{2z^2 - 10z + 8}{\left(z^2 - 4\right)^2}$

$= \dfrac{2\left(z^2 - 5z + 4\right)}{\left(z^2 - 4\right)^2} = \dfrac{2(z - 4)(z - 1)}{\left(z^2 - 4\right)^2}$

29. $y' = \dfrac{\left(x^2 - 5x\right)(16x - 2) - \left(8x^2 - 2x + 1\right)(2x - 5)}{\left(x^2 - 5x\right)^2}$

$= \dfrac{16x^3 - 82x^2 + 10x - \left(16x^3 - 44x^2 + 12x - 5\right)}{\left(x^2 - 5x\right)^2} = \dfrac{-38x^2 - 2x + 5}{\left(x^2 - 5x\right)^2}$

31. $y' = \dfrac{\left(2x^2 - 3x + 2\right)(2x - 4) - \left(x^2 - 4x + 3\right)(4x - 3)}{\left(2x^2 - 3x + 2\right)^2}$

$= \dfrac{4x^3 - 6x^2 + 4x - 8x^2 + 12x - 8 - \left(4x^3 - 16x^2 + 12x - 3x^2 + 12x - 9\right)}{\left(2x^2 - 3x + 2\right)^2}$

$= \dfrac{5x^2 - 8x + 1}{\left(2x^2 - 3x + 2\right)^2}$

33. $g'(x) = \dfrac{\left(x^{100} + 1\right)(0) - (1)\left(100x^{99}\right)}{\left(x^{100} + 1\right)^2}$

$= -\dfrac{100x^{99}}{\left(x^{100} + 1\right)^2}$

35. $u(v) = \dfrac{v^5 - 8}{v} = \dfrac{v^5}{v} - \dfrac{8}{v} = v^4 - 8v^{-1}$

$u'(v) = 4v^3 + 8v^{-2}$

$= 4\left(v^3 + \dfrac{2}{v^2}\right) + \dfrac{4\left(v^5 + 2\right)}{v^2}$

37. $y = \dfrac{3x^2 - x - 1}{\sqrt[3]{x}} = \dfrac{3x^2 - x - 1}{x^{\frac{1}{3}}}$

$= 3x^{\frac{5}{3}} - x^{\frac{2}{3}} - x^{-\frac{1}{3}}$

$y' = 5x^{\frac{2}{3}} - \dfrac{2}{3}x^{-\frac{1}{3}} + \dfrac{1}{3}x^{-\frac{4}{3}}$

$= 5x^{\frac{2}{3}} - \dfrac{2}{3x^{\frac{1}{3}}} + \dfrac{1}{3x^{\frac{4}{3}}}$

$= \dfrac{15x^2 - 2x + 1}{3x^{\frac{4}{3}}}$

39. $y' = -\dfrac{(x-8)(0)-(4)(1)}{(x-8)^2} + \dfrac{(3x+1)(2)-(2x)(3)}{(3x+1)^2}$

$ = \dfrac{4}{(x-8)^2} + \dfrac{2}{(3x+1)^2}$

41. $y' = \dfrac{[(x+2)(x-4)](1)-(x-5)(2x-2)}{[(x+2)(x-4)]^2}$

$ = \dfrac{x^2-2x-8-\left(2x^2-12x+10\right)}{[(x+2)(x-4)]^2}$

$ = \dfrac{-\left(x^2-10x+18\right)}{[(x+2)(x-4)]^2}$

43. $s'(t) = \dfrac{\left[\left(t^2-1\right)\left(t^3+7\right)\right](2t+3)-\left(t^2+3t\right)\left(5t^4-3t^2+14t\right)}{\left[\left(t^2-1\right)\left(t^3+7\right)\right]^2}$

$ = \dfrac{-3t^6-12t^5+t^4+6t^3-21t^2-14t-21}{\left[\left(t^2-1\right)\left(t^3+7\right)\right]^2}$

45. $y = 3x - \dfrac{\dfrac{2}{x}-\dfrac{3}{x-1}}{x-2} = 3x - \dfrac{\dfrac{2(x-1)-3x}{x(x-1)}}{x-2}$

$ = 3x + \dfrac{x+2}{x(x-1)(x-2)} = 3x + \dfrac{x+2}{x^3-3x^2+2x}$

$y' = 3 + \dfrac{(x^3-3x^2+2x)(1)-(x+2)(3x^2-6x+2)}{[x(x-1)(x-2)]^2}$

$ = 3 - \dfrac{2x^3+3x^2-12x+4}{[x(x-1)(x-2)]^2}$

47. $f'(x) = \dfrac{(a+x)(-1)-(a-x)(1)}{(a+x)^2} = -\dfrac{2a}{(a+x)^2}$

49. $y = \left(4x^2+2x-5\right)\left(x^3+7x+4\right)$

$y' = \left(4x^2+2x-5\right)\left(3x^2+7\right)+\left(x^3+7x+4\right)(8x+2)$

$y'(-1) = (-3)(10)+(-4)(-6) = -6$

51. $y = \dfrac{6}{x-1}$

$y' = \dfrac{(x-1)(0)-(6)(1)}{(x-1)^2} = -\dfrac{6}{(x-1)^2}$

$$y'(3) = -\frac{6}{2^2} = -\frac{3}{2}$$

The tangent is $y - 3 = -\frac{3}{2}(x - 3)$, or $y = -\frac{3}{2}x + \frac{15}{2}$.

53. $y = (2x + 3)\left[2\left(x^4 - 5x^2 + 4\right)\right]$

$y' = (2x + 3)\left[2\left(4x^3 - 10x\right)\right] + \left[2\left(x^4 - 5x^2 + 4\right)\right](2)$

$y'(0) = (3)(0) + [2(4)](2) = 16$

The tangent line is $y - 24 = 16(x - 0)$, or $y = 16x + 24$.

55. $y = \dfrac{x}{2x - 6}$

$y' = \dfrac{(2x - 6)(1) - x(2)}{(2x - 6)^2} = \dfrac{-6}{(2x - 6)^2}$

If $x = 1$, then $y = \dfrac{1}{2 - 6} = -\dfrac{1}{4}$ and $y' = \dfrac{-6}{(-4)^2} = \dfrac{-6}{16} = -\dfrac{3}{8}$.

Thus $\dfrac{y'}{y} = \dfrac{-\frac{3}{8}}{-\frac{1}{4}} = \dfrac{3}{2} = 1.5$.

57. $s = \dfrac{2}{t^3 + 1}$. When $t = 1$, then $s = 1$ m.

$v = \dfrac{(t^3 + 1)(0) - 2(3t^2)}{(t^3 + 1)^2} = -\dfrac{6t^2}{(t^3 + 1)^2}$

If $t = 1$, then $v = -\dfrac{6}{4} = -1.5$ m/s.

59. $p = 25 - 0.02q$

$r = pq = 25q - 0.02q^2$

$\dfrac{dr}{dq} = 25 - 0.04q$

61. $p = \dfrac{108}{q + 2} - 3$

$r = pq = \dfrac{108q}{q + 2} - 3q$

$\dfrac{dr}{dq} = \dfrac{(q + 2)(108) - (108q)(1)}{(q + 2)^2} - 3$

$= \dfrac{216}{(q + 2)^2} - 3$

63. $\dfrac{dC}{dI} = 0.672$

65. $C = 2 + 2I^{\frac{1}{2}}$

$\dfrac{dC}{dI} = 0 + 2\left(\dfrac{1}{2}I^{-\frac{1}{2}}\right) = \dfrac{1}{\sqrt{I}}$

When $I = 9$, then $\dfrac{dC}{dI} = \dfrac{1}{\sqrt{9}} = \dfrac{1}{3}$ and $\dfrac{dS}{dI} = 1 - \dfrac{1}{3} = \dfrac{2}{3}$

67. $\dfrac{dC}{dI} = \dfrac{\left(\sqrt{I}+4\right)\left(\dfrac{8}{\sqrt{I}}+1.2\sqrt{I}-0.2\right) - \left(16\sqrt{I}+0.8\sqrt{I^3}-0.2I\right)\left(\dfrac{1}{2\sqrt{I}}\right)}{\left(\sqrt{I}+4\right)^2}$

$\left.\dfrac{dC}{dI}\right|_{I=36} \approx 0.615$, so $\dfrac{dS}{dI} = 1 - 0.615 = 0.385$ when $I = 36$.

69. Simplifying gives $C = 10 + 0.7I - 0.2I^{\frac{1}{2}}$

    a. $\dfrac{dC}{dI} = 0.7 - 0.1I^{-\frac{1}{2}} = 0.7 - \dfrac{0.1}{\sqrt{I}}$

        $\dfrac{dS}{dI} = 1 - \dfrac{dC}{dI} = 0.3 + \dfrac{0.1}{\sqrt{I}}$

        $\left.\dfrac{dS}{dI}\right|_{I=25} = 0.3 + \dfrac{0.1}{5} = 0.32$

    b. $\dfrac{\frac{dC}{dI}}{C}$ when $I = 25$ is $\dfrac{0.7 - \frac{0.1}{5}}{10 + 0.7(25) - 0.2(5)} \approx 0.026$

71. $\dfrac{dc}{dq} = 5 \cdot \dfrac{(q+3)(2q) - q^2(1)}{(q+3)^2} = 5 \cdot \dfrac{q^2 + 6q}{(q+3)^2}$

$= \dfrac{5q(q+6)}{(q+3)^2}$

73. $y = \dfrac{900x}{10 + 45x}$

$\dfrac{dy}{dx} = \dfrac{(10+45x)(900) - (900x)(45)}{(10+45x)^2}$

$\left.\dfrac{dy}{dx}\right|_{x=2} = \dfrac{(100)(900) - (1800)(45)}{(100)^2} = \dfrac{9}{10}$

75. $y = \dfrac{0.7355x}{1 + 0.02744x}$

$\dfrac{dy}{dx} = \dfrac{(1+0.02744x)(0.7355) - (0.7355x)(0.02744)}{(1+0.02744x)^2}$

$= \dfrac{0.7355}{(1+0.02744x)^2}$

77. $\dfrac{d\bar{c}}{dq} = \dfrac{d}{dq}\left(\dfrac{c}{q}\right) = \dfrac{q \cdot \frac{dc}{dq} - c(1)}{q^2}$. When $q = 20$ we have $\dfrac{\frac{d\bar{c}}{dq}}{\bar{c}} = \dfrac{\frac{q \cdot \frac{dc}{dq} - c}{q^2}}{\bar{c}} = \dfrac{\frac{20(125) - 20(150)}{(20)^2}}{150} = -\dfrac{1}{120}$

79. $\dfrac{dy}{dx} = (2x - 1)(x - 2)(1) + (2x - 1)(1)(x + 3) + 2(x - 2)(x + 3)$

$= \left(2x^2 - 5x + 2\right) + \left(2x^2 + 5x - 3\right) + \left(2x^2 + 2x - 12\right)$

$= 6x^2 + 2x - 13$

Principles in Practice 12.6

1. By the chain rule,

$\dfrac{dy}{dt} = \dfrac{dy}{dx} \cdot \dfrac{dx}{dt} = \dfrac{d}{dx}\left(4x^2\right) \cdot \dfrac{d}{dt}(6t)$

$= (8x)(6) = 48x$.

Since $x = 6t$, $\dfrac{dy}{dt} = 48(6t) = 288t$.

Exercise 12.6

1. $\dfrac{dy}{dx} = \dfrac{dy}{du} \cdot \dfrac{du}{dx} = (2u - 2)(2x - 1)$. Expressing the answer in terms of x, we have

$(2u - 2)(2x - 1) = \left[2\left(x^2 - x\right) - 2\right](2x - 1)$

$= \left(2x^2 - 2x - 2\right)(2x - 1)$

$= 4x^3 - 2x^2 - 4x^2 + 2x - 4x + 2$

$= 4x^3 - 6x^2 - 2x + 2$

3. $y = w^{-2}$, so $\dfrac{dy}{dw} = -2w^{-3} = -\dfrac{2}{w^3}$.

$\dfrac{dw}{dx} = -1$. Thus

$\dfrac{dy}{dx} = \dfrac{dy}{dw} \cdot \dfrac{dw}{dx} = \left(-\dfrac{2}{w^3}\right)(-1) = \dfrac{2}{w^3}$

$= \dfrac{2}{(2 - x)^3}$

5. $\dfrac{dw}{dt} = \dfrac{dw}{du} \cdot \dfrac{du}{dt} = (2u)\left[\dfrac{(t - 1) - (t + 1)}{(t - 1)^2}\right]$

$= 2u\left[\dfrac{-2}{(t - 1)^2}\right]$. If $t = 3$, then $u = \dfrac{3 + 1}{3 - 1} = 2$,

so $\dfrac{dw}{dt}\Big|_{t=3} = 2(2)\left[\dfrac{-2}{4}\right] = -2$.

7. $\dfrac{dy}{dx} = \dfrac{dy}{dw} \cdot \dfrac{dw}{dx} = (6w - 8)(6x)$. If $x = 0$, then $\dfrac{dy}{dx} = 0$.

9. $y' = 6(3x + 2)^5 \cdot \dfrac{d}{dx}(3x + 2)$

$= 6(3x + 2)^5 (3) = 18(3x + 2)^5$

11. $y' = 3\left(5 - x^2\right)^2 \cdot \dfrac{d}{dx}\left(5 - x^2\right)$

$= 3\left(5 - x^2\right)^2 (-2x) = -6x\left(5 - x^2\right)^2$

13. y'

$= 3 \cdot 100\left(x^3 - 8x^2 + x\right)^{99} \cdot \dfrac{d}{dx}\left(x^3 - 8x^2 + x\right)$

$= 300\left(x^3 - 8x^2 + x\right)^{99}\left(3x^2 - 16x + 1\right)$

$= 300\left(3x^2 - 16x + 1\right)\left(x^3 - 8x^2 + x\right)^{99}$

15. $y' = -3\left(x^2 - 2\right)^{-4} \cdot \dfrac{d}{dx}\left(x^2 - 2\right)$

$= -3\left(x^2 - 2\right)^{-4}(2x) = -6x\left(x^2 - 2\right)^{-4}$

17. $y' = \left(-\frac{10}{3}\right)\left(2x^2 - 3x - 1\right)^{-\frac{13}{3}}(4x - 3)$

$\quad = -\frac{10}{3}(4x - 3)\left(2x^2 - 3x - 1\right)^{-\frac{13}{3}}$

19. $y = \sqrt{5x^2 - x} = \left(5x^2 - x\right)^{\frac{1}{2}}$

$\quad y' = \frac{1}{2}\left(5x^2 - x\right)^{-\frac{1}{2}}(10x - 1)$

$\quad = \frac{1}{2}(10x - 1)\left(5x^2 - x\right)^{-\frac{1}{2}}$

21. $y = \sqrt[4]{2x - 1} = (2x - 1)^{\frac{1}{4}}$

$\quad y' = \frac{1}{4}(2x - 1)^{-\frac{3}{4}}(2) = \frac{1}{2}(2x - 1)^{-\frac{3}{4}}$

23. $y = 2\sqrt[5]{\left(x^3 + 1\right)^2} = 2\left(x^3 + 1\right)^{\frac{2}{5}}$

$\quad y' = 2\left(\frac{2}{5}\right)\left(x^3 + 1\right)^{-\frac{3}{5}}\left(3x^2\right)$

$\quad = \frac{12}{5}x^2\left(x^3 + 1\right)^{-\frac{3}{5}}$

25. $y = \dfrac{6}{2x^2 - x + 1} = 6\left(2x^2 - x + 1\right)^{-1}$

$\quad y' = 6(-1)\left(2x^2 - x + 1\right)^{-2}(4x - 1)$

$\quad = -6(4x - 1)\left(2x^2 - x + 1\right)^{-2}$

27. $y = \dfrac{1}{\left(x^2 - 3x\right)^2} = \left(x^2 - 3x\right)^{-2}$

$\quad y' = -2\left(x^2 - 3x\right)^{-3}(2x - 3)$

$\quad = -2(2x - 3)\left(x^2 - 3x\right)^{-3}$

29. $y = \dfrac{2}{\sqrt{8x - 1}} = 2(8x - 1)^{-\frac{1}{2}}$

$\quad y' = 2\left(-\frac{1}{2}\right)(8x - 1)^{-\frac{3}{2}}(8) = -8(8x - 1)^{-\frac{3}{2}}$

31. $y = \sqrt[3]{7x} + \sqrt[3]{7}x = (7x)^{\frac{1}{3}} + \sqrt[3]{7}x$

$\quad y' = \frac{1}{3}(7x)^{-\frac{2}{3}}(7) + \sqrt[3]{7}(1) = \frac{7}{3}(7x)^{-\frac{2}{3}} + \sqrt[3]{7}$

33. By the product rule,

$\quad y' = x^2\left[5(x - 4)^4(1)\right] + (x - 4)^5(2x).$

Factoring out $x(x - 4)^4$ from both terms gives

$\quad y' = x(x - 4)^4[5x + 2(x - 4)]$

$\quad = x(x - 4)^4(7x - 8)$

35. $y = 2x\sqrt{6x - 1} = 2x(6x - 1)^{\frac{1}{2}}$ By the product rule,

$\quad y' = 2x\left(\frac{1}{2}(6x - 1)^{-\frac{1}{2}}(6)\right) + \sqrt{6x - 1}(2)$

$\quad = 6x(6x - 1)^{-\frac{1}{2}} + 2\sqrt{6x - 1}$

37. By the product rule,

$\quad y' = \left(x^2 + 2x - 1\right)^3(5) + (5x)\left[3\left(x^2 + 2x - 1\right)^2(2x + 2)\right]$

$\quad = 5\left(x^2 + 2x - 1\right)^2\left[\left(x^2 + 2x - 1\right) + 3x(2x + 2)\right]$

$\quad = 5\left(x^2 + 2x - 1\right)^2\left(7x^2 + 8x - 1\right)$

39. $y' = (8x - 1)^3\left[4(2x + 1)^3(2)\right] + (2x + 1)^4\left[3(8x - 1)^2(8)\right]$

$\quad = 8(8x - 1)^2(2x + 1)^3[(8x - 1) + 3(2x + 1)]$

$\quad = 8(8x - 1)^2(2x + 1)^3(14x + 2)$

$\quad = 16(8x - 1)^2(2x + 1)^3(7x + 1)$

41. $y' = 10\left(\dfrac{x-7}{x+4}\right)^9 \left[\dfrac{(x+4)(1)-(x-7)(1)}{(x+4)^2}\right]$

$= 10\left(\dfrac{x-7}{x+4}\right)^9 \left[\dfrac{11}{(x+4)^2}\right] = \dfrac{110(x-7)^9}{(x+4)^9(x+4)^2} = \dfrac{110(x-7)^9}{(x+4)^{11}}$

43. $y' = \dfrac{1}{2}\left(\dfrac{x-2}{x+3}\right)^{-\frac{1}{2}} \left[\dfrac{(x+3)(1)-(x-2)(1)}{(x+3)^2}\right]$

$= \dfrac{5}{2(x+3)^2}\left(\dfrac{x-2}{x+3}\right)^{-\frac{1}{2}} = \dfrac{5}{2(x+3)^2}\sqrt{\dfrac{x+3}{x-2}}$

45. $y' = \dfrac{\left(x^2+4\right)^3(2)-(2x-5)\left[3\left(x^2+4\right)^2(2x)\right]}{\left(x^2+4\right)^6}$

Factoring out $\left(x^2+4\right)^2$ from the numerator and canceling,

$y' = \dfrac{\left(x^2+4\right)^2 \left\{\left(x^2+4\right)(2)-(2x-5)[3(2x)]\right\}}{\left(x^2+4\right)^6}$

$= \dfrac{\left(x^2+4\right)(2)-(2x-5)(6x)}{\left(x^2+4\right)^4}$

$= \dfrac{2x^2+8-12x^2+30x}{\left(x^2+4\right)^4} = \dfrac{-10x^2+30x+8}{\left(x^2+4\right)^4}$

$= \dfrac{-2\left(5x^2-15x-4\right)}{\left(x^2+4\right)^4}$

47. $y' = \dfrac{(3x-1)^3\left[5(8x-1)^4(8)\right]-(8x-1)^5\left[3(3x-1)^2(3)\right]}{(3x-1)^6}$

$= \dfrac{(3x-1)^2\left[(3x-1)(40)(8x-1)^4-(8x-1)^5(9)\right]}{(3x-1)^6}$

$= \dfrac{(3x-1)(40)(8x-1)^4-(8x-1)^5(9)}{(3x-1)^4}$

$= \dfrac{(8x-1)^4[40(3x-1)-(8x-1)(9)]}{(3x-1)^4}$

$= \dfrac{(8x-1)^4(48x-31)}{(3x-1)^4}$

49. $y = 6(5x^2 + 2)\sqrt{x^4 + 5} = 6\left[(5x^2 + 2)(x^4 + 5)^{\frac{1}{2}}\right]$

$y' = 6\left[(5x^2 + 2) \cdot \frac{1}{2}(x^4 + 5)^{-\frac{1}{2}}(4x^3) + (x^4 + 5)^{\frac{1}{2}}(10x)\right]$

$= 6\left[(5x^2 + 2)(x^4 + 5)^{-\frac{1}{2}}(2x^3) + (x^4 + 5)^{\frac{1}{2}}(10x)\right]$

$= 12x\left[(5x^2 + 2)(x^4 + 5)^{-\frac{1}{2}}(x^2) + (x^4 + 5)^{\frac{1}{2}}(5)\right]$

Factoring out $(x^4 + 5)^{-\frac{1}{2}}$ gives

$y' = 12x(x^4 + 5)^{-\frac{1}{2}}\left[(5x^2 + 2)(x^2) + (x^4 + 5)(5)\right]$

$= 12x(x^4 + 5)^{-\frac{1}{2}}(10x^4 + 2x^2 + 25)$

51. $y' = 8 + \dfrac{(t+4)(1) - (t-1)(1)}{(t+4)^2} - 2\left(\dfrac{8t-7}{4}\right)\left(\dfrac{1}{4} \cdot 8\right)$

$= 8 + \dfrac{5}{(t+4)^2} - (8t - 7) = 15 - 8t + \dfrac{5}{(t+4)^2}$

53. $y' = \dfrac{(x^2 - 7)^4\left[(2x+1)(2)(3x-5)(3) + (3x-5)^2(2)\right] - (2x+1)(3x-5)^2\left[4(x^2-7)^3(2x)\right]}{(x^2 - 7)^8}$

55. $\dfrac{dy}{dx} = \dfrac{dy}{du} \cdot \dfrac{du}{dx}$

$= \left[3(5u+6)^2(5)\right]\left[4(x^2+1)^3(2x)\right]$

When $x = 0$, then $\dfrac{dy}{dx} = 0$.

57. $y' = 3(x^2 - 7x - 8)^2(2x - 7)$

If $x = 8$, then

slope $= y' = 3(64 - 56 - 8)^2(16 - 7) = 0$.

59. $y = (x^2 - 8)^{\frac{2}{3}}$

$y' = \dfrac{2}{3}(x^2 - 8)^{-\frac{1}{3}}(2x) = \dfrac{4x}{3(x^2 - 8)^{\frac{1}{3}}}$

If $x = 3$, then $y' = \dfrac{12}{3(1)} = 4$. Thus the tangent is $y - 1 = 4(x - 3)$, or $y = 4x - 11$.

61. $y' = \dfrac{(x+1)\left(\frac{1}{2}\right)(7x+2)^{-\frac{1}{2}}(7) - \sqrt{7x+2}\,(1)}{(x+1)^2}$

$= \dfrac{(x+1)\left(\frac{7}{2}\right)\frac{1}{\sqrt{7x+2}} - \sqrt{7x+2}}{(x+1)^2}$

If $x = 1$, then $y' = \dfrac{2\left(\frac{7}{2}\right)\left(\frac{1}{3}\right) - 3}{4} = -\dfrac{1}{6}$. The tangent line is $y - \dfrac{3}{2} = -\dfrac{1}{6}(x - 1)$, or

$y = -\dfrac{1}{6}x + \dfrac{5}{3}$.

63. $y = \left(x^2 + 9\right)^3$ and $y' = 6x\left(x^2 + 9\right)^2$. When $x = 4$, then $y = (25)^3$ and $y' = 6(4)(25)^2$, so

$$\frac{y'}{y}(100) = \frac{6(4)(25)^2}{(25)^3}(100)$$

$$= \frac{24}{25}(100) = 96\%$$

65. Given $q = 2m$, $p = -0.5q + 20$; $m = 5$.

$$\frac{dr}{dm} = \frac{dr}{dq} \cdot \frac{dq}{dm}$$

Since $r = pq = -0.5q^2 + 20q$, we have $\frac{dr}{dq} = -q + 20$. For $m = 5$, then

$q = 2(5) = 10$, so $\left.\frac{dr}{dq}\right|_{m=5} = -10 + 20 = 10$. Also, $\frac{dq}{dm} = 2$. Thus $\left.\frac{dr}{dm}\right|_{m=5} = (10)(2) = 20$.

67. $q = \dfrac{10m^2}{\sqrt{m^2 + 9}}$

$p = \dfrac{525}{q + 3}$; $m = 4$

$$\frac{dr}{dm} = \frac{dr}{dq} \cdot \frac{dq}{dm}$$

$r = pq = \dfrac{525q}{q + 3}$, so $\dfrac{dr}{dq} = 525 \cdot \dfrac{(q+3)(1) - q(1)}{(q+3)^2} = \dfrac{1575}{(q+3)^2}$.

If $m = 4$, then $q = 32$, so $\left.\dfrac{dr}{dq}\right|_{m=4} = \dfrac{1575}{1225} = \dfrac{9}{7}$.

$$\frac{dq}{dm} = \frac{\left(m^2+9\right)^{\frac{1}{2}}(20m) - 10m^2 \cdot \frac{1}{2}\left(m^2+9\right)^{-\frac{1}{2}}(2m)}{m^2 + 9}$$

$$= \frac{\left(m^2+9\right)^{-\frac{1}{2}}\left[20m\left(m^2+9\right) - 10m^3\right]}{m^2 + 9}$$

$$= \frac{10m^3 + 180m}{\left(m^2+9\right)^{\frac{3}{2}}}$$

When $m = 4$, then $\dfrac{dq}{dm} = \dfrac{10(64) + 180(4)}{(25)^{\frac{3}{2}}} = \dfrac{1360}{125} = \dfrac{272}{25}$. Thus $\left.\dfrac{dr}{dm}\right|_{m=4} = \dfrac{9}{7} \cdot \dfrac{272}{25} \approx 13.99$.

69. a. $\dfrac{dp}{dq} = 0 - \dfrac{1}{2}\left(q^2 + 20\right)^{-\frac{1}{2}}(2q)$

$$= \frac{-q}{\sqrt{q^2 + 20}}$$

b. $\dfrac{\dfrac{dp}{dq}}{p} = \dfrac{\dfrac{-q}{\sqrt{q^2+20}}}{100 - \sqrt{q^2 + 20}}$

$= -\dfrac{q}{\sqrt{q^2 + 20}\left(100 - \sqrt{q^2 + 20}\right)}$

$= -\dfrac{q}{100\sqrt{q^2 + 20} - q^2 - 20}$

c. $r = pq = 100q - q\sqrt{q^2 + 20}$

$\dfrac{dr}{dq} = 100 - \left[q \cdot \dfrac{1}{2}\left(q^2 + 20\right)^{-\frac{1}{2}}(2q) + \sqrt{q^2 + 20}\,(1) \right]$

$= 100 - \dfrac{q^2}{\sqrt{q^2 + 20}} - \sqrt{q^2 + 20}$

71. $\dfrac{dc}{dp} = \dfrac{dc}{dq} \cdot \dfrac{dq}{dp} = (10 + 0.2q)(-2.5)$

When $p = 80$, then $q = 600$, so $\left.\dfrac{dc}{dp}\right|_{p=80} = -325$.

73. $\dfrac{dc}{dq} = \dfrac{\left(q^2 + 3\right)^{\frac{1}{2}}(10q) - \left(5q^2\right)\left[\frac{1}{2}\left(q^2 + 3\right)^{-\frac{1}{2}}(2q)\right]}{q^2 + 3}$

Multiplying numerator and denominator by $\left(q^2 + 3\right)^{\frac{1}{2}}$ gives $\dfrac{dc}{dq} = \dfrac{\left(q^2 + 3\right)(10q) - 5q^2(q)}{\left(q^2 + 3\right)^{\frac{3}{2}}}$

$= \dfrac{5q^3 + 30q}{\left(q^2 + 3\right)^{\frac{3}{2}}} = \dfrac{5q\left(q^2 + 6\right)}{\left(q^2 + 3\right)^{\frac{3}{2}}}.$

75. $\dfrac{dV}{dt} = \dfrac{dV}{dr} \cdot \dfrac{dr}{dt} = \left(4\pi r^2\right)\left[10^{-8}(2t) + 10^{-7}\right]$. When $t = 10$, then $r = 10^{-8}\left(10^2\right) + 10^{-7}(10)$

$= 10^{-6} + 10^{-6} = 2(10)^{-6}$. Thus

$\left.\dfrac{dV}{dt}\right|_{t=10} = 4\pi\left[2(10)^{-6}\right]^2\left[10^{-8}(2)(10) + 10^{-7}\right]$

$= 4\pi\left[4(10)^{-12}\right]\left[3\left(10^{-7}\right)\right] = 48\pi(10)^{-19}$

77. a. $\dfrac{d}{dx}(l_x) = 2000\left(\dfrac{1}{2}\right)(100-x)^{-\frac{1}{2}}(-1)$

$= -\dfrac{1000}{\sqrt{100-x}}$

If $x = 36$, $\dfrac{d}{dx}(l_x) = -\dfrac{1000}{8} = -125$.

b. If $x = 36$, $\dfrac{\frac{d}{dx}(l_x)}{l} = \dfrac{-125}{2000(8)} = -\dfrac{1}{128}$.

79. By the chain rule, $\dfrac{dc}{dp} = \dfrac{dc}{dq} \cdot \dfrac{dq}{dp}$. We are given that $q = \dfrac{100}{p} = 100p^{-1}$, so $\dfrac{dq}{dp} = -100p^{-2} = \dfrac{-100}{p^2}$.

Thus $\dfrac{dc}{dp} = \dfrac{dc}{dq}\left[\dfrac{-100}{p^2}\right]$. When $q = 200$, then $p = \dfrac{100}{200} = \dfrac{1}{2}$ and we are given that $\dfrac{dc}{dq} = 0.01$. Therefore

$\dfrac{dc}{dp} = 0.01\left[\dfrac{-100}{\left(\frac{1}{2}\right)^2}\right] = -4$.

81. $\dfrac{dy}{dt} = \dfrac{dy}{dx} \cdot \dfrac{dx}{dt} = f'(x)g'(t)$. We are given that $g(2) = 3$, so $x = 3$ when $t = 2$. Thus

$\left.\dfrac{dy}{dt}\right|_{t=2} = \left.\dfrac{dy}{dx}\right|_{x=g(2)} \cdot \left.\dfrac{dx}{dt}\right|_{t=2} = f'(3)g'(2) = 10(4) = 40$.

83. $86,111.22$

Chapter 12 Review Problems

1. $f(x) = 2 - x^2$

$f'(x) = \lim\limits_{h \to 0} \dfrac{f(x+h) - f(x)}{h} = \lim\limits_{h \to 0} \dfrac{\left[2 - (x+h)^2\right] - \left(2 - x^2\right)}{h}$

$= \lim\limits_{h \to 0} \dfrac{\left[2 - x^2 - 2hx - h^2\right] - \left(2 - x^2\right)}{h} = \lim\limits_{h \to 0} \dfrac{-2hx - h^2}{h}$

$= \lim\limits_{h \to 0} \dfrac{-h(2x+h)}{h} = \lim\limits_{h \to 0} -(2x+h) = -2x$

3. $f(x) = \sqrt{3x}$

$f'(x) = \lim\limits_{h \to 0} \dfrac{f(x+h) - f(x)}{h} = \lim\limits_{h \to 0} \dfrac{\sqrt{3(x+h)} - \sqrt{3x}}{h}$

$= \lim\limits_{h \to 0} \dfrac{\sqrt{3(x+h)} - \sqrt{3x}}{h} \cdot \dfrac{\sqrt{3(x+h)} + \sqrt{3x}}{\sqrt{3(x+h)} + \sqrt{3x}}$

$= \lim\limits_{h \to 0} \dfrac{3(x+h) - 3x}{h\left(\sqrt{3(x+h)} + \sqrt{3x}\right)} = \lim\limits_{h \to 0} \dfrac{3h}{h\left(\sqrt{3(x+h)} + \sqrt{3x}\right)}$

$$= \lim_{h \to 0} \frac{3}{\sqrt{3(x+h)} + \sqrt{3x}}$$

$$= \frac{3}{\sqrt{3x} + \sqrt{3x}} = \frac{3}{2\sqrt{3x}} = \frac{\sqrt{3}}{2\sqrt{x}}$$

5. y is a constant function, so $y' = 0$.

7. $y' = 7(4x^3) - 6(3x^2) + 5(2x) + 0$
$$= 28x^3 - 18x^2 + 10x = 2x(14x^2 - 9x + 5)$$

9. $f(s) = s^2(s^2 + 2) = s^4 + 2s^2$
$$f'(s) = 4s^3 + 2(2s) = 4s^3 + 4s = 4s(s^2 + 1)$$

11. $y = \frac{1}{5}(x^2 + 3)$
$$y' = \frac{1}{5}(2x) = \frac{2x}{5}$$

13. $y' = (x^2 + 6x)(3x^2 - 12x) + (x^3 - 6x^2 + 4)(2x + 6)$
$$= 3x^4 + 6x^3 - 72x^2 + (2x^4 + 6x^3 - 12x^3 - 36x^2 + 8x + 24)$$
$$= 5x^4 - 108x^2 + 8x + 24$$

15. $f'(x) = 100(2x^2 + 4x)^{99}(4x + 4)$
$$= 400(x+1)[(2x)(x+2)]^{99}$$

17. $y = (2x + 1)^{-1}$
$$y' = (-1)(2x+1)^{-2}(2) = -\frac{2}{(2x+1)^2}$$

19. y'
$$= (8 + 2x)\left[(4)(x^2 + 1)^3(2x)\right] + (x^2 + 1)^4(2)$$
$$= 2(x^2 + 1)^3\left[4x(8 + 2x) + (x^2 + 1)\right]$$
$$= 2(x^2 + 1)^3(32x + 8x^2 + x^2 + 1)$$
$$= 2(x^2 + 1)^3(9x^2 + 32x + 1)$$

21. $f'(z) = \dfrac{(z^2 + 1)(2z) - (z^2 - 1)(2z)}{(z^2 + 1)^2}$
$$= \frac{4z}{(z^2 + 1)^2}$$

23. $y = (4x - 1)^{\frac{1}{3}}$
$$y' = \frac{1}{3}(4x - 1)^{-\frac{2}{3}}(4) = \frac{4}{3}(4x - 1)^{-\frac{2}{3}}$$

25. $y = (1 - x)^{-\frac{1}{2}}$
$$y' = \left(-\frac{1}{2}\right)(1 - x)^{-\frac{3}{2}}(-1) = \frac{1}{2}(1 - x)^{-\frac{3}{2}}$$

27. $h'(x)$
$$= (x-6)^4 \left[3(x+5)^2\right] + (x+5)^3\left[4(x-6)^3\right]$$
$$= (x-6)^3(x+5)^2[3(x-6)+4(x+5)]$$
$$= (x-6)^3(x+5)^2(7x+2)$$

29. $y' = \dfrac{(x+1)(5)-(5x-4)(1)}{(x+1)^2} = \dfrac{9}{(x+1)^2}$

31. $y' = 2\left(-\dfrac{3}{8}\right)x^{-\frac{11}{8}} + \left(-\dfrac{3}{8}\right)(2x)^{-\frac{11}{8}}(2)$
$$= -\dfrac{3}{4}x^{-\frac{11}{8}} - \dfrac{3}{4}\left(2^{-\frac{11}{8}}\right)x^{-\frac{11}{8}}$$
$$= -\dfrac{3}{4}x^{-\frac{11}{8}}\left(1+2^{-\frac{11}{8}}\right) = -\dfrac{3}{4}\left(1+2^{-\frac{11}{8}}\right)x^{-\frac{11}{8}}$$

33. y'
$$= \dfrac{\left(x^2+5\right)^{\frac{1}{2}}(2x)-\left(x^2+6\right)\left(\frac{1}{2}\right)\left(x^2+5\right)^{-\frac{1}{2}}(2x)}{x^2+5}$$
Multiplying the numerator and denominator
by $\left(x^2+5\right)^{\frac{1}{2}}$ gives
$$y' = \dfrac{\left(x^2+5\right)(2x)-x\left(x^2+6\right)}{\left(x^2+5\right)^{\frac{3}{2}}}$$
$$= \dfrac{x^3+4x}{\left(x^2+5\right)^{\frac{3}{2}}} = \dfrac{x\left(x^2+4\right)}{\left(x^2+5\right)^{\frac{3}{2}}}$$

35. $y' = \dfrac{3}{5}\left(x^3+6x^2+9\right)^{-\frac{2}{5}}\left(3x^2+12x\right)$
$$= \dfrac{3}{5}\left(x^3+6x^2+9\right)^{-\frac{2}{5}}(3x)(x+4)$$
$$= \dfrac{9}{5}x(x+4)\left(x^3+6x^2+9\right)^{-\frac{2}{5}}$$

37. $g(z) = -7z(z-1) = -7\left(z^2-z\right)$
$g'(z) = -7(2z-1) = 7(1-2z)$

39. $y = x^2-6x+4$
$y' = 2x-6$

When $x=1$, then $y=-1$ and $y'=-4$. An equation of the tangent line is
$y-(-1)=-4(x-1)$, or $y=-4x+3$.

41. $y = x^{\frac{1}{3}}$
$y' = \dfrac{1}{3}x^{-\frac{2}{3}}$
When $x=8$, then $y=2$ and $y'=\dfrac{1}{12}$. An equation of the tangent line is
$y-2=\dfrac{1}{12}(x-8)$, or $y=\dfrac{1}{12}x+\dfrac{4}{3}$.

43. $f(x) = 4x^2+2x+8$
$f'(x) = 8x+2$
$f(1)=14$ and $f'(1)=10$. The relative rate of change is $\dfrac{f'(1)}{f(1)} = \dfrac{10}{14} = \dfrac{5}{7} \approx 0.714$, so the percentage rate of change is 71.4%.

45. $r = q(20-0.1q) = 20q-0.1q^2$
$\dfrac{dr}{dq} = 20-0.2q$

47. $\dfrac{dC}{dI} = 0.6-0.25\left(\frac{1}{2}\right)I^{-\frac{1}{2}} = 0.6-\dfrac{1}{8\sqrt{I}}$
$\left.\dfrac{dC}{dI}\right|_{I=16} \approx 0.569$
Thus the marginal propensity to consume is 0.569, so the marginal propensity to save is $1-0.569 = 0.431$.

49. Since $p=-0.5q+450$, then
$r = pq = -0.5q^2+450q$. Thus
$\dfrac{dr}{dq} = 450-q$.

51. $\dfrac{dc}{dq} = 0.125+0.00878q$
$\left.\dfrac{dc}{dq}\right|_{q=70} = 0.7396$

53. $\dfrac{dy}{dx} = 42x^2-34x-16$
$\left.\dfrac{dy}{dx}\right|_{x=2} = 84$ eggs/mm

55. a. $\frac{dt}{dT}$ when $T = 38$ is

$$\frac{d}{dT}\left[\frac{4}{3}T - \frac{175}{4}\right]\bigg|_{T=38} = \frac{4}{3}\bigg|_{T=38} = \frac{4}{3}.$$

b. $\frac{dt}{dT}$ when $T = 35$ is

$$\frac{d}{dT}\left[\frac{1}{24}T + \frac{11}{4}\right]\bigg|_{T=35} = \frac{1}{24}\bigg|_{T=35} = \frac{1}{24}.$$

57. $V' = \frac{1}{2}\pi d^2$. If $d = 4$ ft, then $V' = 8\pi\dfrac{\text{ft}^3}{\text{ft}}$.

59. $c = \bar{c}q = 2q^2 + \dfrac{10,000}{q} = 2q^2 + 10,000q^{-1}$

$$\frac{dc}{dq} = 4q - 10,000q^{-2} = 4q - \frac{10,000}{q^2}$$

61. a. $q = 10\sqrt{m^2 + 3600} - 600$

$p = \sqrt{7200 - 9q}$; $m = 80$

$\dfrac{dr}{dm} = \dfrac{dr}{dq} \cdot \dfrac{dq}{dm}.$

$r = pq = q\sqrt{7200 - 9q}$, so

$\dfrac{dr}{dq}$

$= q\left(\dfrac{1}{2}\right)(7200 - 9q)^{-\frac{1}{2}}(-9) + \sqrt{7200 - 9q}(1).$

If $m = 80$, then $q = 400$, so

$\dfrac{dr}{dq}\bigg|_{m=80} = 30.$

$\dfrac{dq}{dm} = 10 \cdot \dfrac{1}{2}\left(m^2 + 3600\right)^{-\frac{1}{2}}(2m).$

$\dfrac{dq}{dm}\bigg|_{m=80} = 8.$ Thus

$\dfrac{dr}{dm}\bigg|_{m=80} = (30)(8) = 240$

b. $\dfrac{\frac{dr}{dm}\big|_{m=80}}{r} = \dfrac{240}{r}\bigg|_{q=400}$

$= \dfrac{240}{400\sqrt{3600}} = \dfrac{1}{100}$

c. No. The extra cost of \$300 would exceed the extra revenue [approximately \$240, from part (a)].

63. 0.397

65. −0.32

Chapter 13

1. $\dfrac{dq}{dp} = \dfrac{d}{dp}\Big[25 + 2\ln\big(3p^2 + 4\big)\Big]$

   $= 0 + 2\dfrac{d}{dp}\Big[\ln\big(3p^2 + 4\big)\Big]$

   $= 2\Big(\dfrac{1}{3p^2 + 4}\Big)\dfrac{d}{dp}\big(3p^2 + 4\big) = \dfrac{2}{3p^2 + 4}(6p)$

   $= \dfrac{12p}{3p^2 + 4}$

2. With $I_0 = 1$, $R(I) = \log I$.

   $\dfrac{dR}{dI} = \dfrac{d}{dI}[\log I] = \dfrac{d}{dI}\Big[\dfrac{\ln I}{\ln 10}\Big]$

   $= \dfrac{1}{\ln 10}\cdot\dfrac{1}{I} = \dfrac{1}{I\ln 10}$

Exercise 13.1

1. $\dfrac{dy}{dx} = 4\cdot\dfrac{d}{dx}(\ln x) = 4\cdot\dfrac{1}{x} = \dfrac{4}{x}$

3. $\dfrac{dy}{dx} = \dfrac{1}{3x - 4}(3) = \dfrac{3}{3x - 4}$

5. $y = \ln x^2 = 2\ln x$

   $\dfrac{dy}{dx} = 2\cdot\dfrac{1}{x} = \dfrac{2}{x}$

7. $\dfrac{dy}{dx} = \dfrac{1}{1 - x^2}(-2x) = -\dfrac{2x}{1 - x^2}$

9. $f'(p) = \dfrac{1}{2p^3 + 3p}\big(6p^2 + 3\big)$

   $= \dfrac{6p^2 + 3}{2p^3 + 3p} = \dfrac{3\big(2p^2 + 1\big)}{p\big(2p^2 + 3\big)}$

11. $f'(t) = t\Big(\dfrac{1}{t}\Big) + (\ln t)(1) = 1 + \ln t$

13. $\dfrac{dy}{dx} = x^2\Big[\dfrac{1}{4x + 3}(4)\Big] + [\ln(4x + 3)](2x)$

    $= \dfrac{4x^2}{4x + 3} + 2x\ln(4x + 3)$

15. $y = \log_3(2x - 1) = \dfrac{\ln(2x - 1)}{\ln 3}$

    $\dfrac{dy}{dx} = \dfrac{1}{\ln 3}\cdot\dfrac{d}{dx}[\ln(2x - 1)]$

    $= \dfrac{1}{\ln 3}\cdot\dfrac{1}{2x - 1}(2) = \dfrac{2}{(2x - 1)(\ln 3)}$

17. $y = x^2 + \log_2\big(x^2 + 4\big) = x^2 + \dfrac{\ln\big(x^2 + 4\big)}{\ln 2}$

    $\dfrac{dy}{dx} = 2x + \dfrac{1}{\ln 2}\Big[\dfrac{1}{x^2 + 4}(2x)\Big]$

    $= 2x\Bigg[1 + \dfrac{1}{(\ln 2)\big(x^2 + 4\big)}\Bigg]$

19. $f'(z) = \dfrac{z\big(\frac{1}{z}\big) - (\ln z)(1)}{z^2} = \dfrac{1 - \ln z}{z^2}$

21. $\dfrac{dy}{dx} = \dfrac{(\ln x)(2x) - \big(x^2 - 1\big)\big(\frac{1}{x}\big)}{\ln^2 x}$

    $= \dfrac{2x^2\ln(x) - x^2 + 1}{x\ln^2 x}$

23. $y = \ln\big(x^2 + 4x + 5\big)^3 = 3\ln\big(x^2 + 4x + 5\big)$

    $\dfrac{dy}{dx} = 3\cdot\dfrac{1}{x^2 + 4x + 5}(2x + 4)$

    $= \dfrac{3(2x + 4)}{x^2 + 4x + 5} = \dfrac{6(x + 2)}{x^2 + 4x + 5}$

25. $y = \ln\sqrt{1 + x^2} = \dfrac{1}{2}\ln\big(1 + x^2\big)$

    $\dfrac{dy}{dx} = \dfrac{1}{2}\cdot\dfrac{1}{1 + x^2}(2x) = \dfrac{x}{1 + x^2}$

27. $f(l) = \ln\left(\dfrac{1+l}{1-l}\right) = \ln(1+l) - \ln(1-l)$

$f'(l) = \dfrac{1}{1+l} - \dfrac{1}{1-l}(-1)$

$= \dfrac{(1-l)+(1+l)}{(1+l)(1-l)} = \dfrac{2}{1-l^2}$

29. $y = \ln\sqrt[4]{\dfrac{1+x^2}{1-x^2}} = \dfrac{1}{4}\left[\ln\left(1+x^2\right) - \ln\left(1-x^2\right)\right]$

$\dfrac{dy}{dx} = \dfrac{1}{4}\left[\dfrac{2x}{1+x^2} - \dfrac{-2x}{1-x^2}\right]$

$= \dfrac{1}{4}\left[\dfrac{2x\left(1-x^2\right)+2x\left(1+x^2\right)}{\left(1+x^2\right)\left(1-x^2\right)}\right] = \dfrac{x}{1-x^4}$

31. $y = \ln\left[\left(x^2+2\right)^2\left(x^3+x-1\right)\right]$

$= 2\ln\left(x^2+2\right) + \ln\left(x^3+x-1\right)$

$\dfrac{dy}{dx} = 2 \cdot \dfrac{1}{x^2+2}(2x) + \dfrac{1}{x^3+x-1}\left(3x^2+1\right)$

$= \dfrac{4x}{x^2+2} + \dfrac{3x^2+1}{x^3+x-1}$

33. $y = \ln\left(x\sqrt{2x+1}\right) = \ln x + \ln(2x+1)^{\frac{1}{2}}$

$= \ln x + \dfrac{1}{2}\ln(2x+1)$

$\dfrac{dy}{dx} = \dfrac{1}{x} + \dfrac{1}{2} \cdot \dfrac{1}{2x+1}(2) = \dfrac{1}{x} + \dfrac{1}{2x+1}$

$= \dfrac{3x+1}{x(2x+1)}$

35. $\dfrac{dy}{dx} = \left(x^2+1\right)\left[\dfrac{1}{2x+1}(2)\right] + \ln(2x+1) \cdot [2x]$

$= \dfrac{2\left(x^2+1\right)}{2x+1} + 2x\ln(2x+1)$

37. $y = \ln x^3 + \ln^3 x = 3\ln x + (\ln x)^3$

$\dfrac{dy}{dx} = 3 \cdot \dfrac{1}{x} + 3(\ln x)^2 \cdot \dfrac{1}{x} = \dfrac{3}{x} + \dfrac{3(\ln x)^2}{x}$

$= \dfrac{3\left(1+\ln^2 x\right)}{x}$

39. $y = \ln^4(ax) = [\ln(ax)]^4$

$\dfrac{dy}{dx} = 4[\ln(ax)]^3\left(\dfrac{1}{ax} \cdot a\right) = \dfrac{4\ln^3(ax)}{x}$

41. $y = x\ln\sqrt{x-1} = \dfrac{1}{2}x\ln(x-1)$

By the product rule,

$\dfrac{dy}{dx} = \dfrac{1}{2}\left[x\left(\dfrac{1}{x-1}\right) + \ln(x-1) \cdot [1]\right]$

$= \dfrac{x}{2(x-1)} + \ln\sqrt{x-1}$

43. $y = \sqrt{4+\ln x} = (4+\ln x)^{\frac{1}{2}}$

$\dfrac{dy}{dx} = \dfrac{1}{2}(4+\ln x)^{-\frac{1}{2}} \cdot \dfrac{1}{x} = \dfrac{1}{2x\sqrt{4+\ln x}}$

45. $y = \ln\left(x^2-2x-2\right)$

$y' = \dfrac{2x-2}{x^2-2x-2}$

The slope of the tangent line at $x = 3$ is

$y'(3) = \dfrac{6-2}{9-6-2} = 4$. Also, if $x = 3$, then

$y = \ln(9-6-2) = \ln 1 = 0$. Thus an equation of the tangent line is $y - 0 = 4(x-3)$, or

$y = 4x - 12$.

47. $y = \dfrac{x}{\ln x}$

$y' = \dfrac{(\ln x)(1) - x\left(\frac{1}{x}\right)}{\ln^2 x} = \dfrac{\ln x - 1}{\ln^2 x}$

When $x = 2$ the slope is $y'(2) = \dfrac{(\ln 2)-1}{\ln^2 2}$.

49. $c = 25\ln(q+1) + 12$

$\dfrac{dc}{dq} = \dfrac{25}{q+1}$, so $\left.\dfrac{dc}{dq}\right|_{q=6} = \dfrac{25}{7}$.

51. $\dfrac{dq}{dp} = \dfrac{d}{dp}[25 + 10\ln(2p+1)]$

$= 0 + 10\dfrac{d}{dp}[\ln(2p+1)]$

$= 10\left(\dfrac{1}{2p+1}\right)\dfrac{d}{dp}[2p+1]$

$= \dfrac{10}{2p+1}(2) = \dfrac{20}{2p+1}$

53. $A = 6\ln\left(\dfrac{T}{a-T} - a\right)$. Rate of change of A
with respect to T:

$$\frac{dA}{dT} = 6 \cdot \frac{1}{\frac{T}{a-T} - a}\left[\frac{(a-T)(1) - T(-1)}{(a-T)^2}\right]$$

$$= 6 \cdot \frac{1}{\frac{T - a(a-T)}{a-T}}\left[\frac{a}{(a-T)^2}\right]$$

$$= 6 \cdot \frac{a - T}{T - a^2 + aT} \cdot \frac{a}{(a-T)^2}$$

$$= \frac{6a}{\left(T - a^2 + aT\right)(a - T)}$$

55. $\dfrac{d}{dx}\left(\log_b u\right) = \dfrac{d}{dx}\left(\dfrac{\ln u}{\ln b}\right)$

$$= \frac{1}{\ln b} \cdot \frac{d}{dx}(\ln u) = \frac{1}{\ln b}\left(\frac{1}{u} \cdot \frac{du}{dx}\right)$$

$$= \left(\log_b e\right)\left(\frac{1}{u} \cdot \frac{du}{dx}\right) = \frac{1}{u}\left(\log_b e\right)\frac{du}{dx}$$

57. $f'(x) = \dfrac{1 - \ln 2x}{x^2}$
$f'(x) = 0$ for $x \approx 1.36$

Principles in Practice 13.2

1. The rate of change of temperature with
respect to time is $\dfrac{dT}{dt}$. $T(t)$ has the form Ce^u
where C is a constant and $u = kt$.

$$\frac{dT}{dt} = \frac{d}{dt}\left[Ce^{kt}\right] = C\frac{d}{dt}\left[e^{kt}\right]$$

$$= C\left(e^{kt}\right)\frac{d}{dt}[kt] = Ce^{kt}(k) = Cke^{kt}$$

Exercise 13.2

1. $y' = 7 \cdot \dfrac{d}{dx}\left(e^x\right) = 7e^x$

3. $y' = e^{x^2+1}(2x) = 2xe^{x^2+1}$

5. $y' = e^{3-5x} \cdot \dfrac{d}{dx}\left(e^{3-5x}\right) = e^{3-5x}(-5)$
$= -5e^{3-5x}$

7. $f'(r) = e^{3r^2+4r+4}(6r+4)$
$= 2(3r+2)e^{3r^2+4r+4}$

9. By the product rule,
$y' = x\left(e^x\right) + e^x(1) = e^x(x+1)$

11. $y' = x^2\left[e^{-x^2}(-2x)\right] + e^{-x^2}[2x]$
$= 2xe^{-x^2}\left(1 - x^2\right)$

13. $y = \dfrac{1}{2}\left(e^x + e^{-x}\right)$
$y' = \dfrac{1}{2}\left[e^x + e^{-x}(-1)\right] = \dfrac{e^x - e^{-x}}{2}$

15. $\dfrac{d}{dx}\left(4^{3x^2}\right) = \dfrac{d}{dx}\left[e^{(\ln 4)3x^2}\right]$
$= e^{(\ln 4)3x^2}[(\ln 4)(6x)]$
$= (6x)4^{3x^2}\ln 4$

17. $f'(w) = \dfrac{w^2\left[e^{2w}(2)\right] - e^{2w}[2w]}{w^4}$
$= \dfrac{2e^{2w}(w-1)}{w^3}$

19. $y' = e^{1+\sqrt{x}}\left(\dfrac{1}{2}x^{-\frac{1}{2}}\right) = \dfrac{e^{1+\sqrt{x}}}{2\sqrt{x}}$

21. $y = x^3 - 3^x = x^3 - e^{(\ln 3)x}$
$y' = 3x^2 - e^{(\ln 3)x}(\ln 3) = 3x^2 - 3^x\ln 3$

23. $\dfrac{dy}{dx} = \dfrac{\left(e^x + 1\right)\left[e^x\right] - \left(e^x - 1\right)\left[e^x\right]}{\left(e^x + 1\right)^2}$
$= \dfrac{2e^x}{\left(e^x + 1\right)^2}$

25. $y = e^{\ln x} = x$ (by the property $e^{\ln a} = a$).
Thus $y' = 1$.

27. $y' = e^{x \ln x}\left[x \cdot \dfrac{1}{x} + (\ln x)(1)\right] = (1 + \ln x)e^{x \ln x}$

29. $f(x) = ee^x e^{x^2} = e^{1+x+x^2}$

$f'(x) = e^{1+x+x^2}(1+2x) = (1+2x)e^{1+x+x^2}$

$f'(-1) = [1 + 2(-1)]e^{1+(-1)+(-1)^2} = -e$

31. $y = e^x$, $y' = e^x$. When $x = 2$, then $y = e^2$
and $y' = e^2$. Thus an equation of the tangent
line is $y - e^2 = e^2(x-2)$, or $y = e^2 x - e^2$

33. $\dfrac{dp}{dq} = 15e^{-0.001q}(-0.001) = -0.015e^{-0.001q}$

$\left.\dfrac{dp}{dq}\right|_{q=500} = -0.015e^{-0.5}$

35. $\bar{c} = \dfrac{7000e^{\frac{q}{700}}}{q}$, so $c = \bar{c}q = 7000e^{\frac{q}{700}}$. The
marginal cost function is

$\dfrac{dc}{dq} = 7000e^{\frac{q}{700}}\left(\dfrac{1}{700}\right) = 10e^{\frac{q}{700}}$. Thus

$\left.\dfrac{dc}{dq}\right|_{q=350} = 10e^{0.5}$ and $\left.\dfrac{dc}{dq}\right|_{q=700} = 10e$.

37. $w = e^{x^3 - 4x} + x\ln(x-1)$ and $x = \dfrac{t+1}{t-1}$

By the chain rule, $\dfrac{dw}{dt} = \dfrac{dw}{dx} \cdot \dfrac{dx}{dt}$

$= \left[e^{x^3-4x}\left(3x^2 - 4\right) + x\left(\dfrac{1}{x-1}\right) + [\ln(x-1)(1)]\right]$

$\quad \cdot \left[\dfrac{(t-1)(1) - (t+1)(1)}{(t-1)^2}\right]$

$= \left[\left(3x^2 - 4\right)e^{x^3-4x} + \dfrac{x}{x-1} + \ln(x-1)\right]\left[\dfrac{-2}{(t-1)^2}\right]$.

When $t = 3$, then $x = \dfrac{3+1}{3-1} = \dfrac{4}{2} = 2$ and

$\dfrac{dw}{dt} = [8 + 2 + 0]\left[-\dfrac{1}{2}\right] = -5$.

39. $\dfrac{d}{dx}\left(c^x - x^c\right) = \dfrac{d}{dx}\left[\left(e^{\ln c}\right)^x - x^c\right]$

$= \dfrac{d}{dx}\left[e^{(\ln c)x} - x^c\right]$

$= (\ln c)e^{(\ln c)x} - cx^{c-1} = (\ln c)c^x - cx^{c-1}$

When $x = 1$, this derivative is 0. Thus
$(\ln c)c - c = 0$, or $c[\ln(c) - 1] = 0$. Since
$c > 0$, we must have $\ln(c) - 1 = 0$, $\ln c = 1$,
or $c = e$.

41. $q = 500\left(1 - e^{-0.2t}\right)$

$\dfrac{dq}{dt} = 500\left(-e^{-0.2t}\right)(-0.2) = 100e^{-0.2t}$

Thus $\left.\dfrac{dq}{dt}\right|_{t=10} = 100e^{-2}$

43. $P = 20,000e^{0.03t}$

$\dfrac{dP}{dt} = 20,000e^{0.03t}(0.03) = P(0.03)$

$= 0.03P = kP$ for $k = 0.03$.

45. Since $S = Pe^{rt}$, then $\dfrac{dS}{dt} = Pe^{rt}r = rPe^{rt}$.

Thus $\dfrac{\frac{dS}{dt}}{S} = \dfrac{rPe^{rt}}{Pe^{rt}} = r$.

47. $N = 10^A 10^{-bM} = 10^{A-bM} = e^{(\ln 10)(A-bM)}$

$\dfrac{dN}{dM} = e^{(\ln 10)(A-bM)}(\ln 10)(-b)$, so

$\dfrac{dN}{dM} = 10^{A-bM}(\ln 10)(-b)$

$= -b\left(10^{A-bM}\right)\ln 10$

49. $C(t) = C_0 e^{-\left(\frac{r}{V}\right)t}$

$\dfrac{dC}{dt} = C_0 e^{-\left(\frac{r}{V}\right)t}\left(-\dfrac{r}{V}\right)$

$= [C(t)]\left(-\dfrac{r}{V}\right) = -\left(\dfrac{r}{V}\right)C(t)$

51. $f(t) = 1 - e^{-0.008t}$

$f'(t) = 0.008e^{-0.008t}$

$f'(100) = 0.008e^{-0.8} \approx 0.0036$

53. $f'(x) = \left(4x^3 + 4x - 4\right)e^{x^4 + 2x^2 - 4x}$

$f'(x) = 0$ for $x \approx 0.68$

Principles in Practice 13.3

1. Assume that P is a function of t and differentiate both sides of $\ln\left(\frac{P}{1-P}\right) = 0.5t$ with respect to t.

$$\frac{d}{dt}\left[\ln\left(\frac{P}{1-P}\right)\right] = \frac{d}{dt}[0.5t]$$

$$\left(\frac{1}{\frac{P}{1-P}}\right)\frac{d}{dt}\left[\frac{P}{1-P}\right] = 0.5$$

$$\frac{1-P}{P} \cdot \frac{(1)(1-P) - P(-1)}{(1-P)^2} \cdot \frac{dP}{dt} = 0.5$$

$$\frac{1-P+P}{P(1-P)} \cdot \frac{dP}{dt} = 0.5$$

$$\frac{dP}{dt} = 0.5P(1-P)$$

2. $\dfrac{dV}{dt} = \dfrac{d}{dt}\left[\dfrac{4}{3}\pi r^3\right] = \dfrac{4}{3}\pi\left(3r^2\right)\dfrac{dr}{dt} = 4\pi r^2 \dfrac{dr}{dt}$

When $\dfrac{dr}{dt} = 5$ and $r = 12$,

$\dfrac{dV}{dt} = 4\pi(12)^2(5) = 2880\pi$. The balloon is increasing at the rate of 2880π cubic inches/minute.

3. The hypotenuse is the length of the ladder, so $x^2 + y^2 = 100$. Differentiate both sides of the equation with respect to t.

$$\frac{d}{dt}\left[x^2 + y^2\right] = \frac{d}{dt}[100]$$

$$2x\frac{dx}{dt} + 2y\frac{dy}{dt} = 0$$

When $y = 8$, we can find x by using the Pythagorean theorem.

$x^2 + 8^2 = 100$

$x^2 = 100 - 64 = 36$

$x = 6$

When $x = 6$, $y = 8$, and $\dfrac{dx}{dt} = 3$, we have

$$2(6)(3) + 2(8)\frac{dy}{dt} = 0$$

$$36 + 16\frac{dy}{dt} = 0$$

$$\frac{dy}{dt} = -\frac{36}{16} = -\frac{9}{4}$$

$\dfrac{dy}{dt} = -\dfrac{9}{4}$, thus the top of the ladder is sliding down the wall at the rate of $\dfrac{9}{4}$ feet/sec.

Exercise 13.3

1. $2x + 8yy' = 0$

$x + 4yy' = 0$

$4yy' = -x$

$y' = -\dfrac{x}{4y}$

3. $12y^3 y' - 5 = 0$

$y' = \dfrac{5}{12y^3}$

5. $\dfrac{1}{2}x^{-\frac{1}{2}} + \dfrac{1}{2}y^{-\frac{1}{2}}y' = 0$

$x^{-\frac{1}{2}} + y^{-\frac{1}{2}}y' = 0$

$y^{-\frac{1}{2}}y' = -x^{-\frac{1}{2}}$

$y' = -\dfrac{x^{-\frac{1}{2}}}{y^{-\frac{1}{2}}} = -\dfrac{y^{\frac{1}{2}}}{x^{\frac{1}{2}}} = -\dfrac{\sqrt{y}}{\sqrt{x}} = -\sqrt{\dfrac{y}{x}}$

7. $\left(\dfrac{3}{4}\right)x^{-\frac{1}{4}} + \left(\dfrac{3}{4}\right)y^{-\frac{1}{4}}y' = 0$

$y' = -\dfrac{y^{\frac{1}{4}}}{x^{\frac{1}{4}}} = -\left(\dfrac{y}{x}\right)^{\frac{1}{4}}$

9. By the product rule $xy' + y(1) = 0$, $xy' = -y$,

$y' = -\dfrac{y}{x}$

11. $xy' + y(1) - y' - 4 = 0$

$y'(x - 1) = 4 - y$

$y' = \dfrac{4 - y}{x - 1}$

13. $3x^2 + 3y^2 y' - 12(xy' + y) = 0$

$3y^2 y' - 12xy' = 12y - 3x^2$

$y'\left(3y^2 - 12x\right) = 12y - 3x^2$

$y'\left(y^2 - 4x\right) = 4y - x^2$

$y' = \dfrac{4y - x^2}{y^2 - 4x}$

15. $1 = \dfrac{1}{2} y^{-\frac{1}{2}} y' + \dfrac{1}{3} y^{-\frac{2}{3}} y'$

$6 = y'\left(\dfrac{3}{y^{\frac{1}{2}}} + \dfrac{2}{y^{\frac{2}{3}}}\right)$

$6 = y'\left(\dfrac{3y^{\frac{1}{6}} + 2}{y^{\frac{2}{3}}}\right)$

$y' = \dfrac{6y^{\frac{2}{3}}}{3y^{\frac{1}{6}} + 2}$

17. $3x^2\left(3y^2 y'\right) + y^3(6x) - 1 + y' = 0$

$9x^2 y^2 y' + y' = 1 - 6xy^3$

$y'\left(9x^2 y^2 + 1\right) = 1 - 6xy^3$

$y' = \dfrac{1 - 6xy^3}{1 + 9x^2 y^2}$

19. $y\left(\dfrac{1}{x}\right) + (\ln x)y' = x\left(e^y y'\right) + e^y(1)$

$\left[\ln(x) - xe^y\right]y' = e^y - \dfrac{y}{x}$

$\left[\ln(x) - xe^y\right]y' = \dfrac{xe^y - y}{x}$

$y' = \dfrac{xe^y - y}{x\left[\ln(x) - xe^y\right]}$

21. $\left[x\left(e^y y'\right) + e^y(1)\right] + y' = 0$

$xe^y y' + e^y + y' = 0$

$\left(xe^y + 1\right)y' = -e^y$

$y' = -\dfrac{e^y}{xe^y + 1}$

23. $2\left(1 + e^{3x}\right)\left(3e^{3x}\right) = \dfrac{1}{x+y}(1 + y')$

$6e^{3x}\left(1 + e^{3x}\right)(x + y) = 1 + y'$

$y' = 6e^{3x}\left(1 + e^{3x}\right)(x + y) - 1$

25. $1 + [xy' + y(1)] + 2yy' = 0$

$xy' + 2yy' = -1 - y$

$(x + 2y)y' = -(1 + y)$

$y' = -\dfrac{1 + y}{x + 2y}$

At the point (1, 2), $y' = -\dfrac{1 + 2}{1 + 4} = -\dfrac{3}{5}$

27. $8x + 18yy' = 0$

$y' = -\dfrac{8x}{18y} = -\dfrac{4x}{9y}$

Thus at $\left(0, \dfrac{1}{3}\right)$, $y' = 0$; at $\left(x_0, y_0\right)$,

$y' = -\dfrac{4x_0}{9y_0}$.

29. $3x^2 + 2yy' = 0$

$y' = -\dfrac{3x^2}{2y}$

At (−1, 2), $y' = -\dfrac{3}{4}$. The tangent is given by

$y - 2 = -\dfrac{3}{4}(x + 1)$, or $y = -\dfrac{3}{4}x + \dfrac{5}{4}$.

31. $p = 100 - q^2$

$\dfrac{d}{dp}(p) = \dfrac{d}{dp}\left(100 - q^2\right)$

$1 = -2q \cdot \dfrac{dq}{dp}$

$\dfrac{dq}{dp} = -\dfrac{1}{2q}$

33. $p = \dfrac{20}{(q + 5)^2}$

$\dfrac{d}{dp}(p) = \dfrac{d}{dp}\left[\dfrac{20}{(q + 5)^2}\right]$

$\dfrac{d}{dp}(p) = \dfrac{d}{dp}\left[20(q + 5)^{-2}\right]$

$$1 = -\frac{40}{(q+5)^3} \cdot \frac{dq}{dp}$$

$$\frac{dq}{dp} = -\frac{(q+5)^3}{40}$$

35. $\ln\frac{I}{I_0} = -\lambda t$

$\ln I - \ln I_0 = -\lambda t$

$\frac{1}{I}\frac{dI}{dt} = -\lambda$

$\frac{dI}{dt} = -\lambda I$

37. $1.5M = \log\left(\frac{E}{2.5 \times 10^{11}}\right)$

$1.5M = \log E - \log\left(2.5 \times 10^{11}\right)$

$\frac{d}{dM}(1.5M) = \frac{d}{dM}\left[\log E - \log\left(2.5 \times 10^{11}\right)\right]$

$\frac{d}{dM}(1.5M) = \frac{d}{dM}\left[\frac{\ln E}{\ln 10} - \log\left(2.5 \times 10^{11}\right)\right]$

$1.5 = \frac{1}{\ln 10}\left(\frac{1}{E} \cdot \frac{dE}{dM}\right)$

$\frac{dE}{dM} = 1.5E\ln 10$

39. $TV^{0.4} = 1500$. Differentiating implicitly with respect to T:

$T\left(0.4V^{-0.6}\frac{dV}{dT}\right) + V^{0.4}(1) = 0$,

$0.4TV^{-0.6}\frac{dV}{dT} = -V^{0.4}$,

$\frac{dV}{dT} = -\frac{V^{0.4}}{0.4TV^{-0.6}} = -\frac{V}{0.4T} = -2.5\frac{V}{T}$.

41. $S^2 + \frac{1}{4}I^2 = SI + I$. Differentiating implicitly with respect to I:

$2S\frac{dS}{dI} + \frac{1}{2}I = \left[S(1) + I\frac{dS}{dI}\right] + 1$,

$2S\frac{dS}{dI} - I\frac{dS}{dI} = S + 1 - \frac{I}{2}$,

$(2S - I)\frac{dS}{dI} = \frac{2S + 2 - I}{2}$, $\frac{dS}{dI} = \frac{2S + 2 - I}{2(2S - I)}$.

Marginal propensity to consume

$= \frac{dC}{dI} = 1 - \frac{dS}{dI}$. Thus $\frac{dC}{dI} = 1 - \frac{2S + 2 - I}{2(2S - I)}$.

When $I = 16$ and $S = 12$,

$\frac{dC}{dI} = 1 - \frac{24 + 2 - 16}{2(24 - 16)} = 1 - \frac{10}{16} = \frac{6}{16} = \frac{3}{8}$.

Exercise 13.4

1. $y = (x+1)^2(x-1)\left(x^2 + 3\right)$. Taking natural logarithms of both sides gives

$\ln y = \ln\left[(x+1)^2(x-1)\left(x^2 + 3\right)\right]$.

Using properties of logarithms on the right side gives

$\ln y = 2\ln(x+1) + \ln(x-1) + \ln\left(x^2 + 3\right)$.

Differentiating both sides with respect to x,

$\frac{y'}{y} = \frac{2}{x+1} + \frac{1}{x-1} + \frac{2x}{x^2 + 3}$.

Solving for y',

$y' = y\left[\frac{2}{x+1} + \frac{1}{x-1} + \frac{2x}{x^2 + 3}\right]$.

Expressing y in terms of x,

$y' = (x+1)^2(x-1)\left(x^2 + 3\right)\left[\frac{2}{x+1} + \frac{1}{x-1} + \frac{2x}{x^2 + 3}\right]$

3. $\ln y = \ln\left[\left(3x^3 - 1\right)^2 (2x+5)^3\right]$

$= 2\ln\left(3x^3 - 1\right) + 3\ln(2x+5)$

$\dfrac{y'}{y} = 2 \cdot \dfrac{9x^2}{3x^3 - 1} + 3 \cdot \dfrac{2}{2x+5}$

$y' = y\left[\dfrac{18x^2}{3x^3 - 1} + \dfrac{6}{2x+5}\right]$

$y' = \left(3x^3 - 1\right)^2 (2x+5)^3\left[\dfrac{18x^2}{3x^3 - 1} + \dfrac{6}{2x+5}\right]$

5. $y = \sqrt{x+1}\sqrt{x^2 - 2}\sqrt{x+4}$

$\ln y = \ln\left(\sqrt{x+1}\sqrt{x^2 - 2}\sqrt{x+4}\right)$

$\ln y = \dfrac{1}{2}\ln(x+1) + \dfrac{1}{2}\ln\left(x^2 - 2\right) + \dfrac{1}{2}\ln(x+4)$

$\dfrac{y'}{y} = \dfrac{1}{2}\left[\dfrac{1}{x+1} + \dfrac{2x}{x^2 - 2} + \dfrac{1}{x+4}\right]$

$y' = \dfrac{y}{2}\left[\dfrac{1}{x+1} + \dfrac{2x}{x^2 - 2} + \dfrac{1}{x+4}\right]$

$= \dfrac{\sqrt{x+1}\sqrt{x^2 - 2}\sqrt{x+4}}{2}$

$\cdot \left[\dfrac{1}{x+1} + \dfrac{2x}{x^2 - 2} + \dfrac{1}{x+4}\right]$

7. $\ln y = \ln\dfrac{\sqrt{1-x^2}}{1-2x} = \dfrac{1}{2}\ln\left(1-x^2\right) - \ln(1-2x)$

$\dfrac{y'}{y} = \dfrac{1}{2} \cdot \dfrac{-2x}{1-x^2} - \dfrac{-2}{1-2x}$

$y' = y\left[-\dfrac{x}{1-x^2} + \dfrac{2}{1-2x}\right]$

$y' = \dfrac{\sqrt{1-x^2}}{1-2x}\left[\dfrac{x}{x^2 - 1} + \dfrac{2}{1-2x}\right]$

9. $y = \dfrac{\left(2x^2 + 2\right)^2}{(x+1)^2(3x+2)}$

$\ln y = \ln\left[\dfrac{\left(2x^2 + 2\right)^2}{(x+1)^2(3x+2)}\right]$

$= 2\ln\left(2x^2 + 2\right) - 2\ln(x+1) - \ln(3x+2)$

$\dfrac{y'}{y} = 2 \cdot \dfrac{4x}{2x^2 + 2} - 2 \cdot \dfrac{1}{x+1} - \dfrac{3}{3x+2}$

$y' = y\left[\dfrac{8x}{2x^2 + 2} - \dfrac{2}{x+1} - \dfrac{3}{3x+2}\right]$

$= \dfrac{\left(2x^2 + 2\right)^2}{(x+1)^2(3x+2)}\left[\dfrac{4x}{x^2 + 1} - \dfrac{2}{x+1} - \dfrac{3}{3x+2}\right]$

11. $\ln y = \ln\sqrt{\dfrac{(x-1)(x+1)}{3x-4}}$

$= \dfrac{1}{2}[\ln(x-1) + \ln(x+1) - \ln(3x-4)]$

$\dfrac{y'}{y} = \dfrac{1}{2}\left[\dfrac{1}{x-1} + \dfrac{1}{x+1} - \dfrac{3}{3x-4}\right]$

$y' = \dfrac{y}{2}\left[\dfrac{1}{x-1} + \dfrac{1}{x+1} - \dfrac{3}{3x-4}\right]$

y'

$= \dfrac{1}{2}\sqrt{\dfrac{(x-1)(x+1)}{3x-4}}\left[\dfrac{1}{x-1} + \dfrac{1}{x+1} - \dfrac{3}{3x-4}\right]$

13. $y = x^{2x+1}$. Thus

$\ln y = \ln x^{2x+1} = (2x+1)\ln x$.

$\dfrac{y'}{y} = (2x+1)\dfrac{1}{x} + (\ln x)(2)$

$y' = y\left[\dfrac{2x+1}{x} + 2\ln x\right]$

$y' = x^{2x+1}\left[\dfrac{2x+1}{x} + 2\ln x\right]$

15. $y = x^{\frac{1}{x}}$. Thus $\ln y = \dfrac{1}{x}\ln x = \dfrac{\ln x}{x}$.

$\dfrac{y'}{y} = \dfrac{x\left(\frac{1}{x}\right) - (\ln x)(1)}{x^2}$

$y' = y\left[\dfrac{1-\ln x}{x^2}\right]$

$y' = \dfrac{x^{\frac{1}{x}}(1-\ln x)}{x^2}$

17. $y = (3x+1)^{2x}$. Thus

$\ln y = \ln\left[(3x+1)^{2x}\right] = 2x\ln(3x+1)$

$\dfrac{y'}{y} = 2\left\{x\left(\dfrac{3}{3x+1}\right) + [\ln(3x+1)](1)\right\}$

$y' = 2y\left[\dfrac{3x}{3x+1} + \ln(3x+1)\right]$

$= 2(3x+1)^{2x}\left[\dfrac{3x}{3x+1} + \ln(3x+1)\right]$

19. $y = e^x x^{3x}$. Thus

$\ln y = \ln\left(e^x x^{3x}\right) = \ln e^x + \ln x^{3x}$

$= x + 3x\ln x$

$\dfrac{y'}{y} = 1 + 3\left[x\left(\dfrac{1}{x}\right) + (\ln x)(1)\right]$

$y' = y(4 + 3\ln x)$

$y' = e^x x^{3x}(4 + 3\ln x)$

21. $y = (4x-3)^{2x+1}$

$\ln y = \ln(4x-3)^{2x+1} = (2x+1)\ln(4x-3)$

$\dfrac{y'}{y} = (2x+1)\left[\dfrac{4}{4x-3}\right] + [\ln(4x-3)](2)$

$y' = y\left[\dfrac{4(2x+1)}{4x-3} + 2\ln(4x-3)\right]$

When $x = 1$, then $\dfrac{dy}{dx} = 1\left[\dfrac{12}{1} + 2\ln(1)\right] = 12$.

23. $y = (x+1)(x+2)^2(x+3)^2$

$\ln y = \ln(x+1) + 2\ln(x+2) + 2\ln(x+3)$

$\dfrac{y'}{y} = \dfrac{1}{x+1} + \dfrac{2}{x+2} + \dfrac{2}{x+3}$

$y' = y\left[\dfrac{1}{x+1} + \dfrac{2}{x+2} + \dfrac{2}{x+3}\right]$

When $x = 0$, then $y = 36$ and $y' = 96$. Thus
an equation of the tangent line is
$y - 36 = 96(x - 0)$, or $y = 96x + 36$.

25. $y = 3e^x\left(x^2 - x + 1\right)^x$

$\ln y = \ln 3 + \ln e^x + \ln\left(x^2 - x + 1\right)^x$

$= \ln(3) + x + x\ln\left(x^2 - x + 1\right)$

$\dfrac{y'}{y}$

$= 1 + \left[x\left(\dfrac{2x-1}{x^2 - x + 1}\right)\right] + \left[\ln\left(x^2 - x + 1\right)(1)\right]$

$y' = y\left[1 + \dfrac{x(2x-1)}{x^2 - x + 1} + \ln\left(x^2 - x + 1\right)\right]$

When $x = 1$, then $y = 3e$ and
$y' = 3e[1 + 1 + \ln(1)] = 6e$. Thus an equation
of the tangent line is $y - 3e = 6e(x - 1)$, or
$y = 6ex - 3e$.

27. $y = (3x)^{-2x}$

$\ln y = -2x\ln(3x)$

$\dfrac{y'}{y} = -2\left\{x\left[\dfrac{1}{3x}(3)\right] + [\ln(3x)](1)\right\}$

$= -2[1 + \ln(3x)]$

$\dfrac{y'}{y} \cdot 100$ gives the percentage rate of change.

Thus $-2[1 + \ln(3x)](100) = 60$

$1 + \ln(3x) = -0.3$

$\ln(3x) = -1.3$

$3x = e^{-1.3}$

$x = \dfrac{1}{3e^{1.3}}$

Principles in Practice 13.5

1. $\dfrac{dh}{dt} = 0 - 16(2t) = -32t$ ft/sec

$\dfrac{d^2h}{dt^2} = \dfrac{d}{dt}[-32t] = -32$ feet/sec^2

The acceleration of the rock at time t is
-32 feet/sec^2 or 32 feet/sec^2 downward.

2. The rate of change of the marginal cost
function with respect to x is $c''(q)$.

$c'(q) = 14q + 11$

$c'' = 14$

When $x = 3$, the rate of change of the
marginal cost function is 14 dollars/unit^2.

Exercise 13.5

1. $y' = 12x^2 - 24x + 6$

$y'' = 24x - 24$

$y''' = 24$

3. $\dfrac{dy}{dx} = -1$

$\dfrac{d^2 y}{dx^2} = 0$

5. $y' = 3x^2 + e^x$

$y'' = 6x + e^x$

$y''' = 6 + e^x$

$y^{(4)} = e^x$

7. $f(x) = x^2 \ln x$

$f'(x) = x^2 \left(\dfrac{1}{x}\right) + (\ln x)(2x) = x(1 + 2\ln x)$

$f''(x) = x\left(\dfrac{2}{x}\right) + (1 + 2\ln x)(1) = 3 + 2\ln x$

9. $f(p) = \dfrac{1}{6p^3} = \dfrac{1}{6} p^{-3}$

$f'(p) = -\dfrac{1}{2} p^{-4}$

$f''(p) = 2p^{-5}$

$f'''(p) = -10 p^{-6} = -\dfrac{10}{p^6}$

11. $f(r) = \sqrt{1 - r} = (1 - r)^{\frac{1}{2}}$

$f'(r) = -\dfrac{1}{2}(1 - r)^{-\frac{1}{2}}$

$f''(r) = -\dfrac{1}{4}(1 - r)^{-\frac{3}{2}} = -\dfrac{1}{4(1 - r)^{\frac{3}{2}}}$

13. $y = \dfrac{1}{5x - 6} = (5x - 6)^{-1}$

$\dfrac{dy}{dx} = (-1)(5x - 6)^{-2}(5) = -5(5x - 6)^{-2}$

$\dfrac{d^2 y}{dx^2} = -5(-2)(5x - 6)^{-3}(5)$

$= 50(5x - 6)^{-3} = \dfrac{50}{(5x - 6)^3}$

15. $y = \dfrac{x + 1}{x - 1}$

$y' = \dfrac{(x - 1)(1) - (x + 1)(1)}{(x - 1)^2}$

$= -\dfrac{2}{(x - 1)^2} = -2(x - 1)^{-2}$

$y'' = 4(x - 1)^{-3} = \dfrac{4}{(x - 1)^3}$

17. $y = \ln[x(x + 1)] = \ln(x) + \ln(x + 1)$

$y' = \dfrac{1}{x} + \dfrac{1}{x + 1} = x^{-1} + (x + 1)^{-1}$

$y'' = -x^{-2} + (-1)(x + 1)^{-2}$

$= -\left[\dfrac{1}{x^2} + \dfrac{1}{(x + 1)^2}\right]$

19. $f(z) = z^2 e^z$

$f'(z) = z^2\left(e^z\right) + e^z(2z) = \left(ze^z\right)(z + 2)$

$f''(z) = \left(ze^z\right)(1) + (z + 2)\left[ze^z + e^z(1)\right]$

$= e^z\left(z^2 + 4z + 2\right)$

21. $y = e^{2x}$

$\dfrac{dy}{dx} = 2e^{2x}$

$\dfrac{d^2 y}{dx^2} = 4e^{2x}$

$\dfrac{d^3 y}{dx^3} = 8e^{2x}$

$\dfrac{d^4 y}{dx^4} = 16e^{2x}$

$\dfrac{d^5 y}{dx^5} = 32e^{2x}$

$\left.\dfrac{d^5 y}{dx^5}\right|_{x=0} = 32e^0 = 32$

23. $x^2 + 4y^2 - 16 = 0$

$2x + 8yy' = 0$

$8yy' = -2x$

$y' = -\dfrac{x}{4y}$

$$y'' = -\frac{4y(1) - x(4y')}{16y^2}$$

$$= -\frac{4y - 4x\left(-\frac{x}{4y}\right)}{16y^2} = -\frac{4y^2 + x^2}{16y^3}$$

$$= -\frac{16}{16y^3} = -\frac{1}{y^3}$$

25. $y^2 = 4x$

$$2yy' = 4$$

$$y' = \frac{2}{y} = 2y^{-1}$$

$$y'' = -2y^{-2}y' = -2y^{-2}\left(2y^{-1}\right) = -\frac{4}{y^3}$$

27. $\sqrt{x} + 4\sqrt{y} = 4$

$$x^{\frac{1}{2}} + 4y^{\frac{1}{2}} = 4$$

$$\frac{1}{2}x^{-\frac{1}{2}} + 2y^{-\frac{1}{2}}y' = 0$$

$$2y^{-\frac{1}{2}}y' = -\frac{1}{2}x^{-\frac{1}{2}}$$

$$y' = -\frac{1}{2} \cdot \frac{x^{-\frac{1}{2}}}{2y^{-\frac{1}{2}}} = -\frac{1}{4} \cdot \frac{y^{\frac{1}{2}}}{x^{\frac{1}{2}}}$$

$$y'' = -\frac{1}{4}\left[\frac{x^{\frac{1}{2}}\left(\frac{1}{2}y^{-\frac{1}{2}}y'\right) - y^{\frac{1}{2}}\left(\frac{1}{2}x^{-\frac{1}{2}}\right)}{x}\right]$$

$$= -\frac{1}{8}\left[\frac{x^{\frac{1}{2}}\left(-\frac{y^{\frac{1}{2}}}{4x^{\frac{1}{2}}}\right) - \frac{y^{\frac{1}{2}}}{x^{\frac{1}{2}}}}{x}\right] = -\frac{1}{8}\left[\frac{-\frac{1}{4} - \frac{y^{\frac{1}{2}}}{x^{\frac{1}{2}}}}{x}\right]$$

$$= \frac{1}{8}\left[\frac{\frac{1}{4} + \frac{y^{\frac{1}{2}}}{x^{\frac{1}{2}}}}{x}\right] = \frac{1}{8}\left[\frac{x^{\frac{1}{2}} + 4y^{\frac{1}{2}}}{4x^{\frac{3}{2}}}\right]$$

$$= \frac{1}{8}\left[\frac{4}{4x^{\frac{3}{2}}}\right] = \frac{1}{8x^{\frac{3}{2}}}$$

29. $xy + y - x = 4$

$$xy' + y(1) + y' - 1 = 0$$

$$xy' + y' = 1 - y$$

$$(x+1)y' = 1 - y$$

$$y' = \frac{1-y}{1+x}$$

$$y'' = \frac{(1+x)(-y') - (1-y)(1)}{(1+x)^2}$$

$$= \frac{(1+x)\left[-\frac{(1-y)}{(1+x)}\right] - (1-y)}{(1+x)^2}$$

$$= \frac{-(1-y) - (1-y)}{(1+x)^2} = \frac{-2(1-y)}{(1+x)^2} = \frac{2(y-1)}{(1+x)^2}$$

31. $y = e^{x+y}$

$$y' = e^{x+y}(1 + y')$$

$$y' - e^{x+y}y' = e^{x+y}$$

$$y'\left(1 - e^{x+y}\right) = e^{x+y}$$

$$y' = \frac{e^{x+y}}{1 - e^{x+y}}$$

$$y' = \frac{y}{1-y}$$

$$y'' = \frac{(1-y)y' - y(-y')}{(1-y)^2} = \frac{y'}{(1-y)^2}$$

$$= \frac{\frac{y}{1-y}}{(1-y)^2} = \frac{y}{(1-y)^3}$$

33. $x^2 + 8y = y^2$

$$2x + 8y' = 2yy'$$

$$x + 4y' = yy'$$

$$x = yy' - 4y'$$

$$x = y'(y - 4)$$

$$y' = \frac{x}{y-4}$$

$$y'' = \frac{(y-4)(1) - x(y')}{(y-4)^2} = \frac{y - 4 - x\left(\frac{x}{y-4}\right)}{(y-4)^2}$$

$$= \frac{(y-4)^2 - x^2}{(y-4)^3}$$

When $x = 3$ and $y = -1$, then

$$y'' = \frac{(-5)^2 - 3^2}{(-5)^3} = -\frac{16}{125}.$$

35. $f(x) = (5x - 3)^4$

$f'(x) = 20(5x - 3)^3$

$f''(x) = 300(5x - 3)^2$

37. $\dfrac{dc}{dq} = 0.6q + 2$

$\dfrac{d^2c}{dq^2} = 0.6$

$\left. \dfrac{d^2c}{dq^2} \right|_{q=100} = 0.6$

39. $f(x) = x^4 - 6x^2 + 5x - 6$

$f'(x) = 4x^3 - 12x + 5$

$f''(x) = 12x^2 - 12 = 12(x + 1)(x - 1)$

Clearly $f'(x) = 0$ when $x = \pm 1$.

41. $f'(x) = 6e^x - 3x^2 - 30x$

$f''(x) = 6\left(e^x - x - 5\right)$

$f''(x) = 0$ when $x \approx -4.99$ or 1.94.

Chapter 13 Review Problems

1. $y = 2e^x + e^2 + e^{x^2}$

$y' = 2e^x + 0 + e^{x^2}(2x) = 2\left(e^x + xe^{x^2}\right)$

3. $f'(r) = \dfrac{1}{r^2 + 5r}(2r + 5) = \dfrac{2r + 5}{r(r + 5)}$

5. $y = e^{x^2 + 4x + 5}$

$y' = e^{x^2 + 4x + 5}(2x + 4) = 2(x + 2)e^{x^2 + 4x + 5}$

7. $y' = e^x(2x) + \left(x^2 + 2\right)e^x = e^x\left(x^2 + 2x + 2\right)$

9. $y = \sqrt{(x - 6)(x + 5)(9 - x)}$

$\ln y = \ln \sqrt{(x - 6)(x + 5)(9 - x)}$

$= \frac{1}{2}[\ln(x - 6) + \ln(x + 5) + \ln(9 - x)]$

$\dfrac{y'}{y} = \frac{1}{2}\left[\dfrac{1}{x - 6} + \dfrac{1}{x + 5} + \dfrac{-1}{9 - x}\right]$

$y' = \dfrac{y}{2}\left[\dfrac{1}{x - 6} + \dfrac{1}{x + 5} - \dfrac{1}{9 - x}\right]$

$= \dfrac{\sqrt{(x - 6)(x + 5)(9 - x)}}{2}\left[\dfrac{1}{x - 6} + \dfrac{1}{x + 5} + \dfrac{1}{x - 9}\right]$

11. $y' = \dfrac{e^x\left(\frac{1}{x}\right) - (\ln x)\left(e^x\right)}{e^{2x}}$

$= \dfrac{e^x - xe^x \ln x}{xe^{2x}} = \dfrac{1 - x \ln x}{xe^x}$

13. $f(q) = \ln\left[(q+1)^2(q+2)^3\right]$

$= 2\ln(q+1) + 3\ln(q+2)$

$f'(q) = \dfrac{2}{q+1} + \dfrac{3}{q+2}$

15. $y = e^{(2-7x)(\ln 10)}$

$y' = e^{(2-7x)(\ln 10)}(-7\ln 10)$

$= -7(\ln 10)10^{2-7x}$

17. $y = \dfrac{4e^{3x}}{xe^{x-1}} = \dfrac{4e^{2x+1}}{x}$

$y' = 4 \cdot \dfrac{x\left[e^{2x+1}(2)\right] - e^{2x+1}[1]}{x^2}$

$= \dfrac{4e^{2x+1}(2x-1)}{x^2}$

19. $y = \log_2(8x+5)^2 = 2\log_2(8x+5)$

$= 2 \cdot \dfrac{\ln(8x+5)}{\ln 2}$

$y' = 2 \cdot \dfrac{1}{\ln 2} \cdot \dfrac{8}{8x+5} = \dfrac{16}{(8x+5)\ln 2}$

21. $f(l) = \ln\left(1 + l + l^2 + l^3\right)$

$f'(l) = \dfrac{1}{1+l+l^2+l^3}\left[1 + 2l + 3l^2\right]$

$= \dfrac{1 + 2l + 3l^2}{1 + l + l^2 + l^3}$

23. $y = (x+1)^{x+1}$

$\ln y = (x+1)\ln(x+1)$

$\dfrac{y'}{y} = (x+1)\dfrac{1}{x+1} + \ln(x+1)[1]$

$= 1 + \ln(x+1)$

$y' = y[1 + \ln(x+1)]$

$= (x+1)^{x+1}[1 + \ln(x+1)]$

25. $f(t) = \ln\left(t^2\sqrt{1-t}\right) = 2\ln t + \left(\dfrac{1}{2}\right)\ln(1-t)$

$f'(t) = 2\left(\dfrac{1}{t}\right) + \dfrac{1}{2}\left(\dfrac{1}{1-t}\right)(-1)$

$= \dfrac{2}{t} + \dfrac{1}{2(t-1)} = \dfrac{5t-4}{2t(t-1)}$

27. $y = \dfrac{\left(x^2+2\right)^{\frac{3}{2}}\left(x^2+9\right)^{\frac{4}{9}}}{\left(x^3+6x\right)^{\frac{4}{11}}}$

$\ln y$

$= \dfrac{3}{2}\ln\left(x^2+2\right) + \dfrac{4}{9}\ln\left(x^2+9\right) - \dfrac{4}{11}\ln\left(x^3+6x\right)$

$\dfrac{y'}{y} = \dfrac{3}{2}\left(\dfrac{1}{x^2+2}\right)(2x) + \dfrac{4}{9}\left(\dfrac{1}{x^2+9}\right)(2x)$

$\qquad - \dfrac{4}{11}\left(\dfrac{1}{x^3+6x}\right)(3x^2+6)$

$y' = y\left[\dfrac{3x}{x^2+2} + \dfrac{8x}{9(x^2+9)} - \dfrac{12(x^2+2)}{11x(x^2+6)}\right]$

$= \dfrac{\left(x^2+2\right)^{\frac{3}{2}}\left(x^2+9\right)^{\frac{4}{9}}}{\left(x^3+6x\right)^{\frac{4}{11}}}$

$\quad \cdot \left[\dfrac{3x}{x^2+2} + \dfrac{8x}{9(x^2+9)} - \dfrac{12(x^2+2)}{11x(x^2+6)}\right]$

29. $y = \left(x^x\right)^x = x^{x^2}$

$\ln y = \ln x^{x^2} = x^2\ln x$

$\dfrac{y'}{y} = x^2\left(\dfrac{1}{x}\right) + (\ln x)(2x) = x + 2x\ln x$

$y' = y(x + 2x\ln x) = \left(x^x\right)^x(x + 2x\ln x)$

31. $y = (x+1)\ln x^2 = 2(x+1)\ln x$

$y' = 2\left[(x+1)\left(\dfrac{1}{x}\right) + (\ln x)(1)\right]$

$= 2\left[\dfrac{x+1}{x} + \ln x\right]$

When $x = 1$, then $y' = 2\left[\dfrac{2}{1} + \ln 1\right] = 4$.

33. $y = e^{e+x\ln\left(\frac{1}{x}\right)} = e^{e-x\ln x}$

$y' = e^{e-x\ln x}\left(-\left[x\left(\dfrac{1}{x}\right) + (\ln x)(1)\right]\right)$

$= -(1 + \ln x)e^{e-x\ln x}$

When $x = e$, then
$y' = -(1 + \ln e)e^{e - e \ln e} = -(2)e^0 = -2$.

35. $y = e^x$

$y' = e^x$

If $x = \ln 2$, then $y = e^{\ln 2} = 2$ and
$y' = e^{\ln 2} = 2$. An equation of the tangent line is
$y - 2 = 2(x - \ln 2)$, $y = 2x + 2 - 2\ln 2$,
$y = 2x + 2(1 - \ln 2)$. Alternatively, since
$2\ln 2 = \ln 2^2 = \ln 4$, the tangent line can be written as $y = 2x + 2 - \ln 4$.

37. $y = x\left(2^{2 - x^2}\right)$. To find y' we shall use logarithmic differentiation.

$\ln y = \ln\left[x\left(2^{2 - x^2}\right)\right] = \ln x + \left(2 - x^2\right)\ln 2$

$\dfrac{y'}{y} = \dfrac{1}{x} + (-2x)\ln 2$

$y' = y\left[\dfrac{1}{x} - 2(\ln 2)x\right]$

When $x = 1$, then $y = 2$ and $y' = 2(1 - 2\ln 2)$.
Equation of tangent line is
$y - 2 = 2(1 - 2\ln 2)(x - 1)$. The y-intercept of the tangent line corresponds to the point where $x = 0$:
$y - 2 = 2(1 - 2\ln 2)(-1) = -2 + 4\ln 2$
Thus $y = 4\ln 2$ and then y-intercept is $(0, 4\ln 2)$.

39. $y = e^{x^2 - 4}$

$y' = e^{x^2 - 4}[2x] = 2xe^{x^2 - 4}$

$y'' = 2\left(xe^{x^2 - 4}[2x] + e^{x^2 - 4} \cdot 1\right)$

$= 2e^{x^2 - 4}\left(2x^2 + 1\right)$

At $(2, 1)$, $y'' = 2e^0(9) = 18$

41. $y = \ln(2x)$

$y' = \dfrac{1}{2x}(2) = x^{-1}$

$y'' = -1 \cdot x^{-2} = -x^{-2}$

$y''' = -(-2)x^{-3} = \dfrac{2}{x^3}$

At $(1, \ln 2)$, $y''' = \dfrac{2}{1^3} = 2$

43. $2xy + y^2 = 6$

$2(xy' + y) + 2yy' = 0$

$2xy' + 2yy' = -2y$

$(x + y)y' = -y$

$y' = -\dfrac{y}{x + y}$

45. $\ln\left(xy^2\right) = xy$

$\ln x + 2\ln y = xy$

$\dfrac{1}{x} + \dfrac{2}{y}y' = xy' + y$

$y + 2xy' = x^2yy' + xy^2$

$2xy' - x^2yy' = xy^2 - y$

$\left(2x - x^2y\right)y' = xy^2 - y$

$y' = \dfrac{xy^2 - y}{2x - x^2y}$

47. $x + xy + y = 5$

$1 + xy' + y(1) + y' = 0$

$(x + 1)y' = -1 - y$

$y' = -\dfrac{1 + y}{x + 1}$

$y'' = -\dfrac{(x + 1)y' - (1 + y)}{(x + 1)^2}$

At $(2, 1)$, $y' = -\dfrac{1 + 1}{2 + 1} = -\dfrac{2}{3}$ and

$y'' = -\dfrac{3\left(-\frac{2}{3}\right) - 2}{9} = \dfrac{4}{9}$

49. $e^y = (y + 1)e^x$

$e^y y' = (y + 1)e^x + e^x(y')$

$e^y y' - e^x y' = (y + 1)e^x$

$\left(e^y - e^x\right)y' = (y + 1)e^x$

$$y' = \frac{(y+1)e^x}{e^y - e^x} = \frac{(y+1)\left(\frac{e^y}{y+1}\right)}{e^y - \left(\frac{e^y}{y+1}\right)} = \frac{e^y}{e^y - \frac{e^y}{y+1}}$$

$$= \frac{1}{1 - \frac{1}{y+1}} = \frac{y+1}{y}$$

$$y'' = \frac{y(y') - (y+1)(y')}{y^2} = \frac{-y'}{y^2} = -\frac{\frac{y+1}{y}}{y^2}$$

$$= -\frac{y+1}{y^3}$$

51. $f'(t) = \left[0.8e^{-0.0t}(-0.01) - 0.2e^{-0.0002t}(-0.0002)\right]$

$= 0.008e^{-0.0.1t} + 0.00004e^{-0.0002t}$

53. $f'(x) = 12\left(3x^3 + x^2 - 3\right)e^{9x^4 + 4x^3 - 36x}$

$f'(x) = 0$ when $x \approx 0.90$

Chapter 14

Principles in Practice 14.1

1. The graph of $c(q) = 2q^3 - 21q^2 + 60q + 500$ is shown.

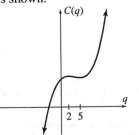

There looks to be a relative maximum at $q = 2$ and a relative minimum at $q = 5$.

$c'(q) = 6q^2 - 42q + 60 = 6(q^2 - 7q + 10)$
$= 6(q - 5)(q - 2)$

$c'(q) = 0$ when $q = 2$ or $q = 5$. If $q < 2$, then $c'(q) = 6(-)(-) = +$, so $c(q)$ is increasing. If $2 < q < 5$, then $c'(q) = 6(+)(-) = -$, so $c(q)$ is decreasing. If $5 < q$, then $c'(q) = 6(+)(+) = +$, so $c(q)$ is increasing. When $q = 2$, there is a relative maximum, since $c'(q)$ changes from + to −. The relative maximum value is

$2(2)^3 - 21(2)^2 + 60(2) + 500 = 552$. When $q = 5$, there is a relative minimum, since $c'(q)$ changes from − to +. The relative minimum value is

$2(5)^3 - 21(5)^2 + 60(5) + 500 = 525$.

2. First, find $C'(t)$, with $C(t) = \dfrac{0.14t}{(t+2)^2}$.

$C'(t) = \dfrac{0.14(t+2)^2 - 0.14t(2)(t+2)}{(t+2)^4}$

$= \dfrac{0.14(t+2) - 0.28t}{(t+2)^3} = \dfrac{0.28 - 0.14t}{(t+2)^3}$

$= \dfrac{0.14(2-t)}{(t+2)^3}$

$C'(t) = 0$ when $t = 2$ and is undefined when $t = -2$. However, since t denotes the number of hours after an injection, negative values of t are not reasonable. If $0 \le t < 2$,

$C'(t) = \dfrac{+}{+} = +$, so $C(t)$ is increasing. If $2 < t$, $C'(t) = \dfrac{-}{+} = -$, so $C(t)$ is decreasing. When $t = 2$, there is a relative maximum, since $C'(t)$ changes from + to −. The drug is at its greatest concentration 2 hours after the injection.

Exercise 14.1

1. Decreasing on $(-\infty, -1)$ and $(3, \infty)$; increasing on $(-1, 3)$; relative minimum $(-1, -1)$; relative maximum $(3, 4)$.

3. Decreasing on $(-\infty, -2)$ and $(0, 2)$; increasing on $(-2, 0)$ and $(2, \infty)$; relative minimum $(-2, 1)$ and $(2, 1)$; no relative maximum.

5. $f'(x) = (x+1)(x-3)$
$f'(x) = 0$ when $x = -1, 3$.
CV: $x = -1, 3$

$$\begin{array}{ccc} + & - & + \\ \hline & -1 \quad\ \ 3 & \end{array}$$

Increasing on $(-\infty, -1)$ and $(3, \infty)$; decreasing on $(-1, 3)$; relative maximum when $x = -1$; relative minimum when $x = 3$.

7. $f'(x) = (x+1)(x-3)^2$
CV: $x = -1, 3$

$$\begin{array}{ccc} - & + & + \\ \hline & -1 \quad\ \ 3 & \end{array}$$

Decreasing on $(-\infty, -1)$; increasing on $(-1, 3)$ and $(3, \infty)$; relative minimum when $x = -1$.

9. $y = x^2 + 2$
$y' = 2x$
CV: $x = 0$

$$\begin{array}{cc} - & + \\ \hline & 0 \end{array}$$

Decreasing on $(-\infty, 0)$; increasing on $(0, \infty)$; relative minimum when $x = 0$.

11. $y = x - x^2 + 2$

$y' = 1 - 2x$

CV: $x = \dfrac{1}{2}$

$$\begin{array}{cc} + & - \\ \hline & \\ \frac{1}{2} & \end{array}$$

Increasing on $\left(-\infty, \dfrac{1}{2}\right)$; decreasing on

$\left(\dfrac{1}{2}, \infty\right)$; relative maximum when $x = \dfrac{1}{2}$.

13. $y = -\dfrac{x^3}{3} - 2x^2 + 5x - 2$

$y' = -x^2 - 4x + 5 = -\left(x^2 + 4x - 5\right)$

$= -(x + 5)(x - 1)$

CV: $x = -5, 1$

$$\begin{array}{ccc} - & + & - \\ \hline & & \\ -5 & 1 & \end{array}$$

Decreasing on $(-\infty, -5)$ and $(1, \infty)$;
increasing on $(-5, 1)$; relative minimum
when $x = -5$; relative maximum when $x = 1$.

15. $y = x^4 - 2x^2$

$y' = 4x^3 - 4x = 4x\left(x^2 - 1\right)$

$= 4x(x + 1)(x - 1)$

CV: $x = 0, \pm 1$

$$\begin{array}{cccc} - & + & - & + \\ \hline & & & \\ -1 & 0 & 1 & \end{array}$$

Decreasing on $(-\infty, -1)$ and $(0, 1)$;
increasing on $(-1, 0)$ and $(1, \infty)$; relative
maximum when $x = 0$; relative minima when
$x = \pm 1$.

17. $y = x^3 - 6x^2 + 9x$

$y' = 3x^2 - 12x + 9 = 3\left(x^2 - 4x + 3\right)$

$= 3(x - 1)(x - 3)$

CV: $x = 1, 3$

$$\begin{array}{ccc} + & - & + \\ \hline & & \\ 1 & 3 & \end{array}$$

Increasing on $(-\infty, 1)$ and $(3, \infty)$; decreasing
on $(1, 3)$; relative maximum when $x = 1$;
relative minimum when $x = 3$.

19. $y = 2x^3 - \dfrac{11}{2}x^2 - 10x + 2$

$y' = 6x^2 - 11x - 10 = (2x - 5)(3x + 2)$

CV: $x = -\dfrac{2}{3}, \dfrac{5}{2}$

$$\begin{array}{ccc} + & - & + \\ \hline & & \\ -\frac{2}{3} & \frac{5}{2} & \end{array}$$

Increasing on $\left(-\infty, -\dfrac{2}{3}\right)$ and $\left(\dfrac{5}{2}, \infty\right)$;

decreasing on $\left(-\dfrac{2}{3}, \dfrac{5}{2}\right)$; relative maximum

when $x = -\dfrac{2}{3}$; relative minimum when

$x = \dfrac{5}{2}$.

21. $y = x^3 + 2x^2 - x - 1$

$y' = 3x^2 + 4x - 1$

Setting $y' = 0$ gives $3x^2 + 4x - 1 = 0$. By
the quadratic formula,

$x = \dfrac{-4 \pm 2\sqrt{7}}{6} = \dfrac{-2 \pm \sqrt{7}}{3}$.

CV: $x = \dfrac{-2 \pm \sqrt{7}}{3}$

$$\begin{array}{ccc} + & - & + \\ \hline & & \\ \frac{-2-\sqrt{7}}{3} & \frac{-2+\sqrt{7}}{3} & \end{array}$$

Increasing on $\left(-\infty, \dfrac{-2-\sqrt{7}}{3}\right)$ and

$\left(\dfrac{-2+\sqrt{7}}{3}, \infty\right)$; decreasing on

$\left(\dfrac{-2-\sqrt{7}}{3}, \dfrac{-2+\sqrt{7}}{3}\right)$; relative maximum

when $x = \dfrac{-2-\sqrt{7}}{3}$; relative minimum when

$x = \dfrac{-2+\sqrt{7}}{3}$.

23. $y = 3x^5 - 5x^3$

$y' = 15x^4 - 15x^2 = 15x^2(x + 1)(x - 1)$

CV: $x = 0, \pm 1$

$$+ \quad - \quad - \quad +$$
$$\overline{\quad\;\;\underset{-1}{\;|\;}\;\;\underset{0}{\;|\;}\;\;\underset{1}{\;|\;}\quad}$$

Increasing on $(-\infty, -1)$ and $(1, \infty)$; decreasing on $(-1, 0)$ and $(0, 1)$; relative maximum when $x = -1$; relative minimum when $x = 1$.

25. $y = -x^5 - 5x^4 + 200$

$y' = -5x^4 - 20x^3 = -5x^3(x + 4)$

CV: $x = 0, -4$

$$- \quad + \quad -$$
$$\overline{\quad\;\;\underset{-4}{\;|\;}\;\;\underset{0}{\;|\;}\quad}$$

Decreasing on $(-\infty, -4)$ and $(0, \infty)$; increasing on $(-4, 0)$; relative minimum when $x = -4$; relative maximum when $x = 0$.

27. $y = 8x^4 - x^8$

$y' = 32x^3 - 8x^7 = 8x^3\left(4 - x^4\right)$

$\quad = 8x^3\left(2 + x^2\right)\left(2 - x^2\right)$

$\quad = 8x^3\left(2 + x^2\right)\left(\sqrt{2} - x\right)\left(\sqrt{2} + x\right)$

CV: $x = 0, \pm\sqrt{2}$

$$+ \quad - \quad + \quad -$$
$$\overline{\quad\;\;\underset{-\sqrt{2}}{\;|\;}\;\;\underset{0}{\;|\;}\;\;\underset{\sqrt{2}}{\;|\;}\quad}$$

Increasing on $\left(-\infty, -\sqrt{2}\right)$ and $\left(0, \sqrt{2}\right)$;

decreasing on $\left(-\sqrt{2}, 0\right)$ and $\left(\sqrt{2}, \infty\right)$;

relative maximum when $x = \pm\sqrt{2}$, relative minimum when $x = 0$.

29. $y = \left(x^3 + 1\right)^3$

$y' = 9x^2\left(x^3 + 1\right)^2$

$\quad = 9x^2(x + 1)^2\left(x^2 - x + 1\right)^2$

CV: $0, -1$

$$+ \quad + \quad +$$
$$\overline{\quad\;\;\underset{-1}{\;|\;}\;\;\underset{0}{\;|\;}\quad}$$

Increasing on $(-\infty, -1)$, $(-1, 0)$, and $(0, \infty)$; never decreasing; no relative extremum.

31. $y = \dfrac{1}{x - 1} = (x - 1)^{-1}$

$y' = -1(x - 1)^{-2} = -\dfrac{1}{(x - 1)^2}$

CV: None, but $x = 1$ must be included in the sign chart because it is a point of discontinuity of y.

$$- \quad - $$
$$\overline{\quad\;\;\underset{\boxed{1}}{\;|\;}\quad}$$

Decreasing on $(-\infty, 1)$ and $(1, \infty)$; no relative extremum.

33. $y = \dfrac{10}{\sqrt{x}} = 10x^{-\frac{1}{2}}$. [Note: $x > 0$]

$y' = -5x^{-\frac{3}{2}} = -\dfrac{5}{\sqrt{x^3}} < 0$ for $x > 0$.

Decreasing on $(0, \infty)$; no relative extremum.

35. $y = \dfrac{x^2}{1 - x}$

$y' = \dfrac{x(2 - x)}{(1 - x)^2}$

CV: $x = 0, 2$, but $x = 1$ must be included in the sign chart because it is a point of discontinuity of y.

$$- \quad + \quad + \quad -$$
$$\overline{\quad\;\;\underset{0}{\;|\;}\;\;\underset{\boxed{1}}{\;|\;}\;\;\underset{2}{\;|\;}\quad}$$

Decreasing on $(-\infty, 0)$ and $(2, \infty)$; increasing on $(0, 1)$ and $(1, 2)$; relative minimum when $x = 0$; relative maximum when $x = 2$.

37. $y = \dfrac{x^2 - 3}{x + 2}$

$y' = \dfrac{(x + 2)(2x) - \left(x^2 - 3\right)(1)}{(x + 2)^2}$

$\quad = \dfrac{x^2 + 4x + 3}{(x + 2)^2} = \dfrac{(x + 1)(x + 3)}{(x + 2)^2}$

CV: $x = -3, -1$, but $x = -2$ must be included in the sign chart because it is a point of discontinuity of y.

$$+ \quad - \quad - \quad +$$
$$\overline{\quad\;\;\underset{-3}{\;|\;}\;\;\underset{\boxed{-2}}{\;|\;}\;\;\underset{-1}{\;|\;}\quad}$$

Increasing on $(-\infty, -3)$ and $(-1, \infty)$; decreasing on $(-3, -2)$ and $(-2, -1)$; relative maximum when $x = -3$; relative minimum when $x = -1$.

39.　$y = \dfrac{5x+3}{x^2+1}$

$$y' = \frac{\left(x^2+1\right)(5) - (5x+3)(2x)}{\left(x^2+1\right)^2}$$

$$= \frac{-5x^2 - 6x + 5}{\left(x^2+1\right)^2}$$

$y' = 0$ when $-5x^2 - 6x + 5 = 0$; by the

quadratic formula, $x = \dfrac{-3 \pm \sqrt{34}}{5}$

CV: $x = \dfrac{-3 \pm \sqrt{34}}{5}$

$$\begin{array}{ccc} - & + & - \\ \hline & & \\ \frac{-3-\sqrt{34}}{5} & \frac{-3+\sqrt{34}}{5} \end{array}$$

Decreasing on $\left(-\infty, \dfrac{-3-\sqrt{34}}{5}\right)$ and

$\left(\dfrac{-3+\sqrt{34}}{5}, \infty\right)$; increasing on

$\left(\dfrac{-3-\sqrt{34}}{5}, \dfrac{-3+\sqrt{34}}{5}\right)$; relative minimum

when $x = \dfrac{-3-\sqrt{34}}{5}$; relative maximum

when $x = \dfrac{-3+\sqrt{34}}{5}$.

41.　$y = (x+2)^3(x-5)^2$

$$y' = (x+2)^3[(2)(x-5)] + (x-5)^2\left[(3)(x+2)^2\right]$$

$$= (x+2)^2(x-5)[2(x+2) + 3(x-5)]$$

$$= (x+2)^2(x-5)(5x-11)$$

CV: $x = -2, 5, \dfrac{11}{5}$

$$\begin{array}{cccc} + & + & - & + \\ \hline & & & \\ -2 & \frac{11}{5} & 5 \end{array}$$

Increasing on $(-\infty, -2)$, $\left(-2, \dfrac{11}{5}\right)$ and $(5, \infty)$;

decreasing on $\left(\dfrac{11}{5}, 5\right)$; relative maximum

when $x = \dfrac{11}{5}$; relative minimum when $x = 5$.

43.　$y = x^3(x-4)^4$

$$y' = x^3\left[4(x-4)^3\right] + (x-4)^4\left(3x^2\right)$$

$$= x^2(x-4)^3[4x + 3(x-4)]$$

$$= x^2(x-4)^3(7x-12)$$

CV: $x = 0, 4, \dfrac{12}{7}$

$$\begin{array}{cccc} + & + & - & + \\ \hline & & & \\ 0 & \frac{12}{7} & 4 \end{array}$$

Increasing on $(-\infty, 0)$, $\left(0, \dfrac{12}{7}\right)$, and $(4, \infty)$;

decreasing on $\left(\dfrac{12}{7}, 4\right)$; relative maximum

when $x = \dfrac{12}{7}$; relative minimum when $x = 4$.

45.　$y = e^{-2x}$

$y' = -2e^{-2x} < 0$ for all x. Thus decreasing on $(-\infty, \infty)$; no relative extremum.

47.　$y = x^2 - 2\ln x$. [Note: $x > 0$.]

$$y' = 2x - \frac{2}{x} = \frac{2x^2 - 2}{x} = \frac{2\left(x^2-1\right)}{x}$$

$$= \frac{2(x+1)(x-1)}{x}$$

CV: $x = 1$

$$\begin{array}{cc} - & + \\ \hline & \\ 0 & 1 \end{array}$$

Decreasing on $(0, 1)$; increasing on $(1, \infty)$; relative minimum when $x = 1$.

49.　$y = e^x + e^{-x}$

$y' = e^x - e^{-x}$

Setting $y' = 0$ gives $e^x - e^{-x} = 0$,

$e^x = e^{-x}$,

$x = -x$, $x = 0$

CV: $x = 0$

$$\begin{array}{cc} - & + \\ \hline & \\ 0 \end{array}$$

Decreasing on $(-\infty, 0)$; increasing on $(0, \infty)$; relative minimum when $x = 0$.

51. $y = x \ln x - x.$ [Note: $x > 0$.]

$$y' = \left[x \cdot \frac{1}{x} + (\ln x)(1) \right] - 1 = \ln x$$

CV: $x = 1$

$$\begin{array}{ccc} & - & + \\ \hline & 0 & 1 \end{array}$$

Decreasing on $(0, 1)$; increasing on $(1, \infty)$; relative minimum when $x = 1$; no relative maximum.

53. $y = x^2 - 6x - 7 = (x - 7)(x + 1)$

Intercepts $(7, 0)$, $(-1, 0)$, $(0, -7)$

$$y' = 2x - 6 = 2(x - 3)$$

CV: $x = 3$

Decreasing on $(-\infty, 3)$; increasing on $(3, \infty)$; relative minimum when $x = 3$.

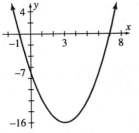

55. $y = 3x - x^3 = x\left(\sqrt{3} + x\right)\left(\sqrt{3} - x\right)$

Intercepts: $(0, 0)$, $\left(\pm\sqrt{3}, 0 \right)$

Symmetric about origin.

$$y' = 3 - 3x^2 = 3(1 + x)(1 - x)$$

CV: $x = \pm 1$

Decreasing on $(-\infty, -1)$ and $(1, \infty)$; increasing on $(-1, 1)$; relative minimum when $x = -1$; relative maximum when $x = 1$.

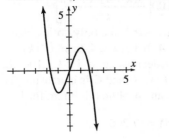

57. $y = 2x^3 - 9x^2 + 12x = x\left(2x^2 - 9x + 12 \right)$

Note that $2x^2 - 9x + 12 = 0$ has no real roots. The only intercept is $(0, 0)$.

$$y' = 6x^2 - 18x + 12 = 6\left(x^2 - 3x + 2 \right)$$

$$= 6(x - 2)(x - 1)$$

CV: $x = 1, 2$

Increasing on $(-\infty, 1)$ and $(2, \infty)$; decreasing on $(1, 2)$; relative maximum when $x = 1$; relative minimum when $x = 2$.

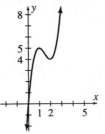

59. $y = x^4 + 4x^3 + 4x^2 = x^2(x + 2)^2$

Intercepts $(0, 0)$, $(-2, 0)$

$$y' = 4x^3 + 12x^2 + 8x = 4x(x + 1)(x + 2)$$

CV: $x = 0, -1, -2$

Increasing on $(-2, -1)$ and $(0, \infty)$; decreasing on $(-\infty, -2)$ and $(-1, 0)$; relative maximum when $x = -1$; relative minimum when $x = -2$ or $x = 0$.

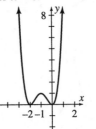

61. $y = (x - 1)^2 (x + 2)^2$

Intercepts: $(1, 0)$, $(-2, 0)$, $(0, 4)$

$$y' = (x - 1)^2 \cdot 2(x + 2) + (x + 2)^2 \cdot 2(x - 1)$$

$$= 2(x - 1)(x + 2)[(x - 1) + (x + 2)]$$

$$= 2(x - 1)(x + 2)(2x + 1)$$

CV: $x = 1, -2, -\frac{1}{2}$

Decreasing on $(-\infty, -2)$ and $\left(-\frac{1}{2}, 1 \right)$;

increasing on $\left(-2, -\frac{1}{2}\right)$ and $(1, \infty)$; relative minimum when $x = -2$ or $x = 1$; relative maximum when $x = -\frac{1}{2}$.

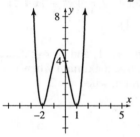

63. $y = 2\sqrt{x} - x = \sqrt{x}\left(2 - \sqrt{x}\right)$. [Note: $x \geq 0$.]

Intercepts $(0, 0)$, $(4, 0)$

$$y' = \frac{1}{\sqrt{x}} - 1 = \frac{1 - \sqrt{x}}{\sqrt{x}}$$

CV: $x = 0, 1$

Increasing on $(0, 1)$; decreasing on $(1, \infty)$; relative maximum when $x = 1$.

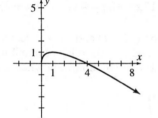

65.

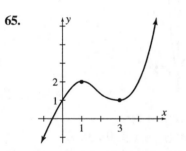

67. $c_f = 25,000$

$$\overline{c}_f = \frac{c_f}{q} = \frac{25,000}{q}$$

$$\frac{d}{dq}\left(\overline{c}_f\right) = -\frac{25,000}{q^2} < 0 \text{ for } q > 0, \text{ so } \overline{c}_f \text{ is a}$$

decreasing function for $q > 0$.

69. $p = 400 - 2q$

Revenue is given by $r = pq = (400 - 2q)q$.

$$= 400q - 2q^2$$

Marginal revenue is $r' = 400 - 4q$. Marginal revenue is increasing when its derivative is positive. But $(r')' = -4 < 0$. Thus marginal revenue is never increasing.

71. $r = 240q + 57q^2 - q^3$

$r' = 240 + 114q - 3q^2 = 0$

$3(40 - q)(2 + q) = 0$

Since $q \geq 0$, we have $q = 40$ as the only CV. Since r is increasing on $(0, 40)$ and decreasing on $(40, \infty)$, r is a maximum when output is 40.

73. $E = 0.71\left(1 - \frac{T_c}{T_h}\right)$

$$\frac{dE}{dT_h} = 0.71\left(\frac{T_c}{T_h^2}\right) > 0, \text{ so as } T_h \text{ increases, } E$$

increases.

75. $C(k) = 100\left[100 + 9k + \frac{144}{k}\right]$, $1 \leq k \leq 100$

  a. $C(1) = 25,300$

  b. $C'(k) = 100\left[9 - \frac{144}{k^2}\right]$

$$= 100\left[\frac{9k^2 - 144}{k^2}\right]$$

$$= 100\left[\frac{9(k + 4)(k - 4)}{k^2}\right]$$

Since $k \geq 1$, the only critical value is $k = 4$. If $1 \leq k < 4$, then $C'(k) < 0$ and C is decreasing. If $4 < k \leq 100$, then $C'(k) > 0$ and C is increasing. Thus C has an absolute minimum for $k = 4$.

  c. $C(4) = 17,200$

77. Relative minimum: $(-4.10, -3.41)$

79. Relative maximum: $(2.74, 2.37)$; relative minimum: $(-2.74, -2.37)$

81. Relative minimum: 0, 1.50, 2.00; relative maximum: 0.57, 1.77

83. a. $f'(x) = 4 - 6x - 3x^2$

b.

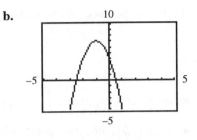

c. $f'(x) > 0$ on $(-2.53, 0.53)$; $f'(x) < 0$ on $(-\infty, -2.53)$, $(0.53, \infty)$, f is inc. on $(-2.53, 0.53)$; f is dec. on $(-\infty, -2.53)$, $(0.53, \infty)$.

d.

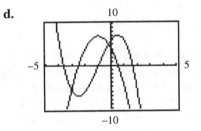

Exercise 14.2

1. $f(x) = x^2 - 2x + 3$ and f is continuous over $[-1, 2]$.
$f'(x) = 2x - 2 = 2(x - 1)$
The only critical value on the interval $(-1, 2)$ is $x = 1$. We evaluate f at this point and at the endpoints: $f(-1) = 6$, $f(1) = 2$, and $f(2) = 3$.
Absolute maximum: $f(-1) = 6$;
absolute minimum: $f(1) = 2$

3. $f(x) = \dfrac{1}{3}x^3 - x^2 - 3x + 1$ and f is
continuous over $[0, 2]$.
$f'(x) = x^2 - 2x - 3 = (x + 1)(x - 3)$
There are no critical values on $(0, 2)$, so we only have to evaluate f at the endpoints:

$f(0) = 1$ and $f(2) = -\dfrac{19}{3}$.
Absolute maximum: $f(0) = 1$;
absolute minimum: $f(2) = -\dfrac{19}{3}$

5. $f(x) = 4x^3 + 3x^2 - 18x + 3$ and f is
continuous over $\left[\dfrac{1}{2}, 3\right]$.
$f'(x) = 12x^2 + 6x - 18 = 6\left(2x^2 + x - 3\right)$
$= 6(2x + 3)(x - 1)$
The only critical value on $\left(\dfrac{1}{2}, 3\right)$ is $x = 1$.
We evaluate f at this point and the
endpoints: $f\left(\dfrac{1}{2}\right) = -\dfrac{19}{4}$; $f(1) = -8$, $f(3) = 84$.
Absolute maximum: $f(3) = 84$;
absolute minimum: $f(1) = -8$

7. $f(x) = -3x^5 + 5x^3$ and f is continuous over
$[-2, 0]$.
$f'(x) = -15x^4 + 15x^2 = 15x^2\left(1 - x^2\right)$
$= 15x^2(1 + x)(1 - x)$
The only critical value on $(-2, 0)$ is
$x = -1$. We have $f(-2) = 56$, $f(-1) = -2$, and
$f(0) = 0$.
Absolute maximum: $f(-2) = 56$;
absolute minimum: $f(-1) = -2$.

9. $f(x) = 3x^4 - x^6$ and f is continuous over
$[-1, 2]$.
$f'(x) = 12x^3 - 6x^5 = 6x^3\left(2 - x^2\right)$
$= 6x^3\left(\sqrt{2} - x\right)\left(\sqrt{2} + x\right)$
The only critical values on $(-1, 2)$ are $x = 0$,
$\sqrt{2}$. We have $f(-1) = 2$, $f(0) = 0$,
$f\left(\sqrt{2}\right) = 4$, and
$f(2) = -16$.
Absolute maximum: $f\left(\sqrt{2}\right) = 4$;
absolute minimum: $f(2) = -16$

11. $f(x) = x^4 - 9x^2 + 2$ and f is continuous over $[-1, 3]$.

$f'(x) = 4x^3 - 18x = 2x(2x^2 - 9)$

$= 2x(\sqrt{2}x - 3)(\sqrt{2}x + 3)$

The only critical values on $(-1, 3)$ are $x = 0$ and $x = \dfrac{3}{\sqrt{2}} = \dfrac{3\sqrt{2}}{2}$. We have $f(-1) = -6$,

$f(0) = 2$, $f\left(\dfrac{3\sqrt{2}}{2}\right) = -\dfrac{73}{4}$, and $f(3) = 2$.

Thus there is an absolute maximum when $x = 0$ or $x = 3$, and an absolute minimum when $x = \dfrac{3\sqrt{2}}{2}$.

Absolute maximum: $f(0) = f(3) = 2$;

absolute minimum: $f\left(\dfrac{3\sqrt{2}}{2}\right) = -\dfrac{73}{4}$

13. $f(x) = x^{\frac{2}{3}}$ and f is continuous over $[-2, 3]$.

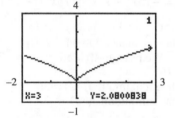

Absolute maximum: $f(3) \approx 2.08$;
absolute minimum: $f(0) = 0$

15.

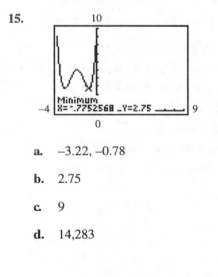

a. $-3.22, -0.78$

b. 2.75

c. 9

d. $14,283$

Exercise 14.3

1. $f(x) = x^4 - 3x^3 + 7x - 5$

$f''(x) = 6x(2x - 3)$

$f''(x)$ is 0 when $x = 0, \dfrac{3}{2}$. Sign chart for f'':

$$\begin{array}{ccc} + & - & + \\ \hline & 0 & \frac{3}{2} \end{array}$$

Concave up on $(-\infty, 0)$ and $\left(\dfrac{3}{2}, \infty\right)$; concave down on $\left(0, \dfrac{3}{2}\right)$. Inflection points when $x = 0, \dfrac{3}{2}$.

3. $f(x) = \dfrac{2 + x - x^2}{x^2 - 2x + 1}$

$f''(x) = \dfrac{2(7 - x)}{(x - 1)^4}$

$f''(x)$ is 0 when $x = 7$. Although f'' is not defined when $x = 1$, f is not continuous at $x = 1$. So there is no inflection point when $x = 1$, but $x = 1$ must be considered in concavity analysis. Sign chart for f'':

$$\begin{array}{ccc} + & + & - \\ \hline & \boxed{1} & 7 \end{array}$$

Concave up on $(-\infty, 1)$ and $(1, 7)$; concave down on $(7, \infty)$. Inflection point when $x = 7$.

5. $f(x) = \dfrac{x^2 + 1}{x^2 - 2}$

$f''(x) = \dfrac{6(3x^2 + 2)}{(x^2 - 2)^3} = \dfrac{6(3x^2 + 2)}{\left[(x - \sqrt{2})(x + \sqrt{2})\right]^3}$

$f''(x)$ is never 0. Although f'' is not defined when $x = \pm\sqrt{2}$, f is not continuous at $x = \pm\sqrt{2}$. So there is no inflection point when $x = \pm\sqrt{2}$, but $x = \pm\sqrt{2}$ must be considered in concavity analysis. Sign chart of f'':

$$\begin{array}{ccc} + & - & + \\ \hline & \boxed{-\sqrt{2}} & \boxed{\sqrt{2}} \end{array}$$

Concave up on $\left(-\infty, -\sqrt{2}\right)$ and $\left(\sqrt{2}, \infty\right)$; concave down on $\left(-\sqrt{2}, \sqrt{2}\right)$. No inflection point.

7. $y = -2x^2 + 4x$

$y' = -4x + 4$

$y'' = -4 < 0$ for all x, so the graph is concave down for all x, that is, on $(-\infty, \infty)$.

9. $y = 4x^3 + 12x^2 - 12x$

$y' = 12x^2 + 24x - 12$

$y'' = 24x + 24 = 24(x + 1)$

Possible inflection point when $x = -1$.
Concave down on $(-\infty, -1)$: concave up on $(-1, \infty)$; inflection point when $x = -1$.

11. $y = 4x^3 - 21x^2 + 5x$

$y' = 12x^2 - 42x + 5$

$y'' = 24x - 42 = 24\left(x - \dfrac{7}{4}\right)$

Possible inflection point when $x = \dfrac{7}{4}$.

Concave down on $\left(-\infty, \dfrac{7}{4}\right)$; concave up on $\left(\dfrac{7}{4}, \infty\right)$; inflection point when $x = \dfrac{7}{4}$.

13. $y = x^4 - 6x^2 + 5x - 6$

$y' = 4x^3 - 12x + 5$

$y'' = 12x^2 - 12 = 12\left(x^2 - 1\right)$

$= 12(x + 1)(x - 1)$

Possible inflection points when $x = \pm 1$.
Concave up on $(-\infty, -1)$ and $(1, \infty)$; concave down on $(-1, 1)$; inflection points when $x = \pm 1$.

15. $y = x^{\frac{1}{5}}$

$y' = \dfrac{1}{5} x^{-\frac{4}{5}}$

$y'' = -\dfrac{4}{25} x^{-\frac{9}{5}} = -\dfrac{4}{25x^{\frac{9}{5}}}$

y'' is not defined when $x = 0$ and y is continuous there. Thus there is a possible

inflection point when $x = 0$. Concave up on $(-\infty, 0)$; concave down on $(0, \infty)$; inflection point when $x = 0$.

17. $y = \dfrac{x^4}{2} + \dfrac{19x^3}{6} - \dfrac{7x^2}{2} + x + 5$

$y' = 2x^3 + \dfrac{19}{2} x^2 - 7x + 1$

$y'' = 6x^2 + 19x - 7 = (3x - 1)(2x + 7)$

Possible inflection points when $x = -\dfrac{7}{2}, \dfrac{1}{3}$.

Concave up on $\left(-\infty, -\dfrac{7}{2}\right)$ and $\left(\dfrac{1}{3}, \infty\right)$; concave down on $\left(-\dfrac{7}{2}, \dfrac{1}{3}\right)$; inflection points when $x = -\dfrac{7}{2}, \dfrac{1}{3}$.

19. $y = \dfrac{1}{20} x^5 - \dfrac{1}{4} x^4 + \dfrac{1}{6} x^3 - \dfrac{1}{2} x - \dfrac{2}{3}$

$y' = \dfrac{1}{4} x^4 - x^3 + \dfrac{1}{2} x^2 - \dfrac{1}{2}$

$y'' = x^3 - 3x^2 + x = x\left(x^2 - 3x + 1\right)$

y'' is 0 when $x = 0$ or $x^2 - 3x + 1 = 0$.
Using the quadratic formula to solve
$x^2 - 3x + 1 = 0$ gives $x = \dfrac{3 \pm \sqrt{5}}{2}$. Thus possible inflection points occur when $x = 0$, $\dfrac{3 \pm \sqrt{5}}{2}$. Concave down on

$(-\infty, 0)$ and $\left(\dfrac{3 - \sqrt{5}}{2}, \dfrac{3 + \sqrt{5}}{2}\right)$; concave up

on $\left(0, \dfrac{3 - \sqrt{5}}{2}\right)$ and $\left(\dfrac{3 + \sqrt{5}}{2}, \infty\right)$;

inflection points when $x = 0$, $\dfrac{3 \pm \sqrt{5}}{2}$.

21. $y = \dfrac{1}{30} x^6 - \dfrac{7}{12} x^4 + 5x^2 + 2x - 1$

$y' = \dfrac{1}{5} x^5 - \dfrac{7}{3} x^3 + 10x + 2$

$y'' = x^4 - 7x^2 + 10 = \left(x^2 - 2\right)\left(x^2 - 5\right)$

$= \left(x + \sqrt{2}\right)\left(x - \sqrt{2}\right)\left(x + \sqrt{5}\right)\left(x - \sqrt{5}\right)$

Possible inflection points when
$x = \pm\sqrt{2}, \pm\sqrt{5}$. Concave up on

$\left(-\infty, -\sqrt{5}\right)$, $\left(-\sqrt{2}, \sqrt{2}\right)$, and $\left(\sqrt{5}, \infty\right)$; concave down on $\left(-\sqrt{5}, -\sqrt{2}\right)$ and $\left(\sqrt{2}, \sqrt{5}\right)$; inflection points when $x = \pm\sqrt{5}, \pm\sqrt{2}$.

23. $y = \dfrac{x+1}{x-1}$

$y' = \dfrac{-2}{(x-1)^2}$

$y'' = \dfrac{4}{(x-1)^3}$

No possible inflection point, but we consider $x = 1$ in the concavity analysis. Concave down on $(-\infty, 1)$; concave up on $(1, \infty)$.

25. $y = \dfrac{x^2}{x^2+1}$

$y' = \dfrac{\left(x^2+1\right)(2x) - x^2(2x)}{\left(x^2+1\right)^2} = \dfrac{2x}{\left(x^2+1\right)^2}$

$y'' = \dfrac{\left(x^2+1\right)^2(2) - 2x(2)\left(x^2+1\right)(2x)}{\left(x^2+1\right)^4}$

$= \dfrac{\left(x^2+1\right)(2) - 8x^2}{\left(x^2+1\right)^3}$

$= \dfrac{2\left(1-3x^2\right)}{\left(x^2+1\right)^3} = \dfrac{2\left(1+\sqrt{3}x\right)\left(1-\sqrt{3}x\right)}{\left(x^2+1\right)^3}$

Possible inflection points when $x = \pm\dfrac{1}{\sqrt{3}}$.

Concave down on $\left(-\infty, -\dfrac{1}{\sqrt{3}}\right)$ and $\left(\dfrac{1}{\sqrt{3}}, \infty\right)$; concave up on $\left(-\dfrac{1}{\sqrt{3}}, \dfrac{1}{\sqrt{3}}\right)$; inflection points when $x = \dfrac{\pm 1}{\sqrt{3}}$.

27. $y = \dfrac{21x+40}{6(x+3)^2}$

$y' = \dfrac{1}{6} \cdot \dfrac{(x+3)^2(21) - (21x+40)[2(x+3)]}{(x+3)^4}$

$= \dfrac{1}{6} \cdot \dfrac{(x+3)(21) - (21x+40)(2)}{(x+3)^3}$

$= \dfrac{1}{6} \cdot \dfrac{-21x-17}{(x+3)^3} = -\dfrac{1}{6} \cdot \dfrac{21x+17}{(x+3)^3}$

y''

$= -\dfrac{1}{6} \cdot \dfrac{(x+3)^3(21) - (21x+17)\left[3(x+3)^2\right]}{(x+3)^6}$

$= -\dfrac{1}{6} \cdot \dfrac{(x+3)(21) - (21x+17)(3)}{(x+3)^4}$

$= -\dfrac{1}{6} \cdot \dfrac{-42x+12}{(x+3)^4} = \dfrac{7x-2}{(x+3)^4}$

Possible inflection point when $x = \dfrac{2}{7}$

($x = -3$ must be considered in concavity analysis). Concave down on $(-\infty, -3)$ and $\left(-3, \dfrac{2}{7}\right)$; concave up on $\left(\dfrac{2}{7}, \infty\right)$; inflection point when $x = \dfrac{2}{7}$.

29. $y = e^x$

$y' = e^x$

$y'' = e^x$

Thus $y'' > 0$ for all x. Concave up on $(-\infty, \infty)$.

31. $y = xe^x$

$y' = xe^x + e^x = e^x(x+1)$

$y'' = e^x(1) + (x+1)e^x + e^x(x+2)$

$y'' = 0$ if $x = -2$. Concave down on $(-\infty, -2)$; concave up on $(-2, \infty)$; inflection point when $x = -2$.

33. $y = \dfrac{\ln x}{x}$.   (Note: $x > 0$.)

$$y' = \frac{x \cdot \frac{1}{x} - (\ln x)(1)}{x^2} = \frac{1 - \ln x}{x^2}$$

$$y'' = \frac{x^2\left(-\frac{1}{x}\right) - (1 - \ln x)(2x)}{x^4}$$

$$= \frac{-x - (1 - \ln x)(2x)}{x^4}$$

$$= \frac{-1 - (1 - \ln x)(2)}{x^3} = \frac{2\ln(x) - 3}{x^3}$$

y'' is 0 if $2\ln(x) - 3 = 0$, $\ln x = \dfrac{3}{2}$, $x = e^{\frac{3}{2}}$.

Concave down on $\left(0, e^{\frac{3}{2}}\right)$; concave up on

$\left(e^{\frac{3}{2}}, \infty\right)$; inflection point when $x = e^{\frac{3}{2}}$.

35. $y = x^2 + 4x + 3 = (x + 3)(x + 1)$

Intercepts $(-3, 0)$, $(-1, 0)$, and $(0, 3)$.

$y' = 2x + 4 = 2(x + 2)$

CV: $x = -2$

Decreasing on $(-\infty, -2)$; increasing on $(-2, \infty)$; relative minimum at $(-2, -1)$.

$y'' = 2$

No possible inflection point. Concave up on $(-\infty, \infty)$.

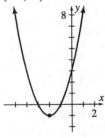

37. $y = 4x - x^2 = x(4 - x)$

Intercepts $(0, 0)$ and $(4, 0)$

$y' = 4 - 2x = 2(2 - x)$

CV: $x = 2$

Increasing on $(-\infty, 2)$; decreasing on $(2, \infty)$; relative maximum at $(2, 4)$.

$y'' = -2$

No possible inflection point. Concave down

on $(-\infty, \infty)$.

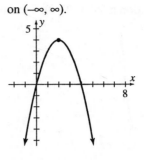

39. $y = x^3 - 9x^2 + 24x - 19$

The x-intercepts are not convenient to find; the y-intercept is $(0, -19)$.

$y' = 3x^2 - 18x + 24 = 3(x - 2)(x - 4)$

CV: $x = 2$ and $x = 4$

Increasing on $(-\infty, 2)$ and $(4, \infty)$; decreasing on $(2, 4)$; relative maximum at $(2, 1)$; relative minimum at $(4, -3)$.

$y'' = 6x - 18 = 6(x - 3)$

Possible inflection point when $x = 3$.
Concave down on $(-\infty, 3)$; concave up on $(3, \infty)$; inflection point at $(3, -1)$.

41. $y = \dfrac{x^3}{3} - 4x = \dfrac{x^3 - 12x}{3}$

$$= \frac{1}{3}x\left(x + 2\sqrt{3}\right)\left(x - 2\sqrt{3}\right)$$

Intercepts $(0, 0)$ and $\left(\pm 2\sqrt{3}, 0\right)$

$y' = x^2 - 4 = (x + 2)(x - 2)$

CV: $x = \pm 2$

Increasing on $(-\infty, -2)$ and $(2, \infty)$; decreasing on $(-2, 2)$; relative maximum at $\left(-2, \dfrac{16}{3}\right)$; relative minimum at $\left(2, -\dfrac{16}{3}\right)$.

$y'' = 2x$

Possible inflection point when $x = 0$.
Concave down on $(-\infty, 0)$; concave up on

$(0, \infty)$; inflection point at $(0, 0)$. Symmetric about the origin.

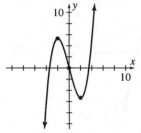

43. $y = x^3 - 3x^2 + 3x - 3$

Intercept $(0, -3)$

$y' = 3x^2 - 6x + 3 = 3(x - 1)^2$

CV: $x = 1$

Increasing on $(-\infty, 1)$ and $(1, \infty)$; no relative maximum or minimum

$y'' = 6(x - 1)$

Possible inflection point when $x = 1$.
Concave down on $(-\infty, 1)$; concave up on $(1, \infty)$; inflection point at $(1, -2)$.

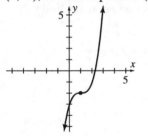

45. $y = 4x^3 - 3x^4 = x^3(4 - 3x)$

Intercepts $(0, 0)$, $\left(\frac{4}{3}, 0\right)$

$y' = 12x^2 - 12x^3 = 12x^2(1 - x)$

CV: $x = 0$ and $x = 1$

Increasing on $(-\infty, 0)$ and $(0, 1)$; decreasing on $(1, \infty)$; relative maximum at $(1, 1)$.

$y'' = 24x - 36x^2 = 12x(2 - 3x)$

Possible inflection points at $x = 0$ and

$x = \frac{2}{3}$. Concave down on $(-\infty, 0)$ and

$\left(\frac{2}{3}, \infty\right)$; concave up on $\left(0, \frac{2}{3}\right)$; inflection

point at $(0, 0)$ and $\left(\frac{2}{3}, \frac{16}{27}\right)$

47. $y = -2 + 12x - x^3$

Intercept $(0, -2)$

$y' = 12 - 3x^2 = 3(2 + x)(2 - x)$

CV: $x = \pm 2$

Decreasing on $(-\infty, -2)$ and $(2, \infty)$; increasing on $(-2, 2)$; relative minimum at $(-2, -18)$; relative maximum at $(2, 14)$.

$y'' = -6x$

Possible inflection point when $x = 0$.
Concave up on $(-\infty, 0)$; concave down on $(0, \infty)$; inflection point at $(0, -2)$.

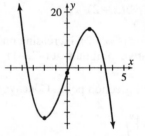

49. $y = x^3 - 6x^2 + 12x - 6$

Intercept $(0, -6)$

$y' = 3x^2 - 12x + 12 = 3(x - 2)^2$

CV: $x = 2$

Increasing on $(-\infty, 2)$ and $(2, \infty)$.

$y'' = 6(x - 2)$

Possible inflection point when $x = 2$.
Concave down on $(-\infty, 2)$; concave up on $(2, \infty)$; inflection point at $(2, 2)$.

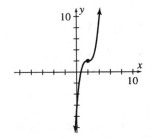

51. $y = 5x - x^5 = x\left(5 - x^4\right)$

$= x\left(\sqrt{5} + x^2\right)\left(\sqrt{5} - x^2\right)$

$= x\left(\sqrt{5} + x^2\right)\left(\sqrt[4]{5} + x\right)\left(\sqrt[4]{5} - x\right)$

Intercepts $(0, 0)$ and $\left(\pm\sqrt[4]{5}, 0\right)$

Symmetric about the origin.

$y' = 5 - 5x^4 = 5\left(1 - x^4\right) = 5\left(1 - x^2\right)\left(1 + x^2\right)$

$= 5(1 - x)(1 + x)\left(1 + x^2\right)$

CV: $x = \pm 1$

Decreasing on $(-\infty, -1)$ and $(1, \infty)$; increasing on $(-1, 1)$; relative minimum at $(-1, -4)$; relative maximum at $(1, 4)$.

$y'' = -20x^3$

Possible inflection point when $x = 0$.
Concave up on $(-\infty, 0)$; concave down on $(0, \infty)$; inflection point at $(0, 0)$.

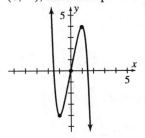

53. $y = 3x^4 - 4x^3 + 1$

Intercepts $(0, 1)$ and $(1, 0)$ [the latter is found by inspection of the equation]. No symmetry.

$y' = 12x^3 - 12x^2 = 12x^2(x - 1)$

CV: $x = 0$ and $x = 1$

Decreasing on $(-\infty, 0)$ and $(0, 1)$; increasing on $(1, \infty)$; relative minimum at $(1, 0)$.

$y'' = 36x^2 - 24x = 12x(3x - 2)$

Possible inflection points at $x = 0$ and $x = \frac{2}{3}$. Concave up on $(-\infty, 0)$ and $\left(\frac{2}{3}, \infty\right)$; concave down on $\left(0, \frac{2}{3}\right)$; inflection points at $(0, 1)$ and $\left(\frac{2}{3}, \frac{11}{27}\right)$.

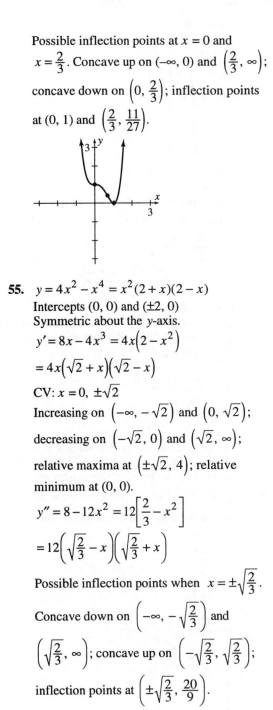

55. $y = 4x^2 - x^4 = x^2(2 + x)(2 - x)$

Intercepts $(0, 0)$ and $(\pm 2, 0)$
Symmetric about the y-axis.

$y' = 8x - 4x^3 = 4x\left(2 - x^2\right)$

$= 4x\left(\sqrt{2} + x\right)\left(\sqrt{2} - x\right)$

CV: $x = 0,\ \pm\sqrt{2}$

Increasing on $\left(-\infty, -\sqrt{2}\right)$ and $\left(0, \sqrt{2}\right)$;

decreasing on $\left(-\sqrt{2}, 0\right)$ and $\left(\sqrt{2}, \infty\right)$;

relative maxima at $\left(\pm\sqrt{2}, 4\right)$; relative minimum at $(0, 0)$.

$y'' = 8 - 12x^2 = 12\left[\frac{2}{3} - x^2\right]$

$= 12\left(\sqrt{\frac{2}{3}} - x\right)\left(\sqrt{\frac{2}{3}} + x\right)$

Possible inflection points when $x = \pm\sqrt{\frac{2}{3}}$.

Concave down on $\left(-\infty, -\sqrt{\frac{2}{3}}\right)$ and

$\left(\sqrt{\frac{2}{3}}, \infty\right)$; concave up on $\left(-\sqrt{\frac{2}{3}}, \sqrt{\frac{2}{3}}\right)$;

inflection points at $\left(\pm\sqrt{\frac{2}{3}}, \frac{20}{9}\right)$.

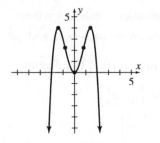

57. $y = x^{1/3}(x - 8)$

Intercepts $(0, 0)$ and $(8, 0)$

Since $y = x^{4/3} - 8x^{1/3}$

$$y' = \frac{4}{3}x^{1/3} - \frac{8}{3}x^{-2/3}$$

$$= \frac{4}{3}\left[x^{1/3} - \frac{2}{x^{2/3}}\right] = \frac{4(x - 2)}{3x^{2/3}}$$

CV: $x = 0, 2$

Decreasing on $(-\infty, 0)$ and $(0, 2)$; increasing on $(2, \infty)$; relative minimum at

$$\left(2, -6\sqrt[3]{2}\right) \approx (2, -7.56).$$

$$y'' = \frac{4}{9}x^{-2/3} + \frac{16}{9}x^{-5/3}$$

$$= \frac{4}{9}\left[\frac{1}{x^{2/3}} + \frac{4}{x^{5/3}}\right] = \frac{4(x + 4)}{9x^{5/3}}$$

Possible inflection points when $x = -4, 0$.
Concave up on $(-\infty, -4)$ and $(0, \infty)$; concave down on $(-4, 0)$; inflection points at $\left(-4, 12\sqrt[3]{4}\right)$ and $(0, 0)$. Observe that at the origin the tangent line exists but it is vertical.

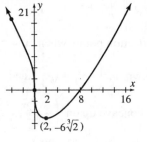

59. $y = 4x^{1/3} + x^{4/3} = x^{1/3}(4 + x)$

Intercepts $(0, 0)$ and $(-4, 0)$

$$y' = \frac{4}{3}x^{-2/3} + \frac{4}{3}x^{1/3} = \frac{4}{3}\left[\frac{1}{x^{2/3}} + x^{1/3}\right]$$

$$= \frac{4(1 + x)}{3x^{2/3}}$$

CV: $x = 0, -1$

Decreasing on $(-\infty, -1)$; increasing on $(-1, 0)$ and $(0, \infty)$; rel. min at $(-1, -3)$

$$y'' = -\frac{8}{9}x^{-5/3} + \frac{4}{9}x^{-2/3}$$

$$= \frac{4}{9}\left[\frac{1}{x^{2/3}} - \frac{2}{x^{5/3}}\right]$$

$$= \frac{4(x - 2)}{9x^{5/3}}$$

Possible inflection points when $x = 0, 2$.
Concave up on $(-\infty, 0)$ and $(2, \infty)$; concave down on $(0, 2)$; inflection point at $(0, 0)$ and $\left(2, 6\sqrt[3]{2}\right)$. Observe that at the origin the tangent line exists but it is vertical.

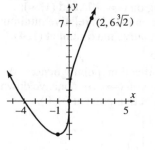

61. $y = 2x + 3x^{2/3} = 2x^{2/3}\left(x^{1/3} + \frac{3}{2}\right)$

Intercepts $(0, 0)$ and $\left(-\frac{27}{8}, 0\right)$

$$y' = 2 + 2x^{-1/3} = 2\left(1 + \frac{1}{\sqrt[3]{x}}\right)$$

$$= 2\left(\frac{\sqrt[3]{x} + 1}{\sqrt[3]{x}}\right)$$

CV: $x = 0, -1$

Increasing on $(-\infty, -1)$ and $(0, \infty)$; decreasing on $(-1, 0)$; relative maximum at $(-1, 1)$; relative minimum at $(0, 0)$.

$$y'' = -\frac{2}{3}x^{-4/3} = -\frac{2}{3x^{4/3}}$$

Possible inflection point at $x = 0$. Concave down on $(-\infty, 0)$ and $(0, \infty)$. Observe that at the origin the tangent line exists but it is vertical.

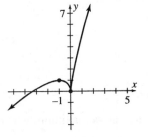

63.

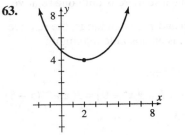

65.

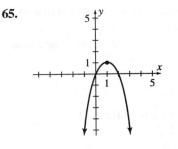

67. $p = \dfrac{100}{q+2}$

$\dfrac{dp}{dq} = -\dfrac{100}{(q+2)^2} < 0$ for $q > 0$, so p is

decreasing. Since $\dfrac{d^2 p}{dq^2} = \dfrac{200}{(q+2)^3} > 0$ for

$q > 0$, the demand curve is concave up.

69. $S = f(A) = 12\sqrt[4]{A}$, $0 \le A \le 625$. For the

given values of A we have $S' = 3A^{-\frac{3}{4}} > 0$

and $S'' = -\left(\dfrac{9}{4}\right)A^{-\frac{7}{4}} < 0$. Thus y is increasing

and concave down.

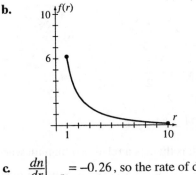

71. $y = 12.5 + 5.8(0.42)^x$

$y' = 5.8(0.42)^x \ln(0.42)$

Since $\ln(0.42) < 0$, we have $y' < 0$, so the function is decreasing.

$y'' = 5.8(0.42)^x \ln^2(0.42) > 0$, so the function is concave up.

73. $n = f(r) = 0.1\ln(r) + \dfrac{7}{r} - 0.8$, $1 \le r \le 10$

a. $\dfrac{dn}{dr} = \dfrac{0.1}{r} - \dfrac{7}{r^2} = \dfrac{0.1r - 7}{r^2}$

$= \dfrac{0.1(r - 70)}{r^2} < 0$

for $1 \le r \le 10$. Thus the graph of f is always falling. Also,

$\dfrac{d^2 n}{dr^2} = -\dfrac{0.1}{r^2} + \dfrac{14}{r^3} = \dfrac{14 - 0.1r}{r^3}$

$= \dfrac{0.1(140 - r)}{r^3} > 0$

for $1 \le r \le 10$. Thus the graph is concave up.

b.

c. $\dfrac{dn}{dr}\bigg|_{r=5} = -0.26$, so the rate of decrease

is 0.26.

75.

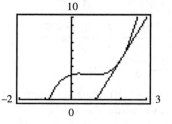

Two inflection points

77. $y = x^3 - 2x^2 + x + 3$

$y' = 3x^2 - 4x + 1$

When $x = 2$, then $y = 5$ and $y' = 5$. Thus an equation of the tangent line at $x = 2$ is $y - 5 = 5(x - 2)$, or $y = 5x - 5$. Graphing the curve and the tangent line indicates that the curve lies above the tangent line around $x = 2$. Thus the curve is concave up at $x = 2$.

79. $f(x) = x^6 + 3x^5 - 4x^4 + 2x^2 + 1$

$f'(x) = 6x^5 + 15x^4 - 16x^3 + 4x$

$f''(x) = 30x^4 + 60x^3 - 48x^2 + 4$

Inflection points of f when $x \approx -2.61, -0.26$.

Exercise 14.4

1. $y = x^2 - 5x + 6$

$y' = 2x - 5$

CV: $x = \dfrac{5}{2}$

$y'' = 2$

$y''\left(\dfrac{5}{2}\right) = 2 > 0$

Thus there is a relative minimum when $x = \dfrac{5}{2}$. Because there is only one relative

extremum and f is continuous, the relative minimum is an absolute minimum.

3. $y = -4x^2 + 2x - 8$

$y' = -8x + 2$

CV: $x = \dfrac{1}{4}$

$y'' = -8$

$y''\left(\dfrac{1}{4}\right) = -8 < 0$

Thus there is a relative maximum when $x = \dfrac{1}{4}$. Because there is only one relative extremum and f is continuous, the relative maximum is an absolute maximum.

5. $y = x^3 - 27x + 1$

$y' = 3x^2 - 27 = 3(x^2 - 9) = 3(x + 3)(x - 3)$

CV: $x = \pm 3$

$y'' = 6x$

$y''(-3) = -18 < 0 \Rightarrow$ relative maximum when $x = -3$

$y''(3) = 18 > 0 \Rightarrow$ relative minimum when $x = 3$

7. $y = -x^3 + 3x^2 + 1$

$y' = -3x^2 + 6x = -3x(x - 2)$

CV: $x = 0, 2$

$y'' = -6x + 6$

$y''(0) = 6 > 0 \Rightarrow$ relative minimum when $x = 0$

$y''(2) = -6 < 0 \Rightarrow$ relative maximum when $x = 2$

9. $y = 2x^4 + 2$

$y' = 8x^3$

CV: $x = 0$

$y'' = 24x^2$

Since $y''(0) = 0$, the second-derivative test fails. Using the first-derivative test, we see that f decreases for $x < 0$ and f increases for $x > 0$, so there is a relative minimum when $x = 0$.

11. $y = 81x^5 - 5x$

$$y' = 81 \cdot 5x^4 - 5 = 5\left(81x^4 - 1\right)$$
$$= 5\left(9x^2 - 1\right)\left(9x^2 + 1\right)$$
$$= 5(3x + 1)(3x - 1)\left(9x^2 + 1\right)$$

CV: $x = \pm\frac{1}{3}$

$$y'' = 81 \cdot 5 \cdot 4x^3$$

$y''\left(-\frac{1}{3}\right) = -60 < 0 \Rightarrow$ relative maximum

when $x = -\frac{1}{3}$

$y''\left(\frac{1}{3}\right) = 60 > 0 \Rightarrow$ relative minimum when

$x = \frac{1}{3}$

13. $y = \left(x^2 + 7x + 10\right)^2$

$$y' = 2\left(x^2 + 7x + 10\right)(2x + 7)$$
$$= 2(x + 2)(x + 5)(2x + 7)$$

CV: $x = -2, -5, -\frac{7}{2}$

$$y'' = 2\left[\left(x^2 + 7x + 10\right)(2) + (2x + 7)(2x + 7)\right]$$

$y''(-5) = 18 > 0 \Rightarrow$ relative minimum when

$x = -5$

$y''\left(-\frac{7}{2}\right) = -9 < 0 \Rightarrow$ relative maximum

when $x = -\frac{7}{2}$

$y''(-2) = 18 > 0 \Rightarrow$ relative minimum when

$x = -2$

Exercise 14.5

1. $y = f(x) = \frac{x}{x + 1}$

When $x = -1$ the denominator is zero but the numerator is not zero. Thus the line $x = -1$ is a vertical asymptote. Testing for horizontal asymptotes,

$$\lim_{x \to \infty} \frac{x}{x + 1} = \lim_{x \to \infty} \frac{x}{x} = \lim_{x \to \infty} 1 = 1.$$

Similarly $\lim_{x \to -\infty} f(x) = 1$. Thus the line

$y = 1$ is a horizontal asymptote.

3. $f(x) = \frac{x - 1}{2x + 3}$

When $x = -\frac{3}{2}$ the denominator is zero but

the numerator is not. Thus $x = -\frac{3}{2}$ is a

vertical asymptote.

$$\lim_{x \to \infty} f(x) = \lim_{x \to \infty} \frac{x}{2x} = \lim_{x \to \infty} \frac{1}{2} = \frac{1}{2}.$$

Similarly $\lim_{x \to -\infty} f(x) = \frac{1}{2}$. Thus $y = \frac{1}{2}$ is a

horizontal asymptote.

5. $y = f(x) = \frac{4}{x}$

When $x = 0$ the denominator is zero but the numerator is not zero, so $x = 0$ is a vertical asymptote. Taking limits at infinity,

$$\lim_{x \to \infty} \left(\frac{4}{x}\right) = 0 = \lim_{x \to -\infty} \left(\frac{4}{x}\right), \text{ so the line } y = 0 \text{ is}$$

a horizontal asymptote.

7. $y = f(x) = \frac{1}{x^2 - 1} = \frac{1}{(x - 1)(x + 1)}$

Vertical asymptotes are $x = 1$ and $x = -1$.

$$\lim_{x \to \infty} \frac{1}{x^2 - 1} = 0. \text{ Similarly, } \lim_{x \to -\infty} f(x) = 0.$$

Thus $y = 0$ is a horizontal asymptote.

9. $y = f(x) = x^2 - 5x + 8$ is a polynomial function, so there are no horizontal or vertical asymptotes.

11. $f(x) = \frac{2x^2}{x^2 + x - 6} = \frac{2x^2}{(x + 3)(x - 2)}$

Vertical asymptotes are $x = -3$ and $x = 2$.

$$\lim_{x \to \infty} f(x) = \lim_{x \to \infty} \frac{2x^2}{x^2} = \lim_{x \to \infty} 2 = 2, \text{ and}$$
$$\lim_{x \to -\infty} f(x) = 2. \text{ Thus } y = 2 \text{ is a horizontal}$$

asymptote.

13. $y = f(x) = \frac{4 + 2x - 7x^2}{x^2 - 5}$

$$= \frac{4 + 2x - 7x^2}{\left(x - \sqrt{5}\right)\left(x + \sqrt{5}\right)}$$

When $x = -\sqrt{5}$ or $x = \sqrt{5}$, the denominator

is zero but the numerator is not. Thus $x = -\sqrt{5}$ and $x = \sqrt{5}$ are vertical asymptotes.

$$\lim_{x \to \infty} f(x) = \frac{-7x^2}{x^2} = \lim_{x \to \infty} -7 = -7.$$

Similarly, $\lim_{x \to -\infty} f(x) = -7$. Thus $y = -7$ is a horizontal asymptote.

15. $y = f(x) = \dfrac{4}{x-6} + 4 = \dfrac{4x-20}{x-6}$

From the denominator we find that the line $x = 6$ is a vertical asymptote. Taking limits at infinity,

$$\lim_{x \to \infty} f(x) = \lim_{x \to \infty} \frac{4x}{x} = \lim_{x \to \infty} 4 = 4, \text{ and}$$

$\lim_{x \to -\infty} f(x) = 4$. Thus $y = 4$ is a horizontal asymptote.

17. $f(x) = \dfrac{3 - x^4}{x^3 + x^2} = \dfrac{3 - x^4}{x^2(x+1)}$

Vertical asymptotes are $x = 0$ and $x = -1$. Because the degree of the numerator (4) is greater than the degree of the denominator (3), there is no horizontal asymptote.

19. $y = f(x) = \dfrac{x^2 - 3x - 4}{1 + 4x + 4x^2} = \dfrac{x^2 - 3x - 4}{(1+2x)^2}$

From the denominator, $x = -\dfrac{1}{2}$ is a vertical asymptote. Also,

$$\lim_{x \to \infty} f(x) = \lim_{x \to \infty} \frac{x^2}{4x^2} = \lim_{x \to \infty} \frac{1}{4} = \frac{1}{4}, \text{and}$$

$\lim_{x \to -\infty} f(x) = \dfrac{1}{4}$, so $y = \dfrac{1}{4}$ is a horizontal asymptote.

21. $y = f(x) = \dfrac{9x^2 - 16}{(3x + 4)^2} = \dfrac{(3x+4)(3x-4)}{(3x+4)^2}$

When $x = -\dfrac{4}{3}$, both the numerator and denominator are zero. Since

$$\lim_{x \to -4/3^+} f(x) = \lim_{x \to -4/3^+} \frac{3x - 4}{3x + 4} = -\infty, \text{ the}$$

line $x = -\dfrac{4}{3}$ is a vertical asymptote.

$$\lim_{x \to \infty} \frac{9x^2 - 16}{(3x + 4)^2} = \lim_{x \to \infty} \frac{9x^2}{9x^2} = \lim_{x \to \infty} 1 = 1.$$

Similarly, $\lim_{x \to -\infty} f(x) = 1$. Thus $y = 1$ is a vertical asymptote.

23. $y = f(x) = 2e^{x+2} + 4$

We have $\lim_{x \to \infty} f(x) = +\infty$ and

$$\lim_{x \to -\infty} f(x) = 2 \cdot \lim_{x \to -\infty} e^x + \lim_{x \to -\infty} 4$$
$$= 2(0) + 4 = 4$$

Thus $y = 4$ is a horizontal asymptote. There is no vertical asymptote because $f(x)$ neither increases nor decreases without bound around any fixed value of x.

25. $y = \dfrac{3}{x}$

Symmetric about the origin. Vertical asymptote is $x = 0$. $\lim_{x \to \infty} \dfrac{3}{x} = 0 = \lim_{x \to -\infty} \dfrac{3}{x}$, so $y = 0$ is a horizontal asymptote.

$$y' = -\frac{3}{x^2}$$

CV: None, however $x = 0$ must be included in the inc.-dec. analysis. Decreasing on $(-\infty, 0)$ and $(0, \infty)$.

$$y'' = \frac{6}{x^3}$$

No possible inflection point, but we include $x = 0$ in the concavity analysis. Concave down on $(-\infty, 0)$; concave up on $(0, \infty)$.

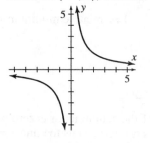

27. $y = \dfrac{x}{x+1}$

Intercept $(0, 0)$

Vertical asymptote is $x = -1$

$\lim_{x \to \infty} y = 1 = \lim_{x \to -\infty} y$, so $y = 1$ is a horizontal asymptote.

$$y' = \frac{(x+1)(1) - x(1)}{(x+1)^2} = \frac{1}{(x+1)^2}$$

CV: None, but $x = -1$ must be included in the inc.-dec. analysis. Increasing on $(-\infty, -1)$ and $(-1, \infty)$.

$$y'' = -\frac{2}{(x+1)^3}$$

No possible inflection point, but $x = -1$ must be included in concavity analysis. Concave up on $(-\infty, -1)$, concave down on $(-1, \infty)$.

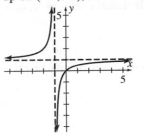

29. $y = x^2 + \frac{1}{x^2} = \frac{x^4 + 1}{x^2}$

$x \neq 0$, so there is no y-intercept. Setting $y = 0 \Rightarrow$ no x-intercept. Replacing x by $-x$ yields symmetry about the y-axis. Setting $x^2 = 0$ gives $x = 0$ as the only vertical asymptote. Because the degree of the numerator is greater than the degree of the denominator, no horizontal asymptote exists.

$$y = x^2 + x^{-2}$$

$$y' = 2x - 2x^{-3} = 2x - \frac{2}{x^3}$$

$$= \frac{2x^4 - 2}{x^3} = \frac{2(x^4 - 1)}{x^3}$$

$$= \frac{2(x^2 + 1)(x+1)(x-1)}{x^3}.$$

CV: $x = \pm 1$, but $x = 0$ must be included in the inc.-dec. analysis. Decreasing on $(-\infty, -1)$ and $(0, 1)$; increasing on $(-1, 0)$ and $(1, \infty)$; relative minima at $(-1, 2)$ and $(1, 2)$,

$$y'' = 2 + \frac{6}{x^4} > 0$$

for all $x \neq 0$. Concave up on $(-\infty, 0)$ and $(0, \infty)$.

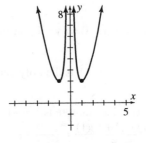

31. $y = \frac{1}{x^2 - 1} = \frac{1}{(x+1)(x-1)}$

Intercept $(0, -1)$
Symmetric about the y-axis.
Vertical asymptotes are $x = -1$ and $x = 1$.

$$\lim_{x \to \infty} \frac{1}{x^2 - 1} = 0 = \lim_{x \to -\infty} \frac{1}{x^2 - 1},$$ so $y = 0$ is a horizontal asymptote.

$$y' = -\frac{2x}{(x^2 - 1)^2}$$

CV: $x = 0$, but $x = \pm 1$ must be included in the inc.-dec. analysis. Increasing on $(-\infty, -1)$ and $(-1, 0)$; decreasing on $(0, 1)$ and $(1, \infty)$; relative maximum at $(0, -1)$.

$$y'' = -2 \cdot \frac{(x^2 - 1)^2 (1) - x\left[4x(x^2 - 1)\right]}{(x^2 - 1)^4}$$

$$= -2 \cdot \frac{(x^2 - 1)\left[(x^2 - 1) - 4x^2\right]}{(x^2 - 1)^4}$$

$$= \frac{2(3x^2 + 1)}{(x^2 - 1)^3} = \frac{2(3x^2 + 1)}{[(x+1)(x-1)]^3}$$

No possible inflection point, but $x = \pm 1$ must be considered in the concavity analysis. Concave up: $(-\infty, -1)$, $(1, \infty)$; concave down: $(-1, 1)$.

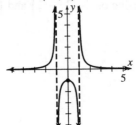

33. $y = \dfrac{1+x}{1-x}$

Intercepts: Setting $x = 0 \Rightarrow y = 1$; setting $y = 0 \Rightarrow x = -1$. Thus the intercepts are $(0, 1)$ and $(-1, 0)$.

Setting $1 - x = 0 \Rightarrow x = 1$ is the only vertical asymptote. Since

$$\lim_{x \to \infty} \frac{1+x}{1-x} = \lim_{x \to \infty} \frac{x}{-x} = \lim_{x \to \infty} -1 = -1$$
$$= \lim_{x \to -\infty} \frac{1+x}{1-x}$$

the only horizontal asymptote is $y = -1$.

$$y' = \frac{(1-x)(1) - (1+x)(1)}{(1-x)^2} = \frac{2}{(1-x)^2}$$

No critical values, but $x = 1$ must be considered in the ind.-dec. analysis. Increasing on $(-\infty, 1)$ and $(1, \infty)$.

$$y'' = \frac{4}{(1-x)^3}$$

No possible inflection point, but $x = 1$ must be included in the concavity analysis. Concave up on $(-\infty, 1)$; concave down on $(1, \infty)$.

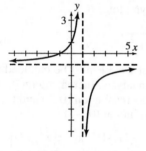

35. $y = \dfrac{x^2}{7x + 4}$

Intercept: $(0, 0)$

Vertical asymptote is $x = -\frac{4}{7}$. Because the degree of the numerator is greater than the degree of the denominator, no horizontal asymptote exists.

$$y' = \frac{(7x+4)(2x) - x^2(7)}{(7x+4)^2}$$
$$= \frac{7x^2 + 8x}{(7x+4)^2} = \frac{x(7x+8)}{(7x+4)^2}$$

CV: $x = 0, -\frac{8}{7}$, but $x = -\frac{4}{7}$ must be included in the inc.-dec. analysis. Increasing on $\left(-\infty, -\frac{8}{7}\right)$ and $(0, \infty)$; decreasing on $\left(-\frac{8}{7}, -\frac{4}{7}\right)$ and $\left(-\frac{4}{7}, 0\right)$; relative maximum at $\left(-\frac{8}{7}, -\frac{16}{49}\right)$; relative minimum at $(0, 0)$.

$$y'' = \frac{\left(7x^2+4\right)^2(14x+8) - \left(7x^2+8x\right)[14(7x+4)]}{(7x+4)^4}$$

$$= \frac{(7x+4)\left[(7x+4)(14x+8) - 14\left(7x^2+8x\right)\right]}{(7x+4)^4}$$

$$= \frac{32}{(7x+4)^3}$$

No possible inflection point but $x = -\frac{4}{7}$ must be included in concavity analysis. Concave down on $\left(-\infty, -\frac{4}{7}\right)$; concave up on $\left(-\frac{4}{7}, \infty\right)$.

37. $y = \dfrac{9}{9x^2 - 6x - 8} = \dfrac{9}{(3x+2)(3x-4)}$

Intercept: $\left(0, -\frac{9}{8}\right)$

Vertical asymptote: $x = -\frac{2}{3}$, $x = \frac{4}{3}$

$$\lim_{x\to\infty} y = \lim_{x\to\infty} \frac{9}{9x^2} = \lim_{x\to\infty} \frac{1}{x^2} = 0 = \lim_{x\to-\infty} y$$

Thus $y = 0$ is a horizontal asymptote. Since $y = 9\left(9x^2 - 6x - 8\right)^{-1}$,

$$y' = 9(-1)\left(9x^2 - 6x - 8\right)^{-2}(18x-6)$$

$$= -\frac{54(3x-1)}{[(3x+2)(3x-4)]^2}$$

CV: $x = \frac{1}{3}$, but $x = -\frac{2}{3}$ and $x = \frac{4}{3}$ must be included in inc.-dec. analysis.

Increasing on $\left(-\infty, -\frac{2}{3}\right)$ and $\left(-\frac{2}{3}, \frac{1}{3}\right)$; decreasing on $\left(\frac{1}{3}, \frac{4}{3}\right)$ and $\left(\frac{4}{3}, \infty\right)$; relative maximum at $\left(\frac{1}{3}, -1\right)$. Finding y'' gives:

$$y'' = -54 \cdot \frac{\left(9x^2 - 6x - 8\right)^2 (3) - (3x-1)\left[2\left(9x^2 - 6x - 8\right)(18x-6)\right]}{\left(9x^2 - 6x - 8\right)^4}$$

$$= -54 \cdot \frac{3\left(9x^2 - 6x - 8\right)\left[\left(9x^2 - 6x - 8\right) - 4(3x-1)(3x-1)\right]}{\left(9x^2 - 6x - 8\right)^4}$$

$$= \frac{-162\left(-27x^2 + 18x - 12\right)}{\left(9x^2 - 6x - 8\right)^3} = \frac{486\left(9x^2 - 6x + 4\right)}{[(3x+2)(3x-4)]^3}$$

Since $9x^2 - 6x + 4 = 0$ has no real roots, y'' is never zero. No possible inflection points, but $x = -\frac{2}{3}$ and $x = \frac{4}{3}$ must be included in concavity analysis. Concave up on $\left(-\infty, -\frac{2}{3}\right)$ and $\left(\frac{4}{3}, \infty\right)$; concave down on $\left(-\frac{2}{3}, \frac{4}{3}\right)$.

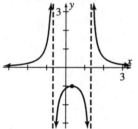

39. $y = \dfrac{2x-3}{(2x-9)^2}$

Intercepts: $\left(\frac{3}{2}, 0\right), \left(0, -\frac{1}{27}\right)$

Vertical asymptote is $x = \frac{9}{2}$.

$$\lim_{x \to \infty} y = \lim_{x \to \infty} \frac{2x}{4x^2} = \lim_{x \to \infty} \frac{1}{2x} = 0 = \lim_{x \to -\infty} y$$

Thus $y = 0$ is horiz. asymptote.

$$y' = \frac{(2x-9)^2(2) - (2x-3)[4(2x-9)]}{(2x-9)^4}$$

$$= \frac{2(2x-9)[(2x-9) - 2(2x-3)]}{(2x-9)^4}$$

$$= \frac{2(-2x-3)}{(2x-9)^3} = -2 \cdot \frac{2x+3}{(2x-9)^3}$$

CV: $x = -\frac{3}{2}$, but $x = \frac{9}{2}$ must be included in inc.-dec. analysis. Decreasing on $\left(-\infty, -\frac{3}{2}\right)$

and $\left(\frac{9}{2}, \infty\right)$; increasing on $\left(-\frac{3}{2}, \frac{9}{2}\right)$; relative minimum at $\left(-\frac{3}{2}, -\frac{1}{24}\right)$.

$$y'' = -2 \cdot \frac{(2x-9)^3(2) - (2x+3)\left[6(2x-9)^2\right]}{(2x-9)^6}$$

$$= -2 \cdot \frac{2(2x-9)^2[(2x-9) - 3(2x+3)]}{(2x-9)^6}$$

$$= -4 \cdot \frac{-4x-18}{(2x-9)^4} = 8 \cdot \frac{2x+9}{(2x-9)^4}$$

Possible inflection point when $x = -\frac{9}{2}$, but $x = \frac{9}{2}$ must be included in concavity analysis. Concave down on $\left(-\infty, -\frac{9}{2}\right)$; concave up on $\left(-\frac{9}{2}, \frac{9}{2}\right)$ and $\left(\frac{9}{2}, \infty\right)$;

inflection point at $\left(-\frac{9}{2}, -\frac{1}{27}\right)$.

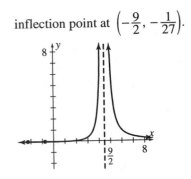

41. $y = \dfrac{x^2 - 1}{x^3} = \dfrac{(x+1)(x-1)}{x^3}$

Intercepts are $(-1, 0)$ and $(1, 0)$.
Symmetric about the origin.
Vertical asymptote $x = 0$.

$\displaystyle\lim_{x \to \infty} \frac{x^2 - 1}{x^3} = \lim_{x \to \infty} \frac{x^2}{x^3} = \lim_{x \to \infty} \frac{1}{x}$

$= 0 = \displaystyle\lim_{x \to -\infty} \frac{1-x}{x^2}$, so $y = 0$ is the only

horizontal asymptote. Since $y = x^{-1} - x^{-3}$,
then

$y' = -x^{-2} + 3x^{-4} = x^{-4}\left(-x^2 + 3\right) = \dfrac{3 - x^2}{x^4}$

CV: $x = \pm\sqrt{3}$, but $x = 0$ must be included in
the inc.-dec. analysis. Increasing on
$\left(-\sqrt{3}, 0\right)$ and $\left(0, \sqrt{3}\right)$; decreasing on
$\left(-\infty, -\sqrt{3}\right)$ and $\left(\sqrt{3}, \infty\right)$; relative

maximum at $\left(\sqrt{3}, \dfrac{2\sqrt{3}}{9}\right)$; relative minimum

at $\left(-\sqrt{3}, -\dfrac{2\sqrt{3}}{9}\right)$.

$y'' = 2x^{-3} - 12x^{-5} = 2x^{-5}\left(x^2 - 6\right)$

$= \dfrac{2\left(x^2 - 6\right)}{x^5}$

Possible inflection points when $x = \pm\sqrt{6}$,
but $x = 0$ must be included in the concavity
analysis. Concave down on $\left(-\infty, -\sqrt{6}\right)$ and

$\left(0, \sqrt{6}\right)$; concave up on $\left(-\sqrt{6}, 0\right)$ and

$\left(\sqrt{6}, \infty\right)$; inflection points at $\left(\sqrt{6}, \dfrac{5\sqrt{6}}{36}\right)$

and $\left(-\sqrt{6}, \dfrac{-5\sqrt{6}}{36}\right)$.

43. $y = x + \dfrac{1}{x+1} = \dfrac{x^2 + x + 1}{x+1}$

Intercepts: Setting $x = 0 \Rightarrow y = 1$; setting
$y = 0$ yields no real roots. Thus the only
intercept is $(0, 1)$. $x = -1$ is the only vertical
asymptote. Because the degree of the
numerator is greater than the degree of the
denominator, there is no horizontal
asymptote.

$y' = \dfrac{(x+1)(2x+1) - \left(x^2 + x + 1\right)}{(x+1)^2}$

$= \dfrac{x^2 + 2x}{(x+1)^2} = \dfrac{x(x+2)}{(x+1)^2}$

CV: 0 and -2, but $x = -1$ must be included in
the inc.-dec. analysis. Increasing on $(-\infty, -2)$
and $(0, \infty)$; decreasing on $(-2, -1)$ and
$(-1, 0)$; relative maximum at $(-2, -3)$;
relative minimum at $(0, 1)$.

$y'' = \dfrac{(x+1)^2(2x+2) - \left(x^2 + 2x\right)[2(x+1)]}{(x+1)^4}$

$= \dfrac{(x+1)(2x+2) - \left(x^2 + 2x\right)[2]}{(x+1)^3} = \dfrac{2}{(x+1)^3}$

No possible inflection point, but $x = -1$ must
be included in the concavity analysis.
Concave down on $(-\infty, -1)$; concave up on
$(-1, \infty)$.

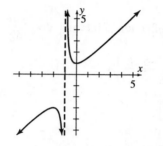

45. $y = \dfrac{-3x^2 + 2x - 5}{3x^2 - 2x - 1} = \dfrac{-3x^2 + 2x - 5}{(3x+1)(x-1)}$

Note that $-3x^2 + 2x - 5$ is never zero.

Intercept: (0, 5)

Vertical asymptotes are $x = -\frac{1}{3}$ and $x = 1$.

$\displaystyle \lim_{x \to \infty} y = \lim_{x \to \infty} \frac{-3x^2}{3x^2} = \lim_{x \to \infty} -1 = -1 = \lim_{x \to -\infty} y$

Thus $y = -1$ is horizontal asymptote.

$y' = \dfrac{\left(3x^2 - 2x - 1\right)(-6x + 2) - \left(-3x^2 + 2x - 5\right)(6x - 2)}{\left(3x^2 - 2x - 1\right)^2}$

$= \dfrac{2(3x-1)\left[\left(3x^2 - 2x - 1\right)(-1) - \left(-3x^2 + 2x - 5\right)\right]}{\left(3x^2 - 2x - 1\right)^2}$

$= \dfrac{12(3x-1)}{\left(3x^2 - 2x - 1\right)^2} = \dfrac{12(3x-1)}{[(3x+1)(x-1)]^2}$

CV: $x = \frac{1}{3}$, but $x = -\frac{1}{3}$ and $x = 1$ must be included in inc.-dec. analysis.

Decreasing on $\left(-\infty, -\frac{1}{3}\right)$ and $\left(-\frac{1}{3}, \frac{1}{3}\right)$; increasing on $\left(\frac{1}{3}, 1\right)$ and $(1, \infty)$; relative minimum at $\left(\frac{1}{3}, \frac{7}{2}\right)$.

$y'' = 12 \cdot \dfrac{\left(3x^2 - 2x - 1\right)^2 (3) - (3x-1)\left[2\left(3x^2 - 2x - 1\right)(6x - 2)\right]}{\left(3x^2 - 2x - 1\right)^4}$

$= 12 \cdot \dfrac{\left(3x^2 - 2x - 1\right)\left[3\left(3x^2 - 2x - 1\right) - 2(3x-1)(6x-2)\right]}{\left(3x^2 - 2x - 1\right)^4}$

$= 12 \cdot \dfrac{-27x^2 + 18x - 7}{\left(3x^2 - 2x - 1\right)^3} = \dfrac{-12\left(27x^2 - 18x + 7\right)}{[(3x+1)(x-1)]^3}$

Since $27x^2 - 18x + 7$ is never zero, there is no possible inflection point, but $x = -\frac{1}{3}$ and $x = 1$ must be included in concavity analysis. Concave down on $\left(-\infty, -\frac{1}{3}\right)$ and $(1, \infty)$; concave up on $\left(-\frac{1}{3}, 1\right)$.

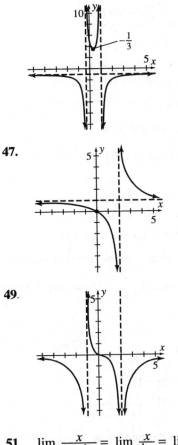

47.

49.

51. $\lim\limits_{x \to \infty} \dfrac{x}{a+bx} = \lim\limits_{x \to \infty} \dfrac{x}{bx} = \lim\limits_{x \to \infty} \dfrac{1}{b} = \dfrac{1}{b}$

Thus $y = \dfrac{1}{b}$ is a horizontal asymptote.

53. $\lim\limits_{t \to \infty}\left(150 - 76e^{-t}\right) = \lim\limits_{t \to \infty}\left(150 - \dfrac{76}{e^t}\right)$

$= 150 - 0 = 150$

Thus $y = 150$ is a horizontal asymptote.

55.

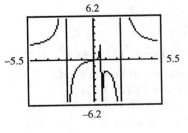

$x \approx \pm 2.45,\ x \approx 0.67,\ y = 2$

57.

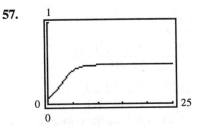

From the graph, it appears that
$\lim\limits_{x \to \infty} y \approx 0.48$. Thus a horizontal asymptote
is $y \approx 0.48$. Algebraically, we have

$$\lim\limits_{x \to \infty} \frac{0.34e^{0.7x}}{4.2 + 0.71e^{0.7x}} = \lim\limits_{x \to \infty} \frac{\frac{0.34e^{0.7x}}{e^{0.7x}}}{\frac{4.2 + 0.71e^{0.7x}}{e^{0.7x}}}$$

$$= \lim\limits_{x \to \infty} \frac{0.34}{\frac{4.2}{e^{0.7x}} + 0.71} = \frac{0.34}{0 + 0.71} \approx 0.48$$

Chapter 14 Review Problems

1. $y = \dfrac{3x^2}{x^2 - 16} = \dfrac{3x^2}{(x+4)(x-4)}$

When $x = \pm 4$ the denominator is zero and the numerator is not zero. Thus $x = 4$ and $x = -4$ are vertical asymptotes.

$$\lim\limits_{x \to \infty} \frac{3x^2}{x^2 - 16} = \lim\limits_{x \to \infty} \frac{3x^2}{x^2} = \lim\limits_{x \to \infty} 3 = 3$$

Similarly, $\lim\limits_{x \to -\infty} y = 3$. Thus $y = 3$ is the only horizontal asymptote.

3. $y = \dfrac{5x^2 - 3}{(3x+2)^2} = \dfrac{5x^2 - 3}{9x^2 + 12x + 4}$

When $x = -\dfrac{2}{3}$, the denominator is zero and the numerator is not zero. Thus $x = -\dfrac{2}{3}$ is a vertical asymptote.

$$\lim\limits_{x \to \infty} y = \lim\limits_{x \to \infty} \frac{5x^2}{9x^2} = \lim\limits_{x \to \infty} \frac{5}{9} = \frac{5}{9}$$

Similarly, $\lim\limits_{x \to -\infty} y = \dfrac{5}{9}$. Thus $y = \dfrac{5}{9}$ is the only horizontal asymptote.

5. $f(x) = \dfrac{x^2}{2-x}$

$f'(x) = \dfrac{(2-x)(2x) - x^2(-1)}{(2-x)^2}$

$= \dfrac{x[2(2-x)+x]}{(2-x)^2} = \dfrac{x(4-x)}{(2-x)^2}$

Thus $x = 0$ and $x = 4$ are the critical values. Note: Although $f'(2)$ is not defined, 2 is not a critical value because 2 is not in the domain of f.

7. $f(x) = \dfrac{\sqrt[3]{x+1}}{3-4x}$

$f'(x) = \dfrac{(3-4x)\left[\frac{1}{3}(x+1)^{-\frac{2}{3}}\right] - (x+1)^{\frac{1}{3}}(-4)}{(3-4x)^2}$

$= \dfrac{\frac{1}{3}(x+1)^{-\frac{2}{3}}[(3-4x)+12(x+1)]}{(3-4x)^2}$

$= \dfrac{8x+15}{3(x+1)^{\frac{2}{3}}(3-4x)^2}$

$f'(x)$ is zero when $x = -\dfrac{15}{8}$; $f'(x)$ is not defined when $x = -1$ or $x = \dfrac{3}{4}$. However $\dfrac{3}{4}$ is not in the domain of f. Thus $x = -\dfrac{15}{8}$ and $x = -1$ are critical values.

9. $f(x) = -x^3 + 6x^2 - 9x$

$f'(x) = -3x^2 + 12x - 9$

$= -3\left(x^2 - 4x + 3\right) = -3(x-1)(x-3)$

CV: $x = 1$ and $x = 3$. Increasing on (1, 3); decreasing on (−∞, 1) and (3, ∞).

11. $f(x) = \dfrac{x^4}{x^2 - 3}$

$f'(x) = \dfrac{\left(x^2-3\right)\left(4x^3\right) - x^4(2x)}{\left(x^2-3\right)^2}$

$\dfrac{2x^3\left[2\left(x^2-3\right)-x^2\right]}{\left(x^2-3\right)^2} = \dfrac{2x^3\left(x^2-6\right)}{\left(x^2-3\right)^2}$

$= \dfrac{2x^3\left(x+\sqrt{6}\right)\left(x-\sqrt{6}\right)}{\left[\left(x+\sqrt{3}\right)\left(x-\sqrt{3}\right)\right]^2}$

CV: $x = 0$, $\pm\sqrt{6}$, but $x = \pm\sqrt{3}$ are also considered in the inc.-dec. analysis. Decreasing on $\left(-\infty, -\sqrt{6}\right)$, $\left(0, \sqrt{3}\right)$, and $\left(\sqrt{3}, \sqrt{6}\right)$; increasing on $\left(-\sqrt{6}, -\sqrt{3}\right)$, $\left(-\sqrt{3}, 0\right)$ and $\left(\sqrt{6}, \infty\right)$.

13. $f(x) = x^4 - x^3 - 14$

$f'(x) = 4x^3 - 3x^2$

$f''(x) = 12x^2 - 6x = 6x(2x - 1)$

$f''(x) = 0$ when $x = 0$ or $x = \dfrac{1}{2}$. Concave up on (−∞, 0) and $\left(\dfrac{1}{2}, \infty\right)$; concave down on $\left(0, \dfrac{1}{2}\right)$.

15. $f(x) = \dfrac{1}{2x-1} = (2x-1)^{-1}$

$f'(x) = -2(2x-1)^{-2}$

$f'' = 8(2x-1)^3 = \dfrac{8}{(2x-1)^3}$

$f''(x)$ is not defined when $x = \dfrac{1}{2}$. Concave down on $\left(-\infty, \dfrac{1}{2}\right)$; concave up on $\left(\dfrac{1}{2}, \infty\right)$.

17. $f(x) = (4x+1)^3(4x+9)$

$f'(x) = (4x+1)^3(4) + (4x+9)\left[12(4x+1)^2\right]$

$= 4(4x+1)^2[(4x+1) + 3(4x+9)]$

$= 4(4x+1)^2(16x+28)$

$= 16(4x+1)^2(4x+7)$

$f''(x)$

$= 16\left\{(4x+1)^2(4) + (4x+7)[8(4x+1)]\right\}$

$= 64(4x+1)[(4x+1) + 2(4x+7)]$

$= 64(4x+1)(12x+15)$

$= 192(4x+1)(4x+5)$

$f''(x) = 0$ when $x = -\dfrac{1}{4}$ or $x = -\dfrac{5}{4}$.

Concave up on $\left(-\infty, -\frac{5}{4}\right)$ and $\left(-\frac{1}{4}, \infty\right)$;

concave down on $\left(-\frac{5}{4}, -\frac{1}{4}\right)$.

19. $f(x) = 2x^3 - 9x^2 + 12x + 7$

$f'(x) = 6x^2 - 18x + 12 = 6\left(x^2 - 3x + 2\right)$

$= 6(x - 1)(x - 2)$

CV: $x = 1$ and $x = 2$

Increasing on $(-\infty, 1)$ and $(2, \infty)$; decreasing on $(1, 2)$. Relative maximum when $x = 1$; relative minimum when $x = 2$.

21. $f(x) = \frac{x^6}{6} + \frac{x^3}{3}$

$f'(x) = x^5 + x^2 = x^2\left(x^3 + 1\right)$

CV: $x = 0$ and $x = -1$

Decreasing on $(-\infty, -1)$; increasing on $(-1, 0)$ and $(0, \infty)$; relative minimum when $x = -1$.

23. $f(x) = x^{\frac{2}{3}}(x + 1) = x^{\frac{5}{3}} + x^{\frac{2}{3}}$

$f'(x) = \frac{5}{3}x^{\frac{2}{3}} + \frac{2}{3}x^{-\frac{1}{3}} = \frac{1}{3}x^{-\frac{1}{3}}(5x + 2)$

$= \frac{5x + 2}{3x^{\frac{1}{3}}}$

CV: $x = 0$ and $x = -\frac{2}{5}$

Increasing on $\left(-\infty, -\frac{2}{5}\right)$ and $(0, \infty)$;

decreasing on $\left(-\frac{2}{5}, 0\right)$. Relative maximum

when $x = -\frac{2}{5}$; relative minimum when

$x = 0$.

25. $y = x^5 - 5x^4 + 3x$

$y' = 5x^4 - 20x^3 + 3$

$y'' = 20x^3 - 60x^2 = 20x^2(x - 3)$

Possible inflection points occur when $x = 0$ or $x = 3$. Concave down on $(-\infty, 0)$ and $(0, 3)$; concave up on $(3, \infty)$. Concavity changes around $x = 3$, so there is an inflection point at $x = 3$.

27. $y = (3x - 5)\left(x^4 + 2\right) = 3x^5 - 5x^4 + 6x - 10$

$y' = 15x^4 - 20x^3 + 6$

$y'' = 60x^3 - 60x^2 = 60x^2(x - 1)$

Possible inflection points occur when $x = 0$ or $x = 1$. Concave down on $(-\infty, 0)$ and $(0, 1)$; concave up on $(1, \infty)$. Inflection point when $x = 1$.

29. $y = \frac{x^2}{e^x} = x^2 e^{-x}$

$y' = x^2\left(-e^{-x}\right) + e^{-x}(2x) = -e^{-x}\left(x^2 - 2x\right)$

$y'' = -\left[e^{-x}(2x - 2) + \left(x^2 - 2x\right)\left(-e^{-x}\right)\right]$

$= e^{-x}\left[-(2x - 2) + \left(x^2 - 2x\right)\right]$

$= e^{-x}\left(x^2 - 4x + 2\right)$

y'' is defined for all x and y'' is zero only

when $x^2 - 4x + 2 = 0$. By the quadratic

formula the only possible points of inflection

occur when $x = 2 \pm \sqrt{2}$. Concave up on

$\left(-\infty, 2 - \sqrt{2}\right)$ and $\left(2 + \sqrt{2}, \infty\right)$; concave

down on $\left(2 - \sqrt{2}, 2 + \sqrt{2}\right)$. Inflection points

when $x = 2 \pm \sqrt{2}$.

31. $f(x) = 3x^4 - 4x^3$ and f is continuous on

$[0, 2]$.

$f'(x) = 12x^3 - 12x^2 = 12x^2(x - 1)$

The only critical value on $(0, 2)$ is $x = 1$.

Evaluating f at this value and at the endpoints

gives $f(0) = 0$, $f(1) = -1$, and $f(2) = 16$.

Absolute maximum: $f(2) = 16$; absolute

minimum $f(1) = -1$.

33. $f(x) = \frac{x}{(5x - 6)^2}$ and f is continuous on

$[-2, 0]$.

$f'(x) = \frac{(5x - 6)^2(1) - x[10(5x - 6)]}{(5x - 6)^4}$

$= \frac{(5x - 6)[(5x - 6) - 10x]}{(5x - 6)^4} = \frac{-5x - 6}{(5x - 6)^3}$

$$= -\frac{5x+6}{(5x-6)^3}$$

The only critical value on $(-2, 0)$ is $x = -\frac{6}{5}$.

Evaluating f at this value and at the endpoints gives

$f(-2) = -\frac{1}{128}$, $f\left(-\frac{6}{5}\right) = -\frac{1}{120}$ and

$f(0) = 0$. Absolute maximum: $f(0) = 0$;

absolute minimum: $f\left(-\frac{6}{5}\right) = -\frac{1}{120}$.

35. $f(x) = \left(x^2 + 1\right)e^{-x}$

a. $f'(x) = \left(x^2 + 1\right)\left(-e^{-x}\right) + e^{-x}(2x)$

$= -e^{-x}\left[\left(x^2 + 1\right) - 2x\right]$

$= -e^{-x}\left(x^2 - 2x + 1\right)$

$= -e^{-x}(x-1)^2$

CV: $x = 1$

Decreasing on $(-\infty, 1)$ and $(1, \infty)$. No relative extrema.

b. $f''(x)$

$= -\left\{e^{-x}[2(x-1)] + (x-1)^2\left(-e^{-x}\right)\right\}$

$= e^{-x}(x-1)[-2 + (x-1)]$

$= e^{-x}(x-1)(x-3)$

Possible inflection points when $x = 1, 3$. Concave up on $(-\infty, 1)$ and $(3, \infty)$; concave down on $(1, 3)$. Inflection

points at $(1, f(1)) = \left(1, 2e^{-1}\right)$ and

$(3, f(3)) = \left(3, 10e^{-3}\right)$.

37. $y = x^2 - 2x - 24 = (x+4)(x-6)$

Intercepts: $(-4, 0)$, $(6, 0)$, $(0, -24)$

No symmetry. No asymptotes.

$y' = 2(x-1)$

CV: $x = 1$

Increasing on $(1, \infty)$; decreasing on $(-\infty, 1)$; relative minimum at

$(1, -25)$.

$y'' = 2$

No possible inflection point. Concave up on

$(-\infty, \infty)$.

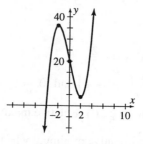

39. $y = x^3 - 12x + 20$

Intercept: $(0, 20)$

No symmetry; no asymptotes

$y' = 3x^2 - 12$

$= 3\left(x^2 - 4\right) = 3(x+2)(x-2)$

CV: $x = \pm 2$

Increasing on $(-\infty, -2)$ and $(2, \infty)$; decreasing on $(-2, 2)$; relative maximum at $(-2, 36)$; relative minimum at $(2, 4)$.

$y'' = 6x$

Possible inflection point when $x = 0$.

Concave up on $(0, \infty)$; concave down on $(-\infty, 0)$; inflection point at $(0, 20)$.

41. $y = x^3 + x = x\left(x^2 + 1\right)$

Intercept $(0, 0)$

Symmetric about the origin. No asymptotes.

$y' = 3x^2 + 1$

CV: None

Increasing on $(-\infty, \infty)$.

$y'' = 6x$

Possible inflection point when $x = 0$.

Concave down on $(-\infty, 0)$; concave up on $(0, \infty)$; inflection point at $(0, 0)$.

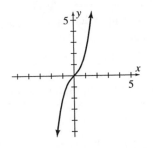

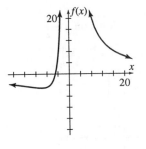

43. $y = f(x) = \dfrac{100(x+5)}{x^2}$

Intercept: $(-5, 0)$

No symmetry.

$x = 0$ is the only vertical asymptote.

$\lim\limits_{x\to\infty} y = 100 \lim\limits_{x\to\infty} \dfrac{x}{x^2} = 100 \lim\limits_{x\to\infty} \dfrac{1}{x} = 0$, and

$\lim\limits_{x\to-\infty} y = 0$, so $y = 0$ is the only horizontal

asymptote.

$y = 100\left[x^{-1} + 5x^{-2} \right]$

$y' = 100\left[-x^{-2} - 10x^{-3} \right] = -100\left[\dfrac{1}{x^2} + \dfrac{10}{x^3} \right]$

$= \dfrac{-100(x+10)}{x^3}$

CV: $x = -10$ but $x = 0$ must be included in analysis for inc-dec. Increasing on $(-10, 0)$; decreasing on $(-\infty, -10)$ and $(0, \infty)$; relative minimum at $(-10, -5)$.

$y'' = 100\left[2x^{-3} + 30x^{-4} \right] = 200\left[\dfrac{1}{x^3} + \dfrac{15}{x^4} \right]$

$= \dfrac{200(x+15)}{x^4}$

Possible inflection point when $x = -15$, but $x = 0$ must also be considered in concavity analysis. Concave up on $(-15, 0)$ and $(0, \infty)$; concave down on $(-\infty, -15)$; inflection point at $\left(-15, -\dfrac{40}{9} \right)$

45. $y = \dfrac{x}{(2x-1)^3}$

Intercept: $(0, 0)$

No symmetry. Vertical asymptote is $x = \dfrac{1}{2}$.

$\lim\limits_{x\to\infty} y = \lim\limits_{x\to\infty} \dfrac{x}{8x^3} = \lim\limits_{x\to\infty} \dfrac{1}{8x^2} = 0$

$= \lim\limits_{x\to-\infty} y$, so $y = 0$ is a horizontal

asymptote.

$y' = \dfrac{(2x-1)^3(1) - x\left[6(2x-1)^2 \right]}{(2x-1)^6}$

$= \dfrac{(2x-1)^2\left[(2x-1) - 6x \right]}{(2x-1)^6}$

$= -\dfrac{4x+1}{(2x-1)^4}$

CV: $x = -\dfrac{1}{4}$, but $x = \dfrac{1}{2}$ must be considered in inc.-dec. analysis. Increasing on $\left(-\infty, -\dfrac{1}{4} \right)$; decreasing on $\left(-\dfrac{1}{4}, \dfrac{1}{2} \right)$ and $\left(\dfrac{1}{2}, \infty \right)$; relative maximum at $\left(-\dfrac{1}{4}, \dfrac{2}{27} \right)$.

$y'' = -\dfrac{(2x-1)^4(4) - (4x+1)\left[8(2x-1)^3 \right]}{(2x-1)^8}$

$= -\dfrac{4(2x-1)^3\left[(2x-1) - 2(4x+1) \right]}{(2x-1)^8}$

$= -\dfrac{4(-6x-3)}{(2x-1)^5} = \dfrac{12(2x+1)}{(2x-1)^5}$

Possible inflection point when $x = -\dfrac{1}{2}$, but

$x = \dfrac{1}{2}$ must be considered in concavity

analysis. Concave up on $\left(-\infty, -\dfrac{1}{2} \right)$ and

$\left(\frac{1}{2}, \infty\right)$; concave down on $\left(-\frac{1}{2}, \frac{1}{2}\right)$;

inflection point at $\left(-\frac{1}{2}, \frac{1}{16}\right)$.

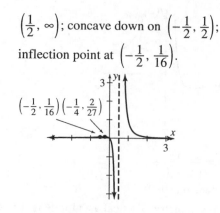

47. $f(x) = \dfrac{e^x + e^{-x}}{2}$

Intercept (0, 1)

Symmetric about the y-axis. No asymptotes.

$f'(x) = \dfrac{e^x - e^{-x}}{2}$

Setting

$f'(x) = 0 \Rightarrow e^x = e^{-x} \Rightarrow x = -x \Rightarrow x = 0$

CV: $x = 0$

Increasing on $(0, \infty)$; decreasing on $(-\infty, 0)$; relative minimum at (0, 1). Finding $f''(x)$

gives: $f''(x) = \dfrac{e^x + e^{-x}}{2}$. $f''(x) > 0$ for all

x. No possible inflection point. Concave up on $(-\infty, \infty)$.

49. a. False. $f'(x_0) = 0$ only indicates the possibility of a relative extremum at x_0, For example, if $f(x) = x^3$, then $f'(x) = 3x^2$ and $f'(0) = 0$. However there is no relative extremum at $x = 0$.

b. False. For example, let $x_1 = -1$ and $x_2 = 1$. Then $x_1 < x_2$ and $f(x_1) = -1 < f(x_2) = 1$.

c. True. The absolute minimum is $f(0) = 0$ and the absolute maximum is $f(1) = 1$.

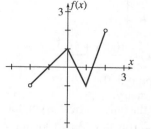

d. False. If concavity does not change around x_0, then $\left(x_0, f(x_0)\right)$ is not an inflection point. For example, consider $f(x) = x^4$. If $x_0 = 0$, then $f''(x_0) = 0$, but $\left(x_0, f(x_0)\right)$ is not an inflection point. See graph in part (c).

e. False. Consider the function f whose graph is shown. On (–2, 2) it has exactly one relative maximum [at the point (0, 1)] but no absolute maximum.

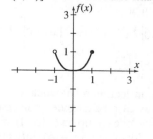

51. $c = q^3 - 6q^2 + 12q + 18$

Marginal cost $= \dfrac{dc}{dq} = 3q^2 - 12q + 12$.

Marginal cost is increasing when its derivative, which is $\dfrac{d^2c}{dq^2}$, is positive.

$\dfrac{d^2c}{dq^2} = 6q - 12 = 6(q - 2)$

$\dfrac{d^2c}{dq^2} > 0$ for $q > 2$. Thus marginal cost is

increasing for $q > 2$.

53. $p = 150 - \dfrac{\sqrt{q}}{10}$, $q > 0$. The revenue function

r is given by

$$r = pq = \left(150 - \dfrac{\sqrt{q}}{10}\right)q = 150q - \dfrac{q^{\frac{3}{2}}}{10}.$$

$$r' = 150 - \dfrac{3}{20}q^{\frac{1}{2}}$$

$$r'' = -\dfrac{3}{40}q^{-\frac{1}{2}} = -\dfrac{3}{40\sqrt{q}}$$

Since $r'' < 0$ for $q > 0$, the graph of the revenue function is concave down for $q > 0$.

55. $f(t) = At^3 + Bt^2 + Ct + D$

$f'(t) = 3At^2 + 2Bt + C$

$f''(t) = 6At + 2B$, which gives an inflection point when $6At + 2B = 0$, that is for

$t_0 = -\dfrac{B}{3A}$. This value of t_0 must be such

that $f'(t_0) = 0$.

$$3A\left(-\dfrac{B}{3A}\right)^2 + 2B\left(-\dfrac{B}{3A}\right) + C = 0$$

$$\dfrac{1}{3}\left(\dfrac{B^2}{A}\right) - \dfrac{2}{3}\left(\dfrac{B^2}{A}\right) + C = 0$$

$$C = \dfrac{1}{3}\left(\dfrac{B^2}{A}\right)$$

$3AC = B^2$,

which was to be shown.

57.

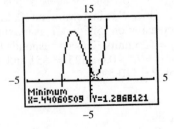

Relative maximum $(-1.32, 12.28)$; relative minimum $(0.44, 1.29)$

59.

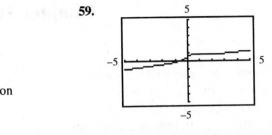

The x-value of the inflection point of f corresponds to the x-intercept of f''. Thus the x-value of the inflection point is $x = -0.60$.

Chapter 15

Exercise 15.1

1. Let the numbers be x and $40 - x$. Then if
$P = x(40 - x) = 40x - x^2$, we have
$P' = 40 - 2x$. Setting $P' = 0 \Rightarrow x = 20$.
Since $P''(20) = -2 < 0$, there is a maximum
when $x = 20$. Because $40 - x = 20$, the
required numbers are 20 and 20.

3. We are given that $5x + 3(2y) = 3000$, or
$y = \dfrac{3000 - 5x}{6}$. We want to maximize area
A, where $A = xy$.
$A = xy = x\left(\dfrac{3000 - 5x}{6}\right) = \dfrac{1}{6}\left(3000x - 5x^2\right)$
$A' = \dfrac{1}{6}(3000 - 10x)$
Setting $A' = 0 \Rightarrow x = 300$. Since
$A''(300) = \dfrac{1}{6}(-10) < 0$, we have a
maximum at $x = 300$. Thus
$y = \dfrac{3000 - 5(300)}{6} = 250$. The dimensions
are 300 ft by 250 ft.

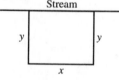

5. $c = 0.05q^2 + 5q + 500$
Avg. Cost per unit
$= \bar{c} = \dfrac{c}{q} = 0.05q + 5 + \dfrac{500}{q}$
$\bar{c}' = 0.05 - \dfrac{500}{q^2}$. Setting $\bar{c}' = 0$ yields
$0.05 = \dfrac{500}{q^2}$, $q^2 = 10,000$, $q = \pm 100$. We
exclude $q = -100$ because q represents the
number of units. Since $\bar{c}'' = \dfrac{1000}{q^3} > 0$ for
$q > 0$, $\bar{c}$ is an absolute minimum when
$q = 100$ units.

7. $p = -5q + 30$
Since total revenue = (price)(quantity),
$r = pq = (-5q + 30)q = -5q^2 + 30q$
Setting $r' = -10q + 30 = 0 \Rightarrow q = 3$. Since
$r'' = -10 < 0$, r is maximum at $q = 3$ units,
for which the corresponding price is
$p = -5(3) + 30 = \$15$.

9. $f(p) = 160 - p - \dfrac{900}{p + 10}$, where $0 \le p \le 100$.
Setting $f'(p) = 0$ gives $-1 + \dfrac{900}{(p + 10)^2} = 0$,
$\dfrac{900}{(p + 10)^2} = 1$,
$(p + 10)^2 = 900$, $p + 10 = \pm 30$, from which
$p = 20$.

  a. Since $f''(p) = \dfrac{-1800}{(p + 10)^3} < 0$ for
$p = 20$, we have an absolute maximum
of $f(20) = 110$ grams.

  b. $f(0) = 70$ and $f(100) = 51\dfrac{9}{11}$, so we
have an absolute minimum of
$f(100) = 51\dfrac{9}{11}$ grams.

11. $p = 72 - 0.04q$
$c = 500 + 30q$
Profit = Total Revenue − Total Cost
$P = pq - c = (72 - 0.04q)q - (500 + 30q)$
$= -\left(0.04q^2 - 42q + 500\right)$
Setting $P' = -(0.08q - 42) = 0$ yields
$q = 525$. Since P is increasing on $[0, 525)$
and decreasing on $(525, \infty)$, P is maximum
when $q = 525$ units. This corresponds to a
price of $p = 72 - 0.04(525) = \$51$ and a
profit of $P = \$10,525$.

13. $p = 42 - 4q$
$\bar{c} = 2 + \dfrac{80}{q}$
Total Cost $= c = \bar{c}q = 2q + 80$
Profit = Total Revenue − Total Cost

$P = pq - c = (42 - 4q)q - (2q + 80)$
$= -\left(4q^2 - 40q + 80\right)$
$P' = -(8q - 40)$
Setting $P' = -(8q - 40) = 0$ gives $q = 5$. We find that $P'' = -8 < 0$, so P has a maximum value when $q = 5$. The corresponding price p is $42 - 4(5) = \$22$.

15. $p = q^2 - 100q + 3200$ on [0, 120]

$\bar{c} = \frac{2}{3}q^2 - 40q + \frac{10,000}{q}$

Profit = Total Revenue – Total Cost
Since total revenue $r = pq$ and
total cost $= c = \bar{c}q$,

$P = pq - \bar{c}q$

$= q^3 - 100q^2 + 3200q - \left(\frac{2}{3}q^3 - 40q^2 + 10,000\right)$

$= \frac{1}{3}q^3 - 60q^2 + 3200q - 10,000$

$P' = q^2 - 120q + 3200 = (q - 40)(q - 80)$

Setting $P' = 0$ gives $q = 40$ or 80.
Evaluating profit at $q = 0, 40, 80,$ and 120
gives $P(0) = -10,000$

$P(40) = \frac{130,000}{3} = 43,333\frac{1}{3}$

$P(80) = \frac{98,000}{3} = 32,666\frac{2}{3}$

$P(120) = 86,000$
Thus the profit maximizing output is
$q = 120$ units, and the corresponding
maximum profit is \$86,000.

17. Total fixed costs = \$1200,
material-labor costs/unit = \$2, and the
demand equation is $p = \dfrac{100}{\sqrt{q}}$.

Profit = Total Revenue – Total Cost
$P = pq - c$
$P = \dfrac{100}{\sqrt{q}} \cdot q - (2q + 1200)$

$= 100\sqrt{q} - 2q - 1200$

$= 2\left(50\sqrt{q} - q - 600\right)$

Setting $P' = 2\left(\dfrac{25}{\sqrt{q}} - 1\right) = 0$ yields $q = 625$.

We see that $P'' = -25q^{-\frac{3}{2}} < 0$ for $q > 0$, so P is maximum when $q = 625$. When MR equals MC, then $\dfrac{50}{\sqrt{q}} = 2$ or, equivalently, $q = 625$. When $q = 625$, then $p = \$4$.

19. If x = number of \$0.50 decreases, where $0 \le x \le 36$, then the monthly fee for each subscriber is $18 - 0.50x$, and the total number of subscribers is $4800 + 150x$. Let r be the total (monthly) revenue.
revenue
= (monthly rate)(number of subscribers)
$r = (18 - 0.50x)(4800 + 150x)$
r'
$= (18 - 0.50x)(150) + (4800 + 150x)(-0.50)$
$= 300 - 150x = 150(2 - x)$
Setting $r' = 0$ yields $x = 2$.
Evaluating r when $x = 0, 2,$ and 36, we find that r is a maximum when $x = 2$. This corresponds to a monthly fee of $18 - 0.50(2) = \$17$ and a monthly revenue r of \$86,700.

21. See Fig. 15.6 in the text. Given that $x^2y = 32$, we want to minimize $S = 4(xy) + x^2$. Since $y = \dfrac{32}{x^2}$, where $x > 0$, we have $S = 4x\left(\dfrac{32}{x^2}\right) + x^2 = \left(\dfrac{128}{x}\right) + x^2$, from which $S' = \left(-\dfrac{128}{x^2}\right) + 2x$. Setting $S' = 0$ gives $2x^3 = 128$, $x^3 = 64$, $x = 4$.
Since $S'' = \left(\dfrac{256}{x^3}\right) + 2$, we get $S''(4) > 0$, so $x = 4$ gives a minimum. If $x = 4$, then $y = \dfrac{32}{16} = 2$. The dimensions are 4 ft $\times$ 4 ft $\times$ 2 ft.

23. $V = x(12 - 2x)^2$
$= 144x - 48x^2 + 4x^3$
$= 4\left(36x - 12x^2 + x^3\right)$
where $0 < x < 6$.

$$V' = 4\left(36 - 24x + 3x^2\right)$$

$$= 12\left(x^2 - 8x + 12\right)$$

$$= 12(x - 6)(x - 2)$$

For $0 < x < 6$, setting $V' = 0$ gives $x = 2$. Since $V' > 0$ on $(0, 2)$ and $V' < 0$ on $(2, 6)$, V is maximum when $x = 2$. Thus the length of the side of the square must be 2 in., which results in a volume of

$$(12 - 4)^2 (2) = 128 \text{ in.}^3.$$

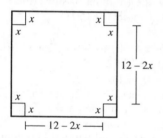

25. See Fig. 15.9 in text.

$$V = K = \pi r^2 h \qquad (1)$$

$$S = 2\pi rh + \pi r^2 \qquad (2)$$

From Equation (1) $h = \dfrac{K}{\pi r^2}$. Thus Equation (2) becomes

$$S = \frac{2K}{r} + \pi r^2$$

$$\frac{dS}{dr} = -\frac{2K}{r^2} + 2\pi r = \frac{2\left(\pi r^3 - K\right)}{r^2}.$$

If $S' = 0$, then $\pi r^3 - K = 0$, $\pi r^3 = K$,

$r = \sqrt[3]{\dfrac{K}{\pi}}$. Thus

$$h = \frac{K}{\pi \left(\frac{K}{\pi}\right)^{\frac{2}{3}}} = \left(\frac{K}{\pi}\right)^{\frac{1}{3}} = \sqrt[3]{\frac{K}{\pi}}.$$

Note that since $S'' = 2\pi + \dfrac{4K}{r^3} > 0$ for $r > 0$, we have a minimum.

27. $p = 600 - 2q$

$c = 0.2q^2 + 28q + 200$

Profit = Total Revenue − Total Cost

$P = pq - c$

$$P = (600 - 2q)q - \left(0.2q^2 + 28q + 200\right)$$

$$= -\left(2.2q^2 - 572q + 200\right)$$

$$P' = -(4.4q - 572)$$

Setting $P' = 0$ yields $q = 130$. Since $P'' = -4.4 < 0$, P is maximum when $q = 130$ units. The corresponding price is $p = 600 - 2(130) = \$340$, and the profit is $P = \$36,980$. If a tax of \$22/unit is imposed on the manufacturer, then the cost equation is

$$c_1 = 0.2q^2 + 28q + 200 + 22q$$

$$= 0.2q^2 + 50q + 200.$$

The demand equation remains the same. Thus

$$P_1 = pq - c_1$$

$$= (600 - 2q)q - \left(0.2q^2 + 50q + 200\right)$$

$$= -\left(2.2q^2 - 550q + 200\right)$$

$$P'_1 = -(4.4q - 550)$$

Setting $P'_1 = 0$ yields $q = 125$. Since $P''_1 = -4.4 < 0$, P_1 is maximum when $q = 125$ units. The corresponding price is $p = \$350$ and the profit is $P_1 = \$34,175$.

29. Let q = number of units in a production run. Since inventory is depleted at a uniform rate, assume that the average inventory is $\dfrac{q}{2}$. The value of average inventory is $10\left(\dfrac{q}{2}\right)$, and carrying costs are $0.128\left[10\left(\dfrac{q}{2}\right)\right]$. The number of production runs per year is $\dfrac{1000}{q}$, and total set-up costs are $40\left(\dfrac{1000}{q}\right)$. We want to minimize the sum C of carry costs and set-up costs.

$$C = 0.128\left[10\left(\frac{q}{2}\right)\right] + 40\left(\frac{1000}{q}\right)$$

$$= 0.64q + \frac{40,000}{q}$$

$$C' = 0.64 - \frac{40,000}{q^2}$$

Setting $C' = 0$ yields

$$q^2 = \frac{40,000}{0.64} = 62,500,$$

$q = 250$ (since $q > 0$). Since

$$C'' = \frac{80,000}{q^3} > 0,$$

C is minimum when $q = 250$. Thus the economic lot size is 250/lot (4 lots).

31. Let x = number of people over the 30.
    Note: $0 \le x \le 10$.
    Revenue = r
    = (number attending)(charge/person)
    = $(30 + x)(50 - 1.25x)$
    = $1500 + 12.5x - 1.25x^2$
    $r' = 12.5 - 2.5x$
    Setting $r' = 0$ yields $x = 5$. Since
    $r'' = -2.5 < 0$, r is maximum when $x = 5$,
    that is, when 35 attend.

33. The cost per mile of operating the truck
    $= 0.11 + \frac{s}{300}$. Driver's salary is $12/hr. The
    number of hours for 700 mi trip is $\frac{700}{s}$.
    Driver's salary for trip is $12\left(\frac{700}{s}\right)$, or $\frac{8400}{s}$.
    The cost of operating the truck for the trip is
    $700\left[0.11 + \frac{s}{300}\right]$.
    Total cost of trip
    $= C = \frac{8400}{s} + 700\left(0.11 + \frac{s}{300}\right)$
    Setting $C' = -\frac{8400}{s^2} + \frac{7}{3} = 0$ yields
    $s^2 = 3600$, or
    $s = 60$ (since $s > 0$). Since $C'' = \frac{16,800}{s^3} > 0$
    for $s > 0$, C is a minimum when $s = 60$ mi/h.

35. Profit P is given by
    P = Total revenue – Total cost
    = Total revenue – (salaries + fixed cost)
    = $50q - (750m + 2500)$
    = $50\left(m^3 - 12m^2 + 60m\right) - 750m - 2500$

$$= 50\left(m^3 - 12m^2 + 45m - 50\right), \text{ where}$$

$0 \le m \le 7$

$$P' = 50\left(3m^2 - 24m + 45\right)$$

$$= 150\left(m^2 - 8m + 15\right) = 150(m - 3)(m - 5)$$

Setting $P' = 0$ gives the critical values 3 and 5. We now evaluate P at these critical values and also at the endpoints 0 and 7.
$P(0) = -2500$
$P(3) = 200$
$P(5) = 0$
$P(7) = 1000$
Thus Ms. Jones should hire 7 salespeople to obtain a maximum weekly profit of $1000.

37. x = tons of chemical A ($x \le 4$),
    $y = \frac{24 - 6x}{5 - x}$ = tons of chemical B, profit on
    A = $2000/ton, and profit on B = $1000/ton.
    Total Profit $= P_T = 2000x + 1000\left(\frac{24 - 6x}{5 - x}\right)$

$$= 2000\left[x + \frac{12 - 3x}{5 - x}\right]$$

$$P'_T = 2000\left[1 + \frac{(5 - x)(-3) - (12 - 3x)(-1)}{(5 - x)^2}\right]$$

$$= 2000\left[1 - \frac{3}{(5 - x)^2}\right]$$

$$= 2000\left[\frac{x^2 - 10x + 22}{(5 - x)^2}\right]$$

Setting $P'_T = 0$ yields (by the quadratic formula)

$$x = \frac{10 \pm 2\sqrt{3}}{2} = 5 \pm \sqrt{3}$$

Because $x \le 4$, choose $x = 5 - \sqrt{3}$. Since P_T is increasing on $\left[0, 5 - \sqrt{3}\right)$ and decreasing on $\left(5 - \sqrt{3}, 4\right]$, P_T is a maximum for $x = 5 - \sqrt{3}$ tons. If profit on A is P/ton and profit on B is $\frac{P}{2}$/ton, then

$$P_T = Px + \frac{P}{2}\left(\frac{24 - 6x}{5 - x}\right) = P\left[x + \frac{12 - 3x}{5 - x}\right]$$

$$P'_T = P\left[\frac{x^2 - 10x + 22}{(5-x)^2}\right]$$

Setting $P'_T = 0$ and using an argument similar to that above, we find that P_T is a maximum when $x = 5 - \sqrt{3}$ tons.

39. $P(j) = Aj\dfrac{L^4}{V} + B\dfrac{V^3L^2}{1+j}$

$$\frac{dP}{dj} = \frac{AL^4}{V} - \frac{BV^3L^2}{(1+j)^2} = 0$$

Solving for $(1+j)^2$ gives $(1+j)^2 = \dfrac{BV^4}{AL^2}$

41. $\bar{c} = \dfrac{c}{q} = 3q + 50 - 18\ln(q) + \dfrac{120}{q},\ q > 0$

$$\frac{d\bar{c}}{dq} = 3 - \frac{18}{q} - \frac{120}{q^2} = \frac{3q^2 - 18q - 120}{q^2}$$

$$= \frac{3\left(q^2 - 6q - 40\right)}{q^2}$$

$$= \frac{3(q-10)(q+4)}{q^2}$$

Critical value is $q = 10$ since $q \geq 0$.
Since $\dfrac{d\bar{c}}{dq} < 0$ for $0 < q < 10$, and $\dfrac{d\bar{c}}{dq} > 0$
for $q > 10$, we have a minimum when $q = 10$ cases. This minimum average cost is $3(10) + 50 - 18\ln 10 + 12 \approx \$50.55$.

Exercise 15.2

1. $y = 3x - 4$
$$dy = \frac{d}{dx}(3x - 4)dx = 3\ dx$$

3. $d[f(x)] = f'(x)dx = \dfrac{1}{2}\left(x^4 + 2\right)^{-1/2}\left(4x^3\right)dx$

$$= \frac{2x^3}{\sqrt{x^4 + 2}}dx$$

5. $u = x^{-2}$
$$du = \frac{d}{dx}\left(x^{-2}\right)dx = -2x^{-3}dx = -\frac{2}{x^3}dx$$

7. $dp = \dfrac{d}{dx}\left[\ln\left(x^2 + 7\right)\right]dx = \dfrac{1}{x^2 + 7}(2x)dx$

$$= \frac{2x}{x^2 + 7}dx$$

9. $dy = y'dx$
$$= \left[(4x+3)e^{2x^2+3}(4x) + e^{2x^2+3}(4)\right]dx$$
$$= 4e^{2x^2+3}[(4x+3)x + 1]dx$$
$$= 4e^{2x^2+3}\left(4x^2 + 3x + 1\right)dx$$

11. $\Delta y = [4 - 7(3.02)] - [4 - 7(3)] = -0.14$
$dy = -7\ dx = -7(0.02) = -0.14$

13. $\Delta y = \left[4(-0.75)^2 - 3(-0.75) + 10\right]$
$$-\left[4(-1)^2 - 3(-1) + 10\right] = -2.5$$
$dy = (8x - 3)\ dx = [8(-1) - 3]\ (0.25) = -2.75$

15. $\Delta y = \sqrt{25 - (2.9)^2} - \sqrt{25 - 3^2} \approx 0.073$
$$dy = \frac{-x}{\sqrt{25 - x^2}}dx = \frac{-3}{\sqrt{16}}(-0.1) = \frac{3}{40}$$
$$= 0.075$$

17. a. $f(x) = \dfrac{x+5}{x+1}$
$$f'(x) = \frac{(x+1)(1) - (x+5)(1)}{(x+1)^2}$$
$$= \frac{-4}{(x+1)^2}$$
$$f'(1) = \frac{-4}{4} = -1$$

b. We use $f(x + dx) \approx f(x) + dy$ with $x = 1$, $dx = 0.1$.
$$f(1.1) = f(1 + 0.1) \approx f(1) + f'(1)dx$$
$$= \frac{6}{2} + (-1)(0.1) = 2.9$$

19. Let $y = f(x) = \sqrt{x}$
$$f(x + dx) \approx f(x) + dy = \sqrt{x} + \frac{1}{2\sqrt{x}}dx$$

If $x = 100$ and $dx = 1$, then
$$\sqrt{101} = f(100 + 1) \approx \sqrt{100} + \frac{1}{2\sqrt{100}} \quad (1)$$
$$= 10.05$$

21. Let $y = f(x) = \sqrt[3]{x}$
$$f(x + dx) \approx f(x) + dy = \sqrt[3]{x} + \frac{1}{3x^{\frac{2}{3}}} dx$$
If $x = 64$ and $dx = -1$, then
$$\sqrt[3]{63} = f(64 + (-1)) \approx \sqrt[3]{64} + \frac{1}{3(\sqrt[3]{64})^2}(-1)$$
$$= 4 + \frac{-1}{3 \cdot 4^2} = 3\frac{47}{48}$$

23. Let $y = f(x) = \ln x$
$$f(x + dx) \approx f(x) + dy = \ln(x) + \frac{1}{x} dx$$
If $x = 1$ and $dx = -0.03$, then
$$\ln(0.97) = f(1 + (-0.03))$$
$$\approx \ln(1) + \frac{1}{1}(-0.03) = -0.03$$

25. Let $y = f(x) = e^x$
$$f(x + dx) \approx f(x) + dy = e^x + e^x dx$$
If $x = 0$ and $dx = 0.01$, then
$$e^{0.01} = f(0 + 0.01) \approx e^0 + e^0(0.01) = 1.01$$

27. $\frac{dy}{dx} = 2$, so $\frac{dx}{dy} = \frac{1}{\frac{dy}{dx}} = \frac{1}{2}$

29. $\frac{dq}{dp} = 6p(p^2 + 5)^2$, so $\frac{dp}{dq} = \frac{1}{6p(p^2 + 5)^2}$

31. $q = p^{-1}$, $\frac{dq}{dp} = -1p^{-2} = \frac{-1}{p^2}$, so $\frac{dp}{dq} = -p^2$

33. $\frac{dx}{dy} = \frac{1}{\frac{dy}{dx}} = \frac{1}{10x + 3}$

If $x = 1$, then $\frac{dx}{dy} = \frac{1}{13}$

35. $p = \frac{500}{q + 2}$
$$\frac{dp}{dq} = \frac{-500}{(q + 2)^2}$$
$$\frac{dq}{dp} = -\frac{(q + 2)^2}{500}$$
$$\left.\frac{dq}{dp}\right|_{q=18} = -\left.\frac{(q + 2)^2}{500}\right|_{q=18} = -\frac{4}{5}$$

37. $P = 396q - 2.2q^2 - 400$, q changes from 80 to 81.
$$\Delta P \approx dP = P' \, dq = (396 - 4.4q)dq$$
Choosing $q = 80$ and $dq = 1$,
$$\Delta P \approx [396 - 4.4(80)](1) = 44.$$
True change is
$$P(81) - P(80) = 17{,}241.80 - 17{,}200 = 41.80$$

39. $p = \frac{10}{\sqrt{q}}$. We approximate p when $q = 24$.
$$p(q + dq) \approx p + dp = \frac{10}{\sqrt{q}} - \frac{5}{\sqrt{q^3}} dq$$
If $q = 25$ and $dq = -1$, then
$$\frac{10}{\sqrt{24}} = p(25 + (-1)) \approx \frac{10}{\sqrt{25}} - \frac{5}{\sqrt{(25)^3}}(-1)$$
$$= 2 + \frac{1}{25} = \frac{51}{25} = 2.04$$

41. $c = \frac{q^4}{2} + 3q + 400$
If $q = 10$ and $dq = 2$,
$$\frac{dc}{c} = \frac{(2q^3 + 3)dq}{\frac{q^4}{2} + 3q + 400} = \frac{(2003)(2)}{5430} \approx 0.7$$

43. $V = \frac{4}{3}\pi r^3$
$$dV = 4\pi r^2 \, dr$$
Now, the change in r is
$$dr = (6.6 \times 10^{-4}) - (6.5 \times 10^{-4})$$
$$= 0.1 \times 10^{-4} = 10^{-5} \text{ Thus}$$
$$dV = 4\pi (6.5 \times 10^{-4})^2 (10^{-5})$$
$$\approx (1.69 \times 10^{-11})\pi \text{ cm}^3.$$

45. a. We substitute $q = 40$ and $p = 20$

$$2 + \frac{40^2}{200} = \frac{4000}{20^2}$$

$$2 + 8 = 10$$

$$10 = 10$$

b. We differentiate implicitly with respect to p.

$$0 + \frac{1}{200}\left(2q\frac{dq}{dp}\right) = -\frac{8000}{p^3}$$

From part (a) $q = 40$ when $p = 20$. Substituting gives

$$\frac{1}{200}\left(2 \cdot 40\frac{dq}{dp}\right) = -\frac{8000}{20^3}$$

$$\frac{dq}{dp} = -2.5$$

c. $q(p + dp) \approx q(p) + dq$

$$= q(p) + q'(p)dp$$

$$q(19.20) = q(20 + (-0.8))$$

$$\approx q(20) + q'(20)dp$$

$$= 40 + (-2.5)(-0.8) = 42 \text{ units}$$

Exercise 15.3

1. $\eta = \dfrac{\frac{p}{q}}{\frac{dp}{dq}} = \dfrac{\frac{p}{q}}{-2}$.

When $q = 5$ then $p = 40 - 2(5) = 30$, so

$$\eta = \frac{\frac{30}{5}}{-2} = -3$$

Because $|\eta| > 1$, demand is elastic.

3. $p = \dfrac{1000}{q} = 1000q^{-1}$

$$\frac{dp}{dq} = -1000q^{-2} = -\frac{1000}{q^2}$$

$$\eta = \frac{\frac{p}{q}}{\frac{dp}{dq}} = \frac{\frac{p}{q}}{-\frac{1000}{q^2}} = \frac{\frac{(1000/q)}{q}}{-\frac{1000}{q^2}} = -1$$

Because $|\eta| = 1$, demand has unit elasticity.

5. $\eta = \dfrac{\frac{p}{q}}{\frac{dp}{dq}} = \dfrac{\frac{p}{q}}{-\frac{500}{(q+2)^2}} = \dfrac{\frac{[500/(q+2)]}{q}}{-\frac{500}{(q+2)^2}} = -\frac{q+2}{q}$

When $q = 100$, then $\eta = -\dfrac{102}{100} = -1.02$.

Because $|\eta| > 1$, demand is elastic.

7. $\eta = \dfrac{\frac{p}{q}}{\frac{dp}{dq}} = \dfrac{\frac{p}{q}}{\frac{-e^{\frac{q}{100}}}{100}}$

When $q = 100$, then $p = 150 - e$ and

$\eta = \dfrac{\frac{150-e}{100}}{-\frac{e}{100}} = -\left(\dfrac{150}{e} - 1\right)$. Because $|\eta| > 1$,

demand is elastic.

9. $q = 600 - 100p$

$$\eta = \frac{\frac{p}{q}}{\frac{dp}{dq}} = \frac{p}{q} \cdot \frac{dq}{dp} = \frac{p}{q}(-100)$$

If $p = 3$, then $q = 600 - 100(3) = 300$, so

$\eta = \dfrac{3}{300}(-100) = -1$. Since $|\eta| = 1$, demand

has unit elasticity.

11. $q = \sqrt{2500 - p}$

$$\eta = \frac{\frac{p}{q}}{\frac{dp}{dq}} = \frac{p}{q} \cdot \frac{dq}{dp}$$

$$\frac{dq}{dp} = \frac{1}{2}(2500 - p)^{-\frac{1}{2}}(-1) = \frac{-1}{2\sqrt{2500 - p}}$$

$$= -\frac{1}{2q}$$

$$\eta = \frac{p}{q}\left(-\frac{1}{2q}\right) = -\frac{p}{2q^2}$$

If $p = 900$, then $q = \sqrt{2500 - 900} = 40$, so

$\eta = -\dfrac{900}{3200} = -\dfrac{9}{32}$. $|\eta| < 1$, so demand is

inelastic.

13. $q = \dfrac{(p-100)^2}{2}$

$\eta = \dfrac{\frac{p}{q}}{\frac{dp}{dq}} = \dfrac{p}{q} \cdot \dfrac{dq}{dp}$

$\dfrac{dq}{dp} = \dfrac{1}{2}(2)(p-100)(1) = p-100$, so

$\eta = \dfrac{p}{q}(p-100)$. If $p = 20$, then

$q = \dfrac{(20-100)^2}{2} = 3200$. Thus

$\eta = \dfrac{20}{3200}(20-100) = -\dfrac{1}{2}$. Demand is inelastic.

15. $p = 13 - 0.05q$

$\eta = \dfrac{\frac{p}{q}}{\frac{dp}{dq}} = -\dfrac{p}{0.05q}$

p	q	η	demand
10	60	$-\dfrac{10}{3}$	elastic
3	200	$-\dfrac{3}{10}$	inelastic
6.50	130	-1	unit elasticity

17. $q = 500 - 40p + p^2$

$\eta = \dfrac{\frac{p}{q}}{\frac{dp}{dq}} = \dfrac{p}{q} \cdot \dfrac{dq}{dp}$

$\dfrac{dq}{dp} = -40 + 2p$, so $\eta = \dfrac{p}{q}(2p-40)$.

When $p = 15$, then

$q = 500 - 40(15) + 15^2 = 125$, so

$\eta|_{p=15} = \dfrac{15}{125}(30-40) = -\dfrac{6}{5} = -1.2$. Now,

(% change in price) $\cdot$ (η) = % change in demand. Thus if the price of 15 increases $\dfrac{1}{2}$%, then the change in demand is

approximately $\left(\dfrac{1}{2}\%\right)(-1.2) = -0.6\%$. Thus demand decreases approximately 0.6%.

19. $p = 500 - 2q$

$\eta = \dfrac{\frac{p}{q}}{\frac{dp}{dq}} = \dfrac{\frac{500-2q}{q}}{-2} = \dfrac{q-250}{q}$

If demand is elastic, then $\eta = \dfrac{q-250}{q} < -1$.

For $q > 0$, we have $q - 250 < -q$, $2q < 250$, so $q < 125$. Thus, if $0 < q < 125$, demand is elastic. If demand is inelastic, then

$\eta = \dfrac{q-250}{q} > -1$. For $q > 0$, the inequality implies $q > 125$. Thus if $125 < q < 250$, then demand is inelastic.
Since Total Revenue

$= r = pq = 500q - 2q^2$, then

$r' = 500 - 4q = 4(125 - q)$. If $0 < q < 125$, then $r' > 0$, so r is increasing. If $125 < q < 250$, then $r' < 0$, so r is decreasing.

21. $p = \dfrac{1000}{q^2}$

$r = pq = \dfrac{1000}{q}$

$\dfrac{dr}{dq} = -1000q^{-2} = -\dfrac{1000}{q^2}$

$\eta = \dfrac{\frac{p}{q}}{\frac{dp}{dq}} = \dfrac{\frac{1000}{q^3}}{-\frac{2000}{q^3}} = -\dfrac{1}{2}$

$p\left(1 + \dfrac{1}{\eta}\right) = \dfrac{1000}{q^2}(1-2) = -\dfrac{1000}{q^2} = \dfrac{dr}{dq}$

23. a. $p = \dfrac{200}{\sqrt{6000 + 10q^2}}$

Substituting $p = 2$ and $q = 20$:

$2 = \dfrac{200}{\sqrt{6000 + 10(20)^2}}$

$2 = \dfrac{200}{100}$

$2 = 2$

b. $\dfrac{dp}{dq} = 200\left(-\dfrac{1}{2}\right)\left(6000 + 10q^2\right)^{-\frac{3}{2}}(20q)$

$= \dfrac{-2000q}{\left(6000 + 10q^2\right)^{\frac{3}{2}}}$

$= \dfrac{200}{\sqrt{6000 + 10q^2}} \cdot \dfrac{-10q}{6000 + 10q^2}$

$= \dfrac{-10pq}{6000 + 10q^2}$

Thus

$\eta = \dfrac{\frac{p}{q}}{\frac{dp}{dq}} = \dfrac{\frac{p}{q}}{\frac{-10pq}{6000+10q^2}} = \dfrac{-\left(6000 + 10q^2\right)}{10q^2}$

When $p = 2$ we have $q = 20$, so

$\eta\big|_{p=2} = \dfrac{-\left[6000 + 10(20)^2\right]}{10(20)^2} = -2.5$

Thus demand is elastic.

c. If the price (when $p = 2$) is decreased by 2%, then the percentage change in demand is $(-2)(-2.5) = 5\%$. Since $q = 20$ when $p = 2$, this means that q will increase approximately by 5% of 20, which is 1. That is, demand increases by 1 unit (approx).

d. Total revenue will increase when the price is lowered because demand is elastic (see the discussion of elasticity and revenue in the text).

25. a. $q = \dfrac{60}{p} + \ln\left(65 - p^3\right)$

$\eta = \dfrac{\frac{p}{q}}{\frac{dp}{dq}} = \dfrac{p}{q}\dfrac{dq}{dp} = \dfrac{p}{q}\left[-\dfrac{60}{p^2} - \dfrac{3p^2}{65 - p^3}\right]$

If $p = 4$, then $q = \dfrac{60}{4} + \ln 1 = 15$, so

$\eta = \dfrac{4}{15}\left[-\dfrac{60}{16} - \dfrac{3(16)}{65 - 64}\right] = -\dfrac{207}{15}$

≈ -13.8, elastic

b. The percentage change in q is $(-2)(-13.8) = 27.6\%$, so q increases by approximately 27.6%.

c. Lowering the price increases revenue because demand is elastic.

27. The percentage change in price is $\dfrac{-5}{80} \cdot 100 = -\dfrac{25}{4}\%$ and the percentage change in quantity is $\dfrac{50}{500} \cdot 100 = 10\%$ thus, since (elasticity)(% change in price) $\approx$ % change in demand,

(elasticity) $\left(-\dfrac{25}{4}\right) \approx 10$

elasticity $\approx -\dfrac{40}{25} = -\dfrac{8}{5} = -1.6$

To estimate $\dfrac{dr}{dq}$ when $p = 80$, we have

$\dfrac{dr}{dq} = p\left(1 + \dfrac{1}{\eta}\right) = 80\left(1 + \dfrac{1}{-\frac{8}{5}}\right) = 30$

29. $\dfrac{dp}{dq} = 200(-1)(q + 5)^{-2} = \dfrac{-200}{(q + 5)^2}$

Thus $\eta = \dfrac{\frac{p}{q}}{\frac{dp}{dq}} = \dfrac{\frac{200}{q(q+5)}}{-\frac{200}{(q+5)^2}} = -\dfrac{q + 5}{q}$.

For $5 \leq q \leq 95$, $|\eta| = \dfrac{q + 5}{q} = 1 + \dfrac{5}{q}$ and $|\eta|' = -\dfrac{5}{q^2}$.

Since $|\eta|' < 0$, $|\eta|$ is decreasing on $[5, 95]$, and thus $|\eta|$ is maximum at $q = 5$ and minimum at $q = 95$.

Principles in Practice 15.4

1. Let $f(x) = 20x - 0.01x^2 - 850 + 3\ln x$, then $f'(x) = 20 - 0.02x + \frac{3}{x}$. $f(10) \approx -644$ and $f(50) \approx 137$,
    so we use 50 to be the first approximation, x_1, to find the break-even quantity between 10 and 50.

$$x_{n+1} = x_n - \frac{f(x_n)}{f'(x_n)} = x_n - \frac{20x_n - 0.01x_n^2 - 850 + 3\ln x_n}{20 - 0.02x_n + 3x_n^{-1}}$$

$$= x_n - \frac{20x_n^2 - 0.01x_n^3 - 850x_n + 3x_n \ln x_n}{20x_n - 0.02x_n^2 + 3}$$

$$= \frac{20x_n^2 - 0.02x_n^3 + 3x_n - \left(20x_n^2 - 0.01x_n^3 - 850x_n + 3x_n \ln x_n\right)}{20x_n - 0.02x_n^2 + 3}$$

$$= \frac{-0.01x_n^3 + 853x_n - 3x_n \ln x_n}{20x_n - 0.02x_n^2 + 3}$$

$$x_2 = 50 - \frac{f(50)}{f'(50)} \approx 42.82602$$

$$x_3 = 42.82602 - \frac{f(42.82602)}{f'(42.82602)} \approx 42.85459$$

$$x_4 = 42.85459 - \frac{f(42.85459)}{f'(42.85459)} \approx 42.85459$$

Since the values of x_3 and x_4 differ by less than 0.0001, we take the first break-even quantity
to be $x \approx 42.85459$ or 43 televisions.
$f(1900) \approx 1073$ and $f(2000) \approx -827$, so we use 2000 to be the first approximation, x_1, for the break-even
quantity between 1900 and 2000.

$$x_2 = 2000 - \frac{f(2000)}{f'(2000)} \approx 1958.63703$$

$$x_3 = 1958.63703 - \frac{f(1958.63703)}{f'(1958.63703)} \approx 1957.74457$$

$$x_4 = 1957.74457 - \frac{f(1957.74457)}{f'(1957.74457)} \approx 1957.74415$$

$$x_5 = 1957.74415 - \frac{f(1957.74415)}{f'(1957.74415)} \approx 1957.74415$$

Since the values of x_4 and x_5 differ by less than 0.0001, we take the second break-even quantity to be
$x \approx 1957.74415$ or 1958 televisions.

Exercise 15.4

1. We want a root of $f(x) = x^3 - 4x + 1 = 0$. We see that $f(0) = 1$ and $f(1) = -2$ have opposite signs, so
    there must be a root between 0 and 1. Moreover, $f(0)$ is closer to 0 than is $f(1)$, so we select $x_1 = 0$ as our
    initial estimate. Since $f'(x) = 3x^2 - 4$, the recursion formula is

$$x_{n+1} = x_n - \frac{f(x_n)}{f'(x_n)} = x_n - \frac{x_n^3 - 4x_n + 1}{3x_n^2 - 4}.$$

Simplifying gives $x_{n+1} = \dfrac{2x_n^3 - 1}{3x_n^2 - 4}$. Thus we obtain:

n	x_n	x_{n+1}
1	0.00000	0.25000
2	0.25000	0.25410
3	0.25410	0.25410

Because $|x_4 - x_3| < 0.0001$, the root is approximately $x_4 = 0.25410$.

3. Let $f(x) = x^3 - x - 1$. We have $f(1) = -1$ and $f(2) = 5$ (note the sign change). Since $f(1)$ is closer to 0 than is $f(2)$, we choose $x_1 = 1$. We have $f'(x) = 3x^2 - 1$, so the recursion formula is

$$x_{n+1} = x_n - \frac{f(x_n)}{f'(x_n)} = x_n - \frac{x_n^3 - x_n - 1}{3x_n^2 - 1}$$
$$= \frac{2x_n^3 + 1}{3x_n^2 - 1}$$

n	x_n	x_{n+1}
1	1.00000	1.50000
2	1.50000	1.34783
3	1.34783	1.32520
4	1.32520	1.32472
5	1.32472	1.32472

Since $|x_6 - x_5| < 0.0001$, the root is approximately $x_6 = 1.32472$.

5. Let $f(x) = x^3 + x + 16$. We have $f(-3) = -14$ and $f(-2) = 6$ (note the sign change). Since $f(-2)$ is closer to 0 than is $f(-3)$, we choose $x_1 = -2$. Since

$f'(x) = 3x^2 + 1$, the recursion formula is

$$x_{n+1} = x_n - \frac{f(x)}{f'(x_n)} = x_n - \frac{x_n^3 + x_n + 16}{3x_n^2 + 1}$$
$$= \frac{2x_n^3 - 16}{3x_n^2 + 1}$$

n	x_n	x_{n+1}
1	-2.00000	-2.46154
2	-2.46154	-2.38977
3	-2.38977	-2.38769
4	-2.38769	-2.38769

Because $|x_5 - x_4| < 0.0001$, the root is approximately $x_5 = -2.38769$.

7. $x^4 = 3x - 1$, so use $f(x) = x^4 - 3x + 1 = 0$. Since $f(0) = 1$ and $f(1) = -1$ (note the sign change), $f(0)$ and $f(1)$ are equally close to 0. We shall choose $x_1 = 0$. Since $f'(x) = 4x^3 - 3$, the recursion formula is

$$x_{n+1} = x_n - \frac{f(x_n)}{f'(x_n)} = x_n - \frac{x_n^4 - 3x_n + 1}{4x_n^3 - 3}$$
$$= \frac{3x_n^4 - 1}{4x_n^3 - 3}$$

n	x_n	x_{n+1}
1	0.00000	0.33333
2	0.33333	0.33766
3	0.33766	0.33767

Because $|x_4 - x_3| < 0.0001$, the root is approximately $x_4 = 0.33767$.

9. Let $f(x) = x^4 - 2x^3 + x^2 - 3$. $f(1) = -3$ and $f(2) = 1$ (note the sign change), so $f(2)$ is closer to 0 than is $f(1)$. We choose $x_1 = 2$. Since $f'(x) = 4x^3 - 6x^2 + 2x$, the recursion formula is

$$x_{n+1} = x_n - \frac{f(x)}{f'(x_n)}$$

$$= x_n - \frac{x_n^4 - 2x_n^3 + x_n^2 - 3}{4x_n^3 - 6x_n^2 + 2x_n}$$

n	x_n	x_{n+1}
1	2.00000	1.91667
2	1.91667	1.90794
3	1.90794	1.90785

Because $|x_4 - x_3| < 0.0001$, the root is approximately $x_4 = 1.90785$.

11. The desired number is x, where $x^3 = 70$, or $x^3 - 70 = 0$. Thus we want to find a root of $f(x) = x^3 - 70 = 0$. Since $4^3 = 64$, the solution should be close to 4, so we choose $x_1 = 4$ as our initial estimate. We have $f'(x) = 3x^2$, so the recursion formula is

$$x_{n+1} = x_n - \frac{f(x_n)}{f'(x_n)} = x_n - \frac{x_n^3 - 70}{3x_n^2}$$

$$= \frac{2x_n^3 + 70}{3x_n^2}$$

n	x_n	x_{n+1}
1	4	4.125
2	4.125	4.121
3	4.121	4.121

Thus to three decimal places, $\sqrt[3]{70} = 4.121$.

13. We want real solutions to $e^x = x + 5$. Thus we want to find roots of $f(x) = e^x - x - 5 = 0$. A rough sketch of the exponential function $y = e^x$ and the line $y = x + 5$ shows that there are two intersection points: one when x is near -5, and the other when x is near 3. Thus we must find two roots. Since $f'(x) = e^x - 1$, the recursion formula is

$$x_{n+1} = x_n - \frac{f(x_n)}{f'(x_n)} = x_n - \frac{e^{x_n} - x_n - 5}{e^{x_n} - 1}$$

If $x_1 = -5$, we obtain

n	x_n	x_{n+1}
1	-5	-4.99
2	-4.99	-4.99

If $x_1 = 3$, we obtain:

n	x_n	x_{n+1}
1	3	2.37
2	2.37	2.03
3	2.03	1.94
4	1.94	1.94

Thus the solutions are -4.99 and 1.94.

15. The break-even quantity is the value of q when total revenue and total cost are equal: $r = c$, or $r - c = 0$. Thus we must find a root of $3q - (250 + 2q - 0.1q^3) = 0$, or $f(q) = q - 250 + 0.1q^3 = 0$, so $f'(q) = 1 + 0.3q^2$. The recursion formula is

$$q_{n+1} = q_n - \frac{f(q_n)}{f'(q_n)} = q_n - \frac{q_n - 250 + 0.1q_n^3}{1 + 0.3q_n^2}$$

We choose $q_1 = 13$, as suggested.

n	x_n	x_{n+1}
1	13	13.33
2	13.33	13.33

Thus $q \approx 13.33$.

17. The equilibrium quantity is the value of q for which supply and demand are equal, that is, it is a root of $2q + 5 = \dfrac{100}{q^2 + 1}$, or of $f(q) = 2q + 5 - \dfrac{100}{q^2 + 1} = 0$. Since

$f'(q) = 2 + \dfrac{200q}{\left(q^2+1\right)^2}$, the recursion

formula is

$q_{n+1} = q_n - \dfrac{f(q_n)}{f'(q_n)} = q_n - \dfrac{2q_n + 5 - \frac{100}{q_n{}^2+1}}{2 + \frac{200q_n}{\left(q_n{}^2+1\right)^2}}$

A rough sketch shows that the graph of the supply equation intersects the graph of the demand equation when q is near 3. Thus we select $q_1 = 3$.

n	x_n	x_{n+1}
1	3	2.875
2	2.875	2.880
3	2.880	2.880

Thus $q \approx 2.880$.

19. For a critical value of

$f(x) = \dfrac{x^3}{3} - x^2 - 5x + 1$, we want a root of

$f'(x) = x^2 - 2x - 5 = 0$. Since

$\dfrac{d}{dx}[f'(x)] = 2x - 2$, the recursion formula is

$x_{n+1} = x_n - \dfrac{x_n{}^2 - 2x_n - 5}{2x_n - 2}$.

For the given interval [3, 4], note that $f'(3) = -2$ and $f'(4) = 3$ have opposite signs. Thus there is a root x between 3 and 4. Since 3 is closer to 0, we shall select $x_1 = 3$.

n	x_n	x_{n+1}
1	3.0	3.5
2	3.5	3.45
3	3.45	3.45

Thus $x \approx 3.45$.

Chapter 15 Review Problems

1. $q = 80m^2 - 0.1m^4$

$\dfrac{dq}{dm} = 160m - 0.4m^3 = 0.4m\left(400 - m^2\right)$

$= 0.4m(20+m)(20-m)$. Setting $\dfrac{dq}{dm} = 0$

yields $m = 0$ or $m = 20$ (for $m \geq 0$). We find that q is increasing on (0, 20) and decreasing on (20, ∞), so q is maximum at $m = 20$.

3. $p = \sqrt{600 - q}$, where $100 \leq q \leq 300$.

Total Revenue $= r = pq = q\sqrt{600 - q}$

$r' = q\left(\dfrac{1}{2}\right)(600 - q)^{-\frac{1}{2}}(-1) + \sqrt{600 - q}\,(1)$

$= \dfrac{1}{2}(600 - q)^{-\frac{1}{2}}[-q + 2(600 - q)]$

$= \dfrac{1200 - 3q}{2\sqrt{600 - q}}$

$= \dfrac{3(400 - q)}{2\sqrt{600 - q}}$

No critical values over [100, 300]. Since $r' > 0$ on [100, 300], r is increasing on [100, 300], so r must have a maximum at $q = 300$.

5. $p = 400 - 2q$

$\bar{c} = q + 160 + \dfrac{2000}{q}$

Total Cost $= c = \bar{c}q = q^2 + 160q + 2000$

Profit = Total Revenue − Total Cost

$P = pq - c$

$= (400 - 2q)q - \left(q^2 + 160q + 2000\right)$

$= -\left(3q^2 - 240q + 2000\right)$

$P' = -(6q - 240) = -6(q - 40)$

Setting $P' = 0$ yields $q = 40$. Since $P'' = -6 < 0$, P is maximum when $q = 40$, and the corresponding profit is

$P = -\left[3 \cdot 40^2 - 240(40) + 2000\right] = \$2800$.

7. $2x + 4y = 800$; thus $x = 400 - 2y$

Area $= A = xy = (400 - 2y)y$

$= 400y - 2y^2$

$\dfrac{dA}{dy} = 400 - 4y = 4(100 - y)$

Setting $\dfrac{dA}{dy} = 0$ gives $y = 100$. Since

$\dfrac{d^2A}{dy^2} = -4 < 0$, A is maximum when

$y = 100$. When $y = 100$, then $x = 200$. The dimensions are 200 ft by 100 ft.

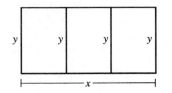

9. a. $c = 2q^3 - 9q^2 + 12q + 20$, where

$\dfrac{3}{4} \le q \le 6$.

$\dfrac{dc}{dq} = 6q^2 - 18q + 12 = 6\left(q^2 - 3q + 2\right)$

$= 6(q - 1)(q - 2)$

Setting $\dfrac{dc}{dq} = 0$ gives $q = 1$ or 2.

Evaluating c at these critical values and the endpoints: $c\left(\dfrac{3}{4}\right) = \dfrac{793}{32} \approx 24.78$,

$c(1) = 25$, $c(2) = 24$, $c(6) = 200$. Thus a minimum occurs at $q = 2$, which corresponds to 200 stands and a total cost of \$24,000. This gives an average

cost per stand of $\dfrac{24,000}{200} = \$120$.

b. There are no critical values of $3 \le q \le 6$, so we only evaluate c at the endpoints: $c(3) = 29$, $c(6) = 200$. Thus a minimum occurs at $q = 3$, which gives 300 stands.

11. $d\left[x^2 \ln(x + 5)\right] = \dfrac{d}{dx}\left[x^2 \ln(x + 5)\right]dx$

$= \left[\dfrac{x^2}{x + 5} + 2x \ln(x + 5)\right]dx$

13. $F = \dfrac{9}{5}C + 32$

$dF = F'dC = \dfrac{9}{5}dC$, so when

$dC = \dfrac{1}{2}°$, $dF = \dfrac{9}{5}\left(\dfrac{1}{2}\right)° = \left(\dfrac{9}{10}\right)°$.

15. Let $y = f(x) = e^x$

$f(x + dx) \approx f(x) + dy = e^x + e^x dx$

If $x = 0$ and $dx = -0.01$, then

$e^{-0.01} = f(0 + (-0.01)) \approx e^0 + e^0(-0.01)$

$= 1 - 0.01 = 0.99$

17. $x = 4y^2 + 7y - 3$

$\dfrac{dy}{dx} = \dfrac{1}{\dfrac{dx}{dy}} = \dfrac{1}{8y + 7}$

19. $p = 900 - q^2$

$\eta = \dfrac{\frac{p}{q}}{\frac{dp}{dq}} = \dfrac{\frac{900-q^2}{q}}{-2q} = -\dfrac{900 - q^2}{2q^2}$

When $q = 10$, then $\eta = -4$. Since $|\eta| > 1$, demand is elastic.

21. $p = 30 - \sqrt{q}$

$\eta = \dfrac{\frac{p}{q}}{\frac{dp}{dq}} = \dfrac{\frac{p}{q}}{-\frac{1}{2\sqrt{q}}} = \dfrac{-2p}{\sqrt{q}} = \dfrac{-2p}{30 - p} = \dfrac{2p}{p - 30}$

a. When $p = 10$, then $\eta = \dfrac{2(10)}{10 - 30} = -1$.

b. $\eta = \dfrac{2p}{p - 30}$

If $0 < p < 10$, then $-1 < \eta < 0$, so $|\eta| < 1$ and demand is inelastic.

23. a. $\eta = \dfrac{\frac{p}{q}}{\frac{dp}{dq}} = \dfrac{p}{q} \cdot \dfrac{dq}{dp}$

$q = \sqrt{100 - p}$, where $0 < p < 100$.

$\dfrac{dq}{dp} = \dfrac{-1}{2\sqrt{100 - p}}$. Thus

$$\eta = \frac{p}{\sqrt{100-p}} \cdot \frac{-1}{2\sqrt{100-p}}$$

$$= \frac{-p}{2(100-p)} = \frac{p}{2p-200}$$

For elastic demand we want

$\frac{p}{2p-200} < -1$. Noting that the denominator is negative for $0 < p < 100$, we multiply both sides of the inequality by $2p - 200$ and reverse the direction of the inequality

$$p > -2p + 200, \; 3p > 200, \; p > \frac{200}{3}$$

Thus $\frac{200}{3} < p < 100$ for elastic demand.

b. $\eta\big|_{p=40} = \frac{40}{80-200} = -\frac{1}{3}$

% change in $q \approx$ (% change in price)(η)

$= 5\left(-\frac{1}{3}\right)\% = -\frac{5}{3}\% = -1.67\%$. Thus demand decreases by approximately 1.67%.

25. We want real solutions of $e^x = 3x$. Thus we want to find roots of $f(x) = e^x - 3x = 0$. A rough sketch of the exponential function $y = e^x$ and the line $y = 3x$ shows that there are two intersection points: one when x is near 0.5, and the other when x is near 1.5. Thus we must find two roots. Since $f'(x) = e^x - 3$, the recursion formula is

$$x_{n+1} = x_n - \frac{f(x_n)}{f'(x_n)} = x_n - \frac{e^{x_n} - 3x_n}{e^{x_n} - 3}$$

If $x_1 = 0.5$, we obtain

n	x_n	x_{n+1}
1	0.5	0.610
2	0.610	0.619
3	0.619	0.619

If $x_1 = 1.5$, we obtain

n	x_n	x_{n+1}
1	1.5	1.512
2	1.512	1.512

Thus the solutions are 0.619 and 1.512.

Chapter 16

Principles in Practice 16.1

1. $\int 28.3\, dq = 28.3q + C$

The form of the cost function is $28.3q + C$.

2. $\int 0.12t^2 dt = 0.12\dfrac{t^3}{3} + C = 0.04t^3 + C$

The revenue function is $R(t) = 0.04t^3 + C$.

3. Let $S(t)$ = the number of subscribers t months after the competition entered the market, then $S'(t) = -\dfrac{480}{t^3}$.

$S(t) = \int -\dfrac{480}{t^3}\, dt = -480\int t^{-3} dt$

$= -480\left(\dfrac{t^{-2}}{-2}\right) + C = 240t^{-2} + C = \dfrac{240}{t^2} + C$

The number of subscribers is $S(t) = \dfrac{240}{t^2} + C$.

4. $\int \left(500 + 300\sqrt{t}\right) dt = \int \left(500 + 300t^{\frac{1}{2}}\right) dt$

$= 500t + \dfrac{t^{\frac{3}{2}}}{\frac{3}{2}} + C = 500t + \dfrac{2}{3}t^{\frac{3}{2}} + C$

The population is $N(t) = 500t + \dfrac{2}{3}t^{\frac{3}{2}} + C$

5. The amount of money saved is $\int \dfrac{dS}{dt}\, dt$.

$\int \left(2.1t^2 - 65.4t + 491.6\right) dt$

$= 2.1\left(\dfrac{t^3}{3}\right) - 65.4\left(\dfrac{t^2}{2}\right) + 491.6t + C$

$= 0.7t^3 - 32.7t^2 + 491.6t + C$

The amount of money saved is

$S(t) = 0.7t^3 - 32.7t^2 + 491.6t + C$

Exercise 16.1

1. $\int 5\, dx = 5x + C$

3. $\int x^8 dx = \dfrac{x^{8+1}}{8+1} + C = \dfrac{x^9}{9} + C$

5. $\int 5x^{-7} dx = 5\int x^{-7} dx = 5 \cdot \dfrac{x^{-7+1}}{-7+1} + C$

$= 5 \cdot \dfrac{x^{-6}}{-6} + C = -\dfrac{5}{6x^6} + C$

7. $\int \dfrac{1}{x^{10}}\, dx = \int x^{-10} dx = \dfrac{x^{-10+1}}{-10+1} + C$

$= \dfrac{x^{-9}}{-9} + C = -\dfrac{1}{9x^9} + C$

9. $\int \dfrac{1}{y^{\frac{11}{5}}}\, dy = \int y^{-\frac{11}{5}} dy = \dfrac{y^{-\frac{11}{5}+1}}{-\frac{11}{5}+1} + C$

$= \dfrac{y^{-\frac{6}{5}}}{-\frac{6}{5}} + C = -\dfrac{5}{6y^{\frac{6}{5}}} + C$

11. $\int (8+u)\, du = \int 8\, du + \int u\, du$

$= 8u + \dfrac{u^{1+1}}{1+1} + C = 8u + \dfrac{u^2}{2} + C$

13. $\int \left(y^5 - 5y\right) dy = \int y^5 dy - \int 5y\, dy$

$= \dfrac{y^{5+1}}{5+1} - 5 \cdot \dfrac{y^{1+1}}{1+1} + C$

$= \dfrac{y^6}{6} - 5 \cdot \dfrac{y^2}{2} + C = \dfrac{y^6}{6} - \dfrac{5y^2}{2} + C$

15. $\int \left(3t^2 - 4t + 5\right) dt$

$= 3\int t^2 dt - 4\int t\, dt + \int 5\, dt$

$= 3 \cdot \dfrac{t^3}{3} - 4 \cdot \dfrac{t^2}{2} + 5t + C = t^3 - 2t^2 + 5t + C$

17. Since $7 + e$ is a constant,

$\int (7+e)\, dx = (7+e)x + C.$

19. $\int\left(\frac{x}{7}-\frac{3}{4}x^4\right)dx = \frac{1}{7}\int x\,dx - \frac{3}{4}\int x^4 dx$

$= \frac{1}{7}\cdot\frac{x^2}{2} - \frac{3}{4}\cdot\frac{x^5}{5} + C$

$= \frac{x^2}{14} - \frac{3x^5}{20} + C$

21. $\int 3e^x dx = 3\int e^x dx = 3e^x + C$

23. $\int\left(x^{8.3} - 9x^6 + 3x^{-4} + x^{-3}\right)dx$

$= \frac{x^{9.3}}{9.3} - 9\cdot\frac{x^7}{7} + 3\cdot\frac{x^{-3}}{-3} + \frac{x^{-2}}{-2} + C$

$= \frac{x^{9.3}}{9.3} - \frac{9x^7}{7} - \frac{1}{x^3} - \frac{1}{2x^2} + C$

25. $\int\frac{-2\sqrt{x}}{3}dx = -\frac{2}{3}\int x^{\frac{1}{2}}dx = -\frac{2}{3}\cdot\frac{x^{\frac{1}{2}+1}}{\frac{1}{2}+1} + C$

$= -\frac{2}{3}\cdot\frac{x^{\frac{3}{2}}}{\frac{3}{2}} + C = -\frac{4x^{\frac{3}{2}}}{9} + C$

27. $\int\frac{1}{4\sqrt[8]{x^7}}dx = \frac{1}{4}\int x^{-\frac{7}{8}}dx = \frac{1}{4}\cdot\frac{x^{\frac{-7}{8}+1}}{\frac{-7}{8}+1} + C$

$= \frac{1}{4}\cdot\frac{x^{\frac{1}{8}}}{\frac{1}{8}} + C = 2\sqrt[8]{x} + C$

29. $\int\left(\frac{x^3}{3} - \frac{3}{x^3}\right)dx = \frac{1}{3}\int x^3 dx - 3\int x^{-3}dx$

$= \frac{1}{3}\cdot\frac{x^{3+1}}{3+1} - 3\cdot\frac{x^{-3+1}}{-3+1} + C$

$= \frac{1}{3}\cdot\frac{x^4}{4} - 3\cdot\frac{x^{-2}}{-2} + C = \frac{x^4}{12} + \frac{3}{2x^2} + C$

31. $\int\left(\frac{3w^2}{2} - \frac{2}{3w^2}\right)dw$

$= \frac{3}{2}\int w^2 dw - \frac{2}{3}\int w^{-2}dw$

$= \frac{3}{2}\cdot\frac{w^3}{3} - \frac{2}{3}\cdot\frac{w^{-1}}{-1} + C = \frac{w^3}{2} + \frac{2}{3w} + C$

33. $\int\frac{2z-5}{7}dz = \frac{1}{7}\int(2z-5)dz$

$= \frac{1}{7}\left(2\int z\,dz - \int 5\,dz\right)$

$= \frac{1}{7}\left(2\cdot\frac{z^{1+1}}{1+1} - 5z\right) + C$

$= \frac{1}{7}\left(2\cdot\frac{z^2}{2} - 5z\right) + C = \frac{1}{7}\left(z^2 - 5z\right) + C$

35. $\int\left(x^e + e^x\right)dx$

$= \int x^e dx + \int e^x dx = \frac{x^{e+1}}{e+1} + e^x + C$

37. $\int\left(2\sqrt{x} - 3\sqrt[4]{x}\right)dx = \int\left(2x^{\frac{1}{2}} - 3x^{\frac{1}{4}}\right)dx$

$= 2\int x^{\frac{1}{2}}dx - 3\int x^{\frac{1}{4}}dx$

$= 2\cdot\frac{x^{\frac{1}{2}+1}}{\frac{1}{2}+1} - 3\cdot\frac{x^{\frac{1}{4}+1}}{\frac{1}{4}+1} + C$

$= 2\cdot\frac{x^{\frac{3}{2}}}{\frac{3}{2}} - 3\cdot\frac{x^{\frac{5}{4}}}{\frac{5}{4}} + C = \frac{4x^{\frac{3}{2}}}{3} - \frac{12x^{\frac{5}{4}}}{5} + C$

39. $\int\left(-\frac{\sqrt[3]{x^2}}{5} - \frac{7}{2\sqrt{x}} + 6x\right)dx$

$= \int\left(-\frac{x^{\frac{2}{3}}}{5} - \frac{7x^{-\frac{1}{2}}}{2} + 6x\right)dx$

$= -\frac{1}{5}\int x^{\frac{2}{3}}dx - \frac{7}{2}\int x^{-\frac{1}{2}}dx + 6\int x\,dx$

$= -\frac{1}{5}\cdot\frac{x^{\frac{5}{3}}}{\frac{5}{3}} - \frac{7}{2}\cdot\frac{x^{\frac{1}{2}}}{\frac{1}{2}} + 6\cdot\frac{x^2}{2} + C$

$= -\frac{3x^{\frac{5}{3}}}{25} - 7x^{\frac{1}{2}} + 3x^2 + C$

41. $\int\left(x^2 + 5\right)(x-3)dx$

$= \int\left(x^3 - 3x^2 + 5x - 15\right)dx$

$= \frac{x^4}{4} - 3\cdot\frac{x^3}{3} + 5\cdot\frac{x^2}{2} - 15x + C$

$= \frac{x^4}{4} - x^3 + \frac{5x^2}{2} - 15x + C$

43. $\int \sqrt{x}(x+3)dx = \int \left(x^{\frac{3}{2}} + 3x^{\frac{1}{2}} \right)dx$

$= \dfrac{x^{\frac{5}{2}}}{\frac{5}{2}} + 3 \cdot \dfrac{x^{\frac{3}{2}}}{\frac{3}{2}} + C$

$= \dfrac{2x^{\frac{5}{2}}}{5} + 2x^{\frac{3}{2}} + C$

45. $\int (2u+1)^2 du = \int \left(4u^2 + 4u + 1 \right)du$

$= 4 \cdot \dfrac{u^3}{3} + 4 \cdot \dfrac{u^2}{2} + u + C$

$= \dfrac{4u^3}{3} + 2u^2 + u + C$

47. $\int v^{-2}\left(2v^4 + 3v^2 - 2v^{-3} \right)dv$

$= \int \left(2v^2 + 3 - 2v^{-5} \right)dv$

$= 2 \cdot \dfrac{v^3}{3} + 3v - 2 \cdot \dfrac{v^{-4}}{-4} + C$

$= \dfrac{2v^3}{3} + 3v + \dfrac{1}{2v^4} + C$

49. $\int \dfrac{z^4 + 10z^3}{5z^2}\,dz = \dfrac{1}{5}\int \left(\dfrac{z^4}{z^2} + \dfrac{10z^3}{z^2} \right)dz$

$= \dfrac{1}{5}\int \left(z^2 + 10z \right)dz$

$= \dfrac{1}{5}\left(\dfrac{z^3}{3} + 10 \cdot \dfrac{z^2}{2} \right) + C = \dfrac{z^3}{15} + z^2 + C$

51. $\int \dfrac{e^x + e^{2x}}{e^x}\,dx = \int \left(\dfrac{e^x}{e^x} + \dfrac{e^{2x}}{e^x} \right)dx$

$= \int \left(1 + e^x \right)dx = x + e^x + C$

53. No, $F(x) - G(x)$ must be a constant.

55. Because an antiderivative of the derivative of a function is the function itself, we have

$$\int \dfrac{d}{dx}\left[\dfrac{1}{\sqrt{x^2+1}} \right]dx = \dfrac{1}{\sqrt{x^2+1}} + C.$$

Principles in Practice 16.2

1. $N(t) = \int \dfrac{dN}{dt}\,dt = \int \left(800 + 200e^t \right)dt$

$= 800t + 200e^t + C$
Since $N(5) = 40{,}000$, we have
$40{,}000 = 800(5) + 200e^5 + C$, so
$C = 40{,}000 - \left(4000 + 200e^5 \right)$
$= 36{,}000 - 200e^5 \approx 6317.37$
$N(t) = 800t + 200e^t + 6317.37$

2. Since $y'' = \dfrac{d}{dt}(y') = 84t + 24$

$y' = \int (84t + 24)dt = 84\left(\dfrac{t^2}{2} \right) + 24t + C_1$

$= 42t^2 + 24t + C_1$
Since $y'(8) = 2891$, we have
$2891 = 42(8)^2 + 24(8) + C_1 = 2880 + C_1$, so
$C_1 = 2891 - 2880 = 11$, and
$y' = 42t^2 + 24t + 11.$

$y(t) = \int y'\,dt = \int \left(42t^2 + 24t + 11 \right)dt$

$= 42\left(\dfrac{t^3}{3} \right) + 24\left(\dfrac{t^2}{2} \right) + 11t + C_2$

$= 14t^3 + 12t^2 + 11t + C_2$
Since $y(2) = 185$, we have
$185 = 14(2)^3 + 12(2)^2 + 11(2) + C_2$
$= 182 + C_2$, so $C_2 = 185 - 182 = 3$.
$y(t) = 14t^3 + 12t^2 + 11t + 3$

Exercise 16.2

1. $\dfrac{dy}{dx} = 3x - 4$

$y = \int (3x - 4)dx = \dfrac{3x^2}{2} - 4x + C$

Using $y(-1) = \dfrac{13}{2}$ gives

$\dfrac{13}{2} = \dfrac{3(-1)^2}{2} - 4(-1) + C$

$\dfrac{13}{2} = \dfrac{11}{2} + C$

Thus $C = 1$, so $y = \dfrac{3x^2}{2} - 4x + 1.$

3. $y' = \dfrac{4}{\sqrt{x}}$

$$y = \int \frac{4}{\sqrt{x}} dx = \int 4x^{-\frac{1}{2}} dx = 4 \cdot \frac{x^{\frac{1}{2}}}{\frac{1}{2}} + C$$

Thus $y = 8x^{\frac{1}{2}} + C$. Now, $y(4) = 10$ implies

$10 = 8 \cdot (4)^{\frac{1}{2}} + C$, $10 = 16 + C$, $C = -6$. Thus

$y = 8\sqrt{x} - 6$. Evaluating at $x = 9$ gives

$y(9) = 8 \cdot 3 - 6 = 18$.

5. $y'' = -x^2 - 2x$

$$y' = \int \left(-x^2 - 2x\right) dx = -\frac{x^3}{3} - x^2 + C_1$$

$y'(1) = 0$ implies $0 = -\dfrac{1}{3} - 1 + C_1$, so

$C_1 = \dfrac{4}{3}$. Thus $y' = -\dfrac{x^3}{3} - x^2 + \dfrac{4}{3}$. Now we

integrate again to find y.

$$y = \int \left(-\frac{x^3}{3} - x^2 + \frac{4}{3}\right) dx$$

$$= -\frac{x^4}{12} - \frac{x^3}{3} + \frac{4x}{3} + C_2$$

$y(1) = 1$, so $1 = -\dfrac{1}{12} - \dfrac{1}{3} + \dfrac{4}{3} + C_2$, from

which $C_2 = \dfrac{1}{12}$. Thus we have

$$y = -\frac{x^4}{12} - \frac{x^3}{3} + \frac{4x}{3} + \frac{1}{12}.$$

7. $y''' = 2x$

$$y'' = \int 2x \, dx = x^2 + C_1$$

$y''(-1) = 3$ implies that $3 = 1 + C_1$, so

$C_1 = 2$.

$$y' = \int \left(x^2 + 2\right) dx = \frac{x^3}{3} + 2x + C_2$$

$y'(3) = 10$ implies $10 = 9 + 6 + C_2$, so

$C_2 = -5$. Thus $y = \int \left(\dfrac{x^3}{3} + 2x - 5\right) dx$

$$= \frac{x^4}{12} + x^2 - 5x + C_3.$$

$y(0) = 2$ implies that $2 = 0 + 0 - 0 + C_3$, so

$C_3 = 2$. Therefore $y = \dfrac{x^4}{12} + x^2 - 5x + 2$.

9. $\dfrac{dr}{dq} = 0.7$

$$r = \int 0.7 dq = 0.7q + C$$

If $q = 0$, r must be 0, so $0 = 0 + C$, $C = 0$.

Thus $r = 0.7q$. Since $r = pq$, we have

$p = \dfrac{r}{q} = \dfrac{0.7q}{q} = 0.7$. The demand function

is $p = 0.7$.

11. $\dfrac{dr}{dq} = 275 - q - 0.3q^2$

Thus

$$r = \int \left(275 - q - 0.3q^2\right) dq$$

$= 275q - 0.5q^2 - 0.1q^3 + C$. When $q = 0$,

r must be 0. Thus $0 = 0 - 0 - 0 + C$, so $C = 0$

and $r = 275q - 0.5q^2 - 0.1q^3$. Since $r = pq$,

then $p = \dfrac{r}{q} = 275 - 0.5q - 0.1q^2$. Thus the

demand function is $p = 275 - 0.5q - 0.1q^2$.

13. $\dfrac{dc}{dq} = 1.35$

$$c = \int 1.35 dq = 1.35q + C$$

When $q = 0$, then $c = 200$, so $200 = 0 + C$, or

$C = 200$. Thus $c = 1.35q + 200$.

15. $\dfrac{dc}{dq} = 0.09q^2 - 1.2q + 4.5$

$$c = \int \left(0.09q^2 - 1.2q + 4.5\right) dq$$

$= 0.03q^3 - 0.6q^2 + 4.5q + C$. If $q = 0$, then

$c = 7700$, from which $C = 7700$. Hence

$c = 0.03q^3 - 0.6q^2 + 4.5q + 7700$. If

$q = 10$, substituting gives $c = 7715$.

17. $G = \int \left[-\dfrac{P}{25} + 2\right] dP = -\dfrac{P^2}{50} + 2P + C$

When $P = 10$, then $G = 38$, so

$38 = -2 + 20 + C$, from which $C = 20$. Thus

$$G = -\frac{1}{50} P^2 + 2P + 20.$$

19. $v = \int -\dfrac{(P_1 - P_2)r}{2l\eta}\, dr = -\dfrac{(P_1 - P_2)r^2}{4l\eta} + C$

Since $v = 0$ when $r = R$, then

$0 = -\dfrac{(P_1 - P_2)R^2}{4l\eta} + C$, so $C = \dfrac{(P_1 - P_2)R^2}{4l\eta}$.

Thus $v = -\dfrac{(P_1 - P_2)r^2}{4l\eta} + \dfrac{(P_1 - P_2)R^2}{4l\eta}$

$= \dfrac{(P_1 - P_2)\left(R^2 - r^2\right)}{4l\eta}$.

21. $\dfrac{dc}{dq} = 0.003q^2 - 0.4q + 40$

$c = \int \left(0.003q^2 - 0.4q + 40\right) dq$

$= 0.003 \cdot \dfrac{q^3}{3} - 0.4 \cdot \dfrac{q^2}{2} + 40q + C$

$= 0.001q^3 - 0.2q^2 + 40q + C$

When $q = 0$, then $c = 5000$, so
$5000 = 0 - 0 + 0 + C$, or $C = 5000$. Thus
$c = 0.001q^3 - 0.2q^2 + 40q + 5000$. When
$q = 100$, then $c = 8000$. Since

Avg. Cost $= \bar{c} = \dfrac{\text{Total Cost}}{\text{Quantity}} = \dfrac{c}{q}$, when

$q = 100$, we have $\bar{c} = \dfrac{8000}{100} = \$80$. (Observe

that knowing $\dfrac{dc}{dq} = 27.50$ when $q = 50$ is not

relevant to the problem.)

Principles in Practice 16.3

1. Using the values given,

$\dfrac{dT}{dt} = -0.5(70 - 60)e^{-0.5t} = -5e^{-0.5t}$

$T(t) = \int \dfrac{dT}{dt}\, dt = \int -5e^{-0.5t}\, dt$

$= 10e^{-0.5t} + C$

2. The number of words memorized is $v(t)$.

$v(t) = \int \dfrac{35}{t+1}\, dt = 35\ln|t+1| + C$ when the

student beings (at $t = 0$), no words are
memorized, so $v(0) = 0$.

$0 = 35\ln|0 + 1| + C = 35(0) + C$, so $C = 0$,
and $v(t) = 35\ln|t + 1|$.

$v(2) = 35\ln|2 + 1| = 35\ln 3 \approx 38.45$

The student would memorize about
38 words.

Exercise 16.3

1. Let $u = x + 5 \Rightarrow du = 1dx = dx$

$\int (x+5)^7 [dx] = \int u^7\, du = \dfrac{u^8}{8} + C$

$= \dfrac{(x+5)^8}{8} + C$

3. Let $u = x^2 + 3 \Rightarrow du = 2x\, dx$

$\int 2x\left(x^2 + 3\right)^5 dx$

$= \int \left(x^2 + 3\right)^5 [2x\, dx] = \int u^5\, du = \dfrac{u^6}{6} + C$

$= \dfrac{\left(x^2 + 3\right)^6}{6} + C$

5. Let $u = y^3 + 3y^2 + 1 \Rightarrow du = \left(3y^2 + 6y\right) dy$

$\int \left(3y^2 + 6y\right)\left(y^3 + 3y^2 + 1\right)^{\frac{2}{3}} dy$

$= \int \left(y^3 + 3y^2 + 1\right)^{\frac{2}{3}}\left[\left(3y^2 + 6y\right) dy\right]$

$= \int u^{\frac{2}{3}}\, du = \dfrac{u^{\frac{5}{3}}}{\frac{5}{3}} + C$

$= \dfrac{3}{5}\left(y^3 + 3y^2 + 1\right)^{\frac{5}{3}} + C$

7. Let $u = 3x - 1 \Rightarrow du = 3\, dx$

$\int \dfrac{3}{(3x-1)^3}\, dx = \int \dfrac{1}{(3x-1)^3} [3\, dx]$

$= \int \dfrac{1}{u^3}\, du = \int u^{-3}\, du$

$= \dfrac{u^{-2}}{-2} + C = -\dfrac{(3x-1)^{-2}}{2} + C$

9. Let $u = 2x - 1 \Rightarrow du = 2\ dx$.

$$\int \sqrt{2x-1}\,dx = \int (2x-1)^{\frac{1}{2}}\,dx$$

$$= \frac{1}{2}\int (2x-1)^{\frac{1}{2}}[2\ dx]$$

$$= \frac{1}{2}\int u^{\frac{1}{2}}\,du = \frac{1}{2}\cdot\frac{u^{\frac{3}{2}}}{\frac{3}{2}} + C = \frac{1}{3}(2x-1)^{\frac{3}{2}} + C$$

11. Let $u = 7x - 6 \Rightarrow du = 7\ dx$

$$\int (7x-6)^4\,dx = \frac{1}{7}\int (7x-6)^4[7\ dx]$$

$$= \frac{1}{7}\int u^4\,du = \frac{1}{7}\cdot\frac{u^5}{5} + C$$

$$= \frac{(7x-6)^5}{35} + C$$

13. Let $u = x^2 + 3 \Rightarrow du = 2x\ dx$

$$\int x\left(x^2+3\right)^{12}\,dx = \frac{1}{2}\int \left(x^2+3\right)^{12}[2x\ dx]$$

$$= \frac{1}{2}\int u^{12}\,du$$

$$= \frac{1}{2}\cdot\frac{u^{13}}{13} + C = \frac{\left(x^2+3\right)^{13}}{26} + C$$

15. Let $u = 27 + x^5 \Rightarrow du = 5x^4\,dx$

$$\int x^4\left(27+x^5\right)^{\frac{1}{3}}\,dx = \frac{1}{5}\int \left(27+x^5\right)^{\frac{1}{3}}\left[5x^4\,dx\right]$$

$$= \frac{1}{5}\int u^{\frac{1}{3}}\,du$$

$$= \frac{1}{5}\cdot\frac{u^{\frac{4}{3}}}{\frac{4}{3}} + C = \frac{3}{20}\left(27+x^5\right)^{\frac{4}{3}} + C$$

17. Let $u = 3x \Rightarrow du = 3\ dx$

$$\int 3e^{3x}\,dx = \int e^{3x}[3\ dx]$$

$$= \int e^u\,du = e^u + C = e^{3x} + C$$

19. Let $u = t^2 + t \Rightarrow du = (2t+1)dt$

$$\int (2t+1)e^{t^2+t}\,dt = \int e^{t^2+t}[(2t+1)\ dt]$$

$$= \int e^u\,du = e^u + C = e^{t^2+t} + C$$

21. $\displaystyle\int xe^{5x^2}\,dx = \frac{1}{10}\int e^{5x^2}[10x\ dx]$

$$= \frac{1}{10}e^{5x^2} + C$$

23. $\displaystyle\int 6e^{-2x}\,dx = 6\left(-\frac{1}{2}\right)\int e^{-2x}[-2\ dx]$

$$= -3e^{-2x} + C$$

25. Let $u = x + 5 \Rightarrow du = dx$

$$\int \frac{1}{x+5}[dx] = \int \frac{1}{u}\,du = \ln|u| + C$$

$$= \ln|x+5| + C$$

27. $\displaystyle\int \frac{3x^2 + 4x^3}{x^3 + x^4}\,dx$

$$= \int \frac{1}{x^3+x^4}\left[\left(3x^2+4x^3\right)dx\right]$$

$$= \ln\left|x^3+x^4\right| + C$$

29. $\displaystyle\int \frac{6z}{\left(z^2-6\right)^5}\,dz = 6\cdot\frac{1}{2}\int \left(z^2-6\right)^{-5}[2z\ dz]$

$$= 3\cdot\frac{\left(z^2-6\right)^{-4}}{-4} + C$$

$$= -\frac{3}{4}\left(z^2-6\right)^{-4} + C$$

31. $\displaystyle\int \frac{4}{x}\,dx = 4\int \frac{1}{x}\,dx = 4\ln|x| + C$

33. $\displaystyle\int \frac{s^2}{s^3+5}\,ds = \frac{1}{3}\int \frac{1}{s^3+5}\left[3s^2ds\right]$

$$= \frac{1}{3}\ln\left|s^3+5\right| + C$$

35. $\displaystyle\int \frac{7}{5-3x}\,dx = 7\left(-\frac{1}{3}\right)\int \frac{1}{5-3x}[-3\ dx]$

$$= -\frac{7}{3}\ln|5-3x| + C$$

37. $\int \sqrt{5x}\,dx = \frac{1}{5}\int (5x)^{\frac{1}{2}}[5\ dx] = \frac{1}{5}\cdot \frac{(5x)^{\frac{3}{2}}}{\frac{3}{2}} + C$

$\qquad = \frac{2}{15}(5x)^{\frac{3}{2}} + C = \frac{2}{15}(5x)(5x)^{\frac{1}{2}} + C$

$\qquad = \frac{2}{3}x\sqrt{5x} + C = \frac{2\sqrt{5}}{3}x^{\frac{3}{2}} + C$

39. $\int \frac{x}{\sqrt{x^2-4}}\,dx = \frac{1}{2}\int (x^2-4)^{-\frac{1}{2}}[2x\ dx]$

$\qquad = \frac{1}{2}\cdot \frac{(x^2-4)^{\frac{1}{2}}}{\frac{1}{2}} + C$

$\qquad = \sqrt{x^2-4} + C$

41. $\int 2y^3 e^{y^4+1}\,dy = 2\int y^3 e^{y^4+1}\,dy$

$\qquad = 2\cdot \frac{1}{4}\int e^{y^4+1}\left[4y^3 dy\right]$

$\qquad = 2\cdot \frac{1}{4}\cdot e^{y^4+1} + C = \frac{1}{2}e^{y^4+1} + C$

43. $\int v^2 e^{-2v^3+1}\,dv = -\frac{1}{6}\int e^{-2v^3+1}\left[-6v^2 dv\right]$

$\qquad = -\frac{1}{6}e^{-2v^3+1} + C$

45. $\int (e^{-5x}+2e^x)\,dx = \int e^{-5x}\,dx + 2\int e^x\,dx$

$\qquad = -\frac{1}{5}\int e^{-5x}[-5\ dx] + 2\int e^x\,dx$

$\qquad = -\frac{1}{5}e^{-5x} + 2e^x + C$

47. $\int (x+1)(3-3x^2-6x)^3\,dx$

$\qquad = -\frac{1}{6}\int (3-3x^2-6x)^3[(-6x-6)dx]$

$\qquad = -\frac{1}{6}\cdot \frac{(3-3x^2-6x)^4}{4} + C$

$\qquad = -\frac{1}{24}(3-3x^2-6x)^4 + C$

49. $\int \frac{x^2+2}{x^3+6x}\,dx = \frac{1}{3}\int \frac{1}{x^3+6x}\left[(3x^2+6)dx\right]$

$\qquad = \frac{1}{3}\ln|x^3+6x| + C$

51. $\int \frac{16s-4}{3-2s+4s^2}\,dx$

$\qquad = 2\int \frac{1}{3-2s+4s^2}[(8s-2)ds]$

$\qquad = 2\ln|3-2s+4s^2| + C$

53. $\int x(2x^2+1)^{-1}\,dx = \int \frac{x}{2x^2+1}\,dx$

$\qquad = \frac{1}{4}\int \frac{1}{2x^2+1}[4x\ dx]$

$\qquad = \frac{1}{4}\ln(2x^2+1) + C$

55. $\int -(x^2-2x^5)(x^3-x^6)^{-10}\,dx$

$\qquad = -\frac{1}{3}\int (x^3-x^6)^{-10}\left[3(x^2-2x^5)\ dx\right]$

$\qquad = -\frac{1}{3}\cdot \frac{(x^3-x^6)^{-9}}{-9} + C$

$\qquad = \frac{1}{27}(x^3-x^6)^{-9} + C$

57. $\int (2x^3+x)(x^4+x^2)\,dx$

$\qquad = \frac{1}{2}\int (x^4+x^2)^1\left[2(2x^3+x)\ dx\right]$

$\qquad = \frac{1}{2}\cdot \frac{(x^4+x^2)^2}{2} + C = \frac{1}{4}(x^4+x^2)^2 + C$

59. $\int \frac{18+12x}{(4-9x-3x^2)^5}\,dx$

$\qquad = -2\int (4-9x-3x^2)^{-5}[(-9-6x)\ dx]$

$\qquad = -2\cdot \frac{(4-9x-3x^2)^{-4}}{-4} + C$

$\qquad = \frac{1}{2}(4-9x-3x^2)^{-4} + C$

61. $u = 4x^3 + 3x^2 - 4$

$du = \left(12x^2 + 6x\right)dx = 6x(2x+1)dx$

$\displaystyle\int x(2x+1)e^{4x^3+3x^2-4}\,dx$

$= \dfrac{1}{6}\displaystyle\int e^{4x^3+3x^2-4}[6x(2x+1)dx]$

$= \dfrac{1}{6}\displaystyle\int e^u\,du = \dfrac{1}{6}e^u + C = \dfrac{1}{6}e^{4x^3+3x^2-4} + C$

63. $\displaystyle\int x\sqrt{\left(7-5x^2\right)^3}\,dx$

$= -\dfrac{1}{10}\displaystyle\int \left(7-5x^2\right)^{\frac{3}{2}}[-10x\,dx]$

$= -\dfrac{1}{10}\cdot\dfrac{\left(7-5x^2\right)^{\frac{5}{2}}}{\frac{5}{2}} + C$

$= -\dfrac{1}{25}\left(7-5x^2\right)^{\frac{5}{2}} + C$

65. $\displaystyle\int\left(\sqrt{2x} - \dfrac{1}{\sqrt{2x}}\right)dx = \int\sqrt{2x}\,dx - \int\dfrac{1}{\sqrt{2x}}\,dx$

$= \dfrac{1}{2}\displaystyle\int (2x)^{\frac{1}{2}}[2\,dx] - \dfrac{1}{2}\int (2x)^{-\frac{1}{2}}[2\,dx]$

$= \dfrac{1}{2}\cdot\dfrac{(2x)^{\frac{3}{2}}}{\frac{3}{2}} - \dfrac{1}{2}\cdot\dfrac{(2x)^{\frac{1}{2}}}{\frac{1}{2}} + C$

$= \dfrac{(2x)^{\frac{3}{2}}}{3} - \sqrt{2x} + C$

$= \dfrac{2\sqrt{2}}{3}x^{\frac{3}{2}} - \sqrt{2}x^{\frac{1}{2}} + C$

67. $\displaystyle\int\left(x^2+1\right)^2 dx = \int\left(x^4 + 2x^2 + 1\right)dx$

$= \dfrac{x^5}{5} + \dfrac{2x^3}{3} + x + C$

69. $\displaystyle\int\left[\dfrac{x}{x^2+1} + \dfrac{x^5}{\left(x^6+1\right)^2}\right]dx$

$= \displaystyle\int\dfrac{x}{x^2+1}\,dx + \int\dfrac{x^5}{\left(x^6+1\right)^2}\,dx$

$= \dfrac{1}{2}\displaystyle\int\dfrac{1}{x^2+1}[2x\,dx] + \dfrac{1}{6}\int\left(x^6+1\right)^{-2}\left[6x^5 dx\right]$

$= \dfrac{1}{2}\ln\left(x^2+1\right) + \dfrac{1}{6}\cdot\dfrac{\left(x^6+1\right)^{-1}}{-1} + C$

$= \dfrac{1}{2}\ln\left(x^2+1\right) - \dfrac{1}{6\left(x^6+1\right)} + C$

71. $\displaystyle\int\left[\dfrac{1}{3x-5} - \left(x^2 - 2x^5\right)\left(x^3 - x^6\right)^{-10}\right]dx$

$= \dfrac{1}{3}\displaystyle\int\dfrac{1}{3x-5}[3\,dx] - \dfrac{1}{3}\int\left(x^3 - x^6\right)^{-10}\left[\left(3x^2 - 6x^5\right)dx\right]$

$= \dfrac{1}{3}\ln|3x-5| - \dfrac{1}{3}\cdot\dfrac{\left(x^3 - x^6\right)^{-9}}{-9} + C$

$= \dfrac{1}{3}\ln|3x-5| + \dfrac{1}{27}\left(x^3 - x^6\right)^{-9} + C$

73. $\int \left[\sqrt{3x+1} - \frac{x}{x^2+3} \right] dx$

$= \int (3x+1)^{\frac{1}{2}} dx - \int \frac{x}{x^2+3} dx$

$= \frac{1}{3} \int (3x+1)^{\frac{1}{2}} [3\ dx] - \frac{1}{2} \int \frac{1}{x^2+3} [2x\ dx]$

$= \frac{1}{3} \cdot \frac{(3x+1)^{\frac{3}{2}}}{\frac{3}{2}} - \frac{1}{2} \ln(x^2+3) + C$

$= \frac{2}{9}(3x+1)^{\frac{3}{2}} - \ln\sqrt{x^2+3} + C$

75. Let $u = \sqrt{x} \Rightarrow du = \frac{1}{2} x^{-\frac{1}{2}} dx = \frac{1}{2\sqrt{x}} dx$.

$\int \frac{e^{\sqrt{x}}}{\sqrt{x}} dx = 2 \int e^{\sqrt{x}} \left[\frac{1}{2\sqrt{x}} dx \right]$

$= 2 \int e^u du = 2e^u + C = 2e^{\sqrt{x}} + C$

77. $\int \frac{1+e^{2x}}{e^x} dx = \int \left(\frac{1}{e^x} + \frac{e^{2x}}{e^x} \right) dx$

$= \int (e^{-x} + e^x) dx$

$= -\int e^{-x}[-1\ dx] + \int e^x dx = -e^{-x} + e^x + C$

79. Let

$u = \ln(x^2+2x) \Rightarrow du = \frac{1}{x^2+2x}(2x+2)dx$

$\int \frac{x+1}{x^2+2x} \ln(x^2+2x) dx$

$= \frac{1}{2} \int \ln(x^2+2x) \left[\frac{2x+2}{x^2+2x} dx \right]$

$= \frac{1}{2} \int u\ du = \frac{1}{2} \cdot \frac{u^2}{2} + C$

$= \frac{1}{4} \ln^2(x^2+2x) + C$

81. $y = \int (3-2x)^2 dx = -\frac{1}{2} \int (3-2x)^2 [-2\ dx]$

$= -\frac{1}{2} \cdot \frac{(3-2x)^3}{3} + C = -\frac{1}{6}(3-2x)^3 + C$

$y(0) = 1$ implies $1 = -\frac{1}{6}(27) + C$, so

$C = \frac{11}{2}$. Thus $y = -\frac{1}{6}(3-2x)^3 + \frac{11}{2}$.

83. $y'' = \frac{1}{x^2}$

$y' = \int x^{-2} dx = -x^{-1} + C_1$

$y'(-1) = 1$ implies $1 = 1 + C_1$, so $C_1 = 0$.

Thus $y' = -x^{-1}$.

$y = \int (-x^{-1}) dx = -\int \frac{1}{x} dx = -\ln|x| + C_2$

$y(1) = 0$ implies that $0 = 0 + C_2$, so $C_2 = 0$.

Thus $y = -\ln|x| = \ln\left|\frac{1}{x}\right|$.

85. $V(t) = \int \frac{dV}{dt} dt = \int 8e^{0.05t} dt$

$= 8\left(\frac{e^{0.05t}}{0.05} \right) + C = 160e^{0.05t} + C$

The house cost \$350,000 to build, so
$V(0) = 350$.

$350 = 160e^0 + C = 160 + C$

$190 = C$

$V(t) = 160e^{0.05t} + 190$

87. Note that $r > 0$.

$C = \int \left[\frac{Rr}{2K} + \frac{B_1}{r} \right] dr = \int \frac{Rr}{2K} dr + \int \frac{B_1}{r} dr$

$= \frac{R}{2K} \int r\ dr + B_1 \int \frac{1}{r} dr$

$= \frac{R}{2K} \cdot \frac{r^2}{2} + B_1 \ln|r| + B_2$

Thus we obtain $C = \frac{Rr^2}{4K} + B_1 \ln|r| + B_2$.

Exercise 16.4

1. $\int \frac{2x^4 + 3x^3 - x^2}{x^3} dx$

$= \int \left(\frac{2x^4}{x^3} + \frac{3x^3}{x^3} - \frac{x^2}{x^3} \right) dx$

$= \int \left(2x + 3 - \frac{1}{x} \right) dx = 2 \cdot \frac{x^2}{2} + 3x - \ln|x| + C$

$= x^2 + 3x - \ln|x| + C$

3. $\int \left(3x^2+2\right)\sqrt{2x^3+4x+1}\,dx$

$= \frac{1}{2}\int \left(2x^3+4x+1\right)^{\frac{1}{2}}\left[2\left(3x^2+2\right)dx\right]$

$= \frac{1}{2}\cdot\frac{\left(2x^3+4x+1\right)^{\frac{3}{2}}}{\frac{3}{2}}+C$

$= \frac{1}{3}\left(2x^3+4x+1\right)^{\frac{3}{2}}+C$

5. $\int \frac{3}{\sqrt{4-5x}}\,dx = 3\int (4-5x)^{-\frac{1}{2}}\,dx$

$= 3\cdot\left(-\frac{1}{5}\right)\int (4-5x)^{-\frac{1}{2}}[-5\,dx]$

$= -\frac{3}{5}\cdot\frac{(4-5x)^{\frac{1}{2}}}{\frac{1}{2}}+C = -\frac{6}{5}\sqrt{4-5x}+C$

7. $\int 4^{7x}\,dx = \int \left(e^{\ln 4}\right)^{7x}\,dx = \int e^{(\ln 4)(7x)}\,dx$

$= \frac{1}{7\ln 4}\int e^{(\ln 4)(7x)}[7\ln 4\,dx]$

$= \frac{1}{7\ln 4}\cdot e^{(\ln 4)(7x)}+C$

$= \frac{1}{7\ln 4}\left(e^{\ln 4}\right)^{(7x)}+C = \frac{4^{7x}}{7\ln 4}+C$

9. $\int 2x\left(7-e^{\frac{x^2}{4}}\right)dx = \int\left(14x-2xe^{\frac{x^2}{4}}\right)dx$

$= 14\int x\,dx - 2\int xe^{\frac{x^2}{4}}\,dx$

$= 14\int x\,dx - 2\cdot 2\int e^{\frac{x^2}{4}}\left[\frac{1}{2}x\,dx\right]$

$= 14\cdot\frac{x^2}{2}-4\cdot e^{\frac{x^2}{4}}+C = 7x^2-4e^{\frac{x^2}{4}}+C$

11. By long division,
$\frac{6x^2-11x+5}{3x-1}=2x-3+\frac{2}{3x-1}$. Thus

$\int\frac{6x^2-11x+5}{3x-1}\,dx = \int\left(2x-3+\frac{2}{3x-1}\right)dx$

$= 2\int x\,dx - \int 3\,dx + 2\cdot\frac{1}{3}\int\frac{1}{3x-1}[3\,dx]$

$= x^2-3x+\frac{2}{3}\ln|3x-1|+C$

13. $\int\frac{3e^{2x}}{e^{2x}+1}\,dx = \frac{3}{2}\int\frac{1}{e^{2x}+1}\left[2e^{2x}dx\right]$

$= \frac{3}{2}\ln\left(e^{2x}+1\right)+C$

15. $\int\frac{e^{\frac{7}{x}}}{x^2}\,dx = \int e^{\frac{7}{x}}\cdot\frac{1}{x^2}\,dx = -\frac{1}{7}\int e^{\frac{7}{x}}\left[-\frac{7}{x^2}\,dx\right]$

$= -\frac{1}{7}e^{\frac{7}{x}}+C$

17. By using long division on the integrand,

$\int\frac{2x^3}{x^2-4}\,dx = \int\left(2x+\frac{8x}{x^2-4}\right)dx$

$= \int 2x\,dx + 4\int\frac{1}{x^2-4}[2x\,dx]$

$= x^2+4\ln\left|x^2-4\right|+C.$

19. $\int\frac{\left(\sqrt{x}+2\right)^2}{3\sqrt{x}}\,dx = \frac{2}{3}\int\left(\sqrt{x}+2\right)^2\left[\frac{1}{2\sqrt{x}}\,dx\right]$

$= \frac{2}{3}\cdot\frac{\left(\sqrt{x}+2\right)^3}{3}+C = \frac{2}{9}\left(\sqrt{x}+2\right)^3+C$

21. $\int\frac{\left(x^{\frac{1}{3}}+2\right)^4}{\sqrt[3]{x^2}}\,dx = 3\int\left(x^{\frac{1}{3}}+2\right)^4\left[\frac{1}{3}x^{-\frac{2}{3}}dx\right]$

$= \frac{3}{5}\left(x^{\frac{1}{3}}+2\right)^5+C$

23. $\int\frac{\ln x}{x}\,dx = \int(\ln x)\left[\frac{1}{x}\,dx\right] = \frac{(\ln x)^2}{2}+C$

$= \frac{1}{2}\left(\ln^2 x\right)+C$

25. $\int\frac{\ln^2(r+1)}{r+1}\,dr = \int[\ln(r+1)]^2\left(\frac{1}{r+1}\,dr\right)$

$= \frac{1}{3}\ln^3(r+1)+C$

27. $\int\frac{3^{\ln x}}{x}\,dx = \int\frac{\left(e^{\ln 3}\right)^{\ln x}}{x}\,dx$

$= \frac{1}{\ln 3}\int e^{(\ln 3)\ln x}\left[\frac{\ln 3}{x}\,dx\right]$

$$= \frac{1}{\ln 3} \cdot e^{(\ln 3)\ln x} + C$$

$$= \frac{1}{\ln 3}\left(e^{\ln 3}\right)^{\ln x} + C = \frac{3^{\ln x}}{\ln 3} + C$$

29. $\displaystyle\int x\sqrt{e^{x^2+3}}\,dx = \int x\left(e^{x^2+3}\right)^{\frac{1}{2}}dx$

$$= \int e^{\frac{\left(x^2+3\right)}{2}}[x\,dx] = e^{\frac{\left(x^2+3\right)}{2}} + C$$

31. $\displaystyle\int \frac{dx}{(x+3)\ln(x+3)} = \int \frac{1}{\ln(x+3)}\left[\frac{1}{x+3}dx\right]$

$$\ln|\ln(x+3)| + C$$

33. By using long division on the integrand,

$$\int \frac{x^3 + x^2 - x - 3}{x^2 - 3}\,dx = \int\left(x + 1 + \frac{2x}{x^2 - 3}\right)dx$$

$$= \int (x+1)dx + \int \frac{1}{x^2 - 3}[2x\,dx]$$

$$= \frac{x^2}{2} + x + \ln|x^2 - 3| + C$$

35. $\displaystyle\int \frac{3x\sqrt{\ln\left(x^2+1\right)^2}}{x^2 + 1}\,dx$

$$= \frac{3}{4}\int\left[2\ln\left(x^2+1\right)\right]^{\frac{1}{2}}\left[\frac{4x}{x^2+1}dx\right]$$

$$= \frac{3}{4} \cdot \frac{\left[2\ln\left(x^2+1\right)\right]^{\frac{3}{2}}}{\frac{3}{2}} + C$$

$$= \frac{1}{2}\ln^{\frac{3}{2}}\left[\left(x^2+1\right)^2\right] + C$$

37. $\displaystyle\int\left[\frac{x^3}{\sqrt{x^4-1}} - \ln 4\right]dx$

$$= \frac{1}{4}\int\left(x^4 - 1\right)^{-\frac{1}{2}}\left[4x^3 dx\right] - \int(\ln 4)dx$$

$$= \frac{1}{4} \cdot \frac{\left(x^4 - 1\right)^{\frac{1}{2}}}{\frac{1}{2}} - (\ln 4)x + C$$

$$= \frac{1}{2}\sqrt{x^4 - 1} - (\ln 4)x + C$$

39. $\displaystyle\int \frac{2x^4 - 8x^3 - 6x^2 + 4}{x^3}\,dx$

$$= \int\left(2x - 8 - \frac{6}{x} + \frac{4}{x^3}\right)dx$$

$$= 2\int x\,dx - \int 8\,dx - 6\int \frac{1}{x}dx + 4\int x^{-3}dx$$

$$= 2 \cdot \frac{x^2}{2} - 8x - 6\ln|x| + 4 \cdot \frac{x^{-2}}{-2} + C$$

$$= x^2 - 8x - 6\ln|x| - \frac{2}{x^2} + C$$

41. By using long division on the integrand,

$$\int \frac{x}{x-1}\,dx = \int\left(1 + \frac{1}{x-1}\right)dx$$

$$= x + \ln|x - 1| + C$$

43. $\displaystyle\int \frac{xe^{x^2}}{\sqrt{e^{x^2}+2}}\,dx = \frac{1}{2}\int\left(e^{x^2}+2\right)^{-\frac{1}{2}}\left[2xe^{x^2}dx\right]$

$$= \frac{1}{2} \cdot \frac{\left(e^{x^2}+2\right)^{\frac{1}{2}}}{\frac{1}{2}} + C = \sqrt{e^{x^2}+2} + C$$

45. $\displaystyle\int \frac{\left(e^{-x}+6\right)^2}{e^x}\,dx = -\int\left(e^{-x}+6\right)^2\left[-e^{-x}dx\right]$

$$= -\frac{\left(e^{-x}+6\right)^3}{3} + C$$

47. $\displaystyle\int\left(x^3 + ex\right)\sqrt{x^2 + e}\,dx$

$$= \int x\left(x^2 + e\right)\left(x^2 + e\right)^{\frac{1}{2}}dx$$

$$= \frac{1}{2}\int\left(x^2 + e\right)^{\frac{3}{2}}[2x\,dx] = \frac{1}{2} \cdot \frac{\left(x^2 + e\right)^{\frac{5}{2}}}{\frac{5}{2}} + C$$

$$= \frac{1}{5}\left(x^2 + e\right)^{\frac{5}{2}} + C$$

49. $\int \sqrt{x}\sqrt{(8x)^{\frac{3}{2}}+3}\,dx = \int \left(8^{\frac{3}{2}}x^{\frac{3}{2}}+3\right)^{\frac{1}{2}}\cdot x^{\frac{1}{2}}dx$

$= \dfrac{2}{3\cdot 8^{\frac{3}{2}}}\int \left(8^{\frac{3}{2}}x^{\frac{3}{2}}+3\right)^{\frac{1}{2}}\left[8^{\frac{3}{2}}\cdot \dfrac{3}{2}\cdot x^{\frac{1}{2}}dx\right]$

$= \dfrac{2}{3\cdot 16\sqrt{2}}\cdot \dfrac{\left(8^{\frac{3}{2}}x^{\frac{3}{2}}+3\right)^{\frac{3}{2}}}{\frac{3}{2}}+C$

$= \dfrac{1}{36\sqrt{2}}\left[(8x)^{\frac{3}{2}}+3\right]^{\frac{3}{2}}+C$

51. $\int \dfrac{\sqrt{s}}{e^{\sqrt{s^3}}}\,ds = -\dfrac{2}{3}\int e^{-s^{\frac{3}{2}}}\left[-\dfrac{3}{2}s^{\frac{1}{2}}ds\right]$

$= -\dfrac{2}{3}e^{-\sqrt{s^3}}+C$

53. $e^{\ln(x+2)}$ is simply $x+2$. Thus

$\int e^{\ln(x+2)}dx = \int (x+2)dx = \dfrac{x^2}{2}+2x+C$

55. $\int \dfrac{\ln\left(xe^x\right)}{x}\,dx = \int \dfrac{\ln x+\ln e^x}{x}\,dx$

$= \int \dfrac{\ln x+x}{x}\,dx = \int \left(\dfrac{\ln x}{x}+1\right)dx$

$= \int (\ln x)\left[\dfrac{1}{x}dx\right]+\int 1\,dx = \dfrac{\ln^2 x}{2}+x+C$

57. $\dfrac{dr}{dq} = \dfrac{200}{(q+2)^2}$

$r = \int 200(q+2)^{-2}\,dq = 200\cdot \dfrac{(q+2)^{-1}}{-1}+C$

$= -\dfrac{200}{q+2}+C$

When $q=0$, then $r=0$, so $0=-100+C$, or

$C=100$. Hence $r=-\dfrac{200}{q+2}+100 = \dfrac{100q}{q+2}$.

Since $r=pq$, then $p=\dfrac{r}{q}=\dfrac{100}{q+2}$.

Answer: $p=\dfrac{100}{q+2}$

59. $\dfrac{dc}{dq} = \dfrac{20}{q+5}$

$c = \int \dfrac{20}{q+5}\,dq = 20\int \dfrac{1}{q+5}\,dq$

$= 20\ln|q+5|+C$

When $q=0$, then $c=2000$, so

$2000=20\ln(5)+C$, or $C=2000-20\ln 5$.

Hence $c=20\ln|q+5|+2000-20\ln 5$

$= 20\left(\ln|q+5|-\ln 5\right)+2000$

$= 20\ln\left|\dfrac{q+5}{5}\right|+2000$

Answer: $c=20\ln\left|\dfrac{q+5}{5}\right|+2000$

61. $\dfrac{dC}{dI} = \dfrac{1}{\sqrt{I}}$

$C = \int I^{-\frac{1}{2}}dI = \dfrac{I^{\frac{1}{2}}}{\frac{1}{2}}+C_1 = 2\sqrt{I}+C_1$

$C(9)=8$ implies that $8=2\cdot 3+C_1$, or

$C_1=2$. Thus $C=2\sqrt{I}+2=2\left(\sqrt{I}+1\right)$.

Answer: $C=2\left(\sqrt{I}+1\right)$

63. $\dfrac{dC}{dI} = \dfrac{3}{4}-\dfrac{1}{6\sqrt{I}}$

$C = \int \left[\dfrac{3}{4}-\dfrac{I^{-\frac{1}{2}}}{6}\right]dI = \int \dfrac{3}{4}dI -\dfrac{1}{6}\int I^{-\frac{1}{2}}dI$

$= \dfrac{3}{4}I-\dfrac{1}{6}\cdot \dfrac{I^{\frac{1}{2}}}{\frac{1}{2}}+C_1 = \dfrac{3}{4}I-\dfrac{\sqrt{I}}{3}+C_1$

Thus $C=\dfrac{3}{4}I-\dfrac{\sqrt{I}}{3}+C_1$. $C(25)=23$ implies

that $23=\dfrac{3}{4}\cdot 25-\dfrac{5}{3}+C_1$, so $C_1=\dfrac{71}{12}$.

Answer: $C=\dfrac{3}{4}I-\dfrac{1}{3}\sqrt{I}+\dfrac{71}{12}$

65. $\dfrac{dc}{dq} = \dfrac{100q^2-4998q+50}{q^2-50q+1}$

a. $\left.\dfrac{dc}{dq}\right|_{q=50} = \dfrac{100(50)^2-4998(50)+50}{(50)^2-50(50)+1}$

$= \$150$ per unit

b. To find c, we integrate $\dfrac{dc}{dq}$ by using long division:

$$c = \int \frac{100q^2 - 4998q + 50}{q^2 - 50q + 1}\, dq$$

$$= \int \left(100 + \frac{2q - 50}{q^2 - 50q + 1} \right) dq$$

$$= \int 100\, dq + \int \frac{1}{q^2 - 50q + 1}[(2q - 50)dq]$$

Thus $c = 100q + \ln\left|q^2 - 50q + 1\right| + C$.

When $q = 0$, then $c = 10{,}000$, so $10{,}000 = 0 + \ln(1) + C$, so $C = 10{,}000$. Hence

$$c = 100q + \ln\left|q^2 - 50q + 1\right| + 10{,}000.$$

When $q = 50$, then
$c = 5000 + \ln(1) + 10{,}000 = \$15{,}000$.

c. If $c = f(q)$, then

$$f(q + dq) \approx g(q) + dc = f(q) + \frac{dc}{dq}\, dq$$

Letting $q = 50$ and $dq = 2$, we have

$$f(52) = f(50 + 2) \approx f(50) + \left.\frac{dc}{dq}\right|_{q=50} \cdot (2)$$

$$= 15{,}000 + 150(2) = \$15{,}300$$

67. $\dfrac{dV}{dt} = \dfrac{8t^3}{\sqrt{0.2t^4 + 8000}}$

$$V = \int \frac{8t^3}{\sqrt{0.2t^4 + 8000}}\, dt$$

$$= \int \left(0.02t^4 + 8000\right)^{-\frac{1}{2}} \cdot 8t^3\, dt$$

$$= 10 \int \left(0.2t^4 + 8000\right)^{-\frac{1}{2}} \left[0.8t^3\right] dt$$

$$= 10 \frac{\left(0.2t^4 + 8000\right)^{\frac{1}{2}}}{\frac{1}{2}} + C$$

Thus $V = 20\sqrt{0.2t^4 + 8000} + C$. If $t = 0$, then
$V = 500$, so $500 = 20\sqrt{8000} + C$,
$500 = 20\sqrt{1600 \cdot 5} + C$, $500 = 800\sqrt{5} + C$,

or $C = 500 - 800\sqrt{5}$. Hence

$$V = 20\sqrt{0.02t^4 + 8000} + 500 - 800\sqrt{5}.$$

When $t = 10$, then

$$V = 20\sqrt{10{,}000} + 500 - 800\sqrt{5}$$

$$= 20(100) + 500 - 800\sqrt{5} \approx \$711 \text{ per acre.}$$

69. $S = \displaystyle\int \frac{dS}{dI}\, dI = \int \frac{5}{(I + 2)^2}\, dI$

$$= 5\int (I + 2)^{-2}\, dI = 5 \cdot \frac{(I + 2)^{-1}}{-1} + C_1$$

Thus $S = -\dfrac{5}{I + 2} + C_1$. If C is the total national consumption (in billions of dollars), then

$C + S = I$, or $C = I - S$. Hence

$C = I + \dfrac{5}{I + 2} - C_1$. When $I = 8$, then

$C = 7.5$, so $7.5 = 8 + \dfrac{1}{2} - C_1$, or $C_1 = 1$.

Thus $S = 1 - \dfrac{5}{I + 2}$. If $S = 0$, then

$$0 = 1 - \frac{5}{I + 2} \Rightarrow \frac{5}{I + 2} = 1 \Rightarrow 5 = I + 2$$

$$\Rightarrow I = 3$$

Exercise 16.5

1. $5 + 6 + 7 + 8 + 9 = 35$

3. $(-1) + 1 + (-1) + 1 + (-1) + 1 + (-1) + 1$
$\qquad + (-1) + 1 = 0$

5. $5 + 20 = 25$

7. $\left(-\dfrac{1}{2}\right) + \dfrac{5}{16} = -\dfrac{3}{16}$

9. $0 + \dfrac{3}{2} + \left(-\dfrac{8}{3}\right) = -\dfrac{7}{6}$

11. $\displaystyle\sum_{k=1}^{15} k$

13. $\displaystyle\sum_{k=1}^{4} (2k - 1)$

15. $\displaystyle\sum_{k=1}^{12} k^2$

17. $\displaystyle\sum_{k=1}^{450} k = \frac{450(451)}{2} = 101,475$

19. $\displaystyle\sum_{j=1}^{6} 4j = 4\sum_{j=i}^{6} j = 4 \cdot \frac{6(7)}{2} = 84$

21. $\displaystyle\sum_{i=1}^{6} 3i^2 = 3\sum_{i=1}^{6} i^2 = 3 \cdot \frac{6(7)(13)}{6} = 273$

23. After n years,

Total maint. cost $= 100 + 200 + \ldots + 100n = 100(1 + 2 + \ldots + n)$

$= 100 \cdot \dfrac{n(n+1)}{2} = 50n(n+1)$

Thus total cost after n years $= 3200 + 50n(n+1)$

Avg. annual total cost is $C = \dfrac{3200 + 50n(n+1)}{n} = \dfrac{3200}{n} + 50(n+1)$

$\dfrac{dC}{dn} = -\dfrac{3200}{n^2} + 50 = \dfrac{50n^2 - 3200}{n^2} = \dfrac{50(n-8)(n+8)}{n^2}$

We want $n > 0$, so the critical point to consider is $n = 8$. Since $\dfrac{dC}{dn} < 0$ for $0 < n < 8$ and $\dfrac{dC}{dn} > 0$ for $n > 8$, then C is minimum when $n = 8$. At this value, $C = 850$.

Answer: 8, \$850

Principles in Practice 16.6

1. Divide the interval $[0, 10]$ into n subintervals of equal length Δx, so $\Delta x = \dfrac{10}{n}$. The endpoints of the subintervals are 0, $\dfrac{10}{n}$, $2\left(\dfrac{10}{n}\right)$, $3\left(\dfrac{10}{n}\right)$, $\ldots$, $(n-1)\left(\dfrac{10}{n}\right)$, and $n\left(\dfrac{10}{n}\right) = 10$. Letting S_n denote the sum of the areas of the rectangles corresponding to right-hand endpoints, we have

$S_n = \dfrac{10}{n} R\left(\dfrac{10}{n}\right) + \dfrac{10}{n} R\left[2\left(\dfrac{10}{n}\right)\right] + \ldots + \dfrac{10}{n} R\left[n\left(\dfrac{10}{n}\right)\right]$

$= \dfrac{10}{n}\left[\left\{600 - 0.5\left(\dfrac{10}{n}\right)\right\} + \left\{600 - 0.5(2)\left(\dfrac{10}{n}\right)\right\} + \ldots + \left\{600 - 0.5(n)\left(\dfrac{10}{n}\right)\right\}\right]$

$= \dfrac{10}{n}\left[600n - 0.5\left(\dfrac{10}{n}\right)\{1 + 2 + \ldots + n\}\right]$

$= \dfrac{10}{n}\left[600n - 0.5\left(\dfrac{10}{n}\right)\dfrac{n(n+1)}{2}\right]$

$= \dfrac{10}{n}[600n - 2.5(n+1)]$

$= 6000 - 25\left(\dfrac{n+1}{n}\right)$

Now take the limit of S_n as $n \to \infty$

$$\lim_{n \to \infty} S_n = \lim_{n \to \infty}\left[6000 - 25\left(\frac{n+1}{n}\right)\right]$$

$$= \lim_{n \to \infty}\left[6000 - 25\left(1+\frac{1}{n}\right)\right] = 6000 - 25$$

$$= 5975$$

The total revenue for selling 10 units is $5975.

Exercise 16.6

1. $f(x) = x, y = 0, x = 1$

$S_3, \Delta x = \frac{1}{3}$

$$S_3 = \frac{1}{3}f\left(\frac{1}{3}\right) + \frac{1}{3}f\left(\frac{2}{3}\right) + \frac{1}{3}f\left(\frac{3}{3}\right) = \frac{1}{3}\left[f\left(\frac{1}{3}\right) + f\left(\frac{2}{3}\right) + f\left(\frac{3}{3}\right)\right]$$

$$= \frac{1}{3}\left[\frac{1}{3} + \frac{2}{3} + \frac{3}{3}\right] = \frac{1}{3} \cdot \frac{6}{3} = \frac{2}{3} \qquad \text{Answer: } \frac{2}{3} \text{ sq unit}$$

3. $f(x) = x^2, y = 0, x = 1$

$S_3, \Delta x = \frac{1}{3}$

$$S_3 = \frac{1}{3}f\left(\frac{1}{3}\right) + \frac{1}{3}f\left(\frac{2}{3}\right) + \frac{1}{3}f\left(\frac{3}{3}\right)$$

$$= \frac{1}{3}\left[\frac{1}{9} + \frac{4}{9} + \frac{9}{9}\right]$$

$$= \frac{1}{3} \cdot \frac{14}{9} = \frac{14}{27}$$

Answer: $\frac{14}{27}$ sq unit

5. $f(x) = 4x; [0, 1]$

$\Delta x = \frac{1}{n}$

$$S_n = \frac{1}{n}f\left(\frac{1}{n}\right) + \ldots + \frac{1}{n}f\left(n \cdot \frac{1}{n}\right)$$

$$= \frac{1}{n}\left[f\left(\frac{1}{n}\right) + \ldots + f\left(n \cdot \frac{1}{n}\right)\right]$$

$$= \frac{1}{n}\left[4 \cdot \frac{1}{n} + \ldots + 4 \cdot \frac{n}{n}\right]$$

$$= \frac{4}{n^2}[1 + \ldots + n] = \frac{4}{n^2} \cdot \frac{n(n+1)}{2}$$

$$= \frac{2(n+1)}{n}$$

7. a. $$S_n = \frac{1}{n}\left[\left(\frac{1}{n}+1\right) + \left(\frac{2}{n}+1\right) + \ldots + \left(\frac{n}{n}+1\right)\right]$$

$$= \frac{1}{n}\left[\frac{1}{n}(1+2+\ldots+n) + n\right]$$

$$= \frac{1}{n}\left[\frac{1}{n} \cdot \frac{n(n+1)}{2} + n\right]$$

$$= \frac{n+1}{2n} + 1$$

b. $$\lim_{n \to \infty} S_n = \lim_{n \to \infty}\left[\frac{n+1}{2n} + 1\right]$$

$$= \lim_{n \to \infty}\left[\frac{1}{2} + \frac{1}{2n} + 1\right]$$

$$= \frac{1}{2} + 0 + 1 = \frac{3}{2}$$

9. $f(x) = x, y = 0, x = 1$

$\Delta x = \frac{1}{n}$

$$S_n = \frac{1}{n}f\left(\frac{1}{n}\right) + \ldots + \frac{1}{n}f\left(n \cdot \frac{1}{n}\right)$$

$$= \frac{1}{n}\left[f\left(\frac{1}{n}\right) + \ldots + f\left(n \cdot \frac{1}{n}\right)\right]$$

$$= \frac{1}{n}\left[\frac{1}{n} + \ldots + \frac{n}{n}\right] = \frac{1}{n^2}[1 + \ldots + n]$$

$$= \frac{1}{n^2} \cdot \frac{n(n+1)}{2}$$

$$= \frac{1}{2} \cdot \frac{n+1}{n} = \frac{1}{2}\left[1 + \frac{1}{n}\right]$$

$$\lim_{n \to \infty} S_n = \frac{1}{2}$$

Answer: $\frac{1}{2}$ sq unit

11. $f(x) = x^2$, $y = 0$, $x = 1$

$$\Delta x = \frac{1}{n}$$

$$S_n = \frac{1}{n} f\left(\frac{1}{n}\right) + \ldots + \frac{1}{n} f\left(n \cdot \frac{1}{n}\right)$$

$$= \frac{1}{n}\left[\left(\frac{1}{n}\right)^2 + \ldots + \left(n \cdot \frac{1}{n}\right)^2\right]$$

$$= \frac{1}{n^3}\left[1^2 + \ldots + n^2\right] = \frac{1}{n^3} \cdot \frac{n(n+1)(2n+1)}{6}$$

$$= \frac{1}{6} \cdot \frac{2n^2 + 3n + 1}{n^2}$$

$$= \frac{1}{6}\left[2 + \frac{3}{n} + \frac{1}{n^2}\right]$$

$$\lim_{n \to \infty} S_n = \frac{1}{3}$$

Answer: $\frac{1}{3}$ sq unit

13. $f(x) = 2x^2$, $y = 0$, $x = 2$

$$\Delta x = \frac{2}{n}$$

$$S_n = \frac{2}{n} f\left(\frac{2}{n}\right) + \ldots + \frac{2}{n} f\left(n \cdot \frac{2}{n}\right)$$

$$= \frac{2}{n}\left[f\left(\frac{2}{n}\right) + \ldots + f\left(n \cdot \frac{2}{n}\right)\right]$$

$$= \frac{2}{n}\left[2\left(\frac{2}{n}\right)^2 + \ldots + 2\left(n \cdot \frac{2}{n}\right)^2\right]$$

$$= \frac{16}{n^3}\left[1^2 + \ldots + n^2\right]$$

$$= \frac{16}{n^3} \cdot \frac{n(n+1)(2n+1)}{6} = \frac{8}{3} \cdot \frac{2n^2 + 3n + 1}{n^2}$$

$$= \frac{8}{3}\left[2 + \frac{3}{n} + \frac{1}{n^2}\right]$$

$$\lim_{n \to \infty} S_n = \frac{16}{3}$$

Answer: $\frac{16}{3}$ sq units

15. $\int_0^2 3x \, dx$

Let $f(x) = 3x$.

$$\Delta x = \frac{2}{n}$$

$$S_n = \frac{2}{n} f\left(\frac{2}{n}\right) + \ldots + \frac{2}{n} f\left(n \cdot \frac{2}{n}\right)$$

$$= \frac{2}{n}\left[3\left(\frac{2}{n}\right) + \ldots + 3\left(n \cdot \frac{2}{n}\right)\right]$$

$$= \frac{12}{n^2}[1 + \ldots + n] = \frac{12}{n^2} \cdot \frac{n(n+1)}{2}$$

$$= 6 \cdot \frac{n+1}{n} = 6\left[1 + \frac{1}{n}\right]$$

$$\int_0^2 3x \, dx = \lim_{n \to \infty} S_n = 6$$

Answer: 6

17. $\int_0^3 -4x \, dx$

Let $f(x) = -4x$.

$$\Delta x = \frac{3}{n}$$

$$S_n = \frac{3}{n} f\left(\frac{3}{n}\right) + \ldots + \frac{3}{n} f\left(n \cdot \frac{3}{n}\right)$$

$$= \frac{3}{n}\left[f\left(\frac{3}{n}\right) + \ldots + f\left(n \cdot \frac{3}{n}\right)\right]$$

$$= \frac{3}{n}\left[-4\left(\frac{3}{n}\right) - \ldots - 4\left(n \cdot \frac{3}{n}\right)\right] = -\frac{36}{n^2}[1 + \ldots + n]$$

$$= -\frac{36}{n^2} \cdot \frac{n(n+1)}{2} = -18 \cdot \frac{n+1}{n} = -18\left[1 + \frac{1}{n}\right]$$

$$\int_0^3 -4x \, dx = \lim_{n \to \infty} S_n = -18$$

Answer: -18

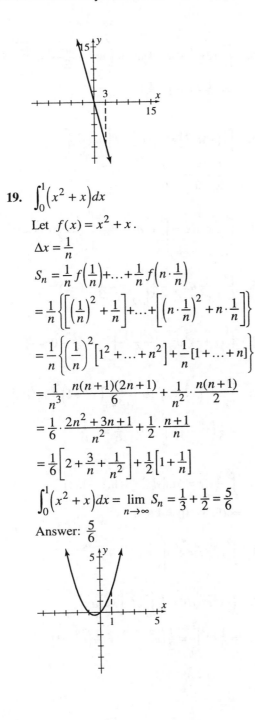

19. $\int_0^1 \left(x^2 + x\right) dx$

Let $f(x) = x^2 + x$.

$\Delta x = \dfrac{1}{n}$

$S_n = \dfrac{1}{n} f\left(\dfrac{1}{n}\right) + \ldots + \dfrac{1}{n} f\left(n \cdot \dfrac{1}{n}\right)$

$= \dfrac{1}{n}\left\{\left[\left(\dfrac{1}{n}\right)^2 + \dfrac{1}{n}\right] + \ldots + \left[\left(n \cdot \dfrac{1}{n}\right)^2 + n \cdot \dfrac{1}{n}\right]\right\}$

$= \dfrac{1}{n}\left\{\left(\dfrac{1}{n}\right)^2 \left[1^2 + \ldots + n^2\right] + \dfrac{1}{n}[1 + \ldots + n]\right\}$

$= \dfrac{1}{n^3} \cdot \dfrac{n(n+1)(2n+1)}{6} + \dfrac{1}{n^2} \cdot \dfrac{n(n+1)}{2}$

$= \dfrac{1}{6} \cdot \dfrac{2n^2 + 3n + 1}{n^2} + \dfrac{1}{2} \cdot \dfrac{n+1}{n}$

$= \dfrac{1}{6}\left[2 + \dfrac{3}{n} + \dfrac{1}{n^2}\right] + \dfrac{1}{2}\left[1 + \dfrac{1}{n}\right]$

$\int_0^1 \left(x^2 + x\right) dx = \lim_{n \to \infty} S_n = \dfrac{1}{3} + \dfrac{1}{2} = \dfrac{5}{6}$

Answer: $\dfrac{5}{6}$

21. $\int_2^3 \sqrt{x^2 + 1}\, dx$ is simply a real number. Thus

$D_x\left[\int_2^3 \sqrt{x^2 + 1}\, dx\right] = D_x \text{ (real number)} = 0.$

Answer: 0

23. $f(x) = \begin{cases} 1 & \text{if} & x \le 1 \\ 2 - x & \text{if} & 1 \le x \le 2 \\ -1 + \frac{x}{2} & \text{if} & x > 2 \end{cases}$

f is continuous and $f(x) \ge 0$ on $[-1, 3]$. Thus

$\int_{-1}^{3} f(x) dx$ gives the area A bounded by

$y = f(x)$,
$y = 0$, $x = -1$, and $x = 3$. From the diagram, this area is composed of three subareas, A_1, A_2, and A_3 and $A = A_1 + A_2 + A_3$.

$A_1 = $ area of rectangle $= (2)(1) = 2$ sq units

$A_2 = $ area of triangle $= \dfrac{1}{2}(1)(1) = \dfrac{1}{2}$ sq unit

$A_3 = $ area of triangle $= \dfrac{1}{2}(1)\left(\dfrac{1}{2}\right) = \dfrac{1}{4}$ sq unit

Since

$A = A_1 + A_2 + A_3 = 2 + \dfrac{1}{2} + \dfrac{1}{4} = \dfrac{11}{4}$ sq units,

we have $\int_{-1}^{3} f(x) dx = \dfrac{11}{4}$.

Answer: $\dfrac{11}{4}$

25. 5.3 sq units

27. 2.4

29. -16.5

Principles in Practice 16.7

1. $\displaystyle\int_3^6 10,000e^{0.02t}\,dt = \left(10,000\,\frac{e^{0.02t}}{0.02}\right)\Big|_3^6$

$= \left(500,000e^{0.02t}\right)\Big|_3^6$

$= 500,000\left(e^{0.02(6)} - e^{0.02(3)}\right)$

$= 500,000\left(e^{0.12} - e^{0.06}\right) \approx 32,830$

The total income for the chain between the third and sixth years was about \$32,830.

2. The total cost for the first 5 years is $M(5)$ or

$M(5) - M(0) = \displaystyle\int_0^5 M'(x)\,dx$

$\displaystyle\int_0^5\left(90x^2 + 5000\right)dx = \left(90\,\frac{x^3}{3} + 5000x\right)\Big|_0^5$

$= \left(30x^3 + 5000x\right)\Big|_0^5 = 30(5)^3 + 5000(5) - 0$

$= 3750 + 25,000 = 28,750$

The total cost for the first 5 years is \$28,750.

Exercise 16.7

1. $\displaystyle\int_0^2 5\,dx = 5x\Big|_0^2 = 5(2) - 5(0) = 10 - 0 = 10$

3. $\displaystyle\int_1^2 7x\,dx = 7\cdot\frac{x^2}{2}\Big|_1^2 = 14 - \frac{7}{2} = \frac{21}{2}$

5. $\displaystyle\int_{-3}^1 (2x-3)\,dx = \left(x^2 - 3x\right)\Big|_{-3}^1$

$= -2 - (18) = -20$

7. $\displaystyle\int_2^3\left(y^2 - 2y + 1\right)dy = \int_2^3 (y-1)^2\,dy$

$= \frac{1}{3}(y-1)^3\Big|_2^3$

$= \frac{8}{3} - \frac{1}{3} = \frac{7}{3}$

9. $\displaystyle\int_{-2}^{-1}\left(3w^2 - w - 1\right)dw = \left(w^3 - \frac{w^2}{2} - w\right)\Big|_{-2}^{-1}$

$= -\frac{1}{2} - (-8) = \frac{15}{2}$

11. $\displaystyle\int_1^2\left(-4t^{-4}\right) = dt = \frac{4}{3}t^{-3}\Big|_1^2 = \frac{4}{3t^3}\Big|_1^2$

$= \frac{1}{6} - \frac{8}{6} = -\frac{7}{6}$

13. $\displaystyle\int_{-1}^1 \sqrt[3]{x^5}\,dx = \int_{-1}^1 x^{\frac{5}{3}}\,dx = \frac{3x^{\frac{8}{3}}}{8}\Big|_{-1}^1 = \frac{3}{8} - \frac{3}{8} = 0$

15. $\displaystyle\int_{1/2}^3 \frac{1}{x^2}\,dx = -\frac{1}{x}\Big|_{1/2}^3 = -\frac{1}{3} - (-2) = \frac{5}{3}$

17. $\displaystyle\int_{-1}^1 (z+1)^5\,dz = \frac{(z+1)^6}{6}\Big|_{-1}^1 = \frac{32}{3} - 0 = \frac{32}{3}$

19. $\displaystyle\int_0^1 2x^2\left(x^3-1\right)^3 dx = \frac{2}{3}\int_0^1\left(x^3-1\right)^3\left[3x^2\,dx\right]$

$= \frac{1}{6}\left(x^3-1\right)^4\Big|_0^1 = 0 - \frac{1}{6} = -\frac{1}{6}$

21. $\displaystyle\int_1^8 \frac{4}{y}\,dy = 4\ln|y|\Big|_1^8 = 4(\ln 8 - \ln 1)$

$= 4(\ln 8 - 0) = 4\ln 8$

23. $\displaystyle\int_0^1 e^5\,dx = e^5 x\Big|_0^1 = e^5 - 0 = e^5$

25. $\displaystyle\int_0^2 x^2 e^{x^3}\,dx = \frac{1}{3}\int_0^2 e^{x^3}\left[3x^2\,dx\right]$

$= \frac{1}{3}e^{x^3}\Big|_0^2 = \frac{1}{3}\left(e^8 - e^0\right) = \frac{1}{3}\left(e^8 - 1\right)$

27. $\displaystyle\int_4^5 \frac{2}{(x-3)^3}\,dx = 2\int_4^5 (x-3)^{-3}\,dx$

$\displaystyle = 2\cdot\frac{(x-3)^{-2}}{-2}\bigg|_4^5$

$\displaystyle = -\frac{1}{(x-3)^2}\bigg|_4^5 = -\frac{1}{4}-(-1) = \frac{3}{4}$

29. $\displaystyle\int_{1/3}^2 \sqrt{10-3p}\,dp = -\frac{1}{3}\int_{1/3}^2 (10-3p)^{\frac{1}{2}}[-3\,dp]$

$\displaystyle = -\frac{2}{9}(10-3p)^{\frac{3}{2}}\bigg|_{1/3}^2 = -\frac{2}{9}(8-27) = \frac{38}{9}$

31. $\displaystyle\int_0^1 x^2\sqrt[3]{7x^3+1}\,dx$

$\displaystyle = \frac{1}{21}\int_0^1 \left(7x^3+1\right)^{\frac{1}{3}}\left[21x^2\,dx\right]$

$\displaystyle = \frac{1}{21}\cdot\frac{\left(7x^3+1\right)^{\frac{4}{3}}}{\frac{4}{3}}\bigg|_0^1 = \frac{\left(7x^3+1\right)^{\frac{4}{3}}}{28}\bigg|_0^1$

$\displaystyle = \frac{16}{28}-\frac{1}{28} = \frac{15}{28}$

33. $\displaystyle\int_0^1 \frac{2x^3+x}{x^2+x^4+1}\,dx$

$\displaystyle = \frac{1}{2}\int_0^1 \frac{1}{x^4+x^2+1}\left[2\left(2x^3+x\right)dx\right]$

$\displaystyle = \frac{1}{2}\ln\left(x^4+x^2+1\right)\bigg|_0^1 = \frac{1}{2}[\ln 3 - \ln 1] = \frac{1}{2}\ln 3$

35. $\displaystyle\int_0^1 \left(e^x - e^{-2x}\right)dx$

$\displaystyle = \int_0^1 e^x\,dx - \left(-\frac{1}{2}\right)\int_0^1 e^{-2x}[-2\,dx]$

$\displaystyle = \left(e^x + \frac{e^{-2x}}{2}\right)\bigg|_0^1 = \left(e + \frac{e^{-2}}{2}\right) - \left(1+\frac{1}{2}\right)$

$\displaystyle = e + \frac{1}{2e^2} - \frac{3}{2}$

37. $\displaystyle\int_1^e \left(x^{-1} + x^{-2} - x^{-3}\right)dx$

$\displaystyle = \left(\ln|x| + \frac{x^{-1}}{-1} - \frac{x^{-2}}{-2}\right)\bigg|_1^e$

$\displaystyle = \left(1 - \frac{1}{e} + \frac{1}{2e^2}\right) - \left(0 - 1 + \frac{1}{2}\right) = \frac{3}{2} - \frac{1}{e} + \frac{1}{2e^2}$

39. $\displaystyle\int_1^3 (x+1)e^{x^2+2x}\,dx$

$\displaystyle = \frac{1}{2}\int_1^3 e^{x^2+2x}[2(x+1)dx]$

$\displaystyle = \frac{1}{2}e^{x^2+2x}\bigg|_1^3 = \frac{1}{2}\left(e^{15} - e^3\right) = \frac{e^3}{2}\left(e^{12} - 1\right)$

41. Using long division on the integrand, we obtain

$\displaystyle\int_0^2 \left[x^3 + x + \frac{3x^2+5}{x^3+5x+1}\right]dx$

$\displaystyle = \left[\frac{x^4}{4} + \frac{x^2}{2} + \ln\left|x^3+5x+1\right|\right]\bigg|_0^2$

$\displaystyle = (6 + \ln 19) - 0 = 6 + \ln 19$

43. $\displaystyle\int_0^2 f(x)\,dx = \int_0^{1/2} 4x^2\,dx + \int_{1/2}^2 2x\,dx$

$\displaystyle = \frac{4x^3}{3}\bigg|_0^{1/2} + x^2\bigg|_{1/2}^2 = \left(\frac{1}{6}-0\right) + \left(4-\frac{1}{4}\right) = \frac{47}{12}$

45. $\displaystyle f(x) = \int_1^x \frac{1}{t^2}\,dt = -\frac{1}{t}\bigg|_1^x = -\frac{1}{x}+1 = 1-\frac{1}{x}$

$\displaystyle \int_e^1 f(x)\,dx = \int_e^1 \left(1-\frac{1}{x}\right)dx = \left(x - \ln|x|\right)\bigg|_e^1$

$\displaystyle = (1-0) - (e-1) = 2 - e$

47. $\displaystyle\int_1^3 f(x)\,dx = \int_1^2 f(x)\,dx + \int_2^3 f(x)\,dx$, so

$\displaystyle\int_1^2 f(x)\,dx = \int_1^3 f(x)\,dx - \int_2^3 f(x)\,dx$

$\displaystyle = \int_1^3 f(x)\,dx + \int_3^2 f(x)\,dx = 4+3 = 7$

49. $\int_1^2 e^{x^2} dx$ is a constant, so $\dfrac{d}{dx}\int_1^2 e^{x^2} dx$ is 0.

Thus $\int_1^2 \left[\dfrac{d}{dx}\int_1^2 e^{x^2} dx \right] dx = \int_1^2 0 \ dx = C\Big|_1^2$

$\qquad = C - C = 0$

51. $\int_0^T \alpha^{\frac{5}{2}} dt = \alpha^{\frac{5}{2}} t \Big|_0^T = \alpha^{\frac{5}{2}} T - 0 = \alpha^{\frac{5}{2}} T$

53. The total number receiving between a and b dollars equals the number $N(a)$ receiving a or more dollars minus the number $N(b)$ receiving b or more dollars. Thus

$N(a) - N(b) = \int_b^a -Ax^{-B} dx$.

55. $\int_0^5 2000 e^{-0.06t} dt$

$= 2000 \cdot \dfrac{1}{-0.06}\int_0^5 e^{-0.06t}[-0.06 \ dt]$

$= -\dfrac{2000}{0.06} e^{-0.06t}\Big|_0^5 = -\dfrac{2000}{0.06}\left(e^{-0.03} - 1\right)$

$\approx \$8639$

57. $\int_{36}^{64} 10{,}000\sqrt{100 - t}\, dt$

$= (-1)(10{,}000)\int_{36}^{64}(100 - t)^{\frac{1}{2}}[(-1)\ dt]$

$= -\dfrac{2}{3}(10{,}000)(100 - t)^{\frac{3}{2}}\Big|_{36}^{64}$

$= -\dfrac{2}{3}(10{,}000)[216 - 512]$

$\approx 1{,}973{,}333$

59. $\int_{60}^{70}(0.2q + 3)dq = \left(0.1q^2 + 3q\right)\Big|_{60}^{70}$

$= 700 - 540 = \$160$

61. $\int_{400}^{900}\dfrac{1000}{\sqrt{100q}} dq = \int_{400}^{900}\dfrac{1000}{10\sqrt{q}} dq$

$= 100\int_{400}^{900} q^{-\frac{1}{2}} dq$

$= 100 \cdot \dfrac{q^{\frac{1}{2}}}{\frac{1}{2}}\Big|_{400}^{900}$

$= 200\sqrt{q}\Big|_{400}^{900}$

$= 200(30 - 20) = \$2000$

63. $\int_0^{12}(8t + 10)dt = \left(4t^2 + 10t\right)\Big|_0^{12}$

$= 696 - 0 = 696$

$\int_6^{12}(8t + 10)dt = \left(4t^2 + 10t\right)\Big|_6^{12}$

$= 696 - 204 = 492$

65. $G = \int_{-R}^{R} i \ dx$

$= ix\Big|_{-R}^{R}$

$= iR - (-iR)$

$= 2Ri$

67. $A = \dfrac{\displaystyle\int_0^R (m + x)[1 - (m + x)]dx}{\displaystyle\int_0^R [1 - (m + x)]dx}$

$= \dfrac{\displaystyle\int_0^R \left(m + x - m^2 - 2mx - x^2\right)dx}{\displaystyle\int_0^R (1 - m - x)dx}$

$= \dfrac{\left[mx + \frac{x^2}{2} - m^2 x - mx^2 - \frac{x^3}{3}\right]\Big|_0^R}{\left[x - mx - \frac{x^2}{2}\right]\Big|_0^R}$

$$= \frac{\left[mR + \frac{R^2}{2} - m^2 R - mR^2 - \frac{R^3}{3} \right] - 0}{\left[R - mR - \frac{R^2}{2} \right] - 0}$$

$$= \frac{R\left[m + \frac{R}{2} - m^2 - mR - \frac{R^2}{3} \right]}{R\left[1 - m - \frac{R}{2} \right]}$$

$$= \frac{m + \frac{R}{2} - m^2 - mR - \frac{R^2}{3}}{1 - m - \frac{R}{2}}$$

69. $\displaystyle\int_0^4 \frac{1}{(4x+4)^2}\, dx = \frac{1}{4}\int_0^4 (4x+4)^{-2}[4\ dx]$

$$= \frac{1}{4} \cdot \left. \frac{(4x+4)^{-1}}{-1} \right|_0^4$$

$$= -\frac{1}{4} \cdot \left. \frac{1}{4x+4} \right|_0^4$$

$$= -\frac{1}{16} \cdot \left. \frac{1}{x+1} \right|_0^4$$

$$= -\frac{1}{16}\left(\frac{1}{5} - 1 \right) = \frac{1}{20} = 0.05$$

71. 3.52

73. 11.08

Exercise 16.8

In Problems 1–34, answers are assumed to be expressed in square units.

  1. $y = 4x, x = 2$

    Area $= \displaystyle\int_0^2 4x\ dx$

    $= \left. 2x^2 \right|_0^2 = 8 - 0 = 8$

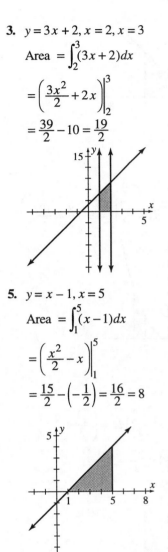

3. $y = 3x + 2, x = 2, x = 3$

  Area $= \displaystyle\int_2^3 (3x+2)dx$

  $= \left. \left(\frac{3x^2}{2} + 2x \right) \right|_2^3$

  $= \frac{39}{2} - 10 = \frac{19}{2}$

5. $y = x - 1, x = 5$

  Area $= \displaystyle\int_1^5 (x-1)dx$

  $= \left. \left(\frac{x^2}{2} - x \right) \right|_1^5$

  $= \frac{15}{2} - \left(-\frac{1}{2} \right) = \frac{16}{2} = 8$

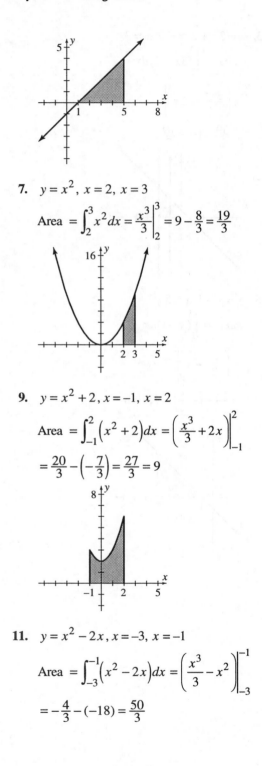

7. $y = x^2$, $x = 2$, $x = 3$

Area $= \int_2^3 x^2\, dx = \dfrac{x^3}{3}\Big|_2^3 = 9 - \dfrac{8}{3} = \dfrac{19}{3}$

9. $y = x^2 + 2$, $x = -1$, $x = 2$

Area $= \int_{-1}^2 \left(x^2 + 2\right) dx = \left(\dfrac{x^3}{3} + 2x\right)\Big|_{-1}^2$

$= \dfrac{20}{3} - \left(-\dfrac{7}{3}\right) = \dfrac{27}{3} = 9$

11. $y = x^2 - 2x$, $x = -3$, $x = -1$

Area $= \int_{-3}^{-1} \left(x^2 - 2x\right) dx = \left(\dfrac{x^3}{3} - x^2\right)\Big|_{-3}^{-1}$

$= -\dfrac{4}{3} - (-18) = \dfrac{50}{3}$

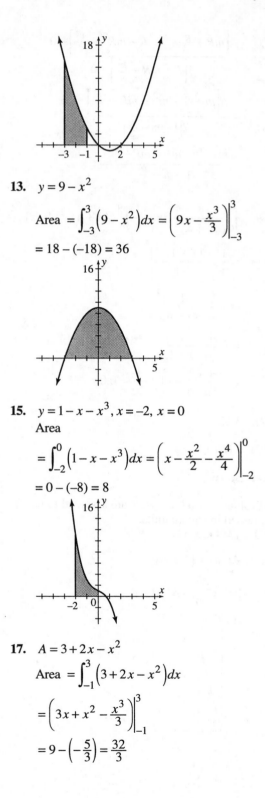

13. $y = 9 - x^2$

Area $= \int_{-3}^3 \left(9 - x^2\right) dx = \left(9x - \dfrac{x^3}{3}\right)\Big|_{-3}^3$

$= 18 - (-18) = 36$

15. $y = 1 - x - x^3$, $x = -2$, $x = 0$

Area

$= \int_{-2}^0 \left(1 - x - x^3\right) dx = \left(x - \dfrac{x^2}{2} - \dfrac{x^4}{4}\right)\Big|_{-2}^0$

$= 0 - (-8) = 8$

17. $A = 3 + 2x - x^2$

Area $= \int_{-1}^3 \left(3 + 2x - x^2\right) dx$

$= \left(3x + x^2 - \dfrac{x^3}{3}\right)\Big|_{-1}^3$

$= 9 - \left(-\dfrac{5}{3}\right) = \dfrac{32}{3}$

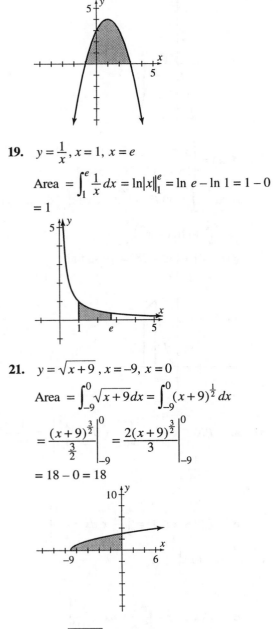

19. $y = \dfrac{1}{x}$, $x = 1$, $x = e$

Area $= \displaystyle\int_1^e \frac{1}{x}\,dx = \ln|x|\Big\|_1^e = \ln e - \ln 1 = 1 - 0$
$= 1$

21. $y = \sqrt{x+9}$, $x = -9$, $x = 0$

Area $= \displaystyle\int_{-9}^0 \sqrt{x+9}\,dx = \int_{-9}^0 (x+9)^{\frac{1}{2}}\,dx$

$= \dfrac{(x+9)^{\frac{3}{2}}}{\frac{3}{2}}\Bigg|_{-9}^0 = \dfrac{2(x+9)^{\frac{3}{2}}}{3}\Bigg|_{-9}^0$

$= 18 - 0 = 18$

23. $y = \sqrt{2x-1}$, $x = 1$, $x = 5$

Area $= \displaystyle\int_1^5 \sqrt{2x-1}\,dx$

$= \dfrac{1}{2}\displaystyle\int_1^5 (2x-1)^{\frac{1}{2}}\,[2\ dx]$

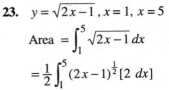

$= \dfrac{(2x-1)^{\frac{3}{2}}}{3}\Bigg|_1^5 = 9 - \dfrac{1}{3} = \dfrac{26}{3}$

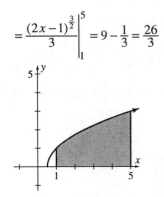

25. $y = \sqrt[3]{x}$, $x = 2$

Area

$= \displaystyle\int_0^2 \sqrt[3]{x}\,dx = \int_0^2 x^{\frac{1}{3}}\,dx = \dfrac{3x^{\frac{4}{3}}}{4}\Bigg|_0^2 = \dfrac{3(2)^{\frac{4}{3}}}{4} - 0$

$= \dfrac{3\left(2\sqrt[3]{2}\right)}{4} = \dfrac{3}{2}\sqrt[3]{2}$

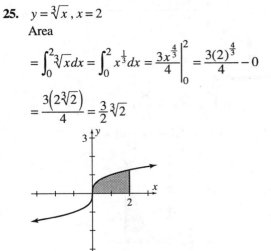

27. $y = e^x$, $x = 0$, $x = 2$

Area $= \displaystyle\int_0^2 e^x\,dx = e^x\Big|_0^2 = e^2 - 1$

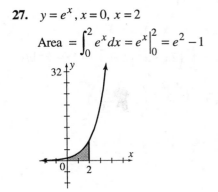

29. $y = x + \dfrac{2}{x}$, $x = 1$, $x = 2$

Area $= \displaystyle\int_1^2 \left(x + \dfrac{2}{x} \right) dx = \left(\dfrac{x^2}{2} + 2\ln|x| \right)\Big|_1^2$

$= (2 + 2\ln 2) - \dfrac{1}{2} = \dfrac{3}{2} + 2\ln 2 = \dfrac{3}{2} + \ln 4$

31. $y = x^3$, $x = -2$, $x = 4$

Area

$= \displaystyle\int_{-2}^0 -x^3\,dx + \int_0^4 x^3\,dx = -\dfrac{x^4}{4}\Big|_{-2}^0 + \dfrac{x^4}{4}\Big|_0^4$

$= [0 - (-4)] + [64 - 0] = 68$

33. $y = 2x - x^2$, $x = 1$, $x = 3$

Area $= \displaystyle\int_1^2 \left(2x - x^2 \right) dx + \int_2^3 -\left(2x - x^2 \right) dx$

$= \left(x^2 - \dfrac{x^3}{3} \right)\Big|_1^2 - \left(x^2 - \dfrac{x^3}{3} \right)\Big|_2^3$

$= \left[\dfrac{4}{3} - \dfrac{2}{3} \right] - \left[0 - \dfrac{4}{3} \right] = \dfrac{6}{3} = 2$

35. $f(x) = \begin{cases} 3x^2 & \text{if} \quad 0 \le x \le 2 \\ 16 - 2x & \text{if} \quad x \ge 2 \end{cases}$

Area $= \displaystyle\int_0^3 f(x)\,dx = \int_0^2 3x^2\,dx + \int_2^3 (16 - 2x)\,dx$

$= x^3\Big|_0^2 + \left(16x - x^2 \right)\Big|_2^3$

$= [8 - 0] + [39 - 28] = 19$ sq units

37. a. $P(0 \le x \le 1) = \displaystyle\int_0^1 \dfrac{1}{8}x\,dx = \dfrac{x^2}{16}\Big|_0^1 = \dfrac{1}{16} - 0$

$= \dfrac{1}{16}$

b. $P(2 \le x \le 4) = \displaystyle\int_2^4 \dfrac{1}{8}x\,dx = \dfrac{x^2}{16}\Big|_2^4$

$= 1 - \dfrac{1}{4} = \dfrac{3}{4}$

c. $P(x \ge 3) = \displaystyle\int_3^4 \dfrac{1}{8}x\,dx = \dfrac{x^2}{16}\Big|_3^4$

$= 1 - \dfrac{9}{16} = \dfrac{7}{16}$

39. a. $P(3 \le x \le 5) = \int_{3}^{5} \frac{1}{x}\,dx = \ln|x|\big\|_{3}^{5}$

$= \ln 5 - \ln 3 = \ln\frac{5}{3}$

b. $P(x \le 4) = \int_{e}^{4} \frac{1}{x}\,dx = \ln|x|\big\|_{e}^{4}$
$= \ln(4) - \ln e = \ln(4) - 1$

c. $P(x \ge 3) = \int_{3}^{e^2} \frac{1}{x}\,dx = \ln|x|\big\|_{3}^{e^2}$
$= \ln e^2 - \ln 3 = 2 - \ln 3$

d. $P\!\left(e \le x \le e^2\right) = \int_{e}^{e^2} \frac{1}{x}\,dx$

$= \ln|x|\big\|_{e}^{e^2} = \ln e^2 - \ln e$
$= 2 - 1 = 1$

41.   1.57 sq units

43.   The *x*-intercept on [1, 3] is $A \approx 2.190327947$

Area $= \int_{1}^{A} -\left(x^4 - 2x^3 - 2\right)dx + \int_{A}^{3}\left(x^4 - 2x^3 - 2\right)dx$

≈ 11.41 sq units.

Exercise 16.9

1.   Area $= \int_{a}^{b}\left(y_{\text{UPPER}} - y_{\text{LOWER}}\right)dx = \int_{-2}^{3}\left[(x+6) - x^2\right]dx$

3.   Intersection points:
$x^2 - x = 2x,\ x^2 - 3x = 0,\ x(x-3) = 0 \Rightarrow x = 0\ \text{or}\ x = 3$

Area $= \int_{0}^{3}\left(y_{\text{UPPER}} - y_{\text{LOWER}}\right)dx + \int_{3}^{4}\left(y_{\text{UPPER}} - y_{\text{LOWER}}\right)dx$

$= \int_{0}^{3}\left[2x - \left(x^2 - x\right)\right]dx + \int_{3}^{4}\left[\left(x^2 - x\right) - 2x\right]dx$

5. The graphs of $y = 1 - x^2$ and $y = x - 1$ intersect when $1 - x^2 = x - 1$,

$0 = x^2 + x - 2$, $0 = (x-1)(x+2) \Rightarrow x = 1$ or $x = -2$. When $x = 1$, then $y = 0$. We use horizontal elements, where y ranges from 0 to 1. Solving $y = x - 1$ for x gives $x = y + 1$, and solving $y = 1 - x^2$ for x gives $x^2 = 1 - y$, $x = \pm\sqrt{1-y}$. We must choose $x = \sqrt{1-y}$ because x is not negative over the given region.

$$\text{Area} = \int_0^1 (x_{\text{RIGHT}} - x_{\text{LEFT}})\,dy$$

$$= \int_0^1 \left[(y+1) - \sqrt{1-y}\right]dy$$

7. The graphs of $y = x^2 - 4$ and $y = 11 - 2x^2$ intersect when $x^2 - 4 = 11 - 2x^2$, $3x^2 = 15$, $x^2 = 5$, so $x = \pm\sqrt{5}$. We use vertical elements.

$$\text{Area} = \int_{-\sqrt{5}}^2 (y_{\text{UPPER}} - y_{\text{LOWER}})\,dx$$

$$= \int_{-\sqrt{5}}^2 \left[\left(11 - 2x^2\right) - \left(x^2 - 4\right)\right]dx$$

In Problems 9–34, the answers are assumed to be expressed in square units.

9. $y = x^2$, $y = 2x$

Region appears below.

Intersection: $x^2 = 2x$, $x^2 - 2x = 0$, $x(x-2) = 0$, so $x = 0$ or 2.

$$\text{Area} = \int_0^2 (2x - x^2)\,dx = \left(x^2 - \frac{x^3}{3}\right)\Big|_0^2$$

$$= \left(4 - \frac{8}{3}\right) - 0 = \frac{4}{3}$$

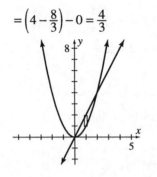

11. $y = x^2$, $x = 0$, $y = 4$ $(x \geq 0)$. Region appears below.

Intersection: $x^2 = 4$, so $x = \pm 2$

$$\text{Area} = \int_0^2 (4 - x^2)\,dx = \left(4x - \frac{x^3}{3}\right)\Big|_0^2$$

$$= \left(8 - \frac{8}{3}\right) - 0 = \frac{16}{3}$$

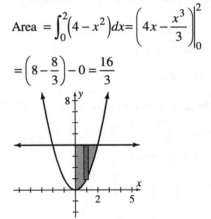

13. $y = x^2 + 3$, $y = 9$. Region appears below.

Intersection: $x^2 + 3 = 9$, $x^2 = 6$, so $x = \pm\sqrt{6}$

$$\text{Area} = \int_{-\sqrt{6}}^{\sqrt{6}} \left[9 - \left(x^2 + 3\right)\right]dx$$

$$= \int_{-\sqrt{6}}^{\sqrt{6}} \left(6 - x^2\right)dx$$

$$= \left(6x - \frac{x^3}{3}\right)\Big|_{-\sqrt{6}}^{\sqrt{6}}$$

$$= \left(6\sqrt{6} - \frac{6\sqrt{6}}{3}\right) - \left(-6\sqrt{6} + \frac{6\sqrt{6}}{3}\right) = 8\sqrt{6}$$

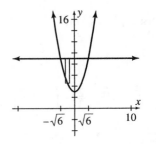

15. $x = 8 + 2y$, $x = 0$, $y = -1$, $y = 3$. Region appears below.

$$\text{Area} = \int_{-1}^{3} (8 + 2y)\,dy = \left(8y + y^2\right)\Big|_{-1}^{3}$$

$$= (24 + 9) - (-8 + 1) = 40$$

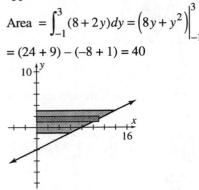

17. $y = 4 - x^2$, $y = -3x$. Region appears below.

Intersection: $-3x = 4 - x^2$, $x^2 - 3x - 4 = 0$, $(x + 1)(x - 4) = 0$, so $x = -1$ or 4.

$$\text{Area} \int_{-1}^{4} \left[\left(4 - x^2\right) - (-3x)\right]dx$$

$$= \left(4x - \frac{x^3}{3} + \frac{3x^2}{2}\right)\Big|_{-1}^{4}$$

$$= \left(16 - \frac{64}{3} + 24\right) - \left(-4 + \frac{1}{3} + \frac{3}{2}\right) = \frac{125}{6}$$

19. $y^2 = x$, $y = x - 2$. Region appears below.

Intersection: $y^2 = y + 2$, $y^2 - y - 2 = 0$, $(y + 1)(y - 2) = 0$, so $y = -1$ or 2.

$$\text{Area} = \int_{-1}^{2} \left[(y + 2) - y^2\right]dy$$

$$= \left(\frac{y^2}{2} + 2y - \frac{y^3}{3}\right)\Big|_{-1}^{2}$$

$$= \left(2 + 4 - \frac{8}{3}\right) - \left(\frac{1}{2} - 2 + \frac{1}{3}\right) = \frac{9}{2}$$

21. $2y = 4x - x^2$, $2y = x - 4$. Region appears below.

Intersection: $x - 4 = 4x - x^2$, $x^2 - 3x - 4 = 0$, $(x + 1)(x - 4) = 0$, so $x = -1$ or 4. Note that the y-values of the curves are given by

$$y = \frac{4x - x^2}{2} \text{ and } y = \frac{x - 4}{2}.$$

$$\text{Area} = \int_{-1}^{4} \left[\left(\frac{4x - x^2}{2}\right) - \left(\frac{x - 4}{2}\right)\right]dx$$

$$= \int_{-1}^{4} \left(\frac{3}{2}x - \frac{x^2}{2} + 2\right)dx$$

$$= \left(\frac{3x^2}{4} - \frac{x^3}{6} + 2x\right)\Big|_{-1}^{4}$$

$$= \left(12 - \frac{64}{6} + 8\right) - \left(\frac{3}{4} + \frac{1}{6} - 2\right)$$

$$= \frac{125}{12}$$

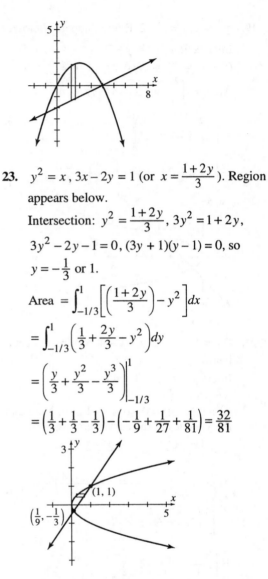

23. $y^2 = x$, $3x - 2y = 1$ (or $x = \dfrac{1+2y}{3}$). Region appears below.

Intersection: $y^2 = \dfrac{1+2y}{3}$, $3y^2 = 1 + 2y$,

$3y^2 - 2y - 1 = 0$, $(3y + 1)(y - 1) = 0$, so

$y = -\dfrac{1}{3}$ or 1.

$$\text{Area} = \int_{-1/3}^{1}\left[\left(\frac{1+2y}{3}\right) - y^2\right]dx$$

$$= \int_{-1/3}^{1}\left(\frac{1}{3} + \frac{2y}{3} - y^2\right)dy$$

$$= \left(\frac{y}{3} + \frac{y^2}{3} - \frac{y^3}{3}\right)\Bigg|_{-1/3}^{1}$$

$$= \left(\frac{1}{3} + \frac{1}{3} - \frac{1}{3}\right) - \left(-\frac{1}{9} + \frac{1}{27} + \frac{1}{81}\right) = \frac{32}{81}$$

25. $y = 8 - x^2$, $y = x^2$, $x = -1$, $x = 1$. Region appears below.

Intersection: $x^2 = 8 - x^2$, $2x^2 = 8$, $x^2 = 4$,

so $x = \pm 2$.

$$\text{Area} = \int_{-1}^{1}\left[\left(8 - x^2\right) - x^2\right]dx$$

$$= \int_{-1}^{1}\left(8 - 2x^2\right)dx$$

$$= \left(8x - \frac{2x^3}{3}\right)\Bigg|_{-1}^{1} = \left(8 - \frac{2}{3}\right) - \left(-8 + \frac{2}{3}\right) = \frac{44}{3}$$

27. $y = x^2$, $y = 2$, $y = 5$. Region appears below.
Area

$$= \int_{2}^{5}\left[\sqrt{y} - \left(-\sqrt{y}\right)\right]dy = \int_{2}^{5} 2\sqrt{y}\,dy = 2 \cdot \frac{y^{\frac{3}{2}}}{\frac{3}{2}}\Bigg|_{2}^{5}$$

$$= \frac{4y^{\frac{3}{2}}}{3}\Bigg|_{2}^{5} = \frac{4 \cdot 5\sqrt{5}}{3} - \frac{4 \cdot 2\sqrt{2}}{3}$$

$$= \frac{4}{3}\left(5\sqrt{5} - 2\sqrt{2}\right)$$

29. $y = x^3$, $y = x$. Region appears below.
Intersection: $x^3 = x$, $x^3 - x = 0$,

$x\left(x^2 - 1\right) = 0$,

$x(x + 1)(x - 1) = 0$, so $x = 0$ or $x = \pm 1$.

$$\text{Area} = \int_{-1}^{0}\left(x^3 - x\right)dx + \int_{0}^{1}\left(x - x^3\right)dx$$

$$= \left(\frac{x^4}{4} - \frac{x^2}{2}\right)\Bigg|_{-1}^{0} + \left(\frac{x^2}{2} - \frac{x^4}{4}\right)\Bigg|_{0}^{1}$$

$$= \left[0 - \left(\frac{1}{4} - \frac{1}{2}\right)\right] + \left[\left(\frac{1}{2} - \frac{1}{4}\right) - 0\right] = \frac{1}{2}$$

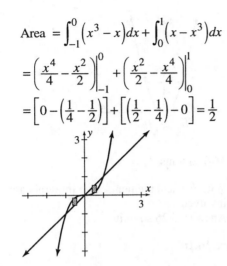

31. $y = \dfrac{-17 - 4x}{4}$, $y = \dfrac{1}{x}$. Region appears

below. Intersection: $\dfrac{-17 - 4x}{4} = \dfrac{1}{x}$,

$-17x - 4x^2 = 4$, $4x^2 + 17x + 4 = 0$, $(4x + 1)(x + 4) = 0$, so $x = -\dfrac{1}{4}$ or -4.

$$\text{Area} = \int_{-4}^{-1/4}\left[\frac{1}{x} - \left(\frac{17 - 4x}{4}\right)\right]dx$$

$$= \left(\ln|x| - \frac{17}{4}x + \frac{x^2}{2}\right)\Bigg|_{-4}^{-1/4}$$

$$= \left(\ln\frac{1}{4} - \frac{17}{16} + \frac{1}{32}\right) - (\ln 4 - 17 + 8)$$

$$= \frac{255}{32} - 4\ln 2$$

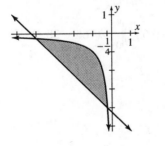

33. $y = x - 1$, $y = 5 - 2x$. Region appears below. Intersection: $x - 1 = 5 - 2x$, $3x = 6$, so $x = 2$.

$$\text{Area} = \int_{0}^{2}[(5 - 2x) - (x - 1)]dx$$

$$+ \int_{2}^{4}[(x - 1) - (5 - 2x)]dx$$

$$= \int_{0}^{2}(6 - 3x)dx + \int_{2}^{4}(3x - 6)dx$$

$$= -\frac{1}{3}\int_{0}^{2}(6 - 3x)[-3\ dx] + \frac{1}{3}\int_{2}^{4}(3x - 6)[3\ dx]$$

$$= -\frac{(6 - 3x)^2}{6}\Bigg|_{0}^{2} + \frac{(3x - 6)^2}{6}\Bigg|_{2}^{4}$$

$$= -[0 - 6] + [6 - 0] = 6 + 6 = 12$$

35. $\dfrac{\text{Area between curve and diag.}}{\text{Area under diagonal}}$

$$= \frac{\int_{0}^{1}\left[x - \left(\frac{20}{21}x^2 + \frac{1}{21}x\right)\right]dx}{\int_{0}^{1}x\ dx}$$

$$\text{Numerator} = \int_{0}^{1}\left[\frac{20}{21}x - \frac{20}{21}x^2\right]dx$$

$$= \frac{20}{21}\int_{0}^{1}\left(x - x^2\right)dx$$

$$= \frac{20}{21}\left(\frac{x^2}{2} - \frac{x^3}{3}\right)\Bigg|_{0}^{1}$$

$$= \frac{20}{21}\left[\left(\frac{1}{2} - \frac{1}{3}\right) - 0\right]$$

$$= \frac{20}{21}\cdot\frac{1}{6} = \frac{10}{63}$$

Denominator $= \int_0^1 x \, dx = \left.\frac{x^2}{2}\right|_0^1 = \frac{1}{2}$

Coefficient of inequality $= \frac{\frac{10}{63}}{\frac{1}{2}} = \frac{20}{63}$

37. $y^2 = 4x$, $y = mx$

Intersection: $(mx)^2 = 4x m^2 x^2 = 4x$,

$m^2 x^2 - 4x = 0$, $x(m^2 x - 4) = 0$, $x = 0$ or

$x = \frac{4}{m^2}$.

If $x = 0$, then $y = 0$; if $x = \frac{4}{m^2}$, then $y = \frac{4}{m}$.

With horizontal elements,

Area $= \int_0^{4/m} \left(\frac{y}{m} - \frac{y^2}{4}\right) dy = \left.\left(\frac{y^2}{2m} - \frac{y^3}{12}\right)\right|_0^{4/m}$

$= \frac{8}{3m^3} - \frac{16}{3m^3} = \frac{8}{3m^3}$ square units

Note: with vertical elements,

Area $= \int_0^{4/m^2} \left(2\sqrt{x} - mx\right) dx$

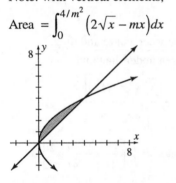

39. $y = x^2$ and $y = k$ intersect when

$x^2 = k$, $x = \pm\sqrt{k}$. Equating areas gives

$\int_{-\sqrt{k}}^{\sqrt{k}} \left(k - x^2\right) dx = \frac{1}{2} \int_{-2}^{2} \left(4 - x^2\right) dx$

$\left.\left(kx - \frac{x^3}{3}\right)\right|_{-\sqrt{k}}^{\sqrt{k}} = \frac{1}{2}\left.\left(4x - \frac{x^3}{3}\right)\right|_{-2}^{2}$

$\frac{4}{3} k^{\frac{3}{2}} = \frac{16}{3}$

$k^{\frac{3}{2}} = 4 \Rightarrow k = 4^{\frac{2}{3}} = \left(2^2\right)^{\frac{2}{3}} = 2^{\frac{4}{3}}$

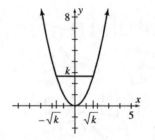

41. 4.76 sq units

43. With vertical elements, two integrals are involved.
Answer: 7.26 sq units

Exercise 16.10

1. $D: p = 20 - 0.8q$
   $S: p = 4 + 1.2q$

   Equilibrium pt. $= (q_0, p_0) = (8, 13.6)$

   $CS = \int_0^{q_0} \left[f(q) - p_0\right] dq$

   $= \int_0^8 [(20 - 0.8q) - 13.6] = \int_0^8 (6.4 - 0.8q) dq$

   $= \left.\left(6.4q - 0.4q^2\right)\right|_0^8 = (51.2 - 25.6) - 0$

   $= 25.6$

   $PS = \int_0^{q_0} \left[p_0 - g(q)\right] dq$

   $= \int_0^8 [13.6 - (4 + 1.2q)] dq$

   $= \int_0^8 (9.6 - 1.2q) dq$

   $= \left.\left(9.6q - 0.6q^2\right)\right|_0^8 = (76.8 - 38.4) - 0$

   $= 38.4$

3. $D: p = \frac{50}{q+5}$
$S: p = \frac{q}{10} + 4.5$

Equilibrium pt. $= (q_0, p_0) = (5, 5)$

$\text{CS} = \int_0^{q_0} [f(q) - p_0]\,dq$

$= \int_0^5 \left[\frac{50}{q+5} - 5\right]dq = \left(50\ln|q+5| - 5q\right)\Big|_0^5$

$= [50\ln(10) - 25] - [50\ln(5)]$

$= 50[\ln(10) - \ln(5)] - 25 = 50\ln(2) - 25$

$\text{PS} = \int_0^{q_0} [p_0 - g(q)]\,dq$

$= \int_0^5 \left[5 - \left(\frac{q}{10} + 4.5\right)\right]dq = \int_0^5 \left(0.5 - \frac{q}{10}\right)dq$

$= \left(0.5q - \frac{q^2}{20}\right)\Big|_0^5 = (2.5 - 1.25) - 0 = 1.25$

5. $D: p = 100(10 - p)$
$S: p = 80(p - 10)$

Equilibrium pt. $= (q_0, p_0) = (400, 6)$

We use horizontal strips and integrate with respect to p.

$\text{CS} = \int_6^{10} 100(10 - p)\,dp$

$= 100\left(10p - \frac{p^2}{2}\right)\Big|_6^{10}$

$= 100[(100 - 50) - (60 - 18)]$

$= 800$

$\text{PS} = \int_1^6 80(p - 1)\,dp$

$= 80\left(\frac{p^2}{2} - p\right)\Big|_1^6$

$= 80\left[(18 - 6) - \left(\frac{1}{2} - 1\right)\right] = 1000$

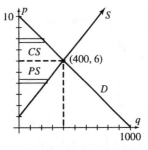

7. We integrate with respect to p. From the demand equation, when $q = 0$, then $p = 100$.

$\text{CS} = \int_{84}^{100} 10\sqrt{100 - p}\,dp$

$= \int_{84}^{100} -10(100 - p)^{\frac{1}{2}}[-dp]$

$= -\frac{20}{3}(100 - p)^{\frac{3}{2}}\Big|_{84}^{100}$

$= -\frac{20}{3}\left[0 - (16)^{\frac{3}{2}}\right] = -\frac{20}{3}(-64)$

$= 426\frac{2}{3} \approx \$426.67$

9. At equilibrium,

$2^{11-q} = 2^{q+1} \Rightarrow 11 - q = q + 1 \Rightarrow q = 5$, so

$p = 2^{11-5} = 64$

$\text{CS} = \int_0^5 \left(2^{11-q} - 64\right)dq = \left(-\frac{2^{11-q}}{\ln 2} - 64q\right)\Big|_0^5$

$= -\frac{64}{\ln 2} - 320 - \left(-\frac{2^{11}}{\ln 2} - 0\right)$

$\approx 2542.307 \text{ hundred} \approx \$254,000$

11. $\text{CS} \approx 1197;\ \text{PS} \approx 477$

Chapter 16 Review Problems

1. $\int \left(x^3 + 2x - 7\right)dx = \frac{x^4}{4} + 2\cdot\frac{x^2}{2} - 7x + C$

$= \frac{x^4}{4} + x^2 - 7x + C$

3. $\int_0^9 \left(\sqrt{x}+x\right)dx = \int_0^9 \left(x^{\frac{1}{2}}+x\right)dx$

$= \left(\dfrac{2x^{\frac{3}{2}}}{3}+\dfrac{x^2}{2}\right)\Bigg|_0^9$

$= \left(18+\dfrac{81}{2}\right) = \dfrac{117}{2}$

5. $\int \dfrac{2}{(x+5)^3}\,dx = 2\int (x+5)^{-3}\,dx$

$= \dfrac{2(x+5)^{-2}}{-2}+C$

$= -(x+5)^{-2}+C$

7. $\int \dfrac{6x^2-12}{x^3-6x+1}\,dx$

$= 2\int \dfrac{1}{x^3-6x+1}\left[\left(3x^2-6\right)dx\right]$

$= 2\ln\left|x^3-6x+1\right|+C$

9. $\int_0^1 \sqrt[3]{3t+8}\,dt = \dfrac{1}{3}\int_0^1 (3t+8)^{\frac{1}{3}}[3\,dt]$

$= \dfrac{1}{3}\cdot\dfrac{(3t+8)^{\frac{4}{3}}}{\frac{4}{3}}\Bigg|_0^1$

$= \dfrac{(3t+8)^{\frac{4}{3}}}{4}\Bigg|_0^1 = \dfrac{11\sqrt[3]{11}}{4}-4$

11. $\int y(y+1)^2\,dy = \int \left(y^3+2y^2+y\right)dy$

$= \dfrac{y^4}{4}+\dfrac{2y^3}{3}+\dfrac{y^2}{2}+C$

13. $\int \dfrac{\sqrt[4]{z}-\sqrt[3]{z}}{\sqrt{z}}\,dz = \int \left(\dfrac{z^{\frac{1}{4}}}{z^{\frac{1}{2}}}-\dfrac{z^{\frac{1}{3}}}{z^{\frac{1}{2}}}\right)dz$

$= \int \left(z^{-\frac{1}{4}}-z^{-\frac{1}{6}}\right)dz$

$= \dfrac{z^{\frac{3}{4}}}{\frac{3}{4}}-\dfrac{z^{\frac{5}{6}}}{\frac{5}{6}}+C = \dfrac{4z^{\frac{3}{4}}}{3}-\dfrac{6z^{\frac{5}{6}}}{5}+C$

15. $\int_1^2 \dfrac{t^3}{2+t^3}\,dt = \dfrac{1}{3}\int_1^2 \dfrac{1}{2+t^3}\left[3t^2\,dt\right]$

$= \dfrac{1}{3}\ln\left|2+t^3\right|\Big\|_1^2$

$= \dfrac{1}{3}(\ln 10-\ln 3) = \dfrac{1}{3}\ln\dfrac{10}{3}$

17. $\int x^2\sqrt{3x^3+2}\,dx = \dfrac{1}{9}\int \left(3x^3+2\right)^{\frac{1}{2}}\left[9x^2\,dx\right]$

$= \dfrac{1}{9}\cdot\dfrac{\left(3x^3+2\right)^{\frac{3}{2}}}{\frac{3}{2}}+C = \dfrac{2}{27}\left(3x^3+2\right)^{\frac{3}{2}}+C$

19. $\int \left(e^{2y}-e^{-2y}\right)dy$

$= \dfrac{1}{2}\int e^{2y}[2\,dy]-\left(-\dfrac{1}{2}\right)\int e^{-2y}[-2\,dy]$

$= \dfrac{1}{2}e^{2y}+\dfrac{1}{2}e^{-2y}+C = \dfrac{1}{2}\left(e^{2y}+e^{-2y}\right)+C$

21. $\int \left(\dfrac{1}{x}+\dfrac{2}{x^2}\right)dx = \int \dfrac{1}{x}\,dx+2\int x^{-2}\,dx$

$= \ln|x|+2\cdot\dfrac{x^{-1}}{-1}+C$

$= \ln|x|-\dfrac{2}{x}+C$

23. $\int_{-2}^1 \left(y^4-y+1\right)dy = \left(\dfrac{y^5}{5}-\dfrac{y^2}{2}+y\right)\Bigg|_{-2}^1$

$= \left(\dfrac{1}{5}-\dfrac{1}{2}+1\right)-\left(-\dfrac{32}{5}-2-2\right) = \dfrac{111}{10} = 11.1$

25. $\int_{\sqrt{3}}^2 7x\sqrt{4-x^2}\,dx = 7\int_{\sqrt{3}}^2 x\left(4-x^2\right)^{\frac{1}{2}}\,dx$

$= 7\cdot\left(-\dfrac{1}{2}\right)\Bigg|_{\sqrt{3}}^2 \left(4-x^2\right)^{\frac{1}{2}}[-2x\,dx]$

$= -\dfrac{7}{2}\cdot\dfrac{\left(4-x^2\right)^{\frac{3}{2}}}{\frac{3}{2}}\Bigg|_{\sqrt{3}}^2$

$= -\dfrac{7}{3}\cdot\left(4-x^2\right)^{\frac{3}{2}}\Bigg|_{\sqrt{3}}^2 = -\dfrac{7}{3}(0-1) = \dfrac{7}{3}$

27. $\int_0^1 \left[2x - \dfrac{1}{(x+1)^{\frac{2}{3}}} \right] dx$

$= 2\int_0^1 x\, dx - \int_0^1 (x+1)^{-\frac{2}{3}} [dx]$

$= \left[2 \cdot \dfrac{x^2}{2} - \dfrac{(x+1)^{\frac{1}{3}}}{\frac{1}{3}} \right]\Big|_0^1 = \left[x^2 - 3(x+1)^{\frac{1}{3}} \right]\Big|_0^1$

$= \left[1 - 3\sqrt[3]{2} \right] - [0 - 3] = 4 - 3\sqrt[3]{2}$

29. $\int \dfrac{\sqrt{t}-3}{t^2}\, dt = \int \left[\dfrac{t^{\frac{1}{2}}}{t^2} - \dfrac{3}{t^2} \right] dt$

$= \int \left(t^{-\frac{3}{2}} - 3t^{-2} \right) dt$

$= \dfrac{t^{-\frac{1}{2}}}{-\frac{1}{2}} - 3 \cdot \dfrac{t^{-1}}{-1} + C = -2t^{-\frac{1}{2}} + 3t^{-1} + C$

$= \dfrac{3}{t} - \dfrac{2}{\sqrt{t}} + C$

31. $\int_{-1}^0 \dfrac{x^2+4x-1}{x+2}\, dx = \int_{-1}^0 \left(x + 2 - \dfrac{5}{x+2} \right) dx$

$= \left(\dfrac{x^2}{2} + 2x - 5\ln|x+2| \right)\Big|_{-1}^0$

$= (-5\ln 2) - \left(\dfrac{1}{2} - 2 - 0 \right)$

$= \dfrac{3}{2} - 5\ln 2$

33. $\int \sqrt{x}\sqrt{x^{\frac{3}{2}}+1}\, dx = \dfrac{2}{3}\int \left(x^{\frac{3}{2}}+1 \right)^{\frac{1}{2}} \left[\dfrac{3}{2}x^{\frac{1}{2}}dx \right]$

$= \dfrac{2}{3} \cdot \dfrac{\left(x^{\frac{3}{2}}+1 \right)^{\frac{3}{2}}}{\frac{3}{2}} + C = \dfrac{4}{9}\left(x^{\frac{3}{2}}+1 \right)^{\frac{3}{2}} + C$

35. $\int_1^e \dfrac{e^{\ln x}}{x^2}\, dx = \int_1^e \dfrac{x}{x^2}\, dx = \int_1^e \dfrac{1}{x}\, dx = \ln|x|\Big|_1^e$

$= \ln e - \ln 1$

$= 1 - 0 = 1$

37. $\int \dfrac{\left(1+e^{3x}\right)^2}{e^{-3x}}\, dx = \dfrac{1}{3}\int \left(1+e^{3x}\right)^2 \left[3e^{3x}dx\right]$

$= \dfrac{\left(1+e^{3x}\right)^3}{9} + C$

39. $\int \sqrt{10^{3x}}\, dx = \int 10^{\frac{3x}{2}}\, dx = \dfrac{2}{3}\int 10^{\frac{3x}{2}} \left[\dfrac{3}{2}dx \right]$

$= \dfrac{2}{3} \cdot \dfrac{10^{\frac{3x}{2}}}{\ln 10} + C = \dfrac{2\sqrt{10^{3x}}}{3\ln 10} + C$

41. $y = \int \left(e^{2x} + 3 \right) dx = \int e^{2x} dx + \int 3\, dx$

$= \dfrac{1}{2}\int e^{2x}[2\, dx] + \int 3\, dx$

$= \dfrac{1}{2}e^{2x} + 3x + C$

$y(0) = -\dfrac{1}{2}$ implies that $-\dfrac{1}{2} = \dfrac{1}{2} + 0 + C$, so

$C = -1$. Thus $y = \dfrac{1}{2}e^{2x} + 3x - 1$

In Problems 43–58, answers are assumed to be expressed in square units.

43. $y = x^2 - 1$, $x = 2$, $y \geq 0$. Region appears below.

$\text{Area } = \int_1^2 \left(x^2 - 1 \right) dx = \left(\dfrac{x^3}{3} - x \right)\Big|_1^2$

$= \left(\dfrac{8}{3} - 2 \right) - \left(\dfrac{1}{3} - 1 \right) = \dfrac{4}{3}$

45. $y = \sqrt{x+4}$, $x = 0$. Region appears below.

$$\text{Area } = \int_{-4}^{0} \sqrt{x+4}\,dx = \int_{-4}^{0} (x+4)^{\frac{1}{2}}\,[dx]$$

$$= \frac{(x+4)^{\frac{3}{2}}}{\frac{3}{2}} \Bigg|_{-4}^{0}$$

$$= \frac{2(x+4)^{\frac{3}{2}}}{3} \Bigg|_{-4}^{0}$$

$$= \frac{16}{3} - 0 = \frac{16}{3}$$

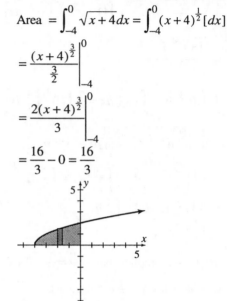

47. $y = 5x - x^2$. Region appears below.

$$\text{Area } = \int_{0}^{5} \left(5x - x^2\right) dx = \left(\frac{5x^2}{2} - \frac{x^3}{3}\right)\Bigg|_{0}^{5}$$

$$= \left(\frac{125}{2} - \frac{125}{3}\right) - 0 = \frac{125}{6}$$

49. $y = \frac{1}{x} + 3$, $x = 1$, $x = 3$. Region appears below.

$$\text{Area } = \int_{1}^{3} \left(\frac{1}{x} + 3\right) dx = \left(\ln|x| + 3x\right)\Bigg|_{1}^{3}$$

$$= [\ln(3) + 9] - 3 = 6 + \ln 3$$

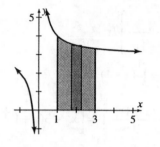

51. $y^2 = 4x$, $x = 0$, $y = 2$. Region appears below.

$$\text{Area } = \int_{0}^{2} \frac{y^2}{4}\,dy = \frac{y^3}{12}\Bigg|_{0}^{2} = \frac{8}{12} - 0 = \frac{2}{3}$$

53. $y = x^2 + 4x - 5$, $y = 0$. Region appears below.

$x^2 + 4x - 5 = 0$, $(x+5)(x-1) = 0$, so $x = -5, 1$.

$$\text{Area } = \int_{-5}^{1} -\left(x^2 + 4x - 5\right) dx$$

$$= -\left(\frac{x^3}{3} + 2x^2 - 5x\right)\Bigg|_{-5}^{1}$$

$$= -\left(\frac{1}{3} + 2 - 5\right) + \left(-\frac{125}{3} + 50 + 25\right) = 36$$

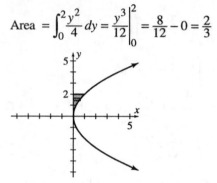

55. $y = x^2 - 2x$, $y = 12 - x^2$. Region appears below.
$x^2 - 2x = 12 - x^2$, $2x^2 - 2x - 12 = 0$,
$2(x + 2)(x - 3) = 0$, so $x = -2, 3$

Area $\int_{-2}^{3}\left[\left(12 - x^2\right) - \left(x^2 - 2x\right)\right]dx$

$= 2\int_{-2}^{3}\left(6 + x - x^2\right)dx$

$= 2\left(6x + \dfrac{x^2}{2} - \dfrac{x^3}{3}\right)\Bigg|_{-2}^{3}$

$= 2\left[\left(18 + \dfrac{9}{2} - 9\right) - \left(-12 + 2 + \dfrac{8}{3}\right)\right] = \dfrac{125}{3}$

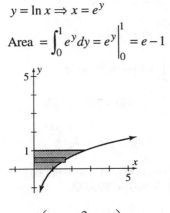

57. $y = \ln x$, $x = 0$, $y = 0$, $y = 1$. Region appears below.

$y = \ln x \Rightarrow x = e^y$

Area $= \int_{0}^{1}e^y dy = e^y\Big|_{0}^{1} = e - 1$

59. $r = \int\left(100 - \dfrac{3}{2}\sqrt{2q}\right)dq$

$= \int 100\, dq - \dfrac{3}{2}\sqrt{2}\int q^{\frac{1}{2}}dq$

$= 100q - \dfrac{3}{2}\sqrt{2}\cdot\dfrac{q^{\frac{3}{2}}}{\frac{3}{2}} + C = 100q - \sqrt{2}q^{\frac{3}{2}} + C$

When $q = 0$, then $r = 0$. Thus $0 = 0 - 0 + C$,

so $C = 0$. Hence $r = 100q - \sqrt{2}q^{\frac{3}{2}}$. Since $r = pq$, then

$p = \dfrac{r}{q} = 100 - \sqrt{2}q^{\frac{1}{2}} = 100 - \sqrt{2q}$. Thus

$p = 100 - \sqrt{2q}$.

61. $\int_{10}^{20}\left(275 - q - 0.3q^2\right)dq$

$= \left(275q - \dfrac{q^2}{2} - \dfrac{0.3q^3}{3}\right)\Bigg|_{10}^{20}$

$= (5500 - 200 - 800) - (2750 - 50 - 100)$

$= \$1900$

63. $\int_{0}^{100}0.008e^{-0.008t}dt$

$= -\int_{0}^{100}e^{0.008t}[-0.008\, dt]$

$= -e^{-0.008t}\Big|_{0}^{100} = -e^{-0.8} + 1 \approx 0.5507$

65. $y = 9 - 2x$, $y = x$; from $x = 0$ to $x = 4$. Region appears below. Intersection: $x = 9 - 2x$, $3x = 9$, so $x = 3$.

Area
$= \int_{0}^{3}[(9 - 2x) - x]dx + \int_{3}^{4}[x - (9 - 2x)]dx$

$= \int_{0}^{3}(9 - 3x)dx + \int_{3}^{4}(3x - 9)dx$

$= \left(9x - \dfrac{3x^2}{2}\right)\Bigg|_{0}^{3} + \left(\dfrac{3x^2}{2} - 9x\right)\Bigg|_{3}^{4}$

$= \left[\left(27 - \dfrac{27}{2}\right) - 0\right] + \left[(24 - 36) - \left(\dfrac{27}{2} - 27\right)\right]$

$= 15$ square units

67. D: $p = 0.01q^2 - 1.1q + 30$
S: $p = 0.01q^2 + 8$

Equil. pt. $= (q_0, p_0) = (20, 12)$

$$CS = \int_0^{q_0} [f(q) - p_0]dq$$

$$= \int_0^{20} \left[(0.01q^2 - 1.1q + 30) - 12\right]dq$$

$$= \int_0^{20} (0.01q^2 - 1.1q + 18)dq$$

$$= \left(\frac{0.01q^3}{3} - \frac{1.1q^2}{2} + 18q\right)\Bigg|_0^{20}$$

$$= \left(\frac{80}{3} - 220 + 360\right) - 0 = 166\frac{2}{3}$$

$$PS = \int_0^{q_0} [p_0 - g(q)]dq$$

$$= \int_0^{20} \left[12 - (0.01q^2 + 8)\right]dq$$

$$= \int_0^{20} (4 - 0.01q^2)dq = \left(4q - \frac{0.01q^3}{3}\right)\Bigg|_0^{20}$$

$$= \left(80 - \frac{80}{3}\right) - 0 = 53\frac{1}{3}$$

69. $$\int_{q_0}^{q_n} \frac{dq}{q - \hat{q}} = -(u+v)\int_0^n dt$$

$$\ln|q - \hat{q}|\Big\|_{q_0}^{q_n} = -(u+v)t\Big|_0^n$$

$$\ln|q_n - \hat{q}| - \ln|q_0 - \hat{q}| = -(u+v)n$$

$$\ln|q_0 - \hat{q}| - \ln|q_n - \hat{q}| = (u+v)n$$

$$\ln\left|\frac{q_0 - \hat{q}}{q_n - \hat{q}}\right| = (u+v)n$$

$$n = \frac{1}{u+v}\ln\left|\frac{q_0 - \hat{q}}{q_n - \hat{q}}\right|$$

as was to be shown.

71. Case 1. $r \neq -1$

$$g(x) = \frac{1}{k}\int_1^{1/x} ku^r du = \int_1^{1/x} u^r du = \frac{u^{r+1}}{r+1}\Bigg|_1^{1/x}$$

$$= \frac{1}{r+1}\left(x^{-r-1} - 1\right)$$

$$g'(x) = \frac{1}{r+1}\left[-(r+1)x^{-r-2}\right] = -\frac{1}{x^{r+2}}$$

Case 2. $r = -1$

$$g(x) = \frac{1}{k}\int_1^{1/x} ku^{-1} du = \int_1^{1/x} \frac{1}{u} du$$

$$= \ln|u|\Big\|_1^{1/x} = \ln\left(\frac{1}{x}\right) - 0 = -\ln x$$

$$g'(x) = -\frac{1}{x} = -\frac{1}{x^{r+2}}$$

73. With vertical elements, two integrals are involved.
Answer: 24.71 sq units

75. $CS \approx 1148$; $PS \approx 251$

Mathematical Snapshot Chapter 16

1. $$\int_0^5 f(t)dt = \int_0^5 (50 - 2t)dt = \left(50t - t^2\right)\Big|_0^5$$

$$= (250 - 25) - 0 = 225$$

$$\int_{10}^{15} f(t)dt = \int_{10}^{15} (50 - 2t)dt = \left(50t - t^2\right)\Big|_{10}^{15}$$

$$= (750 - 225) - (500 - 100) = 125$$

3. a. Total revenue

$$= \int_0^R (m + st)f(t)dt$$

$$= \int_0^{30} (100 + t)(60 - 2t)dt$$

$$= 2\int_0^{30} (100 + t)(30 - t)dt$$

$$= 2\int_0^{30} \left(3000 - 70t - t^2\right)dt$$

$$= 2\left(3000t - 35t^2 - \frac{t^3}{3}\right)\Bigg|_0^{30}$$

$$= 2[(90,000 - 31,500 - 9000) - 0]$$

$$= 2[49,500] = \$99,000$$

b. Total number of units sold

$$= \int_0^R f(t)dt = \int_0^{30} (60 - 2t)dt = 2\int_0^{30} (30 - t)dt$$

$$= 2\left(30t - \frac{t^2}{2}\right)\Bigg|_0^{30}$$

$$= 2[(900 - 450) - 0] = 900$$

  c.   Average delivered price

$$= \frac{\text{total revenue}}{\text{total number of units sold}}$$

$$= \frac{99,000}{900} = \$110$$

Chapter 17

Principles in Practice 17.1

1. $S(t) = \int -4te^{0.1t}\,dt$

Let $u = -4t$ and $dv = e^{0.1t}\,dt$, so $du = -4\,dt$,

and $v = \int e^{0.1t}\,dt = \frac{1}{0.1}e^{0.1t} = 10e^{0.1t}$.

$\int -4te^{0.1t}\,dt$

$= (-4t)\left(10e^{0.1t}\right) - \int \left(10e^{0.1t}\right)(-4)\,dt$

$= -40te^{0.1t} + \int 40e^{0.1t}\,dt$

$= -40te^{0.1t} + 40\dfrac{e^{0.1t}}{0.1} + C$

$= -40te^{0.1t} + 400e^{0.1t} + C$

$S(t) = -40te^{0.1t} + 400e^{0.1t} + C$ and

$S(0) = 5000$

$5000 = 0 + 400e^0 + C$

$C = 4600$

$S(t) = -40te^{0.1t} + 400e^{0.1t} + 4600$

2. $P(t) = \int 0.1t(\ln t)^2\,dt$

Let $u = (\ln t)^2$ and $dv = 0.1t\,dt$, so

$du = 2(\ln t)\left(\frac{1}{t}\right)dt = \dfrac{2\ln t}{t}\,dt$ and

$v = \int 0.1t\,dt = 0.1\dfrac{t^2}{2} = 0.05t^2$

$\int 0.1t(\ln t)^2\,dt$

$= 0.05t^2(\ln t)^2 - \int \left(0.05t^2\right)\left(\dfrac{2\ln t}{t}\right)dt$

$= 0.05(t\ln t)^2 - \int 0.1t\ln t\,dt$

For $\int 0.1t\ln t\,dt$, let $u = \ln t$ and $dv = 0.1t$

dt, so $du = \dfrac{1}{t}\,dt$ and $v = 0.05t^2$.

$\int 0.1t\ln t\,dt = 0.05t^2\ln t - \int \left(0.05t^2\right)\left(\frac{1}{t}\right)dt$

$= 0.05t^2\ln t - \int 0.05t\,dt$

$= 0.05t^2\ln t - 0.05\dfrac{t^2}{2} + C$

$= 0.05t^2\ln t - 0.025t^2 + C$

Thus,

$P(t)$

$= 0.05(t\ln t)^2 - \left(0.05t^2\ln t - 0.025t^2\right) + C$

$= 0.05(t\ln t)^2 - 0.05t^2\ln t + 0.025t^2 + C$

Exercise 17.1

1. $\int f(x)\,dx = uv - \int v\,du$

$= x\cdot\dfrac{2}{3}(x+5)^{\frac{3}{2}} - \int \dfrac{2}{3}(x+5)^{\frac{3}{2}}\,dx$

$= \dfrac{2}{3}x(x+5)^{\frac{3}{2}} - \dfrac{2}{3}\cdot\dfrac{2}{5}(x+5)^{\frac{5}{2}} + C$

$= \dfrac{2}{3}x(x+5)^{\frac{3}{2}} - \dfrac{4}{15}(x+5)^{\frac{5}{2}} + C$

3. $\int xe^{-x}\,dx$

Letting $u = x$, $dv = e^{-x}\,dx$, then $du = dx$,

$v = -e^{-x}$.

$\int xe^{-x}\,dx = -xe^{-x} - \int -e^{-x}\,dx$

$= -xe^{-x} - \int e^{-x}[-dx] = -xe^{-x} - e^{-x} + C$

$= -e^{-x}(x+1) + C$

5. $\int y^3\ln y\,dy$

Letting $u = \ln y$, $dv = y^3\,dy$, then

$du = \left(\dfrac{1}{y}\right)dy$, $v = \dfrac{y^4}{4}$

$$\int y^3 \ln y \, dy = \frac{y^4 \ln y}{4} - \int \frac{y^4}{4}\left(\frac{1}{y}dy\right)$$

$$= \frac{y^4 \ln y}{4} - \int \frac{y^3}{4}dy = \frac{y^4 \ln y}{4} - \frac{y^4}{16} + C$$

$$= \frac{y^4}{4}\left[\ln(y) - \frac{1}{4}\right] + C$$

7. $\int \ln(4x)\, dx$

Letting $u = \ln(4x), dv = dx$, then

$$du = \left(\frac{1}{x}\right)dx,$$

$$v = x.$$

$$\int \ln(4x)dx = x \ln(4x) - \int x\left(\frac{1}{x}dx\right)$$

$$= x \ln(4x) - \int dx = x \ln(4x) - x + C$$

$$= x[\ln(4x) - 1] + C$$

9. $\int x\sqrt{x+1}\, dx$

Let $u = x,\ dv = \sqrt{x+1}\, dx$, then $du = dx$,

$$v = \left(\frac{2}{3}\right)(x+1)^{\frac{3}{2}}$$

$$\int x\sqrt{x+1}\, dx = \frac{2x(x+1)^{\frac{3}{2}}}{3} - \int \frac{2(x+1)^{\frac{3}{2}}}{3}dx$$

$$= \frac{2x(x+1)^{\frac{3}{2}}}{3} - \frac{4}{15}(x+1)^{\frac{5}{2}} + C$$

$$= \frac{2}{15}(x+1)^{\frac{3}{2}}[5x - 2(x+1)] + C$$

$$= \frac{2}{15}(x+1)^{\frac{3}{2}}(3x - 2) + C$$

11. $\int \frac{x}{(2x+1)^2}dx$

Letting $u = x,\ dv = (2x+1)^{-2}dx$, then

$$du = dx,\ v = \frac{(2x+1)^{-1}}{-2} = -\frac{1}{2(2x+1)}$$

$$\int \frac{x}{(2x+1)^2}dx$$

$$= -\frac{x}{2(2x+1)} - \int -\frac{1}{2(2x+1)}dx$$

$$= -\frac{x}{2(2x+1)} + \frac{1}{2}\cdot\frac{1}{2}\int \frac{1}{2x+1}[2\, dx]$$

$$= -\frac{x}{2(2x+1)} + \frac{1}{4}\ln|2x+1| + C$$

13. $\int \frac{\ln x}{x^2}dx$

Letting $u = \ln x,\ dv = x^{-2}dx$, then

$$du = \frac{1}{x}dx,\ v = -x^{-1}.$$

$$\int \frac{\ln x}{x^2}dx = -\frac{\ln x}{x} - \int -x^{-1}\left(\frac{1}{x}dx\right)$$

$$= -\frac{\ln x}{x} + \int x^{-2}dx = -\frac{\ln x}{x} - \frac{1}{x} + C$$

$$= -\frac{1}{x}(1 + \ln x) + C$$

15. $\int_1^2 xe^{2x}dx$

Letting $u = x,\ dv = e^{2x}dx$, then $du = dx$,

$$v = \frac{1}{2}e^{2x}$$

$$\int_1^2 xe^{2x}dx = \left[\frac{xe^{2x}}{2} - \int \frac{1}{2}e^{2x}dx\right]\Bigg|_1^2$$

$$= \left[\frac{xe^{2x}}{2} - \frac{e^{2x}}{4}\right]\Bigg|_1^2 = \frac{e^{2x}}{4}(2x-1)\Bigg|_1^2$$

$$= \frac{e^4}{4}(3) - \frac{e^2}{4}(1) = \frac{e^2}{4}\left(3e^2 - 1\right)$$

17. $\int_0^1 xe^{-x^2}dx = -\frac{1}{2}\int_0^1 e^{-x^2}(-2x\, dx)$

(Form: $\int e^u du$)

$$= -\frac{1}{2}e^{-x^2}\Bigg|_0^1 = -\frac{1}{2}\left(e^{-1} - 1\right) = \frac{1}{2}\left(1 - e^{-1}\right)$$

19. $\int_1^2 \frac{x}{\sqrt{4-x}}dx$

Letting $u = x,\ dv = (4-x)^{-\frac{1}{2}}dx$, then

$$du = dx,\ v = -2(4-x)^{\frac{1}{2}}.$$

$$\int_1^2 \frac{x}{\sqrt{4-x}}dx$$

$$= \left[-2x(4-x)^{\frac{1}{2}} - \int -2(4-x)^{\frac{1}{2}}dx\right]\Bigg|_1^2$$

$$= \left[-2x(4-x)^{\frac{1}{2}} - \frac{4(4-x)^{\frac{3}{2}}}{3}\right]\Bigg|_1^2$$

$$= \left\{ -\frac{2\sqrt{4-x}}{3}[3x + 2(4-x)] \right\}\Big|_1^2$$

$$= \left\{ -\frac{2\sqrt{4-x}}{3}(x+8) \right\}\Big|_1^2$$

$$= -\frac{2}{3}\left(10\sqrt{2} - 9\sqrt{3}\right)$$

$$= \frac{2}{3}\left(9\sqrt{3} - 10\sqrt{2}\right)$$

21. $\int (2x-1)\ln(x-1)dx$

Letting $u = \ln(x-1)$, $dv = (2x-1)dx$, then

$du = \frac{1}{x-1}dx$, $v = x^2 - x = x(x-1)$.

$\int (2x-1)\ln(x-1)dx$

$= x(x-1)\ln(x-1) - \int x(x-1)\frac{1}{x-1}dx$

$= x(x-1)\ln(x-1) - \int x\ dx$

$= x(x-1)\ln(x-1) - \frac{x^2}{2} + C$

23. $\int x^2 e^x dx$

Letting $u = x^2$, $dv = e^x dx$, then $du = 2x\ dx$
and $v = e^x$.

$\int x^2 e^x dx = x^2 e^x - \int e^x (2x\ dx)$

$= x^2 e^x - 2\int xe^x dx$

For $\int xe^x dx$, let $u = x$, $dv = e^x dx$. Then

$du = dx$, $v = e^x$ and

$\int xe^x dx = xe^x - \int e^x dx$

$= xe^x - e^x + C_1$

$= e^x(x-1) + C_1$.

Thus

$\int x^2 e^x dx = x^2 e^x - 2\left[e^x(x-1)\right] + C$

$= e^x\left(x^2 - 2x + 2\right) + C$.

25. $\int \left(x - e^{-x}\right)^2 dx = \int \left(x^2 - 2xe^{-x} + e^{-2x}\right)dx$

$= \frac{x^3}{3} - \frac{e^{-2x}}{2} - 2\int xe^{-x}dx$

Using Problem 3 for $\int xe^{-x}dx$,

$\int \left(x - e^{-x}\right)^2 dx$

$= \frac{x^3}{3} - \frac{e^{-2x}}{2} + 2e^{-x}(x+1) + C$

27. $\int x^3 e^{x^2} dx$

Letting $u = x^2$, $dv = xe^{x^2}dx$, then

$du = 2x\ dx$, $v = \left(\frac{1}{2}\right)e^{x^2}$.

$\int x^3 e^{x^2} dx = \frac{x^2 e^{x^2}}{2} - \int \frac{e^{x^2}}{2}(2x\ dx)$

$= \frac{x^2 e^{x^2}}{2} - \frac{e^{x^2}}{2} + C$

$= \frac{e^{x^2}}{2}\left(x^2 - 1\right) + C$

29. $\int \left(2^x + x\right)^2 dx = \int \left(2^{2x} + 2x2^x + x^2\right)dx$

$= \int 2^{2x}dx + \int x2^{x+1}dx + \int x^2 dx$

For $\int x2^{x+1}dx$, let $u = x$, $dv = 2^{x+1}dx$.

Then $du = dx$, $v = \frac{1}{\ln 2} \cdot 2^{x+1}$ and

$\int x2^{x+1}dx = \frac{x}{\ln 2} \cdot 2^{x+1} - \frac{1}{\ln 2}\int 2^{x+1}dx$

$= \frac{x}{\ln 2} \cdot 2^{x+1} - \frac{1}{\ln^2 2} \cdot 2^{x+1} + C_1$. Thus

$$\int \left(2^x + x\right)^2 dx = \int 2^{2x} dx + \int x 2^{x+1} dx + \int x^2 dx$$

$$= \frac{1}{2} \int 2^{2x} [2 \, dx] + \int x 2^{x+1} dx + \int x^2 dx$$

$$= \frac{1}{2 \ln 2} \cdot 2^{2x} + \frac{x}{\ln 2} \cdot 2^{x+1} - \frac{1}{\ln^2 2} \cdot 2^{x+1} + \frac{x^3}{3} + C$$

$$= \frac{1}{\ln 2} \cdot 2^{2x-1} + \frac{x}{\ln 2} \cdot 2^{x+1} - \frac{1}{\ln^2 2} \cdot 2^{x+1} + \frac{x^3}{3} + C$$

31. area $= \int_1^{e^3} (\ln x) dx$. Letting $u = \ln x$, $dv = dx$,

then $du = \left(\frac{1}{x}\right) dx$, $v = x$.

$$\text{area} = \int_1^{e^3} (\ln x) dx = \left[(x \ln x) - \int x \cdot \frac{1}{x} dx \right]_1^{e^3}$$

$$= \left[(x \ln x) - \int dx \right]_1^{e^3} = [x \ln(x) - x]_1^{e^3}$$

$$= \left[e^3 \cdot 3 - e^3 \right] - [1 \cdot 0 - 1] = 2e^3 + 1$$

Answer: $2e^3 + 1$ sq units

33. area $= \int_0^4 x\sqrt{2x+1} \, dx$. Letting $u = x$,

$dv = (2x+1)^{\frac{1}{2}} dx$, then $du = dx$,

$v = \frac{1}{3}(2x+1)^{\frac{3}{2}}$.

$$\text{area} = \int_0^4 x\sqrt{2x+1} dx$$

$$= \left[\frac{x}{3}(2x+1)^{\frac{3}{2}} - \frac{1}{3}\int (2x+1)^{\frac{3}{2}} dx \right]_0^4$$

$$= \left[\frac{x}{3}(2x+1)^{\frac{3}{2}} - \frac{1}{3} \cdot \frac{1}{2} \int (2x+1)^{\frac{3}{2}}(2 \, dx) \right]_0^4$$

$$= \left[\frac{x}{3}(2x+1)^{\frac{3}{2}} - \frac{1}{15}(2x+1)^{\frac{5}{2}} \right]_0^4$$

$$= \left[\frac{4}{3}(27) - \frac{1}{15}(243) \right] - \left[0 - \frac{1}{15} \right] = \frac{298}{15}$$

Answer: $\frac{298}{15}$ sq units

35. a. Consider $\int p \, dq$. Letting $u = p$,

$dv = dq$, then $du = \frac{dp}{dq} dq$, $v = q$. Thus

$$\int p \, dq = pq - \int q \frac{dp}{dq} dq = r - \int q \frac{dp}{dq} dq$$

(since $r = pq$).

b. From (a), $r = \int p \, dq + \int q \frac{dp}{dq} dq$.

Combining the integrals gives

$$r = \int \left(p + q \frac{dp}{dq} \right) dq.$$

c. From (b), $\frac{dr}{dq} = p + q \frac{dp}{dq}$. Thus

$$\int_0^{q_0} \left(p + q \frac{dp}{dq} \right) dq$$

$$= \int_0^{q_0} \frac{dr}{dq} dq = r(q_0) - r(0) = r(q_0)$$

[since $r(0) = 0$].

Principles in Practice 17.2

1. $r(q) = \int r'(q) dq = \int \frac{5(q+4)}{q^2 + 4q + 3} dq$

Express $\frac{5(q+4)}{q^2 + 4q + 3}$ as a sum of partial

fractions.

$$\frac{5(q+4)}{q^2 + 4q + 3} = \frac{5(q+4)}{(q+1)(q+3)} = \frac{A}{q+1} + \frac{B}{q+3}$$

$5(q+4) = A(q+3) + B(q+1)$

When $q = -3$, we get $5(1) = -2B$, so

$B = -\dfrac{5}{2}$. When $q = -1$, we get $5(3) = A(2)$,

so $A = \dfrac{15}{2}$.

$r(q) = \displaystyle\int \dfrac{5(q+4)}{q^2 + 4q + 3} dx$

$= \displaystyle\int \dfrac{\frac{15}{2}}{q+1} dq - \int \dfrac{\frac{5}{2}}{q+3} dq$

$= \dfrac{15}{2}\ln|q+1| - \dfrac{5}{2}\ln|q+3| + C$

$= \dfrac{5}{2}\ln\left|\dfrac{(q+1)^3}{q+3}\right| + C$

Since $r(0) = 0$, $0 = \dfrac{5}{2}\ln\left|\dfrac{1}{3}\right| + C$ so $C = \dfrac{5}{2}\ln 3$

and $r(q) = \dfrac{5}{2}\ln\left|\dfrac{3(q+1)^3}{q+3}\right|$.

2. $V(t) = \displaystyle\int V'(t)dt = \int \dfrac{300t^3}{t^2 + 6} dt$

Since the degree of the numerator is greater than the degree of the denominator, we first divide $300t^3$ by $t^2 + 6$ to reduce the fraction.

$\dfrac{300t^3}{t^2 + 6} = \dfrac{300t^3 + 1800t - 1800t}{t^2 + 6}$

$= \dfrac{300t\left(t^2 + 6\right) - 1800t}{t^2 + 6} = 300t - \dfrac{1800t}{t^2 + 6}$

$t^2 + 6$ is irreducible. To integrate $\dfrac{1800t}{t^2 + 6}$, let

$u = t^2 + 6$, so $du = 2t\,dt$

$\displaystyle\int \dfrac{300t^3}{t^2 + 6} dt = \int 300t\ dt - \int \dfrac{1800t}{t^2 + 6} dt$

$= 150t^2 - 900\ln\left|t^2 + 6\right| + C$

$V(t) = 150t^2 - 900\ln\left(t^2 + 6\right) + C$

Exercise 17.2

1. $\dfrac{10x}{x^2 + 7x + 6} = \dfrac{10x}{(x+6)(x+1)} = \dfrac{A}{x+6} + \dfrac{B}{x+1}$

$10x = A(x+1) + B(x+6)$

If $x = -1$, then $-10 = 5B$, or $B = -2$. If $x = -6$, then $-60 = -5A$, or $A = 12$.

Answer $\dfrac{12}{x+6} - \dfrac{2}{x+1}$

3. $\dfrac{x^2}{x^2 + 6x + 8} = 1 + \dfrac{-6x - 8}{x^2 + 6x + 8}$

(by long division).

$\dfrac{-6x - 8}{x^2 + 6x + 8} = \dfrac{-6x - 8}{(x+2)(x+4)} = \dfrac{A}{x+2} + \dfrac{B}{x+4}$

$-6x - 8 = A(x+4) + B(x+2)$

If $x = -4$, then $16 = -2B$, or $B = -8$. If $x = -2$, then $4 = 2A$, or $A = 2$.

Answer: $1 + \dfrac{2}{x+2} - \dfrac{8}{x+4}$

5. $\dfrac{4x - 5}{x^2 + 2x + 1} = \dfrac{4x - 5}{(x+1)^2} = \dfrac{A}{x+1} + \dfrac{B}{(x+1)^2}$

$4x - 5 = A(x+1) + B$

If $x = -1$, then $-9 = B$. If $x = 0$, then $-5 = A + B$, $-5 = A - 9$, or $A = 4$.

Answer: $\dfrac{4}{x+1} - \dfrac{9}{(x+1)^2}$

7. $\dfrac{x^2 + 3}{x^3 + x} = \dfrac{x^2 + 3}{x\left(x^2 + 1\right)} = \dfrac{A}{x} + \dfrac{Bx + C}{x^2 + 1}$

$x^2 + 3 = A\left(x^2 + 1\right) + (Bx + C)x$

$x^2 + 3 = (A + B)x^2 + Cx + A$

Thus $A + B = 1$, $C = 0$, $A = 3$. This gives $A = 3$, $B = -2$, $C = 0$.

Answer: $\dfrac{3}{x} - \dfrac{2x}{x^2 + 1}$

9. $\dfrac{5x - 2}{x^2 - x} = \dfrac{5x - 2}{x(x-1)} = \dfrac{A}{x} + \dfrac{B}{x-1}$

$5x - 2 = A(x-1) + Bx$

If $x = 1$, then $3 = B$. If $x = 0$, then $-2 = -A$, or $A = 2$.

$\displaystyle\int \dfrac{5x - 2}{x^2 - x} dx = \int \left(\dfrac{2}{x} + \dfrac{3}{x-1}\right) dx$

Answer:

$2\ln|x| + 3\ln|x - 1| + C = \ln\left|x^2(x-1)^3\right| + C$

11. $\dfrac{x+10}{x^2-x-2}=\dfrac{x+10}{(x+1)(x-2)}=\dfrac{A}{x+1}+\dfrac{B}{x-2}$

$x+10=A(x-2)+B(x+1)$

If $x=2$, then $12=3B$, or $B=4$. If $x=-1$,

then $9=-3A$, or $A=-3$.

$\displaystyle\int\dfrac{x+10}{x^2-x-2}\,dx=\int\left(\dfrac{-3}{x+1}+\dfrac{4}{x-2}\right)dx$

Answer:

$-3\ln|x+1|+4\ln|x-2|+C$

$=\ln\left|\dfrac{(x-2)^4}{(x+1)^3}\right|+C$

13. $\dfrac{3x^3-3x+4}{4x^2-4}=\dfrac{1}{4}\cdot\dfrac{3x^3-3x+4}{x^2-1}$

$=\dfrac{1}{4}\left(3x+\dfrac{4}{x^2-1}\right)$

$\dfrac{4}{x^2-1}=\dfrac{4}{(x-1)(x+1)}=\dfrac{A}{x-1}+\dfrac{B}{x+1}$

$4=A(x+1)+B(x-1)$

If $x=-1$, then $4=-2B$, or $B=-2$. If $x=1$,

then $4=2A$, or $A=2$.

$\displaystyle\int\dfrac{3x^3-3x+4}{4x^2-4}\,dx=\dfrac{1}{4}\int\left(3x+\dfrac{2}{x-1}+\dfrac{-2}{x+1}\right)dx$

Answer:

$\left(\dfrac{1}{4}\right)\left[\left(\dfrac{3x^2}{2}\right)+2\ln|x-1|-2\ln|x+1|\right]+C$

$\left(\dfrac{1}{4}\right)\left[\left(\dfrac{3x^2}{2}\right)+\ln\left|\dfrac{x-1}{x+1}\right|^2\right]+C$

15. $\dfrac{17x-12}{x^3-x^2-12x}=\dfrac{17x-12}{x(x-4)(x+3)}$

$=\dfrac{A}{x}+\dfrac{B}{x-4}+\dfrac{C}{x+3}$

$17x-12$

$=A(x-4)(x+3)+Bx(x+3)+Cx(x-4)$

If $x=0$, then $-12=-12A$, or $A=1$. If $x=4$,

then $56=28B$, or $B=2$. If $x=-3$, then

$-63=21C$, or $C=-3$.

$\displaystyle\int\dfrac{17x-12}{x^3-x^2-12x}\,dx$

$=\displaystyle\int\left(\dfrac{1}{x}+\dfrac{2}{x-4}+\dfrac{-3}{x+3}\right)dx$

Answer:

$\ln|x|+2\ln|x-4|-3\ln|x+3|+C$

$=\ln\left|\dfrac{x(x-4)^2}{(x+3)^3}\right|+C$

17. $\displaystyle\int\dfrac{3x^5+4x^3-x}{x^6+2x^4-x^2-2}\,dx$

$=\dfrac{1}{2}\displaystyle\int\dfrac{1}{x^6+2x^4-x^2-2}\left[2\left(3x^5+4x^3-x\right)dx\right]\left(\text{Form: }\int\left(\dfrac{1}{u}\right)du\right)$ (Partial fractions not required.)

Answer: $\left(\dfrac{1}{2}\right)\ln\left|x^6+2x^4-x^2-2\right|+C$

19. $\dfrac{2x^2-5x-2}{(x-2)^2(x-1)}=\dfrac{A}{x-1}+\dfrac{B}{x-2}+\dfrac{C}{(x-2)^2}$

$2x^2-5x-2$

$=A(x-2)^2+B(x-1)(x-2)+C(x-1)$

If $x = 1$, then $-5 = A$. If $x = 2$, then $-4 = C$.
If $x = 0$, then $-2 = 4A + 2B - C$,
$-2 = -20 + 2B + 4$, or $B = 7$.

$$\int \frac{2x^2 - 5x - 2}{(x-2)^2(x-1)} dx$$

$$= \int \left[\frac{-5}{x-1} + \frac{7}{x-2} + \frac{-4}{(x-2)^2} \right] dx$$

Answer:

$$\left[\frac{4}{(x-2)} \right] - 5\ln|x-1| + 7\ln|x-2| + C$$

$$= \left[\frac{4}{(x-2)} \right] + \ln \left| \frac{(x-2)^7}{(x-1)^5} \right| + C$$

21. $\dfrac{x^2 + 8}{x^3 + 4x} = \dfrac{x^2 + 8}{x(x^2 + 4)} = \dfrac{A}{x} + \dfrac{Bx + C}{x^2 + 4}$

$x^2 + 8 = A(x^2 + 4) + (Bx + C)x$

$x^2 + 8 = (A + B)x^2 + Cx + 4A$

Thus $A + B = 1$, $C = 0$, $4A = 8$. This gives $A = 2$, $B = -1$, $C = 0$.

$$\int \frac{x^2 + 8}{x^3 + 4x} dx = \int \left(\frac{2}{x} + \frac{-x}{x^2 + 4} \right) dx$$

$$= 2\int \frac{1}{x} dx - \frac{1}{2} \int \frac{1}{x^2 + 4} [2\ dx]$$

Answer: $2\ln|x| - \dfrac{1}{2}\ln(x^2 + 4) + C = \dfrac{1}{2}\ln\left[\dfrac{x^4}{(x^2 + 4)} \right] + C$

23. $\dfrac{-x^3 + 8x^2 - 9x + 2}{(x^2 + 1)(x-3)^2} = \dfrac{Ax + B}{x^2 + 1} + \dfrac{C}{x-3} + \dfrac{D}{(x-3)^2} - x^3 + 8x^2 - 9x + 2$

$= (Ax + B)(x-3)^2 + C(x-3)(x^2 + 1) + D(x^2 + 1)$

$= (Ax + B)(x^2 - 6x + 9) + C(x^3 - 3x^2 + x - 3) + D(x^2 + 1)$

$= (A + C)x^3 + (B - 6A - 3C + D)x^2 + (9A - 6B + C)x + (9B - 3C + D)$

Thus $A + C = -1$, $B - 6A - 3C + D = 8$, $9A - 6B + C = -9$, $9B - 3C + D = 2$. This gives $A = -1$, $B = 0$, $C = 0$, $D = 2$.

$$\int \frac{-x^3 + 8x^2 - 9x + 2}{(x^2 + 1)(x-3)^2} dx = \int \left(\frac{-x}{x^2 + 1} + \frac{0}{x-3} + \frac{2}{(x-3)^2} \right) dx$$

Answer: $\left(-\dfrac{1}{2} \right)\ln(x^2 + 1) - \left[\dfrac{2}{(x-3)} \right] + C$

25. $\dfrac{14x^3 + 24x}{\left(x^2 + 1\right)\left(x^2 + 2\right)} = \dfrac{Ax + B}{x^2 + 1} + \dfrac{Cx + D}{x^2 + 2}$

$14x^3 + 24x = \left(x^2 + 2\right)(Ax + B) + \left(x^2 + 1\right)(Cx + D)$

$= (A + C)x^3 + (B + D)x^2 + (2A + C)x + (2B + D)$

Thus $A + C = 14$, $B + D = 0$, $2A + C = 24$,

$2B + D = 0$.

This gives $A = 10$, $B = 0$, $C = 4$, $D = 0$.

$\displaystyle\int \dfrac{14x^3 + 24x}{\left(x^2 + 1\right)\left(x^2 + 2\right)}\,dx = \int\left(\dfrac{10x}{x^2 + 1} + \dfrac{4x}{x^2 + 2}\right)dx$

$= 5\displaystyle\int \dfrac{1}{x^2 + 1}[2\ dx] + 2\int \dfrac{1}{x^2 + 2}[2\ dx]$

Answer:

$5\ln\left(x^2 + 1\right) + 2\ln\left(x^2 + 2\right) + C$

$= \ln\left[\left(x^2 + 1\right)^5\left(x^2 + 2\right)^2\right] + C$

27. $\dfrac{3x^3 + x}{\left(x^2 + 1\right)^2} = \dfrac{Ax + B}{x^2 + 1} + \dfrac{Cx + D}{\left(x^2 + 1\right)^2}$

$3x^3 + x = (Ax + B)\left(x^2 + 1\right) + (Cx + D)$

$= Ax^3 + Bx^2 + (A + C)x + (B + D)$

Thus $A = 3$, $B = 0$, $A + C = 1$, $B + D = 0$.

This gives $A = 3$, $B = 0$, $C = -2$, $D = 0$.

$\displaystyle\int \dfrac{3x^3 + x}{\left(x^2 + 1\right)^2}\,dx = \int\left[\dfrac{3x}{x^2 + 1} + \dfrac{-2x}{\left(x^2 + 1\right)^2}\right]dx$

Answer: $\dfrac{3}{2}\ln\left(x^2 + 1\right) + \dfrac{1}{x^2 + 1} + C$

29. $\dfrac{2 - 2x}{x^2 + 7x + 12} = \dfrac{2 - 2x}{(x + 3)(x + 4)}$

$= \dfrac{A}{x + 3} + \dfrac{B}{x + 4}$

$2 - 2x = A(x + 4) + B(x + 3)$

If $x = -4$, then $10 = -B$, or $B = -10$. If $x = -3$,

then $8 = A$.

$\displaystyle\int_0^1 \dfrac{2 - 2x}{x^2 + 7x + 12}\,dx = \int_0^1\left(\dfrac{8}{x + 3} + \dfrac{-10}{x + 4}\right)dx$

$= \left[8\ln|x + 3| - 10\ln|x + 4|\right]\Big|_0^1$

Answer: $18\ln(4) - 10\ln(5) - 8\ln(3)$

31. Note that $\dfrac{\left(x^2 + 1\right)}{(x + 2)^2} \geq 0$ on $[0, 1]$.

Area $= \displaystyle\int_0^1 \dfrac{x^2 + 1}{(x + 2)^2}\,dx$

$\dfrac{x^2 + 1}{(x + 2)^2} = 1 + \dfrac{-4x - 3}{(x + 2)^2}$ (by long division)

$\dfrac{-4x - 3}{(x + 2)^2} = \dfrac{A}{x + 2} + \dfrac{B}{(x + 2)^2}$

$-4x - 3 = A(x + 2) + B$

If $x = -2$, then $5 = B$. If $x = 0$, then

$-3 = 2A + B$, $-3 = 2A + 5$, or $A = -4$.

Area $= \displaystyle\int_0^1 \dfrac{x^2 + 1}{(x + 2)^2}\,dx$

$= \displaystyle\int_0^1\left[1 + \dfrac{-4}{x + 2} + \dfrac{5}{(x + 2)^2}\right]dx$

$= \left[x - 4\ln|x + 2| - \dfrac{5}{x + 2}\right]\Big|_0^1$

Answer: $\dfrac{11}{6} + 4\ln\dfrac{2}{3}$ sq units

Exercise 17.3

1. Let $u = x$, $a^2 = 9$. Then $du = dx$.
$$\int \frac{dx}{(9-x^2)^{3/2}} = \frac{x}{9\sqrt{9-x^2}} + C$$

3. Let $u = 4x$, $a^2 = 3$. Then $du = 4\,dx$.
$$\int \frac{dx}{x^2\sqrt{16x^2+3}} = 4\int \frac{(4\,dx)}{(4x)^2\sqrt{(4x)^2+3}}$$
$$= 4\left[-\frac{\sqrt{(4x)^2+3}}{3(4x)}\right] + C$$
$$= -\frac{\sqrt{16x^2+3}}{3x} + C$$

5. Formula 5 with $u = x$, $a = 6$, $b = 7$. Then $du = dx$.
$$\int \frac{dx}{x(6+7x)} = \frac{1}{6}\ln\left|\frac{x}{6+7x}\right| + C$$

7. Formula 28 with $u = x$, $a = 3$. Then $du = dx$.
$$\int \frac{dx}{x\sqrt{x^2+9}} = \frac{1}{3}\ln\left|\frac{\sqrt{x^2+9}-3}{x}\right| + C$$

9. Formula 12 with $u = x$, $a = 2$, $b = 3$, $c = 4$, $k = 5$. Then $du = dx$.
$$\int \frac{x\,dx}{(2+3x)(4+5x)}$$
$$= \frac{1}{2}\left[\frac{4}{5}\ln|4+5x| - \frac{2}{3}\ln|2+3x|\right] + C$$

11. Formula 45 with $u = x$, $a = 4$, $b = 3$, $c = 2$. Then $du = dx$.
$$\int \frac{dx}{4+3e^{2x}} = \frac{1}{8}\left(2x - \ln\left[4+3e^{2x}\right]\right) + C$$

13. Formula 9 with $u = x$, $a = 1$, $b = 1$. Then $du = dx$.
$$\int \frac{2\,dx}{x(1+x)^2} = 2\int \frac{dx}{x(1+x)^2}$$
$$= 2\left[\frac{1}{1+x} + \ln\left|\frac{x}{1+x}\right|\right] + C$$

15. Formula 3 with $u = x$, $a = 2$, $b = 1$. Then $du = dx$.
$$\int_0^1 \frac{x\,dx}{2+x} = \left(x - 2\ln|2+x|\right)\Big|_0^1$$
$$= 1 - 2\ln 3 + 2\ln 2$$
$$= 1 - \ln 9 + \ln 4.$$
$$= 1 + \ln\left(\frac{4}{9}\right)$$

17. Formula 23 with $u = x$, $a^2 = 3$. Then $du = dx$.
$$\int \sqrt{x^2-3}\,dx$$
$$= \frac{1}{2}\left(x\sqrt{x^2-3} - 3\ln\left|x+\sqrt{x^2-3}\right|\right) + C$$

19. Formula 38 with $u = x$, $a = 12$. Then $du = dx$.
$$\int_0^{1/12} xe^{12x}\,dx = \frac{e^{12x}}{144}(12x-1)\Big|_0^{1/12}$$
$$= \frac{1}{144}[e(0) - 1(-1)]$$
$$= \frac{1}{144}$$

21. Formula 39 with $u = x$, $n = 2$, $a = 1$. Then $du = dx$.
$$\int x^2 e^x\,dx = x^2 e^x - 2\int xe^x\,dx$$
Applying Formula 38 on $\int xe^x\,dx$ with $u = x$, $a = 1$ (so $du = dx$) gives
$$\int xe^x\,dx = e^x(x-1) + C_1. \text{ Thus}$$
$$\int x^2 e^x\,dx = x^2 e^x - 2\left[e^x(x-1)\right] + C$$
$$= e^x\left[x^2 - 2(x-1)\right] + C$$
$$= e^x\left(x^2 - 2x + 2\right) + C$$

23. Formula 26 with $u = 2x$, $a^2 = 1$. Then $du = 2\,dx$.

$$\int \frac{\sqrt{4x^2+1}}{x^2}\,dx = 2\int \frac{\sqrt{(2x)^2+1}}{(2x)^2}(2\,dx)$$

$$= 2\left(-\frac{\sqrt{4x^2+1}}{2x} + \ln\left|2x + \sqrt{4x^2+1}\right|\right) + C$$

25. Formula 7 with $u = x$, $a = 1$, $b = 3$. Then $du = dx$.

$$\int \frac{x\,dx}{(1+3x)^2} = \frac{1}{9}\left(\ln|1+3x| + \frac{1}{1+3x}\right) + C$$

27. Formula 34 with $u = \sqrt{5}x$, $a = \sqrt{7}$. Then

$$du = \sqrt{5}dx$$

$$\int \frac{dx}{7-5x^2} = \frac{1}{\sqrt{5}}\int \frac{1}{\left(\sqrt{7}\right)^2 - \left(\sqrt{5}x\right)^2}\left(\sqrt{5}dx\right)$$

$$= \frac{1}{\sqrt{5}}\left(\frac{1}{2\sqrt{7}}\ln\left|\frac{\sqrt{7}+\sqrt{5}x}{\sqrt{7}-\sqrt{5}x}\right|\right) + C$$

29. Formula 42 with $u = 3x$, $n = 5$. Then $du = 3\,dx$.

$$\int x^5 \ln(3x)dx = \frac{1}{3^6}\int (3x)^5 \ln(3x)(3\,dx)$$

$$= \frac{1}{3^6}\left[\frac{(3x)^6 \ln(3x)}{6} - \frac{(3x)^6}{36}\right] + C$$

$$= \frac{x^6}{36}[6\ln(3x) - 1] + C$$

31. Formula 13 with $u = x$, $a = 1$, $b = 3$. Then $du = dx$.

$$\int 2x\sqrt{1+3x}dx = 2\int x\sqrt{1+3x}\,dx$$

$$= 2\left[\frac{2(9x-2)(1+3x)^{\frac{3}{2}}}{15\cdot 9}\right] + C$$

$$= \frac{4(9x-2)(1+3x)^{\frac{3}{2}}}{135} + C$$

33. Formula 27 with $u = 2x$, $a^2 = 13$. Then $du = 2\,dx$.

$$\int \frac{dx}{\sqrt{4x^2-13}} = \frac{1}{2}\int \frac{1}{\sqrt{(2x)^2-13}}(2\,dx)$$

$$= \frac{1}{2}\ln\left|2x + \sqrt{4x^2-13}\right| + C$$

35. Formula 21 with $u = 2x$, $a^2 = 9$. Then $du = 2\,dx$.

$$\int \frac{dx}{x^2\sqrt{9-4x^2}} = 2\int \frac{(2\,dx)}{(2x)^2\sqrt{9-(2x)^2}}$$

$$= 2\left[-\frac{\sqrt{9-4x^2}}{9(2x)}\right] + C$$

$$= -\frac{\sqrt{9-4x^2}}{9x} + C$$

37. Formula 45 with
$u = \sqrt{x}$, $a = \pi$, $b = 7$, $c = 4$. Then

$$du = \frac{1}{2\sqrt{x}}\,dx$$

$$\int \frac{dx}{\sqrt{x}\left(\pi + 7e^{4\sqrt{x}}\right)}$$

$$= 2\int \frac{1}{\pi + 7e^{4\sqrt{x}}}\left(\frac{1}{2\sqrt{x}}\,dx\right)$$

$$= 2\left[\frac{1}{4\pi}\left(4\sqrt{x} - \ln\left|\pi + 7e^{4\sqrt{x}}\right|\right)\right] + C$$

$$= \frac{1}{2\pi}\left(4\sqrt{x} - \ln\left|\pi + 7e^{4\sqrt{x}}\right|\right) + C$$

39. Can be put in the form $\int \frac{1}{u} du$.

$$\int \frac{x\,dx}{x^2+1} = \frac{1}{2}\int \frac{1}{x^2+1}(2x\,dx)$$
$$= \frac{1}{2}\ln(x^2+1) + C$$

41. Can be put in the form $\int u^n du$.

$$\int x\sqrt{2x^2+1}\,dx = \frac{1}{4}\int (2x^2+1)^{\frac{1}{2}}(4x\,dx)$$

$$= \frac{1}{4}\cdot\frac{(2x^2+1)^{\frac{3}{2}}}{\frac{3}{2}} + C$$

$$= \frac{1}{6}(2x^2+1)^{\frac{3}{2}} + C$$

43. Formula 11 or partial fractions. For partial fractions,

$$\int \frac{1}{x^2-5x+6}\,dx = \int \left[\frac{1}{x-3} + \frac{-1}{x-2}\right]dx.$$

$$= \ln\left|\frac{x-3}{x-2}\right| + C$$

45. Integration by parts or formula 42. For formula 42, let $u = x$, $n = 3$. Then $du = dx$.

$$\int x^3 \ln x\,dx = \frac{x^4}{4}\left[\ln(x) - \frac{1}{4}\right] + C$$

47. Integration by parts or formula 38. For formula 38, let $u = x$, $a = 2$. Then $du = dx$.

$$\int xe^{2x}\,dx = \frac{e^{2x}}{4}(2x-1) + C$$

49. Integration by parts (applied twice) or formula 43 and then formula 41. For formula 43, let $u = x$, $n = 0$, $m = 2$. Then $du = dx$.

$$\int \ln^2 x\,dx = x\ln^2 x - 2\int \ln x\,dx$$

Now we apply formula 41 to the last integral with $u = x$ (so $du = dx$).

$$\int \ln^2 x\,dx = x(\ln x)^2 - 2x(\ln x) + 2x + C$$

51. Integration by parts or formula 15. For formula 15, let $u = x$, $a = 4$, $b = -1$. Then $du = dx$.

$$\int_1^2 \frac{x\,dx}{\sqrt{4-x}} = \frac{2(-x-8)\sqrt{4-x}}{3}\Bigg|_1^2$$
$$= \frac{2}{3}\left(9\sqrt{3} - 10\sqrt{2}\right)$$

53. Can be put in the form $\int u^n du$.

$$\int_0^1 \frac{2x\,dx}{\sqrt{8-x^2}} = -\int_0^1 (8-x^2)^{-\frac{1}{2}}(-2x\,dx)$$

$$= -\frac{(8-x^2)^{\frac{1}{2}}}{\frac{1}{2}}\Bigg|_0^1$$

$$= -2(8-x^2)^{\frac{1}{2}}\Bigg|_0^1 = -2\left(\sqrt{7}-\sqrt{8}\right)$$

$$= -2\left(\sqrt{7} - 2\sqrt{2}\right)$$

$$= 2\left(2\sqrt{2} - \sqrt{7}\right)$$

55. Integration by parts or formula 42. For formula 42, let $u = 2x$, $n = 1$. Then $du = 2\,dx$.

$$\int_1^2 x\ln(2x)\,dx = \frac{1}{4}\int_1^2 (2x)\ln(2x)[2\,dx]$$

$$= \frac{1}{4}\left[\frac{(2x)^2\ln(2x)}{2} - \frac{(2x)^2}{4}\right]\Bigg|_1^2$$

$$= 2\ln(4) - \frac{1}{2}\ln(2) - \frac{3}{4}$$

$$= 2\ln(2^2) - \frac{1}{2}\ln(2) - \frac{3}{4}$$

$$= 4\ln(2) - \frac{1}{2}\ln(2) - \frac{3}{4}$$

$$= \frac{7}{2}(\ln 2) - \frac{3}{4}$$

57. Partial fractions or formula 5. For formula 5, let $u = q$, $a = 1$, $b = -1$. Then $du = dq$.

$$\int_{q_0}^{q_n} \frac{dq}{q(1-q)} = \ln\left|\frac{q}{1-q}\right|\Bigg|_{q_0}^{q_n}$$

$$= \ln\left|\frac{q_n}{1-q_n}\right| - \ln\left|\frac{q_0}{1-q_0}\right|$$

$$= \ln\left|\frac{q_n(1-q_0)}{q_0(1-q_n)}\right|$$

59. a. For $\int_0^{10} 5000e^{-0.06t}dt$, the form $\int e^u du$ can be applied.

$$\int_0^{10} 5000e^{-0.06t}dt$$

$$= -\frac{5000}{0.06}\int_0^{10} e^{-0.06t}(-0.06\ dt)$$

$$= -\frac{5000}{0.06}e^{-0.06t}\Big|_0^{10} = -\frac{5000}{0.06}\left(e^{-0.6}-1\right)$$

$$\approx \$37,599$$

b. Use formula 38 with $u = t$ and $a = -0.05$, so $du = dt$.

$$\int_0^8 200te^{-0.05t}dt = 200\int_0^8 te^{-0.05t}dt$$

$$= 200\left[\frac{e^{-0.05t}}{0.0025}(-0.05t-1)\right]\Big|_0^8$$

$$= \frac{200}{0.0025}\left[e^{-0.4}(-1.4)+1\right] \approx \$4924$$

61. a. $\int_0^{10} 400e^{0.06(10-t)}dt$

$$= 400\int_0^{10} e^{0.6-0.06t}dt$$

$$= 400\int_0^{10} e^{0.6}e^{-0.06t}dt$$

$$= 400e^{0.6}\int_0^{10} e^{-0.06t}dt$$

$$= 400e^{0.6}\left(\frac{1}{-0.06}\right)\int_0^{10} e^{-0.06t}(-0.06\ dt)$$

$$= \frac{400e^{0.6}}{-0.06}e^{-0.06t}\Big|_0^{10}$$

$$= \frac{400e^{0.6}}{-0.06}\left[e^{-0.6}-1\right]$$

$$\approx \$5481$$

b. Use formula 38 with $u = t$ and $a = -0.04$, so $du = dt$.

$$\int_0^5 40te^{0.04(5-t)}dt = 40\int_0^5 te^{0.2}e^{-0.04t}dt$$

$$= 40e^{0.2}\int_0^5 te^{-0.04t}dt$$

$$= 40e^{0.2}\left[\frac{e^{-0.04t}}{0.0016}(-0.04t-1)\right]\Big|_0^5$$

$$= \frac{40e^{0.2}}{0.0016}\left[e^{-0.2}(-0.2-1)-1(-1)\right] \approx \$535$$

Exercise 17.4

1. $\bar{f} = \frac{1}{4-0}\int_0^4 x^2 dx = \frac{1}{4}\cdot\frac{x^3}{3}\Big|_0^4 = \frac{16}{3}-0 = \frac{16}{3}$

3. $\bar{f} = \frac{1}{2-(-1)}\int_{-1}^2 \left(2-3x^2\right)dx$

$$= \frac{1}{3}\left(2x-x^3\right)\Big|_{-1}^2 = -1$$

5. $\bar{f} = \frac{1}{2-(-2)}\int_{-2}^2 4t^3 dt = \frac{1}{4}t^4\Big|_{-2}^2 = 4-4 = 0$

7. $\bar{f} = \frac{1}{9-1}\int_1^9 \sqrt{x}dx = \frac{1}{8}\left(\frac{2x^{\frac{3}{2}}}{3}\right)\Big|_1^9 = \frac{13}{6}$

9. $\bar{P} = \frac{1}{100-0}\int_0^{100} \left(396q-2.1q^2-400\right)dq$

$$= \frac{1}{100}\left(198q^2-0.7q^3-400q\right)\Big|_0^{100}$$

$$= \frac{1}{100}(1,980,000-700,000-40,000)-0$$

$$= 12,400$$

Answer: $12,400

11. $\dfrac{1}{2-0}\displaystyle\int_0^2 3000e^{0.1t}\,dt$

$=\dfrac{3000}{2}\cdot\dfrac{1}{0.1}\displaystyle\int_0^2 e^{0.1t}[0.1\,dt]$

$=15{,}000e^{0.1t}\Big|_0^2=15{,}000\left(e^{0.2}-1\right)\approx\$3321$

Answer: \$3321

13. Average value $=\dfrac{1}{q_0-0}\displaystyle\int\dfrac{dr}{dq}\,dq$.

$=\dfrac{1}{q_0}\left[r(q_0)-r(0)\right]$

But $r(0)=0$, so avg. value $=\dfrac{r(q_0)}{q_0}$. Since

$r(q_0)$

$=$ [price per unit when q_0 units are sold]$\cdot q_0$,

we have

avg. value $=\dfrac{\begin{bmatrix}\text{price per unit}\\\text{when }q_0\text{ units}\\\text{are sold}\end{bmatrix}\cdot q_0}{q_0}$

$=$ price per unit when $\cdot q_0$ units are sold.

Principles in Practice 17.5

1. In this case, $f(t)=\dfrac{60}{\sqrt{t^2+9}}$, $n=5$, $a=0$,

and $b=5$. Thus $h=\dfrac{b-a}{n}=\dfrac{5-0}{5}=1$. The

terms to be added are

$f(0)=\dfrac{60}{\sqrt{0^2+9}}=\dfrac{60}{3}=20$

$2f(1)=\dfrac{2(60)}{\sqrt{1^2+9}}=\dfrac{120}{\sqrt{10}}\approx37.9473$

$2f(2)=\dfrac{2(60)}{\sqrt{2^2+9}}=\dfrac{120}{\sqrt{13}}\approx33.2820$

$2f(3)=\dfrac{2(60)}{\sqrt{3^2+9}}=\dfrac{120}{\sqrt{18}}\approx28.2843$

$2f(4)=\dfrac{2(60)}{\sqrt{4^2+9}}=\dfrac{120}{5}=24$

$f(5)=\dfrac{60}{\sqrt{5^2+9}}=\dfrac{60}{\sqrt{34}}\approx10.2899$

The sum of the above terms is 153.8035.

The estimate of the radius after 5 seconds is

$\displaystyle\int_0^5\dfrac{60}{\sqrt{t^2+9}}\,dt\approx\dfrac{1}{2}(153.8035)\approx76.90$ feet.

2. In this case, $f(t)=0.3e^{0.2t^2}$, $n=8$, $a=0$,

and $b=4$. Thus, $h=\dfrac{b-a}{n}=\dfrac{4}{8}=0.5$. The

terms to be added are

$f(0)=0.3e^0=0.3$

$4f(0.5)=4(0.3)e^{0.05}\approx1.2615$

$2f(1)=2(0.3)e^{0.2}\approx0.7328$

$4f(1.5)=4(0.3)e^{0.45}\approx1.8820$

$2f(2)=2(0.3)e^{0.8}\approx1.3353$

$4f(2.5)=4(0.3)e^{1.25}\approx4.1884$

$2f(3)=2(0.3)e^{1.8}\approx3.6298$

$4f(3.5)=4(0.3)e^{2.45}\approx13.9060$

$f(4)=0.3e^{3.2}\approx7.3598$

The sum of the above terms is 34.5956. The estimate of the amount the culture grew over the first four hours is

$\displaystyle\int_0^4 0.3e^{0.2t^2}\,dt\approx\dfrac{0.5}{3}(34.5956)\approx5.77$ grams.

Exercise 17.5

1. $f(x)=\dfrac{170}{1+x^2}$, $n=6$, $a=-2$, $b=4$.

Trapezoidal

$h=\dfrac{b-a}{n}=\dfrac{4-(-2)}{6}=\dfrac{6}{6}=1$

$f(-2)=34=34$

$2f(-1)=2(85)=170$

$2f(0)=2(170)=340$

$2f(1)=2(85)=170$

$2f(2)=2(34)=68$

$2f(3)=2(17)=34$

$f(4)=10=\underline{10}$

$\phantom{f(4)=10=}826$

$\displaystyle\int_{-2}^4\dfrac{170}{1+x^2}\,dx\approx\dfrac{1}{2}(826)=413$

3. $f(x) = x^2$, $n = 5$, $a = 0$, $b = 1$
Trapezoidal
$$h = \frac{b-a}{n} = \frac{1-0}{5} = \frac{1}{5} = 0.2$$

$$
\begin{aligned}
f(0) &= \ 0.0000 \\
2f(0.2) &= \ 0.0800 \\
2f(0.4) &= \ 0.3200 \\
2f(0.6) &= \ 0.7200 \\
2f(0.8) &= \ 1.2800 \\
f(1) &= \ \underline{1.0000} \\
&\quad \ 3.4000
\end{aligned}
$$

$$\int_0^1 x^2\,dx \approx \frac{0.2}{2}(3.4000) = 0.340$$

Actual value: $\int_0^1 x^2\,dx = \left.\frac{x^3}{3}\right|_0^1 = \frac{1}{3} \approx 0.333$

5. $f(x) = \frac{1}{x}$, $n = 6$, $a = 1$, $b = 4$
Simpson's
$$h = \frac{b-a}{n} = \frac{4-1}{6} = 0.5$$
Finding the appropriate sum, we have

$$
\begin{aligned}
f(1) &= 1.0000 \\
4f(1.5) &= 2.6667 \\
2f(2) &= 1.0000 \\
4f(2.5) &= 1.6000 \\
2f(3) &= 0.6667 \\
2f(3.5) &= 1.1429 \\
f(4) &= \underline{0.2500} \\
&\quad 8.3263
\end{aligned}
$$

$$\int_1^4 \frac{1}{x}\,dx \approx \frac{0.5}{3}(8.3263) \approx 1.388$$
Actual value:

$$\int_1^4 \frac{1}{x}\,dx = \left.\ln|x|\right|_1^4 = \ln 4 - \ln 1 = \ln 4 - 0$$

$$= \ln 4 \approx 1.386$$

7. $f(x) = \frac{x}{x+1}$, $n = 4$, $a = 0$, $b = 2$
Trapezoidal
$$h = \frac{b-a}{n} = \frac{2}{4} = 0.5$$

$$
\begin{aligned}
f(0) &= 0.0000 \\
2f(0.5) &= 0.6667 \\
2f(1) &= 1.0000 \\
2f(1.5) &= 1.2000 \\
f(2) &= \underline{0.6667} \\
&\quad 3.5334
\end{aligned}
$$

Thus
$$\int_0^2 \frac{x}{x+1}\,dx \approx \frac{0.5}{2}(3.5334) \approx 0.883$$

9. $\int_{15}^{40} l(t)\,dt$, males, $n = 5$, $a = 15$, $b = 40$
$$h = \frac{40-15}{5} = 5$$

$$
\begin{aligned}
l(15) &= \ \ 96,672 \\
2l(20) &= 191,922 \\
2l(25) &= 190,000 \\
2l(30) &= 188,194 \\
2l(35) &= 186,134 \\
l(40) &= \ \underline{91,628} \\
&\quad 944,550
\end{aligned}
$$

$$\int_{15}^{40} l(t)\,dt \approx \frac{5}{2}(944,550) = 2,361,375$$

11. $a = 1$, $b = 5$, $h = 1$

$$
\begin{aligned}
f(1) &= 0.4 &&= 0.4 \\
4f(2) &= 4(0.6) &&= 2.4 \\
2f(3) &= 2(1.2) &&= 2.4 \\
4f(4) &= 4(0.8) &&= 3.2 \\
f(5) &= 0.5 &&= \underline{0.5} \\
&&&\ \ 8.9
\end{aligned}
$$

$$\int_1^5 f(x)\,dx \approx \frac{1}{3}(8.9) \approx 3.0$$
The area is about 3.0 square units.

13. $\int_1^3 f(x)dx$, $n = 4$, $a = 1$, $b = 3$

$h = \dfrac{3-1}{4} = 0.5$

$$\begin{aligned}
f(1) &= 1 & &= 1 \\
4f(1.5) &= 4(2) & &= 8 \\
2f(2) &= 2(2) & &= 4 \\
4f(2.5) &= 4(0.5) & &= 2 \\
f(3) &= 1 & &= \underline{1} \\
& & & \;16
\end{aligned}$$

$\int_1^3 f(x)dx \approx \dfrac{0.5}{3}(16) = \dfrac{8}{3}$

15. $f(x) = \sqrt{1-x^2}$, $a = 0$, $b = 1$, $n = 4$

$h = \dfrac{1-0}{4} = 0.25$

Simpson

$$\begin{aligned}
f(0) &= 1.0000 \\
4f(0.25) &= 3.8730 \\
2f(0.50) &= 1.7321 \\
4f(0.75) &= 2.6458 \\
f(1) &= \underline{0.0000} \\
& \;9.2509
\end{aligned}$$

$\int_0^1 \sqrt{1-x^2}\,dx \approx \dfrac{0.25}{3}(9.2509) \approx 0.771$

17. Let $f(x)$ = distance from near to far shore at point x on highway. Then area $\approx \int_0^4 f(x)dx$.

Using Simpson's rule with $h = 0.5$:

$$\begin{aligned}
f(0) &= 0.5 - 0.5 & &= 0 & &= 0 \\
4f(0.5) &= 4(2.3 - 0.3) &= 4(2) & &= 8 \\
2f(1) &= 2(2.2 - 0.7) &= 2(1.5) & &= 3 \\
4f(1.5) &= 4(3 - 1) & &= 4(2) & &= 8 \\
2f(2) &= 2(2.5 - 0.5) &= 2(2) & &= 4 \\
4f(2.5) &= 4(2.2 - 0.2) &= 4(2) & &= 8 \\
2f(3) &= 2(1.5 - 0.5) &= 2(1) & &= 2 \\
4f(3.5) &= 4(1.3) - 0.8) &= 4(0.5) & &= 2 \\
f(4) &= 1 - 1 & &= 0 & &= \underline{0} \\
& & & & & \;35
\end{aligned}$$

Area $\approx \int_0^4 f(x)dx \approx \dfrac{0.5}{3}(35) = \dfrac{35}{6}\,\text{km}^2$

19. a. $\text{MC} = \dfrac{dc}{dq}$

$\int_0^{120} \dfrac{dc}{dq}\,dq = c(120) - c(0)$

= (total cost of 120 units) − (fixed costs)

= total variable costs of 120 units

Using the trapezoidal rule with $h = 20$ and $f(q) = \dfrac{dc}{dq}$ to estimate the integral:

$$\begin{aligned}
f(0) &= 260 & &= 260 \\
2f(20) &= 2(255) & &= 510 \\
2f(40) &= 2(240) & &= 480 \\
2f(60) &= 2(240) & &= 480 \\
2f(80) &= 2(245) & &= 490 \\
2f(100) &= 2(250) & &= 500 \\
f(120) &= 255 & &= \underline{255} \\
& & & \;2975
\end{aligned}$$

$\int_0^{120} \dfrac{dc}{dq}\,dq \approx \dfrac{20}{2}(2975) = \$29,750$

b. $\text{MR} = \dfrac{dr}{dq}$

$\int_0^{120} \dfrac{dr}{dq}\,dq = r(120) - r(0) = r(120)$

[since $r(0) = 0$]

= total revenue from sale of 120 units

Using Simpson's rule with $h = 20$ and $g(q) = \dfrac{dr}{dq}$ to estimate the integral:

$$\begin{aligned}
g(0) &= 415 & &= 415 \\
4g(20) &= 4(360) & &= 1440 \\
2g(40) &= 2(320) & &= 640 \\
4g(60) &= 4(290) & &= 1160 \\
2g(80) &= 2(270) & &= 540 \\
4g(100) &= 4(260) & &= 1040 \\
g(120) &= 255 = & &= \underline{255} \\
& & & \;5490
\end{aligned}$$

$\int_0^{120} \dfrac{dr}{dq}\,dq \approx \dfrac{20}{3}(5490) = \$36,600$

c. At $q = 120$:
total revenue ≈ 36,600
total cost
= (tot. var. costs) + (fixed costs)
≈ 29,750 + 1500 = 31,250
Thus maximum profit
= (total rev.) − (total costs)
≈ 36,600 − 31,250 = $5350

Principles in Practice 17.6

1. Separating variables, we have
$$\frac{dI}{dx} = -0.0085I$$
$$\frac{dI}{I} = -0.0085dx$$
$$\int \frac{1}{I} dI = -\int 0.0085 \, dx$$
$$\ln|I| + C_1 - 0.0085x$$
To solve for I, we convert to exponential
Formula
$$I = e^{C_1 - 0.0085x} = Ce^{-0.0085x} \text{ since } I = I_0$$
when $x = 0$, $I_0 = Ce^0 = C$, so
$$I(x) = I_0 e^{0.0085x}$$

Exercise 17.6

1. $y' = 2xy^2$
$$\frac{dy}{dx} = 2xy^2$$
$$\frac{dy}{y^2} = 2x \, dx$$
$$\int y^{-2} dy = \int 2x \, dx$$
$$-\frac{1}{y} = x^2 + C$$
$$y = -\frac{1}{x^2 + C}$$

3. $\frac{dy}{dx} - x\sqrt{x^2 + 1} = 0$
$$dy = x\left(x^2 + 1\right)^{\frac{1}{2}} dx$$
$$\int dy = \int x\left(x^2 + 1\right)^{\frac{1}{2}} dx$$

$$\int dy = \frac{1}{2} \int \left(x^2 + 1\right)^{\frac{1}{2}} [2x \, dx]$$
$$y = \frac{1}{2} \cdot \frac{\left(x^2 + 1\right)^{\frac{3}{2}}}{\frac{3}{2}} + C$$
$$y = \frac{1}{3}\left(x^2 + 1\right)^{\frac{3}{2}} + C$$

5. $\frac{dy}{dx} = y$, where $y > 0$.
$$\frac{dy}{y} = dx$$
$$\int \frac{dy}{y} = \int dx$$
$$\ln y = x + C_1$$
$$y = e^{x + C_1} = e^{C_1} e^x = Ce^x, \text{ where } C = e^{C_1}.$$
Thus $y = Ce^x$, where $C > 0$.

7. $y' = \frac{y}{x}$, where $x, y > 0$.
$$\frac{dy}{dx} = \frac{y}{x}$$
$$\frac{dy}{y} = \frac{dx}{x}$$
$$\int \frac{dy}{y} = \int \frac{dx}{x}$$
$$\ln y = \ln x + C_1$$
$$\ln y = \ln x + \ln C, \text{ where } C > 0.$$
$$\ln y = \ln(Cx) \Rightarrow y = Cx, \text{ where } C > 0.$$

9. $y' = \frac{1}{y}$, where $y > 0$ and $y(2) = 2$
$$\frac{dy}{dx} = \frac{1}{y}$$
$$y \, dy = dx$$
$$\int y \, dy = \int dx$$
$$\frac{y^2}{2} = x + C$$

Given $y(2) = 2$, we obtain $\frac{2^2}{2} = 2 + C$, so

$C = 0$. Thus $y^2 = 2x$, $y = \pm\sqrt{2x}$. But given
that $y > 0$, we must choose $y = \sqrt{2x}$.

11. $e^y y' - x^2 = 0$, where $y = 0$ when $x = 0$.

$$e^y \frac{dy}{dx} = x^2$$

$$e^y dy = x^2 dx$$

$$\int e^y dy = \int x^2 dx$$

$$e^y = \frac{x^3}{3} + C$$

Given that $y(0) = 0$, we have $e^0 = 0 + C$, so

$$1 = C \Rightarrow e^y = \frac{x^3}{3} + 1, \ e^y = \frac{x^3 + 3}{3}, \text{ so}$$

$$y = \ln \frac{x^3 + 3}{3}.$$

13. $\left(4x^2 + 3\right)^2 \frac{dy}{dx} - 4xy^2 = 0$

$$\left(4x^2 + 3\right)^2 \frac{dy}{dx} = 4xy^2$$

$$\frac{dy}{y^2} = \frac{4x}{\left(4x^2 + 3\right)^2} dx$$

$$\int \frac{dy}{y^2} = \int \frac{4x}{\left(4x^2 + 3\right)^2} dx$$

$$\int y^{-2} dy = 4 \cdot \frac{1}{8} \int \left(4x^2 + 3\right)^{-2} [8x \ dx]$$

$$-\frac{1}{y} = -\frac{1}{2\left(4x^2 + 3\right)} + C$$

Now, $y(0) = \frac{3}{2}$ implies $-\frac{1}{\frac{3}{2}} = -\frac{1}{2(3)} + C$,

so $C = -\frac{1}{2}$. Thus

$$-\frac{1}{y} = -\frac{1}{2\left(4x^2 + 3\right)} - \frac{1}{2}$$

$$= -\frac{1 + \left(4x^2 + 3\right)}{2\left(4x^2 + 3\right)} = -\frac{4x^2 + 4}{2\left(4x^2 + 3\right)}$$

$$= -\frac{2\left(x^2 + 1\right)}{4x^2 + 3}.$$

Hence $y = \frac{4x^2 + 3}{2\left(x^2 + 1\right)}$.

15. $\frac{dy}{dx} = \frac{3x\sqrt{1 + y^2}}{y}$, where $y > 0$ and $y(1) = \sqrt{8}$.

$$\frac{y \ dy}{\sqrt{1 + y^2}} = 3x \ dx$$

$$\frac{1}{2} \int \left(1 + y^2\right)^{-\frac{1}{2}} [2y \ dy] = 3 \int x \ dx$$

$$\left(1 + y^2\right)^{\frac{1}{2}} = \frac{3x^2}{2} + C$$

$$y(1) = \sqrt{8} \Rightarrow (1 + 8)^{\frac{1}{2}} = \frac{3}{2} + C$$

$$C = \frac{3}{2}$$

Thus

$$\left(1 + y^2\right)^{\frac{1}{2}} = \frac{3x^2}{2} + \frac{3}{2}$$

$$1 + y^2 = \left[\frac{3x^2}{2} + \frac{3}{2}\right]^2$$

$$y^2 = \left[\frac{3x^2}{2} + \frac{3}{2}\right]^2 - 1$$

Since $y > 0$, $y = \sqrt{\left[\frac{3x^2}{2} + \frac{3}{2}\right]^2 - 1}$.

17. $2\frac{dy}{dx} = \frac{xe^{-y}}{\sqrt{x^2 + 3}}$, where $y(1) = 0$.

$$dye^y = \frac{1}{2} x\left(x^2 + 3\right)^{-\frac{1}{2}} dy$$

$$\int e^y dy = \frac{1}{2} \cdot \frac{1}{2} \int \left(x^2 + 3\right)^{-\frac{1}{2}} [2x \ dx]$$

$$e^y = \frac{1}{2}\left(x^2 + 3\right)^{\frac{1}{2}} + C$$

Now, $y(1) = 0 \Rightarrow e^0 = \frac{1}{2}(2) + C$, so $C = 0$.

Thus

$$e^y = \frac{1}{2}\left(x^2 + 3\right)^{\frac{1}{2}} \Rightarrow y = \ln\left(\frac{1}{2}\sqrt{x^2 + 3}\right).$$

19. $(q+1)^2 \dfrac{dc}{dq} = cq$

$$\int \frac{1}{c}\, dc = \int \frac{q}{(q+1)^2}\, dq$$

Using partial fractions or formula 7 for

$\displaystyle\int \frac{q}{(q+1)^2}\, dq$, we obtain

$c = \ln(q+1) + \dfrac{1}{q+1} + C$. Now, fixed cost is

given to be e, which means that $c = e$ when $q = 0$. This implies $1 + 0 = 1 + C$, so $C = 0$. Thus

$$\ln c = \ln(q+1) + \frac{1}{q+1} \Rightarrow c = \frac{e^{\ln(q+1)+1}}{(q+1)},$$

$$c = \frac{e^{\ln(q+1)}e^1}{(q+1)}, \text{ or } c = (q+1)e^{\frac{1}{(q+1)}}.$$

21. $\dfrac{dy}{dt} = -0.05y$

$$\int \frac{1}{y}\, dy = -0.05 \int dt$$

$\ln|y| = -0.05t + C$

Given that $y = 900$ when $t = 0$, we have
$\ln 900 = -0 + C = C$. Thus
$\ln|y| = -0.05t + \ln 900$. To find t when
money is 90% new, we note that y would be
10%(900) = 90. Solving
$\ln 90 = -0.05t + \ln 900$ gives
$t = \dfrac{\ln 900 - \ln 90}{0.05} \approx 46\, \text{weeks}.$

23. Let N be the population at time t, where $t = 0$ corresponds to 1985. Since N follows exponential growth $N = N_0 e^{kt}$. Now, $N = 20{,}000$ when $t = 0$, so $N_0 = 20{,}000$. Therefore $N = 20{,}000 e^{kt}$. Since $N = 24{,}000$ when $t = 10$, we have $24{,}000 = 20{,}000e^{10k}$, $1.2 = e^{10k}$, $\ln 1.2 = 10k$, $k = \dfrac{\ln 1.2}{10}$
Thus

$$N = 20{,}000 e^{\ln(1.2)\left(\frac{t}{10}\right)} \qquad (*)$$

$$N = 20{,}000 e^{0.18\left(\frac{t}{10}\right)}$$

$$N = 20{,}000 e^{0.018t} \qquad \text{(First form)}$$

From (*), we have $N = 20{,}000\left[e^{\ln 1.2}\right]^{\frac{t}{10}}$, so

$$N = 20{,}000(1.2)^{\frac{t}{10}} \qquad \text{(Second form)}$$

At year 2005, $t = 20$ and so

$$N = 20{,}000(1.2)^{\frac{20}{10}} = 20{,}000(1.2)^2$$
$$= 28{,}800.$$

25. Let N be the population (in billions) at time t, where t is the number of years past 1930. N follows exponential growth, so $N = N_0 e^{kt}$. When $t = 0$, then $N = 2$, so $N_0 = 2$. Thus $N = 2e^{kt}$. Since $N = 3$ when $t = 30$, then $3 = 2e^{30k}$

$$\frac{3}{2} = e^{30k}$$

$$30k = \ln\left(\frac{3}{2}\right)$$

$$k = \frac{\ln\frac{3}{2}}{30}$$

Thus

$$N = 2e^{t\ln\frac{3}{2}}{30} \approx 2e^{t\left(\frac{0.40547}{30}\right)} \approx 2e^{(0.013516)t}. \text{ In}$$
2000, $t = 70$ and so
$$N \approx 2e^{(0.013516)70} \approx 2e^{0.946}/\text{billion}$$
$$\approx 5.2 \text{ billion.}$$

27. Let N be amount of sample that remains after t seconds. Then $N = N_0 e^{-\lambda t}$, where N_0 is the initial amount present. When $t = 100$, then $N = 0.3N_0$. Thus
$$0.3N_0 = N_0 e^{-100\lambda}$$
$$0.3 = e^{-100\lambda}$$
$$-100\lambda = \ln 0.3$$
$$\lambda = -\frac{\ln 0.3}{100}$$
Thus $\lambda \approx 0.01204$. The half-life is
$$\frac{\ln 2}{\lambda} = \frac{\ln 2}{-\frac{\ln 0.3}{100}} = -100\frac{\ln 2}{\ln 0.3} \approx 57.57\, \text{s}.$$

29. Let N be the amount of ^{14}C present in the scroll t years after it was made. Then $N = N_0 e^{-\lambda t}$, where N_0 is amount of ^{14}C present when $t = 0$. We must find t when $N = 0.7N_0$.

$0.7 N_0 = N_0 e^{-\lambda t}$

$0.7 = e^{-\lambda t}$

$-\lambda t = \ln 0.7$

so $t = -\dfrac{\ln 0.7}{\lambda}$. By Eq. 15 in text,

$\lambda = \dfrac{\ln 2}{5600}$, so

$t = -\dfrac{\ln 0.7}{\frac{\ln 2}{5600}} = -\dfrac{5600 \ln 0.7}{\ln 2} \approx 2900$ years.

31. $\dfrac{dN}{dt} = kN$

$N = A e^{kt}$

$N_0 = A e^{kt_0}$

$A = \dfrac{N_0}{e^{kt_0}}$

Thus $N = \dfrac{N_0}{e^{kt_0}} \left(e^{kt} \right) = N_0 e^{kt - kt_0}$, or

$N = N_0 e^{k(t - t_0)}$, where $t \ge t_0$.

33. $N = N_0 e^{-\lambda t}$

When $t = 2$, then $N = 10$. Thus

$10 = N_0 e^{-2\lambda}$, $N_0 = 10 e^{2\lambda}$. By Equation 15,

$6 = \dfrac{\ln 2}{\lambda}$

$\lambda = \dfrac{\ln 2}{6}$

Thus $N_0 = 10 e^{2 \frac{\ln 2}{6}} = 10 e^{\frac{\ln 2}{3}} \approx 12.6$ units.

35. $\dfrac{dA}{dt} = 200 - 0.50 A$

$\displaystyle \int \dfrac{dA}{200 - 0.50 A} = \int dt$

$-\dfrac{1}{0.50} \ln(200 - 0.50 A) = t + C_1$

$\ln(200 - 0.50 A) = -0.50 t - 0.50 C_1$

$= -0.50 t + C_2$

Thus

$200 - 0.50 A = e^{-0.50 t + C_2} = e^{-0.50 t} e^{C_2}$

$200 - \dfrac{A}{2} = C e^{-0.50 t}$

Given that $A = 0$ when $t = 0$, we have

$C = 200$, so

$200 - \dfrac{A}{2} = 200 e^{-\frac{t}{2}}$

$200 - 200 e^{-\frac{t}{2}} = \dfrac{A}{2}$

$200 \left(1 - e^{-\frac{t}{2}} \right) = \dfrac{A}{2}$

Thus $A = 400 \left(1 - e^{-\frac{t}{2}} \right)$. If $t = 1$,

$A = 400 \left(1 - e^{-\frac{1}{2}} \right) \approx 157$ gm.

37. a. $\dfrac{dV}{dt} = kV$

$\displaystyle \int \dfrac{1}{V} dV = \int k \, dt$

$\ln V = kt + C_1$

$V = e^{kt} e^{C_1}$

or $V = C e^{kt}$. Now $t = 0$ corresponds to July 1, 1997 where $V = 14,000$, so

$14,000 = C(1)$. Thus $V = 14,000 e^{kt}$.

Also $V = 12,600$ for $t = \dfrac{1}{2}$, so

$12,600 = 14,000 e^{\frac{k}{2}}$

$0.9 = e^{\frac{k}{2}}$

$\dfrac{k}{2} = \ln 0.9$

$k = 2 \ln 0.9$

Thus $V = 14,000 e^{(2 \ln 0.9)t}$.

b. $7000 = 14,000 e^{(2 \ln 0.9)t}$

$\dfrac{1}{2} = e^{(2 \ln 0.9)t}$

$\ln \dfrac{1}{2} = (2 \ln 0.9)t$

$t = \dfrac{\ln \frac{1}{2}}{2 \ln 0.9} \approx 3.289$ yr.

This corresponds to approx. 39.47 months beyond July 1, 1998

$\Rightarrow$ Oct. 2001.

Exercise 17.7

1. $N = \dfrac{M}{1 + be^{-ct}}$

$M = 40,000$

Since $N = 20,000$ at $t = 0$ (1993), we have

$20,000 = \dfrac{40,000}{1+b}$, so $1+b = \dfrac{40,000}{20,000} = 2$,

or $b = 1$. Hence $N = \dfrac{40,000}{1+e^{-ct}}$. If $t = 5$, then

$N = 25,000$, so

$25,000 = \dfrac{40,000}{1+e^{-5c}}$

$1+e^{-5c} = \dfrac{40,000}{25,000} = \dfrac{8}{5}$

$e^{-5c} = \dfrac{8}{5} - 1 = \dfrac{3}{5}$

$e^{-c} = \left(\dfrac{3}{5}\right)^{\frac{1}{5}}$

Hence $N = \dfrac{40,000}{1+\left(\frac{3}{5}\right)^{\frac{t}{5}}}$. In 2003, $t = 10$ so

$N = \dfrac{40,000}{1+\left(\frac{3}{5}\right)^{2}} \approx 29,400$.

3. $N = \dfrac{M}{1+be^{-ct}}$

$M = 3,000,000$, and $N = 50$ when $t = 0$, so

$50 = \dfrac{3,000,000}{1+b}$

$1+b = \dfrac{3,000,000}{50} = 60,000$

$b = 59,999$

Hence $N = \dfrac{3,000,000}{1+59,999e^{-ct}}$. Since

$N = 5000$ when $t = 1$,

$5000 = \dfrac{3,000,000}{1+59,999e^{-c}}$,

$1+59,999e^{-c} = \dfrac{3,000,000}{5000} = 600$

$e^{-c} = \dfrac{599}{59,999}$

Hence $N = \dfrac{3,000,000}{1+59,999\left(\frac{599}{59,999}\right)^{t}}$. If $t = 2$,

then $N = \dfrac{3,000,000}{1+59,999\left(\frac{599}{59,999}\right)^{2}} \approx 430,000$.

5. $N = \dfrac{M}{1+be^{-ct}}$

$M = 100,000$, and since $N = 500$ when $t = 0$, we have

$500 = \dfrac{100,000}{1+b}$

$1+b = \dfrac{100,000}{500} = 200$

$b = 199$

Hence $N = \dfrac{100,000}{1+199e^{-ct}}$. If $t = 1$, then

$N = 1000$. Thus

$1000 = \dfrac{100,000}{1+199e^{-c}}$

$1+199e^{-c} = \dfrac{100,000}{1000} = 100$

$199e^{-c} = 99$

$e^{-c} = \dfrac{99}{199}$

Hence $N = \dfrac{100,000}{1+199\left(\frac{99}{199}\right)^{t}}$. If $t = 2$, then

$N = \dfrac{100,000}{1+199\left(\frac{99}{199}\right)^{2}} \approx 1990$.

7. **a.** $N = \dfrac{375}{1+e^{5.2-2.3t}} = \dfrac{375}{1+e^{5.2}e^{-2.3t}}$

$\approx \dfrac{375}{1+181.27e^{-2.3t}}$

b. $\lim\limits_{t\to\infty} N = \dfrac{375}{1+181.27(0)} = 375$

9. $\dfrac{dT}{dt} = k(T-a)$ where $a = 10$.

$\dfrac{dT}{T-a} = k\,dt$

$\displaystyle\int \dfrac{dT}{T-a} = \int k\,dt$

Thus $\ln(T-10) = kt + C$. At $t = 0$, we have
$T = 32$, so $\ln(32-10) = 0 + C$, $C = \ln 22$, so
$\ln(T-10) = kt + \ln 22$
$\ln(T-10) - \ln 22 = kt$. Hence

$\ln\left(\dfrac{T-10}{22}\right) = kt$. If $t = 1$, then $T = 30$. Thus

$\ln\left(\dfrac{30-10}{22}\right) = k\cdot 1$, so $k = \ln\dfrac{20}{22} = \ln\dfrac{10}{11}$.

Hence $\ln\left(\dfrac{T-10}{22}\right) = \left(\ln\dfrac{10}{11}\right)t$. If $T = 37$, then

$\ln\left(\dfrac{27}{22}\right) = \left(\ln\dfrac{10}{11}\right)t$

$t = \dfrac{\ln\frac{27}{22}}{\ln\frac{10}{11}} \approx -2.15 \text{ hr}$

which corresponds to 2 hr 9 min. Time of murder: 3:15 A.M. $-$ 2 hr 9 min = 1:06 A.M.

11. $\dfrac{dx}{dt} = k(70,000 - x)$

$\displaystyle\int \dfrac{dx}{70,000 - x} = \int k\,dt$

$-\ln(70,000 - x) = kt + C$

$\ln(70,000 - x) = -kt - C$

$70,000 - x = e^{-kt-C} = e^{-C}e^{-kt} = Ae^{-kt}$,

where $A = e^{-C}$. Thus $x = 70,000 - Ae^{-kt}$.
If $t = 0$, then $x = 10,000$, so
$10,000 = 70,000 - A \Rightarrow A = 60,000$. Thus

$x = 70,000 - 60,000e^{-kt}$. If $t = 1$, then
$x = 40,000$, so

$40,000 = 70,000 - 60,000e^{-k}$

$60,000e^{-k} = 30,000$

$e^{-k} = \dfrac{30,000}{60,000} = \dfrac{1}{2}$

Thus $x = 70,000 - 60,000\left(\dfrac{1}{2}\right)^{t}$. If $t = 3$,

then $x = 70,000 - 60,000\left(\dfrac{1}{8}\right) = \$62,500$.

13. $\dfrac{dN}{dt} = k(M - N)$

$\displaystyle\int \dfrac{dN}{M - N} = \int k\,dt$

$-\ln(M - N) = kt + C$

If $t = 0$, then $N = N_0$, so $-\ln(M - N_0) = C$.
Thus we have

$-\ln(M - N) = kt - \ln(M - N_0)$

$\ln(M - N_0) - \ln(M - N) = kt$

$\ln\dfrac{M - N_0}{M - N} = kt$

$\ln\dfrac{M - N}{M - N_0} = -kt$

$\dfrac{M - N}{M - N_0} = e^{-kt}$

$M - N = (M - N_0)e^{-kt}$

$N = M - (M - N_0)e^{-kt}$

Principles in Practice 17.8

1. $\displaystyle\int_0^\infty \left(3e^{-0.1t} - 3e^{-0.3t}\right)dt$

$= \lim_{r\to\infty} \int_0^r \left(3e^{-0.1t} - 3e^{-0.3t}\right)dt$

$= \lim_{r\to\infty} \left(-30e^{-0.1t} + 10e^{-0.3t}\right)\Big|_0^r$

$= \lim_{r\to\infty}\left[-\dfrac{30}{e^{-0.1r}} + \dfrac{10}{e^{0.3r}} - \left(-30e^0 + 10e^0\right)\right]$

$= \lim_{r\to\infty}\left[-\dfrac{30}{e^{0.1r}} + \dfrac{10}{e^{0.3r}} - (-20)\right]$

$= 0 + 0 + 20 = 20$

The total amount of the drug that is eliminated is approximately 20 milliliters.

Exercise 17.8

1. $\displaystyle\int_3^\infty \dfrac{1}{x^2}\,dx = \lim_{r\to\infty}\int_3^r x^{-2}\,dx$

$= \lim_{r\to\infty} \dfrac{x^{-1}}{-1}\Big|_3^r = \lim_{r\to\infty}\left(-\dfrac{1}{x}\right)\Big|_3^r$

$= \lim_{r\to\infty}\left(-\dfrac{1}{r} + \dfrac{1}{3}\right) = 0 + \dfrac{1}{3} = \dfrac{1}{3}$

3. $\displaystyle\int_1^\infty \dfrac{1}{x}\,dx = \lim_{r\to\infty}\int_1^r \dfrac{1}{x}\,dx = \lim_{r\to\infty}\ln|x|\Big|_1^r$

$= \lim_{r\to\infty}\left(\ln|r| - 0\right)$

$= \lim_{r\to\infty}\ln|r| = \infty \Rightarrow \text{diverges}$

5.

$\displaystyle\int_1^\infty e^{-x}\,dx = \lim_{r\to\infty} -\int_1^r e^{-x}[-dx]$

$= \lim_{r\to\infty}(-e^{-x})\Big|_1^r$

$= \lim_{r\to\infty}\left(-e^{-r} + e^{-1}\right) = \lim_{r\to\infty}\left(-\dfrac{1}{e^r} + \dfrac{1}{e}\right)$

$= 0 + \dfrac{1}{e} = \dfrac{1}{e}$

7. $\displaystyle\int_1^\infty \frac{1}{\sqrt{x}}\,dx = \lim_{r\to\infty}\int_1^r x^{-\frac{1}{2}}\,dx = \lim_{r\to\infty} 2x^{\frac{1}{2}}\Big|_1^r$

$\displaystyle = \lim_{r\to\infty}\left(2\sqrt{r}-2\right) = \infty \Rightarrow$ diverges

9. $\displaystyle\int_{-\infty}^{-2}\frac{1}{(x+1)^3}\,dx = \lim_{r\to\infty}\int_r^{-2}(x+1)^{-3}\,dx$

$\displaystyle = \lim_{r\to\infty}\frac{(x+1)^{-2}}{-2}\bigg|_r^{-2}$

$\displaystyle = \lim_{r\to-\infty} -\frac{1}{2(x+1)^2}\bigg|_r^{-2}$

$\displaystyle = \lim_{r\to-\infty}\left[-\frac{1}{2}+\frac{1}{2(r+1)^2}\right]$

$\displaystyle = -\frac{1}{2}+0 = -\frac{1}{2}$

11. $\displaystyle\int_{-\infty}^{\infty} xe^{-x^2}\,dx = \int_{-\infty}^{0} xe^{-x^2}\,dx + \int_0^\infty xe^{-x^2}\,dx$

$\displaystyle\int_{-\infty}^0 xe^{-x^2}\,dx = \lim_{r\to-\infty} -\frac{1}{2}\int_r^0 e^{-x^2}[-2x\ dx]$

$\displaystyle = \lim_{r\to-\infty} -\frac{1}{2}e^{-x^2}\bigg|_r^0$

$\displaystyle = \lim_{r\to-\infty}\left[-\frac{1}{2}+\frac{1}{2e^{r^2}}\right] = -\frac{1}{2}+0 = -\frac{1}{2}$

$\displaystyle\int_0^\infty xe^{-x^2}\,dx = \lim_{r\to\infty} -\frac{1}{2}\int_0^r e^{-x^2}[-2x\ dx]$

$\displaystyle = \lim_{r\to\infty} -\frac{1}{2}e^{-x^2}\bigg|_0^r$

$\displaystyle = \lim_{r\to\infty}\left[-\frac{1}{2e^{r^2}}+\frac{1}{2}\right] = 0+\frac{1}{2}=\frac{1}{2}$

Thus $\displaystyle\int_{-\infty}^\infty xe^{-x^2}\,dx = -\frac{1}{2}+\frac{1}{2}=0$.

13. a. $\displaystyle\int_{800}^\infty \frac{k}{x^2}\,dx = 1$

$\displaystyle\lim_{r\to\infty} k\int_{800}^r x^{-2}\,dx = 1$

$\displaystyle\lim_{r\to\infty} -\frac{k}{x}\bigg|_{800}^r = 1$

$\displaystyle\lim_{r\to\infty}\left(-\frac{k}{r}+\frac{k}{800}\right) = 1$

$\displaystyle 0+\frac{k}{800}=1$

$k = 800$

b. $\displaystyle\int_{1200}^\infty \frac{800}{x^2}\,dx = \lim_{r\to\infty} 800\int_{1200}^r x^{-2}\,dx$

$\displaystyle = \lim_{r\to\infty} -\frac{800}{x}\bigg|_{1200}^r$

$\displaystyle = \lim_{r\to\infty}\left(-\frac{800}{r}+\frac{800}{1200}\right) = 0+\frac{2}{3}=\frac{2}{3}$

15. $\displaystyle\int_0^\infty 240{,}000e^{-0.06t}\,dt$

$\displaystyle = \lim_{r\to\infty}\frac{240{,}000}{-0.06}\int_0^r e^{-0.06t}[-0.06\ dt]$

$\displaystyle = \lim_{r\to\infty} -\frac{240{,}000}{0.06}e^{-0.06t}\bigg|_0^r$

$\displaystyle = \lim_{r\to\infty} -\frac{240{,}000}{0.06}\left(\frac{1}{e^{-0.06r}}-1\right)$

$\displaystyle = -\frac{240{,}000}{0.06}(-1) = 4{,}000{,}000$

17. area $\displaystyle= \int_0^\infty e^{-2x}\,dx = \lim_{r\to\infty} -\frac{1}{2}\int_0^r e^{-2x}[-2\ dx]$

$\displaystyle = \lim_{r\to\infty} -\frac{e^{-2x}}{2}\bigg|_0^r$

$\displaystyle = \lim_{r\to\infty}\left[-\frac{1}{2e^{2r}}+\frac{1}{2}\right] = 0+\frac{1}{2}$

$\displaystyle = \frac{1}{2}$ square unit

19. $\displaystyle\int_0^\infty \frac{10{,}000}{(t+2)^2}\,dt = \lim_{r\to\infty} -\frac{10{,}000}{t+2}\Big|_0^r$

$\displaystyle = \lim_{r\to\infty}\left[-\frac{10{,}000}{r+2}+\frac{10{,}000}{2}\right]$

$\displaystyle = 0 + \frac{10{,}000}{2} = 5000 \text{ increase}$

Chapter 17 Review Problems

1. Integration by parts or formula 42. For integration by parts, let $u = \ln x$, $dv = x\,dx$.

Then $du = \dfrac{1}{x}\,dx$ and $v = \dfrac{x^2}{2}$. Thus

$\displaystyle\int x\ln x\,dx = \ln x\left(\frac{x^2}{2}\right) - \int \frac{x^2}{2}\cdot\frac{1}{x}\,dx$

$\displaystyle = \frac{x^2}{2}\ln(x) - \int\frac{x}{2}\,dx$

$\displaystyle = \frac{x^2}{2}\ln(x) - \frac{x^2}{4} + C = \frac{x^2}{4}[2\ln(x)-1] + C$

[Or, with formula 42, let $u = x$ (so $du = dx$) and $n = 1$.]

3. Formula 23 with $u = 2x$, $a^2 = 9$. Then $du = 2\,dx$.

$\displaystyle\int_0^2 \sqrt{4x^2+9}\,dx = \frac{1}{2}\int_0^2\sqrt{(2x)^2+9}\,(2\,dx)$

$\displaystyle = \frac{1}{2}\left[\frac{1}{2}\left((2x)\sqrt{4x^2+9}+9\ln\left|2x+\sqrt{4x^2+9}\right|\right)\right]_0^2$

$\displaystyle = \left(5 + \frac{9}{4}\ln 9\right) - \left(0 + \frac{9}{4}\ln 3\right)$

$\displaystyle = 5 + \frac{9}{4}\ln 3^2 - \frac{9}{4}\ln 3$

$\displaystyle = 5 + \frac{18}{4}\ln 3 - \frac{9}{4}\ln 3 = 5 + \frac{9}{4}\ln 3$

5. By partial fractions,

$\displaystyle\int\frac{x\,dx}{(2+3x)(3+x)} = \int\left[\frac{-\frac{2}{7}}{2+3x}+\frac{\frac{3}{7}}{3+x}\right]dx$

$\displaystyle = -\frac{2}{21}\ln|2+3x| + \frac{3}{7}\ln|3+x| + C$

$\displaystyle = \frac{1}{21}\left(9\ln|3+x| - 2\ln|2+3x|\right) + C$

Alternatively, by formula 12 with $u = x$ (so $du = dx$), $a = 2$, $b = 3$, $c = 3$, and $k = 1$,

$\displaystyle\int\frac{x\,dx}{(2+3x)(3+x)}$

$\displaystyle = \frac{1}{7}\left[3\ln|3+x| - \frac{2}{3}\ln|2+3x|\right] + C$

$\displaystyle = \frac{1}{21}\left(9\ln|3+x| - 2\ln|2+3x|\right) + C$

7. Partial fractions or formula 9. For formula 9, let $u = x$ (so $du = dx$), $a = 2$, and $b = 1$. For partial fractions,

$\displaystyle\int\frac{dx}{x(x+2)^2} = \int\left[\frac{\frac{1}{4}}{x}+\frac{-\frac{1}{4}}{x+2}+\frac{-\frac{1}{2}}{(x+2)^2}\right]dx$

$\displaystyle = \frac{1}{4}\ln|x| - \frac{1}{4}\ln|x+2| + \frac{1}{2(x+2)} + C$

$\displaystyle = \frac{1}{2(x+2)} + \frac{1}{4}\ln\left|\frac{x}{x+2}\right| + C$

9. Formula 21 with $u = 4x$ (so $du = 4\,dx$) and $a^2 = 9$.

$\displaystyle\int\frac{dx}{x^2\sqrt{9-16x^2}} = 4\int\frac{(4\,dx)}{(4x)^2\sqrt{9-(4x)^2}}$

$\displaystyle = 4\left[-\frac{\sqrt{9-16x^2}}{9(4x)}\right] + C$

$\displaystyle = -\frac{\sqrt{9-16x^2}}{9x} + C$

11. Partial fractions or formula 35. For partial fractions

$\displaystyle\int\frac{9\,dx}{x^2-9} = \int\left[\frac{\frac{3}{2}}{x-3}+\frac{-\frac{3}{2}}{x+3}\right]dx$

$\displaystyle = \frac{3}{2}\ln|x-3| - \frac{3}{2}\ln|x+3| + C$

$\displaystyle = \frac{3}{2}\ln\left|\frac{x-3}{x+3}\right| + C.$

To apply formula 35, first write the integral as $9\displaystyle\int\frac{dx}{x^2-9}$ and then set $u = x$ (so $du = dx$) and $a = 3$.

13. Integration by parts or formula 38. With parts, let $u = x$ and $dv = e^{7x} dx$. Then $du = dx$ and $v = \frac{1}{7} e^{7x}$. Thus

$$\int x e^{7x} dx = x \cdot \frac{1}{7} e^{7x} - \int \frac{1}{7} e^{7x} dx$$

$$= \frac{x}{7} e^{7x} - \frac{1}{7} \cdot \frac{1}{7} \int e^{7x} [7 \; dx]$$

$$= \frac{x}{7} e^{7x} - \frac{1}{49} e^{7x} + C = \frac{e^{7x}}{49}(7x - 1) + C.$$

With formula 38, let $u = x$ (so $du = dx$) and $a = 7$.

15. The integral has the form $\int \frac{1}{u} du$.

$$\int \frac{dx}{2x \ln 2x} = \frac{1}{2} \int \frac{1}{\ln 2x} \left[\frac{2}{2x} dx \right]$$

$$= \frac{1}{2} \ln|\ln 2x| + C$$

17. Long division or formula 3. For long division,

$$\int \frac{2x}{3 + 2x} dx = \int \left[1 - \frac{3}{3 + 2x} \right] dx$$

$$= x - 3 \cdot \frac{1}{2} \int \frac{1}{3 + 2x} [2 \; dx]$$

$$= x - \frac{3}{2} \ln|3 + 2x| + C.$$

To apply formula 3, write the integral as $2 \int \frac{x}{3 + 2x} dx$ and $u = x$ (so $du = dx$), $a = 3$ and $b = 2$.

19. Partial fractions

$$\int \frac{5x^2 + 2}{x^3 + x} dx = \int \left[\frac{2}{x} + \frac{3x}{x^2 + 1} \right] dx$$

$$= 2 \ln|x| + \frac{3}{2} \ln\left(x^2 + 1\right) + C$$

21. Integration by parts
$u = \ln(x + 1)$

$dv = (x + 1)^{-\frac{1}{2}} dx$

Then $du = \frac{1}{x + 1} dx$ and $v = 2(x + 1)^{\frac{1}{2}}$.

$$\int \frac{\ln(x + 1)}{\sqrt{x + 1}} dx$$

$$= 2(x + 1)^{\frac{1}{2}} \ln(x + 1) - 2 \int (x + 1)^{-\frac{1}{2}} dx$$

$$= 2(x + 1)^{\frac{1}{2}} \ln(x + 1) - 4(x + 1)^{\frac{1}{2}} + C$$

$$= 2\sqrt{x + 1}[\ln(x + 1) - 2] + C$$

23. $\bar{f} = \frac{1}{4 - 2} \int_2^4 \left(3x^2 + 2x\right) dx = \frac{1}{2}\left(x^3 + x^2\right)\Big|_2^4$

$$= \frac{1}{2}[(64 + 16) - (8 + 4)] = 34$$

25. $f(x) = \frac{1}{x + 1}$

$n = 6$, $a = 0$, $b = 3$

$h = \frac{b - a}{n} = \frac{3 - 0}{6} = 0.5$

  a.   Trapezoidal

$$f(0) = 1.0000$$
$$2f(0.5) = 1.3333$$
$$2f(1) = 1.0000$$
$$2f(1.5) = 0.8000$$
$$2f(2) = 0.6667$$
$$2f(2.5) = 0.5714$$
$$f(3) = 0.2500$$
$$\overline{ 5.6214}$$

$$\frac{0.5}{2}(5.6214) \approx 1.405$$

  b.   Simpson's

$$f(0) = 1.0000$$
$$4f(0.5) = 2.6667$$
$$2f(1) = 1.0000$$
$$4f(1.5) = 1.6000$$
$$2f(2) = 0.6667$$
$$4f(2.5) = 1.1429$$
$$f(3) = 0.2500$$
$$\overline{ 8.3263}$$

$$\frac{0.5}{3}(8.3263) \approx 1.388$$

27. $y' = 3x^2 y + 2xy, y > 0$

$$\frac{dy}{y} = \left(3x^2 + 2x\right)dx$$

$$\int \frac{dy}{y} = \int \left(3x^2 + 2x\right)dx$$

$\ln y = x^3 + x^2 + C_1$, from which

$y = e^{x^3 + x^2 + C_1}$, $y = Ce^{x^3 + x^2}$, where $C > 0$.

29. $\displaystyle\int_3^\infty \frac{1}{x^3} dx = \lim_{r \to \infty} \int_3^r x^{-3} dx$

$$= \lim_{r \to \infty} \frac{x^{-2}}{-2}\bigg|_3^t = \lim_{r \to \infty} -\frac{1}{2x^2}\bigg|_3^r$$

$$= \lim_{r \to \infty} \left[-\frac{1}{2r^2} + \frac{1}{18}\right] = 0 + \frac{1}{18} = \frac{1}{18}$$

31. $\displaystyle\int_1^\infty \frac{1}{2x} dx = \lim_{r \to \infty} \int_1^r \frac{1}{2x} dx = \lim_{r \to \infty} \frac{1}{2} \ln|x|\bigg|_1^r$

$$= \lim_{r \to \infty}\left[\frac{1}{2}\ln|r| - 0\right] = \infty \Rightarrow \text{diverges}$$

33. $N = N_0 e^{kt}$

Since $N = 100{,}000$ when $t = 0$,
$N_0 = 100{,}000$. Thus $N = 100{,}000e^{kt}$. Since
$N = 120{,}000$ when $t = 15$, then

$120{,}000 = 100{,}000e^{15k}$

$1.2 = e^{15k}$

$\ln 1.2 = 15k$, or $k = \dfrac{\ln 1.2}{15}$. Thus

$N = 100{,}000e^{t\frac{\ln 1.2}{15}} = 100{,}000\left(e^{\ln 1.2}\right)^{\frac{t}{15}}$

$= 100{,}000(1.2)^{\frac{t}{15}}$

For the year 2005 we have $t = 30$ and

$N = 100{,}000(1.2)^{\frac{30}{15}} = 100{,}000(1.2)^2$

$= 144{,}000$

35. $N = N_0 e^{-\lambda t}$, where N_0 is the original
amount present. When $t = 100$, then
$N = 0.95N_0$, so we have

$0.95N_0 = N_0 e^{-100\lambda}$

$0.95 = e^{-100\lambda}$

$100\lambda = \ln 0.95$

$\lambda = -\dfrac{\ln 0.95}{100} \approx 0.0005$ (decay constant).

After 200 years, $N = N_0 e^{-200\lambda}$. Thus

$\dfrac{N}{N_0} = e^{-200\lambda} = e^{-200\left[-\frac{\ln 0.95}{100}\right]} = e^{2\ln 0.95}$

$\approx 0.90 = 90\%$

37. $N = \dfrac{450}{1 + be^{-ct}}$

If $t = 0$, then $N = 2$. Thus $2 = \dfrac{450}{1 + b}$,

$1 + b = \dfrac{450}{2} = 225$, $b = 224$, so

$N = \dfrac{450}{1 + 224e^{-ct}}$. If $t = 6$, then

$N = 300 \Rightarrow 300 = \dfrac{450}{1 + 224e^{-6c}}$

$1 + 224e^{-6c} = \dfrac{450}{300} = \dfrac{3}{2}$

$224e^{-6c} = \dfrac{3}{2} - 1 = \dfrac{1}{2}$

$e^{-6c} = \dfrac{1}{448}$

$e^{6c} = 448$

$6c = \ln 448$

$c = \dfrac{\ln 448}{6} \approx 1.02$

Thus $N \approx \dfrac{450}{1 + 224e^{-1.02t}}$.

39. $\dfrac{dT}{dt} = k(T - 25)$

$\dfrac{dT}{T - 25} = k\,dt$

$\displaystyle\int \frac{dT}{T - 25} = \int k\,dt$

$\ln(T - 25) = kt + C$

If $t = 0$, then $T = 35$. Thus $\ln 10 = C$, so

$\ln\left(\dfrac{T - 25}{10}\right) = kt$. If $t = 1$, then $T = 34$ and

$\ln\left(\dfrac{9}{10}\right) = k$. Thus $\ln\left(\dfrac{T - 25}{10}\right) = (\ln 0.9)t$. If

$T = 37$,

$\ln\dfrac{12}{10} = (\ln 0.9)t$

$\ln 1.2 = (\ln 0.9)t$,

$t = \dfrac{\ln 1.2}{\ln 0.9} \approx -1.73$

Note that 1.73 hr corresponds approximately
to 1 hr 44 min. Thus
6:00 P.M. − 1 hr 44 min = 4:16 P.M.

41. $\displaystyle\int_0^\infty f(x)dx$

$\displaystyle= \lim_{r\to\infty}\int_0^r \left(0.008e^{-0.01x}+0.00004e^{-0.0002x}\right)dx$

$\displaystyle= \lim_{r\to\infty}\left(-0.8e^{-0.01x}-0.2e^{-0.0002x}\right)\Big|_0^r$

$\displaystyle= \lim_{r\to\infty}\left(-\frac{0.8}{e^{0.01r}}-\frac{0.2}{e^{0.0002r}}+0.8+0.2\right)$

$= 0-0+0.8+0.2 = 1$

43. a. Total revenue

$\displaystyle= r(12)-r(0)=\int_0^{12}\frac{dr}{dq}dq.\ f(q)=\frac{dr}{dq}$

$n=4,\ a=0,\ b=12$

$\displaystyle h=\frac{b-a}{n}=\frac{12-0}{4}=3$

Trapezoidal
$f(0)=\ 25$
$2f(3)=\ 44$
$2f(6)=\ 36$
$2f(9)=\ 26$
$f(12)=\ \underline{\ 7\ }$
$\qquad\quad 138$

$TR\approx\frac{3}{2}(138)=207$

Simpson's
$f(0)=\ 25$
$4f(3)=\ 88$
$2f(6)=\ 36$
$4f(9)=\ 52$
$f(12)=\ \underline{\ 7\ }$
$\qquad\quad 208$

$TR\approx\frac{3}{3}(208)=208$

b. Total variable cost

$\displaystyle c(12)-c(0)=\int_0^{12}\frac{dc}{dq}dq$

$\displaystyle f(q)=\frac{dc}{dq}$

$a=0,\ b=12$

Using as little data as possible, we choose $n=1$ for Trapezoidal and $n=2$ for Simpson (n must be even).

Trapezoidal ($n=1$)
$\displaystyle h=\frac{b-a}{n}=\frac{12-0}{1}=12$
$f(0)=15$
$f(12)=\ \underline{\ 7\ }$
$\qquad\quad 22$

$VC\approx\frac{12}{2}(22)=132$

Simpson's ($n=2$)
$\displaystyle h=\frac{b-a}{n}=\frac{12-0}{2}=6$
$f(0)=15$
$4f(6)=48$
$f(12)=\ \underline{\ 7\ }$
$\qquad\quad 70$

$VC\approx\frac{6}{3}(70)=140$

To each of our results we must add on the fixed cost of 25 to obtain total cost. Thus for trapezoidal we get $TC\approx 132+25=157$, and for Simpson we have $TC\approx 140+25=165$.

c. We use the relation

$\displaystyle P(12)=\int_0^{12}\left[\frac{dr}{dq}-\frac{dc}{dq}\right]dq-25.$ First we

determine variable cost for each rule with $n=4$ and $h=\dfrac{b-a}{n}=\dfrac{12-0}{4}=3$.

Trapezoidal
$f(0)=15$
$2f(3)=28$
$2f(6)=24$
$2f(9)=20$
$f(12)=\ \underline{\ 7\ }$
$\qquad\quad 94$

$VC\approx\frac{3}{2}(94)=141$

Simpson's
$f(0)=\ 15$
$4f(3)=\ 56$
$2f(6)=\ 24$
$4f(12)=\ 40$
$f(12)=\ \underline{\ 7\ }$
$\qquad\quad 142$

$$VC \approx \frac{3}{3}(142) = 142$$

Using these results and those of part (a), we have:

Trapezoidal

$$P(12) \approx 207 - 141 - 25 = 41$$

Simpson's

$$P(12) \approx 208 - 142 - 25 = 41$$

Mathematical Snapshot Chapter 17

1. $C = 2000, \ w_0 = 200$

$$w_{eq} = \frac{C}{17.5} = \frac{2000}{17.5} \approx 114$$

$$w(t) = \frac{C}{17.5} + \left(w_0 - \frac{C}{17.5}\right)e^{-0.005t}$$

$$= \frac{2000}{17.5} + \left(200 - \frac{2000}{17.5}\right)e^{-0.005t}$$

Letting $w(t) = 175$ and solving for t gives

$$175 = \frac{2000}{17.5} + \left(200 - \frac{2000}{17.5}\right)e^{-0.005t}$$

$$175 - \frac{2000}{17.5} = \left(200 - \frac{2000}{17.5}\right)e^{-0.005t}$$

$$\frac{175 - \frac{2000}{17.5}}{200 - \frac{2000}{17.5}} = e^{-0.005t}$$

$$-0.005t = \ln\left[\frac{175 - \frac{2000}{17.5}}{200 - \frac{2000}{17.5}}\right]$$

$$t = \frac{\ln\left[\frac{175 - \frac{2000}{17.5}}{200 - \frac{2000}{17.5}}\right]}{-0.005} \approx 69$$

Thus $w_{eq} = 114$ and $t = 69$ days.

3. $w(t) = \frac{C}{17.5} + \left(w_0 - \frac{C}{17.5}\right)e^{-0.005t}$

Since $\frac{C}{17.5} = w_{eq}$, we have

$$w(t) = w_{eq} + \left(w_0 - w_{eq}\right)e^{-0.005t}.$$

Simplifying the equation

$$w(t + d) = w(t) - \frac{1}{2}\left[w(t) - w_{eq}\right] \text{ gives}$$

$$w(t + d) = \frac{1}{2}\left[w(t) + w_{eq}\right]. \text{ Thus}$$

$$w_{eq} + \left(w_0 - w_{eq}\right)e^{-0.005(t+d)}$$

$$= \frac{1}{2}\left[w_{eq} + \left(w_0 - w_{eq}\right)e^{-0.005t} + w_{eq}\right], \text{ or}$$

$$w_{eq} + \left(w_0 - w_{eq}\right)e^{-0.005(t+d)}$$

$$= w_{eq} + \frac{1}{2}\left(w_0 - w_{eq}\right)e^{-0.005t}$$

Solving for d gives

$$e^{-0.005(t+d)} = \frac{1}{2}e^{-0.005t}$$

$$e^{-0.005t}e^{-0.005d} = \frac{1}{2}e^{-0.005t}$$

$$e^{-0.005d} = \frac{1}{2}$$

$$-0.005d = \ln\frac{1}{2} = -\ln 2$$

$$d = \frac{\ln 2}{0.005}$$

as was to be shown.

Chapter 18

Principles in Practice 18.1

1. The uniform density function is given by $f(x) = \begin{cases} \frac{1}{60}, & \text{if } 0 \le x < 60 \\ 0, & \text{otherwise.} \end{cases}$

   The probability of waiting between 25 and 45 minutes is

   $$P(25 \le X \le 45) = \int_{25}^{45} \frac{1}{60} \, dx = \frac{x}{60}\bigg|_{25}^{45}$$
   $$= \frac{45-25}{60} = \frac{20}{60} = \frac{1}{3}.$$

2. The exponential density function is given by $f(x) = \begin{cases} \frac{1}{10} e^{-\frac{x}{10}}, & \text{if } x \ge 0 \\ 0, & \text{if } x < 0. \end{cases}$

   The probability that the break pads will break down after the warranty period is

   $$P(5 < X) = 1 - P(0 \le X \le 5) = 1 - \int_0^5 \frac{1}{10} e^{-\frac{x}{10}} dx = 1 - \left(-e^{-\frac{x}{10}} \bigg|_0^5 \right)$$
   $$= 1 - \left(-e^{-\frac{5}{10}} + e^0 \right) = 1 + e^{-\frac{1}{2}} - 1 = e^{-\frac{1}{2}} \approx 0.607$$

3. The exponential density function is given by $f(x) = \begin{cases} 0.2e^{-0.2x}, & \text{for } x \ge 0 \\ 0, & \text{otherwise.} \end{cases}$

   The mean is given by $\mu = \dfrac{1}{k} = \dfrac{1}{0.2} = 5.$

   The standard deviation is given by $\sigma = \dfrac{1}{k} = \dfrac{1}{0.2} = 5.$

Exercise 18.1

1. **a.** $P(1 < X < 2) = \int_1^2 \frac{1}{6}(x+1)dx$

   $$= \frac{(x+1)^2}{12}\bigg|_1^2$$
   $$= \frac{9}{12} - \frac{4}{12} = \frac{5}{12}$$

   b. $P(X < 2.5) = \int_1^{2.5} \frac{1}{6}(x+1)dx$

   $$= \frac{(x+1)^2}{12}\bigg|_1^{2.5}$$
   $$= \frac{49}{48} - \frac{4}{12} = \frac{11}{16} = 0.6875.$$

   c. $P\left(X \ge \frac{3}{2}\right) = \int_{3/2}^3 \frac{1}{6}(x+1)dx$

   $$= \frac{(x+1)^2}{12}\bigg|_{3/2}^3$$
   $$= \frac{16}{12} - \frac{25}{48} = \frac{13}{16} = 0.8125$$

d.　$\int_1^c \frac{1}{6}(x+1)dx = \frac{1}{2}$

$\left.\frac{(x+1)^2}{12}\right|_1^c = \frac{1}{2}$

$\frac{(c+1)^2}{12} - \frac{1}{3} = \frac{1}{2}$

$(c+1)^2 - 4 = 6$

$(c+1)^2 = 10$

$c+1 = \pm\sqrt{10}$

$c = -1 \pm \sqrt{10}$

We choose $c = -1 + \sqrt{10}$ since $1 < c < 3$.

3. a.　$f(x) = \begin{cases} \frac{1}{3}, & \text{if } 1 \le x \le 4 \\ 0, & \text{otherwise} \end{cases}$

b.　$\frac{3-2}{4-1} = \frac{1}{3}$

c.　$P(0 < X < 1) = \int_0^1 0\,dx = 0$

d.　$P(X \le 3.5) = P(1 \le X \le 3.5)$
$= \frac{3.5-1}{4-1} = \frac{2.5}{3} = \frac{5}{6}$

e.　$P(X > 2) = P(2 < X \le 4) = \frac{4-2}{4-1} = \frac{2}{3}$

f.　0

g.　$P(X < 5) = P(1 \le X \le 4) = \frac{4-1}{4-1} = 1$

h.　$\mu = \int_1^4 x\left(\frac{1}{3}\right)dx = \left.\frac{x^2}{6}\right|_1^4 = \frac{5}{2}$

i.　$\sigma^2 = \int_1^4 x^2\left(\frac{1}{3}\right)dx - \mu^2 = \left.\frac{x^3}{9}\right|_1^4 - \left(\frac{5}{2}\right)^2$

$= \left[\frac{64}{9} - \frac{1}{9}\right] - \frac{25}{4} = 7 - \frac{25}{4} = \frac{3}{4}$

Thus $\sigma = \frac{\sqrt{3}}{2}$.

j.　If $1 \le x \le 4$,

$F(x) = \int_1^x \frac{1}{3}dt = \left.\frac{t}{3}\right|_1^x = \frac{x-1}{3}$

Thus $F(x) = \begin{cases} 0, & \text{if } x < 1 \\ \frac{x-1}{3}, & \text{if } 1 \le x \le 4 \\ 1, & \text{if } x > 4 \end{cases}$

$P(X < 2) = F(2) = \frac{2-1}{3} = \frac{1}{3}$

$P(1 < X < 3) = F(3) - F(1) = \frac{2}{3} - 0 = \frac{2}{3}$

5. a.　$f(x) = \begin{cases} \frac{1}{b-a}, & \text{if } a \le x \le b \\ 0, & \text{otherwise} \end{cases}$

b.　$\mu = \int_a^b x\left(\frac{1}{b-a}\right)dx = \left.\frac{x^2}{2(b-a)}\right|_a^b$

$= \frac{b^2-a^2}{2(b-a)} = \frac{a+b}{2}$

c.　$\sigma^2 = \int_a^b x^2\left(\frac{1}{b-a}\right)dx - \mu^2$

$= \left.\frac{x^3}{3(b-a)}\right|_a^b - \left(\frac{a+b}{2}\right)^2$

$= \frac{b^3-a^3}{3(b-a)} - \frac{(a+b)^2}{4}$

$= \frac{b^2+ab+a^2}{3} - \frac{a^2+2ab+b^2}{4}$

$= \frac{b^2-2ab+a^2}{12} = \frac{(b-a)^2}{12}$

Thus $\sigma = \frac{b-a}{\sqrt{12}}$.

7. $f(x) = \begin{cases} 2e^{-2x}, & \text{if } x \geq 0 \\ 0, & \text{if } x < 0 \end{cases}$

a. $P(1 < X < 3) = \int_1^3 2e^{-2x}\,dx = -e^{-2x}\Big|_1^3$

$= -e^{-6} + e^{-2} \approx 0.133$

b. $P(X < 2) = \int_0^2 2e^{-2x}\,dx = -e^{-2x}\Big|_0^2$

$= -e^{-4} + 1 \approx 0.982$

c. $P(X > 2.5) = 1 - P(X \leq 2.5)$

$= 1 - \int_0^{2.5} 2e^{-2x}\,dx$

$= 1 - \left(-e^{-2x}\right)\Big|_0^{2.5} = 1 - \left(-e^{-5} + 1\right)$

≈ 0.007

d. From the text, $\mu = \sigma = \frac{1}{k} = \frac{1}{2}$

$P(\mu - \sigma < X < \mu + \sigma) = P(0 < X < 1)$

$= \int_0^1 2e^{-2x}\,dx = -e^{-2x}\Big|_0^1$

$= -e^{-2} + 1 \approx 0.865$

e. $\int_0^\infty 2e^{-2x}\,dx = \lim_{r \to \infty} \int_0^r 2e^{-2x}\,dx$

$= \lim_{r \to \infty} -e^{-2x}\Big|_0^r$

$= \lim_{r \to \infty} \left(-e^{-2r} + 1\right) = 0 + 1 = 1$

9. a. $\int_0^4 kx\,dx = 1$

$\frac{kx^2}{2}\Big|_0^4 = 1$

$8k = 1$

$k = \frac{1}{8}$

b. $P(2 < X < 3) = \int_2^3 \frac{x}{8}\,dx = \frac{x^2}{16}\Big|_2^3 = \frac{9}{16} - \frac{4}{16}$

$= \frac{5}{16}$

c. $P(X > 2.5) = \int_{2.5}^4 \frac{x}{8}\,dx = \frac{x^2}{16}\Big|_{2.5}^4$

$= 1 - \frac{25}{64} = \frac{39}{64} \approx 0.609$

d. $P(X > 0) = P(0 \leq X \leq 4) = 1$

e. $\mu = \int_0^4 x\left(\frac{x}{8}\right)dx = \frac{x^3}{24}\Big|_0^4 = \frac{64}{24} - 0 = \frac{8}{3}$

f. $\sigma^2 = \int_0^4 x^2\left(\frac{x}{8}\right)dx - \mu^2 = \frac{x^4}{32}\Big|_0^4 - \left(\frac{8}{3}\right)^2$

$= 8 - \frac{64}{9} = \frac{8}{9}$

Thus $\sigma = \frac{\sqrt{8}}{3} = \frac{2\sqrt{2}}{3}$

g. $P(X < c) = \frac{1}{2}$

$\int_0^c \frac{x}{8}\,dx = \frac{1}{2}$

$\frac{x^2}{16}\Big|_0^c = \frac{1}{2}$

$\frac{c^2}{16} = \frac{1}{2}$

$c^2 = 8$

$c = \pm 2\sqrt{2}$

We choose $c = 2\sqrt{2}$ since $0 < c < 4$.

h. $P(3 < X < 5) = P(3 < X < 4) = \int_3^4 \frac{x}{8}\,dx$

$= \frac{x^2}{16}\Big|_3^4 = \frac{16}{16} - \frac{9}{16} = \frac{7}{16}$

11. $P(X \le 7) = \int_0^7 \frac{1}{10} \, dx = \frac{x}{10}\Big|_0^7 = \frac{7}{10}$

$E(X) = \int_0^{10} x\left(\frac{1}{10}\right) dx = \frac{x^2}{20}\Big|_0^{10} = 5 \text{ min.}$

13. $P(X > 1) = 1 - P(X \le 1)$

$= 1 - \int_0^1 3e^{-3x} dx = 1 - \left(-e^{-3x}\right)\Big|_0^1$

$= 1 - \left(-e^{-3} + 1\right) \approx 0.050$

Exercise 18.2

1. a. $P(0 < Z < 1.8) = A(1.8) = 0.4641$

b. $P(0.45 < Z < 2.81) = A(2.81) - A(0.45)$
$= 0.4975 - 0.1736 = 0.3239$

c. $P(Z > -1.22) = 0.5 + A(1.22)$
$= 0.5 + 0.3888 = 0.8888$

d. $P(Z \le 2.93) = 0.5 + A(2.93)$
$= 0.5 + 0.4983 = 0.9983$

e. $P(-2.61 < Z \le 1.4) = A(2.61) + A(1.4)$
$= 0.4955 + 0.4192 = 0.9147$

f. $P(Z > 0.07) = 0.5 - A(0.07)$
$= 0.5 - 0.0279 = 0.4721$

3. $P(Z < z_0) = 0.5517$

$0.5 + A(z_0) = 0.5517$

$A(z_0) = 0.0517$

$z_0 = 0.13$

5. $P(Z > z_0) = 0.8599$

$0.5 + A(-z_0) = 0.8599$

$A(-z_0) = 0.3599$

$-z_0 = 1.08$

$z_0 = -1.08$

7. $P(-z_0 < Z < z_0) = 0.2662$

$2A(z_0) = 0.2662$

$A(z_0) = 0.1331$

$z_0 = 0.34$

9. a. $P(X < 22) = P\left(Z < \frac{22-16}{4}\right)$
$= P(Z < 1.5) = 0.5 + A(1.5)$
$= 0.5 + 0.4332 = 0.9332$

b. $P(X < 10) = P\left(Z < \frac{10-16}{4}\right)$
$= P(Z < -1.5) = 0.5 - A(1.5)$
$= 0.5 - 0.4332 = 0.0668$

c. $P(10.8 < X < 12.4)$
$= P\left(\frac{10.8-16}{4} < Z < \frac{12.4-16}{4}\right)$
$= P(-1.3 < Z < -0.9) = A(1.3) - A(0.9)$
$= 0.4032 - 0.3159 = 0.0873$

11. $P(X > -2) = P\left(Z > \frac{-2-(-3)}{2}\right)$

$= P\left(Z > \frac{1}{2}\right) = 0.5 - A\left(\frac{1}{2}\right)$

$= 0.5 - 0.1915 = 0.3085$

13. Since $\sigma^2 = 9$, $\sigma = 3$. Thus

$P(19 < X \le 28) = P\left(\frac{19-25}{3} < Z \le \frac{28-25}{3}\right)$

$= P(-2 < Z \le 1) = A(2) + A(1)$

$= 0.4772 + 0.3413 = 0.8185$

15. $P(X > 54) = P(Z > z_0) = 0.0401$

$0.5 - A(z_0) = 0.0401$

$A(z_0) = 0.4599$

$z_0 = 1.75$

Since $\frac{54-40}{\sigma} = 1.75$

$\frac{14}{\sigma} = 1.75$

so $\sigma = \frac{14}{1.75} = 8$.

17. Let X be score on test. Then

$P(X > 630) = P\left(Z > \frac{630-500}{100}\right)$

$= P(Z > 1.3) = 0.5 - A(1.3) = 0.5 - 0.4032$

$= 0.0968 \Rightarrow 9.68\%$

19. Let X be height of an adult. Then
$$P(X < 72) = P\left(Z < \frac{72 - 68}{3}\right) = P(Z < 1.33)$$
$$= 0.5 + A(1.33) = 0.5 + 0.4082 = 0.9082$$
$$\Rightarrow 90.82\%$$

21. Let X be I.Q. of a child in population.

a. $P(X > 125) = P\left(Z > \frac{125 - 100.4}{11.6}\right)$
$$= P(Z > 2.12) = 0.5 - A(2.12)$$
$$= 0.5 - 0.4830 = 0.0170. \text{ Thus } 1.7\% \text{ of}$$
the children have I.Q.'s greater than
125.

b. If x_0 is the value, then
$P(X > x_0) = 0.90$. Thus
$$P\left(Z > \frac{x_0 - 100.4}{11.6}\right) = 0.90 \text{ or}$$
$$0.5 + A\left(-\frac{x_0 - 100.4}{11.6}\right) = 0.90. \text{ Hence}$$
$$A\left(-\frac{x_0 - 100.4}{11.6}\right) = 0.4, \text{ so}$$
$$-\frac{x_0 - 100.4}{11.6} = 1.28 \text{ or}$$
$$x_0 = 85.552 \approx 85.6.$$

Principles in Practice 18.3

1. X is the number of winners and X is
binomial with $n = 60$ and $p = \frac{1}{4}$. To find
$P(X = 20)$, use the normal approximation to
the binomial distribution with
$$\mu = np = 60\left(\frac{1}{4}\right) = 15 \text{ and}$$
$$\sigma\sqrt{npq} = \sqrt{60\left(\frac{1}{4}\right)\left(\frac{3}{4}\right)} = \sqrt{\frac{45}{4}} \approx 3.35.$$
Converting the correct X-values 19.5 and
20.5 to Z-values gives
$$z_1 = \frac{19.5 - 15}{\sqrt{\frac{45}{4}}} \approx 1.34$$
$$z_2 = \frac{20.5 - 15}{\sqrt{\frac{45}{4}}} \approx 1.64$$

Thus $P(X = 20) \approx P(1.34 \le Z \le 1.64)$
$$= A(1.64) - A(1.34) = 0.4495 - 0.4099$$
$$= 0.0396$$
The probability of 20 winners out of 60
contestants is 0.0396.

Exercise 18.3

1. $n = 150$, $p = 0.4$, $q = 0.6$, $\mu = np = 150(0.04)$
$= 60$,
$$\sigma = \sqrt{npq} - \sqrt{150(0.4)(0.6)} = \sqrt{36} = 6$$
$$P(X \le 52) = P(X < 52.5)$$
$$z = \frac{52.5 - 60}{6} = -1.25$$
$$P(X \le 52) = P(X \le 52.5)$$
$$\approx P(Z \le -1.25) = 0.5 - A(1.25)$$
$$= 0.5 - 0.3944 = 0.1056$$
$$P(X \ge 74) = P(X \ge 73.5) \approx P\left(Z \ge \frac{73.5 - 60}{6}\right)$$
$$= P(Z \ge 2.25)$$
$$= 0.5 - A(2.25)$$
$$= 0.5 - 0.4878 = 0.0122$$

3. $n = 200$, $p = 0.6$, $q = 0.4$, $\mu = np = 120$
$$\sigma = \sqrt{npq} = \sqrt{48} = 6.93$$
$$P(X = 125) = P(124.5 \le X \le 125.5)$$
$$\approx P\left(\frac{124.5 - 120}{6.93} \le Z \le \frac{125.5 - 120}{6.93}\right)$$
$$= P(0.65 \le Z \le 0.79)$$
$$= A(0.79) - A(0.65)$$
$$= 0.2852 - 0.2422 = 0.0430$$
$$P(110 \le X \le 135) = P(109.5 \le X \le 135.5)$$
$$\approx P\left(\frac{109.5 - 120}{6.93} \le Z \le \frac{135.5 - 120}{6.93}\right)$$
$$= P(-1.52 \le Z \le 2.24) = A(1.52) + A(2.24)$$
$$= 0.4357 + 0.4875 = 0.9232$$

5. Let X = no. of times 5 occurs. Then X is
binomial with $n = 300$, $p = \frac{1}{6}$, $q = \frac{5}{6}$,
$$\mu = np = 50, \ \sigma = \sqrt{npq} = \sqrt{41.666} = 6.45.$$
$$P(45 \le X \le 60) = P(44.5 \le X \le 60.5)$$
$$\approx P\left(\frac{44.5 - 50}{6.45} \le Z \le \frac{60.5 - 50}{6.45}\right)$$
$$= P(-0.85 \le Z \le 1.63) = A(0.85) + A(1.63)$$
$$= 0.3023 + 0.4484 = 0.7507$$

7. Let X = no. of trucks out of service. Then X can be considered binomial with $n = 60$, $p = 0.1$, $q = 0.9$, $\mu = np = 6$, $\sigma = \sqrt{npq} = \sqrt{5.4} = 2.32$

$$P(X \geq 7) = P(X \geq 6.5) \approx P\left(Z \geq \frac{6.5 - 6}{2.32}\right)$$
$$= P(Z \geq 0.22) = 0.5 - A(0.22)$$
$$= 0.5 - 0.0871 = 0.4129$$

9. Let X = no. of correct answers. Then X is binomial and $p = 0.5$, $q = 0.5$. If $n = 20$, then $\mu = np = 20(0.05) = 10$,

$$\sigma = \sqrt{npq} = \sqrt{20(0.5)(0.5)} = \sqrt{5} = 2.24$$
and $\ P(X \geq 12) = P(X \geq 11.5)$
$$\approx P\left(Z \geq \frac{11.5 - 10}{2.24}\right) = P(Z \geq 0.67)$$
$= 0.5 - A(0.67) = 0.5 - 0.2486 = 0.2514$. If $n = 100$, then $\mu = np = 100(0.5) = 50$,
$$\sigma = \sqrt{npq} = \sqrt{100(0.5)(0.5)} = \sqrt{25} = 5 \text{, and}$$
$$P(X \geq 60) = P(X \geq 59.5)$$
$$\approx P\left(Z \geq \frac{59.5 - 50}{5}\right) = P(Z \geq 1.9)$$
$$= 0.5 - A(1.9)$$
$$= 0.5 - 0.4713 = 0.0287$$

11. Let X = no. of deals consisting of three cards of one suit and two cards of another suit. Then X is binomial with $n = 100$, $p = 0.1$, $q = 0.9$, $\mu = np = 10$, $\sigma = \sqrt{npq} = \sqrt{9} = 3$.
$$P(X \geq 16) = P(X \geq 15.5)$$
$$\approx P\left(Z \geq \frac{15.5 - 10}{3}\right)$$
$$= P(Z \geq 1.83)$$
$$= 0.5 - A(1.83)$$
$$= 0.5 - 0.4664 = 0.0336$$

Chapter 18 Review Problems

1. **a.** $P(0 \leq X \leq 1) = 1$

$$\int_0^1 \left(\frac{1}{3} + kx^2\right) dx = 1$$
$$\left(\frac{x}{3} + \frac{kx^3}{3}\right)\bigg|_0^1 = 1$$
$$\frac{1}{3} + \frac{k}{3} = 1$$
$$\frac{k}{3} = \frac{2}{3}$$
$$k = 2$$

   b. $P\left(\frac{1}{2} < X < \frac{3}{4}\right) = \int_{1/2}^{3/4} \left(\frac{1}{3} + 2x^2\right) dx$

$$= \left(\frac{x}{3} + \frac{2x^3}{3}\right)\bigg|_{1/2}^{3/4} = \frac{1}{3}\left(x + 2x^3\right)\bigg|_{1/2}^{3/4}$$
$$\frac{1}{3}\left[\left(\frac{3}{4} + \frac{27}{32}\right) - \left(\frac{1}{2} + \frac{1}{4}\right)\right] = \frac{9}{32}$$

   c. $P\left(X \geq \frac{1}{2}\right) = \int_{1/2}^1 \left(\frac{1}{3} + 2x^2\right) dx$

$$= \left(\frac{x}{3} + \frac{2x^3}{3}\right)\bigg|_{1/2}^1 = \frac{1}{3}\left(x + 2x^3\right)\bigg|_{1/2}^1$$
$$= \frac{1}{3}\left[(1 + 2) - \left(\frac{1}{2} + \frac{1}{4}\right)\right] = \frac{3}{4}$$

   d. If $0 \leq x \leq 1$, $F(x) = \int_0^x \left(\frac{1}{3} + 2t^2\right) dt$

$$= \left(\frac{t}{3} + \frac{2t^3}{3}\right)\bigg|_0^x = \frac{x}{3} + \frac{2x^3}{3}$$

Therefore,
$$F(x) = \begin{cases} 0, & \text{if } x < 0 \\ \frac{x}{3} + \frac{2x^3}{3}, & \text{if } 0 \leq x \leq 1 \\ 1, & \text{if } x > 1 \end{cases}$$

3. **a.** $\mu = \int_0^3 x\left(\frac{2}{9}x\right) dx = \frac{2x^3}{27}\bigg|_0^3 = 2$

b. $\sigma^2 = \int_0^3 x^2 \left(\frac{2}{9}x\right) dx - \mu^2 = \frac{x^4}{18}\Big|_0^3 - 2^2$

      $= \frac{9}{2} - 4 = \frac{1}{2}$

      Thus $\sigma = \frac{1}{\sqrt{2}} \approx 0.71$.

5. $P(X > 22) = P\left(Z > \frac{22-20}{4}\right)$

      $= P(Z > 0.5) = 0.5 - A(0.5)$

      $= 0.5 - 0.1915 = 0.3085$

7. $P(12 < X < 18) = P\left(\frac{12-20}{4} < Z < \frac{18-20}{4}\right)$

      $= P(-2 < Z < -0.5)$

      $= A(2) - A(0.5) = 0.4772 - 0.1915 = 0.2857$

9. $P(X < 16) = P\left(Z < \frac{16-20}{4}\right)$

      $= P(Z < -1) = 0.5 - A(1)$

      $= 0.5 - 0.3413 = 0.1587$

11. $n = 100$, $p = 0.35$, $q = 0.65$, $\mu = np = 35$,

      $\sigma = \sqrt{npq} = \sqrt{22.75} = 4.77$

      $P(25 \le X \le 47) = P(24.5 \le X \le 47.5)$

      $\approx P\left(\frac{24.5-35}{4.77} \le Z \le \frac{47.5-35}{4.77}\right)$

      $= P(-2.20 \le Z \le 2.62) = A(2.20) + A(2.62)$

      $= 0.4956 + 0.4861 = 0.9817$

13. Let X = height of an individual. X is normally distributed with $\mu = 68$ and $\sigma = 2$.

      $P(X > 72) = P\left(Z > \frac{72-68}{2}\right)$

      $= P(Z > 2) = 0.5 - A(2)$

      $= 0.5 - 0.4772 = 0.0228$

Chapter 19

Principles in Practice 19.1

1. a. $c(500, 700) = 160 + 2(500) + 3(700)$
$= 160 + 1000 + 2100 = 3260$
The cost of manufacturing 500
12-ounce and 700 20-ounce mugs is
$3260.

b. $c(1000, 750) = 160 + 2(1000) + 3(750)$
$= 160 + 2000 + 2250 = 4410$
The cost of manufacturing 1000 12-
ounce mugs and 750 20-ounce mugs is
$4410.

Exercise 19.1

1. $f(2, 1) = 4(2) - (1)^2 + 3 = 8 - 1 + 3 = 10$

3. $g(0, -1, 2) = e^0(2[-1] + 3[2])$
$= 1(-2 + 6) = 4$

5. $h(-3, 3, 5, 4) = \dfrac{-3(3)}{5^2 - 4^2} = \dfrac{-9}{25 - 16}$
$= \dfrac{-9}{9} = -1$

7. $g(4, 8) = 2(4)\left(4^2 - 5\right) = 2(4)(11) = 88$

9. $F(2, 0, -1) = 3$

11. $f(x, y) = 2x - 5y + 4$
$f\left(x_0 + h, y_0\right) = 2\left(x_0 + h\right) - 5y_0 + 4$
$= 2x_0 + 2h - 5y_0 + 4$

13. $f(400, 400, 80) = \dfrac{400(400)}{80} = 2000$

15. A plane parallel to the x, z-plane has the form $y =$ constant. Because $(0, -4, 0)$ lies on the plane, the equation is $y = -4$.

17. A plane parallel to the x, y-plane has the form $z =$ constant. Because $(2, 7, 6)$ lies on the plane, the equation is $z = 6$.

19. $x + y + z = 1$ can be put in the form $Ax + By + Cz + D = 0$, so the graph is a plane. The intercepts are $(1, 0, 0)$, $(0, 1, 0)$, and $(0, 0, 1)$.

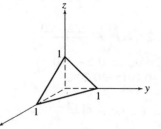

21. $3x + 6y + 2z = 12$ can be put in the form $Ax + By + Cz + D = 0$, so the graph is a plane. The intercepts are $(4, 0, 0)$, $(0, 2, 0)$, and $(0, 0, 6)$.

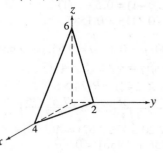

23. $x + 2y = 2$ can be put in the form $Ax + By + Cz + D = 0$, so the graph is a plane. There are only two intercepts: $(2, 0, 0)$ and $(0, 1, 0)$. The x, y-trace is $x + 2y = 2$, which is a line. For any fixed value of z, we obtain the line $x + 2y = 2$.

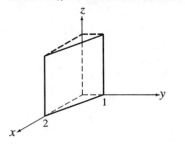

25. $z = 4 - x^2$. The x, z-trace is $z = 4 - x^2$, which is a parabola. For any fixed value of y, we obtain the parabola $z = 4 - x^2$.

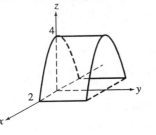

27. $x^2 + y^2 + z^2 = 1$. The x, y-trace is $x^2 + y^2 = 1$, which is a circle. The x, z-trace is $x^2 + z^2 = 1$, which is a circle. The y, z-trace is $y^2 + z^2 = 1$, which is a circle. The surface is a sphere with only the top hemisphere shown in the diagram.

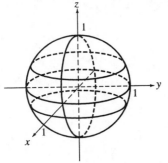

Exercise 19.2

1. $f_x(x, y) = 4(2x) + 0 + 0 = 8x$
$f_y(x, y) = 0 + 3(2y) + 0 = 6y$

3. $f_x(x, y) = 0 + 0 = 0$
$f_y(x, y) = 2(1) + 0 = 2$

5. $g_x(x, y) = \left(3x^2\right)y^2 + 2(2x)y - 3(1)y + 0$
$= 3x^2y^2 + 4xy - 3y$
$g_y(x, y) = x^3(2y) + 2x^2(1) - 3x(1) + 4(1)$
$= 2x^3y + 2x^2 - 3x + 4$

7. $g(p, q) = \sqrt{pq} = (pq)^{\frac{1}{2}}$
$g_p(p, q) = \frac{1}{2}(pq)^{-\frac{1}{2}} \cdot q = \frac{q}{2\sqrt{pq}}$
$g_q(p, q) = \frac{1}{2}(pq)^{-\frac{1}{2}} \cdot p = \frac{p}{2\sqrt{pq}}$

9. $h(s, t) = \frac{s^2 + 4}{t - 3}$
$h_s(s, t) = \frac{1}{t - 3}(2s) = \frac{2s}{t - 3}$
Rewriting $h(s, t)$ as $\left(s^2 + 4\right)(t - 3)^{-1}$, we have
$h_t(s, t) = \left(s^2 + 4\right)\left[(-1)(t - 3)^{-2}(1)\right]$
$= -\frac{s^2 + 4}{(t - 3)^2}$

11. $u_{q_1}(q_1, q_2) = \frac{3}{4} \cdot \frac{1}{q_1} + 0 = \frac{3}{4q_1}$
$u_{q_2}(q_1, q_2) = 0 + \frac{1}{4} \cdot \frac{1}{q_2} = \frac{1}{4q_2}$

13. $h(x, y) = \frac{x^2 + 3xy + y^2}{\sqrt{x^2 + y^2}}$

$h_x(x, y) = \dfrac{\left(x^2 + y^2\right)^{\frac{1}{2}}[2x + 3y] - \left(x^2 + 3xy + y^2\right)\left[\frac{1}{2}\left(x^2 + y^2\right)^{-\frac{1}{2}}(2x)\right]}{\left[\left(x^2 + y^2\right)^{\frac{1}{2}}\right]^2}$

$$= \frac{\left(x^2 + y^2\right)^{-\frac{1}{2}}\left[\left(x^2 + y^2\right)(2x+3y) - \left(x^2 + 3xy + y^2\right)x\right]}{x^2 + y^2}$$

$$= \frac{2x^3 + 3x^2 y + 2xy^2 + 3y^3 - x^3 - 3x^2 y - xy^2}{\left(x^2 + y^2\right)^{\frac{3}{2}}} = \frac{x^3 + xy^2 + 3y^3}{\left(x^2 + y^2\right)^{\frac{3}{2}}}$$

$$h_y(x,\ y) = \frac{\left(x^2 + y^2\right)^{\frac{1}{2}}[3x + 2y] - \left(x^2 + 3xy + y^2\right)\left[\frac{1}{2}\left(x^2 + y^2\right)^{-\frac{1}{2}}(2y)\right]}{\left[\left(x^2 + y^2\right)^{\frac{1}{2}}\right]^2}$$

$$= \frac{\left(x^2 + y^2\right)^{-\frac{1}{2}}\left[\left(x^2 + y^2\right)(3x+2y) - \left(x^2 + 3xy + y^2\right)y\right]}{x^2 + y^2}$$

$$= \frac{3x^3 + 2x^2 y + 3xy^2 + 2y^3 - x^2 y - 3xy^2 - y^3}{\left(x^2 + y^2\right)^{\frac{3}{2}}} = \frac{3x^3 + x^2 y + y^3}{\left(x^2 + y^2\right)^{\frac{3}{2}}}$$

15. $\dfrac{\partial z}{\partial x} = e^{5xy}(5y) = 5ye^{5xy}$; $\dfrac{\partial z}{\partial y} = e^{5xy}(5x) = 5xe^{5xy}$

17. $x = 5x \ln\left(x^2 + y\right)$

$$\frac{\partial z}{\partial x} = 5\left\{x\left[\frac{1}{x^2 + y}(2x)\right] + \ln\left(x^2 + y\right)[1]\right\} = 5\left[\frac{2x^2}{x^2 + y} + \ln\left(x^2 + y\right)\right]$$

$$\frac{\partial z}{\partial y} = 5x\left(\frac{1}{x^2 + y}[1]\right) = \frac{5x}{x^2 + y}$$

19. $f(r,\ s) = (r + 2s)^{\frac{1}{2}}\left(r^3 - 2rs + s^2\right)$

$$f_r(r,\ s) = (r + 2s)^{\frac{1}{2}}\left[3r^2 - 2s\right] + \left(r^3 - 2rs + s^2\right)\left[\frac{1}{2}(r + 2s)^{-\frac{1}{2}}(1)\right]$$

$$= \sqrt{r + 2s}\left(3r^2 - 2s\right) + \frac{r^3 - 2rs + s^2}{2\sqrt{r + 2s}}$$

$$f_s(r,\ s) = (r + 2s)^{\frac{1}{2}}[-2r + 2s] + \left(r^3 - 2rs + s^2\right)\left[\frac{1}{2}(r + 2s)^{-\frac{1}{2}}(2)\right]$$

$$= 2(s - r)\sqrt{r + 2s} + \frac{r^3 - 2rs + s^2}{\sqrt{r + 2s}}$$

21. $f(r, s) = e^{3-r} \ln(7-s)$

$f_r(r, s) = \ln(7-s)\left[e^{3-r}(-1)\right]$

$\quad = -e^{3-r} \ln(7-s)$

$f_s(r, s) = e^{3-r}\left[\dfrac{1}{7-s}(-1)\right] = \dfrac{e^{3-r}}{s-7}$

23. $g_x(x, y, z) = 3y(2x) + 2y^2z(1) + 0$

$\quad = 6xy + 2y^2z$

$g_y(x, y, z) = 3x^2(1) + 2xz(2y) + 0$

$\quad = 3x^2 + 4xyz$

$g_z(x, y, z) = 0 + 2xy^2(1) + 3\left(3z^2\right)$

$\quad = 2xy^2 + 9z^2$

25. $g_r(r, s, t) = e^{s+t}[2r+0] = 2re^{s+t}$

$g_s(r, s, t)$

$\quad = e^{s+t}\left[0 + 21s^2\right] + \left(r^2 + 7s^3\right)\left[e^{s+t}(1)\right]$

$\quad = \left(7s^3 + 21s^2 + r^2\right)e^{s+t}$

$g_t(r, s, t) = \left(r^2 + 7s^3\right)\left[e^{s+t}(1)\right]$

$\quad = e^{s+t}\left(r^2 + 7s^3\right)$

27. $f(x, y) = x^3y + 7x^2y^2$

$f_x(x, y) = 3x^2y + 14xy^2$

$f_x(1, -2) = 50$

29. $g(x, y, z) = e^x\sqrt{y+2z}$

$g_z(x, y, z) = e^x\left[\dfrac{1}{2}(y+2z)^{-\frac{1}{2}}(2)\right]$

$\quad = \dfrac{e^x}{\sqrt{y+2z}}$

$g_z(0, 1, 4) = \dfrac{1}{\sqrt{1+8}} = \dfrac{1}{3}$

31. $h(r, s, t, u) = \left(s^2 + tu\right)\ln(2r+7st)$

$h_s(r, s, t, u) = \dfrac{7t\left(s^2+tu\right)}{2r+7st} + 2s\ln(2r+7st)$

$h_s(1, 0, 0, 1) = 0$

33. $f(r, s, t) = rst\left(r^2 + s^3 + t^4\right)$

$\quad = r^3st + rs^4t + rst^5$

$f_s(r, s, t) = r^3(1)t + r\left(4s^3\right)t + r(1)t^5$

$\quad = r^3t + 4rs^3t + rt^5$

$f_s(1, -1, 2) = 2 + (-8) + 32 = 26$

35. $z = xe^{x-y} - ye^{y-x}$

$\dfrac{\partial z}{\partial x} = \left[xe^{x-y} + e^{x-y}\right] - \left[ye^{y-x}(-1)\right]$

$\dfrac{\partial z}{\partial y} = \left[xe^{x-y}(-1)\right] - \left[ye^{y-x} + e^{y-x}\right]$

Thus $\dfrac{\partial z}{\partial x} + \dfrac{\partial z}{\partial y} = e^{x-y} - e^{y-x}$, as was to be

shown.

37. $F(b, C, T, i) = \dfrac{bT}{C} + \dfrac{iC}{2}$

$\dfrac{\partial F}{\partial C} = \dfrac{\partial}{\partial C}\left[\dfrac{bT}{C}\right] + \dfrac{\partial}{\partial C}\left[\dfrac{iC}{2}\right] = -\dfrac{bT}{C^2} + \dfrac{i}{2}$

39. $R = f(r, a, n) = \dfrac{r}{1+a\left(\frac{n-1}{2}\right)}$

$\quad = r\left[1 + a\left(\dfrac{n-1}{2}\right)\right]^{-1}$

$\dfrac{\partial R}{\partial n} = r(-1)\left[1 + a\left(\dfrac{n-1}{2}\right)\right]^{-2} \cdot \dfrac{a}{2}$

$\quad = -\dfrac{ra}{2\left[1 + a\left(\frac{n-1}{2}\right)\right]^2}$

Exercise 19.3

1. $c = 4x + 0.3y^2 + 2y + 500$

   $\dfrac{\partial c}{\partial y} = 0.6y + 2$

   When $x = 20$ and $y = 30$, then $\dfrac{\partial c}{\partial y} = 0.6(30) + 2 = 20$.

3. $c = 0.03(x + y)^3 - 0.6(x + y)^2 + 4.5(x + y) + 7700$

   $\dfrac{\partial c}{\partial x} = 0.09(x + y)^2 - 1.2(x + y) + 4.5$

   When $x = 50$ and $y = 50$, then $\dfrac{\partial c}{\partial x} = 784.5$.

5. $\dfrac{\partial P}{\partial k} = 1.582(0.764)l^{0.192}k^{-0.236}$

   $= 1.208648 l^{0.192} k^{-0.236}$

   $\dfrac{\partial P}{\partial l} = 1.582(0.192)l^{-0.808}k^{0.764}$

   $= 0.303744 l^{-0.808} k^{0.764}$

7. $\dfrac{\partial q_A}{\partial p_A} = -50$, $\dfrac{\partial q_A}{\partial p_B} = 2$, $\dfrac{\partial q_B}{\partial q_A} = 4$,

   $\dfrac{\partial q_B}{\partial p_B} = -20$

   Since $\dfrac{\partial q_A}{\partial q_B} > 0$ and $\dfrac{\partial q_B}{\partial q_A} > 0$ the products are competitive.

9. $q_A = 100 p_A^{-1} p_B^{-\frac{1}{2}}$

   $q_B = 500 p_B^{-1} p_A^{-\frac{1}{3}}$

   $\dfrac{\partial q_A}{\partial p_A} = 100(-1)p_A^{-2}p_B^{-\frac{1}{2}} = \dfrac{-100}{p_A^2 p_B^{\frac{1}{2}}}$

   $\dfrac{\partial q_A}{\partial p_B} = 100\left(-\dfrac{1}{2}\right)p_A^{-1}p_B^{-\frac{3}{2}} = \dfrac{-50}{p_A p_B^{\frac{3}{2}}}$

   $\dfrac{\partial q_B}{\partial p_A} = 500\left(-\dfrac{1}{3}\right)p_B^{-1}p_A^{-\frac{4}{3}} = \dfrac{-500}{3 p_B p_A^{\frac{4}{3}}}$

   $\dfrac{\partial q_B}{\partial p_B} = 500(-1)p_B^{-2}p_A^{-\frac{1}{3}} = -\dfrac{500}{p_B^2 p_A^{\frac{1}{3}}}$

Since $\dfrac{\partial q_A}{\partial p_B} < 0$ and $\dfrac{\partial q_B}{\partial p_A} < 0$, the products are complementary.

11. $\dfrac{\partial P}{\partial B}$

    $= 0.01 A^{0.27} B^{-0.99} C^{0.01} D^{0.23} E^{0.09} F^{0.27}$

    $\dfrac{\partial P}{\partial C}$

    $= 0.01 A^{0.27} B^{0.01} C^{-0.99} D^{0.23} E^{0.09} F^{0.27}$

13. $\dfrac{\partial z}{\partial x} = 1120$. If a staff manager with an M.B.A. degree had an extra year of work experience before the degree, the manager would receive \$1120 per year in extra compensation.

15. a. $\dfrac{\partial R}{\partial w} = -1.015$; $\dfrac{\partial R}{\partial s} = -0.846$

    b. One for which $w = w_0$ and $s = s_0$ since increasing w by 1 while holding s fixed decreases the reading ease score.

17. $\dfrac{\partial g}{\partial x} = \dfrac{1}{V_F} > 0$ for $V_F > 0$. Thus if x increases and V_F and V_S are fixed, then g increases.

19. a.　$\dfrac{\partial q_A}{\partial p_A} = 30\sqrt{p_B}\left(-\dfrac{2}{3}p_A^{-\frac{5}{3}}\right)$

$\dfrac{\partial q_A}{\partial p_B} = \dfrac{30}{p_A^{\frac{2}{3}}}\left(\dfrac{1}{2}p_B^{-\frac{1}{2}}\right)$

When $p_A = 8$ and $p_B = 64$, then $\dfrac{\partial q_A}{\partial p_A} = 30(8)\left(-\dfrac{2}{3}\cdot\dfrac{1}{32}\right) = -5$

$\dfrac{\partial q_A}{\partial p_B} = \dfrac{30}{4}\left(\dfrac{1}{2}\cdot\dfrac{1}{8}\right) = \dfrac{15}{32}$.

b.　From (a), when $p_A = 8$ and $p_B = 64$, then $\dfrac{\partial q_A}{\partial p_B} = \dfrac{15}{32}$. Hence each \$1 reduction in p_B decreases q_A by approximately $\dfrac{15}{32}$ unit. Thus a \$4 reduction in p_B (from \$64 to \$60) decreases the demand for A by approximately $\dfrac{15}{32}(4) = \dfrac{15}{8}$ units.

21. a.　$\dfrac{\partial R}{\partial E_r} = 2.5945 - 0.1608E_r - 0.0277I_r$

If $E_r = 18.8$ and $I_r = 10$, then $\dfrac{\partial R}{\partial E_r} = -0.70564$. Since $\dfrac{\partial R}{\partial E_r} < 0$,

such a candidate should not be so advised.

b.　$\dfrac{\partial R}{\partial N} = 0.8579 - 0.0122N$

If $\dfrac{\partial R}{\partial N} < 0$, then $N > 70.3 \approx 70\%$

23.　$q_A = 1000 - 50p_A + 2p_B(-50)$

$\eta_{p_A} = \left(\dfrac{p_A}{q_A}\right)\dfrac{\partial q_A}{\partial p_A} = \left(\dfrac{p_A}{q_A}\right) - (50)$

$\eta_{p_B} = \left(\dfrac{p_B}{q_A}\right)\dfrac{\partial q_A}{\partial p_B} = \left(\dfrac{p_B}{q_A}\right)(2)$

When $p_A = 2$ and $p_B = 10$, then

$q_A = 920$, from which $\eta_{p_A} = -\dfrac{5}{46}$ and

$\eta_{p_B} = \dfrac{1}{46}$

25.　$q_A = \dfrac{100}{p_A\sqrt{p_B}}$

$\eta_{p_A} = \left(\dfrac{p_A}{q_A}\right)\dfrac{\partial q_A}{\partial p_A} = \left(\dfrac{p_A}{q_A}\right)\left(\dfrac{-100}{p_A^2\sqrt{p_B}}\right)$

$\eta_{p_B} = \left(\dfrac{p_B}{q_A}\right)\dfrac{\partial q_A}{\partial p_B} = \left(\dfrac{p_B}{q_A}\right)\left(\dfrac{-50}{p_A\sqrt{p_B^3}}\right)$

When $p_A = 1$ and $p_B = 4$, then $q_A = 50$.

This gives $\eta_{p_A} = -1$ and $\eta_{p_B} = -\dfrac{1}{2}$.

Exercise 19.4

1. $2x + 0 + 2z\frac{\partial z}{\partial x} = 0$.

$2z\frac{\partial z}{\partial x} = -2x$, $\frac{\partial z}{\partial x} = -\frac{2x}{2z} = -\frac{x}{z}$

3. $6z^2\frac{\partial z}{\partial y} - 0 - 8y = 0$

$\frac{\partial z}{\partial y} = \frac{8y}{6z^2} = \frac{4y}{3z^2}$

5. $x^2 - 2y - z^2 + y(x^2z^2) = 20$

$2x - 0 - 2z\frac{\partial z}{\partial x} + y\left[x^2 \cdot 2z\frac{\partial z}{\partial x} + z^2 \cdot 2x\right] = 0$

$(2x^2yz - 2z)\frac{\partial z}{\partial x} = -2x - 2xyz^2$

$\frac{\partial z}{\partial x} = \frac{-2x(1 + yz^2)}{2z(x^2y - 1)} = \frac{x(yz^2 + 1)}{z(1 - x^2y)}$

7. $0 + e^y + e^z\frac{\partial z}{\partial y} = 0$

$\frac{\partial z}{\partial y} = -\frac{e^y}{e^z} = -e^{y-z}$

9. $\frac{1}{z}\frac{\partial z}{\partial x} + \frac{\partial z}{\partial x} - y = 0$

$\left(\frac{1}{z} + 1\right)\frac{\partial z}{\partial x} = y$

$\left(\frac{1+z}{z}\right)\frac{\partial z}{\partial x} = y$

$\frac{\partial z}{\partial x} = \frac{yz}{1+z}$

11. $\left(2z\frac{\partial z}{\partial y} + 6x\right)\sqrt{x^3 + 5} = 0$

$2z\frac{\partial z}{\partial y} + 6x = 0$

$\frac{\partial z}{\partial y} = \frac{-6x}{2z} = -\frac{3x}{z}$

13. $\left[x \cdot 2z\frac{\partial z}{\partial x} + z^2 \cdot 1\right] + y\frac{\partial z}{\partial x} - 0 = 0$.

$(2xz + y)\frac{\partial z}{\partial x} = -z^2$

$\frac{\partial z}{\partial x} = -\frac{z^2}{2xz + y}$

If $x = 2$, $y = -2$, $z = 3$, then

$\frac{\partial z}{\partial x} = -\frac{9}{12 - 2} = -\frac{9}{10}$.

15. $e^{yz} \cdot y\frac{\partial z}{\partial x} = -y\left[x\frac{\partial z}{\partial x} + z \cdot 1\right]$.

$\left(ye^{yz} + xy\right)\frac{\partial z}{\partial x} = -yz$

$\frac{\partial z}{\partial x} = -\frac{yz}{y(e^{yz} + x)}$

$\frac{\partial z}{\partial x} = -\frac{z}{e^{yz} + x}$

If $x = -\frac{e^2}{2}$, $y = 1$, $z = 2$, then

$\frac{\partial z}{\partial x} = -\frac{2}{e^2 + \frac{-e^2}{2}} = -\frac{2}{\frac{e^2}{2}} = -\frac{4}{e^2}$.

17. $\frac{1}{z}\frac{\partial z}{\partial x} = 1 + 0$

$\frac{\partial z}{\partial x} = z$

If $x = 5$, $y = -5$, $z = 1$, then $\frac{\partial z}{\partial x} = 1$.

19. $\frac{(rs)\left[2t\frac{\partial t}{\partial r}\right] - (s^2 + t^2)[s]}{(rs)^2} = 0$.

$2rst\frac{\partial t}{\partial r} - s(s^2 + t^2) = 0$

$2rst\frac{\partial t}{\partial r} = s(s^2 + t^2)$

$\frac{\partial t}{\partial r} = \frac{s(s^2 + t^2)}{2rst} = \frac{s^2 + t^2}{2rt}$

If $r = 1$, $s = 2$, $t = 4$, then

$\frac{\partial t}{\partial r} = \frac{4 + 16}{2 \cdot 1 \cdot 4} = \frac{20}{8} = \frac{5}{2}$.

21. $c + \sqrt{c} = 12 + q_A \sqrt{9 + q_B^2}$

a. If $q_A = 6$ and $q_B = 4$, then

$c + \sqrt{c} = 12 + 6(5) = 42$, $\sqrt{c} = 42 - c$,

$c = (42 - c)^2 = 42^2 - 84c + c^2$,

$c^2 - 85c + 1764 = 0$,

$c = \dfrac{85 \pm \sqrt{(-85)^2 - 4(1)(1764)}}{2}$

$= \dfrac{85 \pm \sqrt{169}}{2} = \dfrac{85 \pm 13}{2}$. Thus $c = 49$ or $c = 36$. However $c = 49$ is extraneous but $c = 36$ is not. Thus $c = 36$.

b. Differentiating with respect to q_A:

$\dfrac{\partial c}{\partial q_A} + \dfrac{1}{2\sqrt{c}} \cdot \dfrac{\partial c}{\partial q_A} = \sqrt{9 + q_B^2}$.

$\left(1 + \dfrac{1}{2\sqrt{c}}\right) \dfrac{\partial c}{\partial q_A} = \sqrt{9 + q_B^2}$.

When $q_A = 6$ and $q_B = 4$, then $c = 36$

and $\left(1 + \dfrac{1}{12}\right)\dfrac{\partial c}{\partial q_A} = 5$, $\dfrac{13}{12} \cdot \dfrac{\partial c}{\partial q_A} = 5$, or

$\dfrac{\partial c}{\partial q_A} = \dfrac{60}{13}$.

Differentating with respect to q_B:

$\dfrac{\partial c}{\partial q_B} + \dfrac{1}{2\sqrt{c}} \cdot \dfrac{\partial c}{\partial q_B} = q_A \cdot \dfrac{q_B}{\sqrt{9 + q_B^2}}$

$\left(1 + \dfrac{1}{2\sqrt{c}}\right) \dfrac{\partial c}{\partial q_B} = \dfrac{q_A q_B}{\sqrt{9 + q_B^2}}$

When $q_A = 6$ and $q_B = 4$, then $c = 36$ and

$\left(1 + \dfrac{1}{12}\right)\dfrac{\partial c}{\partial q_B} = \dfrac{24}{5}$, $\dfrac{13}{12} \cdot \dfrac{\partial c}{\partial q_B} = \dfrac{24}{5}$, or

$\dfrac{\partial c}{\partial q_B} = \dfrac{288}{65}$.

Exercise 19.5

1. $f_x(x, y) = 4(2x)y = 8xy$
$f_{xy}(x, y) = 8x$

3. $f_y(x, y) = 3$
$f_{yy}(x, y) = 0$
$f_{yyx}(x, y) = 0$

5. $f_y(x, y) = 4\left[e^{2xy}(2x)\right] = 8xe^{2xy}$
$f_{yx}(x, y) = 8\left[x\left(e^{2xy} \cdot 2y\right) + e^{2xy}(1)\right]$
$= 8e^{2xy}(2xy + 1)$
$f_{yxy}(x, y)$
$= 8\left[e^{2xy}(2x) + (2xy + 1)\left(e^{2xy} \cdot 2x\right)\right]$
$= 8e^{2xy}(2x)[1 + (2xy + 1)]$
$= 8e^{2xy}(2x)[2 + 2xy]$
$= 32x(1 + xy)e^{2xy}$

7. $f(x, y) = (x + y)^2(xy)$
$= \left(x^2 + 2xy + y^2\right)(xy)$
$= x^3y + 2x^2y^2 + xy^3$
$f_x(x, y) = 3x^2y + 4xy^2 + y^3$
$f_y(x, y) = x^3 + 4x^2y + 3xy^2$
$f_{xx}(x, y) = 6xy + 4y^2$
$f_{yy}(x, y) = 4x^2 + 6xy$

9. $\dfrac{\partial z}{\partial x} = \dfrac{1}{2}\left(x^2+y^2\right)^{-\frac{1}{2}}[2x] = x\left(x^2+y^2\right)^{-\frac{1}{2}}$

$\dfrac{\partial^2 z}{\partial x^2} = x\left[-\dfrac{1}{2}\left(x^2+y^2\right)^{-\frac{3}{2}}[2x]\right] + \left(x^2+y^2\right)^{-\frac{1}{2}}[1]$

$= \left(x^2+y^2\right)^{-\frac{3}{2}}\left[-x^2+\left(x^2+y^2\right)\right] = y^2\left(x^2+y^2\right)^{-\frac{3}{2}}$

11. $f_y(x,\,y,\,z) = 0$

$f_{yx}(x,\,y,\,z) = 0$

$f_{yxx}(x,\,y,\,z) = 0$

Thus $f_{yxx}(4,\,3,\,-2) = 0$.

13. $f_k(L,k) = 30L^3k^5 - 7Lk^6$

$f_{kk}(L,\,k) = 150L^3k^4 - 42Lk^5$

$f_{kkL}(L,\,k) = 450L^2k^4 - 42k^5$

Thus

$f_{kkL}(2,\,1) = 450(4)(1) - (42)(1) = 1758$.

15. $f_x(x,\,y) = y^2e^x + \dfrac{1}{x}$

$f_{xy}(x,\,y) = 2ye^x$

$f_{xyy}(x,\,y) = 2e^x$

Thus $f_{xyy}(1,\,1) = 2e$.

17. $\dfrac{\partial c}{\partial q_B} = \dfrac{1}{3}\left(3q_A^2 + q_B^3 + 4\right)^{-\frac{2}{3}}\left(3q_B^2\right)$

$= q_B^2\left(3q_A^2 + q_B^3 + 4\right)^{-\frac{2}{3}}$

$\dfrac{\partial^2 c}{\partial q_A \partial q_B} = -\dfrac{2}{3}q_B^2\left(3q_A^2 + q_B^3 + 4\right)^{-\frac{5}{3}}\left(6q_A\right)$

$= -4q_A q_B^2\left(3q_A^2 + q_B^3 + 4\right)^{-\frac{5}{3}}$

When $p_A = 25$ and $p_B = 4$, then

$q_A = 10 - 25 + 16 = 1$ and

$q_B = 20 + 25 - 44 = 1$, and

$\dfrac{\partial^2 c}{\partial q_A \partial q_B} = -4(8)^{-\frac{5}{3}} = -\dfrac{4}{32} = -\dfrac{1}{8}$.

19. $f_x(x,\,y) = 24x^2 + 4xy^2$

$f_y(x,\,y) = 4x^2y + 20y^3$

$f_{xy}(x,\,y) = 8xy$

$f_{yx}(x,\,y) = 8xy$

Thus $f_{xy}(x,\,y) = f_{yx}(x,\,y)$.

21. $\dfrac{\partial z}{\partial x} = \dfrac{2x}{x^2+y^2}$

$\dfrac{\partial^2 z}{\partial x^2} = \dfrac{\left(x^2+y^2\right)(2) - (2x)(2x)}{\left(x^2+y^2\right)^2}$

$= \dfrac{2\left(y^2-x^2\right)}{\left(x^2+y^2\right)^2}$

$\dfrac{\partial z}{\partial y} = \dfrac{2y}{x^2+y^2}$

$\dfrac{\partial^2 z}{\partial y^2} = \dfrac{\left(x^2+y^2\right)(2) - (2y)(2y)}{\left(x^2+y^2\right)^2}$

$= \dfrac{2\left(x^2-y^2\right)}{\left(x^2+y^2\right)^2}$

$\dfrac{\partial^2 z}{\partial x^2} + \dfrac{\partial^2 z}{\partial y^2} = \dfrac{2\left(y^2-x^2\right)}{\left(x^2+y^2\right)^2} + \dfrac{2\left(x^2-y^2\right)}{\left(x^2+y^2\right)^2} = 0$

23. $2z\dfrac{\partial z}{\partial y} + 2y = 0$

$$\dfrac{\partial z}{\partial y} = -\dfrac{2y}{2z} = -\dfrac{y}{z}$$

$$\dfrac{\partial^2 z}{\partial y^2} = -\dfrac{z(1) - y\cdot\frac{\partial z}{\partial y}}{z^2} = -\dfrac{z - y\left(-\frac{y}{z}\right)}{z^2}$$

$$= -\dfrac{z^2 + y^2}{z^3}$$

From original equation, $z^2 + y^2 = 3x^2$. Thus $\dfrac{\partial^2 z}{\partial y^2} = -\dfrac{3x^2}{z^3}$.

Exercise 19.6

1. $z = 5x + 3y$, $x = 2r + 3s$, $y = r - 2s$

$$\dfrac{\partial z}{\partial r} = \dfrac{\partial z}{\partial x}\dfrac{\partial x}{\partial r} + \dfrac{\partial z}{\partial y}\dfrac{\partial y}{\partial r} = (5)(2) + (3)(1) = 13$$

$$\dfrac{\partial z}{\partial s} = \dfrac{\partial z}{\partial x}\dfrac{\partial x}{\partial s} + \dfrac{\partial z}{\partial y}\dfrac{\partial y}{\partial s} = (5)(3) + (3)(-2) = 9$$

3. $z = e^{x+y}$, $x = t^2 + 3$, $y = \sqrt{t^3}$

$$\dfrac{dz}{dt} = \dfrac{\partial z}{\partial x}\dfrac{dx}{dt} + \dfrac{\partial z}{\partial y}\dfrac{dy}{dt} = e^{x+y}(2t) + e^{x+y}\left(\dfrac{3}{2}t^{\frac{1}{2}}\right)$$

$$= \left(2t + \dfrac{3}{2}\sqrt{t}\right)e^{x+y}$$

5. $w = x^2z^2 + xyz + yz^2$, $x = 5t$, $y = 2t + 3$, $z = 6 - t$

$$\dfrac{dw}{dt} = \dfrac{\partial w}{\partial x}\dfrac{dx}{dt} + \dfrac{\partial w}{\partial y}\dfrac{dy}{dt} + \dfrac{\partial w}{\partial t}\dfrac{dz}{dt}$$

$$= \left(2xz^2 + yz\right)(5) + \left(xz + z^2\right)(2) + \left(2x^2z + xy + 2yz\right)(-1)$$

$$= 5\left(2xz^2 + yz\right) + 2\left(xz + z^2\right) - \left(2x^2z + xy + 2yz\right)$$

7. $z = \left(x^2 + xy^2\right)^3$, $x = r + s + t$, $y = 2r - 3s + t$

$$\dfrac{\partial z}{\partial r} = \dfrac{\partial z}{\partial x}\dfrac{\partial x}{\partial r} + \dfrac{\partial z}{\partial y}\dfrac{\partial y}{\partial r}$$

$$= 3\left(x^2 + xy^2\right)^2\left(2x + y^2\right)[1] + 3\left(x^2 + xy^2\right)^2(2xy)[1]$$

$$= 3\left(x^2 + xy^2\right)^2\left(2x + y^2 + 2xy\right)$$

9. $w = x^2 + xyz + y^3 z^2, \ x = r - s^2, y = rs, z = 2r - 5s$

$$\frac{\partial w}{\partial s} = \frac{\partial w}{\partial x}\frac{\partial x}{\partial s} + \frac{\partial w}{\partial y}\frac{\partial y}{\partial s} + \frac{\partial w}{\partial z}\frac{\partial z}{\partial s}$$

$$= (2x + yz)(-2s) + \left(xz + 3y^2 z^2\right)(r) + \left(xy + 2y^3 z\right)(-5)$$

$$= -2s(2x + yz) + r\left(xz + 3y^2 z^2\right) - 5\left(xy + 2y^3 z\right)$$

11. $y = x^2 - 7x + 5, \ x = 15rs + 2s^2 t^2$

$$\frac{\partial y}{\partial r} = \frac{dy}{dx}\frac{\partial x}{\partial r} = (2x - 7)(15s) = 15s(2x - 7)$$

13. $z = (4x + 3y)^3, \ x = r^2 s, y = r - 2s, r = 0, s = 1$

$$\frac{\partial z}{\partial r} = \frac{\partial z}{\partial x}\frac{\partial x}{\partial r} + \frac{\partial r}{\partial y}\frac{\partial y}{\partial r}$$

$$= 12(4x + 3y)^2 (2rs) + 9(4x + 3y)^2 (1)$$

$$= 3(4x + 3y)^2 (8rs + 3)$$

When $r = 0$, $s = 1$, then $x = 0$, $y = -2$, and $\frac{\partial z}{\partial r} = 324$.

15. $w = e^{3x-y}\left(x^2 + 4z^3\right), x = rs, y = 2s - r, z = r + s, r = 1, s = -1$

$$\frac{\partial w}{\partial s} = \frac{\partial w}{\partial x}\frac{\partial x}{\partial s} + \frac{\partial w}{\partial y}\frac{\partial y}{\partial s} + \frac{\partial w}{\partial z}\frac{\partial z}{\partial s}$$

$$= \left[e^{3x-y}(2x) + \left(x^2 + 4z^3\right)e^{3x-y}(3)\right](r) + \left[e^{3x-y}(-1)\left(x^2 + 4z^3\right)\right](2) + \left[e^{3x-y}\left(12z^2\right)\right](1)$$

$$= e^{3x-y}\left[\left(3x^2 + 2x + 12z^3\right)r - 2\left(x^2 + 4z^3\right) + 12z^2\right]$$

When $r = 1$ and $s = -1$, then $x = -1$, $y = -3$, $z = 0$, and $\frac{\partial w}{\partial s} = -1$.

17. $\dfrac{\partial c}{\partial p_A} = \dfrac{\partial c}{\partial q_A}\dfrac{\partial q_A}{\partial p_A} + \dfrac{\partial c}{\partial q_B}\dfrac{\partial q_B}{\partial p_A}$

$$= \left[\frac{1}{3}\left(3q_A^2 + q_B^3 + 4\right)^{-\frac{2}{3}}(6q_A)\right](-1) + \left[\frac{1}{3}\left(3q_A^2 + q_B^3 + 4\right)^{-\frac{2}{3}}\left(3q_B^2\right)\right](1)$$

$$= \left(3q_A^2 + q_B^3 + 4\right)^{-\frac{2}{3}}\left(-2q_A + q_B^2\right)$$

$$\frac{\partial c}{\partial p_B} = \frac{\partial c}{\partial q_A}\frac{\partial q_A}{\partial p_B} + \frac{\partial c}{\partial q_B}\frac{\partial q_B}{\partial p_B}$$

$$= \left[\frac{1}{3}\left(3q_A^2 + q_B^3 + 4\right)^{-\frac{2}{3}}(6q_A)\right](2p_B) + \left[\frac{1}{3}\left(3q_A^2 + q_B^3 + 4\right)^{-\frac{2}{3}}\left(3q_B^2\right)\right](-11)$$

$$= \left(3q_A^2 + q_B^3 + 4\right)^{-\frac{2}{3}}\left(4q_A p_B - 11q_B^2\right)$$

When $p_A = 25$ and $p_B = 4$, then $q_A = 10 - 25 + 16 = 1$, $q_B = 20 + 25 - 44 = 1$,

and $\dfrac{\partial c}{\partial p_A} = (8)^{-\frac{2}{3}}(-1) = -\dfrac{1}{4}$ and $\dfrac{\partial c}{\partial p_B} = (8)^{-\frac{2}{3}}(5) = \dfrac{5}{4}$.

19. a. $\dfrac{\partial w}{\partial s} = \dfrac{\partial w}{\partial x}\dfrac{\partial x}{\partial s} + \dfrac{\partial w}{\partial y}\dfrac{\partial y}{\partial s}$

b. $\dfrac{\partial w}{\partial s} = \left[3x^2 \cdot \dfrac{1}{x-2y}(1) + \ln(x-2y)[6x]\right]\left(\sqrt{t-2}\right) + \left[3x^2 \cdot \dfrac{1}{x-2y}(-2)\right]\left[-3e^{1-s}(-1)\right]$

$= \left[\dfrac{3x^2}{x-2y} + 6x\ln(x-2y)\right]\sqrt{t-2} - \dfrac{18x^2 e^{1-s}}{x-2y}$

Setting $s = 1$ and $t = 3$ gives $x = 1$, $y = 0$, and $\dfrac{\partial w}{\partial s} = [3+0](1) - \dfrac{18}{1} = -15$

Exercise 19.7

1. $f(x, y) = x^2 + y^2 - 5x + 4y + xy$

$\begin{cases} f_x(x, y) = 2x + y - 5 = 0 \\ f_y(x, y) = x + 2y + 4 = 0 \end{cases}$

Solving the system gives the critical point $\left(\dfrac{14}{3}, -\dfrac{13}{3}\right)$.

3. $f(x, y)$
$= 2x^3 + y^3 - 3x^2 + 1.5y^2 - 12x - 90y$

$\begin{cases} f_x(x, y) = 6x^2 - 6x - 12 = 0 \\ f_y(x, y) = 3y^2 + 3y - 90 = 0 \end{cases}$

Both equations are easily solved by factoring. The critical points are (2, 5), (2, –6), (–1, 5), (–1, –6).

5. $f(x, y, z)$
$= 2x^2 + xy + y^2 + 100 - z(x + y - 200)$

$\begin{cases} f_x(x, y, z) = 4x + y - z = 0 \\ f_y(x, y, z) = x + 2y - z = 0 \\ f_z(x, y, z) = -x - y + 200 = 0 \end{cases}$

Solving gives the critical point (50, 150, 350).

7. $f(x, y) = x^2 + 3y^2 + 4x - 9y + 3$

$\begin{cases} f_x(x, y) = 2x + 4 = 0 \\ f_y(x, y) = 6y - 9 = 0 \end{cases}$

Critical point $\left(-2, \dfrac{3}{2}\right)$

Second-Derivative Test
$f_{xx}(x, y) = 2$, $f_{yy}(x, y) = 6$,

$f_{xy}(x, y) = 0$. At $\left(-2, \dfrac{3}{2}\right)$,

$D = (2)(6) - 0^2 = 12 > 0$ and

$f_{xx}(x, y) = 2 > 0$. Thus at $\left(-2, \dfrac{3}{2}\right)$ there is
a relative minimum.

9. $f(x, y) = y - y^2 - 3x - 6x^2$

$\begin{cases} f_x(x, y) = -3 - 12x = 0 \\ f_y(x, y) = 1 - 2y = 0 \end{cases}$

Critical point $\left(-\dfrac{1}{4}, \dfrac{1}{2}\right)$

Second-Derivative Test
$f_{xx}(x, y) = -12$, $f_{yy}(x, y) = -2$,

$f_{xy}(x, y) = 0$

At $\left(-\dfrac{1}{4}, \dfrac{1}{2}\right)$, $D = (-12)(-2) - 0^2 = 24 > 0$

and $f_{xx}(x, y) = -12 < 0$. Thus $\left(-\dfrac{1}{4}, \dfrac{1}{2}\right)$

there is a relative maximum.

11. $f(x, y) = x^3 - 3xy + y^2 + y - 5$

$$\begin{cases} f_x(x, y) = 3x^2 - 3y = 0 \\ f_y(x, y) = -3x + 2y + 1 = 0 \end{cases}$$

Critical point: (1, 1), $\left(\frac{1}{2}, \frac{1}{4}\right)$

Second-Derivative Test
$f_{xx}(x, y) = 6x$, $f_{yy}(x, y) = 2$,
$f_{xy}(x, y) = -3$
At (1, 1), $D = (6)(2) - (-3)^2 = 3 > 0$ and
$f_{xx}(x, y) = 6 > 0$; thus there is a relative

minimum at (1, 1). At $\left(\frac{1}{2}, \frac{1}{4}\right)$,

$D = (3)(2) - (-3)^2 = -3 < 0$; thus there is
no relative extremum at $\left(\frac{1}{2}, \frac{1}{4}\right)$.

13. $f(x, y) = \frac{1}{3}\left(x^3 + 8y^3\right) - 2\left(x^2 + y^2\right) + 1$

$$\begin{cases} f_x(x, y) = x^2 - 4x = 0 \\ f_y(x, y) = 8y^2 - 4y = 0 \end{cases}$$

Critical points: (0, 0), $\left(4, \frac{1}{2}\right)$, $\left(0, \frac{1}{2}\right)$, (4, 0)

Second-Derivative Test
$f_{xx}(x, y) = 2x - 4$, $f_{yy}(x, y) = 16y - 4$,
$f_{xy}(x, y) = 0$. At (0, 0),

$D = (-4)(-4) - 0^2 = 16 > 0$ and
$f_{xx}(x, y) = -4 < 0$; thus a relative
maximum.
At $\left(4, \frac{1}{2}\right)$, $D = (4)(4) - 0^2 = 16 > 0$ and
$f_{xx}(x, y) = 4 > 0$; thus a relative minimum.
At $\left(0, \frac{1}{2}\right)$, $D = (-4)(4) - 0^2 = -16 > 0$;
thus neither.
At (4, 0), $D = (4)(-4) - 0^2 = -16 < 0$, thus
neither.

15. $f(l, k) = 2lk - l^2 + 264k - 10l - 2k^2$
$$\begin{cases} f_l(l, k) = 2k - 2l - 10 = 0 \\ f_k(l, k) = -4k + 2l + 264 = 0 \end{cases}$$
Critical point: (122, 127)
Second-Derivative Test
$f_{ll}(l, k) = -2$, $f_{kk}(l, k) = -4$, $f_{lk}(l, k) = 2$

At (122, 127), $D = (-2)(-4) - 2^2 = 4 > 0$
and $f_{ll}(l, k) = -2 < 0$; thus there is a relative
maximum at (122, 127).

17. $f(p, q) = pq - \frac{1}{p} - \frac{1}{q}$

$$\begin{cases} f_p(p, q) = q + \dfrac{1}{p^2} = 0 \\ f_q(p, q) = p + \dfrac{1}{q^2} = 0 \end{cases}$$

Critical point: (-1, -1)
Second-Derivative Test
$f_{pp}(p, q) = -\dfrac{2}{p^3}$, $f_{qq}(p, q) = -\dfrac{2}{q^3}$,
$f_{pq}(p, q) = 1$. At (-1, -1),

$D = (2)(2) - 1^2 = 3 > 0$ and
$f_{pp}(p, q) = 2 > 0$; thus there is a relative
minimum at (-1, -1).

19. $f(x, y) = \left(y^2 - 4\right)\left(e^x - 1\right)$

$$\begin{cases} f_x(x, y) = e^x\left(y^2 - 4\right) = 0 & (1) \\ f_y(x, y) = 2y\left(e^x - 1\right) = 0 & (2) \end{cases}$$

From (1), $y = \pm 2$. From (2), $x = 0$, $y = 0$. The
only critical points are (0, -2) and (0, 2).
[$y = 0$ does not give rise to a common
solution of (1) and (2).]
Second-Derivative Test
$f_{xx}(x, y) = e^x\left(y^2 - 4\right)$,

$f_{yy}(x, y) = 2\left(e^x - 1\right)$, $f_{xy}(x, y) = 2ye^x$. At
(0, -2), $D = (0)(0) - (-4)^2 = -16 < 0$; thus
neither. At (0, 2),
$D = (0)(0) - (4)^2 = -16 < 0$; thus neither.

21. $P = f(l, k)$
$= 1.08l^2 - 0.03l^3 + 1.68k^2 - 0.08k^3$
$$\begin{cases} P_l = 2.16l - 0.09l^2 = 0 \\ P_k = 3.36k - 0.24k^2 = 0 \end{cases}$$
Critical points: (0, 0), (0, 14), (24, 0),
(24, 14)
Second-Derivative Test
$P_{ll} = 2.16 - 0.18l$, $P_{kk} = 3.36 - 0.48k$,

$P_{lk} = 0$. At $(0, 0)$, $D = (2.16)(3.36) - 0^2 > 0$ and $P_{ll} = 2.16 > 0$; thus relative minimum.

At $(0, 14)$, $D = (2.16)(-3.36) - 0^2 < 0$; thus no extremum. At $(24, 0)$, $D = (-2.16)(3.36) - 0^2 < 0$; thus no extremum. At $(24, 14)$, $D = (-2.16)(-3.36) - 0^2 > 0$ and $P_{ll} = -2.16 < 0$, so relative maximum Thus $l = 24$, $k = 14$ gives a relative maximum.

23. Profit per lb for A $= p_A - 60$.

Profit per lb for B $= p_B - 70$.

Total Profit $= P = (p_A - 60)q_A + (p_B - 70)q_B$

$P = (p_A - 60)\big[5(p_B - p_A)\big] + (p_B - 70)\big[500 + 5(p_A - 2p_B)\big]$

Thus

$$\begin{cases} \dfrac{\partial P}{\partial p_A} = -10(p_A - p_B + 5) = 0 \\ \dfrac{\partial P}{\partial p_B} = 10(p_A - 2p_B + 90) = 0 \end{cases}$$

Critical point: $p_A = 80$, $p_B = 85$

Second-Derivative Test

$\dfrac{\partial^2 P}{\partial p_A^2} = -10$, $\dfrac{\partial^2 P}{\partial p_B^2} = -20$, $\dfrac{\partial^2 P}{\partial p_B \partial p_A} = 10$. When $p_A = 80$ and $p_B = 85$, then

$D = (-10)(-20) - (10)^2 = 100 > 0$ and $\dfrac{\partial^2 P}{\partial p_A^2} = -10 < 0$; thus relative maximum at $p_A = 80$, $p_B = 85$.

25. $p_A = 100 - q_A$, $p_B = 84 - q_B$, $c = 600 + 4(q_A + q_B)$.

Revenue from market A $= r_A = p_A q_A = (100 - q_A)q_A$.

Revenue from market B $= r_B = p_B q_B = (84 - q_B)q_B$.

Total Profit = Total Revenue – Total Cost

$P = (100 - q_A)q_A + (84 - q_B)q_B - \big[600 + 4(q_A + q_B)\big]$

$$\begin{cases} \dfrac{\partial P}{\partial q_A} = 96 - 2q_A = 0 \\ \dfrac{\partial P}{\partial q_B} = 80 - 2q_B = 0 \end{cases}$$

Critical point: $q_A = 48$, $q_B = 40$

$\dfrac{\partial^2 P}{\partial q_A^2} = -2$, $\dfrac{\partial^2 P}{\partial q_B^2} = -2$, $\dfrac{\partial^2 P}{\partial q_B \partial q_A} = 0$.

At $q_A = 48$ and $q_B = 40$, then $D = (-2)(-2) - 0^2 = 4 > 0$ and $\dfrac{\partial^2 P}{\partial q_A^2} = -2 < 0$; thus relative maximum at

$q_A = 48$, $q_B = 40$. When $q_A = 48$ and $q_B = 40$, then selling prices are $p_A = 52$, $p_B = 44$, and profit = 3304.

27. $c = 1.5q_A^2 + 4.5q_B^2$, $p_A = 36 - q_A^2$, $p_B = 30 - q_B^2$

Total Profit = Total Revenue – Total Cost

$$P = (p_A q_A + p_B q_B) - c$$

$$P = 36q_A - q_A^3 + 30q_B - q_B^3 - (1.5q_A^2 + 4.5q_B^2)$$

$$\begin{cases} \dfrac{\partial P}{\partial q_A} = 36 - 3q_A - 3q_A^2 = 3(4 + q_A)(3 - q_A) \\ \dfrac{\partial P}{\partial q_B} = 30 - 9q_B - 3q_B^2 = 3(5 + q_B)(2 - q_B) \end{cases}$$

Since we want $q_A \geq 0$ and $q_B \geq 0$, the Critical point occurs when $q_A = 3$ and $q_B = 2$.

$$\dfrac{\partial^2 P}{\partial q_A^2} = -3 - 6q_A, \quad \dfrac{\partial^2 P}{\partial q_B^2} = -9 - 6q_B, \quad \dfrac{\partial^2 P}{\partial q_B \partial_A} = 0. \text{ When } q_A = 3 \text{ and } q_B = 2, \text{ then}$$

$$D = (-21)(-21) - 0^2 > 0 \text{ and } \dfrac{\partial^2 P}{\partial q_A^2} = -21 < 0; \text{ thus relative maximum at } q_A = 3, q_B = 2.$$

29. Refer to the diagram in the text.

$xyz = 6$

$C = 3xy + 2[1(xz)] + 2[0.5(yz)]$

Note that $z = \dfrac{6}{xy}$. Thus

$$C = 3xy + 2xz + yz = 3xy + 2x\left(\dfrac{6}{xy}\right) + y\left(\dfrac{6}{xy}\right)$$

$$= 3xy + \dfrac{12}{y} + \dfrac{6}{x}$$

$$\begin{cases} \dfrac{\partial C}{\partial x} = 3y - \dfrac{6}{x^2} = 0 \\ \dfrac{dC}{dy} = 3x - \dfrac{12}{y^2} = 0 \end{cases}$$

A critical point occurs at $x = 1$ and $y = 2$. Thus $z = 3$.

$$\dfrac{\partial^2 C}{\partial x^2} = \dfrac{12}{x^3}, \quad \dfrac{\partial^2 C}{\partial y^2} = \dfrac{24}{y^3}, \quad \dfrac{\partial^2 C}{\partial x \partial y} = 3.$$

When $x = 1$ and $y = 2$, then

$d = (12)(3) - (3)^2 = 27 > 0$ and

$$\dfrac{\partial^2 C}{\partial x^2} = 12 > 0. \text{ Thus we have a minimum.}$$

The dimensions should be 1 ft by 2 ft by 3 ft.

31. $y = \dfrac{3x - 7}{2}$

$$f(x, y) = -2x^2 + 5\left(\dfrac{3x - 7}{2}\right)^2 + 7$$

Setting the derivative equal to 0 gives

$$-4x + 5(2)\left(\dfrac{3x - 7}{2}\right)\left(\dfrac{3}{2}\right) = 0,$$

$$-4x + \dfrac{15}{2}(3x - 7) = 0,$$

$-8x + 15(3x - 7) = 0$, $37x = 105$, or

$x = \dfrac{105}{37}$. The second-derivative is $\dfrac{37}{2} > 0$,

so we have a relative minimum. If $x = \dfrac{105}{37}$,

then $y = \dfrac{28}{37}$. Thus there is a relative

minimum at $\left(\dfrac{105}{37}, \dfrac{28}{37}\right)$.

33. $c = q_A^2 + 3q_B^2 + 2q_A q_B + aq_A + bq_B + d$

We are given that $(q_A, q_B) = (3, 1)$ is a critical point.

$$\begin{cases} \dfrac{\partial c}{\partial q_A} = 2q_A + 2q_B + a = 0 \\ \dfrac{\partial c}{\partial q_B} = 6q_B + 2q_A + b = 0 \end{cases}$$

Substituting the given values for q_A and q_B into both equations gives $a = -8$ and

$b = -12$. Since $c = 15$ when $q_A = 3$ and $q_B = 1$, from the joint-cost function we have

$15 = 3^2 + 3\left(1^2\right) + 2(3)(1) + (-8)(3) + (-12) + d$,

$15 = -18 + d$, $33 = d$. Thus $a = -8$, $b = -12$, $d = 33$.

35. a.   Profit = Total Revenue – Total Cost

$P = p_A q_A + p_B q_B$ – total cost

$$= \left(35 - 2q_A^2 + q_B\right)q_A + \left(20 - q_B + q_A\right)q_B - \left(-8 - 2q_A^3 + 3q_A q_B + 30q_A + 12q_B + \frac{1}{2}q_A^2\right)$$

$$P = 5q_A - \frac{1}{2}q_A^2 - q_A q_B + 8q_B - q_B^2 + 8$$

$$\begin{cases} \dfrac{\partial P}{\partial q_A} = 5 - q_A - q_B = 0 \\ \dfrac{\partial P}{\partial q_B} = -q_A + 8 - 2q_B = 0 \end{cases}$$

Critical point: $q_A = 2$, $q_B = 3$

$$\frac{\partial^2 P}{\partial q_A^2} = -1, \quad \frac{\partial^2 P}{\partial q_B^2} = -2, \quad \frac{\partial^2 P}{\partial q_B \partial q_A} = -1$$

At $q_A = 2$ and $q_B = 3$, then $D = (-1)(-2) - (-1)^2 = 1 > 0$ and $\dfrac{\partial^2 P}{\partial q_A^2} = -1 < 0$; thus there is a relative

maximum profit for 2 units of A and 3 units of B.

b.   Substituting $q_A = 2$ and $q_B = 3$ into the formulas for p_A, p_B, and P gives a selling price for A of 30, a selling price for B of 19, and a relative maximum profit of 25.

37. a. $P = 5T\left(1 - e^{-x}\right) - 20x - 0.1T^2$

b. $\dfrac{\partial P}{\partial T} = 5\left(1 - e^{-x}\right) - 0.2T$

$\dfrac{\partial P}{\partial x} = 5Te^{-x} - 20$

At the point $(T, x) = (20, \ln 5)$,

$\dfrac{\partial P}{\partial T} = 5\left(1 - e^{-\ln 5}\right) - 0.2(20)$

$= 5\left(1 - \dfrac{1}{5}\right) - 4 = 0$

$\dfrac{\partial P}{\partial x} = 5(20)e^{-\ln 5} - 20 = 100\left(\dfrac{1}{5}\right) - 20$

$= 0$

Thus $(20, \ln 5)$ is a critical point. In a similar fashion we verify that $\left(5, \ln\dfrac{5}{4}\right)$ is a critical point.

c. $\dfrac{\partial^2 P}{\partial T^2} = -0.2, \quad \dfrac{\partial^2 P}{\partial x^2} = -5Te^{-x}$,

$\dfrac{\partial^2 P}{\partial T \partial x} = 5e^{-x}$

At $(20, \ln 5)$,

$D = (-0.2)\left[-5(20)e^{-\ln 5}\right] - \left(5e^{-\ln 5}\right)^2$

$= 20\left(\dfrac{1}{5}\right) - \left[5\left(\dfrac{1}{5}\right)\right]^2 = 3 > 0$,

and $\dfrac{\partial^2 P}{\partial T^2} = -0.2 < 0$. Thus we get a

relative maximum at $(20, \ln 5)$.

At $\left(5, \ln\dfrac{5}{4}\right)$,

$$D = (-0.2)\left[-5(5)e^{-\ln\left(\frac{5}{4}\right)}\right] - \left[5e^{-\ln\left(\frac{5}{4}\right)}\right]^2$$

$$= 5\left(\frac{4}{5}\right) - \left[5\left(\frac{4}{5}\right)\right]^2 = -12 < 0\text{, so there is}$$

no relative extremum at $\left(5,\ \ln\frac{5}{4}\right)$.

Exercise 19.8

1. $f(x,\ y) = x^2 + 4y^2 + 6,\ 2x - 8y = 20$

   $F(x,\ y,\ \lambda) = x^2 + 4y^2 + 6 - \lambda(2x - 8y - 20)$

   $$\begin{cases} F_x = 2x - 2\lambda = 0 & (1) \\ F_y = 8y + 8\lambda = 0 & (2) \\ F_\lambda = -2x + 8y + 20 = 0 & (3) \end{cases}$$

   From (1), $x = \lambda$; from (2), $y = -\lambda$.
   Substituting $x = \lambda$ and $y = -\lambda$ into (3)
   gives $-2\lambda - 8\lambda + 20 = 0$, $-10\lambda = -20$, so
   $\lambda = 2$. Thus $x = 2$ and $y = -2$. Critical point
   of F: $(2, -2, 2)$. Critical point of f: $(2, -2)$.

3. $f(x, y, z) = x^2 + y^2 + z^2,\ 2x + y - z = 9$

   $F(x,\ y,\ z,\ \lambda) = x^2 + y^2 + z^2 - \lambda(2x + y - z - 9)$

   $$\begin{cases} F_x = 2x - 2\lambda = 0 & (1) \\ F_y = 2y - \lambda = 0 & (2) \\ F_z = 2z + \lambda = 0 & (3) \\ F_\lambda = -2x - y + z + 9 = 0 & (4) \end{cases}$$

   From (1), $x = \lambda$; from (2), $y = \frac{\lambda}{2}$; from (3),

   $z = -\frac{\lambda}{2}$. Substituting into (4) gives

   $-2\lambda - \frac{\lambda}{2} + \left(\frac{-\lambda}{2}\right) + 9 = 0$, $-6\lambda + 18 = 0$, so

   $\lambda = 3$. Thus $x = 3$, $y = \frac{3}{2}$, $z = -\frac{3}{2}$. Critical

   point of F: $\left(3,\ \frac{3}{2},\ -\frac{3}{2},\ 3\right)$. Critical point of

   f: $\left(3,\ \frac{3}{2},\ -\frac{3}{2}\right)$.

5. $f(x,\ y,\ z) = x^2 + xy + 2y^2 + z^2,\ x - 3y - 4z = 16$

   $F(x,\ y,\ z,\ \lambda)$

   $= x^2 + xy + 2y^2 + z^2 - \lambda(x - 3y - 4z - 16)$

   $$\begin{cases} F_x = 2x + y - \lambda = 0 & (1) \\ F_y = x + 4y + 3\lambda = 0 & (2) \\ F_z = 2z + 4\lambda = 0 & (3) \\ F_\lambda = -x + 3y + 4z + 16 = 0 & (4) \end{cases}$$

   Eliminating x from (1) and (2) yields
   $y = -\lambda$. Substituting $y = -\lambda$ into (2) yields
   $x = \lambda$. From (3), $z = -2\lambda$. Substituting
   $x = \lambda$, $y = -\lambda$, and $z = -2\lambda$ into (4) yields

   $\lambda = \frac{4}{3}$. Critical point of F:

   $\left(\frac{4}{3},\ -\frac{4}{3},\ -\frac{8}{3},\ \frac{4}{3}\right)$. Critical point of f:

   $\left(\frac{4}{3},\ -\frac{4}{3},\ -\frac{8}{3}\right)$.

7. $f(x, y, z) = xyz,\ x + 2y + 3z = 18\ (xyz \neq 0)$

   $f(x,\ y,\ z,\ \lambda) = xyz - \lambda(x + 2y + 3z - 18)$

   $$\begin{cases} F_x = yz - \lambda = 0 & (1) \\ F_y = xz - 2\lambda = 0 & (2) \\ F_z = xy - 3\lambda = 0 & (3) \\ F_\lambda = -x - 2y - 3z + 18 = 0 & (4) \end{cases}$$

   From (1) and (2), $y = \frac{x}{2}$. From (1) and (3),

   $z = \frac{x}{3}$. Hence from (4), $x = 6$, so $y = 3$ and
   $z = 2$. Critical point of f is $(6, 3, 2)$. Note that
   it is not necessary to determine λ.

9. $f(x,\ y,\ z) = x^2 + 2y - z^2,\ 2x - y = 0,$
   $y + z = 0$
   Since there are two constraints, two
   Lagrange multipliers are used.
   $F\left(x,\ y,\ z,\ \lambda_1,\ \lambda_2\right)$

$$= x^2 + 2y - z^2 - \lambda_1(2x - y) - \lambda_2(y + z)$$

$$\begin{cases} F_x = 2x - 2\lambda_1 = 0 & (1) \\ F_y = 2 + \lambda_1 - \lambda_2 = 0 & (2) \\ F_z = -2z - \lambda_2 = 0 & (3) \\ F_{\lambda_1} = -2x + y = 0 & (4) \\ F_{\lambda_2} = -y - z = 0 & (5) \end{cases}$$

From (1), $x = \lambda_1$. From (3), $z = -\frac{\lambda_2}{2}$. From (4) and (5), $2x = -z$, so $\lambda_1 = \frac{\lambda_2}{4}$. Substituting $\lambda_1 = \frac{\lambda_2}{4}$ into (2) yields $\lambda_2 = \frac{8}{3}$. Thus $\lambda_1 = \frac{2}{3}$, $x = \frac{2}{3}$, and $z = -\frac{4}{3}$. From (5), $y = -z$ and hence $y = \frac{4}{3}$. Critical point of f: $\left(\frac{2}{3}, \frac{4}{3}, -\frac{4}{3} \right)$.

11. $f(x, y, z) = xyz$, $x + y + z = 12$, $x + y - z = 0$ $(xyz \neq 0)$
Since there are two constraints, we use two Lagrange multipliers.
$$F(x, y, z, \lambda_1, \lambda_2) = xyz - \lambda_1(x + y + z - 12) - \lambda_2(x + y - z)$$

$$\begin{cases} F_x = yz - \lambda_1 - \lambda_2 = 0 & (1) \\ F_y = xz - \lambda_1 - \lambda_2 = 0 & (2) \\ F_z = xy - \lambda_1 + \lambda_2 = 0 & (3) \\ F_{\lambda_1} = -x - y - z + 12 = 0 & (4) \\ F_{\lambda_2} = -x - y + z = 0 & (5) \end{cases}$$

Subtracting (2) from (1) gives $yz - xz = 0$, so $y = x$. Subtracting (5) from (4) gives $-2z + 12 = 0$, so $z = 6$. Substituting $y = x$ and $z = 6$ in (5) gives $-2x + 6 = 0$, so $x = 3$. Thus $y = 3$. Critical point of f: (3, 3, 6).

13. We minimize $c = f(q_1, q_2) = 0.1q_1^2 + 7q_1 + 15q_2 + 1000$ subject to the constraint $q_1 + q_2 = 100$.

$$F(q_1, q_2, \lambda) = 0.1q_1^2 + 7q_1 + 15q_2 + 1000 - \lambda(q_1 + q_2 - 100)$$

$$\begin{cases} F_{q_1} = 0.2q_1 + 7 - \lambda = 0 & (1) \\ F_{q_2} = 15 - \lambda = 0 & (2) \\ F_\lambda = -q_1 - q_2 + 100 = 0 & (3) \end{cases}$$

From (2), $\lambda = 15$. Substituting $\lambda = 15$ into (1) gives $0.2q_1 + 7 - 15 = 0$, so $q_1 = 40$. Substituting $q_1 = 40$ into (3) gives $-40 - q_2 + 100 = 0$, so $q_2 = 60$. Thus $\lambda = 15$, $q_1 = 40$ and $q = 60$. Thus plant 1 should produce 40 units and plant 2 should produce 60 units.

15. We maximize $f(l, k) = 12l + 20k - l^2 - 2k^2$ subject to the constraint $4l + 8k = 88$.

$$F(l, k, \lambda) = 12l + 20k - l^2 - 2k^2 - \lambda(4l + 8k - 88)$$

$$\begin{cases} F_l = 12 - 2l - 4\lambda = 0 & (1) \\ F_k = 20 - 4k - 8\lambda = 0 & (2) \\ F_\lambda = -4l - 8k + 88 = 0 & (3) \end{cases}$$

Eliminating λ from (1) and (2) yields $k = l - 1$. Substituting $k = l - 1$ into (3) yields $l = 8$, so $k = 7$. Therefore the greatest output is $f(8, 7) = 74$ units (when $l = 8$, $k = 7$).

17. We maximize $P(x, y) = 9x^{\frac{1}{4}}y^{\frac{3}{4}} - x - y$ subject to the constraint $x + y = 60{,}000$.

$$F(x,\ y,\ \lambda) = 9x^{\frac{1}{4}}y^{\frac{3}{4}} - x - y - \lambda(x + y - 60{,}000)$$

$$\begin{cases} F_x = \dfrac{9}{4}x^{-\frac{3}{4}}y^{\frac{3}{4}} - 1 - \lambda = 0 & (1) \\[2mm] F_y = \dfrac{27}{4}x^{\frac{1}{4}}y^{-\frac{1}{4}} - 1 - \lambda = 0 & (2) \\[2mm] F_\lambda = -x - y + 60{,}000 = 0 & (3) \end{cases}$$

Solving (2) for λ and substituting in (1) gives $\dfrac{9}{4}x^{-\frac{3}{4}}y^{\frac{3}{4}} - \dfrac{27}{4}x^{\frac{1}{4}}y^{-\frac{1}{4}} = 0$, $\dfrac{9}{4}x^{-\frac{3}{4}}y^{\frac{3}{4}} = \dfrac{27}{4}x^{\frac{1}{4}}y^{-\frac{1}{4}}$, $y = 3x$.
Substituting for y in (3) $\Rightarrow -4x - 60{,}000 = 0$, so $x = 15{,}000$, from which $y = 45{,}000$. Thus each month $\$15{,}000$ should be spent on newspaper advertising and $\$45{,}000$ on TV advertising.

19. We minimize $B(x,\ y,\ z) = x^2 + y^2 + 2z^2$ subject to $x + y = 20$ and $y + z = 20$.
Since there are two constraints, we use two Lagrange multipliers.

$$F\left(x,\ y,\ z,\ \lambda_1,\ \lambda_2\right) = x^2 + y^2 + 2z^2 - \lambda_1(x + y - 20) - \lambda_2(y + z - 20)$$

$$\begin{cases} F_x = 2x - \lambda_1 = 0 & (1) \\ F_y = 2y - \lambda_1 - \lambda_2 = 0 & (2) \\ F_z = 4z - \lambda_2 = 0 & (3) \\ F_{\lambda_1} = -x - y + 20 = 0 & (4) \\ F_{\lambda_2} = -y - z + 20 = 0 & (5) \end{cases}$$

Eliminating y from (4) and (5) gives $x = z$. From (1) and (3), $\lambda_1 = 2x$ and $\lambda_2 = 4z$. Substituting in (2) we have $2y - 2x - 4z = 0$, $2y - 2x - 4x = 0$, $2y - 6x = 0$, $y = 3x$. Substituting in (5) gives $-(3x) - x + 20 = 0$, so $x = 5$. Thus $z = 5$ and $y = 15$. Therefore, $x = 5, y = 15, z = 5$.

21. $U = x^3y^3,\ p_x = 2,\ p_y = 3, I = 48\ \left(x^3y^3 \neq 0\right)$

We want to maximize $U = x^3y^3$ subject to $2x + 3y = 48$.

$$F(x, y,\ \lambda) = x^3y^3 - \lambda(2x + 3y - 48)$$

$$\begin{cases} F_x = 3x^2y^3 - 2\lambda = 0 & (1) \\ F_y = 3x^3y^2 - 3\lambda = 0 & (2) \\ F_\lambda = -2x - 3y + 48 = 0 & (3) \end{cases}$$

From (1), $\lambda = \dfrac{3}{2}x^2y^3$ and from (2), $\lambda = x^3y^2$. Thus $\dfrac{3}{2}x^2y^3 = x^3y^2$, so $x = \dfrac{3}{2}y$. Substituting this

expression for x into (3) yields $y = 8$. Hence $x = \left(\dfrac{3}{2}\right)8 = 12$.

23. $U = f(x, y, z) = xyz$
$p_x = 2,\ p_y = 1,\ p_z = 4,\ I = 60$
$(xyz \neq 0)$
$F(x,\ y,\ z,\ \lambda) = xyz - \lambda(2x + y + 4z - 60)$

$$\begin{cases} F_x = yz - 2\lambda = 0 & (1) \\ F_y = xz - \lambda = 0 & (2) \\ F_z = xy - 4\lambda = 0 & (3) \\ F_\lambda = -2x - y - 4z + 60 = 0 & (4) \end{cases}$$

From (1) and (2), $\frac{1}{2}yz = xz$, so $y = 2x$.

Similarly, from (1) and (3), $z = \frac{x}{2}$.

Substituting

$y = 2x$ and $z = \frac{x}{2}$ into (4) yields $x = 10$.

Thus
$y = 20$ and $z = 5$.

Exercise 19.9

1. $n = 6$, $\Sigma x_i = 21$, $\Sigma y_i = 18.6$, $\Sigma x_i y_i = 75.7$, $\Sigma x_i^2 = 91$.

$$\hat{a} = \frac{\left(\Sigma x_i^2\right)\left(\Sigma y_i\right) - \left(\Sigma x_i\right)\left(\Sigma x_i y_i\right)}{n\Sigma x_i^2 - \left(\Sigma x_i\right)^2}$$

$$= \frac{91(18.6) - 21(75.7)}{6(91) - (21)^2} = 0.98$$

$$\hat{b} = \frac{n\Sigma x_i y_i - \left(\Sigma x_i\right)\left(\Sigma y_i\right)}{n\Sigma x_i^2 - \left(\Sigma x_i\right)^2}$$

$$= \frac{6(75.7) - 21(18.6)}{6(91) - (21)^2} = 0.61$$

Thus $\hat{y} = 0.98 + 0.61x$. When $x = 3.5$, then $\hat{y} = 3.12$.

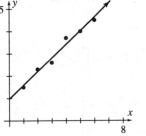

3. $n = 5$, $\Sigma x_i = 22$, $\Sigma y_i = 37$, $\Sigma x_i y_i = 189$, $\Sigma x_i^2 = 112.5$. $\hat{a} = 0.057$, $\hat{b} = 1.67$. Thus $\hat{y} = 0.057 + 1.67x$. When $x = 3.5$, then $\hat{y} = 5.90$.

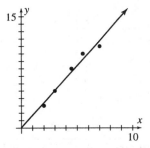

5. $n = 6$,
$\Sigma p_i = 260$, $\Sigma q_i = 329$, $\Sigma p_i q_i = 12,760$,
$\Sigma p_i^2 = 13,600$.

$$\hat{a} = \frac{\left(\Sigma p_i^2\right)\left(\Sigma q_i\right) - \left(\Sigma p_i\right)\left(\Sigma p_i q_i\right)}{n\Sigma p_i^2 - \left(\Sigma p_i\right)^2}$$

$$= \frac{(13,600)(329) - (260)(12,760)}{6(13,600) - (260)^2} = 82.6$$

$$\hat{b} = \frac{n\Sigma p_i q_i - \left(\Sigma p_i\right)\left(\Sigma q_i\right)}{n\Sigma p_i^2 - \left(\Sigma p_i\right)^2}$$

$$= \frac{6(12,760) - (260)(329)}{6(13,600) - (260)^2} = -0.641$$

Thus $\hat{q} = 82.6 - 0.641p$.

7. $n = 4$,
$\Sigma x_i = 160$, $\Sigma y_i = 420.8$, $\Sigma x_i y_i = 16,915.2$,
$\Sigma x_i^2 = 7040$. $\hat{a} = 100$, $\hat{b} = 0.13$. Thus
$\hat{y} = 100 + 0.13x$. When $x = 40$, then
$\hat{y} = 105.2$.

9.

Year (x)	1	2	3	4	5
Production (y)	10	15	16	18	21

$n = 5$,
$\Sigma x_i = 15$, $\Sigma y_i = 80$, $\Sigma x_i y_i = 265$, $\Sigma x_i^2 = 55$.

$$\hat{a} = \frac{\left(\Sigma x_i^2\right)\left(\Sigma y_i\right) - \left(\Sigma x_i\right)\left(\Sigma x_i y_i\right)}{n\Sigma x_i^2 - \left(\Sigma x_i\right)^2}$$

$$= \frac{55(80) - 15(265)}{5(55) - (15)^2} = 8.5$$

$$\hat{b} = \frac{n\Sigma x_i y_i - (\Sigma x_i)(\Sigma y_i)}{n\Sigma x_i^2 - (\Sigma x_i)^2}$$

$$= \frac{5(265) - 15(80)}{5(55) - (15)^2} = 2.5$$

Thus $\hat{y} = 8.5 + 2.5x$

11. a.

Year (x)	1	2	3	4	5
Quantity (y)	35	31	26	24	26

$n = 5$, $\Sigma x_i = 15$, $\Sigma y_i = 142$, $\Sigma x_i y_i = 401$, $\Sigma x_i^2 = 55$. $\hat{a} = 35.9$, $\hat{b} = -2.5$. Thus $\hat{y} = 35.9 - 2.5x$.

b.

Year (x)	−2	−1	0	1	2
Quantity (y)	35	31	26	24	26

$n = 5$, $\Sigma x_i = 0$, $\Sigma y_i = 142$, $\Sigma x_i y_i = -25$, $\Sigma x_i^2 = 10$. $\hat{a} = \dfrac{\Sigma y_i}{n} = 28.4$ and $\hat{b} = \dfrac{\Sigma x_i y_i}{\Sigma x_i^2} = -2.5$. Thus

$\hat{y} = 28.4 - 2.5x$.

Exercise 19.11

1. $\displaystyle\int_0^3 \int_0^4 x\,dy\,dx = \int_0^3 xy\Big|_0^4 dx = \int_0^3 4x\,dx$

$\displaystyle = 2x^2\Big|_0^3 = 18$

3. $\displaystyle\int_0^1 \int_0^1 xy\,dx\,dy = \int_0^1 \frac{x^2 y}{2}\Big|_0^1 dy = \int_0^1 \frac{y}{2}\,dy$

$\displaystyle = \frac{y^2}{4}\Big|_0^1 = \frac{1}{4}$

5. $\displaystyle\int_1^3 \int_1^2 \left(x^2 - y\right)dx\,dy = \int_1^3 \left(\frac{x^3}{3} - xy\right)\Big|_1^2 dy$

$\displaystyle = \int_1^3 \left[\left(\frac{8}{3} - 2y\right) - \left(\frac{1}{3} - y\right)\right]dy = \int_1^3 \left(\frac{7}{3} - y\right)dy$

$\displaystyle = \left(\frac{7}{3}y - \frac{y^2}{2}\right)\Big|_1^3 = \left(7 - \frac{9}{2}\right) - \left(\frac{7}{3} - \frac{1}{2}\right) = \frac{2}{3}$

7. $\displaystyle\int_0^1 \int_0^2 (x + y)dy\,dx = \int_0^1 \left(xy + \frac{y^2}{2}\right)\Big|_0^2 dx$

$\displaystyle = \int_0^1 (2x + 2)dx = \left(x^2 + 2x\right)\Big|_0^1 = 3$

9. $\displaystyle\int_0^6 \int_0^{3x} y\,dy\,dx = \int_0^6 \frac{y^2}{2}\Big|_0^{3x} dx$

$\displaystyle = \int_0^6 \frac{9x^2}{2}\,dx = \frac{3x^3}{2}\Big|_0^6 = 324$

11. $\displaystyle\int_0^1 \int_{3x}^{x^2} 2x^2 y\,dy\,dx = \int_0^1 \left(x^2 y^2\right)\Big|_{3x}^{x^2} dx$

$\displaystyle = \int_0^1 \left(x^6 - 9x^4\right)dx = \left(\frac{x^7}{7} - \frac{9x^5}{5}\right)\Big|_0^1 = -\frac{58}{35}$

13. $\displaystyle\int_0^2\int_0^{\sqrt{4-y^2}} x\,dx\,dy = \int_0^2 \frac{x^2}{2}\bigg|_0^{\sqrt{4-y^2}}dy$

$\displaystyle = \int_0^2 \frac{4-y^2}{2}\,dy$

$\displaystyle = \int_0^2\left(2-\frac{y^2}{2}\right)dy = \left(2y-\frac{y^3}{6}\right)\bigg|_0^2$

$\displaystyle = \left(4-\frac{4}{3}\right)-0 = \frac{8}{3}$

15. $\displaystyle\int_{-1}^{1}\int_x^{1-x}(x+y)\,dy\,dx = \int_{-1}^{1}\left(xy+\frac{y^2}{2}\right)\bigg|_x^{1-x}dx$

$\displaystyle = \int_{-1}^{1}\left[x(1-x)+\frac{(1-x)^2}{2}-\left(x^2+\frac{x^2}{2}\right)\right]dx$

$\displaystyle = \int_{-1}^{1}\left[x-\frac{5x^2}{2}+\frac{(1-x)^2}{2}\right]dx$

$\displaystyle = \left[\frac{x^2}{2}-\frac{5x^3}{6}-\frac{(1-x)^3}{6}\right]\bigg|_{-1}^{1}$

$\displaystyle = \left[\frac{1}{2}-\frac{5}{6}-0\right]-\left[\frac{1}{2}+\frac{5}{6}-\frac{4}{3}\right] = -\frac{1}{3}$

17. $\displaystyle\int_0^1\int_0^y e^{x+y}dx\,dy = \int_0^1 e^{x+y}\bigg|_0^y dy$

$\displaystyle = \int_0^1\left(e^{2y}-e^y\right)dy$

$\displaystyle = \left[\frac{e^{2y}}{2}-e^y\right]\bigg|_0^1 = \frac{e^2}{2}-e-\left(\frac{1}{2}-1\right)$

$\displaystyle = \frac{e^2}{2}-e+\frac{1}{2}$

19. $\displaystyle\int_{-1}^{0}\int_{-1}^{2}\int_1^2 6xy^2z^3\,dx\,dy\,dz$

$\displaystyle = \int_{-1}^{0}\int_{-1}^{2}3x^2y^2z^3\bigg|_1^2 dy\,dz$

$\displaystyle = \int_{-1}^{0}\int_{-1}^{2}9y^2z^3\,dy\,dz = \int_{-1}^{0}3y^3z^3\bigg|_{-1}^2 dz$

$\displaystyle = \int_{-1}^{0}27z^3\,dz = \frac{27z^4}{4}\bigg|_{-1}^0 = -\frac{27}{4}$

21. $\displaystyle\int_0^1\int_{x^2}^{x}\int_0^{xy}dz\,dy\,dx = \int_0^1\int_{x^2}^{x}z\bigg|_0^{xy}dy\,dx$

$\displaystyle = \int_0^1\int_{x^2}^{x}xy\,dy\,dx = \int_0^1 \frac{xy^2}{2}\bigg|_{x^2}^x dx$

$\displaystyle = \int_0^1\left[\frac{x^3}{2}-\frac{x^5}{2}\right]dx = \left[\frac{x^4}{8}-\frac{x^6}{12}\right]\bigg|_0^1 = \frac{1}{24}$

23. $\displaystyle P(0\le x\le 2,\ 1\le y\le 2) = \int_1^2\int_0^2 e^{-(x+y)}dx\,dy$

$\displaystyle = \int_1^2 -e^{-(x+y)}\bigg|_0^2 dy = \int_1^2\left[-e^{-(2+y)}+e^{-y}\right]dy$

$\displaystyle = \left[e^{-(2+y)}-e^{-y}\right]\bigg|_1^2 = e^{-4}-e^{-2}-e^{-3}+e^{-1}$

25. $\displaystyle P(x\ge 1,\ y\ge 2) = \int_2^4\int_1^2 \frac{x}{8}dx\,dy = \int_2^4 \frac{x^2}{16}\bigg|_1^2 dy$

$\displaystyle = \int_2^4\left(\frac{4}{16}-\frac{1}{16}\right)dy = \int_2^4 \frac{3}{16}dy = \frac{3y}{16}\bigg|_2^4$

$\displaystyle = \frac{12}{16}-\frac{6}{16} = \frac{3}{8}$

Chapter 19 Review Problems

1. $2x+3y+z=9$ can be put in the form $Ax+By+Cz+D=0$, so the graph is a plane. The intercepts are $\left(\frac{9}{2},0,0\right)$, $(0,3,0)$, and $(0,0,9)$.

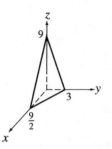

3. $z = y^2$. The y, z-trace is $z = y^2$, which is a parabola. For any fixed value of x, we obtain the parabola $z = y^2$.

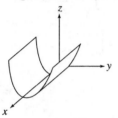

5. $f_x(x, y) = 2(2x) + 3(1)y + 0 - 0 = 4x + 3y$
$f_y(x, y) = 0 + 3x(1) + 2y - 0 = 3x + 2y$

7. $\dfrac{\partial z}{\partial x} = \dfrac{(x + y)(1) - x(1)}{(x + y)^2} = \dfrac{y}{(x + y)^2}$
Because $z = x(x + y)^{-1}$,
$\dfrac{\partial z}{\partial y} = x\left[(-1)(x + y)^{-2}(1)\right] = -\dfrac{x}{(x + y)^2}$.

9. $f(x, y) = \ln\sqrt{x^2 + y^2} = \frac{1}{2}\ln\left(x^2 + y^2\right)$
$\dfrac{\partial}{\partial y}[f(x, y)] = \frac{1}{2} \cdot \dfrac{1}{x^2 + y^2}(2y) = \dfrac{y}{x^2 + y^2}$

11. $w_x(x, y, z) = 2xyze^{x^2yz}$
$w_{xy}(x, y, z) = 2xz\left[y\left(e^{x^2yz} \cdot x^2z\right) + e^{x^2yz} \cdot 1\right]$
$= 2xze^{x^2yz}\left(x^2yz + 1\right)$

13. $\dfrac{\partial}{\partial z}[f(x, y, z)] = (x + y)[2z]$
$\dfrac{\partial^2}{\partial z^2}[f(x, y, z)] = (x + y)[2] = 2(x + y)$

15. $\dfrac{\partial w}{\partial y} = (x \ln z)\left[e^{yz} \cdot z\right] = xze^{yz}\ln z$
$\dfrac{\partial w}{\partial z} = x\left[e^{yz} \cdot \dfrac{1}{z} + (\ln z)\left(e^{yz} \cdot y\right)\right]$
$= xe^{yz}\left[\dfrac{1}{z} + y \ln z\right]$
$\dfrac{\partial^2 w}{\partial x \partial z} = e^{yz}\left[\dfrac{1}{z} + y \ln z\right]$

17. $f(x, y, z) = \dfrac{x + y}{xz} = \dfrac{1}{z} + \dfrac{y}{xz}$
$f_x(x, y, z) = -\dfrac{y}{x^2z}$
$f_{xy}(x, y, z) = -\dfrac{1}{x^2z}$
$f_{xyz}(x, y, z) = \dfrac{1}{x^2z^2}$
$f_{xyz}(2, 3, 4) = \dfrac{1}{2^2 \cdot 4^2} = \dfrac{1}{64}$

19. $\dfrac{\partial w}{\partial r} = \dfrac{\partial w}{\partial x}\dfrac{\partial x}{\partial r} + \dfrac{\partial w}{\partial y}\dfrac{\partial y}{\partial r}$
$= (2x + 2y)\left(e^r\right) + (2x + 6y)\left(\dfrac{1}{r + s}\right)$
$= 2(x + y)e^r + \dfrac{2(x + 3y)}{r + s}$
$\dfrac{\partial w}{\partial s} = \dfrac{\partial w}{\partial x}\dfrac{\partial x}{\partial s} + \dfrac{\partial w}{\partial y}\dfrac{\partial y}{\partial s}$
$= (2x + 2y)(0) + (2x + 6y)\left(\dfrac{1}{r + s}\right)$
$= \dfrac{2(x + 3y)}{r + s}$

21. $2x + 2y - 4z\dfrac{\partial z}{\partial x} + \left[x\dfrac{\partial z}{\partial x} + z(1)\right] + 0 = 0$
$(-4z + x)\dfrac{\partial z}{\partial x} = -(2x + 2y + z)$
$\dfrac{\partial z}{\partial x} = \dfrac{-(2x + 2y + z)}{-4z + x} = \dfrac{2x + 2y + z}{4z - x}$

23. $P = 20l^{0.7}k^{0.3}$. Marginal productivity functions are given by $\dfrac{\partial P}{\partial l} = 20(0.7)l^{-0.3}k^{0.3}$ and

$\dfrac{\partial P}{\partial k} = 20(0.3)l^{0.7}k^{-0.7}$. Thus $\dfrac{\partial P}{\partial l} = 14l^{-0.3}k^{0.3}$ and $\dfrac{\partial P}{\partial k} = 6l^{0.7}k^{-0.7}$.

25. $q_A = 200 - 3p_A + p_B$, $q_B = 50 - 5p_B + p_A$. Since $\dfrac{\partial q_A}{\partial p_B} = 1 > 0$ and $\dfrac{\partial q_B}{\partial p_A} = 1 > 0$, A and B are

competitive products.

27. $f(x, y) = x^2 + 2y^2 - 2xy - 4y + 3$

$\begin{cases} f_x(x, y) = 2x - 2y = 0 \\ f_y(x, y) = 4y - 2x - 4 = 0 \end{cases}$

Critical point: (2, 2)

$f_{xx}(x, y) = 2$, $f_{yy}(x, y) = 4$, $f_{xy}(x, y) = -2$ At (2, 2), $D = (2)(4) - (-2)^2 = 4 > 0$ and

$f_{xx}(x, y) = 2 > 0$; thus relative minimum at (2, 2).

29.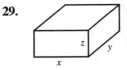

$xyz = 32$. Let S be the amount of cardboard used.

$S = xy + 2yz + 2xz$

$\quad = xy + 2y\left[\dfrac{32}{xy}\right] + 2x\left[\dfrac{32}{xy}\right]$

$\quad = xy + \dfrac{64}{x} + \dfrac{64}{y}$

$\dfrac{\partial S}{\partial x} = y - \dfrac{64}{x^2}$, $\dfrac{\partial S}{\partial y} = x - \dfrac{64}{y^2}$

The critical point occurs when $x = 4$, $y = 4$, and
$z = 2$, which gives a minimum. The dimensions are 4 ft by 4 ft by 2 ft.

31. Profit $= P = (p_A - 50)q_A + (p_B - 60)q_B$

$P = (p_A - 50)[250(p_B - p_A)] + (p_B - 60)[32,000 + 250(p_A - 2p_B)]$.

$\dfrac{\partial P}{\partial p_A} = (p_A - 50)(-250) + [250(p_B - p_A)](1) + 250(p_B - 60)$

$\quad = -500p_A + 500p_B - 250(10) = 500(-p_A + p_B - 5)$

Also, $\dfrac{\partial P}{\partial p_B} = (p_A - 50)(250) + (p_B - 60)(-500) + [32,000 + 250(p_A - 2p_B)]$

$\quad = 500p_A - 1000p_B + 49,500 = 500(p_A - 2p_B + 99)$

Setting $\dfrac{\partial P}{\partial p_A} = 0$ and $\dfrac{\partial P}{\partial p_B} = 0$ gives

$-p_A + p_B - 5 = 0$ (1)

and

$p_A - 2p_B + 99 = 0$ (2)

Adding Equations (1) and (2) gives $-p_B + 94 = 0$. So $p_B = 94$. From Equation (1), $p_A = p_B - 5$, so

$p_A = 94 - 5 = 89$. At $p_A = 89$ and $p_B = 94$, $D = \dfrac{\partial^2 P}{\partial p_A^2} \dfrac{\partial^2 P}{\partial p_B^2} - \dfrac{\partial^2 P}{\partial p_B \partial p_A} = (-500)(-1000) - (500)^2 > 0$

and $\dfrac{\partial^2 P}{\partial p_A^2} = -500 < 0$.

Thus there is a relative maximum profit when A is 89 cents per pound and B is 94 cents per pound.

33. $f(x, y, z) = x^2 + y^2 + z^2,\ 3x + 2y + z = 14$

$F(x, y, z, \lambda) = x^2 + y^2 + z^2 - \lambda(3x + 2y + z - 14)$

$\begin{cases} F_x = 2x - 3\lambda = 0 & (1) \\ F_y = 2y - 2\lambda = 0 & (2) \\ F_z = 2z - \lambda = 0 & (3) \\ F_\lambda = -3x - 2y - z + 14 = 0 & (4) \end{cases}$

From (1), $x = \frac{3\lambda}{2}$; from (2), $y = \lambda$, from (3), $z = \frac{\lambda}{2}$. Substituting into (4) gives

$-3\left(\frac{3\lambda}{2}\right) - 2\lambda - \frac{\lambda}{2} + 14 = 0$, from which $\lambda = 2$. Thus $x = 3$, $y = 2$, and $z = 1$.

Critical point of F: $(3, 2, 1, 2)$, so the critical point of f: $(3, 2, 1)$.

35.

Year (x)	1	2	3	4	5	6
Expenditures (y)	15	22	21	27	26	34

$n = 6,\ \Sigma x_i = 21,\ \Sigma y_i = 145,\ \Sigma x_i y_i = 564,\ \Sigma x_i^2 = 91$

$\hat{a} = \dfrac{\left(\Sigma x_i^2\right)\left(\Sigma y_i\right) - \left(\Sigma x_i\right)\left(\Sigma x_i y_i\right)}{n\Sigma x_i^2 - \left(\Sigma x_i\right)^2} = 12.87$

$\hat{b} = \dfrac{n\Sigma x_i y_i - \left(\Sigma x_i\right)\left(\Sigma y_i\right)}{n\Sigma x_i^2 - \left(\Sigma x_i\right)^2} = 3.23$

Thus $\hat{y} = 12.87 + 3.23x$

37. $\displaystyle\int_0^4 \int_{y/2}^2 xy\,dx\,dy = \int_0^4 \left.\frac{x^2 y}{2}\right|_{y/2}^2 dy = \int_0^4 \left(2y - \frac{y^3}{8}\right) dy = \left.\left(y^2 - \frac{y^4}{32}\right)\right|_0^4 = (16 - 8) - 0 = 8$

39. $\displaystyle\int_0^1 \int_{\sqrt{x}}^{x^2} \left(x^2 + 2xy - 3y^2\right) dy\,dx = \int_0^1 \left.\left(x^2 y + xy^2 - y^3\right)\right|_{\sqrt{x}}^{x^2} dx = \int_0^1 \left[\left(x^4 + x^5 - x^6\right) - \left(x^{\frac{5}{2}} + x^2 - x^{\frac{3}{2}}\right)\right] dx$

$= \left.\left[\frac{x^5}{5} + \frac{x^6}{6} - \frac{x^7}{7} - \frac{2x^{\frac{7}{2}}}{7} - \frac{x^3}{3} + \frac{2x^{\frac{5}{2}}}{5}\right]\right|_0^1 = \left[\frac{1}{5} + \frac{1}{6} - \frac{1}{7} - \frac{2}{7} - \frac{1}{3} + \frac{2}{5}\right] - 0 = \frac{1}{210}$

Mathematical Snapshot Chapter 19

1.

$$y = Ce^{ax} + 5, \quad y - 5 = Ce^{ax}, \quad \ln(y - 5) = ax + \ln C$$

x	y	$y - 5$	$\ln(y - 5)$
0	15	10	2.30259
1	12	7	1.94591
4	9	4	1.38629
7	7	2	0.69315
10	6	1	0.00000

$$n = 5, \ \Sigma x_i = 22, \ \Sigma \ln(y_i - 5) = 6.32794, \ \Sigma \left[x_i \ln(y_i - 5) \right] = 12.34312, \ \Sigma x_i^2 = 166$$

$$a = \frac{n\Sigma \left[x_i \ln(y_i - 5) \right] - \left(\Sigma x_i \right)\left[\Sigma \ln(y_i - 5) \right]}{n\left(\Sigma x_i^2 \right) - \left(\Sigma x_i \right)^2}$$

$$= \frac{5(12.34312) - 22(6.32794)}{5(166) - (22)^2} \approx -0.22399$$

$$\ln C = \frac{\left(\Sigma x_i^2 \right)\left[\Sigma \ln(y_i - 5) \right] - \left(\Sigma x_i \right)\left\{ \Sigma \left[x_i \ln(y_i - 5) \right] \right\}}{n\left(\Sigma x_i^2 \right) - \left(\Sigma x_i \right)^2}$$

$$= \frac{166(6.32794) - 22(12.34312)}{5(166) - (22)^2} \approx 2.25112$$

$$C \approx e^{2.25112} \approx 9.50$$

Thus $y = 9.50e^{-0.22399x} + 5$.

3. Newton's law of cooling: $\frac{dT}{dt} = k(T - a)$, where $a = 45$. Thus $\frac{dT}{dt} = k(T - 45)$, $\frac{dT}{T - 45} = k\, dt$,

$\int \frac{dT}{T - 45} = \int k\, dt$, $\ln|T - 45| = kt + C$. Because $T - 45 > 0$, $\ln(T - 45) = kt + C$. Thus $T - 45 = e^{kt+C}$, or

$T = e^{kt+C} + 45 = e^C e^{kt} + 45 = C_1 e^{kt} + 45$, where $C_1 = e^C$. So $T = C_1 e^{kt} + 45$. When $t = 0$, then $T = 124$.

Hence $124 = C_1 + 45$, or $C_1 = 79$. Thus $T = 79e^{kt} + 45$. When $t = 128$, then $T = 64$, so

$$64 = 79e^{128k} + 45, \ \ 19 = 79e^{128k}, \ \ e^{128k} = \frac{19}{79}, \ 128k = \ln \frac{19}{79}, \ k = \frac{\ln\left(\frac{19}{79} \right)}{128} \approx -0.01113. \ \text{Thus}$$

$$T = 79e^{-0.01113t} + 45.$$

Appendix A: Concepts for Calculus

A.1 Review: Slopes and Equation of Lines

1. $m = \dfrac{y_2 - y_1}{x_2 - x_1} = \dfrac{-1 - 4}{2 - (-6)} = \dfrac{-5}{8} = -\dfrac{5}{8}$

3. In point-slope form we have

$y - 5 = \dfrac{3}{2}(x - 0)$

$y - 5 = \dfrac{3}{2}x$

$3x - 2y + 10 = 0$

5. $m = \dfrac{2 - (-3)}{8 - 4} = \dfrac{5}{4}$

$y - (-3) = \dfrac{5}{4}(x - 4)$

$y + 3 = \dfrac{5}{4}x - 5$

$4y + 12 = 5x - 20$

$5x - 4y - 32 = 0$

7. $2 + x = -3$

$x = -5$

The line is vertical. The slope is undefined.
There is no y-intercept.

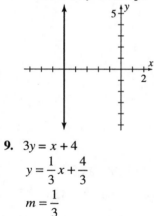

9. $3y = x + 4$

$y = \dfrac{1}{3}x + \dfrac{4}{3}$

$m = \dfrac{1}{3}$

$y - y_1 = m(x - x_1)$

$y - 7 = \dfrac{1}{3}(x - 6)$

$y - 7 = \dfrac{1}{3}x - 2$

$y = \dfrac{1}{3}x + 5$

A.2 Secant Lines and Average Rate of Change

1. Her average rate of growth was

$\dfrac{60 - 42}{12 - 8} = \dfrac{18}{4} = 4.5$ inches per year.

3. a. Average rate $= \dfrac{70 - 49}{14 - 8} = \dfrac{21}{6}$

$= 3.5$ degrees per day

b. Average rate $= \dfrac{65 - 70}{18 - 14} = \dfrac{-5}{4}$

$= -1.25$ degrees per day

c. Average rate $= \dfrac{73 - 57}{21 - 5} = \dfrac{16}{16}$

$= 1$ degree per day

d. Average rate $= \dfrac{79 - 63}{30 - 3} = \dfrac{16}{27}$

≈ 0.59 degrees per day

5.

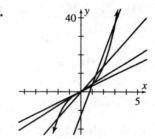

a. Average rate $= \dfrac{g(3) - g(1)}{3 - 1}$

$= \dfrac{3^3 + 3(3) - [1^3 + 3(1)]}{3 - 1} = \dfrac{36 - 4}{2}$

$= \dfrac{32}{2} = 16$

b. Average rate $= \dfrac{g(2) - g(-2)}{2 - (-2)}$

$= \dfrac{2^3 + 3(2) - [(-2)^3 + 3(-2)]}{2 + 2}$

$= \dfrac{14 - (-14)}{4}$

$= \dfrac{28}{4} = 7$

c. Average rate $= \dfrac{g(1) - g(0)}{1 - 0}$

$= \dfrac{1^3 + 3(1) - [(0)^3 + 3(0)]}{1} = \dfrac{4 - 0}{1} = 4$

d. Average rate $= \dfrac{g(0.1) - g(0)}{0.1 - 0}$

$= \dfrac{(0.1)^3 + 3(0.1) - [(0)^3 + 3(0)]}{0.1} = \dfrac{0.301}{0.1}$

$= 3.01$

7. a. Average rate $= \dfrac{g(5) - g(0)}{5 - 0} = \dfrac{5^3 - 0^3}{5}$

$= \dfrac{125}{5} = 25$

b. Average rate $= \dfrac{g(8) - g(3)}{8 - 3} = \dfrac{8^3 - 3^3}{5}$

$= \dfrac{512 - 27}{5} = \dfrac{485}{5} = 97$

c. Average rate $= \dfrac{g(3 + h) - g(3)}{3 + h - 3}$

$= \dfrac{(3 + h)^3 - 3^3}{h}$

$= \dfrac{27 + 27h + 9h^2 + h^3 - 27}{h}$

$= \dfrac{27h + 9h^2 + h^3}{h} = 27 + 9h + h^2$

d. Average rate $= \dfrac{g(x_0 + h) - g(x_0)}{x_0 + h - x_0}$

$= \dfrac{(x_0 + h)^3 - x_0^3}{h}$

$= \dfrac{x_0^3 + 3x_0^2 h + 3x_0 h^2 + h^3 - x_0^3}{h}$

$= \dfrac{3x_0^2 h + 3x_0 h^2 + h^3}{h}$

$= 3x_0^2 + 3x_0 h + h^2$

A.3 Slope of a Curve and Derivative

1. a. $\dfrac{f(0 + h) - f(0)}{h} = \dfrac{h^2 - 0}{h} = h$

As h approaches 0, h approaches 0.

Therefore, the slope is 0, so $\dfrac{df}{dx}(0) = 0$.

b. $\dfrac{f(-4 + h) - f(-4)}{h} = \dfrac{(-4 + h)^2 - (-4)^2}{h}$

$= \dfrac{16 - 8h + h^2 - 16}{h} = \dfrac{-8h + h^2}{h}$

$= -8 + h$

As h approaches 0, $-8 + h$ approaches -8. Therefore the slope is -8, so

$\dfrac{df}{dx}(-4) = -8.$

c. $\dfrac{f(x_0 + h) - f(x_0)}{h} = \dfrac{(x_0 + h)^2 - x_0^2}{h}$

$= \dfrac{x_0^2 + 2x_0 h + h^2 - x_0^2}{h} = \dfrac{2x_0 h + h^2}{h}$

$= 2x_0 + h$

As h approaches 0, $2x_0 + h$ approaches

$2x_0$. Therefore, the slope is $2x_0$, so

$$\frac{df}{dx}(x_0) = 2x_0.$$

3. a. $\dfrac{f(0+h)-f(0)}{h} = \dfrac{\frac{1}{0+h-4} - \frac{1}{0-4}}{h}$

$$= \frac{\frac{1}{h-4} + \frac{1}{4}}{h} = \frac{\frac{1}{h-4} + \frac{1}{4}}{h} \cdot \frac{4(h-4)}{4(h-4)}$$

$$= \frac{4+h-4}{4h(h-4)} = \frac{h}{4h(h-4)} = \frac{1}{4(h-4)}$$

As h approaches 0, $\dfrac{1}{4(h-4)}$

approaches $\dfrac{1}{-16} = -\dfrac{1}{16}$. Thus,

$$\frac{df}{dx}(0) = -\frac{1}{16}.$$

b. $\dfrac{f(10+h)-f(10)}{h} = \dfrac{\frac{1}{10+h-4} - \frac{1}{10-4}}{h}$

$$= \frac{\frac{1}{6+h} - \frac{1}{6}}{h} = \frac{\frac{1}{6+h} - \frac{1}{6}}{h} \cdot \frac{6(6+h)}{6(6+h)}$$

$$= \frac{6-(6+h)}{6h(6+h)} = \frac{-h}{6h(6+h)} = \frac{-1}{6(6+h)}$$

As h approaches 0, $\dfrac{-1}{6(6+h)}$ approaches

$-\dfrac{1}{36}$. Thus $\dfrac{df}{dx}(10) = -\dfrac{1}{36}$.

c. $\dfrac{f(x_0+h)-f(x_0)}{h} = \dfrac{\frac{1}{x_0+h-4} - \frac{1}{x_0-4}}{h}$

$$= \frac{\frac{1}{x_0+h-4} - \frac{1}{x_0-4}}{h} \cdot \frac{(x_0+h-4)(x_0-4)}{(x_0+h-4)(x_0-4)}$$

$$= \frac{x_0-4-(x_0+h-4)}{h(x_0+h-4)(x_0-4)}$$

$$= \frac{-h}{h(x_0+h-4)(x_0-4)}$$

$$= \frac{-1}{(x_0+h-4)(x_0-4)}$$

As h approaches 0,

$\dfrac{-1}{(x_0+h-4)(x_0-4)}$ approaches

$-\dfrac{1}{(x_0-4)^2}$. Thus for $x_0 \neq 4$,

$$\frac{df}{dx}(x_0) = -\frac{1}{(x_0-4)^2}.$$

5. To avoid confusion, we will use k instead of h.

a. $\dfrac{h(0+k)-h(0)}{k} = \dfrac{-16k^2+32k-0}{k}$

$$= -16k+32$$

As k approaches 0, $-16k+32$ approaches 32. Thus, $\dfrac{dh}{dt}(0) = 32$.

b. $\dfrac{h(2+k)-h(2)}{k}$

$$= \frac{-16(2+k)^2 + 32(2+k) - [-16(2)^2 + 32(2)]}{k}$$

$$= \frac{-64 - 64k - 16k^2 + 64 + 32k - (-64 + 64)}{k}$$

$$= \frac{-32k - 16k^2}{k} = -32 - 16k$$

As k approaches 0, $-32 - k$ approaches -32. Thus, $\dfrac{dh}{dt}(2) = -32$.

c. $\dfrac{h(3 + k) - h(3)}{k}$

$$= \frac{-16(3 + k)^2 + 32(3 + k) - [-16(3)^2 + 32(3)]}{k}$$

$$= \frac{-144 - 96k - 16k^2 + 96 + 32k - (-144 + 96)}{k}$$

$$= \frac{-64k - 16k^2}{k} = -64 - 16k$$

As k approaches 0, $-64 - 16k$ approaches -64. Thus $\dfrac{dh}{dt}(3) = -64$.

7. $\dfrac{c(75 + h) - c(75)}{h}$

$$= \frac{0.05(75 + h)^2 + 28(75 + h) + 5000 - [0.05(75)^2 + 28(75) + 5000]}{h}$$

$$= \frac{281.25 + 7.5h + 0.05h^2 + 2100 + 28h + 5000 - [281.25 + 2100 + 5000]}{h}$$

$$= \frac{35.5h + 0.05h^2}{h} = 35.5 + 0.05h$$

As h approaches 0, $35.5 + 0.05h$ approaches 35.5. Thus $\dfrac{dc}{dq}(75) = 35.5$.

9. a. $\dfrac{f(x + h) - f(x)}{h} = \dfrac{11 - 11}{h} = \dfrac{0}{h} = 0$

When $h = 0$, $0 = 0$, thus $\dfrac{dy}{dx} = 0$.

b. $\dfrac{f(x + h) - f(x)}{h} = \dfrac{5(x + h) - 5x}{h}$

$$= \frac{5x + 5h - 5x}{h} = \frac{5h}{h} = 5$$

When $h = 0$, $5 = 5$, thus $\dfrac{dy}{dx} = 5$.

c. $\dfrac{f(x + h) - f(x)}{h}$

$$= \frac{5(x + h) + 11 - (5x + 11)}{h}$$

$$= \frac{5x + 5h + 11 - 5x - 11}{h} = \frac{5h}{5} = 5$$

When $h = 0$, $5 = 5$, thus $\dfrac{dy}{dx} = 5$.

11. a.
$$\frac{f(x+h)-f(x)}{h} = \frac{\frac{1}{5(x+h)+11} - \frac{1}{5x+11}}{h}$$

$$= \frac{\frac{1}{5x+5h+11} - \frac{1}{5x+11}}{h} \cdot \frac{(5x+5h+11)(5x+11)}{(5x+5h+11)(5x+11)}$$

$$= \frac{5x+11-(5x+5h+11)}{h(5x+5h+11)(5x+11)}$$

$$= \frac{-5h}{h(5x+5h+11)(5x+11)}$$

$$= \frac{-5}{(5x+5h+11)(5x+11)}$$

When $h = 0$, $\dfrac{-5}{(5x+5h+11)(5x+11)} = -\dfrac{5}{(5x+11)^2}$, thus $\dfrac{dy}{dx} = -\dfrac{5}{(5x+11)^2}$.

b.
$$\frac{f(x+h)-f(x)}{h} = \frac{\frac{1492}{5(x+h)+11} - \frac{1492}{5x+11}}{h}$$

$$= \frac{\frac{1492}{5x+5h+11} - \frac{1492}{5x+11}}{h} \cdot \frac{(5x+5h+11)(5x+11)}{(5x+5h+11)(5x+11)}$$

$$= \frac{1492(5x+11) - 1492(5x+5h+11)}{h(5x+5h+11)(5x+11)}$$

$$= \frac{-7460h}{h(5x+5h+11)(5x+11)}$$

$$= -\frac{7460}{(5x+5h+11)(5x+11)}$$

When $h = 0$, $-\dfrac{7460}{(5x+5h+11)(5x+11)} = -\dfrac{7460}{(5x+11)^2}$, thus, $\dfrac{dy}{dx} = -\dfrac{7460}{(5x+11)^2}$.

c.
$$\frac{f(x+h)-f(x)}{h} = \frac{\frac{3}{12-5(x+h)} - \frac{3}{12-5x}}{h}$$

$$= \frac{\frac{3}{12-5x-5h} - \frac{3}{12-5x}}{h} \cdot \frac{(12-5x-5h)(12-5x)}{(12-5x-5h)(12-5x)}$$

$$= \frac{3(12-5x) - 3(12-5x-5h)}{h(12-5x-5h)(12-5x)}$$

$$= \frac{15h}{h(12-5x-5h)(12-5x)}$$

$$= \frac{15}{(12-5x-5h)(12-5x)}$$

When $h = 0$, $\dfrac{15}{(12-5x-5h)(12-5x)} = \dfrac{15}{(12-5x)^2}$, thus $\dfrac{dy}{dx} = \dfrac{15}{(12-5x)^2}$.

d. $\dfrac{f(x+h)-f(x)}{h}$

$= \dfrac{\frac{3}{12-5(x+h)}+11-\left(\frac{3}{12-5x}+11\right)}{h}$

$= \dfrac{\frac{3}{12-5x-5h}-\frac{3}{12-5x}}{h}\cdot\dfrac{(12-5x-5h)(12-5x)}{(12-5x-5h)(12-5x)} = \dfrac{3(12-5x)-3(12-5x-5h)}{h(12-5x-5h)(12-5x)}$

$= \dfrac{15h}{h(12-5x-5h)(12-5x)}$

$= \dfrac{15}{(12-5x-5h)(12-5x)}$

When $h=0$, $\dfrac{15}{(12-5x-5h)(12-5x)} = \dfrac{15}{(12-5x)^2}$, thus $\dfrac{dy}{dx} = \dfrac{15}{(12-5x)^2}$.

A.4 Areas of Geometric Shapes

1. The figure consists of a rectangle topped by a triangle. The rectangle is 22 feet by 7 feet, while the triangle has a base of 16 feet and height 12 feet.
   $A_{\text{rectangle}} = bh = (22)(7) = 154$

   $A_{\text{triangle}} = \dfrac{1}{2}bh = \dfrac{1}{2}(16)(12) = 96$
   The area is $154 + 96 = 250$ square feet.

3. The figure consists of a rectangle topped by a trapezoid. The rectangle is 15 in. by 8 in., while the trapezoid has bases of 15 in. and 10 in. and height 3 in.
   $A_{\text{rectangle}} = (15)(8) = 120$

   $A_{\text{trapezoid}} = \dfrac{1}{2}(3)(15+10) = 37.5$
   The area is $120 + 37.5$
   $= 157.5$ square inches.

5. The region consists of three rectangles, each having width 3 units and height of 2, 9, and 6 units, respectively. The area is
   $3(2) + 3(9) + 3(6) = 6 + 27 + 18$
   $= 51$ square units.

7.

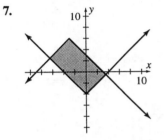

Notice that the slopes of the opposite sides are the same, and that the slopes of adjacent sides are negative reciprocals of one another. Thus, the region is a rectangle. One side extends from
$(-6.5, 2.5)$ to $(-3, 6)$, hence has length
$\sqrt{[-6.5-(-3)]^2 + [2.5-6]^2} = \sqrt{24.5}$
$= \sqrt{\dfrac{49}{2}} = \dfrac{7}{\sqrt{2}}$.
The upper adjacent side extends from $(-3, 6)$ to $(3.5, -0.5)$, hence has length
$\sqrt{[-3-3.5]^2 + [6-(-0.5)]^2} = \sqrt{84.5}$
$= \sqrt{\dfrac{169}{2}} = \dfrac{13}{\sqrt{2}}$.
The region has area
$\left(\dfrac{7}{\sqrt{2}}\right)\left(\dfrac{13}{\sqrt{2}}\right) = \dfrac{91}{2} = 45.5$ square units.

A.5 Sigma Notation

1. The lower limit of summation is 12, upper limit of summation is 17, and the index of summation is t.

3. $\displaystyle\sum_{i=1}^{7} 6i = 6\sum_{i=1}^{7} i = 6 \cdot \frac{7(7+1)}{2} = 6 \cdot 28 = 168$

5. $\displaystyle\sum_{k=3}^{9}(10k+16)$

   $= [10(3)+16] + [10(4)+16] + [10(5)+16] + [10(6)+16] + [10(7)+16] + [10(8)+16] + [10(9)+16]$
   $= 46 + 56 + 66 + 76 + 86 + 96 + 106$
   $= 532$

7. $36 + 37 + 38 + 39 + \cdots + 60 = \displaystyle\sum_{i=36}^{60} i$

9. $5^3 + 5^4 + 5^5 + 5^6 + 5^7 + 5^8 = \displaystyle\sum_{j=3}^{8} 5^j$

11. $\displaystyle\sum_{k=1}^{52} 10 = 10\sum_{k=1}^{52}(1) = 10(52) = 520$

13. $\displaystyle\sum_{k=1}^{n}\left(5 \cdot \frac{1}{n}\right) = \left(5 \cdot \frac{1}{n}\right)\sum_{k=1}^{n}(1) = \left(5 \cdot \frac{1}{n}\right)(n) = 5$

15. $\displaystyle\sum_{k=51}^{100} 10k = 10\sum_{i=1}^{50}(i+50)$

   $= 10\displaystyle\sum_{i=1}^{50} i + (10)(50)\sum_{i=1}^{50}(1)$

   $= 10 \cdot \dfrac{50(51)}{2} + 500(50) = 12{,}750 + 25{,}000$
   $= 37{,}750$

17. $\displaystyle\sum_{k=1}^{20}(5k^2 + 3k) = 5\sum_{k=1}^{20} k^2 + 3\sum_{k=1}^{20} k$

   $= 5 \cdot \dfrac{20(21)(41)}{6} + 3\dfrac{20(21)}{2}$
   $= 5(2870) + 3(210) = 14{,}980$

19. $\displaystyle\sum_{k=51}^{100} k^2 = \sum_{i=1}^{50}(i+50)^2$

   $= \displaystyle\sum_{i=1}^{50}(i^2 + 100i + 2500)$

   $= \displaystyle\sum_{i=1}^{50} i^2 + 100\sum_{i=1}^{50} i + 2500\sum_{i=1}^{50}(1)$

   $= \dfrac{50(51)(101)}{6} + 100\dfrac{50(51)}{2} + 2500(50)$
   $= 42{,}925 + 127{,}500 + 125{,}000 = 295{,}425$

21. $\displaystyle\sum_{k=1}^{10}\left[4 - \left(\frac{2k}{10}\right)^2\right]\frac{2}{10} = \frac{1}{5}\sum_{k=1}^{10}\left(4 - \frac{1}{25}k^2\right)$

   $= \dfrac{1}{5}(4)\displaystyle\sum_{k=1}^{10}(1) - \frac{1}{5}\left(\frac{1}{25}\right)\sum_{k=1}^{10} k^2$

   $= \dfrac{4}{5}(10) - \dfrac{1}{125} \cdot \dfrac{10(11)(21)}{6} = 8 - \dfrac{1}{125} \cdot 385$
   $= 8 - \dfrac{77}{25} = \dfrac{123}{25} = 4\dfrac{23}{25}$

23. $\displaystyle\sum_{k=1}^{n}\left[4-\left(\frac{2}{n}\cdot k\right)^2\right]\frac{2}{n}=\frac{2}{n}\sum_{k=1}^{n}\left(4-\frac{4}{n^2}k^2\right)$

$\displaystyle\qquad=\frac{2}{n}(4)\sum_{k=1}^{n}(1)-\frac{2}{n}\left(\frac{4}{n^2}\right)\sum_{k=1}^{n}k^2$

$\displaystyle\qquad=\frac{8}{n}(n)-\frac{8}{n^3}\cdot\frac{n(n+1)(2n+1)}{6}$

$\displaystyle\qquad=8-\frac{4(n+1)(2n+1)}{3n^2}$

A.6 Riemann Sums and the Definite Integral

1.

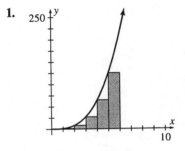

Since the interval length is 1, the number of subintervals is $\dfrac{6}{1}=6$. The subintervals are

[0, 1], [1, 2], [2, 3], [3, 4], [4, 5], and [5, 6]. Using the left-point rule, we must evaluate $f(x)$ at
$x = 0, 1, 2, 3, 4,$ and 5.
Area $\approx 1[f(0)+f(1)+f(2)+f(3)+f(4)+f(5)]$
$= 1(0^3+1^3+2^3+3^3+4^3+5^3)$
$= 1(0+1+8+27+64+125)=225$
This estimate is lower since the top of each rectangle is always on or below the graph.

3.
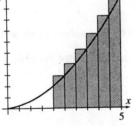

Since the interval length is 0.5, the number of subintervals is $\dfrac{5-2}{0.5}=6$. The subintervals are [2, 2.5],

[2.5, 3], [3, 3.5], [3.5, 4], [4, 4.5], and [4.5, 5]. Using the right-point rule, we must evaluate $h(x)$ at
$x = 2.5, 3, 3.5, 4, 4.5,$ and 5.

Area $\approx 0.5[h(2.5) + h(3) + h(3.5) + h(4) + h(4.5) + h(5)]$

$= 0.5[(2.5^2 + 2.5) + (3^2 + 3) + (3.5^2 + 3.5) + (4^2 + 4) + (4.5^2 + 4.5) + (5^2 + 5)]$

$= 0.5(8.75 + 12 + 15.75 + 20 + 24.75 + 30)$

$= 55.625$

5. Since the interval length is 0.05, the number of subintervals is $\dfrac{3-(-3)}{0.05} = \dfrac{6}{0.05} = 120$. The subintervals

are $[-3 + 0.05(k-1), -3 + 0.05k]$ or $[-3.05 + 0.05k, -3 + 0.05k]$ for

$k = 1, 2, 3, \ldots, 120$. Using the left-point rule, we must evaluate $g(x)$ at $x_k = -3.05 + 0.05k$ for

$k = 1, 2, 3, \ldots, 120$.

Area $\approx 0.05 \sum_{k=1}^{120} g(x_k) = 0.05 \sum_{k=1}^{120} [9 - (-3.05 + 0.05k)^2]$

7.

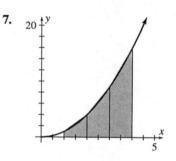

Since the interval length is 1, the number of subintervals is $\dfrac{4-1}{1} = \dfrac{3}{1} = 3$. The subintervals are $[1, 2]$,

$[2, 3]$, and $[3, 4]$.

Area $\approx \dfrac{1}{2} \cdot 1 \cdot [f(1) + f(2)] + \dfrac{1}{2} \cdot 1 \cdot [f(2) + f(3)] + \dfrac{1}{2} \cdot 1 \cdot [f(3) + f(4)]$

$= \dfrac{1}{2}[1^2 + 2^2] + \dfrac{1}{2}[2^2 + 3^2] + \dfrac{1}{2}[3^2 + 4^2]$

$= \dfrac{1}{2}(5) + \dfrac{1}{2}(13) + \dfrac{1}{2}(25) = 21.5$

9. Since the interval length is 0.01, the number of subintervals is $\dfrac{4-1}{0.01} = 300$. The subintervals are

$[1 + 0.01(k-1), 1 + 0.01k]$ or $[0.99 + 0.01k, 1 + 0.01k]$ for $k = 1, 2, 3, \ldots, 300$. Using the left-point rule,

we must evaluate $f(x)$ at $x_k = 0.99 + 0.01k$ for $k = 1, 2, 3, \ldots, 300$.

Area $\approx 0.01 \sum_{k=1}^{300} f(x_k) = 0.01 \sum_{k=1}^{300} (0.99 + 0.01k)^2$.

11. Since the interval length is $\dfrac{3}{N}$, the number of subintervals is $\dfrac{5-2}{\frac{3}{N}} = N$. The intervals are

$\left[2 + \dfrac{3}{N}(k-1), \; 2 + \dfrac{3}{N}k\right]$ for $k = 1, 2, 3, \ldots, N$. Using the right-point rule, we must evaluate $h(x)$ at

$$x_k = 2 + \frac{3}{N}k \text{ for } k = 1, 2, 3, \ldots, N.$$

$$\text{Area} \approx \frac{3}{N}\sum_{k=1}^{N}h(x_k)$$

$$= \frac{3}{N}\sum_{k=1}^{N}\left[\left(2 + \frac{3}{N}k\right)^2 + 2 + \frac{3}{N}k\right]$$

$$= \frac{3}{N}\sum_{k=1}^{N}\left(4 + \frac{12}{N}k + \frac{9}{N^2}k^2 + 2 + \frac{3}{N}k\right)$$

$$= \frac{3}{N}\sum_{k=1}^{N}\left(6 + \frac{15}{N}k + \frac{9}{N^2}k^2\right)$$

$$= \frac{18}{N}\sum_{k=1}^{N}(1) + \frac{45}{N^2}\sum_{k=1}^{N}k + \frac{27}{N^3}\sum_{k=1}^{N}k^2$$

$$= \frac{18}{N}\cdot N + \frac{45}{N^2}\cdot\frac{N(N+1)}{2} + \frac{27}{N^3}\cdot\frac{N(N+1)(2N+1)}{6}$$

$$= 18 + \frac{45(N+1)}{2N} + \frac{9(N+1)(2N+1)}{2N^2}$$

$$= \frac{36N^2 + 45N(N+1) + 9(N+1)(2N+1)}{2N^2}$$

$$= \frac{99N^2 + 72N + 9}{2N^2} = \frac{99}{2} + \frac{36}{N} + \frac{9}{2N^2}$$

13. a.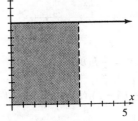

Area $= (3 - 0)(11) = 3 \cdot 11 = 33$ square units

$$\int_0^3 11\,dx = 33$$

b.

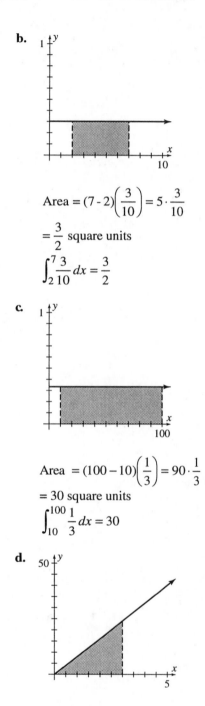

$$\text{Area} = (7 - 2)\left(\frac{3}{10}\right) = 5 \cdot \frac{3}{10}$$

$$= \frac{3}{2} \text{ square units}$$

$$\int_2^7 \frac{3}{10}\, dx = \frac{3}{2}$$

c.

$$\text{Area} = (100 - 10)\left(\frac{1}{3}\right) = 90 \cdot \frac{1}{3}$$

$$= 30 \text{ square units}$$

$$\int_{10}^{100} \frac{1}{3}\, dx = 30$$

d.

$$\text{Area} = \frac{1}{2}(3 - 0)(8 \cdot 3) = \frac{1}{2} \cdot 3 \cdot 24$$

$$= 36 \text{ square units}$$

$$\int_0^3 8x\, dx = 36$$

e.

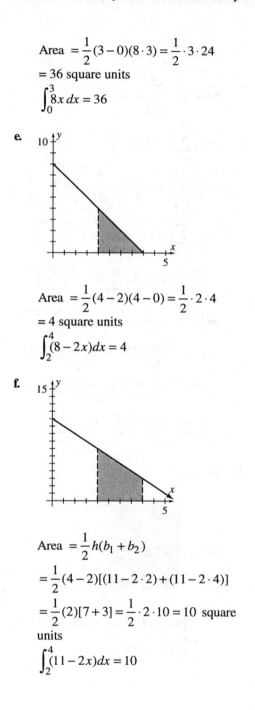

$$\text{Area} = \frac{1}{2}(4 - 2)(4 - 0) = \frac{1}{2} \cdot 2 \cdot 4$$

$$= 4 \text{ square units}$$

$$\int_2^4 (8 - 2x)\, dx = 4$$

f.

$$\text{Area} = \frac{1}{2} h(b_1 + b_2)$$

$$= \frac{1}{2}(4 - 2)[(11 - 2 \cdot 2) + (11 - 2 \cdot 4)]$$

$$= \frac{1}{2}(2)[7 + 3] = \frac{1}{2} \cdot 2 \cdot 10 = 10 \text{ square}$$

units

$$\int_2^4 (11 - 2x)\, dx = 10$$

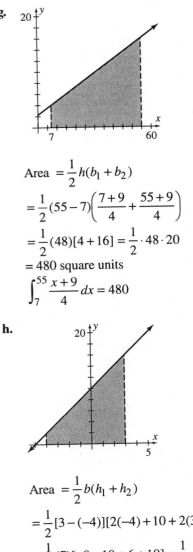

g.

$$\text{Area } = \frac{1}{2}h(b_1 + b_2)$$

$$= \frac{1}{2}(55 - 7)\left(\frac{7+9}{4} + \frac{55+9}{4}\right)$$

$$= \frac{1}{2}(48)[4 + 16] = \frac{1}{2} \cdot 48 \cdot 20$$

$$= 480 \text{ square units}$$

$$\int_7^{55} \frac{x+9}{4}\, dx = 480$$

h.

$$\text{Area } = \frac{1}{2}b(h_1 + h_2)$$

$$= \frac{1}{2}[3 - (-4)][2(-4) + 10 + 2(3) + 10]$$

$$= \frac{1}{2}(7)[-8 + 10 + 6 + 10] = \frac{1}{2} \cdot 7 \cdot 18$$

$$= 63 \text{ square units}$$

$$\int_{-4}^{3}(2x + 10)\, dx = 63$$

15. $\int_0^{100}(40 + 0.3x)\, dx$ is the area of a trapezoid with height $100 - 0 = 100$ units, one base of length $40 + 0.3(0) = 40$ units, and the other base of length $40 + 0.3(100) = 70$ units.

$$\int_0^{100}(40 + 0.3x)\, dx = \frac{1}{2}(100)(40 + 70)$$

$$= \frac{1}{2} \cdot 100 \cdot 110 = 5500$$

Using a graphics calculator,

$$\sum_{k=1}^{100}(40 + 0.3k) = 5515.$$

The summation and integral have values that are close because the sum is a Riemann sum of the area of the region between the graph of $f(x) = 40 + 0.3x$ and the x-axis from $x = 0$ to $x = 100$ using the right-point rule $\Delta x = 1$, while the integral gives the exact value of the area.

A.7 Area Under a Rate-of-Change Curve

1. The graph is of $y = 45$. From $x = 0$ to $x = 6$, the area under this curve is $(6 - 0)(45) = 270$ square units. Thus the train travels 270 miles in six hours.

3. The graph is of $y = 4.95$. From $x = 0$ to $x = 1000$, the area under this curve is $(1000 - 0)(4.95) = 4950$. Thus, the total revenue generate from selling 1000 items is $4950.

5. a. There is no graph until $x = 60$, so parking is free for 60 minutes.

   b. The charge to park for 25 minutes is $(25 - 0)(0) = 0$, so the charge is $0.

   c. Three hours is $3(60) = 180$ minutes. The area from $x = 0$ to $x = 180$ is $(60 - 0)(0) + (180 - 60)(1) = 120$. The charge to park for 3 hours is $1.20.

   d. Nine hours is $9(60) = 540$ minutes. The area from $x = 0$ to $x = 540$ is
$$(60 - 0)(0) + (300 - 60)(1)$$
$$+ (540 - 300)(3)$$
$$= 0 + 240 + 720 = 960.$$
The charge to park for 9 hours is $9.60.

7. a. The distance the rock fell in the first second is the area under the graph of $y = 32x$ from $x = 0$ to $x = 1$, which is

$$\frac{1}{2}(1-0)[32(1)] = 16.$$

The rock fell 16 feet in the first second.

b. The distance the rock fell in 10 seconds is the area under the graph of $y = 32x$ from $x = 0$ to $x = 10$, which is

$$\frac{1}{2}(10-0)[32(10)] = 1600.$$

The rock fell 1600 feet before it hit the ground.

c. The distance the rock fell in the last 3 seconds before hitting the ground is the area of a trapezoid with height $10 - 7 = 3$ units, one base of length $32(7) = 224$ units and the other base of length $32(10) = 320$ units. The area is

$$\frac{1}{2}(3)(224 + 320) = 816.$$ The rock fell

816 feet in the last 3 seconds.

9. The difference in total cost is the area under the graph of $y = 6.75 - 0.00065x$ from $x = 0$ to $x = 4000$. This is the area of a trapezoid with height $4000 - 0 = 4000$ units, one base of length $6.75 - 0.00065(0) = 6.75$ units, and the other base of length $6.75 - 0.00065(4000) = 6.75 - 2.6 = 4.15$ units.
The area is

$$\frac{1}{2}(4000)(6.75 + 4.15) = \frac{1}{2} \cdot 4000 \cdot 10.9$$
$$= 21,800.$$
The difference in total costs is \$21,800.

11. The total revenue can be approximated by the area of the triangle with base of length 100 units and height
$10(50) - 0.1(50)^2 = 250$ units, which is

$$\frac{1}{2}(100)(250) = 12,500$$ square units. Joe

collected approximately \$12,500.

Visual Calculus

Visual Calculus can be run on *any* IBM compatible computer with at least 640K of memory. Visual Calculus can be used with or without a mouse.

To Invoke Visual Calculus from Windows 95 (or later version):
1. Place the diskette in a drive, say drive A.
2. Click the Start button, point to Programs, and click MS-DOS Prompt.
3. If the DOS window does not fill the screen, hold down the Alt key and press the Enter key to enlarge the window.
4. Type A: and press the Enter key.
5. Type CD \VC and press the Enter key.
6. Type VC and press the Enter key.

To Invoke Visual Calculus from Windows 3.1:
1. Place the diskette in a drive, say drive A.
2. From Program Manager, double-click on the DOS icon in the Main program group. Or, exit Windows.
3. Type A: and press the Enter key.
4. Type CD \VC and press the Enter key.
5. Type VC and press the Enter key.

To Invoke Visual Calculus from a computer not containing Windows:
1. Place the diskette in a drive, say drive A.
2. Type A: and press the Enter key.
3. Type CD \VC and press the Enter key.
4. Type VC and press the Enter key.
   (*Note:* If a Hercules adapter is used, the program MSHERC.COM must be run before VC is entered.)

Note: If you are using a slow computer, first copy the files from the diskette into a subdirectory of your hard drive and run VC from that subdirectory. Otherwise, there will be some noticeable delays in the execution of the program.

To select a routine from a menu, do one of the following:

(a) Press the first letter of the routine.

(b) Press the down-arrow and up-arrow keys to highlight the routine, and press Enter.

(c) Double-click the routine with a mouse.

To manage a screen used to display functions:

(a) Use the right- and left-arrow keys to move the crosshairs around the graph – or click on a new point with the mouse. (Notice information about the point at the crosshairs is displayed in the upper-left part of the screen.) Use the down- and up-arrow keys to decrease or increase the distance that the crosshairs moves.

(b) To invoke a bracketed command found in the left column, either press the key surrounded by <>, or click on the command with the mouse.

To manage a screen used to input functions:

(a) Use Tab (or Shift+Tab) to move forward (or backwards) from region to region.

(b) Buttons are activated by pressing Alt+*highlighted letter* or by moving to the button and pressing the Enter key.

(c) With a mouse, you can move to a box (or activate a button) by clicking on the box (or button).

(d) Whenever a function is requested, the user can either type in a function or press F4 to select from lists of functions in the textbook. To select an item from a list, highlight the item by either cursoring down to it, clicking on it, or pressing the first digit of the item one or more times, and then press Enter. (Alternately, double-click on the item.) To remove the lists without making a selection, press F4 again.

(e) A caret (^) must be used for exponentiation. (For example, $x^5 \sin x$ is written x^5 sin x.) The following functions can appear in expressions: log (common log), ln (natural log), sin, cos, tan, cot, csc, sec, arcsin, arccos, arctan, arcsec, arccsc, arccot, exp (same as e^x, but more efficient), sqr (square root), fact (factorial), int, sgn. In the routine "Graphs of Functions", the expression for g(x) can involve f(x), e.g. f(x–2), and the expression for h(x) can involve f(x) and/or g(x), e.g. f(g(x)).

(f) Press P to display π and press I to display ∞. In a numeric input box, press S display $\checkmark$.

To print the graph of a function

The graphing routines have a "Print graph(s)" command that works with most dot-matrix or laser printers and prints a smooth curve. If the command does not work with your printer, you can produce a printout of the screen with one of the following two methods.

Method A: (For computers that have Windows)

Note: This method assumes that you have invoked DOS from the Windows environment; that is, Windows is running.

1. Press the Print Screen key.
2. Return to Windows and invoke Paint from the Accessories program group.
3. Press Ctrl+V to place a copy of the graphics screen in the window.
4. Press Ctrl+ I to invert the colors on the screen. (Otherwise, your printout will appear as white-on-black.)
5. Make sure your printer is turned on and ready to print.
6. Press Ctrl+P to print the contents of the Paint window.

Method B: (Requires DOS only or Windows 3.1)

1. To prepare for graphics screen dumps, you must enter the command GRAPHICS from DOS before invoking Visual Calculus.
2. In Visual Calculus, press Shift+PrintScreen at any time to produce a printout of the screen.

To enter functions:

Mathematical Expression	Computer Expression	Mathematical Expression	Computer Expression
x^2	x^2	$\frac{1}{2x}$	1/(2x)
$\frac{1}{x+1}$	1/(x+1)	$\frac{1}{x} + 1$	1/x + 1
$\sqrt{x}$	sqr(x) or x^(1/2)	$x^{1/3}$	cbr(x)
$\log_e x$	ln x or ln(x)	$\log_{10} x$	log x or log(x)
ln 3x	ln(3x)	$x^2 \ln x$	x^2ln x
x!	fact(x)	[x]	int(x)

Summary of operations for input screen

<Tab>	move around input screen
Shift+<Tab>	move around input screen in reverse order
Alt+*highlighted letter*	push button marked with the letter
Click Mouse	move to input box or activate button
F4	obtain list of appropriate functions from textbook (must be used in a function input box)
P	obtain π
S	obtain √ (cannot be used in input box for a function)
I	obtain ∞ (used only in Limits and Series)

To copy a function from one input box to another:

1. Place the cursor at the beginning of the function.
2. Hold down a shift key and press <End>. (The function is now highlighted.)
3. Press Ctrl+Ins or Ctrl+C. (The function is now saved in the clipboard.)
4. Move to another function input box either in the same routine or in another routine.
5. Press Shift+Ins or Ctrl+V.

Invocation options

When Visual Calculus invoked with the command VC, bw and/or cga can be added to affect the operation of the program. For instance, to obtain the bw option, enter VC bw.

Option	Effect
bw	All graphics will appear in blue and white. This option should be invoked if you are doing screen dumps. (It isn't needed when using the Print command.) This option might be helpful when projecting images onto a large screen or when using a monochrome monitor.
cga	Emulates Color Graphics Adapter. In graphics mode, graphs and text will be thicker. This option might be helpful in a classroom when projecting images onto a large screen.

Main Routines

Analyze a Function and its Derivatives displays the graphs of one or more of f, f', f'' and displays the values of these functions at any point. A Solve command finds zeros, relative extreme points, and inflection points. A Tangent Line command draws a tangent line to $f(x)$ or $f'(x)$ at the crosshairs.

Examine Solutions of Differential Equations graphs the solution of a differential equation of the form $y' = g(t, y)$ with an initial value and determines the coordinates of points on the graph. Graphs with different initial values can be superimposed. Successive Euler approximations may be displayed.

Function Evaluator (1 and 2 variables) displays the value of a function and its derivatives. [1 variable: $f(x)$, $f'(x)$, and $f''(x)$ are displayed. 2 variables: $f(x, y)$, $\partial f / \partial x$, and $\partial f / \partial y$ are displayed.] A single push of a button increases the value of x (and/or y) by an amount input by the user and recomputes.

Graphs of Functions sketches the graphs of 1, 2, or 3 functions. The coordinates of points can be found by moving crosshairs with the arrow keys or clicking on the point with a mouse. A Solve command finds the zeros of a function or the intersection points of two functions. A Zoom command enlarges a rectangular region.

Integrals, Definite calculates the definite integral of a function. Also, illustrates five numerical methods.

Least Squares calculates the line of best fit and also allows the user to move a line around the screen to find the best fit.

Observe Limit of f(x) as x → a evaluates $f(a + h)$ and $f(a - h)$ for $h = .1, .01, .001,$ ... and guesses the limit. Can have a = ∞.

Series and Partial Sums evaluates finite and infinite sums.

Demonstration Routines

Ball Thrown Straight Up shows the connection between the motion of a ball and the graph of its height function.

Car in Motion moves a car across the screen with its position, and hence velocity, determined by a function input by the user.

Garden Fencing Problem shows the connection between a function to be optimized and the corresponding physical problem.

Plot Cosine and Sine Functions traces out the graphs of the sine and cosine functions as a point moves around the unit circle.

Secant Line Approaching Tangent Line moves a secant line closer and closer to a tangent line.

Tangent Line Approaching Curve illustrates the fact that locally a curve looks like its tangent line.

Explorations in Finite Mathematics Software

This software enhances the understanding and visualization of many of the topics covered in the textbook. The self-documented software consists of two programs called FINITE1 and FINITE2.

Part 1 (Execute by entering FINITE1)

Part 1 covers finite math topics involving linear equations, linear inequalities, and matrices. In particular, it contains routines to perform Gaussian elimination, matrix operations, matrix inversion, simplex method, graphical solution of linear programming problems, the method of least-squares, and regular Markov chains. The software follows the conventions of the text.

Part 2 (Execute by entering FINITE2)

Part 2 contains routines for Venn diagrams, Venn diagram counting problems, Venn diagram probability problems, computation of combinations, permutations, and factorials, statistical analysis of data, Galton board, binomial distribution, areas under normal curve, simple interest, compound interest, loan analysis, annuity analysis, and finance tables.

Requirements

The software runs on *any* IBM compatible computer having at least 384 K of memory and a graphics adapter, that is, CGA, EGA, MCGA, VGA, or Hercules.

Technical Support

If you have questions about the software, contact David I. Schneider by e-mail at dis@math.umd.edu.

Matrices On Diskette

Matrices appearing in examples from the text have been saved on the diskette with either suggestive names or names of the form CxSxEx. For instance, the matrix appearing in Chapter 8, Section 3, Example 7 has the name C8S3E7. The list of saved matrices appropriate to the current routine is displayed on the screen whenever you request "Load a matrix saved on disk."

To Invoke Explorations in Finite Mathematics from DOS

1. Place the diskette in a drive, say drive A.
2. Type A: and press the Enter key.
3. Type CD \FINITE and press the Enter key.
4. Type FINITE1 or FINITE2 and press the Enter key.

(*Note:* If a Hercules adapter is used, the program MSHERC.COM must be run before FINITE1 or FINITE2 is entered.)

To Invoke Explorations in Finite Mathematics from Windows 3.1

1. Place the diskette in a drive, say drive A.
2. From Program Manager, double-click on the DOS icon in the Main program group. Or, exit Windows.
3. Type A: and press the Enter key.
4. Type CD \FINITE and press the Enter key.
5. Type FINITE1 or FINITE2 and press the Enter key.

To Invoke Explorations in Finite Mathematics from Windows 95 (or later version)

1. Place the diskette in a drive, say drive A.
2. Click the Start button, point to Programs, and click MS-DOS Prompt.
3. If the DOS window does not fill the screen, hold down the Alt key and press the Enter key to enlarge the window.
4. Type A: and press the Enter key.
5. Type CD \FINITE and press the Enter key.
6. Type FINITE1 or FINITE2 and press the Enter key.